FRAGMENT.

Yes! all is past—swift time has fled away,
  Yet its swell pauses on my sickening mind;
How long will horror nerve this frame of clay?
  I'm dead, and lingers yet my soul behind.
Oh! powerful fate, revoke thy deadly spell,
  And yet that may not ever, ever be,
Heaven will not smile upon the work of hell;
  Ah! no, for heaven cannot smile on me;
Fate, envious fate, has seal'd my wayward destiny.

I sought the cold brink of the midnight surge,
  I sigh'd beneath its wave to hide my woes,
The rising tempest sung a funeral dirge,
  And on the blast a frightful yell arose.

---

148 ST. IRVYNE; OR,

be solemnized as soon as decency would permit, as the poor friendless Eloise wished speedily to quit Geneva. She wrote to announce the fatal event to her sister. Slowly dragged the time. Eloise followed to its latest bed, the corpse of her mother, and was returning from the convent, when a stranger put into her hand a note, and quickly disappeared:—

" Will Eloise de St. Irvyne meet her friend at —— Abbey, to-morrow night, at ten o'clock?"

THE ROSICRUCIAN. 149

CHAP. VIII.

——Why then unbidden gush'd the tear?
. . . .
Then would cold shudderings seize his health,
  As gasping he labour'd for breath;
The strange gaze of his meteor eye,
  Which, beamed, and rolling dreadfully,
Glar'd with hideous gleam,
Would chill like the spectre gaze of Death,
  As, usurp'd by seventh dream,
He seems o'er the sick man's couch to stand,
And shakes the fell lance in his skeleton hand.
                    WANDERING JEW.

Yes;—they fled from Geneva; they had eluded pursuit and justice, but could not escape the torments of an outraged and avenging conscience, which, with stings the most acute, pursued them whithersoever they might go. Fortune even seemed to favour them; for fortune will, sometimes, in

H 3

The Complete Poetry of Percy Bysshe Shelley

A Cat in distress
Nothing more or less
Good folks I must faithfully tell ye
As I am a sinner
It wants for some dinner
To stuff out its own little belly

2

You might'nt easily guess
All the modes of distress
Which torture the tenants of earth
And the various evils
Which like many devils
Attend the poor dogs from their birth

3

Some a living require
And others desire
An old fellow out of the way

The Complete Poetry of Percy Bysshe Shelley

VOLUME ONE

EDITED BY

Donald H. Reiman and Neil Fraistat

The Johns Hopkins University Press
BALTIMORE AND LONDON

This book has been brought to publication
with the generous assistance of
The Carl and Lily Pforzheimer Foundation
and the Office of Graduate Studies and Research
of the University of Maryland.

© 2000 The Johns Hopkins University Press
All rights reserved. Published 2000
Printed in the United States of America on acid-free paper
2 4 6 8 9 7 5 3 1

The Johns Hopkins University Press
2715 North Charles Street
Baltimore, Maryland 21218-4363
www.press.jhu.edu

Library of Congress Cataloging-in-Publication Data will be found at
the end of this book.
A catalog record for this book is available from the British Library.

ISBN 0-8018-6119-5

Endpapers: Left to right: *Song. Sorrow* from *Original Poetry by Victor and Cazire* (1810); *Fragment* from *Posthumous Fragments of Margaret Nicholson* (1810); epigraph to Chapter 8, *St. Irvyne; or, The Rosicrucian* (1811). With kind permission of The Huntington Library.

Frontispiece: "A Cat in distress." Transcript by Elizabeth Shelley, watercolor illustration. With kind permission of The Carl H. Pforzheimer Collection of Shelley and His Circle, The New York Public Library, Astor, Lenox and Tilden Foundations.

For

Shawn and Ann Cleveland Fraistat

"... wonder[s] of this earth,
Where there is little of transcendent worth . . ."
Julian and Maddalo

For

Laurel E. Reiman Henneman and Charles C. Henneman

"... Wit and sense,
Virtue and human knowledge, all that might
Make this dull world a business of delight . . ."
Letter to Maria Gisborne

Contents of Volume One

List of Illustrations	*xi*
Acknowledgments	*xiii*
Editorial Overview	*xix*
Abbreviations	*xli*

TEXTS

Original Poetry: by Victor and Cazire	3
Letter [1] ("Here I sit with my paper, my pen and my ink")	7
Letter [2] (To Miss ——— ——— From Miss ——— ———)	9
Song. ("Cold, cold is the blast when December is howling")	11
Song. ("Come ———! sweet is the hour")	13
Song. Despair.	14
Song. Sorrow.	15
Song. Hope.	16
Song. Translated from the Italian.	17
Song. Translated from the German.	18
The Irishman's Song.	18
Song. ("Fierce roars the midnight storm")	19
Song. To ——— ("Ah! sweet is the moonbeam that sleeps on yon fountain")	20
Song. To ——— ("Stern, stern is the voice of fate's fearfull command")	21
Saint Edmond's Eve.	22
Revenge.	28
Ghasta; or, The Avenging Demon!!!	30
Fragment, or The Triumph of Conscience.	37
The Wandering Jew; or, The Victim of the Eternal Avenger	39
Posthumous Fragments of Margaret Nicholson; Being Poems Found Amongst the Papers of that Noted Female who Attempted the Life of the King in 1786. Edited by John Fitzvictor	89
Advertisement.	92
"Ambition, power, and avarice, now have hurl'd"	93

Fragment. Supposed to be an Epithalamium of Francis Ravaillac and Charlotte Cordé.	95
Despair.	99
Fragment. ("Yes! all is past—swift time has fled away")	100
The Spectral Horseman.	101
Melody to a Scene of Former Times.	102

Poems from *St. Irvyne; or, The Rosicrucian: A Romance* *105*

"'T was dead of the night, when I sat in my dwelling"	109
"Ghosts of the dead! have I not heard your yelling"	110
Ballad. ("The death-bell beats!——")	111
Song. ("How swiftly through heaven's wide expanse")	114
Song. ("How stern are the woes of the desolate mourner")	115
Song. ("Ah! faint are her limbs, and her footstep is weary")	116

The Devil's Walk *119*

The Devil's Walk, a Ballad.	123
Supplement: Letter Version of *The Devil's Walk*	128

Ten Early Poems (1809–1814) *131*

"A Cat in distress"	135
"How swiftly through Heaven's wide expanse"	136
"Oh wretched mortal, hard thy fate!"	138
To Mary who died in this opinion	138
"Why is it said thou canst but live"	139
"As you will see I wrote to you" [1st letter to E. F. Graham]	140
"Dear dear dear dear dear dear Græme!" [2nd letter to E. F. Graham]	142
"Sweet star! which gleaming oer the darksome scene"	144
"Bear witness Erin! when thine injured isle"	145
"Thy dewy looks sink in my breast"	145

COMMENTARIES

Original Poetry by Victor and Cazire	*149*
The Wandering Jew; or, The Victim of the Eternal Avenger	*189*
Posthumous Fragments of Margaret Nicholson	*235*
Poems from *St. Irvyne; or, The Rosicrucian*	*261*
The Devil's Walk	*281*
Ten Early Poems (1809–1814)	*295*

HISTORICAL COLLATIONS

Introduction	*333*
Original Poetry by Victor and Cazire	*335*
The Wandering Jew; or, The Victim of the Eternal Avenger	*355*
Posthumous Fragments of Margaret Nicholson	*375*
Poems from *St. Irvyne; or, The Rosicrucian*	*387*
The Devil's Walk	*403*
Ten Early Poems (1809–1814)	*411*

APPENDIXES

Introduction	*433*
A. Latin School Exercises	435
Epitaphium	435
In Horologium	437
B. Prose Treated as Poems	*438*
"The Ocean rolls between us"	438
"Oh Ireland!"	441
C. Lost Works	*442*
Satirical Poem on "L'infame"	443
Poetical Essay on the Existing State of Things	444
On a Fête at Carlton House	448
Essay on War	451
God Save the King	452
D. Dubia	*453*
Poems in the *Oxford University and City Herald*	453
Ode, to the Breath of Summer.	455
The Grape. From the Greek Anthologia	455
Epigram, from the Greek Anthologia. ("We that were wont")	456
Translation of an Epigram of Vincent Bourne's.	457
On Old Age, from the Greek Anthology	458
Venus and the Muses, from the Same	458
Unattributed Epigraphs to *St. Irvyne*	458
Sadak the Wanderer. A Fragment	460

E. Misattributions • 469

    Epigraph: "If Satan had never fallen" • 469
    Lines, Addressed to His Royal Highness The Prince of Wales,
        on His Being Appointed Regent • 469
    The Modern Minerva; or, The Bat's Seminary for Young Ladies.
        A Satire on Female Education. By Queen Mab • 478
    Anecdotes of Father Murdo • 480
    To the Queen of My Heart • 482

Index of Titles • 487
Index of First Lines • 491

Illustrations

Endpapers	(Left to right) *Song. Sorrow.* from *Original Poetry by Victor and Cazire* (1810); *Fragment.* from *Posthumous Fragments of Margaret Nicholson* (1810); epigraph to Chapter 8, *St. Irvyne; or, The Rosicrucian* (1811)
Frontispiece	"*A Cat in distress.*" Transcript by Elizabeth Shelley.
Page 3	Title page of *Original Poetry by Victor and Cazire* (1810)
Page 39	First page of *The Wandering Jew* (1829)
Page 89	Title page of *Posthumous Fragments of Margaret Nicholson* (1810)
Page 105	Title page of *St. Irvyne; or, The Rosicrucian* (1811)
Page 119	*The Devil's Walk* broadside (1812)
Page 131	"*Oh wretched mortal,*" from Thomas Jefferson Hogg's Oxford notebook
Page 431	Line engraving by E. J. Roberts of John Martin's painting *Sadak in Search of the Waters of Oblivion*.

Acknowledgments

"Is it not a glorious chance, this Shelley editing and biographizing," wrote a delighted William Michael Rossetti to his friend William Allingham, after being invited by the firm of E. Moxon, Son and Company to prepare a new edition of Shelley's poetry in 1868. "Willingly would I not only be doing it for pay, but do it for nothing, or pay to do it." When the Johns Hopkins University Press accepted our proposal in 1990 to undertake a new complete edition of Shelley's poetry, we greeted the "glorious chance" with perhaps more financial restraint than Rossetti, but with something like the same enthusiasm—and the same sense of commitment. Though the years of subsequent labor have impressed upon us the full complexity of the task we then proposed, they have left us no less enthusiastic about both the importance of the project and the pleasure of the work.

Among the chief rewards of this undertaking has been the warm spirit of cooperation that we have experienced from the many individuals and institutions whose help has been necessary to any success it might enjoy. Rossetti, Harry Buxton Forman, and their London contemporaries had nearby access both to all Shelley's books then known to survive and to some of the poet's friends and contemporary acquaintances with whom they discussed his life and works. But any project of this scope and length now depends upon widespread support—financial, intellectual, and emotional. We are delighted to have this opportunity to acknowledge the profoundly social nature of this edition and to thank those who have played important roles in this collaboration.

We could never have undertaken this kind of historical edition without the benefit of released time from other duties, funds to travel to the sites of the primary research materials, or the equipment and staff assistance to gather, collate, and check multiple copies of those authorities. In addition to our personal contributions, most of these resources were provided by the National Endowment for the Humanities (NEH, an independent federal agency), the Carl and Lily Pforzheimer Foundation, Inc., and the University of Maryland. These institutions exhibit human faces through their respective directors, administrators, officers, and consultants: At NEH, we are very grateful to Margot Backas, Alice Hudgins, Steve Veneziani, and David Wallace. At the Pforzheimer Foundation, thanks are due especially to the late Carl H. Pforzheimer, Jr., Carl H. Pforzheimer III, President, and their fellow directors for a matching grant that augmented and facilitated support from NEH and for permitting Donald Reiman's time-sharing arrangement for his work on *Shelley and his Circle* and *The Complete Poetry of Percy Bysshe Shelley* (*CPPBS*). Mary Kitabjan and Anthony L. Ferranti of the Foundation's staff provided practical counsel and liaison. At the University of Maryland, we are grateful for generous support from the College of Arts and Humanities, especially from Deans Robert Griffith, Ira Berlin, and James Harris, as well as Assistant Dean Michele Eastman. Within the English Department, three successive Chairs—Eugene Hammond, Theresa Coletti, and Charles Caramello—have steadfastly supported our work, and Business Manager Irene Sanchez has provided valuable assistance in more ways than we can name. Thanks are also due to the intrepid and (almost always) cheerful staff of the Main English Office, Betty Fern, Lynne Hamilton, Isabella Moulton, Betty Weineke, and, especially, Janet Duncan. Finally, we wish to thank Marion Brown and Dawn Jackson of the Office of Research Advancement and Administration at the University of Maryland, each of whom has offered a warm place to turn when we faced the cold glare of budgets in need of balancing.

Having thus been given the time and the means to access the whole range of the primary evidence, we were aided by a veritable army of knowledgeable scholar-librarians. In 1992–93 skilled professionals at hundreds of libraries around the world filled out (with only a few discernible grumblings) a lengthy questionnaire through which we sought to formulate a preliminary census of authoritative manuscripts, annotated copies, and early editions of Shelley's works outside the well-known principal collections, with indications of their provenances and contemporary annotations. The resulting census of Shelleyan manuscripts, editions, and authorities will be mounted on the *Romantic Circles* website (http://www.rc.umd.edu), together with a record of the institutions and individuals who contributed to it, either in the original effort, or in response to subsequent inquiries. This information has enabled us to focus our research for Volumes I and II upon those locations possessing most of the copies of the poet's earliest and rarest publications, as well as his surviving manuscripts of the period.

Beyond our personal research collections, we have relied where possible on the library resources of the University of Maryland, College Park, recently enhanced in our field through the efforts of Betty Day and rare book librarians Tim Pyatt and Doug McElrath, who have expedited our research in numerous ways; the University of Delaware, where Susan Brynteson, Director of Libraries, and Timothy D. Murray, Head of Special Collections, and their staffs provided special attention to our research needs; and the Library of Congress, to whose obliging staff and superb resources we are much indebted.

Neil Fraistat thanks the always cordial and proficient staff of the Henry E. Huntington Library for ready admission and courteous attention to his research needs while within their walls and gardens, with particular thanks to Thomas Lange, who arranged for the photographs of PBS's early volumes that grace this volume in several places, including the endpapers. Don Reiman is similarly grateful to the efficient staff of the Harry Ransom Humanities Research Center at the University of Texas at Austin, especially to Sally Leach and Cathy Henderson, and for the hospitality of Texan colleagues and friends Warner Barnes, Leah S. Marcus, Terence A. Hoagwood, Theresa M. Kelley, Michael B. Winship, and especially Carl and Mary Woodring, whose company brightened two research trips to Austin. At Harvard, Don remembers the helpfulness of the scholar-librarians of the Houghton Library, especially Rodney G. Dennis, Roger E. Stoddard, Leslie A. Morris, Hugh Amory, and Peter Accardo. In New York, at the Pierpont Morgan Library he thanks especially Anna Lou Ashby, Inge Du Pont, Robert A. Parks, and their staffs; at the New York Public Library, Wayne Furman in the Office of Special Collections and the staff of the Henry W. and Albert A. Berg Collection.

At the Carl H. Pforzheimer Collection of Shelley and His Circle, we are indebted to Stephen Wagner, the Curator, for repeated kindnesses and constant support. He and Doucet Devin Fischer supplied us with facsimiles of the many relevant manuscripts in the Pforzheimer Collection, including the special copies used for illustrations. Since the inception of our work on *CPPBS*, Doucet Devin Fischer, Co-Editor, and Daniel Dibbern, Associate Editor, of Shelley and his Circle have encouraged our work and shared their deep knowledge of matters Shelleyan on a weekly, if not daily, basis, while Elizabeth C. Denlinger has added her specialized knowledge since 1996.

Other librarians have helped from a distance, answering questions about items in their collections or providing us with copies of relevant items. Kate Manners, Assistant Archivist for Manuscripts and Rare Books at University College, London, arranged for us to receive a copy of PBS's letter to Hogg of 16 March 1814, which contains the sole known holograph of "Thy dewy looks sink in my breast"; John F. Guido, Head of Special Collections at Washington State University, went out of his way to microfilm Harriet Shelley's commonplace book of 1812; the Royal Academy of Art helpfully supplied exhibition information about John Martin's painting, *Sadak in Search of the Waters of Oblivion;* while a photo of E. J. Robert's engraving of that painting in the 1828 *Keepsake* was provided by John Lancaster, Curator of Archives and Special Collections of the Amherst College Library; and Anthony Bliss at the Bancroft Library, University of California, Berkeley, kindly produced for us a photocopy of the Dugdale piracy of PBS's *The Wandering Jew.*

Acknowledgments xv

Among our benefactors across the Atlantic, we thank the staff of the British Library and the Public Record Office for their courtesy to us amidst a swarm of impatient American researchers. In addition, we thank the Public Record Office for the photograph of *The Devil's Walk* that appears in this volume. Our gratitude to the staff of the Bodleian Library, Oxford, can be expressed more personally: we thank the entire staff of the Department of Western Manuscripts, led by David C. Vaisey, who then served as Bodley's Librarian, and Mary Clapinson, who succeeded him as the Keeper of Western Manuscripts. Julian Roberts, Keeper of Printed Books during our work there, and his staff provided valuable support. To Bruce C. Barker-Benfield, our colleague, teacher, and friend through years of struggle to bring into reality his vision of *The Bodleian Shelley Manuscripts,* we here cheerfully acknowledge our embarrassingly large debt, for he possesses such wealth of bibliographical and codicological understanding that he may never miss all that he has given to us. Our debts to the other members of the team that edited the Garland Shelley facsimiles—including Charles E. Robinson, Betty T. Bennett, Steven E. Jones, Michael J. Neth, Michael O'Neill, Tatsuo Tokoo, Mary Quinn, Irving Massey, the late E(ugene) B. Murray, P(aul) M. S. Dawson, Timothy Webb, Carlene A. Adamson, Nancy Moore Goslee, and Alan M. Weinberg—are varied and often incalculable, representing as they do years of intellectual exchange and interdependence.

Among other colleagues and friends who have helped shape our understanding and supported this undertaking, we wish to mention especially Marilyn Butler, Vincent Carretta, Stuart Curran, Jerome J. McGann, Leslie A. Marchand, Carl Woodring (again), the late Stuart M. Sperry, Jerrold E. Hogle, William Keach, Susan J. Wolfson, and W. Speed Hill. Desmond Hawkins, Paula Feldman, Barbara Gelpi, and especially James Bieri have aided our work directly by providing specific information or sources specified within the Commentaries in this volume. Kelvin Everest and the late G. M. Matthews, friends with whom we shared personal interchanges on numerous occasions, represent a larger group of Shelley's editors (many of whom had died before either of us was born) from whom collectively we have learned much of what we know about the poet's texts. Matthews and Everest, the most recent editors to precede us in the quest for a complete scholarly edition of Shelley's poetry, join Mary W. Shelley, H. Buxton Forman, and William Michael Rossetti in embodying the best of that Shelleyan editorial tradition both in spirit and technique.

Two colleagues and friends who contributed to our scholarly growth also played a direct role in the contents of the present volume: Jack Stillinger, editor of Keats par excellence, read the entire manuscript of Volume I of *CPPBS* and hundreds of pages that will appear in Volume II, generously sharing his vast knowledge both of textual editing and the Romantic period—and constantly holding our work to the highest scholarly standards.

His detailed response to the manuscript pointed out many places for improvement and helped adjudicate a number of difficult presentational issues for this edition. Nora Crook, fresh from her triumphant editing of Mary Shelley's collected writings, similarly read and sent us detailed notes on the entire typescript of Volume I as it went to the Press; she devoted particular attention to the editorial principles enunciated in our Editorial Overview, with which she will be more intimately involved when she later joins us as the editor of some later volumes of *CPPBS*.

Besides the editors, the people who made the greatest contribution to the present volume up to the time it went to press were the series of splendid Research Assistants drawn from the graduate students of English at the University of Maryland. Linda Brigham, as the first one, not only helped us lay the groundwork for the entire edition, but has since, in effect, provided us with our most recent R.A., David Brookshire, who studied the Romantics with Linda at Kansas State. Jennifer Rush created the database for our census of Shelley manuscripts and first editions, and Matthew Bray, Lorna Ellis, and Eleanor Shevlin diligently and painstakingly helped to create, collate, and proofread the various text files for this edition. Most of all, we are grateful for the unflagging efforts of Melissa J. Sites, whose prodigious talent as a researcher is matched by her superb technological skills; since beginning work on *CPPBS* in 1994, Melissa has made important contributions to virtually every aspect of the edition.

Here we also thank Sally Rogers, a Ph.D. from the Department of Classics, University of Maryland, who aided us in appraising the early translations from the Greek and Latin attributed to PBS, and John Smith and Kathy Russell, who advised us on electronic media, helping us choose computers, scanners, and other peripherals and consulting on various problems during our research and the preparation of copy for the Press. At the University of Delaware, we received advice and encouragement from various members of the Department of English in addition to Charles E. Robinson, especially Carl Dawson and Susan Goodman, George Miller, Marcia Peoples Halio, Lois Potter, and Richard H. Duggan, and from L. Leon Campbell, H. M. Campbell Research Professor of Life and Health Sciences.

If scholarship had really entered a totally electronic age, our naming of this cloud of witnesses might be at an end, but our Texts would not be quite as accurate, our Commentaries would be less consistent and clear, and the presentation would be less readable and aesthetically pleasing. The fine people at the Johns Hopkins University Press, beginning with J. G. Goellner and Eric Halpern, whose enthusiasm for this project made it all possible, have aided us at every stage of our work to transmute a dream into reality. We are indebted to the thoughtful care of Willis Regier, who discerned that our anticipated first-born volume was really twins—and to Wendy Harris, Barbara Lamb, Jacqueline Wehmueller, and latterly Maura Burnett, who became its supervising obstetricians. Kathleen Szawiola designed the book; Valerie Dolan and Dana Battaglia coordinated its production. Most of all, we are indebted to the attentions of Anne Whitmore, whose keen eye and rich experience both improved almost every page of this complicated volume and now guide our planning for Volume II. We are deeply grateful for the happy intervention of these elite publishing professionals.

Last to be acknowledged, but always first, are the friends and family members who have shared the pleasures and supported us through the rigors of this work. For friendships that have meant more than he can ever say, Neil Fraistat wishes to thank Jonathan Auerbach, Bonnie Bernstein, Marijean Berry, Stuart Curran, Joan Goldberg, Len Goldberg, Ivy Goodman, Steve Jones, Bob Levine, Marilee Lindemann, Martha Nell Smith, Carl Stahmer, Orrin Wang, and the ever-irrepressible Joe Wittreich. Always there when it mattered most were Hank Dobin, Sue Lanser, Ted Leinwand, Beth and Bill Loizeaux, and Mick and Zara Mangan. Profound thanks are also due to a truly wonderful and talented family, beginning with Neil's father, Louis Fraistat and his partner Felice Lankasky, Scott and Jennifer Fraistat (and daughters Rachel, Amanda, and Ashley), Rose Ann Cleveland Fraistat, Judy and Terry Silverlight (who make beautiful music together), Bob and Jeff Vilinsky, and Muriel Vilinsky, who remains the dearest aunt that any nephew could hope to have. Although Jack Vilinsky died before this volume was completed, his paintings and his memory remain an abiding inspiration. To Ann Cleveland Fraistat and Shawn Cleveland Fraistat, those funny, charming, and unimaginably bright children who have just turned, respectively, eleven and fifteen years old, Neil dedicates this volume, with great pride and deepest love.

Don Reiman similarly dedicates his efforts in this volume to Laurel E. Reiman Henneman and Charles C. Henneman (his daughter and her husband), while thanking them, Hélène Dworzan (Reiman), and some special friends in addition to the colleagues mentioned above—especially William T. Buice III, Marsha M. Manns, and Robert A. Hartley—for examples of courage under fire, understanding, good counsel, and support that help him persevere through long years toward dimly glimpsed goals.

Editorial Overview

The Complete Poetry of Percy Bysshe Shelley (CPPBS) will, when completed, include critically edited texts of all the poems that Percy Bysshe Shelley (PBS) released for circulation (whether to friends or to the reading public at large) and diplomatic renderings of his uncompleted and fragmentary poetry.[1] The completed and released poems appear in the order and within the volumes and other groupings in which PBS released them to their intended audiences, whereas the poetic fragments that he never released appear either as "Supplements" to related poems that he did release or in groupings based on the draft manuscripts (MSS) in which they survive. Because we shall include more poems and fragments than have hitherto appeared in any single edition, as well as more extensive commentaries and collations than have previously been attempted, it seems likely, at this point, that **CPPBS** will require at least half a dozen volumes comparable in size to this one, or a smaller number of larger volumes.

As we explain below, at this time scholars and students of PBS require a comprehensive edition that recovers the historical status of all of his poetic texts. We attempt this recovery by several means. First, we distinguish between the completed poems in which PBS conveyed his thoughts and feelings in art that he deemed worthy of being shown to his contemporaries and the other drafts and fragmentary efforts that he discarded, withheld from public view, or left unfinished at his death. Second, we retain both the sequential order of release and the internal arrangement of PBS's poetic volumes, to reveal the harmonies (and dissonances) of their interrelationships and of his poetic development. Third, the collations—both the primary variants at the foot of the text page and the Historical Collations at the back of the book—provide a detailed record of changes during the composition and transmission of each poem, showing how our Text of a poem (always capitalized as Text to distinguish it from other texts) relates both to its authoritative copy-text and the texts derived by other editors. Fourth, to foster historical understanding of individual poems and the larger units within which they are grouped, our Commentaries situate PBS's works within their biographical origins, sociopolitical ambiences, and literary traditions, both ideological and generic. Finally, these Commentaries allude to the reception of each poem or fragment and to its cultural development in subsequent textual, literary, and intellectual history. In short, we try to record the inseminating events and influences that led PBS to compose and arrange his poems, his struggle to shape and publish or otherwise circulate them to his intended audience, the reactions to his poems by their early readers and reviewers, their publication and transmission by Mary W. Shelley (MWS) and subsequent editors, and (to a lesser extent) responses to them by writers, critics, and thinkers amid the social and intellectual changes that have both reflected and shaped the reactions of other readers during the nearly two centuries since PBS set them afloat, like his beloved paper boats, upon the stream of Time.

Contents of *CPPBS*

The first three volumes of this edition will contain at least the earliest released poems until his departure with MWS for Italy in April 1818, plus the contemporaneous poetic MSS that PBS never developed or published. In addition, Volume I presents whatever is known about lost works and the texts of some of the early poems that have been attributed to PBS on less than convincing grounds. Beyond the poems in **The Esdaile Notebook** and **Queen Mab,** Volumes II and III will include the poems published in the **Alastor** volume; those written during the summer at Geneva and released during the next year—notably **Hymn to Intellectual Beauty, Mont Blanc, Laon and Cythna,** and the **Rosalind and Helen** volume—with their related supplements and uncompleted fragments from the Bodleian notebooks in which PBS drafted them; and shorter poems that PBS released to friends during the same period. The remaining volumes will be devoted to the mature poems and unreleased fragments of the Italian period, arranged according to the general historical principles that we discuss in the pages that follow.

Although PBS released some fragmentary poetry in letters to his friends, there survive few rough-draft notebooks or MSS of unreleased poems or discarded fragments from the period covered by the early volumes of *CPPBS*—that is, his childhood, youth, and years with Harriet Westbrook Shelley. We shall, of course, present such materials found in his "Geneva Summer Notebook" (Bodleian MS. Shelley adds. e.16), poetic fragments from the notebooks he used when composing and publishing **Laon and Cythna,** and other poetic materials from his papers that predate his final departure for Italy in April 1818—including the Scrope Davies Notebook and the smaller of the two Harvard Shelley Notebooks. But the early volumes of *CPPBS* will be devoted chiefly to poems that PBS himself released, publicly or privately, together with the surviving unreleased versions of such public poems as **Hymn to Intellectual Beauty** and **Mont Blanc.**

Contents of Volume I

CPPBS begins with the four volumes containing poetry that PBS prepared for the press before his expulsion from Oxford in March 1811, namely: ***Original Poetry*** "by Victor and Cazire"; ***The Wandering Jew; or, The Victim of the Eternal Avenger; Posthumous Fragments of Margaret Nicholson;*** and ***St. Irvyne; or, The Rosicrucian.*** Though each of these volumes includes some serious sentimental and political poems by PBS, all but ***The Wandering Jew*** seem to exude the air of schoolboy pranks.

After PBS's elopement in 1811 with Harriet Westbrook Shelley had increased his distance from his family and he had become further disillusioned, first by the attempt of his Oxford friend Thomas Jefferson Hogg to seduce Harriet and then by the condescension of Robert Southey (who tried to persuade PBS to skip his youth by accepting immediately Southey's disillusioned political realism), PBS and Harriet tried their hands as political and social activists in Ireland, Devonshire, and Wales. Though PBS released mainly prose during this period, he also wrote and, in August 1812, tried to circulate ***The Devil's Walk,*** a satiric political broadside ballad aimed at a popular audience, a work immediately suppressed as seditious by local authorities, but surviving in a single copy.

The main part of Volume I concludes with a group of short poems, dating from 1809 through PBS's estrangement from Harriet in March 1814, which the poet sent to friends in letters or gave them in separate transcripts but did not include in his projected volume of "minor poems," which survives as ***The Esdaile Notebook.*** Though these separate, privately released poems include several lyrics, the tone in at least four of them is satirical. These early poems are important not only biographically but also aesthetically, for they provide detailed evidence of how PBS went about learning his craft as a poet, and the differences between their tone and that of his mature short poetry index a radical change in his self-image vis-à-vis other people and, hence, in the tenor of his writings.

The poems in Volume I, then, demonstrate PBS's capacity to write verse in a range of stylistic registers. This early verse, even in its most abandoned forays into Sensibility, the Gothic, political satire, and vulgarity—perhaps especially in these most apparently idiosyncratic gestures—provides telling access to its own cultural moment, as well as to PBS's art and thought in general. Our Commentaries attempt to elucidate the cultural contexts for these poems and to confirm, refute, or modify many debated "facts" relating to PBS's biography. Through the course of our research, we have been able to revise the conventional dates for the completion and publication of several poems and to uncover new information about PBS's theory and practice of composition, as well as his relations with the printers and booksellers with whom he dealt. In this volume we add one new poem to the canon, *"Oh Wretched Mortal,"* and, in Appendixes, we discuss what is known about **God Save the King** and more than twenty other poems, either lost or else dubiously or incorrectly attributed to PBS, of which we include full texts of those that warrant such attention.

History of Shelley's Texts

A primary reason for historicizing the presentation of PBS's poetry lies in its notoriously vexed transmission. Aspects of this story have been detailed by other scholars and in our previous publications; here we can neither repeat this evidence nor discuss the details of our more recent findings (most of which appear in the Commentaries and Collations of this volume). Because a full textual history must necessarily await a reexamination of PBS's entire career and canon, here we simply outline the story from our current knowledge and perspective.

By the time of his drowning, in July 1822, PBS had published under his name (or publicly acknowledged during his maturity) just nine volumes of poetry: **Queen Mab, Alastor, Laon and Cythna** (which he almost immediately reissued as **The Revolt of Islam**), **Rosalind and Helen, The Cenci, Prometheus Unbound, Epipsychidion, Adonais,** and **Hellas.** Only four of these volumes contain shorter poems in addition to their title poems, but PBS had published **Mont Blanc** in **History of a Six Weeks' Tour** (which consists chiefly of prose based on the letters and journals of MWS and PBS) and, besides repeatedly attempting to publish the large body of poems in **The Esdaile Notebook,** had sent to periodicals several short poems that appeared anonymously or under pseudonyms. PBS also had arranged for **Œdipus Tyrannus; or, Swellfoot the Tyrant** to be published anonymously in London (where it was immediately suppressed), and he had sent to Leigh Hunt or Charles Ollier for publication fair copy MSS of **Julian and Maddalo, The Mask of Anarchy, Peter Bell the Third,** and **The Witch of Atlas,** as well as several political and art lyrics that he wished to be published—a few of which did appear in periodicals before or immediately following his death. Finally, he had given to his closest friends and confidants a number of personal lyrics and highly subversive poems on political and religious issues that he felt were not ready for publication.

Soon after PBS's death, MWS wrote to Charles Ollier, his principal publisher, requesting the return of the press copies of PBS's unpublished writings, as well as the unsold stock of his published works. From friends, she similarly gathered manuscripts and copies of his letters. Meanwhile, she pored over the mass of notebooks and loose sheets that represented the workshop remnants of PBS's poetic production. Many of the unpublished fragments are in the roughest of drafts, scrawled nearly indecipherably into notebooks wherever PBS could find space, so that sometimes drafts for different poems are jumbled together on the same page or a single poem is interspersed with others throughout a notebook or even continued in other notebooks without any indication. Working with her intimate and unequaled knowledge of PBS's hand and his habits of composition, MWS transcribed into a copybook now designated Bodleian MS. Shelley adds. d.7 what Irving Massey has described as "any and all interesting scraps from Shelley's papers" that she could glean, ultimately filling the notebook with more than one hundred poems and prose fragments.[2] In a companion notebook, now designated Bodleian MS. Shelley adds. d.9, MWS transcribed another collection, more obviously polished for publication, that includes some items from the first notebook. In still other notebooks she similarly transcribed and organized PBS's unpublished prose.

While preparing PBS's fragmentary and unreleased poetry for the press, MWS often had to decide which of the lines scattered through the MSS belonged to a single poem and in which order the stanzas belonged (since PBS frequently did not draft his poems sequentially). She provided names for untitled poems and polished the drafts that PBS would clearly have reworked before publishing—supplying punctuation, choosing among alternative words, and sometimes filling verbal gaps in the MSS, practices that she had followed while transcribing PBS's work when he was alive and could review her decisions. Without question, no one has had a greater impact on the editing and transmission of PBS's poetry than MWS. Until after 1946, moreover, other editors lacked access to the wide range of MSS from which she worked, leaving them unable to evaluate her editorial decisions or those of PBS's friends and nineteenth-century editors who similarly published poems and fragments that PBS never released during his lifetime from MSS to which they had special access.

Rather than immediately publishing all of PBS's works in a collective edition, MWS instead selected a volume of his more uncontroversial poetry. In *Posthumous Poems* (*1824*), she published not only the poems that survived in polished MSS, such as ***Julian and Maddalo, Prince Athanase, Letter to Maria Gisborne*** (slightly censored), and ***The Witch of Atlas,*** but she also added polished (and often truncated) versions of many poetic drafts and fragments—notably ***The Triumph of Life***—that she had transcribed from his working papers, together with ***Alastor*** and ***Mont Blanc*** (which she reprinted from their original volumes to make them better known).

After brisk early sales, however, ***Posthumous Poems*** was suppressed by order of PBS's father, upon whom MWS depended for money to support and educate her surviving son, and she was unable to fulfill her hopes of editing a collective edition of PBS's poetry until 1839. In the meantime, a series of radical, piratical, or otherwise marginal publishers—notably Richard Carlile, William Benbow, and John Ascham—kept much of PBS's poetry in print in England, while in Paris the English-born Galignani brothers enlisted the journalist Cyrus Redding to obtain the surreptitious help of MWS in correcting and adding to PBS's oeuvre for their collective edition of *The Poetical Works of Coleridge, Shelley, and Keats* (*1829*). The editions of Ascham and the Galignani brothers assumed special importance in the transmission of PBS's poetry when their pages provided MWS with the basis of her press copy for the 1839 edition.[3]

Throughout the 1830s, new poems by PBS were issued by his friends in books or periodicals, a renaissance of interest partly spurred by the publication of a phantom from PBS's youth: *The Wandering Jew,* PBS's earliest major poetic effort, which survived at Edinburgh in a revised holograph manuscript and (as we detail in this volume) appeared in two incomplete versions, first in an Edinburgh periodical in 1829 and then in a London one in 1831. In 1832, a decade after PBS's death, Leigh Hunt edited *The Mask of Anarchy,* Thomas Jefferson Hogg mentioned some of PBS's anonymous early poems in his *New Monthly Magazine* articles entitled "Percy Bysshe Shelley at Oxford," and Thomas Medwin published both a memoir and corrupt texts of some of his cousin's prose and poems, including three of the lyrics that PBS had inscribed to Jane Williams, first in the *Athenæum* and then in book form as *The Shelley Papers* (*1833*).

But MWS, whose foremost aim was to popularize PBS's poetry among early Victorian readers, did not include any of his writings prior to *Queen Mab* in her three basic editions of his *Poetical Works* (*1839, 1840,* and *1847*) or in the one-volume larger format editions that included these texts of the poetry together with a selection of letters and prose from *Essays, Letters from Abroad, Translations and Fragments,* which she originally published in two volumes in 1840. MWS and other early editors and publishers of PBS's writings seem, in fact, to have shared the interests of most editors and publishers of the Victorian period: they tried to enhance the poet's reputation and broaden the audience for his poetry both to spread his liberal ideas and to make as much money as possible. Though MWS and Leigh Hunt obviously believed in the intrinsic aesthetic value of PBS's writings, their first concern was to overcome prejudices against him among the establishment and the middle classes and, thus, to win him a place as a canonical rather than coterie poet. Hunt's introduction to *The Mask* (which he changed to *Masque*) *of Anarchy* attempts to soften PBS's image by recalling his aristocratic Whig background and emphasizing how many of the evils attacked by PBS in that prophetic poem had already been mitigated by the liberalization of British thought between 1819 and 1832, to which both Hunt and PBS had contributed.

MWS's first collective edition of *Poetical Works* (*1839*) continued to omit some of PBS's most outspoken mature political writings, including his attacks in *Queen Mab* on marriage, Christianity, and other established institutions of the age, as well as the entire texts of *Peter Bell the Third* and *Swellfoot the Tyrant*. Only after friends and some reviewers protested her bowdlerization of **Queen Mab** did MWS restore its text and include the two satirical poems in *1840*, but she continued to omit the poems that PBS had written before **Queen Mab**. MWS's monumental editions of the poetry—which begin with a section of major works chronologically ordered, followed by a section of the shorter poems organized by year of composition, and conclude with a section of juvenilia—set the pattern for most editions of PBS's poetry, many of which also include MWS's rich and emotionally compelling biographical notes to the poems.

The next wave of Shelleyan editors, epitomized by William Michael Rossetti (1829–1919) and Henry (Harry) Buxton Forman (1842–1917), were men who had admired PBS from youth and whose close friends were enthusiastic about his art and ideas. By the 1860s, they found that there was no really complete edition in print and that not only the piracies but even MWS's later editions, published by Edward Moxon and his successors, were textually corrupt. Rossetti and Forman both tried to solve these problems by tracking down friends and acquaintances of the poet, gaining insight to his character and ideas through the oral tradition, as well as gaining access to primary documents. But they ultimately chose to resolve textual cruxes in disparate ways. Rossetti, whose father, brother, and sister were poets and many of whose friends were artists and writers associated with the Pre-Raphaelite Brotherhood, was also the more sociable of the two editors. He gained access to otherwise unavailable Shelleyan textual sources and information by becoming friendly with Edward John Trelawny (through whom he met Jane Williams Hogg and received information from Claire Clairmont), through such friends as Richard Garnett and Edward Dowden (both of whom had entrée to the Shelley family collections at Boscombe Manor), and by visiting Italy (where he had relatives) to gain a sense of PBS's life there. But faced with typographical errors and other difficulties in the pages of the later printing of MWS's edition that served as his base text,[4] Rossetti often chose to adopt aesthetic solutions to textual cruxes, emending the texts where he believed that the metrics, diction, or logic were inferior, illogical, or otherwise "un-Shelleyan."

Forman, on the other hand, whenever he could afford to do so, bought first editions, manuscript letters, and some literary MSS of PBS for what eventually became the largest collection of its time relating to PBS, John Keats, and their contemporaries. From his study of these authorities, Forman adopted the conservative scholarly method of correcting the corrupted texts by comparing them with primary editions and (when he encountered them) MSS in the hand of PBS and MWS, the collation of which often enabled him to solve interpretive as well as textual problems. Nevertheless, Rossetti's editions of 1870 (2 vols.) and 1878 (3 vols.), published by the Moxon firm, were received as the official successors to MWS's texts.

Forman, by contrast, had a lesser-known publisher, and his four-volume edition of the poetry (1876–77, corr. 1880) and the four volumes of PBS's prose and letters that he added to complete his Library Edition of 1880 were considered too bulky and professional for general readers. For these and other reasons, Rossetti's text seems to have been far more widely disseminated throughout the last thirty years of the century, although Forman's 1876–77 edition of the **Poetical Works** revealed so many errors and problems in Rossetti's conjectural emendations for *1870* that Rossetti was forced to withdraw a number of them when he reedited it as *1878*. Forman's trimmed down two-volume edition of the poetry (*1882*) became the basis of F. S. Ellis's Shelley *Concordance* (1892) and was reissued with additions as the Aldine Edition (*1892F*).[5]

Later editors seemed unable to decide whether Rossetti's or Forman's editorial methodology was preferable. Although they introduced evidence from whatever new MSS or printings they personally uncovered, even those who understood the value of Forman's methods and claimed to base their texts directly on the best primary authorities generally used as press copy disbound copies of one or more prior editions, altered by introducing a handful of verbal emendations that suited their personal interpretations, while changing the punctuation and orthography on the basis of taste, logical reasoning, or the press's house style. The widely circulated Macmillan edition of Edward Dowden (*1890*), George Edward Woodberry's Centenary Edition (4 vols., *1892W*) and one-volume Cambridge Edition (*1901*), Thomas Hutchinson's Oxford Standard Authors (OSA) Edition (*1904*), C. D. Locock's Methuen editions (1906–8, *1911*), the four poetry volumes in the Julian Edition (1927–28, the work of Roger Ingpen), and many lesser editions from the mid-nineteenth century to the present sometimes resemble the texts of medieval scribes of biblical or Classical MSS who, lacking wide access to authoritative documents, freely emended cruxes according to their best understanding of the authors' intentions.

Shelleyan editors of the Victorian period who desired to check their educated judgments about textual problems against a full range of the documentary evidence were often unable to do so. For throughout the latter half of the nineteenth century, the bulk of PBS's holograph MSS were kept under lock and key by Sir Percy Florence and Jane, Lady Shelley, in a sanctum sanctorum at Boscombe Manor, the evidence from which reached the public only through periodic gleanings sponsored or approved by them, such as *Shelley Memorials* (*1859*), in which PBS's **Essay on Christianity** first appeared; Richard Garnett's *Relics of Shelley* (*1862*), which contained fragments of poetry and prose from a few notebooks, including the so-called "*Prologue to* **Hellas**"; and the archive of censored texts of letters and journals by the Shelleys and their intimates, arranged chronologically and privately printed in a multivolume set entitled *Shelley and Mary* (1886). Even this last was circulated chiefly to the friends of Sir Percy and Lady Shelley, frequently with sections considered too revealing snipped out by scissors and with personal caveats added by Lady Shelley herself. In 1892 (after the death of Sir Percy Florence Shelley in December 1889), Lady Shelley proposed to honor the centennial of PBS's birth by donating both his and MWS's letters, together with selected notebooks and relics, to the Bodleian Library (under restrictions about when and by whom they might be seen).[6] Using that collection, the German scholars Julius Zupitza and Joseph Schick studied the MSS of **Prometheus Unbound** in the 1890s, Locock published *An Examination of the Shelley Manuscripts in the Bodleian Library* (*1903*) and used his findings in the two editions of PBS's poetry mentioned above, and the French scholar André Koszul issued his editions of *Shelley's Prose in the Bodleian Manuscripts* (1910) and MWS's *Proserpine and Midas* (1922).

Between the two world wars and throughout the Modernist ascendancy, PBS's reputation in the academy sank to a low ebb throughout English-speaking nations, and little interest in the study of his MSS was generated. Moreover, the initial bequest to the Bodleian provided a selection of MSS too unrepresentative and inadequate to enable scholars to understand their precise authority vis-à-vis the larger cache of MSS that Lady Shelley simultaneously bequeathed to Sir John Shelley (later Shelley-Rolls, d. 1951). Fortunately, Sir John himself took an interest in them, and he cooperated with Roger Ingpen in producing private printings of an unbowdlerized text of PBS's translation of Plato's *Symposium,* together with PBS's introductory **Discourse on the Manners of the Ancient Greeks** (1931) and *Verse and Prose from the Manuscripts of Percy Bysshe Shelley* (*1934*).

In 1946, B. C. Barker-Benfield notes, Sir John Shelley-Rolls donated "his major run of notebooks to the Bodleian" and arranged for the remainder of the Boscombe Manor trove of papers and relics to be added to the Bodleian's collections after the death of his wife, which occurred in 1961 (*Shelley's Guitar,* xvii). The first person to take an extended interest in the 1946 gift was Neville Rogers, who first publicized the bequest of PBS's draft MSS to the Bodleian in British journals and later made them better known in *Shelley at Work* (1956), a volume that revealed much about a few of the Bodleian's Shelley MSS and the difficulty of deciphering them, though in a context that portrayed PBS as an intuitive Platonic thinker who had little interest in the practical details of life or art. Rogers viewed the chaotic state of the MSS as a vindication of his view (a common prejudice of his day) that PBS cared little for grammar or logic—a poet who grasped misty Platonic ideas but left the details of their articulation to be improved upon by his editors.

Soon after the first volume of Rogers's long-awaited Oxford English Text edition of *The Complete Poetical Works* of PBS appeared (*1972*), its texts were discovered to be chiefly reprints (with some added errors) of the texts in

Thomas Hutchinson's Oxford Standard Authors edition (*1904*), containing little new material besides the poems first published by Kenneth Neill Cameron in *The Esdaile Notebook* (*1964C*). The other poems that Rogers added were chiefly of doubtful authorship (see Appendix D of the present volume). In editing materials not found in Hutchinson, Rogers followed the principle of changing whatever he failed to understand. After a similarly inadequate second volume appeared in 1975, the general outcry against Rogers's edition by scholarly reviewers forced Oxford University Press to suspend its publication. Shelley scholars and critics, thus, have continued to lack a trustworthy complete scholarly edition and have recently relied on *Shelley's Poetry and Prose* (*1977*), the selective Norton Critical Edition edited by Donald H. Reiman and Sharon B. Powers.

The modern fortunes of Shelley's texts improved when G. M. Matthews, after correcting errors in the old Hutchinson OSA edition (corr. ed. *1970*), began reediting all of PBS's poetry for the Longman series of English poets, of which F. W. Bateson was the first General Editor. Matthews, however, was unable to complete the first volume before his untimely death in 1984, after which Kelvin Everest completed the research on Volume I of *The Poems of Shelley* (*1989*). The first of three proposed volumes (the second has not yet appeared), Volume I reflects scholarly care and editorial skill. Matthews and Everest assiduously studied the political, social, and intellectual life of PBS's times, uncovering many new sources and much evidence about the dating and circumstances of the composition of individual poems. They also examined all possible textual authorities (those in the U.K. more intensively than those in America), although Volume I, governed by the rules for the Longman editions (which Bateson conceived as a series of student textbooks), modernizes some of the punctuation and orthography and does not include complete collations of either the primary sources or intervening editions.

Matthews and Everest valuably attempted to publish PBS's poems and fragments in a rigorously chronological order (again, a desideratum in Bateson's conception of the series), thereby demonstrating PBS's development as a poet. As a result, however, *1989* mixes important poems that PBS published with recently recovered fragments that he had rejected and lines of lost poems quoted by his friends from memory decades after his death, thus obscuring the history of the poetic career that PBS had shaped and his contemporaries had witnessed, as well as separating poems that he intended to appear together and modify one another. Moreover, dating PBS's works—especially the early poems and the unreleased fragments—is notoriously difficult and often inconclusive, partly because we often lack sufficient evidence to draw secure conclusions and partly because (as recent studies have shown) PBS sometimes obfuscated the dates of his compositions for personal reasons. Arranging his poems in a suppositional order of composition thus often risks misleading rather than illuminating. Finally, the Longman series places its notes on the same page with the text—a practice that, however convenient for the college students for whom the series is intended, almost buries the texts of PBS's poems under the annotation when that is most comprehensive and helpful.

Whereas Matthews and Everest carried the editing of PBS's poetry as far as it could go using the chronological, reader-centered principles championed by the Longman series, we have undertaken a quite different task. We here present an authorially governed, historically focused, and text-centered edition that highlights the production, reception, and transmission of PBS's poetry. Our approach, based on Forman's example, has not been pursued seriously since 1880 and is best designed not only to address the problematic textual history of PBS's work but also to make effective use of the wealth of new textual evidence made available by the publication of *Shelley and his Circle: 1773–1822*, the catalogue edition of the Carl H. Pforzheimer Collection, New York Public Library (*SC*, 10 vols. to date; 1961–), the Shelley volumes of *Manuscripts of the Younger Romantics* (*MYR: Shelley*, 9 vols., 1985–96), and *The Bodleian Shelley Manuscripts* (*BSM*, 23 vols., 1986–99), which were in the early stages of publication at the time of Matthews's death.

Editing on Historical Principles

CPPBS presents the poems that PBS intended to publish, according to the groupings he arranged and in the chronological order in which he hoped to issue them. Within each such volume or gathering we place the individual poems, wherever possible, in the order that PBS planned for their publication. Those poems that he released only privately to close friends, without attempting publication, are arranged chronologically in separate groupings according to defined periods of his life and, within those groups, in the order that he sent or gave them to friends. We edit the released poems to represent, insofar as the surviving evidence permits, the texts that PBS intended his first reader(s) to see at the time he released them. We correct, according to the principles outlined below, errata in PBS's MSS and first editions, whether or not he is known to have noted them as such, and we attempt to uncover and extirpate errors of the press and later editorial emendations that reflect the judgment of later times and other consciousnesses. Our typical Text will be a critical redaction (sometimes called an "ideal state") of a single version that PBS chose to release to a particular public on a specific occasion. Readers will thus have before them discrete versions that reflect the author's creative thinking about a poetic whole that he intended to release to a historically identifiable audience, rather than a conflation of his judgments at different times, meant for different audiences.

Each released poem, then, will appear in the version in which PBS released it, following his preferred standards of grammar, pointing, and orthography as established by his MSS and published editions. In correcting this base text, we have observed the general principle articulated by Coleridge at the beginning of Chapter 12 of *Biographia Literaria:* "until you understand a writer's ignorance, presume yourself ignorant of his understanding." We have consequently been able to establish the credibility of unusual or doubtful readings in our Text by finding them among the forms and idioms accepted by PBS's contemporaries, as recorded in grammars and dictionaries used during his time, in addition to the *OED* and other scholarly works on the language of his era. In some cases, PBS's supposed errors or eccentricities prove to be merely forms and meanings conventionally correct for a person of his day and class, and we indicate these instances as succinctly as possible. Contemporary editions of the poetry of his peers and predecessors, as well as concordances to their poetry, have also helped us identify the specific sources of some unusual forms, diction, and allusions that he adopted. These sources are sometimes found in the works of writers that PBS is known to have admired during his artistic development, but in other cases our search led to writers and works in whom his interest was formerly a matter of speculation. Aspects of the usage of PBS's time and facets of his intentions are still obscure, and were we to emend without knowledge, we might destroy evidence useful to other readers and researchers in expanding scholarly understanding. Finally, PBS's punctuation was (according to the practice of his time) primarily rhetorical rather than grammatical, and it cannot be modernized without seriously compromising the phrasing and emphases—and, hence, both the metrics and the meaning—of his poems.

In general, therefore, we do not emend the words, orthography, and punctuation of our copy-text unless it contains a reading that cannot be justified through historical research or unless we discover strong evidence against it, either from other extant primary authorities or from PBS's own practices in parallel situations. We are willing to accept as much inconsistency in the spelling and punctuation of his texts as PBS did, judging by variations in his own MSS and in printed texts derived directly from them. Some variants in spelling may provide evidence of authorship—especially in the volume of ***Original Poetry*** "by Victor and Cazire" (***V&C***), where small features of orthography and diction can be important clues to distinguishing compositions by PBS from those by his sister Elizabeth Shelley; sometimes anomalous usage contributes to an understanding of either the nature of the MS underlying the first printed text or the later history of the textual transmission of the work.

We attempt, however, to avoid transmitting obvious errors that PBS elsewhere tried to correct or allowed his amanuenses and printers to correct for him. We have determined over our years of study that he miswrote certain words frequently though not consistently, among them a whole range of words containing *ie* and *ei* (e.g., *thier, feirce, sieze,* and *vermiel*). These were errors that, once discovered, he tried to eliminate from his printed works. In his early MSS and in publications (especially where, as with *V&C*, the compositors seem to have followed his copy blindly), there are many omissions or misplacements of the apostrophe for the possessive case—as well as apostrophes added anomalously to simple plurals. We have emended such solecisms (and noted them as errors) wherever there seemed to be no possibility of another reading of the sentence that would justify PBS's practice.

In his draft MSS, PBS frequently omitted marks of punctuation, including final stops, quotation marks, and commas within a series of three or more nouns. He or his amanuenses usually added these conventional marks during the fair-copying or the printing process; they appear in all the volumes published under his supervision during his maturity, but some are missing in his earliest printed texts, notably *V&C* and **Posthumous Fragments of Margaret Nicholson (PF)**. We try to identify and correct all such readings that the predominance of the surviving evidence shows are erroneous in PBS's terms, not ours. Whenever we emend our copy-text, we signal the change by giving the siglum of the variant at the foot of the page in ***boldface italic*** type (e.g., ***1810***). Also, in the Commentaries we note the emendations and outline our reasons for making them. Where other responsible editors have emended the text but we do not, we explain why we have refrained from doing so. (After making a point a few times for a particular poem, we let these explanations suffice for analogous cases.) In each specific place where a typographical error, rather than a pattern of idiosyncratic usage, mars the sense—sometimes even in those volumes that PBS himself superintended through the printing process (as in line 49 of the second poem in *V&C*, where the compositor typeset "gaol" instead of "goal" in a verse letter probably written by "Cazire," i.e., Elizabeth Shelley)—we emend the text and note our emendation.

Released "Poems" Distinguished from Unreleased "Poetry"

No matter how candid and confessional the poets of the Romantic age might appear when compared with their predecessors, they usually released poetic records of their thoughts and feelings to the world only after they had successfully transmuted those ideas and emotions into artistic forms. When PBS grappled with his material in attempts at composition but failed to resolve the drafts into forms that he considered worthy expressions of his values, he usually abandoned those attempts, though he often recycled images and ideas from such discarded drafts in later poems. Being fully aware of how interesting and how biographically and interpretively revealing these unfinished pieces can be, we include not only such fragments found in other editions but new ones gleaned from the recent work on *The Bodleian Shelley Manuscripts, The Manuscripts of the Younger Romantics, Shelley and his Circle,* and our own researches for **CPPBS**. We edit them, however, not as finished *poems* (as MWS and most subsequent editors have done), but as fragmentary *poetry*—a distinction that PBS himself makes in *A Defence of Poetry,* based upon one that Coleridge earlier proposed in *Biographia Literaria.* These works in progress, sketches, and bits of poetry should not be analyzed or judged on the same terms as polished works of art. Useful as the unreleased fragments are to students of the poet and his age, such unfinished pieces are not part of PBS's self-presentation to his contemporaries and ought to be edited and studied under different rules.

Instead of placing the unreleased fragments in a chronological order that is factitious (many of them cannot be dated relative to one another or to PBS's public poetry and none has a date of completion or release), we plan to arrange them according to the periodical or edition in which they were first published or—if they appear only in transcriptions of MSS in either *The Bodleian Shelley Manuscripts* or *The Manuscripts of the Younger Romantics: Shelley*—to group them with other poetry found in the same MSS or notebooks in which they survive. Thus, all the fragments and smaller, unpolished poems found in Bodleian MS. Shelley adds. e.7 (with the drafts for *Hellas*), except those already published from a later or more finished copy, will appear with the other poetic drafts and fragments found in that notebook (*BSM,* XVI, ed. Reiman and Neth). The Text of each fragment will be the latest extant version that appears to have had PBS's approval, but we may sometimes compare those versions, through selective quotation at the foot of the page or in notes, with other versions of the same fragments that were published, in a polished (sometimes corrupted) form after PBS's death.

By the same general principle, we do not treat as independent works preliminary drafts for—or clearly abandoned or rejected fragments of—finished poems; when we include these false starts or rejected digressions, we label them "Supplements" and print them immediately following the completed, public poems to which they pertain. All such fragments and drafts, like the unreleased poetry in general, will be presented diplomatically to the extent appropriate to each individual case. For some short, undeveloped fragments, all cancellations may be printed along with the uncanceled text. Longer and more substantial independent fragments, such as *The Triumph of Life,* will be given clearer form in hypothesized reading texts, with substantive cancellations and rejected passages presented in collations at the foot of the page or in the Supplements following the poetic fragment.

Like other poets, PBS frequently gave copies of his poems to friends, sometimes using their private reactions to gauge whether the poems were ready to be published. When there exists a later published version (or a later MS prepared for publication), we always include that public version, while treating the privately released version as a way-station toward the public poem by collating it as an authority that may help reveal typographical errors or explain other apparent anomalies in the public text. Where there exist alternative texts that PBS released to the public, or personal poems that he gave in distinctive versions to different friends, we include critical texts of each of the two or three versions, treating them as related poems destined for different audiences and perhaps embodying different meanings. By comparing such multiple versions, released at different times or prepared for distinct audiences, readers will be better able to chart PBS's emerging intentions and the means by which he attempted to reach a public or to perfect his artistry, as well as how he varied the theme or tone of a poem, depending upon the circumstances under which he released it and who his intended readers were.

We seek to avoid, however, separating PBS into two Shelleys—the private person whose inner feelings are documented in his unreleased poems and private letters and the public poet who, during a period of great social and ideological upheaval, was struggling with other writers for the hearts and minds of the British establishment and reading public. To this end, our Commentaries on the various volumes and groupings and on individual passages and lines link these and other facets of the complex individual whose life and ideas, writings and art, we have studied holistically for many years. We also include as Supplements not only those of PBS's drafts that relate most closely to the composition of his completed and released poems but, when feasible (i.e., where these surviving drafts will not overwhelm or dilute the finished poems), we group together such abandoned fragments as fall within the chronological limits of the volume on the basis of their source-manuscripts at chronologically appropriate intervals. (This we can do in the early volumes of ***CPPBS,*** where the surviving drafts of the poems written in England and Switzerland are less voluminous than those of the Italian period.) Our Commentaries on such holograph drafts and rejected fragments will similarly relate these private versions and abandoned attempts to the ways in which PBS made use of similar language, feelings, and ideas in poems that he did release to the public.

Presentation of Texts and Editorial Apparatus

Although the nature of the surviving textual authorities and histories of particular poems will dictate variations in the general pattern, PBS's poems and their apparatus will normally be arranged as follows: the Text of each book-length poem, multi-poem volume arranged by PBS, or group of separate poems gathered by us will be introduced by a brief headnote that identifies the date, nature, origin, and title of the unit and cites the pages in this volume where the reader can find our editorial Commentary, as well as locate the Historical Collations.

So that readers may encounter the living poetry without the weight of scholarly impedimenta, we devote the front of the book to PBS's poetry and the primary authorities that may warrant textual consideration, follow these Texts with our Commentaries in the succeeding section, and place the Historical Collations at the end for the use of analytical readers and textual scholars. Readers of our Commentaries will, we hope, find useful much of the information gathered there from a number of research libraries, but even scholars who attempt to understand the intricacies of PBS's art and thought and, possibly, feel an even deeper appreciation of his genius, may gladly return to his poetry in a format that approximates, if it cannot duplicate, the clarity of presentation in which his works appeared to his first readers.

Collation of Primary Authorities

All *verbal* variants and most variants in orthography, punctuation, and format (e.g., stanza numbers, spacing breaks between stanzas or sections of verse, and patterns of indention) appear in our primary collations, those at the foot of the page containing the poetic Text. Whenever our Text emends the copy-text (or base text), the siglum of the resultant variant appears in ***boldface italic*** type. Primary authorities customarily collated at the foot of the page include:

1. any MS of the poem in the hand of PBS, MSS copied from his holographs by those acting as his amanuenses, and corrections to printed texts supplied either in his own hand or in the hand of MWS acting as his amanuensis

2. all authorized texts of PBS's poems published during his lifetime and MWS's editions of his poems published in 1824, 1839, and 1840 (adding the 1847 edition, when relevant)

3. unauthorized editions that may contain authoritative readings from sources unknown or unavailable to us or that have significantly influenced the textual traditions of a poem; for example, some versions supplied by

Thomas Medwin may be based on contemporary documents now lost, and some pirated editions that MWS used as the base text for *1839* led to errors in her text that were perpetuated by later editors who based their texts on hers, thinking that these errors were purposeful emendations by MWS based on lost authorities

4. the earliest scholarly edition in which a poem was first based on (or significantly corrected from) an authoritative MS

Historical Collations

The Historical Collations, which precede the Appendix section, trace the history of specific readings through significant editions that, though not always based on primary witnesses, deserve attention because of their influence on subsequent texts and criticism. By recording all verbal variants and significant changes in punctuation and orthography in each historical edition collated in Volume I, we aim to provide scholars with concrete evidence about the conventions employed by different editors, clues to the precedents that each followed, their use of (and attitudes toward) the primary textual authorities, a sense of their relative accuracy or reliability, and the sources of the variants that appear in other, derivative editions and in the work of literary critics.

Although we present the materials relevant to a history of editorial work on PBS, we do not aspire to combine with that a history of typographical practice in England and America during the past two centuries. We therefore usually omit from our Historical Collations variants that seem to us purely formal conventions originating with printers or publishers—the length of indentations, the use of full capitals, small capitals, and the appearance of italic or Gothic type in titles and subtitles of poems—practices subject to the selection of fonts available to the printers and the conventions of the compositorial staff and, more recently, to the preferences of publishers, book designers, and their style manuals. Sometimes the start of a new poem, canto, or poetic paragraph has been indicated by indenting the first line, sometimes by placing the first word or two in large capital letters, sometimes in large and small capitals. Unless there is reason to suppose (e.g., through evidence in PBS's underlying manuscript of the poem in question) that these indications are in some way significant to the author's intention, we have not collated such variants. In our Text, however, we try to follow the practice indicated either by PBS's most polished manuscript, or the printing of the work most likely to have received his prior instructions and/or subsequent approval.

In a few cases, where there are doubts about whether the features of a text are authorial, typographical, or editorial, we have collated them to be on the safe side. Forman, the most conservative of our predecessors, announced that he numbered the stanzas of long poems to facilitate reference to specific stanzas and lines. Other editors did also, some using roman numerals, some arabic. Since we (like other recent editors) employ line numbers in the margin, we might merely note the differences and skip the detailed collation of these stanza numbers. But we feel that some of PBS's poems (particularly those in ballad stanzas, such as **The Mask of Anarchy**) had their character somewhat altered by the addition of roman numerals, even in the first edition, published by Leigh Hunt. We therefore collate these features as possible influences upon readers of the poem, especially because later editors (who also employ marginal line numbering) retained the stanza numbers that were originally added simply for ease of reference.

Among the textually or historically important critical editions of PBS's poems that will frequently be cited in the Historical Collations are those edited by Rossetti (*1870, 1878*); Forman (*1876* [pub. 1876–77], *1882,* and *1892F*); Woodberry (*1892W, 1901*); Hutchinson (*1904;* and as revised by Matthews, *1970*); Ingpen and Peck (Julian Edition) I–IV (*1927*); Rogers (*1972*); Reiman and Powers (*1977;* using 3rd issue, pub. 1982); Matthews and Everest (*1989*); and Shelley's **Letters,** edited by Frederick L. Jones (appears as **Letters** in our Commentaries and as *1964J* in our Collations), as well as some recent critical editions of individual poems and small selections of poetry. For a complete listing of textual authorities collated in this volume, see the list of abbreviations that follows.

Commentaries on the Poems: Textual and Informational Notes

PBS's own notes to his public and nonpublic poetry, like his prefaces and the other prose published with the poetry, appear with the Texts of the poems, located according to their placement in the copy-text of the volume or poem in question. The prefaces and notes supplied by MWS in her editions of his poetry dated *1824, 1839, 1840,* and (where relevant) *1847* are reprinted in appendixes to the volumes to which they pertain; they begin in Volume II, since she wrote nothing about poems in the present volume.

Our textual and informational notes appear in the second section of this volume as Commentaries, with running headings that identify the specific pages of the Text to which each page of the notes pertains. An introductory section to each of PBS's volumes or groupings of poems discusses the history of the composition and publication (or other release) of that poem or collection, its original reception, its textual authorities and transmission, and its place in PBS's intellectual and aesthetic development. Following this introductory commentary to the collective unit, our notes to individual poems, sections, and lines explain and support editorial choices made in the Text and point out the implications of the principal deletions, additions, and other revisions by PBS before he either completed or abandoned the work. When citing and quoting particular words of PBS's poems from the Texts in **CPPBS,** we <u>underscore</u> them, rather than using quotation marks, to distinguish references to the Text from variant readings and quotations from other poets and scholars.

Interspersed with our textual notes are informational notes that provide the reader with basic factual information needed to understand the significance of individual words, passages, or poems. Since this is a scholarly edition, to be used primarily by those who intend to exercise their own critical judgment and who, in many cases, may intend (or be required) to write interpretive essays or books on PBS's poetry, we try not to impose our judgment beyond the demonstrable evidence. We both document the sources of the information presented and indicate the degree of doubt inhering in our inferences—including some broad speculations and hypothetical scenarios—that can be usefully drawn from the established facts.

Historical Sources and Perspectives in the Annotation

Our statements on PBS and his immediate circle are based upon more original research than are our statements regarding other contemporary or historical figures and events, for which we often rely on standard authorities. All such research and reference authorities are cited by conventional abbreviations, given in italics. We also consult other sources, earlier than or contemporary with PBS, to see what meaning and associations a person, event, book, or phrase might have evoked in his day and, therefore, what meaning his use of it was likely to have conveyed to his audience within its particular poetic context.

For biographical and historical information we start with the *Annual Register (AR), Dictionary of National Biography (DNB),* and *Encyclopædia Britannica (Encyc. Brit.* + copyright date); for the forms and meaning of words in the poems of PBS, we begin with the *Oxford English Dictionary (OED)* and three contemporary dictionaries begun in the eighteenth century that went through numerous editions and were popularly known as *Bailey's, Johnson's,* or *Entick's Dictionary.* For bibliographical information, we rely on the *National Union Catalogue (NUC),* the *New Cambridge Bibliography of English Literature (NCBEL),* and the *Nineteenth-Century Short Title Catalogue (NSTC),* as well as on information garnered from Online Computer Library Center's WorldCat and other on-line catalogues. Where a book on which we rely is either unique or especially rare, we identify the library in which it is to be found.

Finally, in the last stages of our checking of Volume I, we supplemented the research of our first five years of gathering and checking antecedents and allusions to words and phrases in PBS's verse and notes by using the

Chadwyck-Healey Literature On-Line databases (cited as Chadwyck-Healey *Lion*), a resource that provides a more comprehensive picture of the usage of words and idioms by eighteenth- and nineteenth-century authors—though we frequently concluded that PBS probably derived his interest in and understanding of words or phrases from his Latin studies, Shakespeare, Milton, the Bible, or another obvious source to which other writers owed similar debts.

In referring to PBS and the time when he composed a particular poem, we use the adjective *contemporary* generally to refer to events, people, and attitudes of the period between the French Revolution (1789) and the Reform Bills of 1832–33; events before this period we call *historical*, while those after it are termed *modern* or *recent*. In annotating very specific elements in PBS's poetry, the focus of the "contemporary" period shrinks to the years between the time that PBS (b. 1792) would have become aware of the matter under discussion and the date of the poem or event annotated; conversely, when discussing later editions of his poems and their textual history, we may use *contemporary* in relation, not to PBS himself, but to the editor or the period of textual history under discussion; *contemporary* never refers to our own lives and times—always to those of the people and events being annotated.

NOTES

1. The term *diplomatic* derives from *De re diplomatica* (1681), Dom Jean Mabillon's groundbreaking study of criteria for authenticating medieval charters and other official documents, but it has been neither clearly defined nor consistently used as it pertains to studies of texts from the age of print. The term is not indexed in the introductions to bibliography by R. B. McKerrow (1927) and Philip Gaskell (1972) or in James Thorpe's *Principles of Textual Criticism* (1972). *Webster's Third New International Dictionary* gives as a synonym *paleographic;* "*esp.:* exactly reproducing the original," which is the general sense of its use by G. Thomas Tanselle in his essay "Classical, Biblical, and Medieval Textual Editing and Modern Criticism" (*Studies in Bibliography*, 1983; rpt. in Tanselle's *Textual Criticism and Modern Editing* [1990], 280–81). There are many references to diplomatic transcription in the front matter to various volumes of *The Bodleian Shelley Manuscripts* (e.g., VI, xxxiii, n. 3) and *The Manuscripts of the Younger Romantics*, but because these comments relate to page-by-page transcriptions of notebooks often containing two or more texts on the same page, they do not pertain precisely to our use of the term *diplomatic* in **CPPBS**, a critical edition of individual texts.

In *Textual Scholarship: An Introduction* (Garland, 1992), David C. Greetham usefully distinguishes between a *facsimile* and a *diplomatic transcript* (350): whereas the former "attempts to reproduce the actual physical appearance of the original ... by observing such features as the original lineation, type-size and type-face in the reprint," the latter "dispenses with any attempt at such scrupulous fidelity to appearance, and concentrates primarily on the textual content of the original, reproducing the exact spelling, punctuation, and capitalization (usually) of the *diploma* (the document), but transcribing the text into a different type-face, with different lineation (except in verse, of course)." Our diplomatic editing of PBS's poetic fragments will not only represent the lineation of the verses but indicate blank spaces proportionately and note other features of holograph manuscripts that may be relevant to the author's intention but are not germane to scribal transcripts or historical documents. Diplomatic editors should also exercise critical judgment, because they stand in the same relation to the author (here PBS) as ambassadors do to their governments: their duty is to convey the text of an author's *message* with precise accuracy, even when its essence must be translated into another medium (e.g., from manuscript to print). Thus, our diplomatic transcriptions include not only the verbal text, with its orthography and punctuation, but also such additional evidence as placement, spacing, cancellations, and marginal references that illuminate the development and structure of the poetic draft being represented. But to transmit its meaning faithfully may also require us to omit random marks, blots, and parts of other drafts by PBS that intertwine with the text being transcribed.

2. *Posthumous Poems of Shelley: Mary Shelley's Fair Copy Book* (Montreal: McGill–Queen's University Press, 1969), 7; see also Irving Massey's photofacsimile edition of Bodleian MS. Shelley adds. d.7 in *BSM*, II (1987). Recent students of MWS have advanced alternative analyses that contest some of Massey's conclusions.

3. Charles H. Taylor, Jr., provided the seminal textual analysis of the role of unauthorized or pirated editions in the textual transmission of PBS's poetry in *The Early Collected Editions of Shelley's Poems* (Yale University Press, 1958). For a discussion of the textual and social significance of **Posthumous Poems** and the piracies between 1821 and 1839, see Neil Fraistat, "Illegitimate Shelley: Radical Piracy and the Textual Edition as Cultural Performance," *PMLA* 109 (May 1994): 409–23.

4. The once loose pages of Rossetti's press copy for *1870*, mainly extracted from late reprints of MWS's edition, but supplemented and emended in his hand, were later rebound in two volumes and are now in the Carl H. Pforzheimer Collection of Shelley and His Circle, New York Public Library.

5. For a general discussion of Rossetti and Forman as editors, see Donald H. Reiman, *Romantic Texts and Contexts* (University of Missouri Press, 1987), 86–93.

6. This bequest was actually delivered to the Bodleian in 1893. For a detailed record of the Bodleian's acquisitions of Shelleyan books and manuscripts and their relation to those in other collections, see B. C. Barker-Benfield, *Shelley's Guitar: An Exhibition . . . to Mark the Bicentenary of the Birth of Percy Bysshe Shelley* (Oxford: Bodleian Library, 1992), xvi–xxii.

Abbreviations

Principles of Abbreviation and Citation

To compress the Commentaries, we use PBS and MWS in references to Percy Bysshe Shelley and Mary Wollstonecraft Shelley and we abbreviate the titles of PBS's works and of scholarly sources; but to facilitate comprehension, we employ commonsense methods that the reader can either infer or readily learn. In each Commentary to a major section of Texts, a title of a poem by PBS first appears in full, together with its abbreviated form — for example, ***Queen Mab*** (***QM***) and ***Mont Blanc*** (***MB***). ***Bold italics*** distinguish his titles (whether a separately published volume or a smaller work) from those by other writers, which appear in *light italic*. Readers will thus recognize at once a work of PBS's canon. This rule includes the standard edition of his ***Letters***, edited by F. L. Jones, abbreviated thus in the Commentaries, although the same edition is identified in collations by the siglum *1964J*. The single volume of ***Prose*** (1993) edited by the late E. B. Murray is abbreviated ***Prose***/EBM. (Until that Oxford edition is completed, we must cite and quote texts of PBS's later prose from a variety of sources.)

Major editions of PBS's poetry that we collate or cite frequently, either in the edition as a whole or in a particular volume, are abbreviated by italicized date codes (e.g., *1989*), as listed below. In collations, the cited volume of a multivolume series or edition may be separated from the abbreviation for the work by a slash, as SC/II or *1927*/VII. Scholarly works to which we refer most frequently are identified by abbreviated titles, while others to which we refer repeatedly within a particular Commentary are given nonce abbreviations. Modern scholarly books other than critical editions of PBS's writings are cited by author, title (abbreviated, if this can be done without confusion), and year of publication, their publishers and places of publication being accessible through standard bibliographies and catalogues. In general, sources in literary or scholarly periodicals will be cited by author and by date, volume, abbreviated title, and relevant page(s) of the periodical; the title of the cited article, note, letter, or review will be given only when the authorship is anonymous, or identification might otherwise be difficult (e.g., when references to the same topic appear in multiple articles within an issue or volume).

Each volume of ***CPPBS*** will contain its own list of editions of PBS's poetry and reference materials relevant to the Texts and Commentaries therein. When referring to a unique or specific authority—a manuscript (MS—plural, MSS), or an annotated or especially rare printed edition—we identify it by its location, using a code for the institution or collection in which it can be found—for example, Bod for Bodleian Library, Oxford. When citing both a manuscript and a printed edition held by the same collection and we refer to the former, we add "MS" to the code (e.g., MS Pfz). Unique textual authorities belonging to individuals or institutions that are not represented in our list of abbreviations will receive nonce codes within the Commentaries that discuss them.

In our transcriptions of MSS, words canceled with strikeover lines indicate authorial deletions, letters or blank spaces enclosed by square brackets ([ ]) indicate partially or wholly illegible characters, spaces enclosed by angle brackets (< >) represent words or characters missing because of damage to the paper. When quoting such transcriptions by other scholars, we sometimes retain or modify their editorial symbols with appropriate explanations.

Abbreviations Used in Volume One

LIBRARIES

Berg	Henry W. and Albert A. Berg Collection, New York Public Library
BL	British Library
Bod	Bodleian Library, Oxford University
Cam	Cambridge University Library
Del	University of Delaware Library
Harv	Houghton Library, Harvard University
Htn	The Huntington Library, San Marino, California
JHU	Johns Hopkins University Libraries
LC	Library of Congress
Md	University of Maryland, College Park
NYPL	New York Public Library
PMgn	Pierpont Morgan Library
Pfz	Carl H. Pforzheimer Collection of Shelley and His Circle, New York Public Library
Tx	Humanities Research Center, University of Texas at Austin
UCL	University College, London

EDITIONS OF AND TEXTUAL SOURCES FOR SHELLEY'S POETRY

DW	*The Devil's Walk* (1812)
Esd	*The Esdaile Notebook* (released 1813)
Laon	*Laon and Cythna; or, The Revolution of the Golden City: A Vision of the Nineteenth Century in the Stanza of Spenser* (1817; revised and reissued in 1818 as *The Revolt of Islam*)
PF	*Posthumous Fragments of Margaret Nicholson* (1810)
QM	*Queen Mab; A Philosophical Poem: with Notes* (1813)
R&H	*Rosalind and Helen: A Modern Eclogue* (1819)
St.Irv	*St. Irvyne; or, The Rosicrucian: A Romance* (1811)
To EFG#1	First verse letter to Edward Fergus Graham: "As you will see I wrote to you" (14 May 1811)
To EFG#2	"Dear dear dear dear dear dear Græme!" (7 June 1811)
V&C	*Original Poetry* "by Victor and Cazire" (1810)
WJ	*The Wandering Jew; or, The Victim of the Eternal Avenger* (1810)
1810	*Original Poetry* "by Victor and Cazire." London: J. J. Stockdale, 1810.
1810PF	*Posthumous Fragments of Margaret Nicholson: Being Poems Found Amongst the Papers of That Noted Female Who Attempted the Life of the King in 1786.* Oxford: J. Munday, 1810.
1811	*St. Irvyne; or, The Rosicrucian: A Romance.* By A Gentleman Of The University Of Oxford. London: Printed For J. J. Stockdale, 41, Pall Mall. 1811.
1812	*The Devil's Walk: A Ballad.* Public Record Office, England: File number: H.O. 42/127, f. 426.
1813	*Queen Mab; A Philosophical Poem: with Notes.*
1824	*Posthumous Poems of Percy Bysshe Shelley* [ed. Mary W. Shelley]. London: John and Henry L. Hunt, 1824.
1829	*The Poetical Works of Coleridge, Shelley, and Keats* [ed. Cyrus Redding]. Paris: A. and W. Galignani, 1829.
1833	*The Shelley Papers: Original Poems and Papers by Percy Bysshe Shelley*, ed. Thomas Medwin. London: Whittaker, Treacher & Co., 1833.
1834	*Works of Percy Bysshe Shelley, with His Life.* 2 vols. London: John Ascham, 1834.
1839	*The Poetical Works of Percy Bysshe Shelley*, ed. Mrs. Shelley. 4 vols. London: Edward Moxon, 1839.

1840 The Poetical Works of Percy Bysshe Shelley, ed. Mrs. Shelley. London: Edward Moxon, 1840 (on printed title page; engraved title page reads: 1839).

1847 The Poetical Works of Percy Bysshe Shelley, ed. Mrs. Shelley. 3 vols. London: Edward Moxon, 1847.

1859 Shelley Memorials, from Authentic Sources, ed. Lady Shelley [assisted by Edmund Ollier]. London: Smith, Elder & Co., 1859.

1862 Relics of Shelley, ed. Richard Garnett. London: Edward Moxon, 1862.

1870 The Poetical Works of Percy Bysshe Shelley, ed. William Michael Rossetti. 2 vols. London: E. Moxon, Son, & Co., 1870.

c. 1870PF Type facsimile of **Posthumous Fragments of Margaret Nicholson** [prepared by R. H. Shepherd, circa 1870].

1876 The Poetical Works of Percy Bysshe Shelley, ed. H[arry] Buxton Forman. 4 vols. London: Reeves & Turner, 1876–77.

1878 The Poetical Works of Percy Bysshe Shelley, ed. William Michael Rossetti. 3 vols. London: E. Moxon, Son & Co., 1878.

1880 The Works of Percy Bysshe Shelley in Verse and Prose, ed. H[arry] Buxton Forman. 8 vols. London: Reeves & Turner, 1880.

1882 The Poetical Works of Percy Bysshe Shelley, ed. H[arry] Buxton Forman. 2 vols. London: Reeves & Turner, 1882.

1888 The Poetical Works of Percy Bysshe Shelley, ed. Richard Herne Shepherd. 3 vols. London: Chatto & Windus, 1888.

1890 The Poetical Works of Percy Bysshe Shelley, ed. Edward Dowden. London: Macmillan & Co., 1890.

1892F The Poetical Works of Percy Bysshe Shelley, ed. H[arry] Buxton Forman. 5 vols. [Aldine Edition] London and New York: George Bell & Sons, 1892.

1892W The Complete Poetical Works of Percy Bysshe Shelley, ed. George Edward Woodberry. Centenary Edition. 4 vols. Boston and New York: Houghton, Mifflin, 1892.

1898 Type facsimile of **Original Poetry** "by Victor and Cazire," with an introduction by Richard Garnett. London and New York: John Lane, 1898.

1901 The Complete Poetical Works of Shelley, ed. George Edward Woodberry. Cambridge Edition. Cambridge, Mass.: Houghton, Mifflin, 1901.

1903 C[harles] D. Locock. *An Examination of the Shelley*

	Manuscripts in the Bodleian Library. Oxford: Clarendon Press, 1903.
1904	*The Complete Poetical Works of Percy Bysshe Shelley*, ed. Thomas Hutchinson. Oxford: Clarendon Press, 1904. (Reset 1905 and 1934 as Oxford Standard Authors Edition; corrected by G. M. Matthews and reset, 1970).
1911	*The Poems of Percy Bysshe Shelley*, ed. C[harles] D. Locock. 2 vols. London: Methuen, 1911.
1927	*The Complete Works of Percy Bysshe Shelley*, ed. Roger Ingpen and Walter E. Peck. 10 vols. Julian Edition. London: Ernest Benn; New York: Charles Scribner's Sons, 1926–30.
1934	*Verse and Prose from the Manuscripts of Percy Bysshe Shelley*, ed. Sir John C. E. Shelley-Rolls, Bart., and Roger Ingpen. London: privately printed, 1934.
1959	*Shelley's* **Prometheus Unbound**: *A Variorum Edition*, ed. Lawrence John Zillman. Seattle: University of Washington Press, 1959.
1964C	**The Esdaile Notebook:** *A Volume of Early Poems, by Percy Bysshe Shelley*, edited by Kenneth Neill Cameron from the Original Manuscript in The Carl H. Pforzheimer Library. New York: Alfred A. Knopf, 1964.
1964J	See **Letters,** below.
1964M	*Shelley: Selected Poems and Prose*, ed. G[eoffrey] M. Matthews. London: Oxford University Press, 1964.
1968	*Shelley's* **Prometheus Unbound**: *The Text and the Drafts; Toward a Modern Definitive Edition*, ed. Lawrence John Zillman. New Haven: Yale University Press, 1968.
1970	*The Complete Poetical Works of Percy Bysshe Shelley*, ed. Thomas Hutchinson, corrected by G. M. Matthews. Oxford Standard Authors Edition. Oxford: Oxford University Press, 1970. (This text, which corrects *1904* locally, is cited as *1970* only where it departs from that parent edition.)
1972	*The Complete Poetical Works of Percy Bysshe Shelley*, ed. Neville Rogers. Volume I, 1802–1813; Volume II, 1814–1817. Oxford: Clarendon Press, 1972 (Vol. I), 1975 (Vol. II).
1972C	Judith Chernaik. *The Lyrics of Shelley.* Cleveland: Case Western Reserve University Press, 1972.
1977	*Shelley's Poetry and Prose*, ed. Donald H. Reiman and Sharon B. Powers. New York: Norton, 1977 (3rd printing, corrected, 1982).
1977W	*Percy Bysshe Shelley: Selected Poems*, ed. Timothy Webb. Everyman's University Library. London: Dent, 1977.

1989   *The Poems of Shelley,* ed. G. M. Matthews and Kelvin Everest. 1 vol. to date. London: Longman, 1989.

ADDITIONAL SIGLA USED IN VOLUME ONE

TT1   "The Black Canon of Elmham; or, Saint Edmond's Eve." In *Tales of Terror.* London: printed for J. Bell by Bulmer & Co., 1801.

TT2   "The Black Canon of Elmham; or, Saint Edmond's Eve." In *Tales of Terror.* London: printed for J. Bell by Bulmer & Co., 1808.

TT   Represents agreement of *TT1* and *TT2* in collations.

1829E   "The Poet Shelley—His Unpublished Work, 'The Wandering Jew.'" *The Edinburgh Literary Journal; or, Weekly Register of Criticism and Belles Lettres,* no. 33 (27 June 1829), 43–45, and no. 34 (4 July 1829), 57–60.

1829Inc   "An Incantation Scene.—A poem, hitherto unpublished by Percy Bysshe Shelley." *The Edinburgh Literary Journal; or, Weekly Register of Criticism and Belles Lettres,* no. 59 (26 Dec. 1829), 425–26.

1831F   "The Wandering Jew. A Poem. By the late Percy Bysshe Shelley." *Fraser's Magazine for Town and Country* 3, no. 18 (July 1831), 666–77.

1835   Robert Montgomery. *Oxford, a Poem.* 4th ed. Oxford: Slatter, 1835.

1847M   Thomas Medwin. *The Life of Percy Bysshe Shelley.* 2 vols. London: Newby, 1847.

1858   Thomas Jefferson Hogg. *The Life of Percy Bysshe Shelley.* 2 vols. London: Moxon, 1858.

1871   "The Devil's Walk," ed. W. M. Rossetti. *Fortnightly Review* (n.s., 9 [15 of full sequence], no. 49 (Jan. 1871), 67–85.

1872   See Mac-Carthy, *Early Life,* below.

1886   In Historical Collations for Ten Poems, lines 13–15 of **"Sweet star!,"** from a letter to Hogg, dated "Bracknell, March 16, 1814." In Dowden, *Life* I, 409–10.

1887D   *The Wandering Jew. A Poem,* ed. Bertram Dobell. London: Reeves & Turner, 1887.

1890W   *The Letters from Percy Bysshe Shelley to Elizabeth Hitchener,* ed. T. J. Wise. 2 vols. London: privately printed, 1890.

1909   H[arry] Buxton Forman. "More Shelley Crumbs." *Athenæum,* no. 4258 (5 June 1909), 674.

1913   See Medwin *Life,* ed. Forman.

1917   *Letters about Shelley Interchanged by Three Friends—Edward*

	Dowden, Richard Garnett, and William Michael Rossetti, ed. R[obert] S. Garnett. London: Hodder & Stoughton, 1917.
1922/LMer	"Biographical Notes and News." *London Mercury* 6 (Aug. 1922), 417–18.
KSMB/1973	Neville Rogers. "An Unpublished Shelley Letter." *Keats-Shelley Memorial Bulletin* 24 (1973), 20–24.

SHORT TITLES OF RESEARCH AND REFERENCE WORKS

Anderson, *Legend/WJ*	George Kumler Anderson. *The Legend of the Wandering Jew*. Providence: Brown University Press, 1965.
AR	*Annual Register*
BSM	*The Bodleian Shelley Manuscripts*, ed. Donald H. Reiman et al. 23 vols. New York: Garland Publishing, 1986–99.
Byron, *CPW*	*The Complete Poetical Works of Lord Byron*, ed. Jerome J. McGann. Oxford: Clarendon Press, 1980–93.
Chadwyck-Healey *Lion*	Chadwyck-Healey Literature On-Line databases at <http://lion.chadwyck.com>.
DNB	*Dictionary of National Biography*
Dowden, *Life*	Edward Dowden. *The Life of Percy Bysshe Shelley*. 2 vols. London: Kegan Paul, Trench & Co., 1886.
ELJ	*Edinburgh Literary Journal*; see also *1829E* and *1829Inc*.
Encyc. Brit.	*Encyclopædia Britannica* (+ copyright date).
ESTC	*English Short Title Catalogue*. London: British Library, 1998 (CD-ROM and on-line editions). (Incorporates the *Eighteenth-Century Short-Title Catalogue* [also *ESTC*], available in print.)
FM	*Fraser's Magazine for Town and Country*; see also *1831F*.
Hawkins, *First Love*	Desmond Hawkins. *Shelley's First Love*. London: Kyle Cathie; Hamden, Conn.: Archon, 1992.
Hogg *Life*, ed. Wolfe	*The Life of Percy Bysshe Shelley as Comprised in* The Life of Percy Bysshe Shelley *by Thomas Jefferson Hogg,* The Recollections of Shelley & Byron *by Edward John Trelawny,* Memoirs of Shelley *by Thomas Love Peacock*, ed. Humbert Wolfe. 2 vols. London: J. M. Dent, 1933.
Hughes, *Nascent Mind*	A. M. D. Hughes. *The Nascent Mind of Shelley*. Oxford: Clarendon Press, 1947.
Letters	*The Letters of Percy Bysshe Shelley*, ed. Frederick L. Jones. 2 vols. Oxford: Clarendon Press, 1964. (Cited in collations as *1964J*.)
Mac-Carthy, *Early Life*	Denis Florence Mac-Carthy. *Shelley's Early Life from Original Sources with Curious Incidents, Letters, and*

	Writings, Now First Published or Collected. London: John Camden Hotten, 1872. (Cited in collations as *1872*.)
Medwin *Life*, ed. Forman	*The Life of Percy Bysshe Shelley By Thomas Medwin. A New Edition printed from a copy copiously amended and extended by the Author and left unpublished at his death, with an Introduction and Commentary by H. Buxton Forman.* New York: Oxford University Press, 1913.
MLR	*Modern Language Review* (English quarterly)
MYR: Shelley	*The Manuscripts of the Younger Romantics: Percy Bysshe Shelley*, ed. Donald H. Reiman et al. 9 vols. New York: Garland Publishing, 1985–97.
NCBEL	*New Cambridge Bibliography of English Literature*, ed. George Watson. 4 vols. Cambridge: Cambridge University Press, 1969–71.
NSTC	*Nineteenth-Century Short Title Catalogue.* Cambridge: Chadwyck-Healey, 1985–(print and CD-ROM editions).
NUC	*National Union Catalogue of Printed Books*
OED	*Oxford English Dictionary*
OxH	*The Oxford Herald*
Peck, *Shelley*	Walter Edwin Peck. *Shelley: His Life and Work.* 2 vols. Boston and New York: Houghton Mifflin, 1927.
PL	*Paradise Lost,* by John Milton.
Prose/EBM	*The Prose Works of Percy Bysshe Shelley,* ed. E. B. Murray. Oxford: Clarendon Press, 1993. (Only volume published before Murray's death.)
RR	*The Romantics Reviewed; Contemporary Reviews of British Romantic Writers.* 9 vols. in 3 parts, A–C, ed. Donald H. Reiman. New York: Garland Publishing, 1972.
SC	*Shelley and his Circle: 1773–1822.* Volumes I–IV, ed. Kenneth Neill Cameron; V–VI, ed. Donald H. Reiman; VII–X, ed. Reiman and Doucet Devin Fischer. Cambridge: Harvard University Press, 1961–.
Shelley Concordance	*A Lexical Concordance to the Poetical Works of Percy Bysshe Shelley,* comp. and ed. F. S. Ellis. London: Bernard Quaritch, 1892.
White, *Shelley*	Newman Ivey White. *Shelley.* 2 vols. New York: Alfred A. Knopf, 1940; London: Secker & Warburg, 1947.
Wise	T[homas] J. Wise. *A Shelley Library.* London: for private circulation, 1924.
YS	Kenneth Neill Cameron. *The Young Shelley: Genesis of a Radical.* New York: Macmillan, 1950.

TEXTS

ORIGINAL POETRY;

BY

VICTOR AND CAZIRE.

CALL IT NOT VAIN:—THEY DO NOT ERR,
WHO SAY, THAT, WHEN THE POET DIES,
MUTE NATURE MOURNS HER WORSHIPPER.
Lay of the Last Minstrel.

WORTHING:
PRINTED BY C. AND W. PHILLIPS,
FOR THE AUTHORS;
AND SOLD BY J. J. STOCKDALE, 41, PALL-MALL,
AND ALL OTHER BOOKSELLERS.

1810.

Title page of *Original Poetry by Victor and Cazire* (1810). With kind permission of The Huntington Library.

ORIGINAL POETRY

by Victor and Cazire

Most of the seventeen poems and fragments in this collection (***V&C***) were written by Percy Bysshe Shelley (PBS), but five were probably written, in whole or in part, by his eldest sister, Elizabeth Shelley, and the longest poem in the volume was plagiarized from Matthew G. ("Monk") Lewis. The volume was printed in Sussex during the summer of 1810 under PBS's supervision and published with authorial pseudonyms early in the autumn of that year by John Joseph Stockdale, an established London bookseller. When Stockdale became aware of the plagiarism from Lewis, the edition was suppressed and most copies destroyed. Though ***V&C*** was reviewed in a few contemporary periodicals, the texts of its poems did not come to light again till 1898, when a copy was located and a type-facsimile was printed in London.

The copy-text, or base text, for our edition is the original edition of *1810*, as established through a comparison of the three known surviving copies. Below our critical Text, we record its variants from *1810* and the facsimile (*1898*). On pages 335–53, we collate historically important publications that involve texts from ***V&C***. Detailed historical, textual, and informational commentary can be found on pages 149–87.

Of the PBS volumes presented in the first volume of this edition, only *V&C* had a table of contents, and we reproduce that page below.

CONTENTS.

	PAGE.
Letter,	5
Letter,	10
Song,	14
Song,	17
Despair,	19
Sorrow,	21
Hope,	24
Song, translated from the Italian,	26
Song, translated from the German,	27
The Irishman's Song,	29
Song,	31
Song,	33
Song,	35
St. Edmond's Eve,	37
Revenge	45
Ghasta, or the avenging Demon,	50
Fragment,	63

LETTER [1]

A Person complained that whenever he began to write, he never could arrange his ideas in grammatical order. Which occasion suggested the idea of the following lines:

HERE I sit with my paper, my pen and my ink,
First of this thing, and that thing, and t'other thing think;
Then my thoughts come so pell-mell all into my mind,
That the sense or the subject I never can find:
This word is wrong placed,—no regard to the sense,   5
The present and future, instead of past tense,
Then my grammar I want; O dear! what a bore,
I think I shall never attempt to write more,
With patience I then my thoughts must arraign,
Have them all in due order like mutes in a train,   10
Like them too must wait in due patience and thought,
Or else my fine works will all come to nought,
My wit too's so copious, it flows like a river,
But disperses its waters on black and white never;
Like smoke it appears independent and free,   15
But ah luckless smoke! it all passes like thee—
Then at length all my patience entirely lost,
My paper and pens in the fire are tost;
But come, try again—you must never despair
Our Murray's or Entick's are not all so rare,   20
Implore their assistance—they'll come to your aid,
Perform all your business without being paid,
They'll tell you the present tense, future and past,
Which should come first, and which should come last,
This Murray will do—then to Entick repair,   25
To find out the meaning of any word rare.
This they friendly will tell, and ne'er make you blush,
With a jeering look, taunt, or an O fie! tush!
Then straight all your thoughts in black and white put,
Not minding the if's, the be's, and the but,   30
Then read it all over, see how it will run,
How answers the wit, the retort, and the pun,
Your writings may then with old Socrates vie,

Text collated with *1810* and *1898*.
Title. *omitted* **1810** *1898*
12 nought,] nought. *1898*
19 despair] despair, *1898*

  May on the same shelf with Demosthenes lie,
35 May as Junius be sharp, or as Plato be sage,
  The pattern or satire to all of the age;
  But stop—a mad author I mean not to turn,
  Nor with thirst of applause does my heated brain burn,
  Sufficient that sense, wit, and grammar combined,
40 My letters may make some slight food for the mind;
  That my thoughts to my friends I may freely impart,
  In all the warm language that flows from the heart,
  Hark! futurity calls! it loudly complains,
  It bids me step forward and just hold the reins,
45 My excuse shall be humble, and faithful, and true,
  Such as I fear can be made but by few—
  Of writers this age has abundance and plenty,
  Three score and a thousand, two millions and twenty,
  Three score of them wits who all sharply vie,
50 To try what odd creature they best can belie,
  A thousand are prudes who for *Charity* write,
  And fill up their sheets with spleen, envy, and spite,
  One million are bards, who to heaven aspire,
  And stuff their works full of bombast, rant, and fire,
55 T'other million are wags who in Grub-street attend,
  And just like a cobler the old writings mend,
  The twenty are those who for pulpits indite,
  And pore over sermons all Saturday night.
  And now my good friends—who come after I mean,
60 As I ne'er wore a cassoc, or dined with a dean,
  Or like coblers at mending I never did try,
  Nor with poets in lyrics attempted to vie;
  As for prudes these good souls I both hate and detest,
  So here I believe the matter must rest.—
65 I've heard your complaint—my answer I've made,
  And since to your calls all the tribute I've paid,
  Adieu my good friend; pray never despair,
  But grammar and sense and every thing dare,
  Attempt but to write dashing, easy, and free,
70 Then take out your grammar and pay him his fee,
  Be not a coward, shrink not a tense,
  But read it all over and make it out sense.

---

52 spite,] spite *1898*
71 not a tense,] not to a tense, *1898*

What a tiresome girl!—pray soon make an end,
Else my limited patience you'll quickly expend.
Well adieu, I no longer your patience will try— 75
So swift to the post now the letter shall fly.
                    JANUARY, 1810.

                    LETTER [2]
                To Miss ——— ———
            From Miss ————— —————

For your letter, dear ————, accept my best thanks,
Rendered long and amusing by virtue of franks,
Tho' concise they would please, yet the longer the better,
The more news that's crammed in, more amusing the letter,
All excuses of etiquette nonsense I hate, 5
Which only are fit for the tardy and late,
As when converse grows flat, of the weather they talk,
How fair the sun shines—a fine day for a walk,
Then to politics turn, of Burdett's reformation,
One declares it would hurt, t'other better the nation, 10
Will ministers keep? sure they've acted quite wrong,
The burden this is of each morning-call song.
So ———— is going to ———— you say,
I hope that success her great efforts will pay
That the Colonel will see her, be dazzled outright, 15
And declare he can't bear to be out of her sight.
Write flaming epistles with love's pointed dart,
Whose sharp little arrow struck right on his heart,
Scold poor innocent Cupid for mischevious ways,
He knows not how much to laud forth her praise, 20
That he neither eats, drinks or sleeps for her sake,
And hopes her hard heart some compassion will take,
A refusal would kill him, so desperate his flame,
But he fears, for he knows she is not common game,
Then praises her sense, wit, discernment and grace, 25
He's not one that's caught by a sly looking face,
Yet that's *too* divine—such a black sparkling eye,
At the bare glance of which near a thousand will die;

Dateline. 1810.] *period omitted* *1898*   12 morning-call] morning—call
                                                    1810 1898
Text collated with *1810* and *1898*.   15 the Colonel] ———— *1898*

> Thus runs he on meaning but one word in ten,
> More than is meant by most such kind of men,
> For they're all alike, take them one with another,
> Begging pardon—with the exception of my brother.
> Of the drawings you mention much praise I have heard,
> Most opinion's the same, with the difference of word,
> Some get a good name by the voice of the croud,
> Whilst to poor humble merit small praise is allowed,
> As in parliament votes, so in pictures a name,
> Oft determines a fate at the altar of fame.—
> So on Friday this City's gay vortex you quit,
> And no longer with Doctors and Johnny cats sit—
> Now your parcel's arrived ——'s letter shall go,
> I hope all your joy mayn't be turned into woe,
> Experience will tell you that pleasure is vain,
> When it promises sun shine how often comes rain,
> So when to fond hope every blessing is nigh,
> How oft when we smile it is checked with a sigh,
> When Hope, gay deceiver, in pleasure is drest,
> How oft comes a stroke that may rob us of rest.
> When we think ourselves safe, and the goal near at hand,
> Like a vessel just landing, we're wrecked near the strand,
> And tho' memory forever the sharp pang must feel,
> 'Tis our duty to bear, and our hardship to steel—
> May misfortunes dear Girl, ne'er thy happiness cloy,
> May thy days glide in peace, love, comfort and joy,
> May thy tears with soft pity for other woes flow,
> Woes, which thy tender heart never may know,
> For hardships our own, God has taught us to bear,
> Tho' sympathy's soul to a friend drops a tear.
> Oh dear! what sentimental stuff have I written,
> Only fit to tear up and play with a kitten.
> What sober reflections in the midst of this letter!
> Jocularity sure would have suited much better;
> But there are exceptions to all common rules,
> For this is a truth by all boys learnt at schools.
> Now adieu my dear —— I'm sure I must tire,

---

35 croud,] crowd,   *1898*
41 parcel's] parcels   ***1810*** *1898*
44 rain,] rain.   *1898*
49 goal] gaol   ***1810*** *1898*

For if I do, you may throw it into the fire,
So accept the best love of your cousin and friend,
Which brings this nonsensical rhyme to an end.

        APRIL 30, 1810.

SONG.

COLD, cold is the blast when December is howling,
 Cold are the damps on a dying Man's brow,—
Stern are the seas when the wild waves are rolling,
 And sad is the grave where a loved one lies low;
But colder is scorn from the being who loved thee,   5
More stern is the sneer from the friend who has proved thee,
More sad are the tears when their sorrows have moved thee,
 Which mixed with groans anguish and wild madness flow.—

And ah! poor [Louisa] has felt all this horror,
 Full long the fallen victim contended with fate: 10
'Till a destitute outcast abandoned to sorrow,
 She sought her babe's food at her ruiner's gate—
Another had charmed the remorseless betrayer,
He turned laughing aside from her moans and her prayer,

---

68 end.] end *1898*

Text collated with *1810*, Pfz, and *1898*. MS Pfz is one of three parts of *V&C* that PBS wrote out for Hogg on the same MS sheet. This poem is followed by fragments of *Song: To ————* ("*Ah! sweet is the moonbeam*") and *Song: To ————* ("*Stern, stern is the voice*"), below.

Title. SONG.] *omitted* Pfz
1 COLD,] Cold Pfz
 howling,] howling Pfz
2 Man's brow,—] mans brow Pfz
3 rolling,] rolling Pfz
4 is] *omitted* Pfz
 low;] low Pfz
5 thee,] thee Pfz
6 thee,] thee Pfz
7 their] these Pfz
 thee,] thee Pfz
8 mixed] mixèd Pfz
 groans] groans, Pfz
 and] & Pfz

flow.—] flow. Pfz
 flow— *1898*
9 [Louisa]] ———— *1810 1898*
 Louisa Pfz
 horror,] horror Pfz
10 fate:] fate Pfz
11 'Till] Till Pfz
 sorrow,] sorrow Pfz
12 ruiner's] ruiners *1810 1898*
 gate—] gate Pfz
13 betrayer,] betrayer Pfz
14 laughing] callous Pfz
 and] & Pfz
 prayer,] prayer Pfz

15   She said nothing, but wringing the wet from her hair,
            Crossed the dark mountain side, tho' the hour it was late.

      'Twas on the wild height of the dark Penmanmawr,
            That the form of the wasted [Louisa] reclined;
      She shrieked to the ravens that croaked from afar,
20   And she sighed to the gust of the wild sweeping wind.—
      "I call not yon rocks where the thunder peals rattle,
      "I call not yon clouds where the elements battle,
            "But thee, cruel [Henry] I call thee unkind!—"

      Then she wreathed in her hair the wild flowers of the mountain,
25   And deliriously laughing, a garland entwined,
      She bedewed it with tears, then she hung o'er the fountain,
            And laving it, cast it a prey to the wind.
      "Ah! go," she exclaimed, "when the tempest is yelling,
      "'Tis unkind to be cast on the sea that is swelling,
30   "But I left, a pityless outcast, my dwelling,
            "My garments are torn, so they say is my mind—"

---

15 She] She^d *probable reading* Pfz
    nothing,] nothing   Pfz
    hair,] hair   Pfz
16 side,] side   Pfz
    tho'] tho   Pfz
    late.] late   Pfz
17 wild . . . dark dark summit of
        huge   Pfz
    Penmanmawr,] Penmanmawr   Pfz
18 [Louisa]] ———   *1810 1898*
                Louisa Pfz   [*"L" may be super-
                imposed on "H" (as SC says) or
                "L" may be "El" for Elouisa.*]
    reclined;] reclined,   Pfz
19 afar,] afar   Pfz
20 gust] gusts   Pfz *1898*
    wind.—] wind   Pfz
21 "I] I   Pfz
    rocks] ~~rocks~~ *inserted* clouds   Pfz
    rattle,] rattle   Pfz
22 "I] I   Pfz
    clouds] rocks   Pfz
    battle,] battle   Pfz
23 "But] But   *1810* Pfz *1898*
    thee,] thee   Pfz

    cruel [Henry]] perjured Henry   Pfz
        cruel ———
                1810 1898
    unkind!—"] unkind!—   *1810 1898*
        unkind   Pfz
24 mountain,] mountain   Pfz
25 laughing,] laughing   Pfz
    entwined,] entwined   Pfz
26 o'er] oer   Pfz
    fountain,] fountain   Pfz
27 laving] leaving   *1810 1898*
    wind.] wind   Pfz
28 "Ah! go,"] "Ah! go"   Pfz
    exclaimed,] exclaimed   Pfz
    "when . . . yelling,]
        "where . . . yelling   Pfz
29 "'Tis] 'Tis   Pfz
    swelling,] swelling   Pfz
30 "But I left, a pityless outcast,]
        But I left a pityless outcast   Pfz
    dwelling,] dwelling   Pfz
31 "My] My   Pfz
    torn,] torn   Pfz
    mind—"] mind"   Pfz
    stanza break follows

Not long lived [Louisa], but over her grave
    Waved the desolate form of a storm-blasted yew,
Around it no demons or ghosts dare to rave,
    But spirits of peace steep her slumbers in dew.   35
Then stay thy swift steps mid the dark mountain heather,
Tho' chill blow the wind and severe is the weather,
For perfidy, traveller! cannot bereave her,
    Of the tears, to the tombs of the innocent due.—

JULY, 1810.

SONG.

Come ———! sweet is the hour,
    Soft Zephyrs breathe gently around,
The anemone's night-boding flower,
    Has sunk its pale head on the ground.

'Tis thus the world's keenness hath torn,   5
    Some mild heart that expands to its blast,
'Tis thus that the wretched forlorn,
    Sinks poor and neglected at last.—

The world with its keenness and woe,
    Has no charms or attraction for me,   10
Its unkindness with grief has laid low,
    The heart which is faithful to thee.

The high trees that wave past the moon,
    As I walk in their umbrage with you,
All declare I must part with you soon,   15
    All bid you a tender adieu!—

---

32 [Louisa], but] ———, but
        1810 1898
        Louisa—but   Pfz
33 yew,] yew   Pfz
34 rave,] rave   Pfz
35 peace] Peace   Pfz
    dew.] dew   Pfz
36 heather,] heather   Pfz
37 Tho'] Tho   Pfz
    and] &   Pfz
    is] be   Pfz

38 perfidy,] perfidy   Pfz
    traveller!] traveller   Pfz
    her,] her   Pfz
39 tears,] tears   Pfz
    due.—] due   Pfz
    Dateline. JULY, 1810.] *omitted*   Pfz

Text collated with *1810* and *1898*.
No variants appear.

Then ───────! dearest farewell,
      You and I love, may ne'er meet again;
   These woods and these meadows can tell
      How soft and how sweet was the strain.—
               April, 1810.

SONG.
DESPAIR.

Ask not the pallid stranger's woe,
   With beating heart and throbbing breast,
Whose step is faultering, weak, and slow,
   As tho' the body needed rest.—

Whose wildered eye no object meets,
   Nor cares to ken a friendly glance,
With silent grief his bosom beats,—
   Now fixed, as in a deathlike trance.

Who looks around with fearful eye,
   And shuns all converse with mankind,
As tho' some one his griefs might spy,
   And sooth them with a kindred mind.

A friend or foe to him the same,
   He looks on each with equal eye;
The difference lies but in the name,
   To none for comfort can he fly.—

'Twas deep despair, and sorrow's trace,
   To him too keenly given,
Whose memory, time could not efface—
   His peace was lodged in Heaven.—

He looks on all this world bestows,
   The pride and pomp of power,
As trifles best for pageant shows
   Which vanish in an hour.—

Text collated with *1810* and *1898*.
12 sooth] soothe   *1898*
24 hour.—] hour.   *1898*

14   *Victor and Cazire*

When torn is dear affection's tie, 25
    Sinks the soft heart full low;
It leaves without a parting sigh,
    All that these realms bestow.
              JUNE, 1810.

SONG.
SORROW.

To me this world's a dreary blank,
    All hopes in life are gone and fled,
My high strung energies are sank,
    And all my blissfull hopes lie dead.—

The world once smiling to my view, 5
    Shewed scenes of endless bliss and joy;
The world I then but little knew,
    Ah! little knew how pleasures cloy:

All then was jocund, all was gay,
    No thought beyond the present hour, 10
I danced in pleasure's fading ray,
    Fading alas! as drooping flower.

Nor do the heedless in the throng,
    One thought beyond the morrow give,
They court the feast, the dance, the song, 15
    Nor think how short their time to live.

The heart that bears deep sorrow's trace,
    What earthly comfort can console,
It drags a dull and lengthened pace,
    'Till friendly death its woes enroll.— 20

The sunken cheek, the humid eyes,
    E'en better than the tongue can tell;

---

25 affection's] affections *1810 1898*
Dateline. JUNE,] JUNE *1898*

Text collated with ***1810*** and *1898*.

8 cloy:] cloy; *1898*
11 pleasure's] pleasures ***1810*** *1898*
14 give,] give *1898*
17 sorrow's] sorrows ***1810*** *1898*

In whose sad breast deep sorrow lies,
   Where memory's rankling traces dwell.—

25   The rising tear, the stifled sigh,
   A mind but ill at ease display,
Like blackening clouds in stormy sky,
   Where fiercely vivid lightening's play.

Thus when souls' energy is dead,
30   When sorrow dims each earthly view,
When every fairy hope is fled,
   We bid ungrateful world adieu.

                              AUGUST, 1810.

SONG.
HOPE.

AND said I that all hope was fled,
   That sorrow and despair were mine,
That each enthusiast wish was dead,
   Had sank beneath pale Misery's shrine.—

5   Seest thou the sunbeam's yellow glow,
   That robes with liquid streams of light
Yon distant Mountain's craggy brow,
   And shews the rocks so fair,—so bright——

'Tis thus sweet expectation's ray,
10   In softer view shews distant hours,
And portrays each succeeding day,
   As dressed in fairer, brighter flowers,—

The vermeil tinted flowers that blossom,
   Are frozen but to bud anew.

Dateline. AUGUST,] AUGUST *1898*

Text collated with *1810* and *1898*.
6 light] light: *1810*
    light; *1898*
7 Mountain's] Mountains *1810*
    brow,] brow. *1810 1898*

9 expectation's] expectations *1810 1898*
13 vermeil] vermiel *1810 1898*
    blossom,] blossom; *1810 1898*
14 anew.] anew, *1810 1898*

Then sweet deceiver calm my bosom,   15
    Although thy visions be not true,—

Yet true they are,—and I'll believe,
    Thy whisperings soft of love and peace,
God never made thee to deceive,
    'Tis sin that bade thy empire cease.   20

Yet tho' despair my life should gloom,
    Tho' horror should around me close,
With those I love, beyond the tomb,
    Hope shews a balm for all my woes.
                    AUGUST, 1810.

SONG,
TRANSLATED FROM THE ITALIAN.

Oh! what is the gain of restless care,
    And what is ambitious treasure?
And what are the joys that the modish share,
    In their sickly haunts of pleasure?

My husband's repast with delight I spread,   5
    What tho' 'tis but rustic fare,
May each guardian angel protect his shed,
    May contentment and quiet be there.

And may I support my husband's years,
    May I soothe his dying pain,   10
And then may I dry my fast falling tears,
    And meet him in Heaven again.
                    JULY, 1810.

---

15 deceiver] deceivers *1810 1898*
Dateline. AUGUST,] AUGUST *1810*

Text collated with *1810* and *1898*.
5 husband's] husbands *1810 1898*
9 husband's] husbands *1810 1898*

SONG.

TRANSLATED FROM THE GERMAN.

Ah! grasp the dire dagger and couch the fell spear,
If vengeance and death to thy bosom be dear,
The dastard shall perish, death's torment shall prove,
For fate and revenge are decreed from above.

Ah! where is the hero, whose nerves strung by youth,
Will defend the firm cause of justice and truth;
With insatiate desire whose bosom shall swell,
To give up the oppressor to judgment and Hell—

For him shall the fair one twine chaplets of bays,
To him shall each warrior give merited praise,
And triumphant returned from the clangor of arms,
He shall find his reward in his loved maiden's charms.

In extatic confusion the warrior shall sip,
The kisses that glow on his love's dewy lip,
And mutual, eternal, embraces shall prove,
The rewards of the brave are the transports of love.

OCTOBER, 1809.

THE IRISHMAN'S SONG.

THE stars may dissolve, and the fountain of light
May sink into ne'er ending chaos and night,
Our mansions must fall, and earth vanish away,
But thy courage O Erin! may never decay.

See! the wide wasting ruin extends all around,
Our ancestors' dwellings lie sunk on the ground,
Our foes ride in triumph throughout our domains,
And our mightiest heroes lie stretched on the plains.

Ah! dead is the harp which was wont to give pleasure,
Ah! sunk is our sweet country's rapturous measure,

Text collated with *1810* and *1898*.
3 death's] deaths *1810 1898*
12 maiden's] maidens *1810 1898*

Text collated with *1810* and *1898*.
6 ancestors'] ancestors *1810 1898*

But the war note is waked, and the clangor of spears,
The dread yell of Sloghan yet sounds in our ears.

Ah! where are the heroes! triumphant in death,
Convulsed they recline on the blood sprinkled heath,
Or the yelling ghosts ride on the blast that sweeps by,   15
And "my countrymen! vengeance!" incessantly cry.
       OCTOBER, 1809.

SONG.

FIERCE roars the midnight storm,
 O'er the wild mountain,
Dark clouds the night deform,
 Swift rolls the fountain—

See! o'er yon rocky height,   5
 Dim mists are flying—
See by the moon's pale light,
 Poor Laura's dying!

Shame and remorse shall howl,
 By her false pillow—   10
Fiercer than storms that roll,
 O'er the white billow;

No hand her eyes to close,
 When life is flying,
But she will find repose,   15
 For Laura's dying!

Then will I seek my love,
 Then will I cheer her,
Then my esteem will prove,
 When no friend is near her.   20

On her grave I will lie,
 When life is parted,

Text collated with *1810* and *1898*.
1 storm,] storm *1898*

On her grave I will die,
For the false hearted.

DECEMBER, 1809.

SONG.
To ⸺⸺⸺⸺

Ah! sweet is the moonbeam that sleeps on yon fountain,
   And sweet the mild rush of the soft-sighing breeze,
And sweet is the glimpse of yon dimly-seen mountain,
   'Neath the verdant arcades of yon shadowy trees.

5   But sweeter than all was thy tone of affection,
   Which scarce seemed to break on the stillness of eve,
Though the time it is past!—yet the dear recollection,
   For aye in the heart of thy ⸺⸺⸺ must live.

Yet he hears thy dear voice in the summer winds sighing,
10   Mild accents of happiness lisp in his ear,
When the hope-winged moments athwart him are flying,
   And he thinks of the friend to his bosom so dear.—

And thou dearest friend in his bosom for ever
   Must reign unalloyed by the fast rolling year,
15   He loves thee, and dearest one never, Oh! never
   Canst thou cease to be loved by a heart so sincere.

AUGUST, 1810.

Text collated with *1810*, Pfz, and *1898*. MS Pfz consists of lines 1–5 only; it is one of three excerpts of *V&C* that PBS wrote out for Hogg on the same sheet. This fragment is preceded by *Song* ("Cold, cold is the blast") and is followed directly by a fragment of *Song. To* ⸺⸺⸺ ("Stern, stern is the voice").

Title. SONG.] *omitted* Pfz
Subtitle. To ⸺⸺⸺⸺]
    omitted Pfz
1 Ah!] Ah Pfz
    fountain,] fountain Pfz
2 soft-sighing] soft sighing Pfz
    breeze,] breeze Pfz

3 dimly-seen] dimly seen Pfz
    mountain,] mountain Pfz
4 trees.] trees Pfz
stanza break] *omitted* Pfz
5 all] all⸺ Pfz
    was . . . affection,] *omitted* Pfz
Dateline. AUGUST,] AUGUST *1810*

SONG.
To ——————

    Stern, stern is the voice of fate's fearfull command,
        When accents of horror it breathes in our ear,
    Or compels us for aye bid adieu to the land,
        Where exists that loved friend to our bosom so dear,
    'Tis sterner than death o'er the shuddering wretch bending,   5
    And in skeleton grasp his fell sceptre extending,
    Like the heart-stricken deer to that loved covert wending,
        Which never again to his eyes may appear—

    And ah! he may envy the heart-stricken quarry,
        Who bids to the friend of affection farewell,   10
    He may envy the bosom so bleeding and gory,
        He may envy the sound of the drear passing knell,
    Not so deep is his grief on his death couch reposing,
        When on the last vision his dim eyes are closing!
    As the outcast whose love-raptured senses are losing,   15
        The last tones of thy voice on the wild breeze that swell!

    Those tones were so soft, and so sad, that ah! never,
        Can the sound cease to vibrate on Memory's ear,

Text collated with *1810*, MS Pfz, and *1898*. For MS Pfz, consisting of only lines 9–15 and 17–18 of this poem, see headnote to the collation of primary authorities for the previous poem.

Title. SONG.] *omitted* Pfz
Subtitle. To ———————] *omitted* Pfz
1 fate's] fates *1810 1898*
9 he] she Pfz
   heart-stricken quarry,]
      heart [?] quarry
      The medial word may be streaked *but is*
      more likely stricted *(i.e.,* stricken *given*
      as weak past participle). Pfz
10 friend] scenery Pfz
   affection] childhood Pfz
   farewell,] farewell Pfz
11 He] She Pfz
   so] all Pfz
   and] & Pfz
   gory,] gory Pfz
12 He] She Pfz
   knell,] knell Pfz
13 is] are Pfz
   grief] woes Pfz
   reposing,] reposing Pfz
14 closing!] closing Pfz
15 outcast] outcast— Pfz
   whose . . . losing,] *omitted* Pfz
17 tones] notes Pfz
   soft,] soft Pfz
   and] & Pfz
   sad,] sad Pfz
   never,] never Pfz
18 Can] May Pfz
   Memory's] memory's Pfz
   ear,] ear Pfz

In the stern wreck of Nature for ever and ever,
20   The remembrance must live of a friend so sincere.
                                    AUGUST, 1810.

                    SAINT EDMOND'S EVE.

        Oh! did you observe the black Canon pass,
            And did you observe his frown?
        He goeth to say the midnight mass,
            In holy St. Edmond's town.

5   He goeth to sing the burial chaunt,
            And to lay the wandering sprite,
        Whose shadowy, restless form doth haunt,
            The Abbey's drear aisle this night.

        It saith it will not its wailings cease,
10   'Till that holy man come near,
        'Till he pour o'er its grave the prayer of peace,
            And sprinkle the hallowed tear.

        The Canon's horse is stout and strong,
            The road is plain and fair,
15   But the Canon slowly wends along,
            And his brow is gloomed with care.

Dateline. AUGUST, 1810.] *omitted* Pfz

Text collated with *1810*, *TT1*, *TT2*, and *1898*. *TT (Tales of Terror)* is used when the reading of the 1801 (*TT1*) and 1808 (*TT2*) editions agree.
Title. SAINT . . .] THE BLACK CANON OF ELMHAM;* OR, AN OLD ENGLISH BALLAD.
        double rule—Hic Niger est! Horat. *double rule*   *TT*

1 Oh!] Oh, *TT*	10 'Till] Till *TT*
black] Black *TT*	come] comes *TT*
pass,] pass? *TT*	near,] near; *TT*
3 mass,] mass *TT*	11 'Till] Till *TT*
6 wandering] wand'ring *TT*	pour] breathes *TT*
7 shadowy,] shadowy *TT*	12 sprinkle] sprinkles *TT*
haunt,] haunt *TT*	hallowed] hallow'd *TT*
8 Abbey's] abbey's *TT*	13 strong,] strong *1898*
aisle] isle *TT1*	16 gloomed] gloom'd *TT*
9 wailings] wailing *1898*	
cease,] cease *TT*	

22   *Victor and Cazire*

Who is it thus late at the Abbey-gate?
    Sullen echoes the portal bell,
It sounds like the whispering voice of fate,
    It sounds like a funeral knell.   20

The Canon his faultering knee thrice bowed,
    And his frame was convulsed with fear,
When a voice was heard distinct and loud,
    "Prepare! for thy hour is near."

He crosses his breast, he mutters a prayer,   25
    To Heaven he lifts his eye,
He heeds not the Abbot's gazing stare,
    Nor the dark Monks who murmured by.

Bare-headed he worships the sculptured saints
    That frown on the sacred walls,   30
His face it grows pale,—he trembles, he faints,
    At the Abbot's feet he falls.

And strait the father's robe he kissed,
    Who cried, "Grace dwells with thee,
"The spirit will fade like the morning mist,   35
    "At your benedicite.

"Now haste within! the board is spread,
    "Keen blows the air, and cold,

---

17 Abbey-gate?] abbey gate? *TT*
18 bell,] bell— *TT*
20 knell.] knell! *TT*
21 faultering] faltering *TT2*
    bowed,] bow'd, *TT*
22 And . . . convulsed]
    His body it shook *TT*
    fear,] fear; *TT*
23 When . . . heard]
    And a voice he heard cry *TT*
24 "Prepare!] —"Prepare! *TT*
    near."] near."— *TT*
26 eye,] eye; *TT*
27 Abbot's] abbot's *TT*
28 Monks] monks *TT*
    murmured] murmur'd *TT*

29 Bare-headed] Bareheaded *TT*
    sculptured] sculptur'd *TT*
31 pale,—he] pale, he *TT*
32 Abbot's] abbot's *TT*
    falls.] falls! *TT*
33 strait] straight *TT*
    kissed,] kiss'd, *TT*
34 cried, "Grace] cried—"Grace *TT*
    thee,] thee! *TT*
35 spirit] sprite *TT*
    fade] fade, *TT2*
    like] like, *TT1*
36 benedicite.] Benedicite. *TT*
37 within! the] within—the *TT*
    spread,] spread— *TT*
38 cold,] cold; *TT*

       "The spectre sleeps in its earthy bed,
40   "'Till St. Edmond's bell hath tolled,—

       "Yet rest your wearied limbs to night,
         "You've journeyed many a mile,
       "To-morrow lay the wailing sprite,
         "That shrieks in the moonlight aisle."

45   "Oh! faint are my limbs and my bosom is cold,
         "Yet to-night must the sprite be laid,
       "Yet to-night when the hour of horror's told,
         "Must I meet the wandering shade.

       "Nor food, nor rest may now delay,—
50   "For hark! the echoing pile,
       "A bell loud shakes!—Oh haste away,
         "O lead to the haunted aisle."

       The torches slowly move before,
         The cross is raised on high,
55   A smile of peace the Canon wore,
         But horror dimmed his eye—

       And now they climb the footworn stair,
         The chapel gates unclose,

---

39 bed,] bed   *TT*
40 "'Till] 'Till   *TT*
    bell] eve   *TT*
    tolled,—] toll'd.   *TT*
41 wearied] weary   *TT*
    to night,] to-night,   *TT 1898*
42 journeyed] journey'd   *TT*
    mile,] mile;   *TT*
44 moonlight] moon-light   *TT*
    aisle."] aisle."—   *TT*
        aisle.   *1898*
45 limbs] limbs,   *TT*
    is] *omitted*   *TT*
    cold,] cold!   *TT*
46 to-night] to night   *TT*
    laid,] laid;—   *TT*

47 to-night] to night   *TT*
    told,] toll'd,   *TT*
48 shade.] shade!   *TT*
49 rest] rest,   *TT2*
    may] can   *TT*
    delay,—] delay,   *TT*
50 pile,] pile   *TT*
51 shakes!—Oh] shakes! Oh!   *TT*
52 "O] "Oh!   *TT*
    aisle."] aisle."—   *TT*
54 raised] rear'd   *TT*
    high,] high;   *TT*
56 dimmed] fix'd   *TT*
    eye—] eye.   *TT*
57 footworn] foot-worn   *TT*
58 unclose,] unclose;   *TT*

Now each breathed low a fervent prayer,
    And fear each bosom froze—— 60

Now paused awhile the doubtful band
    And viewed the solemn scene,—
Full dark the clustered columns stand,
    The moon gleams pale between—

"Say father, say, what cloisters gloom 65
    "Conceals the unquiet shade,
"Within what dark unhallowed tomb,
    "The corse unblessed was laid."

"Through yonder drear aisle alone it walks,
    And murmurs a mournful plaint, 70
Of thee! Black Canon, it wildly talks,
    And calls on thy patron saint—

"The pilgrim this night with wondering eyes,
    "As he prayed at St. Edmond's shrine,
"From a black marble tomb hath seen it rise, 75
    "And under yon arch recline."—

"Oh! say upon that black marble tomb,
    "What memorial sad appears."—

---

60 froze——] froze. *TT*
61 band] band, *TT*
62 viewed] view'd *TT*
    scene,—] scene; *TT*
63 clustered] cluster'd *TT*
64 pale] bright *TT*
    between—] between. *TT*
65 "Say] —"Say, *TT*
    father,] Father, *TT*
    cloisters] cloister's *TT*
66 shade,] shade? *TT*
67 unhallowed] unhallow'd *TT*
    tomb,] tomb *TT*
68 unblessed] unbless'd *TT*
    laid."] laid?"— *TT*
69 "Through] —"Through *TT*

70 And] "And *TT*
    plaint,] plaint; *TT*
71 Of] "Of *TT*
    Canon,] Cannon, *TT1*
72 And] "And *TT*
    calls] call *TT 1898*
    saint—] saint. *TT*
73 night] night, *TT*
74 "As] "When *TT*
    prayed] prays *TT*
75 black marble] black-marble *TT*
77 "Oh!] —"Oh! *TT*
    black marble] black-marble *TT*
    tomb,] tomb *TT*
78 appears."—] appears?"— *TT*

80   "Undistinguished it lies in the chancels gloom,
           "No memorial sad it bears"—

         The Canon his paternoster reads,
            His rosary hung by his side,
         Now swift to the chancel door he leads,
            And untouched they open wide,

85   Resistless, strange sounds his steps impel,
            To approach to the black marble tomb,
         "Oh! enter Black Canon" a whisper fell,
            "Oh! enter, thy hour is come."

         He paused, told his beads, and the threshold passed,
90   Oh! horror, the chancel doors close,
         A loud yell was borne on the rising blast,
            And a deep, dying groan arose.

         The Monks in amazement shuddering stand,
            They burst thro' the chancels gloom,
95   From St. Edmond's shrine, lo! a skeletons hand,
            Points to the black marble tomb.

---

79 "Undistinguished]
     —"Undistinguish'd   *TT*
   chancels] chancel's   *TT*
80 bears"—] bears!"—   *TT*
81 paternoster] pater-noster   *TT*
82 side,] side;   *TT*
83 swift] straight   *TT*
   door] doors   *TT*
84 untouched] untouch'd   *TT*
   wide,] wide!   *TT*
85 Resistless, . . . impel,] —"Oh! enter,
     Black Canon!" a whisper fell,   *TT*
86 To . . . tomb,] "Oh! enter! thy hour
     is come!"—   *TT*
87 "Oh! . . . fell,] The sounds irresistless
     his steps impel   *TT*
88 "Oh! . . . come."]
     To approach the marble tomb.   *TT*

89 paused, told] paused—told   *TT*
   beads, and] beads—and   *TT*
   passed,] pass'd,   *TT1*
            pass'd—   *TT2*
90 Oh!] Oh,   *TT*
   horror,] horror!   *TT*
   close,] close;—   *TT*
91 borne] born   *TT1*
   rising] howling   *TT*
92 deep,] deep   *TT*
93 Monks] monks   *TT*
94 thro'] through   *TT*
   chancels] chancel's   *TT*
   gloom,] gloom!   *TT*
95 skeletons] wither'd   *TT*
96 black marble] black-marble   *TT*

26   *Victor and Cazire*

Lo! deeply engraved, an inscription blood red,
    In characters fresh and clear——
"The guilty black Canon of Elmham's dead,
    "And his wife lies buried here!"   100

In Elmham's tower he wedded a Nun,
    To St. Edmond's his bride he bore,
On this eve her noviciate here was begun,
    And a monks grey weeds she wore;—

O! deep was her conscience dyed with guilt,   105
    Remorse she full oft revealed,
Her blood by the ruthless black Canon was spilt,
    And in death her lips he sealed;

Her spirit to penance this night was doomed,
    'Till the Canon atoned the deed,   110
Here together they now shall rest entombed,
    'Till their bodies from dust are freed—

Hark! a loud peal of thunder shakes the roof,
    Round the altar bright lightnings play,
Speechless with horror the monks stand aloof,   115
    And the storm dies sudden away—

---

97 blood red,] blood-red, *TT*
98 clear——] clear; *TT*
    clear— *1898*
99 "The] —"The *TT*
  black] Black *TT*
  dead,] dead! *TT*
101 In] "In *TT*
  Nun,] nun, *TT*
102 To] "To *TT*
  Edmond's] Edmonds *TT*
  bore,] bore; *TT*
103 On] "On *TT*
  here was] was here *TT*
104 And] "And *TT*
  monks] friar's *TT*
  wore;—] wore. *TT*
105 O!] "Oh! *TT*

106 Remorse] "Remorse *TT*
  revealed,] reveal'd; *TT*
107 Her . . . spilt,] "The Black Canon
  her blood relentless spilt, *TT*
108 And] "And *TT*
  sealed;] seal'd! *TT*
109 Her] "Her *TT*
  doomed,] doom'd, *TT*
110 'Till] "Till *TT*
  deed,] deed; *TT*
111 Here] "Here *TT*
112 'Till] "Till *TT*
  freed—] freed!"— *TT*
114 play,] play; *TT*
115 aloof,] aloof— *TT*
116 away—] away! *TT*

The inscription was gone! a cross on the ground,
　　And a rosary shone thro' the gloom,
But never again was the Canon there found,
120　　Or the Ghost on the black marble tomb.

REVENGE.

"Ah! quit me not yet, for the wind whistles shrill,
"Its blast wanders mournfully over the hill,
"The thunder's wild voice rattles madly above,
"You will not then, cannot then, leave me my love.—"

5　"I must dearest Agnes, the night is far gone—
"I must wander this evening to Strasburg alone,
"I must seek the drear tomb of my ancestors' bones,
"And must dig their remains from beneath the cold stones.

"For the spirit of Conrad there meets me this night,
10　"And we quit not the tomb 'till dawn of the light,
"And Conrad's been dead just a month and a day!
"So farewell dearest Agnes for I must away,—

"He bid me bring with me what most I held dear,
"Or a month from that time should I lie on my bier,
15　"And I'd sooner resign this false fluttering breath,
"Than my Agnes should dread either danger or death,

"And I love you to madness my Agnes I love,
"My constant affection this night will I prove,
"This night will I go to the sepulchre's jaw,
20　"Alone will I glut its all conquering maw"—

"No! no loved Adolphus thy Agnes will share,
"In the tomb all the dangers that wait for you there,

117　gone! a] gone.—A　*TT*
118　thro'] through　*TT*
　　gloom,] gloom;　*TT*
120　Or] Nor　*TT*
　　Ghost] ghost　*TT*
　　black marble] black-marble　*TT*

Text collated with *1810* and *1898*.
1　whistles] whitsles　*1810 1898*
3　thunder's] thunders　*1810 1898*
7　ancestors'] ancestors　*1810 1898*
19　sepulchre's] sepulchres　*1810 1898*

"I fear not the spirit,—I fear not the grave,
"My dearest Adolphus I'd perish to save—

"Nay seek not to say that thy love shall not go,   25
"But spare me those ages of horror and woe,
"For I swear to thee here that I'll perish ere day,
"If you go unattended by Agnes away"—

The night it was bleak the fierce storm raged around,
The lightning's blue fire-light flashed on the ground,   30
Strange forms seemed to flit,—and howl tidings of fate,
As Agnes advanced to the sepulchre gate.—

The youth struck the portal,—the echoing sound
Was fearfully rolled midst the tombstones around,
The blue lightning gleamed o'er the dark chapel spire,   35
And tinged were the storm clouds with sulphurous fire.

Still they gazed on the tombstone where Conrad reclined,
Yet they shrank at the cold chilling blast of the wind,
When a strange silver brilliance pervaded the scene,
And a figure advanced—tall in form—fierce in mien.   40

A mantle encircled his shadowy form,
As light as a gossamer borne on the storm,
Celestial terror sat throned in his gaze,
Like the midnight pestiferous meteor's blaze.—

SPIRIT.

Thy father, Adolphus! was false, false as hell,   45
And Conrad has cause to remember it well,
He ruined my Mother, despised me his son,
I quitted the world ere my vengeance was done.

I was nearly expiring—'twas close of the day,—
A demon advanced to the bed where I lay,   50
He gave me the power from whence I was hurled,
To return to revenge, to return to the world,—

---

24 save—] save"—   *1810 1898*
30 lightning's] lightnings   *1810 1898*
44 meteor's] meteors   *1810 1898*

55   Now Adolphus I'll seize thy best loved in my arms,
       I'll drag her to Hades all blooming in charms,
       On the black whirlwind's thundering pinion I'll ride,
       And fierce yelling fiends shall exult o'er thy bride—

       He spoke, and extending his ghastly arms wide,
       Majestic advanced with a swift noiseless stride,
       He clasped the fair Agnes—he raised her on high,
60   And cleaving the roof sped his way to the sky—

       All was now silent,—and over the tomb,
       Thicker, deeper, was swiftly extended a gloom,—
       Adolphus in horror sank down on the stone,
       And his fleeting soul fled with a harrowing groan.
                                  DECEMBER, 1809.

GHASTA;
OR, THE AVENGING DEMON!!!

The idea of the following tale was taken from a few unconnected German Stanzas.—The principal Character is evidently the Wandering Jew, and although not mentioned by name, the burning Cross on his forehead undoubtedly alludes to that superstition, so prevalent in the part of Germany called the Black Forest, where this scene is supposed to lie.

        Hark! the owlet flaps her wing,
           In the pathless dell beneath,
        Hark! night ravens loudly sing,
           Tidings of despair and death.—

5   Horror covers all the sky,
           Clouds of darkness blot the moon,
        Prepare! for mortal thou must die,
           Prepare to yield thy soul up soon—

        Fierce the tempest raves around,
10   Fierce the volleyed lightnings fly,

---

53 seize] sieze *1810*
55 whirlwind's] whirlwinds *1810 1898*
62 gloom,—] gloom, *1898*

Dateline. DECEMBER,] DECEMBER *1898*

Text collated with *1810* and *1898*.

30   *Victor and Cazire*

Crashing thunder shakes the ground,
   Fire and tumult fill the sky.—

Hark! the tolling village bell,
   Tells the hour of midnight come,
Now can blast the powers of Hell,   15
   Fiend-like Goblins now can roam—

See! his crest all stained with rain,
   A warrior hastening speeds his way,
He starts, looks round him, starts again,
   And sighs for the approach of day.   20

See! his frantic steed he reins,
   See! he lifts his hands on high,
Implores a respite to his pains,
   From the powers of the sky.—

He seeks an Inn, for faint from toil,   25
   Fatigue had bent his lofty form,
To rest his wearied limbs awhile,
   Fatigued with wandering and the storm.—
   *   *   *   *   *   *   *
   *   *   *   *   *   *   *

Slow the door is opened wide—
   With trackless tread a stranger came,   30
His form Majestic, slow his stride,
   He sate, nor spake,—nor told his name—

Terror blaunched the warrior's cheek,
   Cold sweat from his forehead ran,
In vain his tongue essayed to speak,——   35
   At last the stranger thus began:

"Mortal! thou that saw'st the sprite,
   "Tell me what I wish to know,

---

16 Fiend-like] Fiend—like   *1810*
    Goblins] goblins   *1898*
21 reins,] reigns,   *1898*
28 storm.—] storm.   *1898*

40   "Or come with me before 'tis light,
            "Where cypress trees and mandrakes grow.

        "Fierce the avenging Demon's ire,
           "Fiercer than the wintry blast,
        "Fiercer than the lightning's fire,
           "When the hour of twilight's past—"

45   The warrior raised his sunken eye,
           It met the stranger's sullen scowl,
        "Mortal! Mortal! thou must die,"
           In burning letters chilled his soul.—

              WARRIOR.
        Stranger! whosoe'er you are,
50   I feel impelled my tale to tell—
        Horrors stranger shalt thou hear,
           Horrors drear as those of Hell.

        O'er my Castle silence reigned,
           Late the night and drear the hour,
55   When on the terrace I observed,
           A fleeting shadowy mist to lower.—

        Light the cloud as summer fog,
           Which transient shuns the morning beam;
        Fleeting as the cloud on bog,
60   That hangs or on the mountain stream.—

        Horror seized my shuddering brain,
           Horror dimmed my starting eye,
        In vain I tried to speak,—In vain
           My limbs essayed the spot to fly—

65   At last the thin and shadowy form,
           With noiseless, trackless footsteps came,—

---

43 lightning's] lightnings   *1810 1898*
44 twilight's] twilights   *1810 1898*
    past—"] past—   *1810 1898*
48 soul.—] soul—   *1810*
      soul.   *1898*

49 Stranger!] "Stranger!   *1810 1898*
    whosoe'er] whoso'er   **1810** *1898*
64 limbs] limb's   *1810 1898*

Its light robe floated on the storm,
    Its head was bound with lambent flame.

In chilling voice drear as the breeze
    Which sweeps along th' autumnal ground,   70
Which wanders thro' the leafless trees,
    Or the mandrake's groan which floats around.

"Thou art mine and I am thine,
    "'Till the sinking of the world,
"I am thine and thou art mine,   75
    "'Till in ruin death is hurled——

"Strong the power and dire the fate
    "Which drags me from the depths of Hell,
"Breaks the tomb's eternal gate,
    "Where fiendish shapes and dead men yell,   80

"Haply I might ne'er have shrank
    "From flames that rack the guilty dead,
"Haply I might ne'er have sank
    "On pleasure's flowry, thorny bed—

—"But stay! no more I dare disclose,   85
    "Of the tale I wish to tell,
"On Earth relentless were my woes,
    "But fiercer are my pangs in Hell—

"Now I claim thee as my love,
    "Lay aside all chilling fear,   90
"My affection will I prove,
    "Where sheeted ghosts and spectres are!

"For thou art mine, and I am thine,
    "'Till the dreaded judgment day,
"I am thine, and thou art mine—   95
    "Night is past—I must away."

---

72 mandrake's] mandrakes   *1810 1898*
79 tomb's] tombs   *1810 1898*
84 pleasure's] pleasures   *1810 1898*

                Still I gazed, and still the form
                    Pressed upon my aching sight,
                Still I braved the howling storm,
100   When the ghost dissolved in night.—

                Restless, sleepless fled the night,
                    Sleepless as a sick man's bed,
                When he sighs for morning light,
                    When he turns his aching head,—

105   Slow and painful passed the day,
                    Melancholy seized my brain,
                Lingering fled the hours away,
                    Lingering to a wretch in pain.—

                At last came night, ah! horrid hour,
110   Ah! chilling time that wakes the dead,
                When demons ride the clouds that lower,
                    —The phantom sat upon my bed.

                In hollow voice, low as the sound
                    Which in some charnel makes it moan,
115   What floats along the burying ground,
                    The phantom claimed me as her own.

                Her chilling finger on my head,
                    With coldest touch congealed my soul—
                Cold as the finger of the dead,
120   Or damps which round a tombstone roll—

                Months are passed in lingering round,
                    Every night the spectre comes,
                With thrilling step it shakes the ground,
                    With thrilling step it round me roams—

125   Stranger! I have told to thee,
                    All the tale I have to tell—

---

102 man's] mans *1810 1898*
106 seized] siezed *1810*

Stranger! canst thou tell to me,
    How to scape the powers of Hell—

        STRANGER.

Warrior! I can ease thy woes,
    Wilt thou, wilt thou, come with me—   130
Warrior! I can all disclose,
    Follow, follow, follow me.

Yet the tempest's duskiest wing,
    Its mantle stretches o'er the sky,
Yet the midnight ravens sing,   135
    "Mortal! Mortal thou must die."

At last they saw a river clear,
    That crossed the heathy path they trode,
The Stranger's look was wild and drear,
    The firm Earth shook beneath his nod—   140

He raised a wand above his head,
    He traced a circle on the plain,
In a wild verse he called the dead,
    The dead with silent footsteps came.

A burning brilliance on his head,   145
    Flaming filled the stormy air,
In a wild verse he called the dead,
    The dead in motley crowd were there.—

"Ghasta! Ghasta! come along,
    "Bring thy fiendish crowd with thee,   150
"Quickly raise th' avenging Song,
    "Ghasta! Ghasta! come to me."

Horrid shapes in mantles grey,
    Flit athwart the stormy night,
"Ghasta! Ghasta! come away,   155
    "Come away before 'tis light."

---

128 scape] 'scape *1898*
    Hell—] Hell"— ***1810** 1898*
133 tempest's] tempests ***1810** 1898*

See! the sheeted Ghost they bring,
 Yelling dreadful o'er the heath,
Hark! the deadly verse they sing,
160   Tidings of despair and death!

The yelling Ghost before him stands,
 See! she rolls her eyes around,
Now she lifts her bony hands,
 Now her footsteps shake the ground.

    STRANGER.
165 Phantom of Theresa say,
 Why to earth again you came,
Quickly speak, I must away!
 Or you must bleach for aye in flame,—

    PHANTOM.
"Mighty one I know thee now,
170 "Mightiest power of the sky,
"Know thee by thy flaming brow,
 "Know thee by thy sparkling eye.

"That fire is scorching! Oh! I came,
 "From the caverned depth of Hell,
175 "My fleeting false Rodolph to claim,
 "Mighty one! I know thee well."—

    STRANGER.
Ghasta! seize yon wandering sprite,
 Drag her to the depth beneath,
Take her swift, before 'tis light,
180 Take her to the cells of death!

Thou that heardst the trackless dead,
 In the mouldering tomb must lie,
Mortal! look upon my head,
 Mortal! Mortal! thou must die.

185 Of glowing flame a cross was there,
 Which threw a light around his form,

---

177 seize] sieze *1810*

>   Whilst his lank and raven hair,
>   Floated wild upon the storm.—
>
>   The warrior upwards turned his eyes,
>   Gazed upon the cross of fire,   190
>   There sat horror and surprise,
>   There sat God's eternal ire.—
>
>   A shivering through the Warrior flew,
>   Colder than the nightly blast,
>   Colder than the evening dew,   195
>   When the hour of twilight's past.—
>
>   Thunder shakes th' expansive sky,
>   Shakes the bosom of the heath,
>   "Mortal! Mortal! thou must die"—
>   The warrior sank convulsed in death.   200
>   JANUARY, 1810.

FRAGMENT,
OR THE TRIUMPH OF CONSCIENCE.

> 'Twas dead of the night when I sate in my dwelling,
>   One glimmering lamp was expiring and low,—
> Around the dark tide of the tempest was swelling,
> Along the wild mountains night-ravens were yelling,
>   They bodingly presaged destruction and woe!   5
>
> 'Twas then that I started, the wild storm was howling,
>   Nought was seen, save the lightning that danced
>   on the sky,
> Above me the crash of the thunder was rolling,
>   And low, chilling murmurs the blast wafted by.—
>
> My heart sank within me, unheeded the jar   10
>   Of the battling clouds on the mountain tops broke,
> Unheeded the thunder-peal crashed in mine ear,

---

196 twilight's] twilights   *1810 1898*

Text collated with *1810* and *1898*.
No variants appear.

    This heart hard as iron was stranger to fear,
        But conscience in low noiseless whispering spoke.

15   'Twas then that her form on the whirlwind uprearing,
        The dark ghost of the murdered Victoria strode,
    Her right hand a blood reeking dagger was bearing,
        She swiftly advanced to my lonesome abode.—

    I wildly then called on the tempest to bear me!
     *   *   *   *   *   *   *   *
 *   *   *   *   *   *   *   *

PHILLIPS, PRINTERS, WORTHING.

THE EDINBURGH LITERARY JOURNAL;

OR,

WEEKLY REGISTER OF CRITICISM AND BELLES LETTRES.

No. 33.   SATURDAY, JUNE 27, 1829.   Price 6d.

LITERARY CRITICISM.

THE POET SHELLEY—HIS UNPUBLISHED WORK, "THE WANDERING JEW."

We now proceed to redeem the promise we made last Saturday, to give our readers a more detailed account of this exceedingly interesting poem. There can be little doubt that, with the single exception of Lord Byron, no poet of our day has evinced a more strikingly powerful and original genius than Shelley,—indeed, in so far as originality is concerned, he is probably entitled to claim precedency even of Lord Byron. Hardly, therefore, could there have come into our possession any literary curiosity upon which we should have placed a greater value than an unpublished work by the author of the "Cenci;" for, much as we regret the fallacious and unhappy principles which Shelley was induced to adopt, and whose spirit he was too much in the habit of infusing into his writings, we hesitate not to own the great admiration we have ever entertained for his profound abilities.

We have already mentioned that the whole of the manuscript of "The Wandering Jew," now in our possession—and which, we have every reason to believe, is the only copy extant—is written in Shelley's own hand, and that it must have been composed about twenty years ago. This latter fact is sufficiently established by the date affixed to the Preface, which is "January 1811;" and the Preface bears internal marks of having been written after the poem, which may therefore be set down as belonging to the year 1810. It is, consequently, in all likelihood, the very earliest production of Shelley's pen; for that wild and astonishing poem, "Queen Mab," was not written till 1811, and was not given to the public till 1815. In 1811, Shelley was only eighteen, and he himself, writing from Pisa in 1821, says,—"A poem, entitled *Queen Mab*, was written by me at the age of eighteen, I daresay in a sufficiently intemperate spirit," &c. It thus appears, that "The Wandering Jew" must have been written when the poet was only seventeen, and when his talents were entirely unknown. It may possibly have been offered to one or two booksellers, both in London and Edinburgh, without success, and this may account for the neglect into which the author allowed it to fall, when new cares crowded upon him, and new prospects opened round him. Certain it is, that it has been carefully kept by the literary gentleman to whom he intrusted its perusal when he visited Edinburgh in 1811, and would have been willingly surrendered by him at any subsequent period, had any application to that effect been made. A poem written by a lad of seventeen would, in most cases, possess little attraction; but when it is recollected that the same individual produced "Queen Mab" at eighteen, and afterwards, during his brief career, stood in the very first place of intellectual superiority, the case is altered, and the *primitiæ* of such a mind become perhaps still more interesting than its most matured efforts.

Mr Shelley appears to have had some doubts whether to call his poem "The Wandering Jew," or "The Victim of the Eternal Avenger." Both names occur in the manuscript; but had the work been published, it is to be hoped that he would finally have fixed on the former, the more especially as the poem itself contains very little calculated to give offence to the religious reader. The motto on the title-page is from the 22d chapter of St John,—"If I will that he tarry till I come, what is that to thee?—follow thou me." Turning over the leaf, we meet with the following dedication:—"To Sir Francis Burdett, bart. M. P., in consideration of the active virtues by which both his public and private life is so eminently distinguished, the following poem is inscribed by the Author." Again turning the leaf, we meet with the

PREFACE.

"The subject of the following Poem is an imaginary personage, noted for the various and contradictory traditions which have prevailed concerning him—The Wandering Jew. Many sage monkish writers have supported the authenticity of this fact, the reality of his existence. But as the quoting them would have led me to annotations perfectly uninteresting, although very fashionable, I decline presenting to the public any thing but the bare poem, which they will agree with me not to be of sufficient consequence to authorize deep antiquarian researches on its subject. I might, indeed, have introduced, by anticipating future events, the no less grand, although equally groundless, superstitions of the battle of Armageddon, the personal reign of J— C—, &c.; but I preferred, improbable as the following tale may appear, retaining the old method of describing past events: it is certainly more consistent with reason, more interesting, even in works of imagination. With respect to the omission of elucidatory notes, I have followed the well-known maxim of ' Do unto others as thou wouldest they should do unto thee.'

"*January*, 1811."

The poem introduced by the above Preface is in four cantos; and, though the octosyllabic verse is the most prominent, it contains a variety of measures, like Sir Walter Scott's poetical romances. The incidents are simple, and refer rather to an episode in the life of the Wandering Jew, than to any attempt at a full delineation of all his adventures. We shall give an analysis of the plot, and intersperse, as we proceed, some of the most interesting passages of the poem. It opens thus, in a strain of subdued and tranquil beauty:

"The brilliant orb of parting day
Diffused a rich and a mellow ray
 Above the mountain's brow;
It tinged the hills with lustrous light,
It tinged the promontory's height
 Still sparkling with the snow;
And, as aslant it threw its beam,
Tipp'd with gold the mountain stream
 That laved the vale below.
Long hung the eye of glory there,
And linger'd as if loth to leave
A scene so lovely and so fair,
 'Twere there even luxury to grieve;
So soft the clime, so balm the air,
 So pure and genial were the skies,
In sooth 'twas almost Paradise,—

First page of the first installment of *The Wandering Jew*, 27 June 1829 issue of *Edinburgh Literary Journal*. With kind permission of The Carl H. Pforzheimer Collection of Shelley and His Circle, The New York Public Library, Astor, Lenox, and Tilden Foundations.

THE WANDERING JEW;
or, The Victim of the Eternal Avenger

Begun by the winter of 1809/10 and first released to a publisher the following summer, ***The Wandering Jew; or, The Victim of the Eternal Avenger (WJ)*** was PBS's earliest completed book-length poem and remains one of his most textually perplexing works. No version of the poem appeared in print during PBS's lifetime, despite his several attempts to find an interested publisher. And although PBS produced at least two MS versions of ***WJ***, the whereabouts of neither one has been known since the 1830s. Consequently, we see this poem through a glass darkly, as presented in two periodicals that published versions of ***WJ*** after PBS's death: the *Edinburgh Literary Journal; or, Weekly Register of Criticism and Belles Lettres* (*ELJ*), which published a version of ***WJ*** in the summer of 1829 (*1829E*); and *Fraser's Magazine for Town and Country* (*FM*), which published its own version of the poem in 1831 (*1831F*). Each of these sources offers an abridged version of ***WJ*** that differs textually from the other in important ways, creating formidable difficulties for textual scholars, who have disagreed about the relationship between the two published texts themselves and about the source from which each was drawn. Further difficulties in understanding the textual history of ***WJ*** have arisen because, after PBS's death, his cousin Thomas Medwin claimed co-authorship of the poem, raising questions about how much of ***WJ*** was actually written by PBS himself.

Our investigation of these issues suggests that ***WJ*** as transmitted through the early periodical versions was written entirely by PBS and that both of these versions derive from the same MS, most probably a fair copy of ***WJ*** revised heavily in some places (esp. Canto IV) that PBS left with the Edinburgh publisher James Ballantyne in the summer of 1811. Although the version of ***WJ*** published in *FM* is more complete, it appears to be based on *ELJ*, wherever possible, resorting directly to a transcription of the safekeeping MS (also now lost) for the parts of ***WJ*** that the editor of *FM* could not find in *ELJ*. Our own text similarly follows *ELJ* (which appears to us to be more accurately produced) as its copy-text for all of the portions of ***WJ*** that it includes, and turns to *FM* for the rest of the text. For Commentary see pages 189–234; for Historical Collations see pages 355–74.

THE WANDERING JEW;

OR, THE VICTIM OF THE ETERNAL AVENGER

"If I will that he tarry till I come, what is that to thee?—follow thou me." *St. John,* xxi.22.

To Sir Francis Burdett, bart. M. P., in consideration of the active virtues by which both his public and private life is so eminently distinguished, the following poem is inscribed by the Author.

PREFACE.

The subject of the following Poem is an imaginary personage, noted for the various and contradictory traditions which have prevailed concerning him—The Wandering Jew. Many sage monkish writers have supported the authenticity of this fact, the reality of his existence. But as the quoting them would have led me to annotations perfectly uninteresting, although very fashionable, I decline presenting to the public any thing but the bare poem, which they will agree with me not to be of sufficient consequence to authorize deep antiquarian researches on its subject. I might, indeed, have introduced, by anticipating future events, the no less grand, although equally groundless, superstitions of the battle of Armageddon, the personal reign of J—C—, &c.; but I preferred, improbable as the following tale may appear, retaining the old method of describing past events: it is certainly more consistent with reason, more interesting, even in works of imagination. With respect to the omission of elucidatory notes, I have followed the well-known maxim of 'Do unto others as thou wouldest they should do unto thee.'

January, 1811

Text collated with *1811* (II, III), *1829E*, *1829Inc* (IV), and *1831F*. The siglum *1831F* appears in boldface for those sections of Text for which it serves as copy-text. The epigraph in *1829E* appears after the dedication and preface. In *1831F* the epigraph appears after the title, and the dedication and preface are omitted.

In Canto I, *1829E* omits lines 58–89, 102–49, 168–341; and *1831F* omits 14–18, 25–28, 39–40, 43–57, 98–101, and 150–61.

Title. The . . . Avenger]
    THE WANDERING JEW *1831F*
Epigraph. —follow] Follow *1831F*
    St. John, xxi.22.] 22d chapter
    of St John *1829E*

Dedication. To . . . Author.]
    omitted *1831F*
Preface. *Text of Preface*] omitted *1831F*

Canto I.

> "Me miserable, which way shall I fly?
> Infinite wrath and infinite despair—
> Which way I fly is hell—myself am hell;
> And in this lowest deep a lower deep,
> To which the hell I suffer seems a heaven."
>
> *Paradise Lost.*

    The brilliant orb of parting day
    Diffused a rich and a mellow ray
      Above the mountain's brow;
    It tinged the hills with lustrous light,
5   It tinged the promontory's height
      Still sparkling with the snow;
    And, as aslant it threw its beam,
    Tipp'd with gold the mountain stream
      That laved the vale below.
10   Long hung the eye of glory there,
      And linger'd as if loth to leave
    A scene so lovely and so fair,
    'Twere there even luxury to grieve;
    So soft the clime, so balm the air,
15   So pure and genial were the skies,
      In sooth 'twas almost Paradise,—
    For ne'er did the sun's splendour close
    On such a picture of repose;—
    All, all was tranquil, all was still,
20   Save when the music of the rill,
      Or a distant waterfall,
    At intervals broke on the ear,
    Which Echo's self was pleased to hear,
      And ceased her babbling call.
25   With every charm the landscape glow'd

Canto marker. CANTO I.] *omitted* ***1829E***
Epigraph. *omitted* ***1829E***
2 a mellow] a *omitted* *1831F*
    ray] ray, *1831F*
5 height] height, *1831F*
7 And,] And *1831F*
8 Tipp'd] Tipt *1831F*
9 below.] below; *1831F*
13 there even luxury to grieve;]
    luxury even, there to grieve. *1831F*

14–18 *omitted* *1831F*
20 when] where ***1829E***
21 a distant] a *omitted* *1831F*
23 Echo's] echo's *1831F*
    pleased] charmed *1831F*
24 stanza break added *1831F*
25–28 *omitted* *1831F*

Which partial Nature's hand bestow'd;
Nor could the mimic hand of art
Such beauties or such hues impart.

Light clouds, in fleeting livery gay,
Hung painted in grotesque array   30
   Upon the western sky;
Forgetful of the approaching dawn,
The peasants danced upon the lawn,
   For the vintage time was nigh;
How jocund to the tabor's sound,   35
The smooth turf trembling as they bound,
In every measure light and free,
The very soul of harmony!
Grace in each attitude, they move,
   They thrill to amorous ecstasy,   40
Light as the dew-drops of the morn
That hang upon the blossom'd thorn,
Subdued by the pow'r of resistless Love.

Ah! days of innocence, of joy,
Of rapture that knows no alloy,   45
   Haste on,—ye roseate hours,
Free from the world's tumultuous cares,
From pale distrust, from hopes and fears,
Baneful concomitants of time,—
'Tis yours, beneath this favour'd clime, 50
   Your pathway strewn with flowers,
Upborne on pleasure's downy wing,
To quaff a long unfading spring,
And beat with light and careless step the ground;
The fairest flowers too soon grow sere, 55
Too soon shall tempests blast the year,
And sin's eternal winter reign around.

---

29 clouds,] clouds   *1831F*
30 Hung] Hung,   *1831F*
31 sky;] sky: *1831F*
34 nigh;] nigh: *1831F*
36 The . . . as] O'er the smooth,
    trembling turf   *1831F*
38 harmony!] harmony;   *1831F*
39–40 *omitted*   *1831F*

41 dew-drops] dewdrops   *1831F*
    morn] morn,   *1831F*
42 blossom'd] blossomed   *1831F*
    thorn,] thorn.   *1831F*
    stanza break added   *1831F*
43–57 *omitted*   *1831F*
57 *stanza break follows*

>
> But see, what forms are those,
> Scarce seen by glimpse of dim twilight,
> 60   Wandering o'er the mountain's height?
> They swiftly haste to the vale below:
> One wraps his mantle around his brow,
> As if to hide his woes;
> And as his steed impetuous flies,
> 65   What strange fire flashes from his eyes!
> The far off city's murmuring sound
> Was borne on the breeze which floated around;
> Noble Padua's lofty spire
> Scarce glow'd with the sunbeam's latest fire,
> 70   Yet dashed the travellers on—
> Ere night o'er the earth was spread,
> Full many a mile they must have sped,
> Ere their destined course was run.
> Welcome was the moonbeam's ray,
> 75   Which slept upon the towers so grey.
> But, hark! a convent's vesper bell—
> It seemed to be a very spell—
> The stranger checked his courser's rein,
> And listened to the mournful sound:
> 80   Listened—and paused—and paused again:
> A thrill of pity and of pain
> Through his inmost soul had past,
> While gushed the tear-drops silently and fast.
>
> A crowd was at the convent gate,
> 85   The gate was opened wide;
> No longer on his steed he sate,
> But mingled with the tide.
> He felt a solemn awe and dread,
> As he the chapel entered;
> 90   Dim was the light from the pale moon beaming,
>   As it fell on the saint-cipher'd panes,
> Or, from the western window streaming,
>   Tinged the pillars with varied stains.

58–59 *omitted* *1829E*
91 saint-cipher'd] saint-cyphered   *1831F*
   panes,] panes;   *1831F*
92 Or,] Or   *1831F*

To the eye of enthusiasm strange forms were gliding,
    In each dusky recess of the aisle,   95
And indefined shades in succession were striding
    O'er the coignes[1] of the pillar'd pile;—
The pillars to the vaulted roof
    In airy lightness rose;
Now they mount to the rich Gothic ceiling aloof,   100
    And exquisite tracery disclose.

The altar illumined now darts its bright rays,
The train past in brilliant array;
On the shrine Saint Pietro's rich ornaments blaze,
And rival the brilliance of day.   105
Hark!—now the loud organ swells full on the ear—
So sweetly mellow, chaste, and clear;
Melting, kindling, raising, firing,
Delighting now, and now inspiring,
Peal upon peal the music floats—   110
Now they list still as death to the dying notes;
Whilst the soft voices of the choir,
Exalt the soul from base desire;
Till it mounts on unearthly pinions free,
Dissolved in heavenly ecstasy.   115

Now a dead stillness reigned around,
Uninterrupted by a sound;
Save when in deadened response ran,
The last faint echoes down the aisle,
Reverberated through the pile,   120
As within the pale the holy man,
With voice devout and saintly look,
Slow chaunted from the sacred book,
Or pious prayers were duly said,
For spirits of departed dead.   125
With beads and crucifix and hood,

---

[1] Buttress nor coigne of 'vantage.—*Macbeth.*

94 gliding,] gliding   *1831F*
95 aisle,] aisle;   *1831F*
96 striding] striding,   *1831F*
97 pillar'd pile;—]
    gothic pile. *stanza break*   *1831F*
Footnote. *omitted*   *1829E*

98–101 *omitted*   *1831F*
102–49 *omitted*   **1829E**

   Close by his side the abbess stood;
   Now her dark penetrating eyes
   Were raised in suppliance to heaven,
130 And now her bosom heaved with sighs,
   As if to human weakness given.
   Her stern, severe, yet beauteous brow
   Frowned on all who stood below;
   And the fire which flashed from her steady gaze,
135 As it turned on the listening crowd its rays,
    Superior virtue told,—
   Virtue as pure as heaven's own dew,
   But which, untainted, never knew,
    To pardon weaker mould.
140 The heart though chaste and cold as snow—
   'Twere faulty to be virtuous so.

   Not a whisper now breathed in the pillared aisle—
   The stranger advanced to the altar high—
   Convulsive was heard a smothered sigh!
145 Lo! four fair nuns to the altar draw near,
   With solemn footstep, as the while
   A fainting novice they bear—
   The roses from her cheek are fled,
   But there the lily reigns instead;
150 Light as a sylph's, her form confest,
   Beneath the drapery of her vest,
    A perfect grace and symmetry;
   Her eyes, with rapture form'd to move,
   To melt with tenderness and love,
155   Or beam with sensibility,
   To Heaven were raised in pious prayer,
    A silent eloquence of woe;
   Now hung the pearly tear-drop there,
   Sate on her cheek a fix'd despair;
160 And now she beat her bosom bare,
    As pure as driven snow.
   Nine graceful Novices around
   Fresh roses strew'd upon the ground,
    In purest white array'd;

150–61 *omitted* *1831F*   163 strew'd] strew *1831F*
162 Novices] novices *1831F*   ground,] ground: *1831F*
              164 array'd;] arrayed, *1831F*

Three spotless vestal virgins shed 165
Sabean incense o'er the head
   Of the devoted maid.

They dragged her to the altar's pale,
The traveller leant against the rail,
And gazed with eager eye,— 170
His cheek was flushed with sudden glow,
On his brow sate a darker shade of woe,
As a transient expression fled by.

The sympathetic feeling flew
Thro' every breast, from man to man, 175
Confused and open clamours ran,
Louder and louder still they grew;
When the abbess waved her hand,
A stern resolve was in her eye,
And every wild tumultuous cry 180
Was stilled at her command.

The abbess made the well known sign—
The novice reached the fatal shrine,
And mercy implored from the power divine;
At length she shrieked aloud, 185
She dashed from the supporting nun,
Ere the fatal rite was done,
And plunged amid the crowd.
Confusion reigned throughout the throng,
Still the novice fled along, 190
Impelled by frantic fear,
When the maddened traveller's eager grasp
In firmest yet in wildest clasp
Arrested her career.
As fainting from terror she sank on the ground, 195
Her loosened locks floated her fine form around;
The zone which confined her shadowy vest
No longer her throbbing bosom prest,
Its animation dead;

---

165 Three] Nine *1831F*
166 Sabean] Sabæan *1831F*
168–*end of Canto I.*] *omitted* ***1829E***

200   No more her feverish pulse beat high,
      Expression dwelt not in her eye,
      Her wildered senses fled.
              *   *   *   *   *

      Hark! hark! the demon of the storm!
      I see his vast expanding form
205   Blend with the strange and sulphurous glare
      Of comets through the turbid air.
      Yes, 'twas his voice, I heard its roar,
      The wild waves lashed the caverned shore
      In angry murmurs hoarse and loud,
210   Higher and higher still they rise;
      Red lightnings gleam from every cloud
      And paint wild shapes upon the skies;
      The echoing thunder rolls around,
      Convulsed with earthquake rocks the ground.

215   The traveller yet undaunted stood,
      He heeded not the roaring flood;
      Yet Rosa slept, her bosom bare,
      Her cheek was deadly pale,
      The ringlets of her auburn hair
220   Streamed in a lengthened trail,
      And motionless her seraph form;
      Unheard, unheeded raved the storm.
      Whilst, borne on the wing of the gale,
      The harrowing shriek of the white sea mew
225   As o'er the midnight surge she flew;
      The howlings of the squally blast
      As o'er the beetling cliffs it past;
      Mingled with the peals on high,
      That, swelling louder, echoed by,
230   Assailed the traveller's ear.
      He heeded not the maddened storm
      As it pelted against his lofty form,
      He felt no awe, no fear.
      In contrast, like the courser pale[1]

---

[1] "Behold a pale horse, and his name that sate upon him was Death, and Hell followed with him."—*Revelation*, vi. 8.

Footnote for 234.
   Revelation] *Revelations*   *1831F*

That stalks along Death's pitchy vale 235
With silent, with gigantic tread,
Trampling the dying and the dead.

Rising from her death-like trance,
Fair Rosa met the stranger's glance;
She started from his chilling gaze, 240
Wild was it as the tempest's blaze,
It shot a lurid gleam of light.
A secret spell of sudden dread,
A mystic, strange, and harrowing fear,
As when the spirits of the dead, 245
Drest in ideal shapes appear,
And hideous glance on human sight—
Scarce could Rosa's frame sustain,
The chill that pressed upon her brain.

Anon, that transient spell was o'er, 250
Dark clouds deform his brow no more,
But rapid fled away;
Sweet fascination dwelt around,
Mixed with a soft, a silver sound,
As soothing to the ravished ear, 255
As what enthusiast lovers hear;
Which seems to steal along the sky,
When mountain mists are seen to fly,
Before the approach of day.
He seized on wondering Rosa's hand, 260
"And, ah!" cried he, "be this the band
Shall join us, till this earthly frame,
Sinks convulsed in bickering flame—
When around the demons yell,
And drag the sinful wretch to hell, 265
Then, Rosa, will we part—
Then fate, and only fate's decree,
Shall tear thy lovely soul from me,
And rend thee from my heart.
Long has Paulo sought in vain, 270
A friend to share his grief;—
Never will he seek again,
For the wretch has found relief,
Till the Prince of Darkness bursts his chain,
Till death and desolation reign— 275

Rosa, wilt thou then be mine?
Ever fairest, I am thine!"

He ceased, and on the howling blast,
Which wildly round the mountain past,
280 Died his accents low;
Yet fiercely howled the midnight storm,
As Paulo bent his awful form,
And leaned his lofty brow.

ROSA

"Stranger, mystic stranger, rise;
285 Whence do these tumults fill the skies?
Who conveyed me, say, this night,
To this wild and cloud-capped height?
Who art thou? and why am I
Beneath Heaven's pityless canopy?
290 For the wild winds roar around my head;
Lightnings redden the wave;—
Was it the power of the mighty dead,
Who live beneath the grave?
Or did the Abbess drag me here,
295 To make yon swelling surge my bier?"

PAULO

"Ah, lovely Rosa! cease thy fear,
It was thy friend who bore thee here—
I, thy friend, till this fabric of earth,
Sinks in the chaos that gave it birth;
300 Till the meteor-bolt of the God above,
Shall tear its victim from his love,—
That love which must unbroken last,
Till the hour of envious fate is past;
Till the mighty basements of the sky
305 In bickering hell-flames heated fly:
E'en then will I sit on some rocky height,
Whilst around lower clouds of eternal night,
E'en then will I loved Rosa save
From the yawning abyss of the grave.—
310 Or, into the gulf impetuous hurled—
If sinks with its latest tenants the world,
Then will our souls in union fly

Throughout the wide and boundless sky:
Then, free from th' ills that envious fate
Has heaped upon our mortal state,   315
We'll taste etherial pleasure;
Such as none but thou canst give, —
Such as none but I receive,
And rapture without measure."

As thus he spoke, a sudden blaze   320
Of pleasure mingled in his gaze:
Illumined by the dazzling light,
He glows with radiant lustre bright;
His features with new glory shine,
And sparkle as with beams divine.   325
"Strange, awful being," Rosa said,
"Whence is this superhuman dread,
That harrows up my inmost frame?
Whence does this unknown tingling flame,
Consume and penetrate my soul?   330
By turns with fear and love possessed,
Tumultuous thoughts swell high my breast;
A thousand wild emotions roll,
And mingle their resistless tide;
O'er thee some magic arts preside;   335
As by the influence of a charm,
Lulled into rest my griefs subside,
And safe in thy protecting arm,
I feel no power can do me harm:
But the storm raves wildly o'er the sea,   340
Bear me away! I confide in thee!"

Canto II.

"I could a tale unfold, whose slightest word
Would harrow up thy soul, freeze thy young blood,
Make thy two eyes, like stars, start from their spheres;

In this canto, *1811* consists of lines 94 and 102–10, which appear as an epigraph to Chapter 8 of *St.Irv* identified as being from "WANDERING JEW. 1811." *1829E* provides the text of only lines 79–192, the rest of this canto originating in *1831F*.
Canto marker. CANTO II] *omitted*   *1829E*
Epigraph. *omitted*   *1829E*

>   Thy knotted and combined locks to part,
>   And each particular hair to stand on end,
>   Like quills upon the fretful porcupine."
>   *Hamlet.*

    THE horrors of the nightly blast,
The lowering tempest clouds were past,
Had sunk beneath the main;
Light baseless mists were all that fled,
5   Above the weary traveller's head,
As he left the spacious plain.

Fled were the vapours of the night,
Faint streaks of rosy tinted light
Were painted on the matin grey;
10   And as the sun began to rise,
To pour his animating ray,
Glowed with his fire the eastern skies,
The distant rocks—the far-off bay,
The ocean's sweet and lovely blue,
15   The mountain's variegated breast,
Blushing with tender tints of dawn,
Or with fantastic shadows drest.
The waving wood, the opening lawn,
Rose to existence, waked anew,
20   In colours exquisite of hue.
Their mingled charms Victorio viewed,
And lost in admiration stood.

From yesternight how changed the scene,
When howled the blast o'er the dark cliff's side,
25   And mingled with the maddened roar
Of the wild surge that lashed the shore.
To-day—scarce heard the whispering breeze,
And still and motionless the seas
Scarce heard the murmuring of their tide;
30   All, all is peaceful and serene,
Serenely on Victorio's breast

1–78 omitted *1829E*
24 cliff's] cliffs *1831F*

It breathed a soft and tranquil rest,
Which bade each wild emotion cease,
And hushed the passions into peace.

Along the winding Po he went, 35
His footsteps to the spot were bent
Where Paulo dwelt, his wandered friend,
For thither did his wishes tend.
Noble Victorio's race was proud,
From Cosmo's blood he came; 40
To him a wild untutored crowd
Of vassals, in allegiance bowed,
Illustrious was his name;
Yet vassals and wealth he scorned, to go
Unnoticed with a man of woe: 45
Gay hope and expectation sate,
Throned in his eager eye,
And ere he reached the castle gate,
The sun had mounted high.

Wild was the spot where the castle stood, 50
Its towers embosomed deep in wood,
Gigantic cliffs, with craggy steeps,
Reared their proud heads on high,
Their bases were washed by the foaming deeps,
Their summits were hid in the sky; 55
From the valley below they excluded the day,
That valley ne'er cheered by the sunbeam's ray;
Nought broke on the silence drear,
Save the hungry vultures darting by,
Or eagles yelling fearfully, 60
As they bore to the rocks their prey,
Or when the fell wolf ravening prowled,
Or the gaunt wild boar fiercely howled
His hideous screams on the night's dull ear.

Borne on pleasure's downy wing, 65
Downy as the breath of spring,
Not thus fled Paulo's hours away,
Though brightened by the cheerful day:
Friendship or wine, or softer love,
The sparkling eye, the foaming bowl, 70

>   Could with no lasting rapture move,
>   Nor still the tumults of his soul.
>   And yet there was in Rosa's kiss
>   A momentary thrill of bliss;
> 75 Oft the dark clouds of grief would fly,
>   Beneath the beam of sympathy;
>   And love and converse sweet bestow,
>   A transient requiem from woe.—
>
>   Strange business, and of import vast,
> 80 On things which long ago were past,
>   Drew Paulo oft from home;
>   Then would a darker, deeper shade,
>   By sorrow traced, his brow o'erspread,
>   And o'er his features roam.
> 85 Oft as they spent the midnight hour,
>   And heard the wintry wild winds rave
>   Midst the roar and spray of the dashing wave,
>   Was Paulo's dark brow seen to lour.
>   Then, as the lamp's uncertain blaze
> 90 Shed o'er the hall its partial rays,
>   And shadows strange were seen to fall,
>   And glide upon the dusky wall,
>   Would Paulo start with sudden fear.
>   Why then unbidden gush'd the tear,
> 95 As he mutter'd strange words to the ear?—
>   Why frequent heaved the smother'd sigh?—
>   Why did he gaze on vacancy,
>   As if some strange form was near?
>   Then would the fillet of his brow
> 100 Fierce as a fiery furnace glow,
>   As it burn'd with red and lambent flame;
>   Then would cold shuddering seize his frame,
>   As gasping he labour'd for breath.
>   The strange light of his gorgon eye,
> 105 As, frenzied and rolling dreadfully,

---

94 Why] ———Why *1811*
    tear,] tear? *1811*
102 shuddering] shudderings *1811*
    frame,] brain, *1811*
103 breath.] breath; *1811*
104 light] gaze *1811*
    gorgon] meteor *1811*
105 As,] Which, *1811*
    As *1831F*
    frenzied] frenzied, *1811*

It glared with terrific gleam,
Would chill like the spectre gaze of death,
　　As, conjured by feverish dream,
He seems o'er the sick man's couch to stand,
And shakes the dread lance in his skeleton hand.　　　110

But when the paroxysm was o'er,
And clouds deform'd his brow no more,
Would Rosa soothe his tumults dire,
　　Would bid him calm his grief,
Would quench reflection's rising fire,　　　115
　　And give his soul relief.
As on his form with pitying eye,
　　The ministering angel hung,
And wiped the drops of agony,
　　The music of her siren tongue　　　120
Lull'd forcibly his griefs to rest.
Like fleeting visions of the dead,
Or midnight dreams, his sorrows fled:
Waked to new life, through all his soul
A soft delicious languor stole,　　　125
And lapt in heavenly ecstasy
He sank and fainted on her breast.

'Twas on an eve, the leaf was sere,
Howl'd the blast round the castle drear,
The boding night-bird's hideous cry　　　130
Was mingled with the warning sky;
Heard was the distant torrent's dash,
Seen was the lightning's dark red flash,
　　As it gleam'd on the stormy cloud;
Heard was the troubled ocean's roar,　　　135
As its wild waves lash'd the rocky shore;
　　The thunder mutter'd loud,
As wilder still the lightnings flew;
Wilder as the tempest blew,
More wildly strange their converse grew.　　　140

106　It . . . terrific]
　　　Glar'd with hideous　*1811*
107　death,] Death,　*1811*
108　As,] As　*1831F*
　　　conjured] conjur'd　*1811*
110　dread] fell　*1811*

120　siren] syren　*1831F*
121　rest.] rest,　*1831F*
124　life,] life　*1831F*
133　flash,] flash.　*1831F*
140　*stanza break follows*

They talk'd of the ghosts of the mighty dead,
If, when the spark of life were fled,
    They visited this world of woe?
Or, were it but a phantasy,
145   Deceptive to the feverish eye,
When strange forms flash'd upon the sight,
And stalk'd along at the dead of night?
    Or if, in the realms above,
They still, for mortals left below,
150   Retain'd the same affection's glow,
    In friendship or in love?—
Debating thus, a pensive train,
    Thought upon thought began to rise;
Her thrilling wild harp Rosa took;
155   What sounds in softest murmurs broke
    From the seraphic strings!
Celestials borne on odorous wings,
    Caught the dulcet melodies,
The life-blood ebb'd in every vein,
160   As Paulo listen'd to the strain.

SONG.

What sounds are those that float upon the air,
    As if to bid the fading day farewell,—
What form is that so shadowy, yet so fair,
    Which glides along the rough and pathless dell?

165   Nightly those sounds swell full upon the breeze,
    Which seems to sigh as if in sympathy;
They hang amid yon cliff-embosom'd trees,
    Or float in dying cadence through the sky.

Now rests that form upon the moonbeam pale,
170   In piteous strains of woe its vesper sings;
Now—now it traverses the silent vale,
    Borne on transparent ether's viewless wings.

Oft will it rest beside yon Abbey's tower,
    Which lifts its ivy-mantled mass so high;

---

173 Abbey's] abbey's *1831F*

Rears its dark head to meet the storms that lour, 175
    And braves the trackless tempests of the sky.

That form, the embodied spirit of a maid,
    Forced by a perjured lover to the grave;
A desperate fate the madden'd girl obey'd,
    And from the dark cliff plunged into the wave. 180

There the deep murmurs of the restless surge,
    The mournful shriekings of the white sea-mew,
The warring waves, the wild winds, sang her dirge,
    And o'er her bones the dark red coral grew.

Yet though that form be sunk beneath the main, 185
    Still rests her spirit where its vows were given;
Still fondly visits each loved spot again,
    And pours its sorrows on the ear of Heaven.

That spectre wanders through the Abbey dale,
    And suffers pangs which such a fate must share; 190
Early her soul sank in death's darken'd vale,
    And ere long all of us must meet her there.

She ceased, and on the listening ear
Her pensive accents died;
So sad they were, so softly clear, 195
It seemed as if some angel's sigh
Had breathed the plaintive symphony;
So ravishingly sweet their close,
The tones awakened Paulo's woes;
Oppressive recollections rose, 200
And poured their bitter tide.

Absorbed awhile in grief he stood;
At length he seemed as one inspired,
His burning fillet blazed with blood—
A lambent flame his features fired. 205

---

180 plunged] plung'd   *1831F*
189 Abbey] abbey   *1831F*
193–*end of Canto II.*] *omitted*   **1829E**

"The hour is come, the fated hour;
Whence is this new, this unfelt power?—
Yes, I've a secret to unfold,
And such a tale as ne'er was told,
210   A dreadful, dreadful mystery!
Scenes, at whose retrospect e'en now,
Cold drops of anguish on my brow,
The icy chill of death I feel:
Wrap, Rosa, bride, thy breast in steel,
215   Thy soul with nerves of iron brace,
As to your eyes I darkly trace,
My sad, my cruel destiny.

"Victorio, lend your ears, arise,
Let us seek the battling skies,
220   With o'er our heads the thunder crashing,
And at our feet the wild waves dashing;
As tempest, clouds, and billows roll,
In gloomy concert with my soul.
Rosa, follow me—
225   For my soul is joined to thine,
And thy being's linked to mine—
Rosa, list to me."

Canto III.

"His form had not yet lost
All its original brightness, nor appeared
Less than archangel ruined, and the excess
Of glory obscured; but his face
Deep scars of thunder had intrenched, and care
Sate on his faded cheek."
Paradise Lost.

In Canto III, *1811* consists of lines 213 and 215–23, which appear as an epigraph to Chapter 10 of ***St.Irv***. *1829E* omits lines 1–8, 58–159, 232–71, 300–349, 429–55; and *1831F* omits lines 9–12, 22, 38, 42–48, 50–52, 56–57, 160, 163, 165–67, 173, 178–79, 189–91, 195–96.
Canto marker. CANTO III.] *omitted* ***1829E***
Epigraph. *omitted* ***1829E***

PAULO.

"'Tis sixteen hundred years ago,
Since I came from Israel's land;
Sixteen hundred years of woe!—
With deep and furrowing hand,
God's mark is painted on my head;   5
Must there remain until the dead
Hear the last trump, and leave the tomb,
And earth spouts fire from her riven womb.

"How can I paint that dreadful day,
That time of terror and dismay,   10
When, for our sins, a Saviour died,
And the meek Lamb was crucified!
'Twas on that day, as borne along
To slaughter by the insulting throng,
Infuriate for Deicide,   15
I mock'd our Saviour, and I cried,
'Go! go!' 'Ah! I will go,' he said,
'Where scenes of endless bliss invite,
To the blest regions of the light;
I go—but thou shalt here remain,   20
    Nor see thy dying day
Till I return again."
E'en now, by horror traced, I see
His perforated feet and hands;
The madden'd crowd around him stands,   25
Pierces his side the ruffian spear,
Big rolls the bitter anguish'd tear;
Hark that deep groan! He dies, he dies!
And breathes, in death's last agonies,
Forgiveness to his enemies!   30

1–8 *omitted* *1829E*
9–12 *omitted* *1831F*
13 'Twas on that day, as]
  "As dread that day, when *1831F*
16 mock'd] mocked *1831F*
17 'Go! go!'] Go, go, *1831F*
  go,' he said,] go,' said he, *1831F*
18 invite,] invite; *1831F*
19 light;] light *1831F*
20 go—but] go, but *1831F*
  remain,] remain— *1831F*

21 Nor . . . day] Thou diest not till
  I come again'— *1831F*
22 Till . . . again."] *omitted* *1831F*
25 stands,] stands. *1831F*
27 tear;] tear. *1831F*
28 Hark] Hark, *1831F*
  groan! He dies, he dies!]
    groan!—he dies—he dies. *1831F*
30 enemies!] enemies. *1831F*

        Then was the noonday glory clouded,
        The sun in pitchy darkness shrouded;
        Then were strange forms through the darkness gleaming,
        And the red orb of night on Jerusalem beaming,
35   Which faintly, with ensanguined light,
        Dispersed the thickening shades of night;
        Convulsed, all nature shook with fear,
        As if the very end was near;
           Earth to her centre trembled;
40   Rent in twain was the temple's vail,
           The graves gave up their dead;
        Whilst ghosts and spirits, ghastly pale,
           Glared hideous on the sight,
        Seen through the dark and lurid air,
45   As fiends array'd in light,
        Threw on the scene a frightful glare,
        And, howling, shriek'd with hideous yell—
        They shriek'd in joy, for a Saviour fell!
        'Twas then I felt the Almighty's ire;
50   Then full on my remembrance came
        Those words despised, alas! too late!
        The horrors of my endless fate
           Flash'd on my soul and shook my frame;
           They scorch'd my breast as with a flame
55   Of unextinguishable fire;
        An exquisitely torturing pain
        Of frenzying anguish fired my brain.
        By keen remorse and anguish driven,
        I called for vengeance down from Heaven.
60   But, ah! the all-wasting hand of Time,
        Might never wear away my crime!

---

31 noonday] noon-day *1831F*
32 shrouded;] shrouded. *1831F*
34 beaming,] beaming; *1831F*
36 night;] night. *1831F*
38 *omitted* *1831F*
39 to . . . trembled;] trembled as if the end was near. *1831F*
40 in twain . . . vail,] was the Temple's vail in twain— *1831F*
41 dead;] dead again. *1831F*
42–48 *omitted* *1831F*

49 ire;] ire— *1831F*
50–52 *omitted* *1831F*
53 Flash'd . . . frame;] Those words flashed on my soul, my frame, *1831F*
54 They . . . breast] Scorched breast and brain *1831F*
55 fire;] fire! *1831F*
56–57 *omitted* *1831F*
58–159 *omitted* **1829E**

I scarce could draw my fluttering breath—
Was it the appalling grasp of death?
I lay entranced, and deemed he shed
His dews of poppy o'er my head; 65
But though the kindly warmth was dead,
The self-inflicted torturing pangs
Of conscience lent their scorpion fangs,
Still life prolonging, after life was fled.

"Methought, what glories met my sight, 70
As burst a sudden blaze of light,
Illumining the azure skies,
I saw the blessed Saviour rise.
But how unlike to him who bled!
Where then his thorn-encircled head? 75
Where the big drops of agony
Which dimmed the lustre of his eye?
Or deathlike hue that overspread
The features of that heavenly face?
Gone now was every mortal trace; 80
His eyes with radiant lustre beamed—
His form confessed celestial grace,
And with a blaze of glory streamed.
Innumerable hosts around,
Their brows with wreaths immortal crowned, 85
With amaranthine chaplets bound,
As on their wings the cross they bore,
Deep dyed in the Redeemer's gore,
Attune their golden harps, and sing
Loud hallelujahs to their King. 90

"But, in an instant, from my sight,
Fled were the visions of delight.
Darkness had spread her raven pall;
Dank, lurid duskness covered all.
All was as silent as the dead; 95
I felt a petrifying dread,
Which harrowed up my frame;
When suddenly a lurid stream
Of dark red light, with hideous gleam,
Shot like a meteor through the night, 100
And painted Hell upon the skies—
The Hell from whence it came.

What clouds of sulphur seemed to rise!
What sounds were borne upon the air!
105 The breathings of intense despair—
The piteous shrieks—the wails of woe—
The screams of torment and of pain—
The red-hot rack—the clanking chain!
I gazed upon the gulf below,
110 Till, fainting from excess of fear,
My tottering knees refused to bear
My odious weight. I sink—I sink!
Already had I reached the brink.
The fiery waves disparted wide,
115 To plunge me in their sulphureous tide;
When, racked by agonizing pain,
I started into life again.

"Yet still the impression left behind
Was deeply graven on my mind,
120 In characters whose inward trace
No change or time could e'er deface;
A burning cross illumed my brow,
I hid it with a fillet grey,
But could not hide the wasting woe
125 That wore my wildered soul away,
And ate my heart with living fire.
I knew it was the avenger's sway,
I felt it was the avenger's ire!

"A burden on the face of earth,
130 I cursed the mother who gave me birth;
I cursed myself—my native land.
Polluted by repeated crimes,
I sought in distant foreign climes
If change of country could bestow
135 A transient respite from my woe.
Vain from myself the attempt to fly,
Sole cause of my own misery.

"Since when, in deathlike trance I lay,
Past, slowly past, the years away
140 That poured a bitter stream on me,
When once I fondly longed to see
Jerusalem, alas! my native place.

Jerusalem, alas! no more in name,
No portion of her former fame
Had left behind a single trace.   145
Her pomp—her splendour—was no more.
Her towers no longer seem to rise,
To lift their proud heads to the skies.
Fane and monumental bust,
Long levelled even with the dust.   150
The holy pavements were stained with gore.
The place where the sacred temple stood
Was crimson-dyed with Jewish blood.
Long since, my parents had been dead,
All my posterity had bled   155
Beneath the dark Crusader's spear,
No friend was left my path to cheer,
To shed a few last setting rays
Of sunshine on my evening days!

"Rack'd by the tortures of the mind,   160
   How have I long'd to plunge beneath
   The mansions of repelling death!
And strove that resting place to find
   Where earthly sorrows cease.
Oft, when the tempest-fiends engaged,   165
And the warring winds tumultuous raged,
   Confounding skies with seas,
Then would I rush to the towering height
   Of the gigantic Teneriffe,
   Or some precipitous cliff,   170
All in the dead of the silent night.

"I have cast myself from the mountain's height,
Above was day—below was night;
The substantial clouds that lower'd beneath

---

160 *omitted* *1831F*
161 long'd] longed *1831F*
162 death!] death *1831F*
163 *omitted* *1831F*
164 cease.] cease! *1831F*
165–67 *omitted* *1831F*
168 Then ... rush]
   Oft have I rushed *1831F*

171 silent] stormy *1831F*
   night.] night, *1831F*
   stanza break] *omitted* *1831F*
172. "I ... height,]
   And flung me to the seas. *1831F*
173 *omitted* *1831F*
174 beneath] beneath, *1831F*

175   Bore my detested form;
              They whirl'd it above the volcanic breath,
                  And the meteors of the storm;
              The torrents of electric flame
              Scorch'd to a cinder my fated frame.
180   Hark to the thunder's awful crash—
                  Hark to the midnight lightning's hiss!
              At length was heard a sullen dash,
              Which made the hollow rocks around
              Rebellow to the awful sound;
185   The yawning ocean opening wide,
                  Received me in its vast abyss,
              And whelm'd me in its foaming tide.
              Though my astounded senses fled,
              Yet did the spark of life remain;
190   Then the wild surges of the main
              Dash'd and left me on the rocky shore.
              Oh! would that I had waked no more!
              Vain wish! I lived again to feel
              Torments more fierce than those of hell!
195   A tide of keener pain to roll,
              And the bruises to enter my inmost soul.

              "I cast myself in Etna's womb,[1]
              If haply I might meet my doom

---

[1] "I cast myself from the overhanging summit of the gigantic Teneriffe into the wide weltering ocean. The clouds which hung upon its base below, bore up my odious weight; the foaming billows, swoln by the fury of the northern blast, opened to receive me, and, burying in a vast abyss, at length dashed my almost inanimate frame against the crags. The bruises entered into my soul, but I awoke to life and all its torments. I precipitated myself into the crater of Vesuvius, the bickering flames and melted lava vomited me up again, and though I felt the tortures of the damned, though the sulphureous bitumen scorched the blood within my veins, parched up my flesh, and burnt it to a cinder, still did I live to drag the galling chain of existence on. Repeatedly have I exposed myself to the tempestuous battling of the elements; the clouds

---

177 storm;] storm.   *1831F*
178–79 *omitted*   *1831F*
180 crash—] crash!   *1831F*
184 sound;] sound,   *1831F*
187 tide.] tide—   *1831F*
188 Though my] My   *1831F*
     fled,] fled!   *1831F*
189–91 *omitted*   *1831F*
192 Oh! would] Oh—would   *1831F*
     more!] more,   *1831F*

193 Vain . . . feel] But the wild surge
         swept my corpse ashore—   *1831F*
194 Torments . . . hell!] I was not with
         the dead! *stanza break*   *1831F*
195–96 *omitted*   *1831F*
Footnote. *omitted*   **1829E**
198 doom] doom,   *1831F*

> In torrents of electric flame;
> Thrice happy had I found a grave 200
> 'Mid fierce combustion's tumults dire,
> 'Mid oceans of volcanic fire,
> Which whirl'd me in their sulphurous wave,
>   And scorch'd to a cinder my hated frame,
> Parch'd up the blood within my veins, 205
> And rack'd my breast with damning pains;
> Then hurl'd me from the mountain's entrails dread.
> With what unutterable woe
> Even now I feel this bosom glow—
> I burn—I melt with fervent heat— 210
> Again life's pulses wildly beat—
> What endless throbbing pangs I live to feel!
> The elements respect their Maker's seal,—
> That seal deep printed on my fated head.
>
> "Still like the scathed pine-tree's height, 215
> Braving the tempests of the night
>   Have I 'scaped the bickering fire.
> Like the scathed pine which a monument stands
> Of faded grandeur, which the brands
>   Of the tempest-shaken air 220
> Have riven on the desolate heath,
> Yet it stands majestic even in death,
>   And rears its wild form there.
> Thus have I 'scaped the ocean's roar,
> The red-hot bolt from God's right hand, 225

which burst upon my head in crash terrific and exterminating, and the flaming thunderbolt hurled headlong on me its victim, stunned but not destroyed me. The lightning, in bickering coruscation, blasted me; and like the scattered oak, which remains a monument of faded grandeur, and outlives the other monarchs of the forest, doomed me to live for ever. Nine times did this dagger enter into my heart—the ensanguined tide of existence followed the repeated plunge; at each stroke, unutterable anguish seized my frame, and every limb was convulsed by the pangs of approaching dissolution. The wounds still closed, and still I breathe the hated breath of life."

I have endeavoured to deviate as little as possible from the extreme sublimity of idea which the *style* of the German author, of which this is a translation, so forcibly impresses.

---

213 seal,—] seal! *1811*
214 *omitted* *1811*
215 "Still] Still *1811*
216 night] night, *1811*
217 'scaped] 'scap'd *1811*

fire.] flame. *1811*
218 scathed] scath'd *1811*
 pine] pine, *1811*
219 grandeur,] grandeur; *1831F*
221 heath,] heath; *1811*

The flaming midnight meteor brand,
    And Etna's flames of bickering fire.
Thus am I doom'd by fate to stand,
    A monument of the Eternal's ire;
230 Nor can this being pass away,
Till time shall be no more.

"I pierce with intellectual eye,
Into each hidden mystery;
I penetrate the fertile womb
235 Of nature; I produce to light
The secrets of the teeming earth,
And give air's unseen embryos birth:
The past, the present, and to come,
Float in review before my sight:
240 To me is known the magic spell,
To summon e'en the Prince of Hell;
Awed by the Cross upon my head,
His fiends would obey my mandates dread,
To twilight change the blaze of noon,
245 And stain with spots of blood the moon.
But that an interposing hand
Restrains my potent arts, my else supreme command."

He raised his passion-quivering hand,
He loosed the grey encircling band,
250 A burning cross was there;
Its colour was like to recent blood,
Deep marked upon his brow it stood,
And spread a lambent glare.
Dimmer grew the taper's blaze,
255 Dazzled by the brighter rays,
Whilst Paulo spoke—'twas dead of night—
Fair Rosa shuddered with affright;
Victorio, fearless, had braved death
Upon the blood-besprinkled heath;
260 Had heard, unmoved, the cannon's roar,
Echoing along the Wolga's shore,

232–71 *omitted* *1829E*
261 shore,] shore. *1831F*

When the thunder of battle was swelling,
When the birds for their dead prey were yelling,
When the ensigns of slaughter were streaming,
And falchions and bayonets were gleaming, 265
And almost felt death's chilling hand,
Stretched on ensanguined Wolga's strand;
And, careless, scorned for life to cry.
Yet now he turned aside his eye,
Scarce could his death-like terror bear, 270
And owned now what it was to fear.

"Once a funeral met my aching sight,
It blasted my eyes at the dead of night,
When the sightless fiends of the tempests rave,
And hell-birds howl o'er the storm-blacken'd wave. 275
Nought was seen, save at fits, but the meteor's glare,
And the lightnings of God painting hell on the air;
Nought was heard save the thunder's wild voice in the sky,
And strange birds who, shrieking, fled dismally by.
'Twas then from my head my drench'd hair that I tore, 280
And bid my vain dagger's point drink my life's gore;
'Twas then I fell on the ensanguined earth,
And cursed the mother who gave me birth!
My madden'd brain could bear no more—
Hark! the chilling whirlwind's roar; 285
The spirits of the tombless dead
Flit around my fated head,—
Howl horror and destruction round,
As they quaff my blood that stains the ground,
And shriek amid their deadly stave,— 290
'Never shalt thou find the grave!
Ever shall thy fated soul
In life's protracted torments roll,
Till, in latest ruin hurl'd,
And fate's destruction, sinks the world! 295
Till the dead arise from the yawning ground,
   To meet their Maker's last decree,
Till angels of vengeance flit around,
   And loud yelling demons seize on thee!'

---

281 bid] bade   *1831F*   299 *stanza break follows*

300   "Ah! would were come that fated hour,
       When the clouds of Chaos around shall lower;
       When this globe calcined by the fury of God
       Shall sink beneath his wrathful nod!"

       As thus he spake, a wilder gaze
305   Of fiend-like horror lit his eye
       With a most unearthly blaze,
       As if some phantom-form passed by.
       At last he stilled the maddening wail
       Of grief, and thus pursued his tale:—

310   "Oft I invoke the fiends of hell,
       And summon each in dire array—
       I know they dare not disobey
       My stern, my powerful spell.
       —Once on a night, when not a breeze
315   Ruffled the surface of the seas,
       The elements were lulled to rest,
       And all was calm, save my sad breast,
       On Death resolved—intent,
       I marked a circle round my form;
320   About me sacred reliques spread,
       The reliques of magicians dead,
       And potent incantations read—
       I waited their event.

       "All at once grew dark the night,
325   Mists of swarthiness hung o'er the pale moonlight.
       Strange yells were heard, the boding cry
       Of the night raven that flitted by,
       Whilst the silver winged mew
       Startled with screams o'er the dark wave flew.
330   'Twas then I seized a magic wand,
       The wand by an enchanter given,
       And deep dyed in his heart's red blood.
       The crashing thunder pealed aloud;
       I saw the portentous meteor's glare,
335   And the lightnings gleam o'er the lurid air;
       I raised the wand in my trembling hand,
       And pointed Hell's mark at the zenith of Heaven.

300–349 *omitted* *1829E*   337 *stanza break follows*

"A superhuman sound
Broke faintly on the listening ear,
Like to a silver harp the notes,   340
And yet they were more soft and clear.
I wildly strained my eyes around—
Again the unknown music floats.
Still stood Hell's mark above my head—
In wildest accents I summoned the dead—   345
And through the insubstantial night,
It diffused a strange and fiendish light;
Spread its rays to the charnel-house air,
And marked mystic forms on the dark vapours there.
The winds had ceased—a thick dark smoke   350
From beneath the pavement broke;
 Around ambrosial perfumes breathe
A fragrance, grateful to the sense,
And bliss, past utterance, dispense.
 The heavy mists, encircling, wreath,   355
Disperse, and gradually unfold
 A youthful female form;—she rode
 Upon a rosy-tinted cloud;
Bright stream'd her flowing locks of gold;
She shone with radiant lustre bright,   360
And blazed with strange and dazzling light;
A diamond coronet deck'd her brow,
Bloom'd on her cheek a vermeil glow;
 The terrors of her fiery eye
Pour'd forth insufferable day,   365
And shed a wildly lurid ray.
A smile upon her features play'd,
 But there, too, sate pourtray'd
The inventive malice of a soul
Where wild demoniac passions roll;   370
Despair and torment on her brow
Had mark'd a melancholy woe
 In dark and deepen'd shade.
Under those hypocritic smiles,

---

353 fragrance,] fragrance *1831F*
355 mists,] mists *1831F*
 encircling,] encircling *1831F*
361 light;] light. *1831F*

375 Deceitful as the serpent's wiles,
     Her hate and malice were conceal'd;
   Whilst on her guilt-confessing face,
   Conscience, the strongly printed trace
     Of agony betray'd,
380 And all the fallen angel stood reveal'd.
   She held a poniard in her hand,
   The point was tinged by the lightning's brand;
   In her left a scroll she bore,
   Crimson'd deep with human gore;
385 And, as above my head she stood,
   Bade me smear it with my blood.
     She said, that then it was my doom
   That every earthly pang should cease;
   The evening of my mortal woe
390   Would close beneath the yawning tomb;
   And, lull'd into the arms of death,
   I should resign my labouring breath;
   And in the sightless realms below
   Enjoy an endless reign of peace.
395 She ceased—oh, God, I thank thy grace,
   Which bade me spurn the deadly scroll;
   Uncertain for a while I stood—
   The dagger's point was in my blood.
     Even now I bleed!—I bleed!
400 When suddenly what horrors flew,
   Quick as the lightnings through my frame;
     Flash'd on my mind the infernal deed,
   The deed which would condemn my soul
   To torments of eternal flame.
405 Drops colder than the cavern dew
   Quick coursed each other down my face,
     I labour'd for my breath;
   At length I cried, 'Avaunt! thou fiend of Hell,
   Avaunt! thou minister of death!'
410 I cast the volume on the ground,
   Loud shriek'd the fiend with piercing yell,

---

385 And,] And   *1831F*
395 God,] God!   *1831F*
401 lightnings] lightnings,   *1831F*
405 dew] dew,   *1831F*

And more than mortal laughter peal'd around.
The scatter'd fragments of the storm
Floated along the Demon's form,
Dilating till it touch'd the sky; 415
The clouds that roll'd athwart his eye,
Reveal'd by its terrific ray,
Brilliant as the noontide day,
   Gleam'd with a lurid fire;
Red lightnings darted around his head, 420
Thunders hoarse as the groans of the dead,
   Pronounced their Maker's ire;
A whirlwind rush'd impetuous by,
Chaos of horror fill'd the sky;
I sunk convulsed with awe and dread. 425
When I waked the storm was fled,
But sounds unholy met my ear,
And fiends of hell were flitting near.

"Here let me pause—here end my tale,
My mental powers begin to fail; 430
At this short retrospect I faint:
Scarce beats my pulse—I lose my breath,
I sicken even unto death.
Oh! hard would be the task to paint
And gift with life past scenes again; 435
To knit a long and linkless chain,
Or strive minutely to relate
The varied horrors of my fate.
Rosa! I could a tale disclose,
So full of horror—full of woes, 440
Such as might blast a demon's ear,
Such as a fiend might shrink to hear—
But, no."—

Here ceased the tale. Convulsed with fear,
The tale yet lived in Rosa's ear— 445
She felt a strange mysterious dread,

---

414 Demon's] demon's   *1831F*
424 sky;] sky: *1831F*
429–*end of Canto III omitted* **1829E**

           A chilling awe as of the dead;
           Gleamed on her sight the demon's form.
           Heard she the fury of the storm?
450   The cries and hideous yells of death?
           Tottered the ground her feet beneath?
           Was it the fiend before her stood?
           Saw she the poniard drop with blood?
           All seemed to her distempered eye
455   A true and sad reality.
                    *   *   *   *   *

                         CANTO IV.
              Οὔτοι γυναῖχας, ἀλλὰ Γοζγόνας λέγω·
              οὐδ' αὖτε Γοζγείοισιν εἰχάσω τύποις·
              ——— μέλαιναι δ'ἐς τὸ πᾶν βδελύχτζοποι·
              ρέγχουσι δ' οὐ πλαστοῖσι φυσιάμασιν·
              ἐχ δ' ὀμμάτων λείβουσι δυσφιλῆ βίαν.
                              Æschylus. Eumenides, v. 48.

           "———What are ye
           So withered and so wild in your attire,
           That look not like th' inhabitants of earth,
           And yet are on 't?—Live you, or are you aught
           That man may question?"
                                           Macbeth.

           Ah! why does man, whom God has sent
           As the Creation's ornament,
           Who stands amid his works confest
           The first—the noblest—and the best;
5   Whose vast—whose comprehensive eye,
           Is bounded only by the sky,
           O'erlook the charms which Nature yields,
           The garniture of woods and fields,
           The sun's all vivifying light,

In Canto IV *1829E* omits lines 38–85, 149–270, 332–402; and *1831F* omits lines 28–29, 292–93, 298–300, 318–31, and 424–28; and lines 419–23 are given in the following order: 419, 423, 421, 422, 420. *1829Inc* consists of lines 271–331.
Canto marker. CANTO IV.] *omitted* *1829E*
Epigraph 1. *omitted* *1829E*
Epigraph 2. *omitted* *1829E*

The glory of the moon by night, 10
And to himself alone a foe,
Forget from whom these blessings flow?
And is there not in friendship's eye,
Beaming with tender sympathy,
An antidote to every woe, 15
And cannot woman's love bestow
An heav'nly paradise below?
Such joys as these to man are given,
And yet you dare to rail at Heaven,
Vainly oppose the Almighty Cause, 20
Transgress His universal laws,
Forfeit the pleasures that await
The virtuous in this mortal state,
Question the goodness of the Power on high,
In misery live, despairing die. 25
What then is man, how few his days,
And heighten'd by what transient rays,
Made up of plans of happiness,
Of visionary schemes of bliss,
The varying passions of his mind 30
Inconstant, varying as the wind,
Now hush'd to apathetic rest,
Now tempested with storms his breast,
Now with the fluctuating tide
Sunk low in meanness, swoln with pride, 35
Thoughtless, or overwhelm'd with care,
Hoping, or tortured by despair!

The sun had sunk beneath the hill,
Soft fell the dew, the scene was still;
All nature hailed the evening's close. 40
Far more did lovely Rosa bless
The twilight of her happiness.

---

15 woe,] woe? *1831F*
19 Heaven,] Heaven; *1831F*
21 laws,] laws; *1831F*
23 state,] state; *1831F*
27 rays,] rays; *1831F*

28–29 *omitted* *1831F*
31 wind,] wind; *1831F*
33 breast,] breast; *1831F*
35 pride,] pride; *1831F*
38–85 *omitted* **1829E**

       Even Paulo blest the tranquil hour
       As in the aromatic bower,
45   Or wandering through the olive grove,
       He told his plaintive tale of love;
       But welcome to Victorio's soul
       Did the dark clouds of evening roll!
       But, ah! what means his hurried pace,
50   Those gestures strange, that varying face;
       Now pale with mingled rage and ire,
       Now burning with intense desire;
       That brow where brood the imps of care,
       That fixed expression of despair,
55   That haste, that labouring for breath—
       His soul is madly bent on death.
       A dark resolve is in his eye,
       Victorio raves—I hear him cry,
       "Rosa is Paulo's eternally."

60   But whence is that soul-harrowing moan,
       Deep drawn and half supprest—
       A low and melancholy tone,
       That rose upon the wind?
       Victorio wildly gazed around,
65   He cast his eyes upon the ground,
       He raised them to the spangled air,
       But all was still—was quiet there.
       Hence, hence, this superstitious fear;
       'Twas but the fever of his mind
70   That conjured the ideal sound,
       To his distempered ear.

       With rapid step, with frantic haste,
       He scoured the long and dreary waste;
       And now the gloomy cypress spread
75   Its darkened umbrage o'er his head;
       The stately pines above him high,
       Lifted their tall heads to the sky;
       Whilst o'er his form, the poisonous yew

---

60 soul-harrowing] soul harrowing   *1831F*

And melancholy nightshade threw
Their baleful deadly dew.   80
At intervals the moon shone clear;
Yet, passing o'er her disk, a cloud
Would now her silver beauty shroud.
The autumnal leaf was parched and sere;
It rustled like a step to fear.   85
The precipice's battled height
Was dimly seen through the mists of night,
   As Victorio moved along.
At length he reach'd its summit dread,
The night-wind whistled round his head,   90
   A wild funereal song.
A dying cadence swept around
   Upon the waste of air,
It scarcely might be call'd a sound,
   For stillness yet was there,   95
Save when the roar of the waters below
Was wafted by fits to the mountain's brow.
Here for a while Victorio stood
Suspended o'er the yawning flood,
And gazed upon the gulf beneath.   100
No apprehension paled his cheek,
No sighs from his torn bosom break,
   No terror dimm'd his eye.
"Welcome, thrice welcome, friendly death,"
In desperate harrowing tone he cried,   105
"Receive me, ocean, to your breast,
Hush this ungovernable tide,
   This troubled sea to rest.
Thus do I bury all my grief—
This plunge shall give my soul relief,   110
   This plunge into eternity!"
I see him now about to spring
   Into the watery grave:
Hark! the death angel flaps his wing
   O'er the blacken'd wave.   115

---

90 head,] head   *1831F*
94 call'd] called   *1831F*
99 o'er] on   **1829E**

Hark! the night-raven shrieks on high
　　To the breeze which passes on;
　Clouds o'ershade the moonlight sky—
　　The deadly work is almost done—
120　When a soft and silver sound,
　　Softer than the fairy song,
　　Which floats at midnight hour along
　The daisy-spangled ground,
　　Was borne upon the wind's soft swell.
125　　Victorio started—'twas the knell
　Of some departed soul;
　　Now on the pinion of the blast,
　　Which o'er the craggy mountain past,
　The lengthen'd murmurs roll—
130　　Till lost in ether, dies away
　　The plaintive, melancholy lay.
　'Tis said congenial sounds have power
　To dissipate the mists that lower
　　Upon the wretch's brow—
135　To still the maddening passions' war—
　To calm the mind's impetuous jar—
　　To turn the tide of woe.
　Victorio shudder'd with affright,
　Swam o'er his eyes thick mists of night;
140　Even now he was about to sink
　　Into the ocean's yawning womb,
　But that the branches of an oak,
　Which, riven by the lightning's stroke,
　O'erhung the precipice's brink,
145　　Preserved him from the billowy tomb;
　Quick throbb'd his pulse with feverish heat,
　He wildly started on his feet,
　And rush'd from the mountain's height.

　The moon was down, but thro' the air
150　Wild meteors spread a transient glare,
　Borne on the wing of the swelling gale,
　Above the dark and woody dale,
　Thick clouds obscured the sky.

149–270 *omitted* **1829E**

All was now wrapped in silence drear,
Not a whisper broke on the listening ear,   155
Not a murmur floated by.

In thought's perplexing labyrinth lost
The trackless heath he swiftly crost.
Ah! why did terror blanch his cheek?
Why did his tongue attempt to speak,   160
And fail in the essay?
Through the dark midnight mists, an eye,
Flashing with crimson brilliancy,
Poured on his face its ray.
What sighs pollute the midnight air?   165
What mean those breathings of despair?
Thus asked a voice, whose hollow tone
Might seem but one funereal moan.
Victorio groaned, with faltering breath,
"I burn with love, I pant for death!"   170

Suddenly a meteor's glare,
With brilliant flash illumed the air;
Bursting through clouds of sulphurous smoke,
As on a Witch's form it broke,
Of herculean bulk her frame   175
Seemed blasted by the lightning's flame;
Her eyes that flared with lurid light,
Were now with bloodshot lustre filled.
They blazed like comets through the night,
And now thick rheumy gore distilled;   180
Black as the raven's plume, her locks
Loose streamed upon the pointed rocks,
Wild floated on the hollow gale,
Or swept the ground in matted trail;
Vile loathsome weeds, whose pitchy fold   185
Were blackened by the fire of Hell,
Her shapeless limbs of giant mould
Scarce served to hide—as she the while
"Grinned horribly a ghastly smile"
And shrieked with demon yell.   190

---

182 rocks,] rocks; *1831F*   190 *stanza break follows*

　　　　 Terror unmanned Victorio's mind,
　　　　 His limbs, like lime leaves in the wind,
　　　　 Shook, and his brain in wild dismay
　　　　 Swam—Vainly he strove to turn away.
195　　 "Follow me to the mansions of rest,"
　　　　 The weird female cried;
　　　　 The life-blood rushed thro' Victorio's breast
　　　　 In full and swelling tide.
　　　　 Attractive as the eagle's gaze,
200　　 And bright as the meridian blaze,
　　　　 Led by a sanguine stream of light,
　　　　 He followed through the shades of night—
　　　　 Before him his conductress fled,
　　　　 As swift as the ghosts of the dead,
205　　 When on some dreadful errand they fly,
　　　　 In a thunderblast sweeping the sky.

　　　　 They reached a rock whose beetling height
　　　　 Was dimly seen thro' the clouds of night;
　　　　 Illumined by the meteor's blaze,
210　　 Its wild crags caught the reddened rays,
　　　　 And their refracted brilliance threw
　　　　 Around a solitary yew,
　　　　 Which stretched its blasted form on high,
　　　　 Braving the tempests of the sky.
215　　 As glared the flame—a caverned cell,
　　　　 More pitchy than the shades of hell,
　　　　 Lay open to Victorio's view.
　　　　 Lost for an instant was his guide;
　　　　 He rushed into the mountain's side.
220　　 At length with deep and harrowing yell
　　　　 She bade him quickly speed,
　　　　 For that ere again had risen the moon
　　　　 'Twas fated that there must be done
　　　　 A strange—a deadly deed.

225　　 Swift as the wind Victorio sped;
　　　　 Beneath him lay the mangled dead;
　　　　 Around dank putrefaction's power
　　　　 Had caused a dim blue mist to lower.
　　　　 Yet an unfixed, a wandering light
230　　 Dispersed the thickening shades of night;
　　　　 Yet the weird female's features dire

Gleamed thro' the lurid yellow air:
With a deadly livid fire,
Whose wild, inconstant, dazzling light
Dispelled the tenfold shades of night,   235
Whilst her hideous fiendlike eye
Fixed on her victim with horrid stare,
Flamed with more kindled radiancy;
More frightful far than that of Death,
When exulting he stalks o'er the battle heath;   240
Or of the dread prophetic form,
Who rides the curled clouds in the storm,
And borne upon the tempest's wings,
Death, despair, and horror brings.
Strange voices then and shrieks of death   245
Were borne along the trackless heath;
Tottered the ground his steps beneath;
Rustled the blast o'er the dark cliff's side,
And their works unhallowed spirits plied,
As they shed their baneful breath.   250

Yet Victorio hastened on—
Soon the dire deed will be done.
"Mortal," the female cried, "this night
Shall dissipate thy woe;
And, ere return of morning light   255
The clouds that shade thy brow,
Like fleeting summer mists shall fly
Before the sun that mounts on high.
I know the wishes of thy heart—
A soothing balm I could impart: 260
Rosa is Paulo's—can be thine,
For the secret power is mine."

          VICTORIO.
"Give me that secret power—Oh! give
To me fair Rosa—I will live
To bow to thy command.   265
Rosa but mine—and I will fly
E'en to the regions of the sky,
Will traverse every land."

WITCH.

"Calm then those transports and attend,
270   Mortal, to one, who is thy friend—
      The charm begins."

                  —An ancient book
      Of mystic characters she took;
      Her loose locks floated on the air,
      Her eyes were fix'd in lifeless stare;
275   She traced a circle on the floor,
      Around, dark chilling vapours lower;
      A golden cross on the pavement she threw;
      'Twas tinged by a flame of lambent blue,
      From which bright scintillations flew;—
280   By it she cursed her Saviour's soul!—
      Then savage laughter round did roll,
      A hollow, wild, and frightful sound,
      In air above, and under ground.

      She utter'd then, in accents dread,
285   Some maddening rhyme that wakes the dead,
      And forces every shivering fiend
      To her their demon-forms to bend.
      At length a wild and piercing shriek,
      As the dark mists disperse and break,
290   Announced the coming Prince of Hell!
      But when his form obscured the cell,
      What words could paint, what tongue could tell,

---

271 The charm begins." | —An ancient book] THE charm begins,—an ancient book   *1829Inc*
    —An] An   *1831F*
273 air,] air;   *1831F*
274 fix'd] fixed   *1831F*
    stare;] stare: *1831F*
276 Around,] Around   *1831F*
    dark] dank   *1831F*
    lower;] lower: *1831F*
277 threw;] threw,   *1831F*
278 by] with   *1831F*
279 flew;—] flew;   *1831F*
280 soul!—] soul;   *1831F*

281 Then . . . round] Around strange fiendish laughs   *1831F*
283 In . . . ground.] At fits was heard to float around.   *1831F*
284 utter'd] uttered   *1831F*
286 fiend] fiend,   *1831F*
287 demon-forms to bend.] demon forms to bend;   *1831F*
288 length] length,   *1831F*
290 Hell!] Hell—   *1831F*
291 But . . . his] His horrid   *1831F*
    cell,] cell.   *1831F*
292–93] *omitted*   *1831F*

82   *The Wandering Jew*

    The terrors of his look!
The witch's heart, unused to shrink
Even at extremest danger's brink,   295
    With deadliest terror shook!
And with their Prince were seen to rise
Spirits of every shape and hue,—
A hideous and infernal crew,
With hell-fires flashing from their eyes.   300
The cavern bellows with their cries,
Which, echoing through a thousand caves,
Sound like as many tempest-waves.

Inspired and wrapt in bickering flame,
The strange and wild enchantress stood;—   305
Words unpremeditated came,
In unintelligible flood,
From her black tumid lips—array'd
In livid, fiendish smiles of joy—
Lips, which now dropp'd with deadly dew,   310
And now, extending wide, display'd
Projecting teeth of mouldy blue.
As with a loud and piercing cry,
A mystic, harrowing lay she sang,
The rocks, as with a death-peal, rang,   315

---

294 The . . . heart,]
    Victorio shrunk,   *1831F*
    shrink] shrink,   *1831F*
295 Even] E'en   *1831F*
    brink,] brink;   *1831F*
296 With . . . shook!] The witch then pointed to the ground, | Infernal shadows flitted around,   *1831F*
297 Prince] prince   *1831F*
    rise] rise,   *1831F*
298–300] *omitted*   *1831F*
302 Which,] Which   *1831F*
303 tempest-waves.]
    tempest waves.   *1831F*
305 strange] strange,   *1831F*
    and . . . enchantress]
        the awful being   *1831F*
    stood;—] stood.   *1831F*

306 Words] Words,   *1831F*
    unpremeditated]
        unpremeditated,   *1831F*
308 lips—array'd] lips,—arrayed   *1831F*
309 livid,] livid   *1831F*
    joy—] joy;   *1831F*
310 dropp'd] dropped   *1831F*
311 now,] now   *1831F*
    wide,] wide   *1831F*
    display'd] displayed,   *1831F*
312 blue.] hue,   *1831F*
314 mystic,] mystic   *1831F*
315 The . . . with]
    Along the rocks   *1831F*
    death-peal,] death-peal   *1831F*
    rang,] rang.   *1831F*

    And the dread accents, deep and drear,
    Struck terror on the dark night's ear!

    As ceased the soul-appalling verse,
    Obedient to its power, grew still
320 The hellish shrieks;—the mists disperse;—
    Satan—a shapeless, hideous beast—
    In all his horrors stood confest!
    And as his vast proportions fill
    The lofty cave, his features dire
325 Gleam with a pale and sulphurous fire;
    From his fixed glance of deadly hate
    Even *she* shrunk back, appall'd with dread—
    For there contempt and malice sate,
    And from his basiliskine eye
330 Sparks of living fury fly,
    Which wanted but a being to strike dead.

    A wilder, a more awful spell
    Now echoed through the long-drawn cell;
    The demon bowed to its mandates dread.
335 "Receive this potent drug," he cried,
    "Whoever quaffs its fatal tide,
    Is mingled with the dead."
    Swept by a rushing sulphurous blast,
    Which wildly through the cavern past,
340 The fatal word was borne.
    The cavern trembled with the sound,[1]
    Trembled beneath his feet the ground,
    With strong convulsions torn,
    Victorio, shuddering, fell;
345 But soon awakening from his trance,

---

[1]   "Death!
  Hell trembled at the hideous name and sighed
  From all its caves, and back resounded death."
      —*Paradise Lost.*

---

316 And . . . accents,]
   In accents hollow, *1831F*
   deep] deep, *1831F*
317 Struck terror on the dark night's]
   They struck upon Victorio's *1831F*
   ear!] ear. *1831F*

318–31 *omitted* *1831F*
331 [five asterisks] *added* ***1829Inc***
332–402 *omitted* ***1829E***
Footnote. *omitted* ***1829E***

He cast around a fearful glance,
Yet gloomy was the cell,
Save where a lamp's uncertain flare
Cast a flickering, dying glare.

WITCH.

"Receive this dear-earned drug—its power 350
Thou, mortal, soon shalt know:
This drug shall be thy nuptial dower,
This drug shall seal thy woe.
Mingle it with Rosa's wine,
Victorio—Rosa then is thine." 355

She spake, and, to confirm the spell,
A strange and subterranean sound
Reverberated long around,
In dismal echoes—the dark cell
Rocked as in terror—thro' the sky 360
Hoarse thunders murmured awfully,
And winged with horror, darkness spread
Her mantle o'er Victorio's head.
He gazed around with dizzy fear,
No fiend, no witch, no cave, was near; 365
But the blasts of the forest were heard to roar,
The wild ocean's billows to dash on the shore.
The cold winds of Heaven struck chill on his frame;
For the cave had been heated by hell's blackening flame,
And his hand grasped a casket—the philtre was there! 370
*   *   *   *   *

Sweet is the whispering of the breeze
Which scarcely sways yon summer trees;
Sweet is the pale moon's pearly beam,
Which sleeps upon the silver stream,
In slumber cold and still: 375
Sweet those wild notes of harmony,
Which on the blast that passes by,
Are wafted from yon hill:
So low, so thrilling, yet so clear,
Which strike enthusiast fancy's ear; 380
Which sweep along the moonlight sky,
Like notes of heavenly symphony.

SONG.

      See yon opening flower
      Spreads its fragrance to the blast;
385   It fades within an hour,
      Its decay is pale, is fast.
      Paler is yon maiden;
      Faster is her heart's decay;
      Deep with sorrow laden,
390   She sinks in death away.

          *   *   *   *   *

      'Tis the silent dead of night—
      Hark! hark! what shriek so low yet clear,
      Breaks on calm rapture's pensive ear,
      From Lara's castled height?
395   'Twas Rosa's death-shriek fell!
      What sound is that which rides the blast,
      As onward its fainter murmurs past?
      'Tis Rosa's funeral knell!
      What step is that the ground which shakes?
400   'Tis the step of a wretch, nature shrinks from his tread;
      And beneath their tombs tremble the shuddering dead;
      And while he speaks the churchyard quakes.

PAULO.

      "Lies she there for the worm to devour,
      Lies she there till the judgment hour,
405   Is then my Rosa dead!
      False fiend! I curse thy futile power!
      O'er her form will lightnings flash,
      O'er her form will thunders crash,
        But harmless from my head
410   Will the fierce tempest's fury fly,
      Rebounding to its native sky.—
      Who is the God of Mercy?—where
        Enthroned the power to save?
      Reigns he above the viewless air?
415   Lives he beneath the grave?

---

403 "Lies] Lies *1831F*   405 dead!] dead? *1831F*
    devour,] devour? *1831F*   411 sky.—] sky. *1831F*
404 hour,] hour? *1831F*   413 Enthroned] Enthrones *1831F*

To him would I lift my suppliant moan,
That power should hear my harrowing groan;—
Is it then Christ's terrific Sire?
Ah! I have felt his burning ire,
    I feel,—I feel it now,—   420
His flaming mark is fix'd on my head,
And must there remain in traces dread;
    Wild anguish glooms my brow;
Oh! Griefs like mine that fiercely burn,
    Where is the balm can heal!   425
Where is the monumental urn
Can bid to dust this frame return,
    Or quench the pangs I feel!"
As thus he spoke grew dark the sky,
Hoarse thunders murmured awfully,   430
"O Demon! I am thine!" he cried.
A hollow fiendish voice replied,
"Come! for thy doom is misery."

---

417 groan;—] groan;   *1831F*
419 ire,] ire,—   *1831F*
    line 423 inserted here, followed by 421,
    422, and 420   *1831F*
420 feel,—I] feel—I   *1831F*
    now,—] now!' *stanza break*   *1831F*

421 fix'd] fixed   *1831F*
424–28 *omitted*   *1831F*
431 cried.] cried,   *1831F*
432 hollow] hollow,   *1831F*
433 misery."] misery!"   *1831F*

Title page of *Posthumous Fragments of Margaret Nicholson* (1810). With kind permission of The Huntington Library.

POSTHUMOUS FRAGMENTS OF MARGARET NICHOLSON;

Being Poems Found Amongst the Papers of that Noted Female who Attempted the Life of the King in 1786.

Edited by John Fitzvictor

A slim quarto volume, **Posthumous Fragments of Margaret Nicholson** (**PF**) was published in an edition of 250 copies in the third week of November 1810 by J. Munday in Oxford. The first of the publications that PBS originated after taking up residence at University College, Oxford, it is a student prank that mixes antiestablishment rhetoric with sexual double entendres, all wrapped in the protective fiction that the six poems were emotional outpourings by a mad laundress who had attempted to kill King George III in 1786, collected and edited by her nephew. Individual passages in the volume show, however, that PBS had begun to find various aspects of his mature lyric voice. He also used specialized typography to achieve expressive effects. For instance, the heading "Symphony" on page 98 was set in shadow type in the first edition. For Commentary, see pages 235–59; for Historical Collations, see pages 375–86.

ADVERTISEMENT.

THE energy and native genius of these Fragments, must be the only apology which the Editor can make for thus intruding them on the Public Notice. The FIRST I found with no title, and have left it so. It is intimately connected with the dearest interests of universal happiness; and much as we may deplore the fatal and enthusiastic tendency which the ideas of this poor female had acquired, we cannot fail to pay the tribute of unequivocal regret to the departed memory of genius, which, had it been rightly organized, would have made that intellect, which had since become the victim of phrenzy and despair, a most brilliant ornament to society.

In case the sale of these Fragments evinces that the Public have any curiosity to be presented with a more copious collection of my unfortunate Aunt's Poems, I have other papers in my possession, which shall, in that case, be subjected to their notice. It may be supposed they require much arrangement; but I send the following to the press in the same state in which they came into my possession.

J. F.

Text collated with *1810PF* and *c.1870PF*. No variants occur between our Text and the primary witnesses.

"Ambition, power, and avarice, now have hurl'd"

AMBITION, power, and avarice, now have hurl'd
Death, fate, and ruin, on a bleeding world.
See! on yon heath what countless victims lie,
Hark! what loud shrieks ascend thro' yonder sky;
Tell then the cause, 'tis sure the avenger's rage   5
Has swept these myriads from life's crowded stage:
Hark to that groan, an anguish'd hero dies,
He shudders in death's latest agonies;
Yet does a fleeting hectic flush his cheek,
Yet does his parting breath essay to speak—   10

"Oh God! my wife, my children—Monarch thou
"For whose support this fainting frame lies low;
"For whose support in distant lands I bleed,
"Let his friends' welfare be the warrior's meed.
"He hears me not—ah! no—kings cannot hear,   15
"For passion's voice has dull'd their listless ear.
"To thee, then, mighty God, I lift my moan,
"Thou wilt not scorn a suppliant's anguish'd groan.
"Oh! now I die—but still is death's fierce pain—
"God hears my prayer—we meet, we meet again."   20
He spake, reclin'd him on death's bloody bed,
And with a parting groan his spirit fled.

Oppressors of mankind to *you* we owe
The baleful streams from whence these miseries flow;
For you how many a mother weeps her son,   25
Snatch'd from life's course ere half his race was run!
For you how many a widow drops a tear,
In silent anguish, on her husband's bier!

"Is it then thine, Almighty Power," she cries,
"Whence tears of endless sorrow dim these eyes?   30
"Is this the system which thy powerful sway,
"Which else in shapeless chaos sleeping lay,
"Form'd and approv'd?—it cannot be—but oh!
"Forgive me Heaven, my brain is warp'd by woe."

Text collated with *1810PF* and *c.1870PF*.
24 baleful] hateful   *c.1870PF*

35   'Tis not—he never bade the war-note swell,
       He never triumph'd in the work of hell—
       Monarchs of earth! thine is the baleful deed,
       Thine are the crimes for which thy subjects bleed.
       Ah! when will come the sacred fated time,
40   When man unsullied by his leaders' crime,
       Despising wealth, ambition, pomp, and pride,
       Will stretch him fearless by his foemen's side?
       Ah! when will come the time, when o'er the plain
       No more shall death and desolation reign?
45   When will the sun smile on the bloodless field,
       And the stern warrior's arm the sickle wield?
       Not whilst some King, in cold ambition's dreams,
       Plans for the field of death his plodding schemes;
       Not whilst for private pique the public fall,
50   And one frail mortal's mandate governs all.
       Swell'd with command and mad with dizzying sway;
       Who sees unmov'd his myriads fade away.
       Careless who lives or dies—so that he gains
       Some trivial point for which he took the pains.
55   What then are Kings?—I see the trembling crowd,
       I hear their fulsome clamours echoed loud;
       Their stern oppressor pleas'd appears awhile,
       But April's sunshine is a Monarch's smile—
       Kings are but dust—the last eventful day
60   Will level all and make them lose their sway;
       Will dash the sceptre from the Monarch's hand,
       And from the warrior's grasp wrest the ensanguin'd brand.

       Oh! Peace, soft peace, art thou for ever gone,
       Is thy fair form indeed for ever flown?
65   And love and concord hast thou swept away,
       As if incongruous with thy parted sway?
       Alas I fear thou hast, for none appear.
       Now o'er the palsied earth stalks giant Fear,
       With War, and Woe, and Terror, in his train;
70   List'ning he pauses on the embattled plain,
       Then speeding swiftly o'er the ensanguin'd heath,
       Has left the frightful work to hell and death.
       See! gory Ruin yokes his blood-stain'd car,

---

41 pride,] pride *c.1870PF*

He scents the battle's carnage from afar;
Hell and destruction mark his mad career, 75
He tracks the rapid step of hurrying Fear;
Whilst ruin'd towns and smoking cities tell,
That thy work, Monarch, is the work of hell.
It is thy work! I hear a voice repeat,
Shakes the broad basis of thy blood-stained seat; 80
And at the orphan's sigh, the widow's moan,
Totters the fabric of thy guilt-stained throne—
"It is thy work, O Monarch;" now the sound
Fainter and fainter yet is borne around,
Yet to enthusiast ears the murmurs tell 85
That heaven, indignant at the work of hell,
Will soon the cause, the hated cause remove,
Which tears from earth peace, innocence, and love.

FRAGMENT.
SUPPOSED TO BE AN EPITHALAMIUM OF FRANCIS RAVAILLAC AND CHARLOTTE CORDÉ.

'Tis midnight now—athwart the murky air,
    Dank lurid meteors shoot a livid gleam;
From the dark storm-clouds flashes a fearful glare,
    It shews the bending oak, the roaring stream.
I ponder'd on the woes of lost mankind, 5
    I ponder'd on the ceaseless rage of Kings;
My rapt soul dwelt upon the ties that bind
    The mazy volume of commingling things,
When fell and wild misrule to man stern sorrow brings.

I heard a yell—it was not the knell, 10
    When the blasts on the wild lake sleep,
That floats on the pause of the summer gale's swell,
    O'er the breast of the waveless deep.

I thought it had been death's accents cold
    That bade me recline on the shore; 15

Text collated with *1810PF* and *c.1870PF.*
6 Kings;] Kings, *c.1870PF*

I laid mine hot head on the surge-beaten mould,
And thought to breathe no more.

But a heavenly sleep
That did suddenly steep
In balm my bosom's pain,
Pervaded my soul,
And free from control,
Did mine intellect range again.

Methought enthron'd upon a silvery cloud,
Which floated 'mid a strange and brilliant light;
My form upborne by viewless æther rode,
And spurn'd the lessening realms of earthly night.
What heavenly notes burst on my ravish'd ears,
What beauteous spirits met my dazzled eye!
Hark! louder swells the music of the spheres,
More clear the forms of speechless bliss float by,
And heavenly gestures suit æthereal melody.

But fairer than the spirits of the air,
More graceful than the Sylph of symmetry,
Than the enthusiast's fancied love more fair,
Were the bright forms that swept the azure sky.
Enthron'd in roseate light, a heavenly band
Strew'd flowers of bliss that never fade away;
They welcome virtue to its native land,
And songs of triumph greet the joyous day
When endless bliss the woes of fleeting life repay.

Congenial minds will seek their kindred soul,
E'en though the tide of time has roll'd between;
They mock weak matter's impotent control,
And seek of endless life the eternal scene.
At death's vain summons *this* will never die,
In nature's chaos *this* will not decay—
These are the bands which closely, warmly, tie
Thy soul, O Charlotte, 'yond this chain of clay,
To him who thine must be till time shall fade away.

Yes Francis! thine was the dear knife that tore
A tyrant's heart-strings from his guilty breast,

Thine was the daring at a tyrant's gore,
    To smile in triumph, to contemn the rest;
And thine, lov'd glory of thy sex! to tear   55
    From its base shrine a despot's haughty soul,
To laugh at sorrow in secure despair,
    To mock, with smiles, life's lingering control,
And triumph 'mid the griefs that round thy fate did roll.

Yes! the fierce spirits of the avenging deep   60
    With endless tortures goad their guilty shades.
I see the lank and ghastly spectres sweep
    Along the burning length of yon arcades;
And I see Satan stalk athwart the plain;
    He hastes along the burning soil of hell.   65
"Welcome thou despots to my dark domain,
    "With maddening joy mine anguish'd senses swell
"To welcome to their home the friends I love so well."

*   *   *   *   *   *   *   *
*   *   *   *   *   *   *   *
Hark! to those notes, how sweet, how thrilling sweet
They echo to the sound of angels' feet.   70
*   *   *   *   *   *   *   *
Oh haste to the bower where roses are spread,
For there is prepared thy nuptial bed.
Oh haste—hark! hark!—they're gone.
*   *   *   *   *   *   *   *

        CHORUS OF SPIRITS.
STAY ye days of contentment and joy,
    Whilst love every care is erasing,   75
Stay ye pleasures that never can cloy,
    And ye spirits that can never cease pleasing.

And if any soft passion be near,
    Which mortals, frail mortals, can know,
Let love shed on the bosom a tear,   80
    And dissolve the chill ice-drop of woe.

---

70 angels'] angels   *1810PF*

SYMPHONY.
FRANCIS.

"SOFT, my dearest angel stay,
"Oh! you suck my soul away;
"Suck on, suck on, I glow, I glow!
85 "Tides of maddening passion roll,
"And streams of rapture drown my soul.
"Now give me one more billing kiss,
"Let your lips now repeat the bliss,
"Endless kisses steal my breath,
90 "No life can equal such a death."

CHARLOTTE.
"Oh! yes I will kiss thine eyes so fair,
    "And I will clasp thy form;
"Serene is the breath of the balmy air,
    "But I think, love, thou feelest me warm.
95 "And I will recline on thy marble neck
    "Till I mingle into thee.
"And I will kiss the rose on thy cheek,
    "And thou shalt give kisses to me.
"For here is no morn to flout our delight,
100   "Oh! dost thou not joy at this?
"And here we may lye an endless night,
    "A long, long night of bliss."

Spirits! when raptures move,
Say what it is to love,
105 When passion's tear stands on the cheek,
    When bursts the unconscious sigh;
And the tremulous lips dare not speak
    What is told by the soul-felt eye.
Bu t wa t is sweeter to revenge's ea r
110   Than the fell tyrant's last expiring yell?
Yes! than love's sweetest blisses 'tis more dear
    To drink the floatings of a despot's knell.
I wake—'tis done—'tis o'er. *   *
  *   *   *   *   *   *   *   *
    *   *   *   *   *   *   *   *

DESPAIR.

AND can'st thou mock mine agony, thus calm
    In cloudless radiance, Queen of silver night?
Can you, ye flow'rets, spread your perfumed balm
    'Mid pearly gems of dew that shine so bright?
And you wild winds, thus can you sleep so still   5
    Whilst throbs the tempest of my breast so high?
Can the fierce night-fiends rest on yonder hill,
    And, in the eternal mansions of the sky,
Can the directors of the storm in powerless silence lie?

Hark! I hear music on the zephyr's wing,   10
    Louder it floats along the unruffled sky;
Some fairy sure has touch'd the viewless string—
    Now faint in distant air the murmurs die,
Awhile it stills the tide of agony.
    Now—now it loftier swells—again stern woe   15
Arises with the awakening melody.
    Again fierce torments, such as demons know,
In bitterer, feller tide, on this torn bosom flow.

Arise ye sightless spirits of the storm,
    Ye unseen minstrels of the aërial song,   20
Pour the fierce tide around this lonely form,
    And roll the tempest's wildest swell along.
Dart the red lightning, wing the forked flash,
    Pour from thy cloud-form'd hills the thunder's roar;
Arouse the whirlwind—and let ocean dash   25
    In fiercest tumult on the rocking shore,
Destroy this life or let earth's fabric be no more.

Yes! every tie that links me here is dead;
    Mysterious fate thy mandate I obey,
Since hope and peace, and joy, for aye are fled,   30
    I come, terrific power, I come away.
Then o'er this ruin'd soul let spirits of hell,
    In triumph, laughing wildly, mock its pain;
And though with direst pangs mine heart-strings swell,

Text collated with **1810PF** and *c.1870PF*.
22 tempest's] tempests   **1810PF** *c.1870PF*

35   I'll echo back their deadly yells again,
            Cursing the power that ne'er made aught in vain.

FRAGMENT.

    Yes! all is past—swift time has fled away,
        Yet its swell pauses on my sickening mind;
    How long will horror nerve this frame of clay?
        I'm dead, and lingers yet my soul behind.
5   Oh! powerful fate, revoke thy deadly spell,
        And yet that may not ever, ever be,
    Heaven will not smile upon the work of hell;
        Ah! no, for heaven cannot smile on me;
    Fate, envious fate, has seal'd my wayward destiny.

10 I sought the cold brink of the midnight surge,
        I sigh'd beneath its wave to hide my woes,
    The rising tempest sung a funeral dirge,
        And on the blast a frightful yell arose.
    Wild flew the meteors o'er the madden'd main,
15   Wilder did grief athwart my bosom glare;
    Still'd was the unearthly howling, and a strain,
        Swell'd 'mid the tumult of the battling air,
    'Twas like a spirit's song, but yet more soft and fair.

    I met a maniac, like he was to me,
20   I said—"Poor victim wherefore dost thou roam?
    "And canst thou not contend with agony,
        "That thus at midnight thou dost quit thine home?"
    "Ah there she sleeps: cold is her bloodless form,
        "And I will go to slumber in her grave;
25 "And then our ghosts, whilst raves the madden'd storm,
        "Will sweep at midnight o'er the wilder'd wave;
    "Wilt thou our lowly beds with tears of pity lave?"

    "Ah! no, I cannot shed the pitying tear,
        "This breast is cold, this heart can feel no more;

Text collated with *1810PF* and *c.1870PF.*
22 home?"] home? *1810PF*

>"But I can rest me on thy chilling bier,   30
>"Can shriek in horror to the tempest's roar."
*   *   *   *   *   *   *   *

THE SPECTRAL HORSEMAN.

WHAT was the shriek that struck fancy's ear
As it sate on the ruins of time that is past?
Hark! it floats on the fitful blast of the wind,
And breathes to the pale moon a funeral sigh.
It is the Benshie's moan on the storm,   5
Or a shivering fiend that thirsting for sin,
Seeks murder and guilt when virtue sleeps,
Wing'd with the power of some ruthless king,
And sweeps o'er the breast of the prostrate plain.
It was not a fiend from the regions of hell   10
That poured its low moan on the stillness of night;
It was not a ghost of the guilty dead,
Nor a yelling vampire reeking with gore;
But aye at the close of seven years' end,
That voice is mixed with the swell of the storm   15
And aye at the close of seven years' end,
A shapeless shadow that sleeps on the hill
Awakens and floats on the mist of the heath.
It is not the shade of a murdered man,
Who has rushed uncalled to the throne of his God, 20
And howls in the pause of the eddying storm.
This voice is low, cold, hollow, and chill,
'Tis not heard by the ear, but is felt in the soul.
'Tis more frightful far than the death-demon's scream,
Or the laughter of fiends when they howl o'er the
    corpse   25
Of a man who has sold his soul to hell.
It tells the approach of a mystic form,
A white courser bears the shadowy sprite;
More thin they are than the mists of the mountain,
When the clear moonlight sleeps on the waveless lake. 30

Text collated with *1810PF* and *c.1870PF*. *No variants occur between our Text and the primary witnesses.*

More pale *his* cheek than the snows of Nithona
When winter rides on the northern blast,
And howls in the midst of the leafless wood.
Yet when the fierce swell of the tempest is raving,
35   And the whirlwinds howl in the caves of Inisfallen,
Still secure 'mid the wildest war of the sky,
The phantom courser scours the waste,
And his rider howls in the thunder's roar.
O'er him the fierce bolts of avenging heaven
40   Pause, as in fear, to strike his head.
The meteors of midnight recoil from his figure,
Yet the wildered peasant that oft passes by,
With wonder beholds the blue flash thro' his form:
And his voice, though faint as the sighs of the dead,
45   The startled passenger shudders to hear,
More distinct than the thunder's wildest roar.
Then does the dragon, who chain'd in the caverns
To eternity, curses the champion of Erin,
Moan and yell loud at the lone hour of midnight,
And twine his vast wreathes round the forms of the
50   demons;
Then in agony roll his death-swimming eye-balls,
Though wilder'd by death, yet never to die!
Then he shakes from his skeleton folds the nightmares,
Who, shrieking in agony, seek the couch
55   Of some fevered wretch who courts sleep in vain;
Then the tombless ghosts of the guilty dead
In horror pause on the fitful gale.
They float on the swell of the eddying tempest,
And scared seek the caves of gigantic * *
60   Where their thin forms pour unearthly sounds
On the blast that sweeps the breast of the lake,
And mingles its swell with the moonlight air.

MELODY TO A SCENE OF FORMER TIMES.

A<small>RT</small> thou indeed for ever gone,
    For ever, ever, lost to me?
Must this poor bosom beat alone,

Text collated with ***1810PF*** and *c.1870PF.*

  Or beat at all, if not for thee?
Ah! why was love to mortals given,   5
To lift them to the height of heaven,
Or dash them to the depths of hell?
  Yet I do not reproach thee dear!
Ah! no, the agonies that swell
   This panting breast, this frenzied brain   10
  Might wake my ————'s slumb'ring tear.
  Oh! heaven is witness I did love,
And heaven does know I love thee still,
Does know the fruitless sick'ning thrill,
  When reason's judgment vainly strove   15
To blot thee from my memory;
But which might never, never be.
Oh! I appeal to that blest day
When passion's wildest ecstacy
Was coldness to the joys I knew,   20
When every sorrow sunk away.
Oh! I had never liv'd before,
But now those blisses are no more.
  And now I cease to live again,
I do not blame thee love; ah no!   25
The breast that feels this anguish'd woe
Throbs for thy happiness alone.
Two years of speechless bliss are gone,
I thank thee dearest for the dream.
'Tis night—what faint and distant scream   30
Comes on the wild and fitful blast?
It moans for pleasures that are past,
It moans for days that are gone by.
Oh! lagging hours how slow you fly!
  I see a dark and lengthen'd vale,   35
The black view closes with the tomb;
But darker is the lowering gloom
  That shades the intervening dale.
In visioned slumber for awhile
I seem again to share thy smile,   40
I seem to hang upon thy tone.
  Again you say, "confide in me,
"For I am thine, and thine alone,

---

11 slumb'ring] slumbering *c.1870PF*

45
"And thine must ever, ever be."
But oh! awak'ning still anew,
Athwart my enanguish'd senses flew
A fiercer, deadlier agony!

FINIS.

MUNDAY, PRINTER, OXFORD.

ST. IRVYNE;

OR,

THE ROSICRUCIAN:

A ROMANCE.

BY
A GENTLEMAN
OF THE UNIVERSITY OF OXFORD.

LONDON:
PRINTED FOR J. J. STOCKDALE,
41, PALL MALL.
1811.

Title page of *St. Irvyne; or, The Rosicrucian* (1811). With kind permission of The Huntington Library.

POEMS FROM
St. Irvyne; or, The Rosicrucian: A Romance

The six poems below appeared scattered through PBS's second Gothic romance (hereafter ***St.Irv***), which was printed in December 1810 by Samuel Gosnell and published with the date 1811 by John Joseph Stockdale in London. In 1822, the book was reissued by Stockdale with a new title page and label dated 1822 (H. B. Forman, *The Shelley Library* [1886], 14–15). For Commentary, including the context of each poem within PBS's Gothic romance in prose and the relationships of the texts of ***St.Irv*** with PBS's other versions of some of them, see pages 261–79; for the Historical Collations of these texts, see pages 387–401.

"'T was dead of the night, when I sat in my dwelling"

'T was dead of the night, when I sat in my dwelling;
    One glimmering lamp was expiring and low;
Around, the dark tide of the tempest was swelling,
Along the wild mountains night-ravens were yelling,—
    They bodingly presag'd destruction and woe.   5

'T was then that I started!—the wild storm was howling,
    Nought was seen, save the lightning, which danc'd in the sky;
Above me, the crash of the thunder was rolling,
    And low, chilling murmurs, the blast wafted by.

My heart sank within me—unheeded the war   10
    Of the battling clouds, on the mountain-tops, broke;—
Unheeded the thunder-peal crash'd in mine ear—
This heart, hard as iron, is stranger to fear;
    But conscience in low, noiseless whispering spoke.

'T was then that her form on the whirlwind upholding,   15
    The ghost of the murder'd Victoria strode;

Text collated with *1811* (**St.Irv**) and *1810* (**V&C**). Unlike the other poems in *1811*, opening and closing quotation marks surround this poem. These are a feature of the novel, not the poem, and are omitted from our Text.

Title. none] FRAGMENT, OR THE TRIUMPH
    OF CONSCIENCE. *1810*
1 'T was] 'Twas *1810*
    night,] night *1810*
    sat] sate *1810*
    dwelling;] dwelling, *1810*
2 low;] low,— *1810*
3 Around,] Around *1810*
4 yelling,—] yelling, *1810*
5 presag'd] presaged *1810*
    woe.] woe! *1810*
6 'T was] 'Twas *1810*
    started!—the] started, the *1810*
7 lightning, which danc'd in the sky;]
    lightning that danced on the sky,
    1810
8 me,] me *1810*
9 murmurs,] murmurs *1810*
    by.] by.— *1810*
10 me—unheeded]
    me, unheeded *1810*
    war] jar *1810*
11 clouds,] clouds *1810*
    mountain-tops,] mountain tops *1810*
    broke;—] broke, *1810*
12 crash'd] crashed *1810*
    ear—] ear, *1810*
13 heart,] heart *1810*
    iron,] iron *1810*
    is] was *1810*
    fear;] fear, *1810*
14 low,] low *1810*
15 'T was] 'Twas *1810*
    upholding,] uprearing, *1810*
16 The ghost] The dark ghost *1810*
    murder'd] murdered *1810*
    strode;] strode, *1810*

In her right hand, a shadowy shroud she was holding,
    She swiftly advanc'd to my lonesome abode.

I wildly then call'd on the tempest to bear me——

"Ghosts of the dead! have I not heard your yelling"

Ghosts of the dead! have I not heard your yelling
    Rise on the night-rolling breath of the blast,
When o'er the dark ether the tempest is swelling,
    And on eddying whirlwind the thunder-peal past?

5   For oft have I stood on the dark height of Jura,
    Which frowns on the valley that opens beneath;
Oft have I brav'd the chill night-tempest's fury,
    Whilst around me, I thought, echo'd murmurs of death.

And now, whilst the winds of the mountain are howling,
10   O father! thy voice seems to strike on mine ear;
In air whilst the tide of the night-storm is rolling,
    It breaks on the pause of the elements' jar.

On the wing of the whirlwind which roars o'er the mountain
    Perhaps rides the ghost of my sire who is dead;
15 On the mist of the tempest which hangs o'er the fountain,
    Whilst a wreath of dark vapour encircles his head.

---

17 In her] Her   *1810*
   hand,] hand   *1810*
   shadowy . . . holding,] blood reeking
      dagger was bearing,   *1810*
18 advanc'd] advanced   *1810*
   abode.] abode.—   *1810*
19 call'd] called   *1810*
   me——]
      me!**************   *1810*

Text collated with *1811* and *1835*
(Montgomery, *Oxford*).
1 Ghosts] "Ghosts   *1835*
7 brav'd] braved   *1835*
8 echo'd] echoed   *1835*
11 air] air,   *1835*
13 mountain] mountain,   *1835*
16 head.] head!"   *1835*

BALLAD.

I.

The death-bell beats!—
The mountain repeats
The echoing sound of the knell;
And the dark monk now
Wraps the cowl round his brow,　　　　　5
As he sits in his lonely cell.

II.

And the cold hand of death
Chills his shuddering breath,
As he lists to the fearful lay
Which the ghosts of the sky,　　　　　10
As they sweep wildly by,
Sing to departed day.
And they sing of the hour
When the stern fates had power
To resolve Rosa's form to its clay.　　　　　15

III.

But that hour is past;
And that hour was the last
Of peace to the dark monk's brain.
Bitter tears, from his eyes, gush'd silent and fast;
And he strove to suppress them in vain.　　　　　20

IV.

Then his fair cross of gold he dash'd on the floor,
When the death-knell struck on his ear.
Delight is in store
For her evermore;
But for me is fate, horror, and fear.　　　　　25

V.

Then his eyes wildly roll'd,
When the death-bell toll'd,
And he rag'd in terrific woe.
And he stamp'd on the ground,—

Text collated with *1811*.

No variants occur between our Text and *1811*.

But when ceas'd the sound,
Tears again began to flow.

VI.

And the ice of despair
Chill'd the wild throb of care,
And he sate in mute agony still;
   Till the night-stars shone through the cloudless air,
   And the pale moon-beam slept on the hill.

VII.

Then he knelt in his cell:—
And the horrors of hell
Were delights to his agoniz'd pain.
   And he pray'd to God to dissolve the spell,
Which else must for ever remain.

VIII.

And in fervent pray'r he knelt on the ground,
   Till the abbey bell struck One:
His feverish blood ran chill at the sound:
   A voice hollow and horrible murmur'd around—
   "The term of thy penance is done!"

IX.

Grew dark the night;
The moon-beam bright
Wax'd faint on the mountain high;
   And, from the black hill,
   Went a voice cold and still,—
"Monk! thou art free to die."

X.

Then he rose on his feet,
And his heart loud did beat,
And his limbs they were palsied with dread;
   Whilst the grave's clammy dew
   O'er his pale forehead grew;
And he shudder'd to sleep with the dead.

XI.

And the wild midnight storm
Rav'd around his tall form,

As he sought the chapel's gloom:
   And the sunk grass did sigh
   To the wind, bleak and high,
As he search'd for the new-made tomb.

XII.
And forms, dark and high,   65
   Seem'd around him to fly,
And mingle their yells with the blast:
   And on the dark wall
   Half-seen shadows did fall,
As enhorror'd he onward pass'd.   70

XIII.
And the storm-fiend's wild rave
   O'er the new-made grave,
And dread shadows, linger around.
   The Monk call'd on God his soul to save,
And, in horror, sank on the ground.   75

XIV.
Then despair nerv'd his arm
   To dispel the charm,
And he burst Rosa's coffin asunder.
   And the fierce storm did swell
   More terrific and fell,   80
And louder peal'd the thunder.

XV.
And laugh'd, in joy, the fiendish throng,
   Mix'd with ghosts of the mouldering dead:
And their grisly wings, as they floated along,
   Whistled in murmurs dread.   85

XVI.
And her skeleton form the dead Nun rear'd,
   Which dripp'd with the chill dew of hell.
In her half-eaten eyeballs two pale flames appear'd,
And triumphant their gleam on the dark Monk glar'd,
   As he stood within the cell.   90

XVII.

And her lank hand lay on his shuddering brain;
   But each power was nerv'd by fear.—
"I never, henceforth, may breathe again;
Death now ends mine anguish'd pain.—
95   The grave yawns,—we meet there."

XVIII.

And her skeleton lungs did utter the sound,
   So deadly, so lone, and so fell,
That in long vibrations shudder'd the ground;
And as the stern notes floated around,
100   A deep groan was answer'd from hell.

SONG.

How swiftly through heaven's wide expanse
   Bright day's resplendent colours fade!
How sweetly does the moonbeam's glance
   With silver tint St. Irvyne's glade!

5   No cloud along the spangled air,
   Is borne upon the evening breeze;
How solemn is the scene! how fair
   The moonbeams rest upon the trees!

  Yon dark gray turret glimmers white,
10   Upon it sits the mournful owl;
Along the stillness of the night,
   Her melancholy shriekings roll.

Text collated with *1811* and MS PMgn (an earlier version of the poem in a letter from PBS to E. F. Graham, 22 April 1810, which contains only some of the stanzas found in ***St.Irv***).

Title. SONG.] *omitted* PMgn
1 heaven's] Heaven's PMgn
2 colours] colors PMgn
  fade!] fade PMgn
4 tint] teint PMgn
  St.] St PMgn
  glade!] glade PMgn
5 air,] air PMgn
6 breeze;] breeze, PMgn

7 scene!] scene, PMgn
8 moonbeams] moonbeam's PMgn
  trees!] trees PMgn
9 glimmers] glimmer's PMgn
  white,] white PMgn
10 owl;] owl PMgn
11 night,] night PMgn
12 roll.] roll PMgn
    stanza break] *page break* PMgn

But not alone on Irvyne's tower,
    The silver moonbeam pours her ray;
It gleams upon the ivied bower,   15
    It dances in the cascade's spray.

"Ah! why do dark'ning shades conceal
    The hour, when man must cease to be?
Why may not human minds unveil
    The dim mists of futurity?   20

"The keenness of the world hath torn
    The heart which opens to its blast;
Despis'd, neglected, and forlorn,
    Sinks the wretch in death at last."

SONG.

How stern are the woes of the desolate mourner,
    As he bends in still grief o'er the hallowed bier,
As enanguish'd he turns from the laugh of the scorner,
    And drops, to perfection's remembrance, a tear;
When floods of despair down his pale cheek are streaming,   5
When no blissful hope on his bosom is beaming,

---

13 tower,] tower PMgn
14 silver moonbeam pours her ray;]
    moonbeam pours it's silver ray;
    PMgn
15 gleams] gleam's PMgn
    bower,] bower PMgn
16 spray.] spray PMgn
16–17 *Between lines 16 and 17,* PMgn *contains five additional stanzas. See the Historical Collations to this poem.*
17 "Ah!] Ah PMgn
    dark'ning] darkning PMgn
    line 37 PMgn
18 hour,] hour PMgn
20 dim mists] dark shade PMgn
    stanza break] *poem ends here* PMgn

Text collated with ***1811*** and MS Bod (PBS to Graham, 14 Sept. 1810).
Title. SONG.] *omitted* Bod
Stanza marker. *none*] 1 Bod
1 mourner,] mourner Bod
2 o'er] oer Bod
  bier,] bier Bod
3 enanguish'd] enanguished Bod
  scorner,] scorner Bod
4 drops,] drops Bod
  perfection's] Perfection's Bod
  remembrance,] remembrance Bod
  tear;] tear Bod
5 streaming,] streaming Bod
6 on] oer Bod
  beaming,] beaming Bod

Or, if lull'd for a while, soon he starts from his dreaming,
    And finds torn the soft ties to affection so dear.

Ah! when shall day dawn on the night of the grave,
    Or summer succeed to the winter of death?
Rest awhile, hapless victim, and Heaven will save
    The spirit, that faded away with the breath.
Eternity points in its amaranth bower,
Where no clouds of fate o'er the sweet prospect lower,
Unspeakable pleasure, of goodness the dower,
    When woe fades away like the mist of the heath.

SONG.

I.

Ah! faint are her limbs, and her footstep is weary,
    Yet far must the desolate wanderer roam;
Though the tempest is stern, and the mountain is dreary,
    She must quit at deep midnight her pitiless home.
I see her swift foot dash the dew from the whortle,
As she rapidly hastes to the green grove of myrtle;
And I hear, as she wraps round her figure the kirtle,
    "Stay thy boat on the lake,—dearest Henry, I come."

II.

High swell'd in her bosom the throb of affection,
    As lightly her form bounded over the lea,
And arose in her mind every dear recollection:
    "I come, dearest Henry, and wait but for thee."

---

7 Or,] Or   Bod
  lull'd] lulled   Bod
  while,] time,   Bod
  dreaming,] dreaming   Bod
8 dear.] dear   Bod
Stanza marker. *none*] 2   Bod
9 Ah!] Oh!   Bod
  grave,] grave   Bod
10 death?] Death   Bod
11 awhile,] awhile   Bod
  victim,] victim   Bod
12 spirit,] spirit   Bod
  breath.] breath   Bod

13 bower,] bower   Bod
14 o'er] oe'r   Bod
  lower,] <*text missing*>   Bod
15 pleasure,] pleasure   Bod
  dower,] dower   Bod
16 When] Where   Bod
  of] on   Bod
  heath.] heath   Bod

Text collated with *1811*.
    No variants occur between our Text and *1811*.

How sad, when dear hope every sorrow is soothing,
When sympathy's swell the soft bosom is moving,
And the mind the mild joys of affection is proving,   15
    Is the stern voice of fate that bids happiness flee!

III.
Oh! dark lower'd the clouds on that horrible eve,
    And the moon dimly gleam'd through the tempested air;
Oh! how could fond visions such softness deceive?
    Oh! how could false hope rend a bosom so fair?   20
Thy love's pallid corse the wild surges are laving,
O'er his form the fierce swell of the tempest is raving;
But, fear not, parting spirit; thy goodness is saving,
    In eternity's bowers, a seat for thee there.

The Devil's Walk,

A BALLAD.

ONCE, early in the morning,
  Beelzebub arose,
With care his sweet person adorning,
  He put on his Sunday clothes.

He drew on a boot to hide his hoof,
  He drew on a glove to hide his claw,
His horns were concealed by *Bras Chapeau*,
  And the Devil went forth as natty a *Beau*;
  As Bond-street ever saw.

He sate him down, in London town,
  Before earth's morning ray
With a favourite imp he began to chat,
On religion, and scandal, this and that,
  Until the dawn of day.

And then to St. James's court he went,
  And St. Paul's Church he took in his way,
He was mighty thick with every Saint,
  Tho' they were formal and he was gay.

The Devil was an agriculturist,
  And as bad weeds quickly grow,
In looking over his farm, I wist
  He would'nt find cause for woe.

He peeped in each hole, to each chamber stole,
  His promising live stock to view,
Grinning applause, he just shewed them his claws,
And they shrunk with affright from his ugly sight,
  Whose works they delighted to do.

Satan poked his red nose into crannies so small,
  Once would think that the innocents fair,
Poor lambkins! were just doing nothing at all,
But settling some dress or arranging some ball,
  But the Devil saw deeper there.

A Priest, at whose elbow the Devil during prayer,
  Sate familiarly, side by side,
Declared, that if the tempter were there,
  His presence he would not abide:
Ah!Ah! thought Old Nick, that's a very stale trick,
  For without the Devil, O! favourite of evil,
  In your carriage you would not ride.

Satan next saw a brainless King,
  Whose house was as lot at his own,
Many imps in attendance were there on the wing,
  They flapped the pennon and twisted the sting,
  Close by the very Throne.

Ah, ha! thought Satan, the pasture is good,
  My Cattle will here thrive better than others,
They dine on news of human blood,
  They sup on the groans of the dying and dead,
  And supperless never will go to bed;
  Which will make them as fat as their brothers.

Fat as the fiends that feed on blood,
  Fresh and warm from the fields of Spain,
  Where ruin ploughs her gory way,
When the shoots of earth are nipped in the bud,
  Where Hell is the Victor's prey,
  Its glory the meed of the slain.

Fat—as the death birds on Erin's shore,
  That glutted themselves in her dearest gore,
  And flitted round Castlereagh,
When they snatched the Patriot's heart, that *his* grasp
  Had torn from its widow's maniac clasp,
  And fled at the dawn of day.

Fat—as the reptiles of the tomb,
  That riot in corruption's spoil,
That fret their little hour in gloom,
  And creep, and live the while.

Fat as that Prince's maudlin brain,
  Which addled by some gilded toy,
Tired, gives his sweetmeat, and again
  Cries for it, like a humoured boy.

For he is fat, his waistcoat gay,
  When strained upon a levee day,
  Scarce meets across his princely paunch,
And pantaloons are like half moons,
  Upon each brawny haunch.

How vast his stock of calf! when plenty
  Had filled his empty head and heart,
Enough to satiate foplings twenty,
  Could make his pantaloon seams start.

The Devil, (who sometimes is called nature,)
  For men of power provides thus well,
Whilst every change, and every feature,
  Their great original can tell.

Satan saw a lawyer, a viper slay,
  That crawled up the leg of his table,
It reminded him most marvellously,
  Of the story of Cain and Abel.

The wealthy yeoman, as he wanders,
  His fertile fields among,
And on his thriving cattle ponders,
  Counts his sure gains, and hums a song;
Thus did the Devil, thro' earth walking,
  Hum low a hellish song.

For they thrive well, whose garb of gore,
  Is Satan's choicest livery,
And they thrive well, who from the poor,
  Have snatched the bread of penury,
And heap the houseless wanderer's store,
  On the rank pile of luxury.

The Bishops thrive, tho' they are big,
  The Lawyers thrive, tho' they are thin;
For every gown, and every wig,
  Hides the safe thrift of Hell within.

Thus pigs were never counted clean,
  Altho' they dine on finest corn;
And cormorants are, sin-like lean,
  Altho' they eat from night to morn.

Oh! why is the Father of Hell in such glee,
  As he grins from ear to ear?
Why does he doff his clothes joyfully,
  As he skips, and prances, and flaps his wing,
  As he sidles, leers, and twirls his sting,
  And dares, as he is, to appear?

A Statesman pass'd—alone to him,
  The Devil dare his whole shape uncover,
To show each feature, every limb,
  Secure of an unchanging lover.

At this known sign, a welcome sight,
  The watchful demons sought their King,
And every fiend of thy Stygian night,
  Was in an instant on the wing.

Pale Loyalty, his guilt steeled brow,
  With wreaths of gory laurel crowned;
The hell-hounds, Murder, Want and Woe,
  For ever hungering flocked around;
From Spain had Satan sought their food,
  'Twas human woe and human blood!

Hark the earthquake's crash I hear,
  Kings turn pale, and Conquerors start,
Ruffians tremble in their fear,
  For their Satan doth depart.

This day fiends give to revelry,
  To celebrate their King's return,
And with delight its sire to see,
  Hell's adamantine limits burn.

But were the Devil's sight as keen,
  As Reason's penetrating eye,
His sulphurous Majesty I ween,
  Would find but little cause for joy.

For the sons of Reason see,
  That ere fate consume the Pole,
The false Tyrant's cheek shall be,
  Bloodless as his coward soul.

The Devil's Walk (1812). With kind permission of the Public Record Office Image Library, London. The original sheet is 18 1/16 × 14 7/8 inches.

THE DEVIL'S WALK,
A Ballad

PBS sent an early draft of **The Devil's Walk** (**DW**) in a mid-January 1812 letter to Elizabeth Hitchener. Although this draft was far from a finished poem, PBS by August 1812 had prepared for distribution a fully developed satire of thirty stanzas and had it printed as a broadsheet (arranged in three columns of ten stanzas apiece) entitled **The Devil's Walk, A Ballad**. This poem, printed in Barnstaple—perhaps by PBS himself—treats several topics that are absent from his draft in the January letter, some of more recent date.

The sole textual authority for the broadside version of **DW** remains the single extant copy in the Public Record Office (PRO), London (H.O. 42/127, f. 426), which serves as our copy-text (*1812*). Following the text of the broadside, we provide as a supplement the text of the letter version, transcribed diplomatically from the MS in the BL (Add. MS 37,496, f. 80). Below the critical text of the broadside, we record its variants from *1812*. We collate historically important editions of the broadside on pages 403–7, and historically important editions of the draft on pages 407–10. Commentary for both versions can be found on pages 281–93.

THE DEVIL'S WALK,
A BALLAD.

ONCE, early in the morning,
    Beelzebub arose,
With care his sweet person adorning,
    He put on his Sunday clothes.

He drew on a boot to hide his hoof,   5
    He drew on a glove to hide his claw,
His horns were concealed by *Bras Chapeau*,
And the Devil went forth as natty a *Beau*,
    As Bond-street ever saw.

He sate him down, in London town,   10
    Before earth's morning ray,
With a favourite imp he began to chat,
On religion, and scandal, this and that,
    Until the dawn of day.

And then to St. James's court he went,   15
    And St. Paul's Church he took in his way,
He was mighty thick with every Saint,
    Tho' they were formal and he was gay.

The Devil was an agriculturist,
    And as bad weeds quickly grow,   20
In looking over his farm, I wist
    He wouldn't find cause for woe.

He peeped in each hole, to each chamber stole,
    His promising live stock to view;
Grinning applause, he just shewed them his claws,   25
And they shrunk with affright from his ugly sight,
    Whose works they delighted to do.

Text collated with *1812*.

Title in gothic type; both lines of title centered. Beneath title is elaborate swell rule. Text is divided into three columns. *1812* (See page *119*.)
11 ray,] ray *1812*
22 wouldn't] would'nt *1812*
24 view;] view, *1812*

Satan poked his red nose into crannies so small,
    One would think that the innocents fair,
30   Poor lambkins! were just doing nothing at all,
But settling some dress or arranging some ball,
    But the Devil saw deeper there.

A Priest, at whose elbow the Devil during prayer,
    Sate familiarly, side by side,
35   Declared, that if the tempter were there,
    His presence he would not abide;
Ah! Ah! thought Old Nick, that's a very stale trick,
For without the Devil, O! favourite of evil,
    In your carriage you would not ride.

40   Satan next saw a brainless King,
    Whose house was as hot as his own,
Many imps in attendance were there on the wing,
They flapped the pennon and twisted the sting,
    Close by the very Throne.

45   Ah, ha! thought Satan, the pasture is good,
    My Cattle will here thrive better than others,
They dine on news of human blood,
They sup on the groans of the dying and dead,
And supperless never will go to bed;
50   Which will make them as fat as their brothers.

Fat as the fiends that feed on blood,
    Fresh and warm from the fields of Spain,
    Where ruin ploughs her gory way,
When the shoots of earth are nipped in the bud,
55   Where Hell is the Victor's prey,
    Its glory the meed of the slain.

Fat—as the death birds on Erin's shore,
That glutted themselves in her dearest gore,
    And flitted round Castlereagh,

---

37 Ah! Ah!] Ah!Ah! *1812*
41 as] at *1812*
50 their] thier *1812*
    end column one; begin column two *1812*

When they snatched the Patriot's heart, that *his* grasp   60
Had torn from its widow's maniac clasp,
    And fled at the dawn of day.

Fat—as the reptiles of the tomb,
    That riot in corruption's spoil,
That fret their little hour in gloom,   65
    And creep, and live the while.

Fat as that Prince's maudlin brain,
    Which addled by some gilded toy,
Tired, gives his sweetmeat, and again
    Cries for it, like a humoured boy.   70

For he is fat, his waistcoat gay,
When strained upon a levee day,
    Scarce meets across his princely paunch,
And pantaloons are like half moons,
    Upon each brawny haunch.   75

How vast his stock of calf! when plenty
    Had filled his empty head and heart,
Enough to satiate foplings twenty,
    Could make his pantaloon seams start.

The Devil, (who sometimes is called nature,)   80
    For men of power provides thus well,
Whilst every change, and every feature,
    Their great original can tell.

Satan saw a lawyer, a viper slay,
    That crawled up the leg of his table,   85
It reminded him most marvellously,
    Of the story of Cain and Abel.

The wealthy yeoman, as he wanders,
    His fertile fields among,
And on his thriving cattle ponders,   90
    Counts his sure gains, and hums a song;

---

61 clasp,] claps, *1812*

Thus did the Devil, thro' earth walking,
    Hum low a hellish song.

For they thrive well, whose garb of gore,
    Is Satan's choicest livery,
And they thrive well, who from the poor,
    Have snatched the bread of penury,
And heap the houseless wanderer's store,
    On the rank pile of luxury.

The Bishops thrive, tho' they are big,
    The Lawyers thrive, tho' they are thin;
For every gown, and every wig,
    Hides the safe thrift of Hell within.

Thus pigs were never counted clean,
    Altho' they dine on finest corn;
And cormorants are sin-like lean,
    Altho' they eat from night to morn.

Oh! why is the Father of Hell in such glee,
    As he grins from ear to ear?
Why does he doff his clothes joyfully,
        As he skips, and prances, and flaps his wing,
        As he sidles, leers, and twirls his sting,
    And dares, as he is, to appear?

A Statesman pass'd—alone to him,
    The Devil dare his whole shape uncover,
To show each feature, every limb,
    Secure of an unchanging lover.

At this known sign, a welcome sight,
    The watchful demons sought their King,
And every fiend of thy Stygian night,
    Was in an instant on the wing.

Pale Loyalty, his guilt steeled brow,
    With wreaths of gory laurel crowned:

---

99 *end column two; begin column three* 1812
106 are] are, 1812

The hell-hounds, Murder, Want and Woe,
    For ever hungering flocked around;   125
From Spain had Satan sought their food,
'Twas human woe and human blood!

Hark, the earthquake's crash I hear,
    Kings turn pale, and Conquerors start,
Ruffians tremble in their fear,   130
    For their Satan doth depart.

This day fiends give to revelry,
    To celebrate their King's return,
And with delight its sire to see,
    Hell's adamantine limits burn.   135

But were the Devil's sight as keen,
    As Reason's penetrating eye,
His sulphurous Majesty I ween,
    Would find but little cause for joy.

For the sons of Reason see,   140
    That ere fate consume the Pole,
The false Tyrant's cheek shall be,
    Bloodless as his coward soul.

---

128 Hark,] Hark *1812*

SUPPLEMENT
Letter Version of *The Devil's Walk*

This is a literal transcription of the text in BL Add. MS. 37,496, f. 80 verso, except that letters partially worn away by damage to, or repair of, the paper have been included as if whole and the line indentations that PBS seems to have intended have been accentuated.

[FIRST COLUMN]

      The Devil went out a walking one day
         Being tired of staying in Hell
      He dressed himself in his Sunday array
      And the reason that he was drest so gay
5   Was to cunningly pry, whether under the sky
         The affairs of earth went well
          —

      He poked his hot nose into corners so small
         One w^d. think that the innocents there
      Poor creatures were just doing nothing at all
10   But settling some dress or arranging some ball
        —The Devil saw deeper there
          —

      He peeped in each hole, to each chamber stole
         His promising live-stock to view
      Grinning applause, he just shews his claws
15   And Satan laughed in the mirth of his soul
      That they started with fright, from <u>his</u> ugly sight
         Whose works they delighted to do
          —

      A Parson with whom in the house of prayer
         The devil sate side by side
20   Bawled out that if the devil were
         His presence he couldnt abide,   trick
      Ha ha thought old Nick, thats a very stale $_\wedge$
      For without the Devil, ô favorite of evil
         In thy carriage thou wouldst not ride
          —

25   He saw the Devil a viper slay
         Under his brief-covered table

Text collated with MS BL and *MYR*/VIII.
14 Grinning] Receiving *MYR*/VIII
16 they] <u>they</u> (*underline stricken through*) *MYR*/VIII

26 his] this/his *"his" superimposed on "this"* *MYR*/VIII

It reminded the Devil marvellously
   Of the story of Cain and Abel

           —

[SECOND COLUMN]
Satan next saw a Brainless King
   In a house as hot as his own   30
Many imps he saw near there on the wi[ng]
They flapped the black pennon and twiste[d]
                        the sting
   Close to the very throne

           —

Ah! Ah cried Satan the pasture is go[od]
   My cattle will <u>here</u> thrive better than oth[ers]   35
They will have for their food, news of
                        humans blood
They will drink the groans of the dying
                        & dead
And supperless never will go to bed
   W^{ch} will make 'em as fat as their
                        brothers .

           —

The Devil was walking in the Park   40
   Dressed like a bond Street beau
For ~~al~~tho his visage was rather dark
And his mouth was wide his chin came
                        out
And something like Castlereagh was his
                        snout
   He might be calld so, so . .   45

           —

Why does the Devil grin so wide
   & shew the hore teeth within
Nine and ninety on each side
   By the clearest reckoning—

           —

---

31 wi[ng]] wing   *MYR*/VIII
32 twiste[d]] twirle<d>   *MYR*/VIII
34 go[od]] good   *MYR*/VIII
35 <u>here</u>] here   *MYR*/VIII
   oth[ers]] other<s>   *MYR*/VIII

39 brothers .] brothers.   *MYR*/VIII
   W^{ch}] W^{ch}.   *MYR*/VIII
45 so . .] so.   *MYR*/VIII
47 hore] Iron   *MYR*/VIII

Oh wretched mortal hard thy fate
Stern misery frowns on every state

Text of *"Oh wretched mortal, hard thy fate!"* written in a notebook belonging to Thomas Jefferson Hogg while a student at Oxford. With kind permission of The Carl H. Pforzheimer Collection of Shelley and His Circle, The New York Public Library, Astor, Lenox and Tilden Foundations.

Ten Early Poems (1809–1814)

The following ten short poems by PBS—some of which may be excerpts from poems otherwise lost—were written and released between 1809 or early 1810 and March 1814 but were never later revised for publication. They are drawn from manuscripts—letters, notebooks, and a copy by his sister—that preserve the scattered survivors of a larger body of poetry that PBS undoubtedly wrote and either handed or mailed to members of his circle before his elopement with Mary W. Godwin (MWS) on 27 July 1814. PBS collected and revised a number of such poems, which he copied into ***The Esdaile Notebook (Esd)*** between 1812 and 1814, and in Volume II of ***CPPBS*** the privately released texts of those poems will be discussed and collated with the revised texts in ***Esd***. The ten poems below, however, are ones that PBS either lost track of by 1812, did not choose to include in the ***Esd*** collection, or composed after he had abandoned ***Esd***.

As usual, we collate the primary textual authorities for each poem at the bottom of the pages upon which the relevant text appears; in the Commentary (pages 295–329) we discuss the significance of each poem or fragment for PBS's life, thought, and poetic development, provide factual annotation and information on the approximate date and the occasion of its composition, trace the provenance of its primary textual authorities and its textual history, and outline our editorial procedures with regard to it. Variants between our Texts and other significant editions appear on pages 411–28, among the Historical Collations. The poems are arranged in the order of their original private release, insofar as we can establish that sequence.

1. "A Cat in distress"
2. "How swiftly through Heaven's wide expanse"
3. "Oh wretched mortal, hard thy fate!"
4. To Mary who died in this opinion
5. "Why is it said thou canst but live"
6. "As you will see I wrote to you" (1st letter to E. F. Graham)
7. "Dear dear dear dear dear dear Græme!" (2nd letter to E. F. Graham)
8. "Sweet star! which gleaming oer the darksome scene"
9. "Bear witness Erin! when thine injured isle"
10. "Thy dewy looks sink in my breast"

"A Cat in distress"

1.

A Cat in distress
Nothing more or less,
Good folks I must faithfully tell ye,
    As I am a sinner
    It wants for some dinner   5
To stuff out its own little belly.

2.

You migh'n't easily guess
All the modes of distress
Which torture the tenants of earth,
    And the various evils   10
    Which like many devils
Attend the poor dogs from their birth:

3.

Some a living require
And others desire
An old fellow out of the way,   15
    And which is the best
    I leave to be guessed
For I cannot pretend to say.

4.

One wants society
T'other variety   20
Others a tranquil life;
    Some want food
    Others as good
Only require a wife.

Text collated with **MS Pfz** and *SC/IV*.
Stanza marker. 1] *omitted* **Pfz** *SC/IV*
2 less,] less **Pfz** *SC/IV*
3 ye,] ye **Pfz** *SC/IV*
6 belly.] belly **Pfz** *SC/IV*
Stanza marker. 2.]
    2 ——— **Pfz** *SC/IV*
9 earth,] earth **Pfz** *SC/IV*
12 birth:] birth **Pfz** *SC/IV*

Stanza marker. 3.]
    3 ——— **Pfz** *SC/IV*
15 way,] way **Pfz** *SC/IV*
18 say.] say **Pfz** *SC/IV*
Stanza marker. 4.] 4 **Pfz** *SC/IV*
20 T'other] Tother **Pfz** *SC/IV*
21 life;] life **Pfz** *SC/IV*
24 wife.] wife **Pfz** *SC/IV*

5.

25   But this poor little Cat
            Only wanted a rat
        To stuff out its own little maw,
            And 'twere as good
            Had some people such food
30   To make them hold their jaw.

"How swiftly through Heaven's wide expanse"

How swiftly through Heaven's wide expanse
    Bright day's resplendent colors fade,
How sweetly does the moonbeam's glance
    With silver teint St. Irvyne's glade.

5   No cloud along the spangled air
        Is borne upon the evening breeze,
    How solemn is the scene, how fair
        The moonbeams rest upon the trees.

    Yon dark grey turret glimmers white,
10   Upon it sits the mournful owl;
    Along the stillness of the night
        Her melancholy shriekings roll.

    But not alone on Irvyne's tower
        The moonbeam pours its silver ray;
15 It gleams upon the ivied bower,
        It dances in the cascade's spray.

Stanza marker. 5.]
  5 ——— **Pfz** *SC/IV*
27 maw,] maw **Pfz** *SC/IV*
28 'twere] twere **Pfz**
        t'were *SC/IV*
30 jaw.] jaw **Pfz** *SC/IV*

Text collated with **MS PMgn.**
2 fade,] fade **PMgn**
4 St.] St **PMgn**
  glade.] glade **PMgn**

8 moonbeams] moonbeam's **PMgn**
  trees.] trees **PMgn**
9 glimmers] glimmer's **PMgn**
  white,] white **PMgn**
10 owl;] owl **PMgn**
12 roll.] roll **PMgn**
14 its] it's **PMgn**
15 gleams] gleam's **PMgn**
  bower,] bower **PMgn**
16 spray.] spray **PMgn**

For there a youth with darken'd brow
    His long lost love is heard to mourn:
He vents his swelling bosom's woe—
    "Ah! when will hours like those return?"   20

O'er this torn soul, o'er this frail form
    Let feast the fiends of tortured love—
Let lower dire fate's terrific storm,
    I would the pangs of death to prove.

Ah! why do prating priests suppose,   25
    That God can give the wretch relief,
Can stop the bosom's bursting woes
    Or calm the tide of frantic grief?

Within me burns a raging Hell;
    Fate I defy thy farther power,   30
Fate I defy thy fiercer spell
    And long for stern death's welcome hour.

No power of Earth, of Hell or Heaven,
    Can still the tumult of my brain:
The power to none save ———'s given   35
    To calm my bosom's frantic pain.

Ah why do darkning shades conceal
    The hour when man must cease to be?
Why may not human minds unveil
    The dark shade of futurity?"   40

---

17 darken'd] dark'ned   **PMgn**
18 mourn:] mourn   **PMgn**
19 bosom's] bosoms   **PMgn**
20 return?] return   **PMgn**
22 love—] love   **PMgn**
24 prove.] prove[.]   **PMgn**
28 calm] s̶t̶i̶l̶l̶ stem   **PMgn**
    grief?] grief   **PMgn**
29 Hell;] Hell   **PMgn**
30 power,] power   **PMgn**
34 brain:] brain   **PMgn**
36 calm] t̶a̶k̶e̶ calm   **PMgn**
40 futurity?"] futurity?   **PMgn**

"Oh wretched mortal, hard thy fate!"

Oh wretched mortal, hard thy fate!
Stern misery frowns on every state
To thee assigned—— Who can express
The varying forms of thy distress?
5   Ah say, what is adversity
If sorrow be prosperity—
Say, cynic, what can glory be,
If high renown be infamy?
Who can be free if liberty
10   Be aye the basest slavery?
What tongue the infernal woes can tell,
What mind conceive if heaven be hell?
Sure, wretched mortal! hard thy fate—
Keen misery is thy happiest state.
15   The sentence hear which wisdom gave:
"The lover is the vilest slave."

To Mary who died in this opinion

Maiden, quench the glare of sorrow
   Struggling in thine haggard eye:
Firmness dare to borrow
   From the wreck of destiny;
5   For the ray morn's bloom revealing
   Can never boast so bright an hue

Text collated with **MS Pfz.**
1 mortal,] mortal **Pfz**
   fate!] fate **Pfz**
4 distress?] distress **Pfz**
5 say,] say **Pfz**
6 prosperity—] prosperity **Pfz**
7 Say,] Say **Pfz**
   cynic,] cynic **Pfz**
   be,] be **Pfz**
8 infamy?] infamy[.] **Pfz**
10 slavery?] slavery **Pfz**
11 tell,] tell **Pfz**
12 hell?] hell **Pfz**
13 Sure,] Sure **Pfz**

mortal!] mortal **Pfz**
   fate—] fate **Pfz**
14 state.] state **Pfz**
15 which] w^ch **Pfz**
   wisdom] wisdom **Pfz**
   gave:] gave **Pfz**
16 slave."] slave" **Pfz**
   single rule added **Pfz**

Text collated with **MS BL** and *MYR/* VIII.
2 eye:] eye **BL** *MYR/* VIII
4 destiny;] destiny **BL** *MYR/* VIII
5 morn's] morns **BL** *MYR/* VIII

As that which mocks concealing
    And sheds its loveliest light on you.

                    2
Yet is the tie departed
    Which bound thy lovely soul to bliss: 10
Has it left thee broken hearted
    In a world so cold as this?
Yet tho fainting, fair one
    (Sorrow's self thy cup has given),
Dream thou'lt meet thy dear one   15
    Never more to part in Heaven.

                    3
Existence would I barter
    For a dream so dear as thine,
And smile to die a martyr
    On affection's bloodless shrine: 20
Nor would I change for <u>pleasure</u>
    That withered hand and ashy cheek
If my heart enshrined a treasure
    [Such as] forces thine to break.

       "Why is it said thou canst but live"

Why is it said thou canst but live
    In a youthful breast and fair:
Since thou eternal life canst give,

---

8   you.] you   **BL** *MYR/*VIII
10 bliss:] bliss   **BL** *MYR/*VIII
12 In] <I>n   **BL** *MYR/*VIII
    this?] this   **BL** *MYR/*VIII
13 fainting,] fainting   **BL** *MYR/*VIII
14 (Sorrow's . . . given),] Sorrows . . . given   **BL** *MYR/*VIII
16 Heaven.] Heaven   **BL** *MYR/*VIII
17 would] w.ᵈ   **BL**
    wᵈ.   *MYR/*VIII
18 thine,] thine   **BL** *MYR/*VIII
20 affection's]
        affections   **BL** *MYR/*VIII
    shrine:] shine   **BL** *MYR/*VIII

21 would] w.ᵈ   **BL**
        wᵈ.   *MYR/*VIII
23 enshrined]
        enshined   **BL** *MYR/*VIII
24 [Such as]] *omitted*   **BL** *MYR/*VIII
    break.] break   **BL** *MYR/*VIII

Text collated with **MS Pfz** and *SC/*II.
2   and] &   **Pfz** *SC/*II
    fair:] fair   **Pfz** *SC/*II
3   give,] give   **Pfz**
        ~~ga~~give   *SC/*II

                    Canst bloom forever there,
5   Since withering pain no power possesses
                    Nor Age to blanch thy vermeil hue,
                Since time's dread victor death confesses
                    Tho bathed with his poison dew,
                Still thou retainst unchanging bloom
10   Fixed tranquil even in the tomb.—
                And oh! when on the blest reviving
                    The day star dawns of love,
                Each energy of soul surviving
                    More vivid soars above.———
15   Hast thou ne'er felt a rapturous thrill
                    Like June's warm breath athwart thee fly
                Oer each idea then to steal
                    When other passions die—
                Felt it in some wild noonday dream
20   When sitting by the lonely stream
                Where Silence says mine is the dell,
                    And not a murmur from the plain
                And not an echo from the fell
                    Disputes her silent reign?

          "*As you will see I wrote to you*"
                    [To EFG #1]

                As you will see I wrote to you
                As is most fitting, right and due
                With Killjoy's frank, old Killjoy he
                Is eaten up with Jealousy,
5   His brows so dark, his ears so blue!
                And all this fury is for you.
                Yes Graham, thine is sure the name

---

4 there,] there   **Pfz** *SC/*II
           possesses
5 possesses] [   ]   *SC/*II
6 hue,] hue   **Pfz** *SC/*II
8 dew,] dew   **Pfz** *SC/*II
12 love,] love   **Pfz** *SC/*II
14 above.———]
          above ———   **Pfz** *SC/*II
18 When] <u>When</u>   *SC/*II
       die—] die   **Pfz** *SC/*II
21 dell,] dell   **Pfz** *SC/*II

23 the fell] the [?] fell   *SC/*II
24 reign?] reign   **Pfz** *SC/*II

Text collated with **MS Berg** and *MYR/* VIII.
2 fitting,] fitting   **Berg** *MYR/* VIII
   and] &   **Berg** *MYR/* VIII
4 Jealousy,]
       Jealousy   **Berg** *MYR/* VIII
5 dark,] dark   **Berg** *MYR/* VIII
6 you.] you   **Berg** *MYR/* VIII

On Spanish fields so dear to fame
Which sickening Killjoy scarce can hear
Without a mingled pang of fear.   10
Fear, hatred cowards always have
But Gratitude usurps the brave
And therefore Graham I will tell
You if you don't as yet know well
Before I tell this tale to you   15
That Killjoy, hot with envy blue,
Can neither bear Græme me or you.
A good man bears his heaven about him,
An idiot's pride won't move without him,
And pride may justly be called Hell,   20
Since 'twas from Pride that Satan fell,
From pride the mighty conquerors strode
Oer half the globe, from pride the abode
Of Peace, becomes the poisoned cell
Where the fiends of Hatred dwell: 25
Suspicion always tracks its way,
Around the wretch what horrors play
And on his poisoned vitals prey.
Hence you my Fargy when we know
That you are never used to go   30
In courtship to the ancient dames
Who reverence claim instead of flames,
Since but once in an age is seen
Of forty eight a peerless queen
Like Ninon famed, that girl of France   35
Who at ninety two could dance
With such a grace as did impart
Improper flames to Grandson's heart,

---

10 fear.] fear **Berg** *MYR/* VIII
11 Fear,] Fear- **Berg**
    Fear *MYR/* VIII
14 don't] dont **Berg** *MYR/* VIII
16 Killjoy,] Killjoy **Berg** *MYR/* VIII
   blue,] blue **Berg** *MYR/* VIII
17 you.] you **Berg** *MYR/* VIII
18 him,] him **Berg** *MYR/* VIII
19 idiot's] idiots **Berg** *MYR/* VIII
   won't] wont **Berg** *MYR/* VIII
   him,] him **Berg** *MYR/* VIII
20 justly be]
    be justly be **Berg** *MYR/* VIII

Hell,] Hell **Berg** *MYR/* VIII
21 'twas] twas **Berg** *MYR/* VIII
   Satan] Satian **Berg**
25 dwell:] dwell **Berg** *MYR/* VIII
26 Suspicion] Supicion **Berg**
   its] it's **Berg** *MYR/* VIII
   way,] way **Berg** *MYR/* VIII
31 courtship] courtsip **Berg** *MYR/* VIII
32 flames,] flames **Berg** *MYR/* VIII
38 heart,] heart **Berg** *MYR/* VIII

40 　　　We fairly may acquit your soul
　　　(Tho your life's pulses fiercely roll)
　　　Of having let one wild wish glow
　　　Of cornuting old Killjoy's brow;
　　　Heaven knows 'twere a corageous horn
　　　That would this frowning brow adorn:
45 　　　Oh! not the fiercest antler dare
　　　To stretch its fell luxuriance there.
　　　Safe mayst thou sin altho' there's none
　　　Of what is called temptation
　　　And I should think 'twere no mistake
50 　　　To say you sinned for sinning sake.
　　　Yet as this place no news affords
　　　But secret damns and glossy words
　　　Before your face, I bid adieu
　　　And wish my Græme, good night to you.

　　　　　　　———

55 　　　P.S.
　　　　The wind is high and I have been
　　　With little Jack upon the green,
　　　A dear delightful red faced brute,
　　　And setting up a parachute;
　　　The wind beneath its bosom played
60 　　　Oh! Fargy wonderous sport we made.
　　　Are not human minds just like this little poem

"Dear dear dear dear dear dear Græme!"
[To EFG #2]

Dear dear dear dear dear dear Græme!
When back from Cuckfield here I came

---

40 (Tho . . . roll)]
　　Tho . . . roll **Berg** *MYR/*VIII
42 Killjoy's] Killjoys **Berg** *MYR/*VIII
43 'twere] twere **Berg** *MYR/*VIII
44 adorn:] adorn **Berg** *MYR/*VIII
46 there.] there **Berg** *MYR/*VIII
47 sin] sin; **Berg** *MYR/*VIII
　　there's] theres **Berg** *MYR/*VIII
48 temptation] temtation **Berg**
49 'twere] twere **Berg** *MYR/*VIII
50 sake.] sake **Berg** *MYR/*VIII
52 But] [But] **Berg** *MYR/*VIII
　　and] & **Berg** *MYR/*VIII

53 Before] [Before] **Berg**
　　　　[?Before] *MYR/*VIII
　　your] yours **Berg** *MYR/*VIII
　　face,] [face], **Berg** *MYR/*VIII
55 and] & **Berg** *MYR/*VIII
56 green,] green **Berg** *MYR/*VIII
58 parachute;]
　　　parachute **Berg** *MYR/*VIII
60 Fargy] fargy **Berg** *MYR/*VIII
　　made.] made **Berg** *MYR/*VIII

Text collated with **MS Pfz.**

    I found your penitential letter,
But sackcloth cannot now prevail
Nor even ashes aught avail,   5
For I can see there's no relenting—
Indeed I fear that all repenting
    Would act but as a temper-whetter,
For the more you repent, the more tears he demands
The more you submit, the more the commands   10
The more sighs that you breathe, the joy's so divine
The more will he want you to groan, gnash and whine.
They are food to his soul, and when the notes fall
'Tis like your beloved Catalani's squall—
The murmurs of grief are the music he hears   15
And discontent's groanings are balm to his ears.
What wonder then happiness sounds to him woe
What wonder that mirth bid satire to flow,
That his blue visage gleams with a blueness intenser
[?When] happiness acts as a passion condenser?   20
But give him a prison, and give him a throne
And give him a world to reign in alone:
Full of death-groaning nations let it be crammed
And I wish no worse place for the souls of the damned;
Or give him a daughter and give him a wife,   25
I'll engage he'll torment 'em just out of their life
If so be't their peculiar wish lies this way,
With exactness our squire will their wishes obey.
Have you found yet the horn, that dares to adorn

---

3 letter,] letter **Pfz**
5 avail,] avail **Pfz**
6 there's no] there's i̶s̶ no **Pfz**
  relenting—] relenting **Pfz**
8 temper-whetter,]
  temper-whetter **Pfz**
10 submit,] submit **Pfz**
11 so] [ ]o **Pfz**
12 and] & **Pfz**
13 and] & **Pfz**
14 Catalani's] Calatani's **Pfz**
  squall—] squall **Pfz**
      mirth
18 mirth] l̶a̶u̶g̶h̶t̶e̶r̶ [∧] **Pfz**
  flow,] flow **Pfz**

20 [?When]] *omitted* **Pfz**
  happiness] [ ] happiness **Pfz**
  condenser?] condenser **Pfz**
21 But] [ ]! **Pfz**
  and] & **Pfz**
22 alone:] alone **Pfz**
23 death-groaning nations let]
      nations
    death-groaning ∧ let **Pfz**
24 damned;] damned **Pfz**
25 and] & **Pfz**
  wife,] wife **Pfz**
26 their] thier **Pfz**
27 their] thier **Pfz**
  way,] way **Pfz**

30　　　　A brow which no daring horn yet has attempted?
　　　　　And I will engage, for the rest of his age
　　　　　　　That from all further duty he shall be exempted:
　　　　　I think that our squire, does mainly desire
　　　　　　　That an horn on his dark frowning brow were implanted—
35　　　　I've hit it exactly, he'd get one directly
　　　　　　　But the worst is that things will not come when they're wanted.
　　　　　He wishes to drive, from her own native hive
　　　　　　　His wife who so merrily laughs at each odd whim.
　　　　　And now I have done, for they say that this fun
40　　　　Would look worse on the side of this letter than Godwin.

"Sweet star! which gleaming oer the darksome scene"

　　Sweet star! which gleaming oer the darksome scene
　　Thro' fleecy clouds of silvery radiance fling'st
　　Spanglets of light on evening's shadowy veil
　　Which shrouds the day beam from the waveless lake,
5　　Lighting the hour of sacred love, more sweet
　　Than the expiring morn-star's paly fires—
　　Sweet star! when wearied nature sinks to sleep
　　And all is hushed,—all save the voice of love,
　　Whose broken murmurings swell the balmy blast
10　　Of soft Favonius, which at intervals
　　Sighs in the ear of stillness,—art thou aught but love
　　Lulling the slaves of interest to repose
　　With that mild pitying gaze . . oh! I could look
　　On thy dear beam 'till every bond of sense
15　　Became unnerved. . . . .

30　attempted?] attempted　**Pfz**
32　exempted:] exempted　**Pfz**
34　implanted—] implanted　**Pfz**
36　they're] there　**Pfz**
　　wanted.] wanted　**Pfz**
38　whim.] whim　**Pfz**
39　And now] A̶n̶d̶ And now　**Pfz**
40　Godwin.] Godwin　**Pfz**

Text collated with **MS Pfz** and *SC*/II.
2　fling'st] fli̶g̶hng'st　**Pfz** *SC*/II
3　veil] viel　**Pfz** *SC*/II
4　lake,] lake　**Pfz** *SC*/II
6　fires—] fires　**Pfz** *SC*/II
11　stillness,—art] stillness.—art　*SC*/II
　　aught] ought　**Pfz** *SC*/II
13　could] cd.　**Pfz** *SC*/II

"Bear witness Erin! when thine injured isle"

Bear witness Erin! when thine injured isle
Sees summer on its verdant pastures smile,
Its cornfields waving in the winds that sweep
The billowy surface of thy circling deep—
Thou tree whose shadow oer the Atlantic gave 5
Peace wealth and beauty to its friendly wave
——————its blossoms fade
And blighted are the leaves that cast its shade
Whilst the cold hand gathers its scanty fruit
Whose chillness struck a canker to its root. 10

"Thy dewy looks sink in my breast"

Thy dewy looks sink in my breast,
    Thy gentle words stir poison there:
Thou hast disturbed the only rest
    That was the portion of despair.

Subdued to Duty's hard control 5
    I could have borne my wayward lot:
The chains that bind this ruined soul
    Had cankered then—but crushed it not.

Text collated with **MS BL** and *MYR*/VIII.
1 Bear witness] Be<   >tness **BL**
              Be<   >ess *MYR*/VIII
2 smile,] smile *MYR*/VIII
4 deep—] deep - *MYR*/VIII
              beauty
6 and beauty] and freshness
    BL *MYR*/VIII
10 its] it's **BL**
    its' *MYR*/VIII

Text collated with **MS UCL.**
1 breast,] breast **UCL**
2 there:] there. **UCL**
4 despair.] despair **UCL**
5 Duty's] Dutys **UCL**
8 then—but] then— but **UCL**

COMMENTARIES

Original Poetry
by Victor and Cazire

Much of what is known about this volume's history appears in two publications by Richard Garnett. In the first, entitled "Shelley in Pall Mall," in *Macmillan's Magazine* (2 [June 1860]: 100–110), Garnett announced that he had verified the existence of the book (though he had not located a copy of it) from his reading of *Stockdale's Budget*, a short-lived periodical (Dec. 1826–Feb. 1827). The London publisher John Joseph Stockdale (1770–1847, *DNB*) was ruined by libel suits in 1826 for publishing—and probably writing—the memoirs of the famous courtesan Harriette Wilson (1789–1846, *DNB*). At the end of 1826, Stockdale sought revenge on "polite" society by publishing his *Budget*, filled with scandalous stories about the upper classes. There he printed serially an extended account of his experiences as PBS's early publisher, which appeared as the first substantive articles in the first two issues (13 and 20 Dec. 1826) and continued in the third through ninth issues (the last dated 7 Feb. 1827); in these he quoted eleven letters from PBS to him, dated between 6 September 1810 and 1 August 1811, and told how the young man had come to him "early in the autumn of 1810," requesting that Stockdale "extricate him from a pecuniary difficulty, in which he was involved, with a printer . . . who resided at Horsham, near to which Timothy Shelley Esquire M.P. . . . had a seat, called Field Place." Stockdale agreed to take over the sale of the printed work, and "on the 17th September 1810 . . . received fourteen hundred and eighty copies of a thin royal 8vo. volume, in sheets, and not gathered. It was entitled Original Poetry, by Alonzo and Cazire, or two names, something like them. The Author told me that the poems were the joint production of himself and a friend, whose name was forgotten by me as soon as I heard it" (*Budget*, 13 Dec. 1826, 1–2; note the density of Stockdale's punctuation, a style to which PBS conformed in ***St. Irvyne***). This was the bulk, at least, of the first edition of ***Original Poetry*** (***V&C***). Stockdale's account of his involvement with ***V&C*** is very circumstantial, apparently based upon his own business records as well as PBS's letters to him and his own memory, but a few demonstrable errors show that his facts cannot be taken as gospel. Though Stockdale recorded correctly the book's title (which he may have copied from his invoice or receipt for the shipment), he seems not to have had a copy of the work itself available when he wrote, for he misremembered not only the pseudonyms of the authors but also the format of the volume, which Stockdale calls "a thin royal 8vo volume" (but is actually a quarto of 32 leaves—64 pages) that was delivered to him "in sheets, and not gathered."

Thirty-eight years after Garnett announced the existence of the volume, he (by then Keeper of Printed Books in the British Museum) wrote the Introduction to a type-facsimile edition of the volume (London: John Lane, 1898) (*1898*) that was based on the very first copy of *V&C* to surface, one belonging to a grandson of PBS's cousin Charles Henry Grove. Though Garnett, who thus rescued Shelley's first volume of published poetry from oblivion, was judicious in his estimate both of what it has to teach us and of its limitations, he also added a memorable yet condescending judgment on the poetry that may have discouraged others from giving the volume a fair hearing. The crucial paragraph in Garnett's Introduction is this:

[N]ot more than five pieces in the volume, including the plagiarised poem, can be attributed to Elizabeth Shelley. The book is consequently a more important document for the mental history of Shelley than might have been expected, and enlarges our conception of Shelley's range at this early period, both of thought and of metrical practice. Childishly immature as it is, it offers nothing to forbid the anticipation of eventual excellence, and something to encourage it. It shows, at all events, that the youthful Shelley could write better verse than can be found in his novels, and that he even then possessed the feeling for melody which is rarely dissociated from more or less of endowment with the poetical faculty. Biographically, it contributes something to illustrate an obscure period of his life, and strengthens the belief that his attachment for his fair cousin was more than a passing fancy. It is, therefore, of considerable interest, apart from the romantic history [of its loss and rediscovery] which constitutes its chief claim to celebrity, and the rarity which gives it a unique place among Shelley's extant writings. Fervently as we hoped that a copy might one day be found, we must now hope with equal fervour that no one may ever find another. (*1898*, xxv–xxvi)

Suppression and Survival

Because **Original Poetry** "by Victor and Cazire" was not available until 1898, Harry Buxton Forman and other early editors never had a chance to explore the textual problems that the original volume presents. Garnett, proud of his efforts in identifying and searching for the lost publication, may have believed that one original copy and the facsimile to which he contributed were sufficient for the world. In fact, however, that copy was textually imperfect, since the Groves had erased a reference that Charlotte Grove considered an invasion of her privacy (see below), and as the collations attest, the facsimile edition introduced several other textual errors.

Luckily, two uncensored copies have since come to light. Stockdale says that soon after he began to sell the newly bound volume of poems, "I happened to be perusing them, with more attention . . . , when I recognised, in the collection, one, which I knew to have been written by Mr. M. G. Lewis, the Author of The Monk" (*Budget*). Stockdale confronted PBS, who apologized, blamed his coadjutor, and asked the bookseller to destroy the unsold copies. But, Stockdale noted, this happened only after he had "advertised the work in nearly all the London papers" and "through the author and me, about one hundred, in the whole, have been put into circulation" (*Budget*, 2). Considering how many of the owners of these copies would have been friends and relatives of PBS himself, it is mildly surprising that of the fifteen hundred or so copies and those one hundred distributed by PBS and Stockdale, just three have been identified.

The copy that PBS gave to Harriet Grove, from which *1898* was printed, was purchased by T. J. Wise, who sold it after he bought a second, much taller copy; that Grove family copy, now in the Humanities Research Center, University of Texas at Austin (Tx), shows exactly what irritated the Groves about the volume, for the words "the Colonel" are erased from **line 15** of the second poem (see **Letter [2], lines 13–30,** and its commentary). Wise's second copy, now with his Ashley Collection in the British Library (BL), originally belonged to "William Wellesley, fourth Earl of Mornington, a cousin of the Duke of Wellington," who had inscribed it: "Given to me at Eton by the Author | Percy Bysse [*sic*] Shelley, my friend | and schoolfellow — 1810" (Wise, 30). The third copy, now in the Huntington Library (Htn), shows that the printer was not ashamed of the volume, for it is inscribed: "To | Mr Perry | this Poem is given with respectful | compliments of | Chas Phillips." Perry was probably James Perry, editor of the Whig *Morning Chronicle*, PBS's early admiration of whom E. B. Murray discusses in *Studies in Romanticism* (17 [1978]: 35–49). Perry was a notable book collector, in whose posthumous book sale (four sessions from March 1822 to March 1823 at "Mr. Evans, No. 93 Pall-Mall"; copy in Pfz) were listed at least two titles by Thomas Love Peacock and PBS's ***Revolt of Islam***, but not ***V&C***, suggesting that Perry may have given it to someone else to examine for possible review in the *Morning Chronicle*.

Site of Printing

Most scholars have accepted without comment the evidence of the book's colophon that it was printed by C. and W. Phillips in Worthing, on the south coast of Sussex, some twenty miles directly south of Horsham (Paterson's *Roads* [1808], 32), but the evidence is mixed. Supporting the Worthing site is Samuel J. Looker's local history study *Shelley, Trelawny, and Henley: A Study of Three Titans* (pub. in Worthing, 1950), which places PBS among the worthies of Worthing chiefly on the basis of his having printed there both *V&C* and **The Necessity of Atheism** (see Looker, 24–31, and 67–145, where both these rare editions are reproduced in high-quality photofacsimile). Looker says that in the year 1807 James Phillips, a printer of Horsham, began

printing playbills for the New Theatre at Worthing, and his imprint may be found upon them. Three years later he had established a printery in the town at what was then number 12, Warwick Street, to which he sent his sons Charles and William. James Phillips, however, seems to have been the sole proprietor of the business, for there is in existence a letter written by him on December 10, 1810, addressed to Thomas Medwin [actually, Thomas Charles Medwin, the father of Shelley's second cousin and schoolfellow] stating that money was due to him from Shelley for printing carried out at Worthing, and asking for a loan until he could secure payment from the poet himself. This debt was for the printing of the Victor and Cazire book. (Looker, 25)

Contrary evidence appears not only in Stockdale's statement that the "printer . . . resided at Horsham," but in additional facts garnered by James Bieri from his researches at Horsham: "James Phillips, the father of C. & W. Phillips, had a printing firm (and bindery) in Horsham, did printing for [Thomas] Medwin senior as early as 1800, and acted as sort of a clerk to him." Bieri has also provided us with a full transcript of the same note that Looker cites, from James Phillips to the elder Medwin and dated 10 December 1810; it does not state *where* the printing was done: "Sir I should esteem it a favor if you would be pleased to lend me a pound note to send to London until the 15th of this month as I shall then have the 75£ to take of P. B. Shelley Esq. for printing done for him. Jas. Phillips" (Horsham Museum, #437; Bieri to Reiman: letter of 23 Apr. 1994 and e-mail of 14 Sept. 1996). James Phillips's claim conforms to Stockdale's reference to PBS's troubles with a *Horsham* printer and PBS's more casual statement about "Philipps the Horsham printer" (**Letters** I, 13). Bieri further suggests that the use of the Phillips sons' Worthing imprint may have been a blind to disguise the identity of the young authors.

On the other hand, the idea that the printing itself took place at Worthing is supported not only by the colophon, but also by the inscription of the Huntington copy to Perry by "Cha⁵ Phillips," one of the two sons at Worthing. By December 1810, when James Phillips wrote to Thomas Medwin, Sr., *V&C* had already been suppressed and destroyed, and the Phillips family, father at Horsham and sons at Worthing alike, may have been concerned with receiving payment for the printing. The request from James Phillips, owner of both printshops, to borrow £1 from Medwin, kinsman of PBS's mother and the local agent for the Duke of Norfolk, might be merely an oblique way to remind Timothy Shelley and his father Sir Bysshe, who were dependent allies of the duke, of their family's debt. The mystery of the payment of the Phillipses' bill may be complicated further by Stockdale's statement: "I am not quite certain how the difference, between the poet, and the printer, was arranged; but, after I had looked over the account, I know that it was paid; though, whether I assisted in the payment by money or acceptance, I cannot remember" (*Budget*, 1). Stockdale's use of the word "acceptance" indicates that he may have agreed to "accept" (redeem at face value) a post-dated promissory note payable to Phillips by a third party— probably either Timothy or Sir Bysshe—that would come due on 15 December 1810, almost exactly three months after the likely date on which the printers shipped the ungathered sheets of *V&C* to Stockdale that he received on 17 September. Since PBS's letter requesting Stockdale to intervene on his behalf is dated 16 September 1810, this shows that Stockdale came to his rescue immediately (**Letters** I, 15; *SC* II, 633–34).

The quality of the Phillipses' printing in *V&C* (and in **The Necessity of Atheism** the following spring) becomes an issue because of a letter that Barclay Phillips wrote: when his aunt Philadelphia Phillips, who had worked as a printer with the family firm, lived with his family at Brighton, he "frequently heard her talk of Shelley. She said he took great interest in the art of printing, and would often come in and spend hours in the printing office learning to set up the types, and help my cousin (the daughter)" (see Ingpen, *Shelley in England* [1917], 188–89). Ingpen goes on to speculate whether PBS "actually set up the type for the *Necessity of Atheism*" (189). Looker, who assumes that Philadelphia Phillips worked in the Worthing rather than the Horsham printshop, imagines that PBS might have become "interested in a young woman who, by all accounts which we possess [i.e., one], was undoubtedly much in advance of most members of her sex" (Looker, 27), and his book's frontispiece is an imagined portrait of her as a fashionably dressed Austen heroine, sitting in the Worthing printing house with a bouquet of flowers in her lap and looking over a proofsheet with PBS, whose hand is on her shoulder. If Philadelphia Phillips was, however, a skilled printer—likely a daughter of James Phillips—she probably remained at Horsham to help him after his two sons moved away to start the new business. Because of some features in the text of the first edition of *V&C*, we suspect that PBS may have helped typeset parts of it. This would have been far more likely if it was printed at Horsham, rather than Worthing, an additional twenty miles away from Field Place (although Worthing was close to Castle Goring, the unfinished mansion of PBS's grandfather), but the available evidence on the location remains inconclusive.

Distribution of the Type

While collating the three known copies of *1810*, we noted that in the BL copy some lines of type have begun to work themselves loose, leaving a few letters out of line. This deterioration, which does not appear in Htn, suggests that BL was printed later in the press run than Htn; but in spite of this and some egregious typographical errors (the most notable being "gaol" for "goal" in **line 49** of Elizabeth Shelley's second verse letter), the typographic formalities of *V&C* do not suggest an amateur compositor throughout. (The frequent omission of apostrophes in the possessive case merely signals an alternative usage defended in the grammatical summary of *Entick's New Spelling Dictionary,* a work cited as an authority in the first poem of *V&C*.) On the other hand, the typography of *1810* may give us a clue as to the printing process. The text of the volume contains an unusually large proportion of capital Ws, which seem to have been in short supply in the font of eleven-point type used throughout *1810*. At least three different Ws in the font seem to be badly and distinctively malformed, and one such malformed *W* appears first on page 19 and then again on page 57 of *1810* (the two other malformed Ws also appear in signature "H" on 54 and 60); such a reappearance of this single type piece indicates that some early sheets of *V&C* were typeset, printed, and their types distributed before the compositor set the final signatures. This evidence, in turn, supports the idea that there was a break between the printing of the early poems and the final ones—evidence that bears upon our explanation of PBS's blatant plagiarism of **Saint Edmond's Eve** from *Tales of Terror.*

Plagiarisms, Authorship, Pseudonyms, and Title

Garnett left unanswered the question of what plagiarism scuttled the publication of *1810*, but Edward Dowden wrote on 20 October 1898, immediately after Garnett had sent him a copy, "I fancy at the first glance that if any poem is stolen it may be Saint Edmonds Eve" (*Letters about Shelley,* 195); Dowden may have noted, as Lisa M. Wilson observes in "Shelley's Early Career in Print" (an unpublished paper), that **Saint Edmond's Eve** is the only poem in *V&C* except the concluding fragment that has no date of composition at the end. In 1906, A. B. Young noted (*MLR* 1 [July 1906]: 323; see also Wise, 30, 96) that **Saint Edmond's Eve** was copied from *The Black Canon of Elmham; or, Saint Edmond's Eve,* the fifteenth poem in the anonymous *Tales of Terror* (London: printed for J. Bell by Bulmer & Co., 1801). Other poems "by Victor and Cazire" have also been identified as containing plagiarisms and echoes of contemporary poets (as noted below), rendering it unlikely that the inclusion of **Saint Edmond's Eve** in a volume entitled **Original Poetry** was accidental, or that PBS was innocent of responsibility. After listing plagiarisms identified up to 1950, Kenneth Neill Cameron observes: "it seems likely that Shelley intended the insertion of a long poem . . . as a hoax . . . and was indicating this in his title" (*YS,* 306). But as we suggest in the note to **Saint Edmond's Eve** (below), PBS may have been forced into the plagiarism by his lack of original material to complete the volume, and his "hoax" may have been an attempt to make a virtue of necessity. If he was hoaxing by entitling the volume ***Original Poetry***, he may also have known that even that title itself was not original; *NSTC* lists several earlier publications entitled *Original Poems* or *Original Poetry*, the most famous being a volume by William Cowper's cousin Maria F. C. Cowper, revised by Cowper himself and often reprinted early in the nineteenth century.

The authorship of the seventeen individual poems in *V&C* has never been fully explored, apart from the identification of plagiarisms. Garnett, who rightly assumed that PBS's sister Elizabeth Shelley was the youth's coauthor, assigned the first two verse letters to her ("Cazire") and thought that the eighth poem—***Song, Translated from the Italian***—was also likely to be hers; the rest he judged to be either by "Victor" or else plagiarisms. After the editors of *1904* and *1927* and the biographies by Peck, White, and Blunden had echoed Garnett, Cameron declared in *YS* that three other poems were by Elizabeth Shelley, because PBS gave them to Thomas Jefferson Hogg as samples of her poetry. Later, however, while editing ***The Esdaile Notebook*** (***Esd***), where these and other poems attributed to Elizabeth in PBS's dealings with Hogg are included as PBS's own, Cameron concluded that PBS had fooled Hogg about their authorship. In *1989*, Matthews and Everest include all but three of the poems from *V&C* as being by PBS, the exceptions being the first two verse letters and ***Saint Edmond's Eve***, all attributed to Elizabeth Shelley (I, 587) and therefore omitted from their edition.

Barbara Charlesworth Gelpi, in a paper entitled "Sentimental Exchanges: Percy Bysshe Shelley and Charlotte Dacre," read in 1992 at the Shelley Bicentennial Conference at Gregynog, Wales (but not published), first identified the source of the name *Cazire* as that of the narrator-heroine of Charlotte Dacre's three-volume sentimental romance, *Confessions of the Nun of St. Omer* (London: Hughes, 1805), which seems also to have influenced some passages in ***St.Irv***. Victor, PBS's nom-de-plume, asserts PBS's youthful sense of his power and importance and seems to require no literary source. Clearly he then liked the name well enough to play off it when he named the "editor" of ***Posthumous Fragments of Margaret Nicholson*** John Fitzvictor. That the overreaching truth-seeker who sets the plot in motion in MWS's *Frankenstein* (and in whom most critics have seen elements of PBS's personality) is named Victor in a novel that MWS discussed with him at every stage of its creation may suggest that, by 1817, PBS, while still valuing the name, in retrospect saw flaws in the persona that he had adopted during his ill-fated year at Oxford. He did not use the name in his own writings after 1810.

Gelpi's paper also proposed that all the poems in *V&C* were written by PBS, employing ventriloquism in some of them to sound like a woman.

This suggestion challenged us to assign individual responsibility for the authorship of each specific poem to PBS or Elizabeth Shelley on the basis of style, diction, and orthography, though the evidence on Elizabeth's side is much less helpful, since there are no other extant poems by her. Moreover, some of the poems that are of doubtful authorship contain plagiarisms, while the texts of others may have been cross-fertilized by suggestions that PBS made to his younger sister (born 10 May 1794) before the poems went to press, orthographic changes that Elizabeth Shelley (whose handwriting was superior) may have made while transcribing some of PBS's poems for the press, or substantive changes that PBS may have made in poems by her while correcting proofs (or, possibly, even setting type). Still, after collecting and sifting the available contemporary evidence, we are fully convinced that both PBS and Elizabeth Shelley contributed poetry to *V&C*.

The title-page notice "Printed . . . for the Author*s*" is supported by other contemporary testimony. First, PBS wrote in a postscript to his letter to Edward Fergus Graham on Friday [14 Sept.] 1810: "What think you of *our* Poetry—" (***Letters*** I, 17; italics added). Next, on 17 September 1810, Harriet Grove (1791-1867), the Shelleys' cousin—and PBS's beloved, with whom PBS and Elizabeth Shelley were both in regular communication throughout the period of the volume's gestation and publication—wrote: "Received the Poetry of Victor & Cazire, Charlotte [Grove] offended & with reason as I think *they* have done very wrong in publishing what *they* have of her" (*SC* II, 590; italics added). If PBS had ventriloquized the verse letters from Elizabeth Shelley to Grove, the latter would surely have been the first to recognize and comment on the subterfuge—and Elizabeth would probably also have resisted his assumption of her identity. Additional evidence supporting joint authorship comes from Hellen Shelley, a younger sister of PBS and Elizabeth, who later wrote: "At one time, he [PBS], with my eldest sister [Elizabeth], wrote a play secretly, and sent it to Matthews, the comedian [Charles Mathews (1776-1835, *DNB*)]; who, after a time, returned it, with the opinion that it would not do for acting. I wonder whether Matthews knew the age of the boy and girl who ventured upon writing a play. The subject was never known to me; and most likely the youthful authors made a good blaze with the MS" (Hogg, *Life*, ed. Wolfe, I, 26). This reminiscence from Hellen Shelley's childhood (probably reinforced by later conversations with Elizabeth Shelley) is also confirmed by contemporary evidence, for PBS, in a letter of (?) August 1810, asks Graham for the addresses of the managers of the Covent Garden and Lyceum theaters, to whom he planned to send a tragedy that he was writing and "a farce which my friend is composing" (***Letters*** I, 14); Hellen Shelley's story informs us that PBS's "friend" was Elizabeth Shelley, who is thus confirmed to be at this period an author collaborating with her brother. Their secrecy about their writings may have been maintained even more closely in the case of

V&C, since that attempt was both successful and unlikely to win plaudits from the authors' parents.

We can confidently attribute to Elizabeth Shelley the first two verse letters, which probably derive from letters actually sent by her to Harriet Grove earlier in 1810, though the texts of the letters published in *V&C* were presumably revised late in the summer of 1810 before they were sent to press; they seem to refer to events earlier or later than the dates subscribed at the end of each and the dates at which Grove's 1810 diary seems to record their receipt. (The discrepancies in these dates may arise from Elizabeth Shelley's inexact dating of the versions she sent to press, which were probably revised weeks afterwards from her undated draft-copies.) These verse letters, though hardly literature, are respectable occasional verse, especially when one recalls that their composition coincided with Elizabeth Shelley's sixteenth birthday. They clearly belong to the tradition of familiar verse letters written by both men and women stretching back into the seventeenth century, which in the eighteenth developed into a strong contemporary use of anapestic tetrameter for both humorous verse and light social satire in such popular works as Christopher Anstey's *New Bath Guide* (1766, with new editions through the 1830s). In the poems that Thomas Moore later wrote as "Thomas Brown the Younger," including *Intercepted Letters; or, The Twopenny Post-Bag* and *The Fudge Family in Paris,* the letters in anapestic tetrameter couplets are assigned to the female characters, confirming the observation that this meter, whether used by male or female poets, "had strong associations with the informal female pen" (see Nora Crook in *Evaluating Shelley,* ed. Clark and Hogle [1996], 155). Other poems that seem assignable to Elizabeth Shelley on the basis of their subject matter, versification, and diction include the sixth, seventh, and eighth poems—that is, the "songs" subtitled **Sorrow** and **Hope** and that said to be **Translated from the Italian** (the opening stanza of which has also been identified as a plagiarism). The detailed notes to each poem give our reasons for attributing its primary authorship to PBS or to Elizabeth Shelley.

The Black Canon of Elmham; or, Saint Edmond's Eve, is the fifteenth poem in an anonymous volume entitled *Tales of Terror* (1801), which partially parodies the two-volume *Tales of Wonder,* edited by Matthew G. ("Monk") Lewis, that appeared the same year. The *Tales of Terror* volume was also plausibly attributed to Lewis because it was originally printed for J. Bell, Lewis's publisher, with a single leaf of advertisements listing six titles by Lewis and just two other works (both translations from German). Though Louis F. Peck says that its authorship—including that of *The Black Canon*—has never been settled (see *Life of Matthew G. Lewis* [1961], 132–33), in 1808, a second edition of *Tales of Terror* was "Printed by S[amuel] Hamilton, Weybridge, Surry [*sic*]," and distributed by eight London publishers, including Longmans. When Stockdale very specifically states, "I recognised, in the collection, one [poem], which I knew to have been written by Mr. M. G. Lewis, the Author of The Monk" (*Budget*, 2), we can assume that he knew from colleagues in the book trade that Lewis was the author of *Tales of Terror.*

The collation of the *V&C* text with *The Black Canon* should put to rest any doubt about PBS's responsibility for the plagiarism. Although **Saint Edmond's Eve** in *V&C* generally replicates *The Black Canon*, with no effort to disguise its origins in *Tales of Terror* (either one of the almost identical texts of that poem in 1801 and 1808), several verbal variants from Lewis's text and almost total disregard for the orthography and punctuation of the original suggest that the plagiarist wrote out **Saint Edmond's Eve** from memory, rather than copying it from a printed text. PBS is more likely than Elizabeth Shelley to have admired *Tales of Terror* enough to memorize *The Black Canon*. In any case, he can hardly have been ignorant of the theft, even if the poem were copied out for the press by Elizabeth.

But *why* did PBS instigate (or condone) the plagiarism? Only those who have seen the original *1810* edition of *V&C* can realize how slender and insufficient the volume would have been without this lengthy poem, occupying pages 37–44 in the large quarto, in which the type is so large and heavily leaded as to limit each printed page to a few lines of text. Even with Elizabeth Shelley's contributions and the inclusion of his own inchoate **Fragment, or The Triumph of Conscience** at the end, the really original poetry in the manuscript failed to add up to a viable quarto volume. Now aware that this work was printed by a firm with its origins at Horsham, near PBS's home, we can speculate that PBS, having contracted with the Phillipses to publish a volume of a certain size, did not wish to admit that he and his "friend" together did not have enough poetry to fill such a slim volume. He probably submitted part of his copy at once, promising more, when or if it were needed. He had clearly set his sights on writing in the tradition of such prolific or facile authors as Scott, Southey, and Lewis, the last of whom had finished *The Monk* at age nineteen and published its three volumes, enhanced with skillful poems, before his twenty-first birthday. Actually, of course, it was no disgrace for PBS (just eighteen in Aug. 1810) to possess only a few poems that he felt were worth printing. In 1797, Charles Lamb and Charles Lloyd (both b. 1775) had found it necessary to piggyback their slender stocks of poetry onto the second edition of Coleridge's *Poems*. And Lewis, it has been discovered, translated two-thirds of *The Monk* "almost word for word, from a German romance" (J. M. S. Tompkins, *The Popular Novel in England, 1770–1800* [1932; rpt. 1962], 245fn.). As we noted in discussing the printing, type seems to have been distributed during a hiatus between the setting and printing of the early sheets of *V&C* and the typesetting of the later sheets; this gap may mark the time during which PBS, scurrying to try to fill up the volume, resorted to his memorial "composition" of *Saint Edmond's Eve.*

Contemporary Reception

Stockdale recalled, "I advertised the work, which was to be retailed at 3s. 6d., in nearly all the London papers of the day, seventeen in number; but I was told that, though paid for, it did not appear in the Times.... In many papers however, I saw it.... few, if any were sold, in consequence, as I intimated was not unlikely...; though, even in these boyish trifles, assisted by my personal intercourse with the author, I, at once, formed the opinion that [the author] was not an every day-character [*sic*]" (*Budget*, 2). Stockdale wrote that he received 1,480 copies of ***V&C*** from the printer on 17 September 1810; the next day, an advertisement for it appeared in Perry's *Morning Chronicle* (see *SC* II, 635). From the Htn copy, which the printer Phillips sent to Perry's *Morning Chronicle*, we surmise that many review copies were sent out addressed to periodical editors whom those connected with the volume either knew or admired, but ultimately three of the four reviews of the suppressed volume appeared in Tory publications that ridiculed it, while one treated it with more sympathetic humor. In October 1810 the *Literary Panorama*, a monthly that later gave positive reviews to Leigh Hunt's *The Story of Rimini* and Godwin's *Mandeville*, reviewed ***V&C***'s Gothic horrors with amused condescension and ended its page and a half notice by quoting ten of the final sixteen lines from Elizabeth Shelley's second verse letter, concluding, "Which brings this nonsensical rhyme to an end" (*RR*, Part C, 540–41). The same month, a short paragraph in the *Antijacobin Review* quoted just three bad lines from Elizabeth's verse letters and the dates given for some of the poems and then closed sarcastically, "if the reader wishes more we must refer to this elegant volume" (*RR*, C, 31). The *British Critic*, another moralistic Tory monthly, waited until April 1811 to notice ***V&C*** (after attacking ***St.Irv*** in January), again quoting lines from Elizabeth Shelley's verse letters and concluding: "Two epistles, in this exquisite style, begin this volume, which is filled up by songs of sentimental nonsense, and very absurd tales of horror.... whatever we may say in favour of the poetry of this time, such volumes as this have no share in the commendation. One thing may be said in its favour, that the printer has done his task well: would he had been employed on something better!" (*RR*, C, 204–5). Finally, in the annual *Poetical Register* for 1810–11—which was not actually published till 1814!—there appeared this belated epitaph, which reads in full:

There is no "original *poetry*" in this volume; there is nothing in it but downright scribble. It is really annoying to see the waste of paper which is made by such persons as the putters together of these sixty-four pages. There is, however, one consolation for the critics, who are obliged to read all this sort of trash. It is, that the crime of publishing is generally followed by condign punishment, in the shape of bills from the stationer and printer, and in the chilling tones of the bookseller, when, to the questions of the anxious rhymer, how the book sells, he answers that not more than half a dozen copies have been sold. (*RR*, C, 750)

Epigraph *(See facsimile of title page of* **V&C**.*)*

Scott's lines from *The Lay of the Last Minstrel* (1805), V.i.1–3, claim that since the poet keeps alive the memory of the past, his death brings "a second death" (V.ii.8) to those whose deeds and sufferings he has recounted: "The phantom knight, his glory fled, | Mourns o'er the field he heaped with dead; | Mounts the wild blast that sweeps amain, | And shrieks along the battle-plain:" (V.ii.13–16). The epigraph's text also accords with the ninth edition of *Last Minstrel,* printed by James Ballantyne (for Longmans in London and Constable in Edinburgh, 1808). Late in 1810 PBS, who greatly admired Scott's poetry, submitted **The Wandering Jew** to the firm of Ballantyne, which had recently issued *The Lady of the Lake.*

Letter [1] ("Here I sit with my paper")

The two verse letters that open the volume seem to have been based on two (or more) actual letters sent by Elizabeth Shelley to Harriet Grove. PBS may have placed these poems first (as **History of a Six Weeks' Tour** begins with journal entries by MWS) in order to attract ordinary readers before they encountered PBS's more "metaphysical" poems of love, liberty, and revenge. References to Elizabeth Shelley in Grove's diaries for 1809 and 1810 (*SC* II, 475–540 and 564–98) portray her from the ages of fourteen to sixteen as habitually loud, boisterous, and high-spirited; Thomas Medwin, the Shelleys' kinsman, said that Elizabeth also "possessed a talent for oil-painting that few artists have acquired" (*Life,* ed. Forman, 18). Though this verse letter discusses grammar, its punctuation is chiefly rhetorical rather than syntactical, most marks paralleling the natural pauses at the ends of lines and couplets. Notable is the dearth of full stops: there are just six periods and one terminal exclamation point in the poem's 76 lines; when we include colons, semicolons, and dashes that mark the end of syntactical units, there are breaks in thought—all at the ends of lines and most at the ends of couplets—at **lines 2, 4, 14, 16, 18, 26, 28, 36, 40, 46, 58, 62, 64, 72, 74, 75,** and **76,** with their increasing frequency at the end signaling Elizabeth Shelley's efforts to achieve closure as she neared the end of her letter paper. In the second **Letter,** two of the first three full stops—after

lines 12 and **32**—appear at the ends of printed pages 10 and 11 in *1810*, suggesting that some of this meager pointing may have been added to the poem in proof. Such light pointing was typical of contemporary informal verse epistles and humorous poems, even by mature poets. Compare an exchange between Talleyrand and Napoleon, with the same metrics that Elizabeth Shelley uses, in Sir John Carr's *Poems* (1809, 165–69) and the blank verse of William Hayley's *The Triumphs of Temper* (13th ed., 1807).

line 10. mutes in a train: Besides indicating someone "dumb" or "silent," mute as a noun used in reference to a person could signify (in dialect) a variant of mule—"in some districts applied to the offspring of a mare and an ass (the 'mule' properly so called), and in others to that of a she-ass and stallion (the 'hinny')"; but by mute Elizabeth Shelley undoubtedly means "a professional attendant at a funeral, a hired mourner" (*OED*, sb. B.3.e, sb.4).

PBS himself uses mutes as a substantive only at **Laon** XII.v and xiv, with a more literal meaning that may derive from the thirty-sixth note to William Beckford's *Vathek: An Arabian Tale*, which first quotes from Habesci's *State of the Ottoman Empire:* "It has been usual, in Eastern courts . . . to retain a number of mutes. These are not only employed to amuse the monarch, but also to instruct his pages in an art to us little known, of communicating everything by signs, lest the sound of their voices should disturb the sovereign." Beckford then adds: "The mutes are also the secret instruments of his private vengeance, in carrying the fatal string" (i.e., the bowstring, used to strangle the ruler's distrusted deputies).

line 12. works: Though conjectural emendation to *words* is an option, works remains a possible reading. The final comma might also be changed to a semicolon or period (as *1898* alters the line, in spite of its claim of reproducing *1810* precisely), but the sense is clear without emending the punctuation.

line 13. copious: used in the rhetorical sense of "having a plentiful command of language" (*OED* 2.b).

line 20. American-born Lindley Murray (1745–1826, *DNB*) first published his popular *English Grammar, Comprehending the Principles and Rules of the Language* in 1795; John Entick (?1703–73, *DNB*) was an antiministerial journalist and advocate of a free press, as well as the compiler of Latin-English dictionaries and author of *A New Spelling Dictionary, Teaching to Write and Pronounce the English Tongue with Ease and Propriety* (1764 et seq.); by 1810, *Entick's New Spelling Dictionary*, edited with a grammatical summary by William Crakelt, a Kent clergyman (1741–1812, *DNB*), was a standard school text, co-published by several leading London booksellers; in our research, we have used printings of *Entick's* dated 1795 (BL) and 1805 (Reiman's copy).

line 28. Does this line suggest Elizabeth Shelley's resentment at her older brother's superior manner when he gave her advice?

lines 33–35. Though the classical names may sound as if they were suggested by PBS, Medwin reports that his "elder sisters" (i.e., Elizabeth, Mary, and perhaps Hellen Shelley) "received the same education" as he did, "being instructed in the rudiments of Latin and Greek by Mr. [Evan] Edwards, the clergyman of Warnham" (*Life*, ed. Forman, 14). They later attended a boarding school in Clapham Common, Surrey, run by a Mrs. Fenning (Louise Schutz Boas, *Harriet Shelley* [1962], 11).

lines 37–58. When Elizabeth Shelley lists the kinds of authors whom she does *not* wish to emulate, she asserts that the majority write lyric poetry, which loomed large in the Shelley household. Most writings published during this period, however, involved neither epic, dramatic, narrative, nor lyric poetry that the Romantics were then reestablishing according to the Græco-Latin and Renaissance hierarchy of genres, but consisted of satirical and didactic verse (both comic and sober), prose histories, biographies, and treatises, including a generous number of sermons and religious tracts. In the title index to *NSTC* (*1801–1815*), a page listing about fifty titles beginning "A Serious," exhorting people to specific religious, political, or social behavior, is followed by twenty-five pages (over 1,250 titles) beginning "Sermon" or "Sermons," a section matched by a similar number of (usually) secular didactic or controversial works beginning "A Letter" and almost as many titles beginning "Reflections," "Remarks," "Remonstrance," "Reply," and "Report," besides many "Accounts," "Addresses," "Proposals," "Strictures," "Vindications," and the like. Given this plethora, we cannot know which specific works Elizabeth Shelley may have had in mind.

lines 55, 56, 61. cobler: This word, in a variant spelling acceptable until late in the nineteenth century (*OED*), means someone who patches badly and alludes to poorly paid editors and translators employed to prepare classic and foreign works for English readers—very low-status work (as a wag was an inferior "wit") that was often satirized in eighteenth-century poems and novels under the rubric of Grub-street, which was proverbially their cheap place of residence.

line 59. good friends (i.e., the reading public or posterity) identifies the intended audience of Elizabeth Shelley's published poem, since Harriet Grove knew that Elizabeth had "ne'er worn a cassoc," the outer garment worn by a priest (and so spelled in *Entick's*).

line 71. shrink not a tense] shrink not to a tense *1898* through *1972*. Metrical tightening reinforces the imperative mood, and the emendation (or error) in other editions is based on a misunderstanding of Elizabeth Shelley's meaning here: the line urges Grove not to shrink back from writing for fear of making errors in verb tense forms and sequences (cf. *OED* 14.b, where a transitive usage deriving from "to shrink in the neck" means "to flinch, recoil"). If a word were added, it should be *from* rather than *to*.

lines 73–74. tiresome girl!: either Elizabeth Shelley's anticipation of Grove's response to her letter as she finished writing it, or lines added before publication, based on Grove's actual reaction.

Letter [2] To Miss ⎯⎯⎯ ⎯⎯⎯ From Miss ⎯⎯⎯ ⎯⎯⎯

In *1810*, the title did not include the name of writer (Elizabeth Shelley) or recipient (Harriet Grove), dashes being substituted in both the title and other lines. This convention marked the decorous reticence characteristic of authors of the period who turned private verse to public use. (Earlier poets tended to supply classical pseudonyms, as Lord Byron does in several early poems.) To supply the actual names in the text is to distort ahistorically the sense of decorum in these poems and in the age.

line 1. The blank in this line could be filled with either *Harriet* (pronounced in two syllables) or, possibly, *Hattie*.

line 2. During the early nineteenth century, when British postal rates—charged by both distance and weight—were raised to help finance the French wars, the cost of sending or (since the recipient usually paid the postage) receiving letters reached its highest level in history. Many in the upper classes avoided the cost by sending their letters enclosed in franks—address-sheets signed by Members of Parliament, such as Timothy Shelley, and other government officials. In spite of attempts to restrict franking, the abuses continued until high postal rates were abolished through the introduction of the National Uniform Penny Post in 1839–40. (See *SC* II, 914–25; V, xxxii–xxxiv. For additional context, see James E. Tierney, "Eighteenth-Century Authors and the Abuse of the Franking System," *Studies in Bibliography* 48 [1995]: 112–20.)

lines 9–11. These lines reflect the political concerns of the Shelley family in early 1810. Parliament had opened in January with attacks on the military bungling of the King's ministers, particularly the failed campaign at Walcheren in the Netherlands, where a British army had suffered heavy losses, mainly from disease, before withdrawing with little accomplished. Popular fury was fueled by the King's refusal to hear a petition from the London common council requesting a parliamentary investigation into the conduct of the ministers, who were further disgraced in September 1809, when George Canning and Robert Stewart (by courtesy, Viscount Castlereagh), both members of the cabinet, fought a duel over their differences about the conduct of the war.

In the House of Lords, the attack on the government was initiated by the aging naval hero John Jervis, Earl of St. Vincent (1735–1823, *DNB*), while Lord Grenville blasted Lord Chatham for sending troops into "the Walcheren," the climate of which standard military textbooks cited as especially unhealthy, and for failing to send money to support the troops there. On 26 January 1810, after the defeat of various motions in both houses to investigate ministerial blunders, Sir Francis Burdett (1770–1844, *DNB*) declared that Parliament's failure to rebuke the ministers' incompetence and corruption showed that the entire political system needed reformation. Burdett told the M.P.s (according to the *Edinburgh Annual Register*) that he "could see in that room the root of all the evil. Here was the root; and the branches spread over and extended to every extremity of the country. Under their shade flourished no useful plants, nothing but noxious weeds. The fruits upon the boughs were tempting to the eye, but to the taste they [like the fruits tasted by the devils in Milton's Pandaemonium] betrayed the bitterness of ashes" (*EAR, 1810,* 22). When the Tory ministers, led by Spencer Percival and the Earl of Liverpool, thought that public outrage had subsided, Parliament voted to imprison Burdett for insulting the Members; but on 9 April 1810, the soldiers who arrested Burdett and conducted him to the Tower of London were stoned by a mob of angry citizens in what became known as the "Burdett riot."

PBS probably knew Burdett's widely discussed speech well, for not only did he dedicate to Burdett ***The Wandering Jew*** (q.v.), which he wrote or revised during the summer of 1810 and sent out for publication near the time that ***V&C*** was printed, but later, in ***Queen Mab*** (***QM***), he also echoes Burdett's allusion to the poisonous "Upas tree" during his attack on "kings who rule, and cowards who crouch": "Let the axe I Strike at the root, the poison-tree will fall" (IV.77, 82–83). Here, on the other hand, Elizabeth Shelley's reference to Burdett's reformation is general and abstract, deriving from family conversation, not quotations from his speeches in newspapers. On the relationship of Burdett and his ideas to the Foxite Whigs supported by Timothy Shelley and his patron the Duke of Norfolk, see P. M. S. Dawson, *Unacknowledged Legislator* (1980), 36–40.

line 12. burden: the "refrain" or "chorus" (*OED* 10): that is, the constant topic of conversation during morning social calls at the time.

lines 13–32. [the blanks]: A year earlier, at the age of twenty-six, Harriet Grove's elder sister [Charlotte] had been introduced by Timothy Shelley to Col. Warden Sergison of Cuckfield Place, near [Cuckfield], Sussex, the village where Capt. John Pilfold, Royal Navy, a brother of PBS's and Grove's mothers, also lived. On 19 April 1810, Charlotte began a visit to her uncle (presumably to see more of the Colonel), a visit possibly planned before the 10 April date given for the poem. Though Charlotte enjoyed her visit and did not return home till 13 August (Grove's Diary, *SC* II, 586–87), she had no romance with Sergison (who died the following year). On 17 September 1810, a month after the events indiscreetly teased about in **lines 13–15** et seq., Grove wrote: "Received the Poetry of Victor & Cazire, Charlotte offended & with reason as I think they have done very wrong in publishing what they have of her" (see *SC* II, 590; and Hawkins, *First Love*, 14–17, 26–27, 33–35, 45–51). As we observe in the headnote, the Tx copy of *V&C 1810*, on which *1898* based its text, descended from a member of the Grove family who had scratched out the words the Colonel (**15**); these words were thus omitted from *1898* and subsequent texts based on this flawed "facsimile."

line 19. mischevious: Though some editors emend this spelling, the *OED* lists *mischevious* as a dialectal variant of *mischievous* from the seventeenth century on.

line 32. Elizabeth Shelley excepts PBS from her jocular denigration of men because of Grove's fondness for him.

line 33. drawings: On 11 May 1810, Grove mentions "figures by McFee [a name we have not located in reference books on British artists] & landscapes by [John] Glover" (1767–1849, *DNB*) in a watercolor exhibition (Grove's Diary, *SC* II, 578); this reference, like that to Charlotte's visit to Cuckfield, suggests that the text of the verse letter may have been revised after 30 April 1810, its date as given in the printed text. However, Elizabeth Shelley (herself a budding artist) may have recommended the exhibition to Harriet Grove in advance of the Groves' visit; by July or August, when she recopied the letter from her draft for publication, she may have misremembered when she had sent the original letter to Grove, thus misdating it rather than adding anachronisms.

line 35. croud: variant of *crowd* in sixteenth–eighteenth centuries (*OED*); upper-class orthography was consistently more conservative than that of the middle classes.

line 40. Grove and her family stayed in London at 49 Lincoln's Inn Fields with her brother Johnny, who was Elizabeth Shelley's suitor; John, a student of medicine, owned at least one cat (see Hawkins, *First Love*, 9; and Grove's Diary for 21 April 1810, *SC* II, 576).

line 41. your parcel's arrived] your parcels arrived *1810*. The omission of this apostrophe relates, not to the possessive case, as it frequently does in *V&C*, but to Elizabeth Shelley's failure to signal the contraction of "parcel has arrived" (or, possibly, "parcel is arrived").

The blank represents "Percy" or "Bysshe," either of which in the possessive case would be pronounced in two syllables.

line 47. Hope, gay deceiver parallels a reference to Hope as a "sweet deceiver" in **Song. Hope** (line 15), a poem probably also by Elizabeth Shelley.

line 49. goal: misprinted "gaol" (jail) in *1810*.

lines 56–61. These lines exhibit a conventional religious outlook likely to be used by Elizabeth Shelley in a letter to the pious Grove, but uncharacteristic of PBS even at this early date.

line 65. The blank once again probably originally contained either "Harriet" or "Hattie."

Song ("Cold, cold is the blast")

There are two basic versions of this poem, *V&C* and, heavily revised, the forty-fifth poem in the **Esdaile Notebook** (**Esd**, which will appear in Volume II). MS Pfz, which PBS transcribed from his memory of the *V&C* text (*SC* II, 625–26), contains a few explicable substantive variants that, though most are probably errors of memory, may in some instances identify errors in *1810*. MS Pfz shows how PBS all but ignored punctuation when releasing his early poems to close friends, though he generally added pointing for the benefit of miscellaneous readers, either when sending his poems to press or while proofreading them in type. The rhyme scheme and the anapestic tetrameter of both this poem and the final two poems in **St.Irv** follow those of Scott's *Helvellyn*, a favorite poem of young PBS (see Medwin, *Life*, 52; and the Commentary for **St.Irv**).

Before the discovery of the revised version in **Esd**, scholars had doubts about its authorship, because in 1810–11, while trying to interest Hogg in his sister Elizabeth, PBS wrote out from memory this poem and parts of two others as examples of her poetry (see Hogg, *Life*, ed. Wolfe, I, 126). Cameron argued, when he edited MS Pfz for *SC* (II, 625–31), that Hogg's account of these poems established Elizabeth Shelley as their author; but he later concluded, while editing the revised version in **Esd**, that—as *1989* and we agree—PBS himself wrote those poems that he had told Hogg were by his sister, presumably to impress Hogg with Elizabeth Shelley's exceptional talent: "Shelley," wrote Cameron, "was simply pulling Hogg's leg" (**Esd** *1965*, 259). Psychoanalytic critics may probe PBS's use of his poetry to arouse in his closest friend a romantic interest in his look-alike sister. Captain Kennedy, who saw PBS and Elizabeth Shelley together during PBS's last visit to Field Place, later wrote: "His resemblance to his sister,

Elizabeth, was as striking as if they had been twins" (Hogg, *Life*, ed. Wolfe, II, 153).

line 9. MS Pfz supplies the name *Louisa* here and in **lines 18** and **32.** Henry Tilney in *Northanger Abbey* (Chap. 14) alludes to the ubiquity of Louisa as a name for fictional heroines: "Do not imagine that you can cope with me in a knowledge of Julias and Louisas" (Austen, *Novels*, ed. R. W. Chapman [1926] V, 107). Whatever PBS's source, he probably deleted this name from *V&C* because Harriet Grove's fourteen-year-old sister Louisa Grove had just died on 19 June 1810 of a fever, compounded by medical bloodletting.

line 10. fallen: To make the line metrical, PBS probably intended this word to be pronounced as a single syllable. The first edition of **Laon** (1817) uses the spelling "fall'n" at I.iii.9 (as did Milton in *PL* VII.25–26) to indicate such a monosyllabic pronunciation, but in PBS's intermediate fair copy MS of **Laon** I, the word is "fallen," as PBS usually spelled it, whether the scansion required one or two syllables.

line 12. ruiner's: Though this word lacks an apostrophe in *1810*, the appearance of the apostrophe both in babe's here and in "ruiner's" in MS Pfz establishes PBS's intention.

line 17. Penmanmawr: "Penmaen Mawr Mountain" in Paterson's *Roads* (1808), col. 132; "Penmaenmawr" in Shell Roadmap 4. Wales ("Based upon the Ordinance Survey map, Crown Copyright," ca. 1985): a steep peak (1,500 ft.) in the Snowdonian complex, on the edge of Conway Bay in the far northwest corner of Wales (then Caernarvonshire, now Gwynedd). In PBS's day, the place where the main road from Bangor to Conway crosses this mountain was the scene of many accidents. PBS's grandfather Bysshe Shelley had been High Sheriff of Radnorshire in 1784 and PBS's cousins the Groves had made Cwm Ellan in that county of Wales their retreat since the 1790s (Hawkins, *First Love*), but we cannot determine that PBS had ever visited Snowdonia by 1810. His awareness of Penmanmawr could have come either from the tales of family members or from his reading; *1989* quotes a description (*Monthly Magazine* 14 [1802]: 304) of the "huge, bare, overhanging rock, rising almost perpendicular from the sea" and cites poetic references in John Philips's *Cyder* (1708), where the barren "cliffy Height | Of *Penmenmaur*, and that Cloud-piercing Hill, | *Plinlimmon*" demonstrate by their support of "hardy Men" who "Cut Sampire" that no land is useless to humanity (I, 105–9); James Thomson's *The Seasons* (1730, 1744; Birmingham, 1804, 73): "from the rude rocks | Of Penmanmaur heap'd hideous to the sky | Tumble the smitten cliffs" (*Summer,* 163–65); and Southey's *Madoc* I.i.26–27 (1805, 1808): "the naked crags | Of Penmanmawr." In MS Pfz, before writing the Welsh name in the poem, PBS (or possibly Hogg) wrote it out in large block letters near the bottom of page 3 of that MS—probably to check the spelling (*SC* II, 627).

line 20. gust: PBS wrote the plural "gusts" in MS Pfz, but the reading in *1810* also makes perfect sense.

lines 21–22. PBS reverses clouds (21) and rocks (22) in MS Pfz, but not only do the readings in *1810* seem to us to make more sense, but the printed text has greater authority; as Hogg wrote, "Bysshe wrote down these verses for me at Oxford from memory. I was to have a complete and more correct copy of them some day" (*Life*, ed. Wolfe, I, 126).

line 23. In MS Pfz, the blank is filled by *Henry*, a name that PBS often used for his heroes and surrogates in his early poems (e.g., **Henry and Louisa** and *QM*). Here, of course, "Henry" is a villain; but PBS used the name to represent his alter ego in a variety of self-dramatizations. His use of this name might derive from either contemporary poems, in which *Henry* was a common name for lover-heroes, or from historical sources—such as Henry "Hotspur" Percy (1364–1403, *DNB*), in Shakespeare's *2 Henry IV* (PBS echoed a speech by Hotspur in an angry letter to his father; see John Freeman, *Keats-Shelley Memorial Bulletin* 34: 8), or the poet Henry Howard, Earl of Surrey (?1517–47, *DNB*), beheaded by Henry VIII, who was a forebear of Charles Howard, 11th Duke of Norfolk (1746–1815, *DNB*), the political patron of PBS's father and grandfather. See also the note to **Song. To ——— ("Ah! sweet is the moonbeam")**, line 8.

unkind: The *OED* sense 5—"unnaturally cruel, severe, or hostile"—was archaic or obsolete in general usage by 1810, but literary parallels in Shakespeare (e.g., "more than kin, and less than kind"—*Hamlet* I.ii.65) and Milton ("Abortive, monstrous, or unkindly mixt"—*PL* III.456) among others, kept that meaning alive for poets.

line 27. laving (MS Pfz), that is, washing it (i.e., the garland in **line 25**): Louisa first entwined the garland, bedewed it with tears, then leaned over the fountain (**26**), and (after) laving the garland to remove her tears, cast it over the cliff to be carried into the sea by the wind (**27**). PBS used forms of the verb "lave" in comparable contexts in other early poems: See *PF, Fragment ("Yes! all is past")*, line 27; *St.Irv, Song ("Ah! faint are her limbs")*, line 21; and *WJ*, I.9. The reading "leaving" (*1810*), which makes no sense in this context, is probably a typographical error.

line 28. when *1810*] where MS Pfz. These two words are frequently indistinguishable in PBS's MSS, and context often guides the choice. Here it is difficult to be certain whether or not the compositor chose wrong and PBS failed to catch the typo. By telling the garland to go and then casting it from the height, Louisa may be directing *where* (on the sea—**29**) rather than *when* it should go, that having been determined as she cast it into the wild sweeping wind (**20**). Yet she, emulating King Lear, may instead tell the garland to go while the tempest is yelling, because that is *when* Nature echoes her state of mind. We retain the reading of *1810*.

Song. ("Come ————! sweet is the hour")

PBS almost certainly wrote this poem to Harriet Grove during or immediately after her family's visit to Sussex and London in April 1810. His authorship is supported by the classical Zephyrs/anemone allusion in **lines 2–4**: not only does *anemone* mean "daughter of the wind" in Greek, but as *1989* notes, Pliny's *Natural History*, part of which PBS translated at Eton, says that anemones open their petals only when the wind blows (XXI.165)—a reference also noted by Erasmus Darwin in *Botanic Garden, Part II* (2nd ed., 1790, II, 33n), another of PBS's favorite books. (His copy survives at Harvard.) See also the note to **line 14**.

line 1. *Harriet*, pronounced trisyllabically, fits the blanks both here and in **line 17**.

line 14. PBS's authorship is further suggested by the Latinate usage of umbrage, even though it does not appear in *Shelley Concordance*. *OED* gives as its sole contemporary example of its meaning 2.c, "Shade or shadow cast by trees or the like," PBS's parallel use in Chapter 11 of **St.Irv**, where during a crucial love scene between Eloise and Fitzeustace, "The tall ash and oak, in mingled umbrage, sighed far above their heads" (*1811*, 214–15), and on 26 July 1811, PBS wrote to Elizabeth Hitchener of "waterfalls midst the umbrage of a thousand shadowy trees" (**Letters** I, 128).

The word appears with this usage in *PL* IX.1087 and is common among classically trained male poets of the late eighteenth and early nineteenth centuries, who account for a huge majority of pre-1810 uses we checked via Chadwyck-Healey *Lion* in such poets as M. Akenside, J. Beattie, W. L. Bowles, Egerton Brydges, S. T. Coleridge, J. Dyer, E. Darwin, J. Keate, J. Montgomery, R. Polwhele, and W. Wordsworth, as well as in poems by at least three female poets—Anna Seward, Sydney Owenson, and Mary Tighe.

Song. Despair

Both contemporary comments on Elizabeth Shelley (especially in the diaries of Harriet Grove and her sister Charlotte) and the tone of her verse letters, above, present her as gregarious and mirthful, apparently contrasting with her moody brother. One reason that we believe her to be author of the three Songs subtitled Despair, Sorrow, and Hope is that they are all so abstract and conventional in their expressions of these emotions that they seem the work of one who had little first-hand experience of them. Since we know from the testimony of Hellen Shelley that when she was ten years old or younger, PBS set topics for her to write poems on and then had the poems printed (see Hogg, *Life*, ed. Wolfe, I, 26), it is not unlikely that he suggested that Elizabeth Shelley write on these three emotions when he urged her to contribute to the volume he wished to prepare for press, as schoolmasters of the time set rhetorical recitations on similar topics. These three poems share diction and sentiments that suggest a mild, uncritical religiosity that was not PBS's mode even at this early period, for he had already conceived and begun to write ***The Wandering Jew*** (see *WJ* Commentary).

If PBS did guide Elizabeth Shelley's choice of subject, or quote lines to start off her contributions, and especially if he revised her poems to improve or polish them—identifying a primary author becomes very difficult; rather than specifying PBS or Elizabeth Shelley as sole author for some poems, it is prudent to adopt Jack Stillinger's concept of a collective "authorship" (see *Multiple Authorship and the Myth of the Solitary Genius,* 1991).

line 5. Though other editors emend wildered to "'wildered," as if the word were truncated from *bewildered, Entick's New Spelling Dictionary* gives *wilder* as a verb, meaning "to lose, to puzzle in an unknown track."

line 6. ken: to discern, recognize by sight (now dialect; *Webster's III*). Though S. T. Coleridge uses *ken* thus in *Ancient Mariner* (57), it does not appear elsewhere in PBS's canon and may be a word favored by Elizabeth Shelley.

line 12. sooth was a variant spelling of the verb "to soothe" from the sixteenth into the nineteenth century (*OED*); it is so spelled in *Bailey's Dictionary* (1733) and *Entick's* (1805).

line 23. In *Bailey's Dictionary shew* is given as the preferred spelling for both verb and noun; in a pocket dictionary of 1803, based on Johnson's *Dictionary*, both meanings are spelled "show"; and in *Entick's* (1805) the word *shew* is cross-referenced to *show*, where both verb and noun appear. Both spellings were frequently used by PBS's contemporaries—perhaps interchangeably by most; but a preliminary analysis of texts based on PBS's MSS and first editions suggests that he may have preferred to use show (as here) when the word was a noun, while spelling the verb "shew," as Elizabeth Shelley or he did in **line 6** of the next poem and in **lines 8, 10,** and **24** of *Song: Hope.*

Song. Sorrow

This artificial expression of "sorrow," filled with clichés (dreary blank, drooping flower, humid eyes, fairy hope), comes most likely from Elizabeth Shelley, who seems not to have suffered from the same *Weltschmerz* that afflicted PBS and therefore expressed its ravages with less personal conviction. The spelling "shew" for the verb may also have been taught to Elizabeth Shelley, or PBS could have introduced this spelling when he saw the poem through the press.

line 3. are sank: *Sank* served as a variant form of the past participle during this period, when *sunk* had become a common past tense form (*OED*); see also Had sank in the following poem, line 4, and parallel usages in **Ghasta**, 81 and 83; **Laon** I.xiii.2, and *A Vision of the Sea*, 8.

line 11. I danced: a phrase uncharacteristic of PBS, who seems never to have written "I dance(d)" when speaking in his own persona; spirits of the universe, nature's creatures, and the madding crowd do the dancing in his poetry. (See also **line 15.**)

pleasure's: The apostrophe, lacking in *1810*, has been added both here and in sorrow's, **line 17** below. (See next note.)

line 28. PBS and Elizabeth Shelley at this time followed the argument in the unconventional grammatical notes of *Entick's New Spelling Dictionary*, which declared that the use of the apostrophe for the possessive case was a corruption of native English grammar, based on a misconception that the *s* in the possessive case was a contraction of *his* or *hers*. PBS soon accepted the conventional formation of the possessive case, but for a number of years his manuscripts show that he remained uncertain of its correct formation. This uncertainty appears in Elizabeth Shelley's or PBS's use of the apostrophe in what they intended as plural nouns, such as lightening's. Putting an *e* in this word was a conventional way of indicating how many syllables "lightnings" should add to the poetic line.

line 29. souls': perhaps an error for *soul's*, but here not so clearly one as to require conjectural emendation of the text (as in **11** and **17**).

line 32. bid ungrateful] bid the ungrateful   *1989*. This novelty apparently resulted from a simple mistranscription or typo.

Song. Hope

This, like the two previous poems, may also have been authored by Elizabeth Shelley. Whoever originally wrote it probably did so hastily (note the August 1810 date appended to it). Perhaps the printer then made some erroneous changes and PBS compounded them while revising the proofs of his sister's poem. As Matthews and Everest note in *1989* (101), **lines 5–10** echo the idea of the opening lines of Thomas Campbell's *The Pleasures of Hope* (1801 et seq.), the heart of which reads: "Why do those cliffs of shadowy tint appear | More sweet than all the landscape smiling near? | 'Tis distance lends enchantment to the view, | And robes the mountain in its azure hue" (I, 5–8). If PBS suggested the subject to Elizabeth Shelley, she, with or without PBS's suggestion, turned for inspiration to the period's best-known poem on the subject of hope.

lines 6–7. In *1810* the punctuation ending these two lines makes no sense, for the sentence that begins at **line 5** continues at least to the end of **8**. We have removed a colon from the end of **line 6** and changed the period after brow to a comma, while also supplying a needed apostrophe to Mountains.

line 9. expectation's: emended from "expectations" (*1810*) to the possessive singular because expectation (i.e., hope) is addressed in **line 15** as [a] sweet deceiver(s) (see note below) and the pronouns referring to that word are singular.

lines 13–14. vermeil: misspelled "vermiel" in *1810* (PBS's characteristic transposition of *i* and *e*). We have also emended the erroneous punctuation of these lines, changing the semicolon at the end of **13** (*1810*) to a comma and the comma ending **14** to a period.

line 15. deceiver: emended from "deceivers" (*1810*) because the pronouns referring to this word are singular: thy (**16, 20**) and thee (**19**). Though the apparent grammatical antecedent of deceivers is flowers (**13**), perhaps leading PBS to change deceiver to "deceivers" in proof, its logical antecedent is expectation (**9**). As noted above, the reference to expectation's ray (i.e., hope) as a sweet deceiver parallels "Hope, gay deceiver" in line 47 of the second verse letter, and the similar phrases suggest that both poems were originally written by Elizabeth Shelley, although this one was probably then revised—and muddled—in proof by PBS.

line 19. The use of God in this line and sin in **20** may signal Elizabeth Shelley's authorship. The infrequent appearances of the latter word in PBS's poetry usually occur either in speeches by villains or in sardonic comments on popular superstitions.

Song, Translated from the Italian

The first stanza of this poem is plagiarized, as André Koszul noted in 1929 (*Modern Language Notes* 44:42–43), from a quite different "Song" in *English Lyrics* by William Smyth, a prominent Cambridge don (1765–1849, *DNB*).

The first and second editions of Smyth's collection came out in 1797 and 1798, but the song in question first appeared in Volume II of an expanded edition published in 1805 and reissued in 1806 and 1815. In the BL copy of the 1806 edition, Smyth's "Song" (two stanzas, 16 lines) appears on II, 40; its first four lines are identical to the first stanza in *V&C* except for the words underscored:

> Oh! what is the gain of restless care,
>   And what is <u>ambition's</u> treasure,
> And what are the joys <u>which</u> the modish share,
>   In their <u>haunts of sickly</u> pleasure.

Smyth's "Song" goes on to praise the beauties of nature, while that in *V&C* concerns home, hearth, and husband, suggesting that it was written by Elizabeth Shelley. PBS wished to manage or reform the world, and in his poems he usually scorned a life of unambitious retirement; if he had added a poem to the thematic introduction from Smyth, he would have been more likely to take up the theme of nature versus society found in Smyth's original. Perhaps PBS quoted Smyth's opening lines to Elizabeth Shelley to help get her started on a poem.

Song. Translated from the German

PBS is almost certainly the author of this piece. The German literary tradition fascinated him at this period, and though Hogg claims that he did not learn the language till 1815, Medwin dates this study much earlier. Leland R. Phelps argues that PBS's literal translations from *Faust*, which Phelps describes as written on paper watermarked with a posthorn in a crowned shield and countermarked "C Wilmott | 1810"—paper used by PBS only at Field Place and at Eton—date from 1810 or 1811 ("Goethe's *Faust* and the Young Shelley," in *Wege der Worte*, ed. D. C. Riechel, 1978, 310–11). In *BSM*, Murray opts for a later date (XXI, 476), but we note that E. F. Graham's friend Joseph Gibbons Merle, in his "A Newspaper Editor's Reminiscences, IV" (*Fraser's Magazine* 23 [June 1841]), tells of seeing PBS after his expulsion from Oxford, when he was trying to get London publishers to purchase two of his "translations from the German, which were written in a common school copying book" (703).

In any case, the sentiments in **lines 5–8** could almost be taken as PBS's credo in 1810, and **13–16** depict the reward of love that he hoped for. We emend *1810* only by providing apostrophes for the possessives in **lines 3** and **12,** which PBS probably omitted due to the influence of the theory propounded in *Entick's New Spelling Dictionary* (see the general Commentary on *V&C*, page 154).

The Irishman's Song

This poem is clearly by PBS, whose signature may be seen in both its subject matter and its militant political rhetoric. His model here was Scott's early patriotic poetry, but the cosmic, apocalyptic sweep of the language is his own. PBS's inspirations (as *1989* notes) also include Moore's *Irish Melodies* (1808) and particular poems of "Ossian" (i.e., James Macpherson, 1736–96, *DNB*). Textually we have added one apostrophe to *1810:* for <u>ancestors'</u> in **line 6**.

line 12. <u>The dread yell of Sloghan</u>: "Slogan" or "slughorn" (from the Gaelic *sluagh-ghairm,* or "host-shout") was a war cry of Gaelic-speaking clans of both Scotland and Ireland. One likely poetic source for PBS is Scott's *Lay of the Last Minstrel:* "To heaven the Border slogan rung, | 'St Mary for the young Buccleuch!'" (5th ed. [1805] IV.xxiv; 9th ed. [1808] IV.xxvii), but we have not identified an exact precedent for PBS's spelling <u>Sloghan</u>. According to Chadwyck-Healey *Lion,* the word appears as "slogan" twice in Scott's edition of *Minstrelsy of the Scottish Border* (1802; Scott's original poems not yet being in the database) as a clan war-cry, but all four uses by Chatterton that are listed are modernizations of Chatterton's word "slughorne" or "slugghorne"—defined in *Poems supposed to have been written at Bristol by Thomas Rowley* (Cambridge: printed by B. Flowers, 1794) as "Warlike instrument of music" (92) or "A kind of claryon, or war trumpet" (139). PBS, while taking his meaning from *Minstrelsy* or Scott's *Lay,* may have changed the spelling through misremembering Chatterton's archaism.

line 15. <u>Or</u>] As *1989*. Matthews and Everest emend on the presumption that <u>Or</u> is "a printer's misreading," but it seems to us to be correct: the fallen <u>heroes</u> are either still <u>convulsed</u> in the agony of dying, <u>or</u> are already <u>ghosts cry</u>ing for <u>vengeance</u>.

Song ("Fierce roars the midnight storm")

The subject matter—a man vows to be faithful to a woman who has been seduced and abandoned by a false lover—might be attributed to either Elizabeth Shelley or PBS (who employs it in the subplot of **St.Irv**), but its relatively sophisticated metrics and rhetoric (perhaps deriving, as *1989* suggests, from Fitz-Eustace's song in Canto III.x–xi of Scott's *Marmion,* one of PBS's favorite poems) and its gory denouement, in which the woman dies and the forsaken man vows to expire on her grave, point to PBS as the likely author.

Song. To ——— ("Ah! sweet is the moonbeam")

This poem was written by PBS to Harriet Grove during the height of their correspondence following the Grove family's visit to Field Place and London in April and May 1810. It recalls the "walk in the evening to Strood by moonlight" that PBS and Grove took on 17 April and that PBS first commemorated in *Song* ("*Come ———! sweet is the hour*"), which treats in the present tense what the poet here recollects with emotion as he later revisits the scene of the lovers' walk.

When PBS wrote out the first four and a half lines of *Song. To ———* for Hogg, pretending that it was an example of verse written by his sister (MS Pfz; see *SC* II, 627), he stopped just before the part that reveals it is a love poem, for he did not wish Hogg to think that Elizabeth Shelley already had a lover. There are no substantive differences between *1810* and the fragment in MS Pfz, though the latter is more lightly punctuated.

lines 1–5. The rhetoric of these opening lines, which name three things that are <u>sweet</u>, only to top them with a fourth that is <u>sweeter</u>, probably derives, either directly or through other poets, from PBS's favorite passage in Lucretius's *De rerum natura*, the opening of Book II, which PBS quotes in a note to *QM* V.58 (*1813*, 137; emphasis added):

> *Suave* mari magno turbantibus æquora ventis
> E terrâ magnum alterius spectare laborem;
> Non quia vexari quemquam 'st jucunda voluptas,
> Sed quibus ipse malis careas quia cernere *suave'st*.
> *Suave* etiam belli certamina magna tueri,
> Per campos instructa, tua sine parte pericli;
> Sed nil *dulcius* est bene quam munita tenere
> Edita doctrina sapientum templa serena; . . .

<u>Ah! sweet is the moonbeam that sleeps</u> (**line 1**) also echoes *Merchant of Venice* (V.i.54), in the love scene between Lorenzo and Jessica, a subject of PBS's lifelong interest: in 1812, Harriet Westbrook Shelley copied ten lines from this scene (including this one) on fol. 17 verso of her commonplace book (MS, Washington State University), and in a reported debate with Byron in 1822 on the nature of poetry, PBS used "How sweet the moonlight sleeps upon this bank" to exemplify how a line of poetry, as well as a drama, can be "a whole, beautiful in itself" (see Peck, *Shelley* II, 424). One parallel between Shakespeare's lovers and PBS's romances with both Harriet Grove and Harriet Westbrook was that the fathers of the young women opposed their daughters' suitors. For this situation as a stimulant to PBS's romantic and literary interest, see Reiman on *"The waters are flashing"* (*The Fugitives*), in *MYR: Shelley* VIII (1997, 109–12).

line 8. ———: The metrics require two syllables; at the beginning of the PBS-Grove relationship, all the Groves referred to PBS as "Bysshe" (pronounced "Bish"), as he was called at home; but after an evening tête-à-tête at the Groves' London lodgings on 27 April 1810, Harriet Grove's diary began to refer to PBS as "Percy" or "P" rather than "Bysshe" or "B" (*SC* II, 577; Hawkins, *First Love,* 38). PBS became "Shelley" only after his elopement with Harriet Shelley and his break with his family, who shared that name.

line 9. winds sighing: Though an apostrophe might be added to make winds into a possessive (singular or plural), the text makes perfect sense as it stands.

line 13. dearest friend: This phrase and dearest one (**15**), both vocatives, would conventionally be preceded by commas and followed by exclamation marks. PBS may have neglected to punctuate this poem formally because he originally wrote it as a personal expression sent to Grove; or he may have felt that such internal punctuation impeded the rhythms of his verse. Since throughout his career PBS continued to punctuate more lightly than was customary, presumably to facilitate the flow of his verse, it seems more important to call attention to his departures from standard practice and their possible significance (or lack thereof) than to attempt to regularize the punctuation of his released texts.

Dateline. An apparent error in *1810* omits the comma after August. We have inserted the comma to make this dateline conform with the others in the volume.

Song. To ——— ("Stern, stern is the voice")

PBS probably wrote this poem; one piece of inverse evidence for his authorship is that he transcribed for Hogg eight and a half lines of it from memory, along with **"Cold, cold is the blast"** (above), which is certainly by PBS, who told Hogg that these lines were the work of Elizabeth Shelley in order to impress his new friend with his sister's poetic ability (see Hogg, *Life,* ed. Wolfe, I, 126; *SC* II, 627, which transcribes MS Pfz). The MS in Pfz—not part of a letter—dates from the autumn of 1810, probably in late October or November, early in the college friendship of the two young men. Since PBS was writing down fragments of this poem from memory, as well as altering words in order to make Hogg believe that Elizabeth Shelley was the author (e.g., changing some pronouns from masculine to feminine), the text in *1810* is the only proper textual authority, but since the corrupt version in MS Pfz was published by Hogg in his *Life of PBS* decades before *V&C*

was discovered, the version in MS Pfz was followed by several early editors, and we collate MS Pfz as one primary textual authority.

The subject and tone of *"Stern, stern is the voice"* approximate those of the love poem preceding it in *V&C*, which is surely by PBS; the poem also contains the image of the wounded deer, on which PBS drew throughout his career, as well as Gothic touches characteristic of his early work. Though we believe that this composition was mainly by PBS, this may be another place where he completed or revised a poem with some lines composed by Elizabeth Shelley and where Jack Stillinger's concept of collective "authorship" should come into play.

The theme of the poem—that death is better than banishment from a beloved—suggests that it was written by PBS after Grove or her family became angry with him over some offense in one of his letters. PBS may here be equating his suffering in his estrangement from Grove to her sorrow over the recent death of her sister Louisa (see *"Cold, cold . . . ,"* **9**, note).

line 1. fate's fearfull command: We have added the apostrophe to fate's but have left fearfull as it appears in *1810*. As with the word *blissfull* in **Song. Sorrow,** line 4, the final doubled consonant in fearfull is uncharacteristic of PBS's mature orthography. Perhaps the Phillips printing family (who may have fought to keep the double *l* in their name) spelled words ending in *-full* with the final consonant doubled, or perhaps Elizabeth Shelley did so. In the second case, there is still a question as to whether the poems in which these variant forms appear were composed by Elizabeth or were merely transcribed by her from PBS's rough copies. We know from her transcription of PBS's *A Cat in Distress* (see frontispiece) that she had a much more legible copying hand than did PBS at this age.

line 7. heart-stricken deer: The tone of this image (which PBS used at *Cenci* I.ii.12–13; *Epipsychidion,* 272; and *Adonais* xxxiii.9) relates it closely to Cowper's *Task* iii.108–11—"I was a stricken deer, that left the herd | Long since . . . | To seek a tranquil death in distant shades"—rather than to Cowper's probable source, *As You Like It* II.i, where Duke Senior's courtiers joke about Jaques's moralizing over "a poor sequest'red stag, | That from the hunter's aim had ta'en a hurt" and report with glee his "weeping and commenting | Upon the sobbing deer" ("Sweep on, you fat and greasy citizens"). But the issue of PBS's source is complicated by sentimental paintings of "Jacques and the Wounded Stag" produced by contemporary artists to illustrate Shakespeare's plays. In *The Boydell Shakespeare Gallery,* edited by Frederick Burwick and Walter Pape (1996), Burwick discusses not only William Hodges' painting, which hung in John Boydell's Shakespeare Gallery in Pall Mall, and prints of it, which appeared in Boydell's edition of

Shakespeare's works (1802–5), but also subsequent oil paintings of the subject by Sir George Beaumont and John Constable (12–14).

line 18. <u>Memory's ear</u>: Though it may not be the "source" for a phrase that could grow naturally out of the context of this poem, there is a parallel use of "Memory's ear" in line 22 of Charles Lamb's *To Charles Lloyd, An Unexpected Visitor*, first published in 1797 with the second edition of Coleridge's *Poems*, where PBS could conceivably have seen it.

Saint Edmond's Eve

On PBS's plagiarism of *The Black Canon of Elmham; or, Saint Edmond's Eve*, see the "Plagiarisms, Authorship, and Title" section of the introduction to *V&C*. PBS probably chose to pad his volume with the poem by M. G. Lewis because he had memorized it and could copy it out as though it were his own composition. But, if so, why had he memorized this particular poem? Any answer, however conjectural, should recognize that *Tales of Terror* (both in 1801 and 1808) opens with a seven-page verse dialogue between "Author" and "Friend" on the taste for Gothic literature; when "Friend" attacks it, "Author" replies in this vein (4):

> My mind unalter'd views, with fix'd delight,
> The wreck of learning snatch'd from Gothic night;
> Changed by no time, unsettled by no place,
> It feels the Grecian Fire, the Roman grace;
> . . . .
> Yet still the soul for *various* pleasure form'd
> By Pity melted, and by Terror storm'd,
> Loves to roam largely through each distant clime,
> And "leap the flaming bounds of space and time!"

By lifting a prominent poem from *Tales of Terror* that defended the Gothic mode as a mind-liberating force, PBS would thus (if readers recognized his plagiarism) provide a vindication of his own Gothic poems that follow it.

The plot of *The Black Canon*—vengeance by the ghost of a nun upon an ecclesiastical superior who had first seduced and then murdered her—accords not only with Gothic conventions but with PBS's general sense of justice, as well as tensions within his own family, since Timothy and Bysshe Shelley, both of whom he despised, had fathered illegitimate children. (For the relationship of PBS's temperamental predispositions to his continuing interest in Gothic literature, see Reiman, *Romantic Texts and Contexts* [1987], 347–53.) But probably the main reasons PBS included *The Black Canon* in the volume were that PBS had memorized it (and could, therefore, fake its composition in front of a witness, such as Elizabeth Shelley) and that it was thematically related to the poems of his that follow it in *V&C* (or, rather, his poems relate to *The Black Canon*, one of their models).

Since the *V&C* text of **Saint Edmond's Eve** is a nearly literal transcription of the work of another poet, we have simply transcribed the text as it appears in *1810* and collated that against *The Black Canon* in two editions of *Tales of Terror* (1801 and 1808) and the "facsimile" of *V&C* (*1898*). The Historical Collations of **Saint Edmond's Eve** are briefer, because the poem did not appear in any edition of PBS's poetry published before *1898*, and since Matthews and Everest omit this poem from *1989* on the grounds that it was not written by PBS, the only authorities are *1904* (with Matthews's updating of that edition in *1970*), *1927*, and *1972*.

line 1. black Canon: Gilbert White describes "*Black-Canons* of the order of *St. Augustine*, called also *Canons-Regular*" as "a kind of religious" who lived communally and "were bound by vows to observe the rules and statutes of their order . . . whose discipline was less rigid than the *monks*" (*The Natural History and Antiquities of Selborne* [1789]; ed. L. C. Miall and W. W. Fowler [1901], 257–58n).

line 11. pour o'er its grave: PBS's substitution of this wording for the text in *The Black Canon* ("breathes o'er its grave"), his similar verbal substitutions in **lines 22, 40, 49, 56, 64, 83, 91, 95, 104,** and **107,** and his more substantial garbling of the text of **lines 85–88** are more likely to have resulted from imperfect memorization than from faulty transcription. Together with the numerous variants in punctuation and orthography, they show that PBS was quoting *The Black Canon* from memory, rather than copying a printed text.

lines 71–72. it wildly talks, | And calls: The second edition of *Tales of Terror* (1808), *1898*, and the historical editions we collate—*1904*, *1927*, *1970*, and *1972*—all substitute "call" for calls, leaving the ungrammatical: "Of thee! Black Canon, it wildly talks, | And call on thy patron saint— "

Revenge

This dramatic narrative, largely in dialogue, follows the pattern of the Gothic tales in verse of M. G. Lewis, Scott, and other British poets of the first decade of the century, a form that they, in turn, derived from Bishop Percy's collection *Reliques of Ancient Poetry* (1765 ff.) and the art ballads of German writers of the late eighteenth century, which were translated by Lewis, Scott, and others. PBS presumably wrote this poem, there being nothing in subject, style, diction, or orthography to link it with Elizabeth Shelley.

As *1989* details, the names and some incidents in the poem have direct parallels in Lewis's *The Monk* (1796) and *Tales of Wonder* (1801), and with Charlotte Dacre's *Zofloya; or, The Moor* (1806); the meter (as *1989* notes) is that of *The Wanderer of the Wold* in Scott's earlier *Apology for Tales of Terror* (Kelso, 1799). An Agnes not only figures in the plot of *The Monk*, but she— like PBS's heroine here—remains etymologically correct by becoming a sacrificial *lamb*.

The plot of **Revenge** traces the vengeance of an illegitimate half-brother (PBS had one) on the legitimate heir for their father's betrayal of the avenger's mother—a pattern paralleled in PBS's **Zastrozzi** (published in Dec. 1809, but dated 1810). Though Cameron dates the composition of that novel between March and August 1809 (*YS*, 303) and Matthews and Everest date its completion in September 1809 (*1989* I, 26), both datings are conjectural. In fact, a letter from PBS dated 7 May 1809 to "Messrs. Longman & Co—" speaks of a novel in progress (**Letters** I, 4–5) and an unpublished one dated 13 July 1809 to an unnamed publisher (which will appear in the Retrospective that will open *SC* IX) refers to a novel then finished and ready to submit. Unless that novel was a lost work, **Zastrozzi** was completed long before this poem (datelined December, 1809.) and may well have provided a scenario for it. The innocent woman killed soon after her wedding as a vengeance upon her husband would reappear more memorably in *Frankenstein*.

line 1. whistles: emended from "whitsles" (*1810*). No dictionary or usage known to us includes "whitsles" as either a valid word or a variant spelling.

line 3. thunder's: emended from "thunders" (*1810*). Though William Crakelt, the editor of later editions of *Entick's New Spelling Dictionary*, objected in a note that an apostrophe for the genitive case should be unnecessary, in the 1805 edition, the rule appears: "the *genitive* case is formed by adding *s*, with an *apostrophe*, to the *nominative:* as, men, men*'s;* ox, ox*'s*" (ix).

line 4. love.—": Several editors (or their copyeditors or compositors) move the end quotation marks from the end of the line, placing them between the period and the dash. Because we do not fully understand the conventions on the placement of quotation marks in PBS's day—and thus do not know whether such a change affects PBS's intention—we follow *1810* here.

line 6. Strasburg: This spelling of the name of the Alsatian capital, the scene of an adventure in Lewis's *The Monk*, is an English form (found in the first edition of *Encyclopædia Britannica*, 1771) that differs from the contemporary French and German spellings of that name.

line 7. ancestors': emended to possessive plural; note their remains (8).

line 10. 'till dawn: Though the metrics might seem to require *the* before dawn, the pause required by the caesura before 'till would fill out the metrical line, just as in music a rest fills out the measure.

line 17. Though *1989* suggests emending the final I love, to *my love*, (without actually doing so), the repetition effectively intensifies the emotion of Adolphus's declaration.

line 20. maw"—: The dash and lack of a full stop in *1810* may suggest that Adolphus has not finished speaking before Agnes breaks in with her equally emotional response.

lines 21, 24, 53. Vocatives, or phrases of direct address, such as loved Adolphus and dearest Adolphus (or similar addresses to Agnes in **5**, **12**, and **17**) would conventionally be set off from what precedes with a comma and followed by an exclamation mark, but PBS may have intended to omit such punctuation in hurried, emotion-filled exchanges, while including it in **line 45**, at the solemn and measured opening of the speech by Conrad's Spirit. We delete the quotation marks that appear at the end of **line 24** in *1810* because Agnes continues speaking in the next stanza.

line 30. lightning's: We have emended *1810*'s reading to the possessive singular (rather than plural) because in **35** lightning is characterized as singular.

blue fire-light: Though carrying benign connotations when associated with eyes, sky, or sea, blue was conventionally related to death or the supernatural when a body or a light turned blue; *1989* cites examples from Gothic works and *Richard III* (V.iii.180); see also S. T. Coleridge's "famine or blue plague" in *Fears in Solitude,* 91. Parallel uses by PBS include **QM** I.4; *Alastor,* 216; and **Laon** III.xxvi.1, VI.xlviii.9, and X.xx.1. As can be seen in PBS's verse letters to Edward Fergus Graham (see pp. 140–44 and Commentary), *blue* carried strongly negative personal associations for PBS.

line 42. On his family estates, PBS would have observed "gossamers"—the tiny filaments of broken spider webs that autumn breezes stretch out from vegetation and blow across the fields, and the word *gossamer* became a prominent literary word in the nineteenth century. It was employed before 1810 by such poets as Charlotte Smith, in the titles of two of her *Elegiac Sonnets;* Coleridge, in the 1798 version of *Ancient Mariner;* and both Anna Laetitia Aiken (later Barbauld) and Mary Robinson in poems addressed to Coleridge. The word was also used in poems by Robert Bloomfield, Southey, Henry Kirke White, and several others before PBS used it here, in **QM** I, 120, in **Laon** XII.xxxii.6, and in his letter of 15 February 1821 to Peacock, where PBS calls himself "the Knight of the Shield of shadow &

the lance of Gossamere"—perhaps an allusion to himself as a Don Quixote figure (see **Letters** II, 261, and *SC* X).

line 43. Here PBS uses <u>sat</u>, rather than his preferred spelling, "sate," perhaps to avoid creating assonance with <u>gaze</u> so strong as to suggest an internal rhyme.

line 44. We emend "meteors" to a possessive, judging from the syntax of the previous line (<u>terror</u> is <u>Like</u> . . . <u>blaze</u>) that <u>blaze</u> is a noun; the text of *1810* would not need emendation here if *blaze* were intended as a verb, with *meteors* as its plural subject. In PBS's day *meteor* referred to any meteorological phenomenon—not necessarily matter from outer space flaming through the Earth's atmosphere, but here PBS's use seems close to the modern meaning.

line 45. PBS's change in the method of identifying the speakers, from hints in the dialogue to a centered designation of each new speaker above his or her speech, changes the nature of the dialogue (both in this poem and **Ghasta**, which follows) from the genre of the ballad, connoting the historical past, to the immediacy of a drama played out before the reader's eyes. In *1989*, Matthews and Everest add quotation marks in the dramatic speeches, producing quotation marks within quotation marks.

line 48. The end punctuation is a period; in the BL copy of *1810*, the ink is smeared, and in photocopies it could appear as a comma—though it does not in the facsimile of the same copy of *1810* that appears in Looker, *Shelley, Trelawny, and Henley.*

line 53. <u>seize</u>: corrected from "sieze" *1810* (a characteristic PBS error).

line 55. <u>whirlwind's</u>: apostrophe added to *1810* text.

line 60. <u>to the sky—</u>: This seems an important early example of PBS's transvaluation of traditional symbolism; instead of carrying the innocent victim *down* to <u>Hades</u> (**line 54**), the demon carries her *up*, toward the seat of traditional theocratic power (cf. Jupiter in **Prometheus Unbound**).

line 62. The comma and dash at the end of this line in *1810*, like the dash at the end of **60,** do the rhetorical work of periods, colons, and other fixed punctuation, while maintaining the sense of movement and excitement. PBS seems to have known what effect he wanted here, even though—or because—it is *not* conventional.

Ghasta; or, The Avenging Demon!!!

This strange and confusing poem employs the meter of *The Sword of Angantyr,* one of Lewis's translations from the German in *Tales of Wonder.* (Thematically this translation relates closely to PBS's **Revenge,** above.) **Ghasta** is the first poem that PBS published on the legend of the Wandering Jew, who remained a central focus of his imagination—in some sense his personal surrogate—from this time through **Hellas,** his final major published work (1822). In the Commentary to **WJ,** we discuss PBS's interest in the myth stimulated by an English translation of Christian Friedrich Daniel Schubart's *Der ewige Jude. Eine lyrische Rhapsodie,* an unrhymed poetic fragment (111 lines of varying length), written in 1783 and published in 1786, which PBS probably encountered in a prose translation in the London monthly *La Belle Assemblée* (Jan. 1809, 19–20), where it had been reprinted—with errors—from an 1801 issue of another London periodical. Though January 1809 thus marks the earliest date by which PBS encountered this German source of the legend, on which he was also writing his much larger poem **WJ,** PBS presumably recognized its protagonist from his earlier reading of Lewis's *The Monk.* As Helene Richter pointed out in 1899 (*Englische Studien* XXVI, 138–44), much of **Ghasta** derives from Don Raymond's tale of the Bleeding Nun in *The Monk* (Chap. 4), on which see **WJ** Commentary.

Those unfamiliar with *The Monk* may welcome an outline of **Ghasta**'s tangled plot. A medieval Warrior, who seeks shelter at an inn from a storm and Fiend-like Goblins, confronts a stranger, to whom he feels impelled to relate his encounter with a mist-like spirit who claims him as her love and comes every night to embrace him. The stranger leads the warrior to a heath and casts a spell that raises evil spirits, including the ghost of Theresa, once the betrayed love and now the succubus of the warrior Rodolph. The Stranger (who proves to be the Wandering Jew) commands Ghasta, chief of the avenging demons, to send the ghost of Theresa to the cells of death; as Rodolph gazes upon the fiery cross on the stranger's brow, he is struck by the cold wind of death and (we are left to imagine) his spirit joins Theresa's to await the Last Judgment.

In *1989,* Matthews and Everest judge PBS's poem to be very severe in punishing mere sexual weakness or betrayal (I, 31–32), but *The Monk* and other Gothic novels and poems of the period are full of similar terroristic retributions, probably designed both to add a dimension of irrational excitement for readers and to highlight (from a post-Enlightenment perspective) the harshness of medieval "superstition"; moreover, PBS's poetry (like W. Wordsworth's) usually judges such betrayals harshly. There is, as yet, no evidence that PBS had at this date any reason (as Wordsworth did) to feel personal guilt about a young woman whom he had seduced and then abandoned.

PBS's headnote. Though the note ends with a period in *1810*, smeared ink in both BL and Htn could mislead readers into supposing the mark to be a comma; in Tx the character is lightly inked, but clearly a period.

line 1. owlet flaps: Medwin identified this phrase and stanza as "almost taken" from Chatterton (*Life*, ed. Forman, 45); *1989* identified the poem as "The Mynstrelle's Songe" in *Ælla* (lines 885 ff.), and much this same phrase appears in Chatterton's *The Tournament*, line 56: "The flemed owlett flapps herr eve-speckte wynge," with "flemed owlett" defined as "Frighted owl" (*Poems . . . by Thomas Rowley* [1794], 141).

line 16. Fiend-like: In *1810* the hyphen is misprinted as a dash; *1898* misprints Goblins with a lowercase g.

line 21. reins: misprinted as "reigns" in *1898* (a good example of why one cannot trust type-facsimiles).

line 33. blaunched: Perhaps PBS intentionally used this older form to add to the archaic flavor, à la Chatterton; in *QM* the word is spelled "blanched" (VII.158).

lines 36–47. Note that it is the stranger (the Wandering Jew) who does all the talking to this point, addressing the warrior as Mortal!.

line 40. cypress trees and mandrakes: These Mediterranean plants, neither one native to the British Isles, came to British writers from classical and Italian literature. The cypress, sacred to Hecate, goddess of witchcraft and queen of Hades, became a standard feature of literary funerals and cemeteries (e.g., "Come away, come away, death | And in sad cypress let me be laid"—*Twelfth Night* II.iv.51–52; Milton's sorcerer dwells "Immur'd in cypress shades"—*Comus* 521).

Magical powers were attributed to the mandrake (or *mandragora*, of the family *Solanaceæ*), which had been used as a strong narcotic since ancient times (see *Othello* III.iii.330, *Antony and Cleopatra* I.v.4). The roots of the plant, which has male and female forms, often resemble human figures and were thought to embody unquiet spirits who cried out when the plants were pulled from the ground and could render "barren women fruitful" (*Encyc. Brit.*, 1771; see also *Cruden's Concordance to the Bible*).

lines 43, 44. We have added apostrophes to lightning's and twilight's and the quotation marks required to close the Stranger's speech at the end of **44**.

line 47. The Wandering Jew, who cannot die, emphasizes the mortality of others.

lines 49ff. From here to **line 136,** the direct speeches of the Warrior and the Stranger (Wandering Jew) are introduced by speech headings (as in a dramatic text), while their reports of the speeches of others (such as that of the succubus in **73–96**) are indicated by quotation marks before each line. We have, therefore, removed the opening quotation marks at **line 49** and closing quotation marks at **128,** which do not follow this pattern and are probably vestigial remains of an earlier system of reference in the MS that PBS had abandoned but failed to eliminate consistently. See note to **lines 169–76** below.

line 49. We have emended *1810*'s "whoso'er" to whosoe'er.

lines 53, 55. These lines do not rhyme—a common enough occurrence with the first and third lines of ballad stanzas generally, but unique in this poem.

lines 59–60. These lines mean to say: "Fleeting as the cloud that hangs on bog or on mountain stream." The inversions that complicate the early poems of PBS and his contemporaries result ultimately from their training in Latin composition: in a highly inflected language like Latin, which can accommodate such inversions without confusion, they were prized for adding sophisticated variety to the versification. Milton and other Latin masters reinforced the practice in English, but young or untalented poets often overused inversions, simply to help them maintain the rhyme scheme.

line 64. limbs: corrected from "limb's" *1810*.

line 70. th' autumnal: Such earlier poets as Pope, Cowper, and the young W. Wordsworth and S. T. Coleridge (or their printers), when manipulating the number of syllables in their poetic lines, elided neutral vowels with other vowels that immediately preceded or followed, signaling such elisions (as in French) by replacing the vowels with apostrophes. PBS used this convention sparingly throughout his career to clarify the meter of particular poetic lines (see also **151** and **197**).

line 72. mandrake's: apostrophe added to "mandrakes" *1810;* see the note to **40.**

lines 73–76, 93–96. Thou art mine and I am thine, etc.: These formulaic incantations derive from Lewis's *The Monk*. See the note to *WJ* I.276–77.

line 79. tomb's: corrected from "tombs" *1810*.

line 84. pleasure's: corrected from "pleasures" *1810*.

line 94. Till . . . judgment day: In nineteenth-century Anglican doctrine, which prided itself on returning to early apostolic Christianity, the souls of the dead were believed neither to go directly to Heaven or Hell (as in Lutheran and Reformed theology) nor to pass through Purgatory (as most of the redeemed must do according to Roman Catholic doctrine). Instead, they were thought to lie in their graves (the cells of death in **line 180**), awaiting the coming of Christ and the resurrection of the body on the Day of Judgment, when the archangel would sound his trumpet and the just and the unjust would assemble before the throne of God to be redeemed or damned. For more detail, see the note to *WJ* III.387.

line 102. man's: corrected from "mans" *1810*.

line 106. seized: corrected from "siezed" *1810*.

lines 112–28. A succubus (female equivalent of incubus) was a demon in female shape who forced sexual intercourse upon men in their sleep— clearly a theological explanation of erotic dreams.

line 114. Other editors change it to "its"; but the Warrior seems to be saying that the phantom who sat on his bed spoke in a hollow voice that was as low as the sound in some charnel (made by air rushing through its chambers) that made it—that is, the charnel—seem to moan. We defer to PBS's knowledge of the environment and follow his text. As MWS writes in her fragmentary "Life of Shelley" (begun in 1822 and consisting of Bodleian MS. Shelley adds. c. 5, folios 113v–118r): "At his father's house where his influence was of course great among the dependants, he got admission to the charnel house & sat harrowed by fear yet trembling with expectation to see one of the spiritual possessors of the bones piled around him" (f. 116r; *BSM* XXII, ed. Alan M. Weinberg, 1997, Part 2, 271). See also ***Alastor***, where PBS claims that he had made his "bed | In charnels and on coffins" (lines 23–24).

line 115. In *1810* the initial *W* of this line (on 57) is a malformed type that seems identical with the initial *W* in line 5 of **Song. Despair** (19), suggesting that the type of page 19 had been distributed before that of page 57 was set.

line 128. scape: Though 1898 adds an initial apostrophe, *OED* gives this form—both with and without the apostrophe—as a poetic form of *escape*.

line 132. Follow, follow: an early premonition of ***Prometheus*** II.i.132.

line 133. tempest's: emended from "tempests" *1810*.

line 136. The Stranger's speech ends with his quotation of the ravens reciting his own earlier words (**47**).

line 138. PBS rhymes trode with nod (**140**). Though *OED* gives *trode* as an alternative past tense of *tread* (fourteenth through nineteenth centuries), pronounced as though rhymed with *mode*, John Walker's *Critical Pronouncing Dictionary and Expositor of the English Language* (1823) lists *trode* as the preterit of *tread*, to be pronounced the same as *trod* (*o* as in *not*).

line 166. In *1810* the initial *W* is not just badly inked but is a broken or malformed type character, yet different from that at **line 115.**

lines 169–76. PBS throughout this poem (and his career) had trouble recording consistently the beginnings and ends of quotations, but here the meaning is clear: he merely mixes two systems of reference, providing the speech of the Phantom with both a belt and suspenders.

line 171. flaming brow: that is, the fiery cross mentioned in PBS's headnote.

line 177. seize: corrected from "sieze" *1810*.

line 185. The poet's narrative resumes, following the final speech of the Stranger, whose refrain is echoed by the thunder at the Warrior's death.

line 196. twilight's: emended from "twilights" *1810*.

dateline. In January, 1810 PBS was probably at Field Place, on holiday from Eton, engaged in writing **WJ** and (perhaps) **Zastrozzi**. Since **Ghasta** relates to both works in subject and theme, the subscribed date is plausible and shows that PBS was seeking material to fill this volume among much earlier poems that he may not have planned to include.

Fragment, or The Triumph of Conscience

It seems almost too pat that PBS should end his first poetic volume with a fragment called ***The Triumph of Conscience*** and end his poetic career with a fragment entitled ***The Triumph of Life***. PBS's authorship of this early fragment is clear. Not only does it embody all his interests and stylistic tricks, but he soon republished it in the first chapter of ***St.Irv***. Our notes to that reprinting comment on the minor differences between the two texts.

The Wandering Jew;
or, The Victim of the Eternal Avenger

Textual History

PBS's earliest references to **The Wandering Jew** (*WJ*) appear in his recently discovered pocket diary for 1810 (Pfz); the page listing the week of 26 February contains a memo in which passages from Revelation 6:8 and 6:12 (see note at "I.234.Footnote" below) have been copied out under the heading "wandering Jew" (*sic*). On the lower part of the space for Thursday (1 March) are the words "Parcel to Harriet." Harriet Grove's diary for 1810 alludes to the arrival of "a Parcel & letter from my Greatest Friend" on 5 March, and in a partly canceled entry for 8 March mentions that she "Shewed the Poem <———?———> They <———?———> think it nonsense <———?———>." On 10 March, Grove wrote: "sent B[ysshe's] Poem away" (*SC* II, 571–72). These notations about a substantial (parcel size) single poem probably allude to an early form of *WJ*, a conclusion further supported by an entry in Grove's diary for 3 April 1810, in which she notes reading "Raymond & Agnes" (*SC* II, 574), probably the play based on the same subplot in the fourth chapter of M. G. Lewis's *The Monk* that powerfully influenced *WJ* as we now have it (see "Sources and Influences," below). However, the relation between the version of *WJ* that PBS sent her in March 1810 and the poem as it finally appeared remains obscure.

After PBS's death, Medwin claimed that he and PBS together wrote *WJ* during the winter of 1809/10, presumably during PBS's Christmas holiday from Eton. If so, the unnamed poem sent to Grove in March 1810 may have been a version to which Medwin contributed. Perhaps after the negative reactions of his Grove cousins and, it is said, an equally unflattering appraisal by the poet Thomas Campbell (see "Medwin's Claims," below), PBS revised the work completely, in the process eliminating or submerging Medwin's contributions.

Convinced that the version of *WJ* that survives is substantially PBS's composition, we shall trace its textual history before appraising in detail Medwin's claims to co-authorship. PBS first mentioned plans to publish *WJ* in his letter of 1 April 1810 to his friend Edward Fergus Graham, saying that he intended to bargain with "Jock" (Robinson, of G. Wilkie and J. Robinson, publishers of ***Zastrozzi***) to obtain "a devil of a price for my Poem & at least 60£ for my new Romance in three volumes"—that is, ***St.Irv*** (***Letters*** I, 6). But since Wilkie and Robinson were apparently unwilling to publish ***WJ*** on his terms, PBS may have revised it again before sending it, near the end of the summer of 1810, to the Ballantyne brothers in Edinburgh, printers and publishers of the poems of Scott. A letter from John Ballantyne dated 24 September 1810 tactfully declined "the honour" of publishing it, while indirectly warning PBS of the grounds for the refusal: "it is perhaps, better suited to the . . . liberal feeling of the English, than the bigoted narrow spirit . . . in this country. Even Walter Scott, is assailed . . . for having promulgated atheistical doctrines in the Lady of the Lake." PBS immediately forwarded this letter to John Joseph Stockdale and, denying that his poem contained "Atheistical principles," invited him to publish it (***Letters*** I, 17–18). In subsequent letters from Oxford on 14, 19, and 21 November 1810, PBS first asked Stockdale whether he had received the MS of ***WJ*** from Ballantyne, next offered to send Stockdale a second MS copy (presumably a safekeeping copy to which he added further revisions), and then mentioned this complication to Graham. On 2 December 1810, PBS requested of Stockdale: "if you have got two copies of the Wandering Jew send one of them to me, as I have thought of some corrections which I wish to make" (***Letters*** I, 23–24).

These references make clear that PBS had sent his second MS copy of ***WJ*** to Stockdale in 1810, but when publishing in *Stockdale's Budget* for 3 January 1827 the letter about ***WJ*** that PBS had sent to him and one that Ballantyne had sent to PBS, Stockdale declared that "the poem of The Wandering Jew never reached my hands, nor have I either seen or heard of it." He also wrote that he "much regretted" that Ballantyne had expressed his concern with PBS's religious opinions "in a way far from discouraging to their promulgation." Stockdale's motive for publishing his articles on PBS in *Stockdale's Budget* was to shame Sir Timothy Shelley into repaying Stockdale for his early losses from PBS's publications; denying that he had seen and (perhaps) agreed to publish ***WJ*** may have been part of Stockdale's effort to create the impression that in 1810–11 he had discouraged any unorthodox tendency in the writings of PBS and his friend T. J. Hogg. (All of Stockdale's statements are quoted or abstracted from *Stockdale's Budget* at BL.)

Common wisdom holds that Stockdale published *Stockdale's Budget* to discredit the hypocritical British establishment for lawsuits that had driven him into bankruptcy for publishing the *Memoirs of Harriette Wilson*, remembrances by a courtesan to the upper classes. But if the financial collapse in 1826 of Ballantyne, Constable, and their London partners, which ruined many London publishers, was a proximate cause of Stockdale's bankruptcy, he may have targeted the Ballantyne brothers and Scott, whom he could embarrass simply by quoting publicly the Ballantyne letter that impugned the taste of the Scottish reading public. Though John Ballantyne had died in 1821, readers in publishing circles very likely brought the account in *Stockdale's Budget* to the attention of his brother James. Not long after Stockdale published this account of the Scottish firm's involvement with PBS and **WJ**, there surfaced a MS of **WJ** still held by James Ballantyne. Thus, Stockdale's account of the poem may have stimulated the unearthing of this MS and led to the first publication of **WJ**.

On Saturday, 20 June 1829, the *Edinburgh Literary Journal; or, Weekly Register of Criticism and Belles Lettres* (*ELJ*) announced:

There has recently been put into our hands a manuscript volume, which we look upon as one of the most remarkable literary curiosities extant. It is a poem in four cantos, by the late poet Shelley, and written entirely in his own hand. It is entitled "The Wandering Jew," and contains many passages of great power and beauty. It was composed upwards of twenty years ago, and brought by the poet to Edinburgh, which he visited about that period. It has since lain in the custody of a literary gentleman of this town [identified elsewhere as James Ballantyne], to whom it was then offered for publication. (*ELJ*, no. 32, p. 41)

The next two issues of *ELJ* (27 June and 4 July 1829) contain selected passages of **WJ**, with prose summaries of sections omitted. Six months later, on 26 December 1829, *ELJ* published "An Incantation Scene" (i.e., Canto IV, lines 271–331) as "a poem, hitherto unpublished, by Percy Byshe [*sic*] Shelley" (no. 59, pp. 425–26). These lines, perhaps added hastily as a filler from a transcription made earlier by the editor of *ELJ* (rather than from the original MS), may have less textual authority than the passages quoted in June and July.

Two years after the selection appeared in *ELJ*, **WJ** resurfaced in the June and July 1831 issues of the brash young London monthly *Fraser's Magazine for Town and Country* (*FM*) (3, nos. 17 and 18), where it was billed as a previously unpublished poem. The June issue of *FM* contains a critical essay on PBS's poetry and his influence entitled "New Poem.—By Percy Bysshe Shelley: The Wandering Jew. Introduction" (*529–536; the pages numbered *529–*532 in this issue are extra pages inserted between 532 and 533. Perhaps the essay on PBS, delayed or altered because of the dispute with *ELJ* discussed below, turned out to be longer than planned when that issue of *FM* first went into page proof.) Although a remonstrance against this publication appeared in the 9 July issue of *ELJ* (see next section below), *FM* for July 1831 (3, no. 18, pp. 666–77) contains what purports to be the entire text of PBS's poem as a work newly discovered. But this text in *FM* (*1831F*) actually omits many lines that appear in the *ELJ* text (*1829E*).

Analysis of the Textual Status

Bertram Dobell first compared *1829E* and *1831F* in *The Wandering Jew. A Poem*, an edition sponsored by the Shelley Society (London: Reeves & Turner, 1887; hereafter cited as *1887D*). Observing that each early text contains lines or passages omitted from the other version, Dobell noted PBS's mentions of his two MSS of *WJ* and inferred from verbal differences between *1829E* and *1831F* that they derived from these two distinct MSS— *1829E* from the final copy and *1831F* from the rough draft (xxxi). Dobell's argument for a text that conflates what he believed to be different versions, based upon two discrete MSS, was accepted, rejected, or modified by successive editors: in *1892W*, Woodberry went back to the periodical texts and distinguished their respective contributions by printing in *italics* those lines found only in *1829E* and printing in roman type those first published in *1831F*, the authority that he preferred. Harry Buxton Forman continued to accept Medwin's tale that he was a primary author of *WJ* and did not add to his Aldine Edition (*1892F*) a poem to which he had denied entry in two earlier editions (see his rationale in *1876*, IV, 317–18). Thomas Hutchinson, who often followed Forman mechanically, omitted *WJ* from *1904,* as did both C. D. Locock from *1911* and G. M. Matthews from his *1970* redaction of *1904*. Though Ingpen included *WJ* in an appendix to Volume IV of *1927*, he followed *1892W* in reversing Dobell's preference by using *1831F* as his basic text and printing lines found only in *1829E* within square brackets. In *1972*, Neville Rogers adopted *1927*'s (erroneous) evaluation of the authority of the two primary texts and *1892W*'s practice of differentiating the two texts through typography: *1972* followed *1831F* as copy-text, printing in italics the lines unique to *1829E*.

Such editorial confusion should have been unnecessary by 1972, for three decades earlier Adaline E. Glasheen, who wrote a thesis on *WJ*, had analyzed and (with the help of her husband F. J. Glasheen) discussed the nature of the differences between the two texts in "The Publication of 'The Wandering Jew'" (*Modern Language Review* 38 [1943]:12–17). That article showed that both *1829E* and *1831F* relied upon a single MS source. The Glasheens quote the editor of *ELJ*, who noted that his predecessor, Henry Glassford Bell (identified in *DNB* as having "started and conducted" *ELJ*), after publishing excerpts from the MS in 1829, lent this MS "to a gentleman who was writing an essay on the genius of Shelley, with permission to make a few extracts. That person copied the whole poem, and transmitted it to Fraser. Upon [Bell's] remonstrance that the poem was Mrs. Shelley's property, he wrote to Fraser requesting him not to print it. The bibliopole, however, or his editor, persisted" (*ELJ*, 9 July 1831, p. 24; quoted by Glasheens, "Publication of WJ," 14). Bell, we might further note, in a speech made at the Scott Centenary Banquet in 1871, prided himself on being "the means of first giving to the world an unpublished poem of Shelley, which he had left and forgotten in the hands of James Ballantyne, of Edinburgh" (*Memoirs and Portraits of One Hundred Glasgow Men* [Glasgow: James Maclehose, 1886], I, 30).

The verso of the table of contents of Volume 3 of *FM* contains the following notice: "An obscure cotemporary [*sic*] has accused us of announcing for publication Shelley's Poem without proper authority.—We beg to assure him, that we have the sanction of Mrs. Shelley. O.Y." (i.e., "Oliver Yorke," the pseudonym of *FM*'s editor). MWS, who was busy during 1831 putting Trelawny's *Adventures of a Younger Son* through the press and negotiating with Sir Timothy Shelley about money for her son's education, gave no public sanction to the publication (possibly because he had threatened to cut off her income if she brought PBS's name before the public) and left no record of such a request or permission in her letters or journals. But with MWS living in London, it seems unlikely that a magazine published there would make such a statement unless it were true.

In *1989*, Matthews and Everest suggest that the "essay on the genius of Shelley" by the literary gentleman who borrowed the MS might be articles entitled "Percy Bysshe Shelley" published in *Tait's Edinburgh Magazine* in October and December 1832 (2: 92–103, 331–42). However, not only do the antithetical political stances of *Tait's* and *Fraser's* make the linkage less likely than might otherwise appear, but also the essay in *Tait's* mentions **WJ** only in a brief footnote that displays no greater knowledge of the original MS than what could be gleaned from the introduction in *1831F*. The most likely candidate for the unknown literary gentleman is John Abraham Heraud (1799–1887, *DNB*), the assistant editor of *Fraser's* and a poet himself, who appears to have written the introductory essay to **WJ** and edited *1831F*, with the possible assistance of William Maginn, the editor of *Fraser's*. For the attribution, see Miriam M. H. Thrall, *Rebellious "Fraser's": Nol Yorke's Magazine in the Days of Maginn, Thackeray, and Carlyle* (1934; New York, AMS Press, 1966), 284–85, an attribution that is accepted in the *Wellesley Index to Victorian Periodicals* (II, 327). The "unknown essay" may well have taken the form of Heraud's extensive introductory essay evaluating PBS's life and thought that appears in *1831F* itself and that addresses **WJ** only briefly at its end. Heraud later published an even longer essay entitled "The Poetry of Shelley" in *Fraser's* for June 1838 (17:653–76).

The Glasheens show that *1831F* includes many verse passages that *1829E* had summarized in prose, while *1831F* truncates other passages to condense **WJ**, several times revising or rearranging words in the text to maintain the rhymes or to avoid omitting elements necessary to the plot. Our collations confirm the Glasheens' conclusions. In the opening 100 lines of **WJ**, for example, while *ELJ* substitutes a prose redaction for **I.58–89** and omits PBS's footnote, *FM* silently tightens and polishes the text by omitting words (**I.2, 21**) and lines (**I.14–18, 25–28, 39–40, 43–57, 98–101**), correcting syntax (**I.13**), and replacing *pleased* in **I.23** with *charmed* from the omitted **I.25**. Instead of amalgamating two versions drawn from different manuscripts, editors must, therefore, compare two texts abridged from the same MS to posit the nature of their common original. The Glasheens further argue that the underlying MS was not that originally sent to the Ballantynes in 1810 but a revised version of the poem that PBS carried to Edinburgh when he eloped there with Harriet Westbrook Shelley in August 1811. (As the notice in *ELJ* of 20 June 1829 put it, the MS was "brought by the poet to Edinburgh . . . upwards of twenty years ago.") The Glasheens give as PBS's motive for approaching Ballantyne again his lack of money during the elopement journey; this is a possible but not necessary cause, for PBS could have opened his visit by asking what had happened to the MS that Ballantyne had promised to return a year earlier, and after a friendly exchange he could have offered his revised—probably less antireligious—text in place of that version.

Cameron in *YS* (1950) endorsed the Glasheens' arguments. Although *1989* was the first text of ***WJ*** to be based on their analysis, Matthews and Everest contend that PBS did not give the Ballantynes a revised version of ***WJ*** during his elopement journey in the fall of 1811, because the date subscribed to the Preface ("January 1811") would have been prospective rather than retrospective. According to the *ELJ* description, however, "the Preface bears internal marks of having been written after the poem" (27 June 1829), and because PBS revised the text in the late fall of 1810, the date of that added Preface to his revised copy would naturally have read "January 1811," inasmuch as books printed and released in the December book-buying season were (like ***St.Irv***) regularly postdated to January of the following year. Conversely, the preface of a copy that PBS submitted to the Ballantynes in August or September 1810 was more likely to bear an 1810 date. PBS did not thoroughly revise the poem again in 1811, we conjecture, but carried the text that he had revised for Stockdale late in 1810, exchanging it for his earlier version when he met Ballantyne in 1811, in the hope that he might like it better and publish it.

Additional evidence supports the Glasheens' scenario: besides textual evidence cited below, we note that *ELJ* three times describes the MS as being a bound notebook: (1) its 20 June 1829 advertisement for the forthcoming ***WJ*** begins: "There has recently been put into our hands a *manuscript volume*" (italics added); (2) its description of the contents of the MS on 27 June makes clear that the "volume" was a bound one—the pages of which turned like a book; (3) in attacking *FM* for publishing the poem without permission (9 July 1831), *ELJ* again calls the MS "the book" (24). The phrase "a manuscript volume" describes bound notebooks, such as the **Esdaile Notebook**, the **Scrope Davies Notebook**, the larger **Harvard Shelley**

Notebook, and the three Bodleian notebooks containing his (heavily revised) fair draft of **Prometheus Unbound** (**Prom**), in which PBS customarily both drafted his works and transcribed the initial coherent versions of his poems that he retained as safekeeping copies. The MS used by *FM*, on the other hand, may have been on loose sheets, since it was a transcription (now lost or destroyed) made by the literary critic to whom the editor of *ELJ* lent "this book."

MSS that PBS sent to press were, however, customarily copied on loose sheets, or else were, like the MS of **Laon and Cythna** (and MWS's *Frankenstein*), made up of leaves removed from the notebooks in which they were first copied. Thus, the "manuscript book" was probably PBS's safekeeping copy, which he sent to and then retrieved from Stockdale in 1810 so that he could revise it. This could, then, be the revised text that PBS gave to Ballantyne in 1811 in exchange for the unrevised fair copy, presumably on loose sheets, that he had originally sent to Edinburgh ca. 1 September 1810. After PBS retrieved this MS, it then became his new safekeeping copy.

Other Attempts to Publish

Hidden from clear view may be an occasion earlier in 1811 when PBS tried to publish *WJ*: Thornton Hunt, in his memoirs of PBS (reprinted in Ingpen's 1903 edition of Leigh Hunt, *Autobiography* II, 27–28), reported that PBS and Hunt met (in May 1811) after the young man, recently expelled from Oxford, had submitted a "manuscript poem" to Hunt's kinsman Rowland Hunter, the bookseller who succeeded to the St. Paul's Churchyard bookshop of Joseph Johnson, Mary Wollstonecraft's friend. Though Hunter found that the poem "by no means suited," he sent PBS to discuss the matter with Hunt, and their first meeting involved a long discussion of their respective religious beliefs (**Letters** I, 76–78; *SC* II, 769–75). As Cameron notes, PBS had earlier written to Hunt, who may have been anxious to meet the young man after hearing his story from Hunter (*SC* II, 772–73) — or, perhaps, he had acted as Hunter's reader for the unnamed poem. At this date, *WJ* was PBS's only poem of book length that had not already been published, and if Thornton Hunt's reminiscence is accurate, then the approach to Hunter must have involved it.

As late as 5 October 1814, after his elopement with Mary Godwin (later MWS), PBS asked Harriet Shelley to "send . . . the Wandering Jew if it is with you" (**Letters** I, 405). This, apparently PBS's last surviving reference to *WJ*, suggests that he may still have been interested in revising and trying to publish it from the version on loose sheets as late as 1814, though if this was the version that Ballantyne had rejected as atheistic, PBS may simply have been trying to retrieve the MS from his estranged wife and her family, either to avoid future legal problems or to use it as a source book for the legend of the Wandering Jew that he was then evoking in his fragmentary prose fiction known as **The Assassins** (1814–15), for, as E. B. Murray points out, PBS jotted down the following note on the first page of the holograph MS of **On the Vegetable System of Diet** (?late 1814–late 1815): "To write the Wandering Jew. A Novel" (***Prose*** I, 394). Though Murray suggests no candidate, **The Assassins** is a fragmentary prose fiction that seems to have been developing in this direction (see ***Prose*** I, 133–39).

The cited and inferred references to ***WJ*** make clear that PBS submitted various versions of this poem for publication on at least three—and possibly six—different occasions, if we count his sending to Campbell the text that he and Medwin had written jointly (see below). PBS also drew upon both the words and ideas of ***WJ*** in later works. He probably would have been pleased, then, to learn that in 1829 it finally reached an audience (albeit in abridged form), perhaps because Ballantyne was trying to help a struggling young liberal periodical (*ELJ* was published only 1828–32). Since we cannot be certain whether the MS underlying the publications in *ELJ* and *FM* was one PBS completed and sent to Ballantyne in August or September 1810, a version revised while he negotiated with Stockdale in December 1810, or a later redaction given to Ballantyne during a visit to Edinburgh, we place the poem's date of release as ca. 1 September 1810, when he first sent the poem off to the Edinburgh publisher.

Medwin's Claims to Joint Authorship

While tracing the textual and publication history of the version of ***WJ*** that we include among PBS's poems, we have dismissed Medwin's claims to be the co-author of these cantos. Now we must analyze and evaluate his assertions. In *The Shelley Papers* (*1833*), Medwin declared that shortly after PBS was fifteen,

we wrote, in conjunction, six or seven cantos on the story of the Wandering Jew, of which the first four, with the exception of a very few lines, were exclusively mine. It was a thing, such as boys usually write, a *cento* from different favourite authors; the crucifixion scene altogether a plagiary from a volume of Cambridge prize poems. The part which I contributed I have still, and was surprised to find *totidem verbis* in *Fraser's Magazine*. The Wandering Jew continued to be a favourite subject of Shelley's. In the notes of "Queen Mab" he gives the Legend, probably a translation from the German, from which Byron took that splendid idea in Manfred—

> Back,
> Back by a single hair, I could not die.

Shelley also introduces Ahasuerus in his "Hellas." Voltaire did the same in the "Henriade."

As might be shown by the last cantos of that poem, which *Fraser* did not think worth publishing, his ideas were, at that time, strange and incomprehensible, mere elements of thought—images wild, vast, and Titanic. (7–9)

Medwin extended this account in his *Life of Percy Bysshe Shelley* (1847), which we cite from Medwin's revised version for a prospective new edition (finally edited and published in 1913 by Forman). There Medwin said that he and PBS first began writing alternate chapters of "a wild and extravagant romance," featuring "a hideous witch . . . whose portrait—not a very inviting one—is given in *The Wandering Jew*, . . . almost versified from a passage in our *Nightmare*" (Medwin, *Life,* ed. Forman, 39). After quoting the passage (IV.171–90), Medwin writes: "Shelley having abandoned prose for poetry, now formed a *grand* design, to write a metrical romance on the subject of the Wandering Jew, of which the first three cantos were, with a few additions and alterations, almost entirely mine" (40). After repeating what he had said in *Shelley Papers* down to the plagiarism of the Crucifixion scene, he adds:

The part which I supplied is still in my possession. After seven or eight cantos were *perpetrated*, Shelley sent them to Campbell for his opinion on their merits, with a view to publication. The author of *The Pleasures of Hope* returned the MS. with the remark, that there were only two good lines in it:

> It seemed as if an angel's sigh
> Had breathed the plaintive symphony [i.e., II.196–97]

This criticism of Campbell's gave a death-blow to our hopes of immortality, and so little regard did Shelley entertain for the production, that he left it at his lodgings in Edinburgh, where it was disinterred by some correspondent of *Fraser's*, and in whose magazine, in 1831, four of the cantos appeared. The others he very wisely did not think worth publishing. (40–41)

Medwin goes on to confess that "Shelley's contributions to this juvenile attempt were far the best" and prove "thus early he had imbibed opinions which were often the subject of our controversies. We differed also about the conduct of the poem" (41). He subsequently describes the translation of Schubart's poem on the Wandering Jew as "the fragment, which I, not Shelley, picked up in Lincoln's-Inn-Fields (as mentioned in my preface to *Ahasuerus*), and which was not found till some of the cantos had been written" (42) and discusses PBS's use of the Wandering Jew in his later works. He then mentions that "after Shelley had been matriculated, on his visit to the Bodleian, the first question he put to the librarian, was, whether he had *The Wandering Jew*. He supposed Shelley meant the Periodical so entitled, edited, I believe, by the Marquis d'Argens, who formed one of the wits composing the literary court of Frederick the Great, but told him he knew of no book in German by that name. . . . He was not aware that the fragment which I had accidentally found was not a separate publication, but mixed up with the works of Schubard [*sic*], and had been copied, I believe, from a Magazine of the day" (39–43).

Scholars have pointed to the many errors and contradictions in Medwin's various accounts; for a summary of the arguments against Medwin's claims, see Cameron, *YS*, 309–10. But the strongest evidence against Medwin's authorship of any part of the present text of **WJ** is his own volume *Ahasuerus, The Wanderer: A Dramatic Legend, in six parts* (London: G. & W. B. Whittaker, 1823), published anonymously as "By the Author of Sketches in Hindoostan, and Other Poems." This volume, dedicated to Byron "by his friend," includes in the Preface a version of the legend that closely resembles the prose translation of Schubart's German poem that PBS quotes both in **WJ** and in the notes to **Queen Mab** (**QM**). Medwin claims that at Pisa in the spring of 1822, while PBS, Byron, and he were discussing the note on the Wandering Jew in **QM**, PBS credited Medwin with having found the translation of Schubart's poem; but, writes Medwin, "Though I perfectly remembered the circumstance of having given the note in question to Mr. Shelley, some fifteen years ago, I had a very vague recollection of what it contained, nor at this distance of time can I trace its origin. Whether it was translated by a German master who at that time attended me, from his own language, or was partly his composition, and partly mine, or what its real history is, I am at this moment entirely ignorant" (*Ahasuerus,* viii). By 1847, however, Medwin miraculously remembered far more about this and everything else regarding the early history of PBS's poem on the Wandering Jew, including their joint authorship of it.

Medwin's *Ahasuerus* exhibits none of the special *angst* or intensity of PBS's **WJ** and other early poetry, though it does share enough similarities in plot with **WJ** for S. G. Andrews to claim that in 1847 Medwin's memory of **WJ** became confused with the memory of his own poem, which is in fact a cento from different favorite authors and does have six cantos and a vision in the third canto taken from *The Monk*. Andrews points to the following similarities in plot: in both poems the Wandering Jew falls in love with a woman recently "rescued" from a convent to whom he confesses his true identity in a dramatic scene and who eventually dies, and in both poems an additional central character threatens the Wandering Jew's happiness (*Keats-Shelley Journal* 20 [1971]: 81–82). Set in the Greek Isles, Medwin's poem is light, escapist entertainment similar to a number of oriental tales written by imitators of Byron's early Mediterranean romances. Stylistically it is a pastiche, with several works of PBS besides **WJ** careening through it. The opening lines of Part II (p. 9) resemble the last third of **Epipsychidion:**

> It was an isle, the last of those that lie
> Under the clear light of the Ionian sky,

> Blue as the sea that laves it, all the strand
> With crags is girt as with a cestus, and
> For ever there the breakers leap and bound,
> They sport and play with dolphin gambols round,
> Exultingly—as if it were their own.
> One little creek is there, one cove alone,
> Save for a Suliote fisherman unknown,
> Whose shatter'd bark in storms once found a home
> Worn by the refluence of those waves of foam.

By page 15, couplets have given way to a flaccid blank verse with echoes reminiscent of *Alastor* and sentiments stolen straight from PBS's fragmentary essay **On Love** (for Medwin's early familiarity with and use of this text, see *SC* VI, 633–47):

> He thirsted for his likeness, and he found
> No bosom that could sympathise with his,
> Or dive into the fountains of his mind's
> Deep mysteries; none who could hold intercourse
> Or commune with his soul. There language seem'd
> As of a distant and a savage land,
> Sounds unintelligible, that could make
> No music to his ear, awake no chord
> Of music in his thoughts; he spoke—and lips
> Of mute and motionless ice replied to lips
> Quivering and burning with the heart's best fires.

The derivative quality of Medwin's mature "original" poetry eliminates him as a serious contender for co-author of *WJ*, and his reputation as a literary jackal, earned by his gossipy writings on his younger cousin and Byron, may have been the catalyst that provoked him into claiming that he himself had been the originator of the most ambitious of PBS's juvenile poems. Medwin (who was four years older than PBS) may well have begun a novel with PBS, and the two schoolboys may even have composed jointly such a seven- or eight-canto *prose* romance on the subject of the Wandering Jew as he describes. But the diction, the pace, and quality of the verse, the metaphysical, religious, and psychological concerns, and the great intensity of the four-canto poem published as *WJ*, together with all the external evidence except Medwin's own testimony, point to PBS as its sole author. If he began to write a poem on the legend of the Wandering Jew jointly with Medwin, he certainly recast and recomposed it from new ideas that arose in the course of that juvenile joint effort. If PBS really submitted the joint version to the judgment of Campbell and received a discouraging verdict, he probably looked critically at the initial attempt, decided that Medwin's contributions were inferior, and discarded or rewrote them.

Sources and Influences

PBS's first attempt to publish a substantial poem that would occupy an entire volume has as its tragic hero the mythic figure whom PBS also introduced in his poetry in **Ghasta; or, The Avenging Demon!!!**, the final complete poem in **Original Poetry** "by Victor and Cazire" (**V&C**). That poem depends on information about the Wandering Jew available in M. G. Lewis's *The Monk,* but we cannot be sure whether **Ghasta** was written earlier than **WJ**, or was a spin-off needed to fill out **V&C** (of which it is the penultimate poem), as PBS revised the early version of **WJ** during the summer of 1810. In any case, **WJ** suggests a much wider range of knowledge about the pan-European legend of the Wandering Jew.

George K. Anderson's *The Legend of the Wandering Jew* (Providence, R.I.: Brown UP, 1965; hereafter *Legend/WJ*) traces the legend from its roots in folk myths beginning in the fourth or fifth century A.D., through its full incarnation in the thirteenth-century English chronicles of Roger Wendover and Matthew Paris (both of the Abbey of St. Albans and the "sage monkish writers" that PBS may have consulted). Paris is mentioned in a note on the poem entitled *The Wandering Jew* in Bishop Thomas Percy's *Reliques of Ancient English Poetry* (1765 et seq.), which draws upon the accounts of Matthew Paris, Calmet's *Dictionary of the Bible,* and Volume II, Book 3, Letter 1 of *The Turkish Spy,* an oft reprinted satire on European religion and culture, disguised as a travel book, entitled *Letters Writ by a Turkish Spy,* which first appeared as a whole in English in 1694 and which also contains anti-Cartesian philosophical and humanitarian themes that would have interested PBS.

In any case, PBS knew enough of the tradition to comment on the contradictory aspects of the legend, which Anderson, in *Legend/WJ*, traces to two biblical texts from the Gospel of John and their elaboration in oral tradition: one, based on John 18:4–10, concerns Malchus, a servant of the High Priest, who came to arrest Jesus but whose ear was cut off by Simon Peter and restored by Jesus; the other, based on John 21:20–22 (from which PBS draws his first epigraph to **WJ**), turns on Jesus's saying that John might "tarry" till the Second Coming. Over centuries of cross-fertilization and moralistic elaboration, there grew up various traditions about a witness to Christ's Passion who was immortal and expiated his guilt for rejecting or harassing him by wandering the world (like Cain), sometimes witnessing to Christ's power by prophesying or healing, but in other cases suffering endless tortures without being able to die. In most of the versions, the figure—who eventually assumed the identity of a Jewish shoemaker of Jerusalem named Ahasuerus in *Kurtze Beschreibung und Erzehlung von einem Juden mit Namen Ahasverus* (1602)—was remorseful and longed only for rest.

George Crabbe in *The Parish Register* (1807) notes that among the "valued tomes . . . the pedlar's pack supplied . . . The Wandering Jew has found his way to fame" (*The Poetical Works of the Rev. George Crabbe* [London: John Murray, 1838], II, 146). And, indeed, by the early nineteenth century there were numerous popular English writings, both comic and serious, drawing upon the legend of the Wandering Jew that PBS could have known. Andrew Franklin's *The Wandering Jew: or, Love's Masquerade* (1797), is a routine stage comedy of intrigue and disguise in which the young hero courts his beloved disguised as "the rich Wandering Jew" to impress her avaricious father. There survive also several eighteenth- and early-nineteenth-century English chapbooks recording encounters with the Wandering Jew at Hull and at Portsmouth. Some were published with the title *The Wandering Jew, or The Shoemaker of Jerusalem, who lived when our Lord and saviour Jesus Christ was crucified,* one adding at the end of a long subtitle "*to which is added, his true description of Christ*"; while another, published in London between 1800 and 1809, contains "*a discourse with some clergymen about the end of the world.*" Still another chapbook (ca. 1792–1800) announces the arrival from Canada of a Captain Williams and his ship, the Dolphin, carrying the Wandering Jew and giving the text of a hymn that he sang when alone. Some of these publications were doubtless based on the regular appearances in England of charlatans who pretended to be the Wandering Jew, a contemporary instance being described by Southey in Letter LV of his *Letters from England* (1807 et seq.). Coleridge, who contemplated writing a romance on the Wandering Jew, instead played upon the Wandering Jew tradition in creating the character of his Ancient Mariner (first published in *Lyrical Ballads* [1798]). And even W. Wordsworth published a (forgettable) poem entitled *Song for the Wandering Jew* in the second edition of *Lyrical Ballads* (1800). All these instances and more popular dramas and chapbooks (the largest collections being at Brown University, where Anderson taught, and at Cleveland Public Library) indicate that PBS's interest in the legend was neither singular nor recondite, but his repeated uses of it throughout his career show clearly both that the Wandering Jew had great personal resonance for him and that he did not view the myth as being either humorous or edifying for pious Christians. For the relationship of the myth of the Wandering Jew as the Romantics knew it to stereotypes of itinerant Jewish pedlars in eighteenth- and nineteenth-century England, see Chapter 4, "Wandering Jews, Vagabond Jews," in Frank Felsenstein, *Anti-Semitic Stereotypes: A Paradigm of Otherness in English Popular Culture, 1660–1830* (Johns Hopkins UP, 1995), 58–89, 275–81.

Though Medwin, as we have seen, cited Voltaire's introduction of Ahasuerus in *La Henriade* (his epic about Henri IV, "Henry of Navarre") and though many others have noted the elements of the legend of the Wandering Jew in Godwin's novel *St. Leon* (1799 et seq.; by 1812 one of PBS's favorite works), the strongest literary influences on his early conception of the figure originated in Germany—notably *Der ewige Jude: Eine lyrische Rhapsodie,* by Christian Friedrich Daniel Schubart (1739–91), a poem that focuses on Ahasuerus's persistent defiance in the face of unspeakable tortures and suffering inflicted by an implacable God. PBS quotes one prose version of this unrhymed poetic fragment (111 lines of varying length, written in 1783 and published in 1786) in his note to III.197 of *WJ,* another version in a MS he apparently sent to Hogg from Field Place over the Oxford holidays in late December 1810 or early January 1811 (see MS Pfz; *SC* II, 649–59), and a third in the notes to ***QM*** (q.v.).

Schubart himself had been driven from one German principality to another for his attacks on feudal abuses and in 1777 was kidnapped and imprisoned for ten years without trial by the Duke of Württemberg for his "ridicule of one of the Duke's mistresses" (Victor Lange, *The Classical Age of German Literature, 1740–1815* [New York: Holmes & Meier, 1982], 84). He thus must have put much of himself into his portrayal of the persecuted outcast. PBS encountered this outcry by a kindred soul in a prose translation of (most of) Schubart's poem in the London monthly *La Belle Assemblée* (Jan. 1809, 19–20), where it had been reprinted—with errors—from another London periodical of 1801. In ***Queen Mab,*** PBS claims to have picked up just a fragment of this text in Lincoln's Inn Fields, near which his cousin John Grove lived, but was unable to discover either its title or its author's name. He had reasons, however, for not wishing to quote the whole document in his note to ***QM,*** and the single page of his holograph copy published by Hogg contains portions that, in ***QM,*** he claimed were missing from the text he had seen. Medwin, who claimed credit for finding the fragment from the periodical and giving it to PBS, perhaps owed his knowledge of its discovery from PBS's note to ***QM.***

As Cameron shows in his analysis of the variant published texts (*SC* II, 649–59) and as our collations confirm, PBS's source was the issue of *La Belle Assemblée,* thus making January 1809 the earliest date by which PBS could have encountered Schubart's version of the legend. But he had earlier been impressed by the mythic character in Lewis's *The Monk* (a work largely plagiarized from a German novel). He cribbed from the portrayal of the necromancer in *The Monk* before the influence of the Titanic victim-resister of Schubart's *Der ewige Jude* appears in his work (see the notes to ***Ghasta*** in *V&C*). Medwin names other possible sources of information on the Wandering Jew both in his *Ahasuerus* volume (1824) and in his articles on PBS in the *Athenæum* (1832), and we feel that the portrayal of the rather lonely, domestic Wandering Jew in *WJ* differs so much from the enemy of the Deity's injustice in ***QM*** that the character in *WJ* may well have been conceived before PBS (or Medwin) discovered the translation of Schubart's poem. Possibly PBS's desire to revise *WJ* late in 1810 arose when he first encountered that version, for the attitudes represented there appear chiefly in *WJ*'s fourth and final canto—the part with which the transcribers of PBS's MS seem to have had the greatest difficulty and which was, therefore, very likely the most heavily revised.

Without question, then, the single most influential work on PBS's conception of *WJ* is Lewis's *The Monk*. Whereas local notes in our Commentary point out various resemblances between the two works, one particular subplot is so important to *WJ* that it requires some discussion here. The Wandering Jew appears in the fourth chapter of the novel (Vol. II, Chap. 1) in a plot about Don Raymond, who has fallen in love with Agnes, a woman promised to the Church and about to enter her novitiate. Raymond instead persuades the girl to elope with him during the night when the ghost of the Bleeding Nun is said to walk the castle. Disguised as the ghost, Agnes is to meet Raymond outside of the castle grounds. Ultimately, however, Raymond unwittingly elopes with the ghost herself, to whom he vows eternal love in a refrain that echoes throughout the chapter and is also echoed in *WJ*:

> "Agnes! Agnes! thou art mine!
> Agnes! Agnes! I am thine!
> In my veins while blood shall roll,
> Thou art mine!
> I am thine!
> Thine my body! Thine my soul."
> (ed. Howard Anderson [London: Oxford UP, 1973], 155–56)

The ghost subsequently has the succubus-like power to drain him of life, until the Wandering Jew appears upon the scene to exorcise her, a feat he can accomplish only by unbinding the band of black velvet around his forehead to reveal a burning cross impressed upon his brow. PBS appears to have borrowed and collapsed the novitiate plot (perhaps by way of Radcliffe's *The Italian;* see Commentary to **I.183–202**) so that the Wandering Jew himself runs off with the novice. The Wandering Jew's supernatural powers and his hidden burning cross were also taken from Lewis, who seems to be the first writer to use the device of the burning cross.

The Ghost of the Bleeding Nun subplot was so popular that it was reproduced independently of the novel in several different forms, including a two-act play written by Henry W. Grossette and performed during 1809 in London under the title: *Raymond and Agnes, The Travellers Benighted; or, The Bleeding Nun of Lindenberg*. Perhaps this play, produced in the same year in which PBS began composing *WJ*, drew his attention to the possibilities of adapting the plot for his own purposes. Moreover, in the same issue of *La Belle Assemblée* in which PBS found the translation of Schubart's poem about the Wandering Jew, the immediately preceding story is "Laurenstein Castle; or, The Ghost of the Nun," another adaptation of the Bleeding Nun story—including the "I am thine" refrain—in which Raymond and Agnes are replaced by Frederic and Emily, and a mysterious "old Lieutenant" who performs the exorcism. In the Advertisement to *The Monk*, Lewis mentions that the Bleeding Nun story is "a tradition still credited in many parts of Germany; and I have been told, that the ruins of the Castle of *Lauenstein*, which She is supposed to haunt, may yet be seen upon the borders of *Thuringia*" (6). In pairing "Laurenstein Castle" with Schubart's poem, the editor of *La Belle Assemblée* was obviously recalling the connection in *The Monk* of the Bleeding Nun story with that of the Wandering Jew. Indeed, the translation of Schubart, titled "The Wandering Jew," not only begins on the bottom of the page in which "Laurenstein Castle" ends (p. 19), but is prefaced by the following note: "Our Readers are acquainted with the uses to which Mr. Lewis, in his Novel of the Monk, has converted the ancient legend of the Wandering Jew.—The original story was the invention of the celebrated Schubart, and is as follows." PBS, who was so impressed with the Bleeding Nun subplot that he also uses it in **Ghasta**, would certainly have noted the significance of the pairing in *La Belle Assemblée*.

Stylistically, both the structure and meter of **WJ** are modeled on the popular poetic romances of Scott. Besides debts to the poetry of Scott, Lewis, Campbell (especially *Gertrude of Wyoming*) and, probably, Southey for the handling of the narrative, PBS—as his epigraphs suggest—drew themes, imagery, and diction from the Bible and the writings of Shakespeare (especially *Hamlet* and *Macbeth*) and Milton. In spite of PBS's choice of acceptable models of the time, the poem's versification, though varied, suffers (as the first editors of **WJ** noted) from repetitions of words and phrases designed to maintain the rhyme scheme but adding little to the meaning. The only contemporary notice of **WJ** that we have found, by Maria Jane Jewsbury in the *Athenæum* for 16 July 1831, finds the publication of **WJ** in *Fraser's* "to all intents and purposes, as important, in point of length, as Lord Byron's early poems; and we do not see why the accidental form of publication should militate against its lying equally open to criticism" (456). Jewsbury judges **WJ** to be "a 'wonderful attempt' [quoting from *Fraser's*], containing, with all its schoolboyism, the germ of the 'Prometheus,'" noting further, "One thing surprises us—there is very little promise of Shelley's after *versification;* and there is a good deal of Sir Walter Scott's manner in the descriptions" (457).

Editorial Analysis, Copy-Text, and Emendations

Modern Shelleyans must be grateful to the editors of *1829E* and *1831F* for preserving from oblivion the outlines and much of the text of **WJ**, enabling us to glimpse the lineaments of PBS's earliest surviving ambitious poem. But without access to the original MS of **WJ** (which may still survive in some attic in Scotland), we cannot be sure how closely our two sources follow the poet's text. We are left, at present, with a muddled transmission that shows us mainly how PBS's early admirers encountered what he intended as his first major poetic effort.

We judge that *1829E*—especially its original articles of 27 June and 4 July 1829—is more accurate in its textual details for the portions of the poem that it includes than is the more nearly complete text published in *1831F*; where the two texts coincide, *1831F* follows the text of *1829E* in most minor textual features, such as commas at the ends of lines and apostrophes to elide past participles from *ed* to *'d*. These correspondences appear only, however, in the lines of *1829E* in the main articles of 27 June and 4 July; there are much greater discrepancies between the two texts in the additional section of Canto IV (**IV.271–331**) that appeared in *ELJ* on 26 December (425–26). This difference suggests that the unanimity between the two texts on minor matters of punctuation and orthography must have originated in *1829E* and been copied by *1831F*, rather than residing in PBS's underlying MS, which—if we are right in thinking that it was a safekeeping copy like the notebook containing the Esdaile poems (**Esd** MS Pfz)—would lack much necessary punctuation throughout. This hypothesis is further borne out by the presence of closing quotation marks at the end of II.192 in both texts: in *1829E* these quotation marks signal the end of an excerpt, but they have no functional role whatsoever in *1831F*, where they seem to be an uncaught error derived from *1829E*. Thus we infer that the literary man (probably Heraud) who borrowed PBS's MS from H. G. Bell also had clippings of the June and July *ELJ* articles and used the text of *1829E*, rather than PBS's MS itself, as press copy for the corresponding passages in *1831F*. On the other hand, the December 1829 publication of **IV.271–331** as "AN INCANTATION SCENE.—A POEM, HITHERTO UNPUBLISHED, *By Percy Byshe* [sic] *Shelley*" apparently did not come to the attention of the editor of *1831F*, for in the two texts those lines differ markedly in words as well as orthography and punctuation.

Differences elsewhere in the poem can be explained (the Glasheens note) by citing the need in *1831F* to maintain rhyme patterns and include all plot elements, while abridging the text slightly to keep within the allotted space; but the quantity and nature of the verbal divergences in **IV.271–331** suggest that in the case of those lines two transcribers were working independently to decipher a passage of the MS complicated either by alternative versions of some lines or by partially illegible cancellations and interlineations, from which each transcriber tried to construct a coherent text as best he could. Both possibilities suggest a heavily revised text, like those found in such revised safekeeping copies as the Bod MSS of **Prom** and a few poems in the larger Harvard Shelley Notebook, thus not only supporting the Glasheens (against *1989*) on Shelley's delivery of a revised MS to Edinburgh in 1811 but also suggesting why both published texts are incomplete. The editor of *1829E* probably found transcribing the whole poem so difficult or burdensome that he contented himself with those passages that were most fully legible; later, when the editor of *1831F*, to assert that he had gone beyond his predecessor, attempted to transcribe text that he did not find in *ELJ*, he was forced to omit passages and to improvise when presenting those that proved too difficult to transcribe with precision. Modern editors of PBS's literary drafts and intermediate copies will sympathize with these working journalists, trying to transcribe nearly illegible passages quickly to meet their deadlines. The editor of *1831F*, forced to improvise, began to guess at some readings and to invent where he could not decipher—expedients that, once adopted, tend to become habitual.

To summarize our analysis of the two primary textual authorities: Agreement of the two texts suggests not so much the state of PBS's underlying MS as it does the reliance of *1831F* on *1829E*. Unless either PBS's MS notebook that was held successively by the Ballantynes and H. G. Bell or the (doubtless imperfect) copy made from that MS and submitted to *FM* should resurface, there is no way to critique the individual readings of either periodical text. At present we have no choice but to follow them, giving preference to textual details in *1829E*. After considering the textual evidence (available in our apparatus) and the logical inferences drawn from parallels with PBS's other MSS, we must rely (as did *1831F*) on *1829E* for the passages transcribed there. Though the editor of *1829E* abridged the poem, he did not (so far as we can determine) alter the words, and in only one instance (**IV.271**) did he misrepresent the syntax, in order to begin "An Incantation Scene" without syntactical connection to the previous lines. Where *1831F* provides the sole witness to the lost authority, we perforce follow its readings, but we know that the text has been abridged more than we can identify, for as the Glasheens point out ("Publication of WJ," 13), the Introduction to *WJ* in the June 1831 issue of *FM* (536) quotes three lines from "the end of the fourth canto" that do not otherwise appear in either text of the poem we have. These lines, which seem to contain a personal note, read:

> 'Tis mournful when the deadliest hate
> Of friends, of fortune, and of fate
> Is levelled at one fated head.

The literary man who wrote that article and apparently edited the *1831F* version may have omitted the passage in which these lines appear on critical grounds, for just after quoting these lines, he comments on the poem's "poverty of rhymes" and we observe that both **III.214** and **III.287** also end with the words "fated head."

If *Esd* MS Pfz is taken as an example of the state of PBS's safekeeping notebooks of the period, much of the punctuation in *1829E* and *1831F* must represent editorial additions, but we accept most of it, because those periodicals clearly incorporate *some* of PBS's punctuation and follow conventions closer to his time and milieu than have subsequent editors. Similarly, although PBS characteristically indented lines in his poetic MSS to show variations in the rhyme scheme, his original indentations for the sometimes complicated rhyme schemes of *WJ* are not recoverable through the interventions of *ELJ* and *FM*. In the absence of the MS, we follow the indentations in our copy-text, which, for the lines contained in *ELJ*, remains the best witness to PBS's practice in his MS. *FM* had to forgo indentations, because it printed *WJ* in a reasonably large type and in double columns so narrow as to cause many awkward runover lines even without frequent indentations. In general, we rarely emend our two copy-text authorities, discussing, as usual, our decisions in the notes.

Collation

To illustrate the main lines of textual transmission of *WJ*, we collate at the foot of the page *1829E, 1829Inc* ("An Incantation Scene"), and *1831F*, to which we add the portions of the text used as epigraphs in *St.Irv* (collated as *1811*). We do not include as variants the quotation marks in *1829E* that indicate the beginning and ending of excerpts from PBS's MS.

WJ appears in the second volume of William Dugdale's piracy, *The Works of Percy Bysshe Shelley* (London, 1839), but was not included in the other major pirated editions of the 1830s or in the editions of MWS. We do not provide collations of Dugdale's text, which was based directly upon *FM*, with the mistaken omission of **I.103** and the epigraph from *Eumenides* to Canto IV, as well as the introduction of several typos. Dugdale also freely alters the spelling and punctuation of *Fraser's*, often omitting the punctuation at the end of the line or even at the end of a verse paragraph. To illustrate the later transmission of *WJ*, we collate at the back of the book the following significant editions: *1887D, 1892W, 1927, 1972*, and *1989*, to which we add the quotations of the text in Medwin's *Life*, ed. Forman (collated as *1913*).

WJ did not appear in *1870, 1876, 1878, 1904,* and *1970*, all of which instead provide two excerpts from the poem: **III.215–23,** which also was used as an epigraph to Chapter 10 of *St.Irv,* appearing as "Fragment from the Wandering Jew" ("The Elements respect their Maker's seal!"), and **IV. 383–90,** which appears as "Song from the Wandering Jew" ("See yon opening flower," or "See yon opening rose"). *1911* provides neither *WJ*, nor the fragments, but *1927* gives both.

PBS's notes, which *1831F* first published, appear as footnotes to the text and are discussed below.

Title. According to *ELJ* (27 June 1829), "Mr Shelley appears to have had some doubts whether to call his poem 'The Wandering Jew,' or 'The Victim of the Eternal Avenger.' Both names occur in the manuscript; . . . it is to be hoped that he would finally have fixed on the former, . . . as the poem itself contains very little calculated to give offense to the religious reader" (43). If PBS did gain a new conception of *WJ* from Schubart's poem after he had completed the text he first sent to Ballantyne, he may well have added the "Eternal Avenger" when he revised Canto IV, and it would thus represent his latest intention. This point cannot be settled, however, without access to the MS.

Epigraph. In the final chapter of the Gospel according to St. John, after the Resurrection "Jesus shewed himself again to the disciples at the sea of Tiberius" while they were fishing. After they had landed the Miraculous Draught of Fishes and had eaten, Jesus questioned Peter about his loyalty, and when Peter asked him about John ("the disciple whom Jesus loved"), Jesus replied, "If I will that he tarry till I come, what is that to thee? follow thou me" (21:22). This verse, as noted above, is one of the two key scriptural passages that were embroidered in the legend of the Wandering Jew.

Dedication. Sir Francis Burdett, Baronet (1770–1844) was an able and fearless spokesman for the Foxite Whigs in the House of Commons. (See the note to **line 9** of the second poem in *V&C*). During the summer of 1812, PBS was apparently writing regularly to Burdett (whose son Robert was the poet's classmate at Eton), a correspondence that brought PBS under the suspicious eyes of the local constabulary and that was reported to Lord Sidmouth, the Home Secretary, by Henry Drake, Town Clerk of Barnstaple on 20 August 1812 (Public Record Office, H.O. 42/127; see Commentary to *Devil's Walk*).

Preface. Though it is not clear that PBS actually did consult any "sage monkish writers," he most likely refers to the chronicles of Roger of Wendover (d. 1236) and Matthew Paris (ca. 1200–1259), both English Benedictine monks at the Abbey of St. Albans (in Hertfordshire). Roger recorded the first known British sighting of the Wandering Jew in his *Chronica sive, Flores historiarum* (ca. 1235, which was also the source of Lady Godiva's famous ride). Matthew Paris appropriated, revised, and continued Roger's chronicle, embellishing it with notes and broadening its scope (see Anderson, *Legend/WJ*, 18–21). The chronicle, first printed in London in 1571, was subsequently transmitted as Paris's work, and it is so cited in Percy's *Reliques*, where it may have come to PBS's attention.

PBS's jab at the folly of anticipating future events, including superstitions of the battle of Armageddon suggests not only that he was aware of popular publications such as that in which the Wandering Jew prophesied "about the end of the world" (see "Sources," above) but that by the time he released this version of *WJ*, he regarded the Bible as a source of superstition, for there is a clear scriptural basis in Revelation 16:16 for this final, apocalyptic struggle between God's power and the forces of evil at Armageddon (Greek: Harmagedon, a transliteration of the Hebrew for "Mountain of Megiddo[n]"—perhaps a corrupted allusion to the *plain* of Meggido[n], the site of several crucial Old Testament battles).

In the Introduction to *1887D*, Dobell remarks that PBS's comment about the absence of annotations "is a side-blow at Sir Walter Scott, and rather an unfair one, considering that *The Wandering Jew* bears evident tokens that its author had diligently studied Scott's poetical romances" (xxii). PBS was to more than make up for the paucity of annotations in *WJ* while writing **QM**. By June 1811, PBS had lost patience with Scott's poetry: "I am not very enthusiastic in the cause of Walter Scott—the aristocratical tone which his writings assume does not prepossess me in his favor, since my opinion is that all poetical beauty ought to be subordinate to the inculcated moral—that metaphorical language ought to be a pleasing vehicle for useful & momentous instruction" (***Letters*** I, 98).

Medwin claims that both ***St.Irv*** and ***WJ*** were influenced by PBS's reading of Godwin's *St. Leon,* "which Shelley . . . read . . . till he believed that there was truth in Alchymy, and the *Elixir Vitæ,* which indeed entered into the plot of *The Wandering Jew,* of which I possess a preface by him, intended for the poem, had it been published" (*Life,* ed. Forman, 49). We provide the portion of this supposed Preface that Medwin actually quotes, but there is no supporting evidence that it relates directly to ***WJ***:

> The opinion that gold can be made, passed from the Arabs to the Greeks, and from the Greeks to the rest of Europe; those who professed it, gradually assumed the form of a sect, under the name of Alchymists. These Alchymists laid it down as a first principle, that all metals are composed of the same materials, or that the substances at least that form gold, exist in all metals, contaminated indeed by various impurities, but capable of being brought to a perfect state, by purification; and hence that considerable quantities of gold might be extracted from them. The generality of this belief in the eastern provinces of the Roman empire, is proved by a remarkable edict of Dioclesian [*sic*], quoted by Gibbon from the authority of two ancient historians, &c. (*Life,* ed. Forman, 49–50)

Neither PBS's bona fide Preface, nor the Dedication appears in *1831F.*

Epigraph to Canto I. Although this passage from *Paradise Lost* (*PL*) (IV.73–76, 78) is part of Satan's internal debate before he confirms himself in evil and betrays Eve and Adam, PBS seems to have extracted it to characterize the psychological misery, rather than corrupted nature, of his own protagonist. Perhaps PBS cited this passage from memory: his epigraph omits IV.77 ("Still threat'ning to devour me opens wide"). Satan's lines are later echoed by the Wandering Jew at **III.136–37**.

I.1–28. Scott's poetic narratives also begin with natural descriptions but ones more integrated with the plots of his poems (e.g., the chase of the stag that opens *The Lady of the Lake*). The opening of *WJ*, on the other hand, displays PBS's diction, tone, and perspective that continually enlist the denotations and connotations of words and the mellifluous quality of their sounds to transform solid physical objects into transient, etherial states of moral significance. These qualities can be exemplified briefly without reference to compulsory rhyme words: Diffused (**2**), tinged (**4, 5**), aslant (**7**), laved (**9**), luxury to grieve (**13**), pure and genial . . . skies (**15**).

I.1. orb of parting day: "Orb of day" was a conventional poeticism for the sun and was a particular favorite of Southey, who uses it in such poems as *Joan of Arc, Thalaba the Destroyer,* and *Madoc* (all greatly admired by PBS), as well as in several shorter pieces.

I.14. so balm the air: the air was fragrant and soothing. Though *balm* does not appear as an adjective in the *OED* or dictionaries contemporary with PBS, he was probably following the poetic license that allows *chill* to appear in place of *chilly* when the metrics require it. (Cf. Byron's use of *chill* and *mirk* in the note to **II.1**, below.)

I.20. when: This reading in *1831F*, which emphasizes the temporal over the spatial "where" in *1829E*, better fits the passage—which concerns "intervals" of sound that punctuate the tranquil silence—and probably represents a more acute deciphering of PBS's hand, in which *when* and *where* can look very similar.

I.35. tabor's sound: One likely source of this phrase is Wordsworth's *Ode . . . Immortality,* where the exact phrase "tabor's sound" appears in the third and tenth stanzas; it may evidence PBS's early reading of Wordsworth's *Poems; in Two Volumes* (1807). After the word *drum* came into use (16th cen.), *tabor* was used to describe a small drum without snares, usually associated with pipes and other peasant instruments. Used by Spenser once (*Epithalamion,* line 131) and by Shakespeare in six plays (most notably at the beginning of *Twelfth Night* III.i), *tabor* had become archaic and relatively rare by the end of the eighteenth century, though the word appears in "The Scenes of Conway" in *Poems* (1808) by Felicia Dorothea Browne (later Hemans). Medwin, who subscribed to Browne's 1808 volume, "made her and her works the frequent subject of conversation with Shelley" and claimed that the volume "made a powerful impression" on PBS, who promptly began a correspondence with her (see *Life*, ed. Forman, 58–59). PBS wrote the latter portions of this correspondence under the pseudonym of "Philippe Sidney" (see B. C. Barker-Benfield, *Shelley's Guitar* [Oxford: Bodleian Library, 1992], 26). He later mentions her in a letter written to Hogg ca. 28 July 1811: "Now there is Miss F. D. Browne . . . [who] surpasses my sister in poetical talents, this your dispassionate criticism *must* allow—that lovely extract of her poems *certainly* surpasses any of Eliza's . . ." (**Letters** I, 129).

I.48. pale distrust: Edward Young invokes "Pale distrust" as the "assistant" of "Experience" in disabusing innocent youth's claim to joy (*The Complaint; or, Night Thoughts on Life, Death, and Immortality* [1742; London: Longman, 1796]: VIII.310–11).

I.58–89. *1829E* omits these lines and provides the following summary: "Amidst the sights and sounds of the scene thus described, a traveller is seen descending the hills in the vicinity of Padua. He is attracted by the tolling of a convent bell, and seeing a crowd assembled at the gate, he enters, along with others, the convent chapel, after the sun has already set and vespers are over: . . ."

I.90–101. Dim . . . tracery disclose: Curt R. Zimansky calls attention to the resemblance between the chapel in *WJ* and the Church of the Capuchins in *The Monk* ("Shelley's *Wandering Jew:* Some Borrowings from Lewis and Radcliffe," *Studies in English Literature* 18 [1978]: 604): "The faint beams of the rising Moon scarcely could pierce through the gothic obscurity of the Church. . . . The Moon-beams darting into the Church through painted windows, tinged the fretted roofs and massy pillars with a thousand various tints of light and colours . . ." (*The Monk*, 26).

I.91. saint-cipher'd panes: stained-glass windows that illustrate the lives of the saints.

I.97. Footnote. coigne . . . pile: *1831F* supplies a footnote, presumably from PBS, that cites a line from *Macbeth*. The full sentence, spoken by Banquo, reads: "No jutty, frieze, | Buttress, nor coign of vantage, but this bird | Hath made his pendant bed and procreant cradle" (I.vi.6–8).

As the *OED* points out, the use of *coign* to mean a projecting corner or point from which observation can be safely made descends from this passage in *Macbeth*, which was later used by Scott in both *Heart of Midlothian* and *Quentin Durward*.

I.102–49. *1829E* omits these lines and supplies the following summary: "A young novice is about to take the veil, or rather, it is about to be forced upon her. She is thus spoken of: . . ."

I.104. Saint Pietro's rich ornaments blaze: The chapel contains a shrine to Saint Peter, which is probably ornamented with large golden keys (diagonally crossed), the icon with which he is most closely associated (Matthew 16:19: "I will give unto thee the keys of the kingdom of Heaven"). Other associated icons with which the shrine might be decorated include an inverted cross, a crozier with triple transverses (representing the papacy), a book (representing the gospels), a cock, a ship, or a fish.

PBS's Anglo-Italian hybridization of the name, Saint Pietro, was not uncommon in his day.

I.108–9. Melting . . . inspiring: As *1887D* suggests, these lines may recall Pope's "The Dying Christian to his Soul, Ode," Part II of "Adaptations of the Emperor Hadrian": "Trembling, hoping, ling'ring, flying, | Oh the pain, the bliss of dying!" (lines 3–4), which themselves are based on Thomas Flatman's earlier translation of Hadrian's lines: "Fainting, gasping, trembling, crying, | Panting, groaning, speechless, dying . . ." (*Poems and Songs* [London: Benjamin Took, 1674]).

I.140–41. The heart . . . virtuous so: Cf. PBS's attack on "Monkish" chastity as false virtue in *QM,* note 9.

I.166. Sabean: Sabà (biblical Sheba), a land in pre-Islamic southwestern Arabia, in what is now Yemen, was famous since antiquity for its aromatic spices. The spelling "Sabæan" in *1831F* was an alternative in PBS's day. A common poeticism, the adjective appears in poems by Sidney, Milton, Pope, Seward, Southey, and Hemans.

I.168–II.78. *1829E* omits this long portion of the poem, substituting the following summary:

Just as the ceremony is about to be performed, the intended victim, by a sudden impulse, throws herself among the crowd, and rushes from the chapel. The stranger, who has already felt interested in her fate, flies to her assistance, catches her in his arms, and bears her away through the gathering twilight beyond the reach of pursuit. A storm comes on; they seek shelter, and briefly inform each other who they are. The nun's name is Rosa, and the stranger is Paulo—the Wandering Jew. They conceive, strangely enough, a sudden affection for each other, and the first canto closes with the expression of Rosa's consent to share the future fortunes of Paulo. It is curious to observe, before proceeding to the second canto, that, in illustration of something said by Paulo, Shelley quotes, in the margin, the following line from Æschylus, so remarkably applicable to his own future fate,—
("Εμε θανοντος γαια μιχθητο ποζι").
In canto second, we are introduced to Paulo's castle on the banks of the Po, where he lives in deep retirement with Rosa, visited only by Victorio, an Italian of noble birth, who resides in the neighbourhood. Some bold and vigorous descriptions of Alpine scenery follow. But it is evident that Paulo is not happy, and he spends a wild, uneasy life: . . .

The line of Greek can be translated: "When I die the earth is mingled with fire," and it can be found as Fragment 430 (Adespota) in Augustus Nauck's *Tragicorum Graecorum Fragmenta* (Leipzig: Teubner, 1856; it is absent from the most recent edition of the *Tragicorum Graecorum Fragmenta*, ed. Bruno Snell [1971]). This line, which was widely used in antiquity and collected in florilegia, is discussed by Cicero in *de Finibus* (3, 19, 64). Rather than attributing it to Aeschylus, Cicero indicates that it was a cliché: "the claim of those who declare that they care not if when they themselves are dead the universal conflagration follows (as is usually proclaimed in a certain popular Greek verse) is considered wicked and inhuman." Given its proverbial status, PBS could have seen the line in several different sources (e.g., both Nero and Tiberius quote it, and it is discussed by Seneca the Younger in *de Clementia*, II, sec. 2). It is unclear whether PBS himself or the editor of *ELJ* attributes the line to Aeschylus.

I.183–202. The novice . . . senses fled: Although the Agnes–Don Raymond subplot of *The Monk* underlies this scene, Zimansky suggests as an intermediate source, Chapter 11 of Radcliffe's *The Italian* (1797), which, in a scene based on *The Monk*, portrays an unwilling novice (Ellena) refusing to take the veil (resisting an imperious abbess) and fainting into the arms of her lover Vivaldi, who has entered the chapel just in time to witness the ceremony ("Borrowings," 608). Zimansky speculates that PBS took the name Rosa from the character Ellena Rosalba and the name Paulo from Vivaldi's servant Paulo, but see note to **I.217**, below.

I.202–3. Here and throughout we follow *1831F* in supplying a row of asterisks to indicate a lacuna in the text.

I.203–14. Hark! . . . earthquake rocks the ground: PBS may have considered glossing this passage about violent disturbances in the earth and sky with the passage from Revelation 6:12 that he copied into his pocket diary for the week of 26 February–1 March 1810 under the title "wandering Jew": "& I behel[d] when he had opened the 6th seal there was a great Earthquake & the sun becam[e] black as sackcloth & the moon as red as blood." For the other passage from Revelation in this diary entry, see the Commentary below to PBS's **footnote** to **I.234**.

I.204. I see: the first of only a few references to the narrator in the first person (see also **I.207, IV.58, IV.112**).

I.217. Rosa: Beyond Zimansky's suggestion that PBS took the name Rosa from *The Italian*, PBS may have had in mind Maddalena Rosa, the heroine of William Henry Ireland's *The Abbess. A Romance* (1799), a convent boarder who is victimized by an evil abbess. The name could also derive from "Rosa Matilda" (Charlotte Dacre), the author of two of PBS's favorite romances,

Confessions of a Nun of St. Omer's (whose heroine, Cazire, provided the Cazire of ***V&C***) and *Zofloya, or, The Moor: A Romance of the Fifteenth Century,* which influenced much of his early work in both poetry and fiction (see Commentary to **Revenge**, p. 180). Medwin calls both ***Zastrozzi*** and ***St.Irv*** "Rosa-Matilda-like production[s]" (*Life,* ed. Forman, 49).

PBS's **Ballad** *("The death-bell beats!—"),* published in ***St.Irv*** and written at about the same time as ***WJ****,* features a monk tormented by remorse for his role in the death of his beloved Rosa (a nun, like the novice Rosa in ***WJ***), who also longs for death. Like the Wandering Jew, the monk is cursed by a spell that prevents him from dying; unlike the Wandering Jew, the monk is permitted to die at the end of the poem. Of course, **"The death-bell beats!—"** and ***WJ*** follow conventional Gothic plots with important roots in Lewis's *The Monk.* Cf. also Lewis's *The Black Canon of Elmham* in ***V&C****.*

I.224. The: The change to "Came the" in *1972* is conjectural and unsupported by the primary witnesses.

I.227. beetling cliffs: Cf. *Hamlet* I.iv.69–71: "What if it tempt you toward the flood, my lord, | Or to the dreadful summit of the cliff | That beetles o'er his base into the sea. . . ."

I.234. Footnote: PBS copied this passage from Revelation in his pocket diary entry for the week of 26 February–1 March 1810 under the heading "wandering Jew" (see "Textual History," above). We have corrected *"Revelations"* in *1831F* to *Revelation.*

I.239–49. stranger's glance . . . her brain: In *The Monk,* the Wandering Jew explains, "Such is the curse imposed on me. . . . I am doomed to inspire all who look on me with terror and detestation" (Lewis, ed. H. Anderson, 170). PBS's Wandering Jew is also apparently able to inspire love.

I.262–65. this earthly frame . . . hell: a reference to Judgment Day (see note to **III.387,** below).

I.263. bickering flame: quivering, flashing. PBS would have found this phrase (which appears several times in ***WJ***) in Milton's description of the "Chariot of Paternal Deity," about which "roll'd | . . . smoke and bickering flame" (*PL* VI.765–66), a description on which PBS drew often throughout his poetic career.

I.276–77. mine . . . I am thine: As *1887D* pointed out (p. 108), these lines echo a refrain in Chapter 4 of Lewis's *The Monk,* where they are first inadvertently addressed by Don Raymond to the ghost of the Bleeding Nun, who he thinks is Agnes in disguise. PBS echoes this same passage in **II.225–27** and in **Ghasta** in ***V&C****,* lines 73–76 and 93–96.

I.300. meteor-bolt: lightning bolt. PBS characteristically uses *meteor* to signify any atmospheric phenomenon, its primary contemporary meaning.

I.304. basements: foundations.

I.322–25. Illumined ... beams divine: This description of Paulo's face is echoed in his later vision of the face of the resurrected Christ, **III.81–83**.

I.335. thee: *1989* provides no rationale for changing thee to "these," an apparent error.

II. Epigraph. These lines are addressed to Hamlet by the ghost of his father, who would render such a harrowing tale, were he not "forbid | To tell the secrets of my prison-house ... To ears of flesh and blood" (I.v.13–22).

II.1. nightly blast: *1887D* initiated an influential but unnecessary change to "mighty blast."

Cf. **Ghasta**, line 194, and Byron, "Chill and mirk is the nightly blast, | Where Pindus' mountains rise, | And angry clouds are pouring fast | The vengeance of the skies" ("Stanzas," lines 1–4; *CPW* I, 275). Although Byron's lyric was written in October 1809, it was not published until the first edition of *Childe Harold's Pilgrimage* (1812).

II.21. Victorio: For PBS's use in various forms of the name Victor, see Commentary to *V&C*, p. 155.

II.24. cliff's side: In *1831F*, the apostrophe in "cliff's" is either missing or obscured by the top of the preceding *f*, leading perhaps to the reading "cliffs'" in *1989*. There is, however, a clear space left for the apostrophe between the *f* and *s*.

II.35. winding Po: Paulo's castle is located on the banks of the Po, which descends from the Cottian Alps in the northwest through northern Italy to the Adriatic Sea, some sixty miles southeast of Padua. Since the castle is located both on the banks of the Po and within sight of the ocean, it must be near the Foci del Po (the mouths of the Po). The only such location that is both on a "mountain" and within sight of the Adriatic Sea may be Monte Rua', the highest of the Colli Euganei, from which PBS was later to look down upon Venice, Padua, and the sea when he drafted his **Lines written among the Euganean Hills**—apparently near the imagined site of Paulo's castle.

II.40. Cosmo's blood: Victorio descends from Cosimo de Medici (1389–1464; known posthumously as "The Father of his Country"), who along with his brother Lorenzo founded the famous line of the Medici family. Lorenzo's great-great-grandson Cosimo de Medici (1519–74) became

Duke of Florence and Grand Duke of Tuscany, ultimately reigning as Cosimo I; his descendants (including Cosimo II and III) ruled Florence into the mid-eighteenth century.

PBS's contemporaries commonly referred to Cosimo as "Cosmo." Cf. Byron's, *Childe Harold* IV: "Our veneration for the Medici begins with Cosmo and expires with his grandson; that stream is pure only at the source; and it is in search of some memorial of the virtuous republicans of the family, that we visit the church of St. Lorenzo at Florence (IV.532 note; *CPW* II, 244).

II.64. night's dull ear: This phrase, from the Prologue to Act IV of Shakespeare's *Henry V* ("Steed threatens steed, in high and boastful neighs | Piercing the night's dull ear") appeared also in the work of PBS's contemporaries Charles Lloyd ("Oswald, A Poem," I.96) and Charlotte Smith ("On the Departure of the Nightingale," 4), both of whom place quotation marks around it.

In omitting the stanza break after this line, *1892W* and *1927* are following *1887D*, where the line break comes at the bottom of a page.

II.76. beam: *1887D* initiated an unnecessary change to "beams."

II.78. A transient requiem from woe: rephrased in **III.135:** "A transient respite from my woe."

II.94, 102–10. Why then unbidden . . . | Then would cold . . . skeleton hand: These lines were excerpted as an epigraph for Chapter 8 of *St.Irv* and are collated as *1811* (p. 149):

> —— Why then unbidden gush'd the tear?
> * * * * * * *
> Then would cold shudderings seize his brain,
>   As gasping he labour'd for breath;
> The strange gaze of his meteor eye,
> Which, frenzied, and rolling dreadfully,
>   Glar'd with hideous gleam,
> Would chill like the spectre gaze of Death,
>   As, conjur'd by feverish dream,
> He seems o'er the sick man's couch to stand,
> And shakes the fell lance in his skeleton hand.

For the depiction of death in this passage, see the note to **IV.114–15.**

II.97–98. gaze . . . strange form was near: In *The Monk*, the Wandering Jew has the ability to see spirits and ghosts invisible to others.

II.99. fillet: a band of material worn around his forehead. In *The Monk*, at the crucial point of his exorcism, the Wandering Jew unbinds "the sable band from his fore-head. . . . [revealing] a burning Cross impressed upon his brow" (172).

II.118–19. <u>The ministering angel . . . agony</u>: *1887D* suggests a borrowing from Scott's *Marmion* (1808) VI.xxxi.5–6: "When pain and anguish wring the brow, | A ministering angel thou"—which itself echoes Laertes's speech in *Hamlet:* "I tell thee, churlish priest, | A minist'ring angel shall my sister be | When thou liest howling" (V.i.240–42).

II.127. <u>He sank . . . breast</u>: After this line, *1829E* comments, without omitting any text: "These and similar passages naturally prepare the mind of the reader for the history of the Wandering Jew,—to which indeed they are merely introductory. We can afford room for only one other extract from this canto; it is a passage immediately preceding the commencement of Paulo's narrative, and is one not unworthy the future author of 'Prometheus': . . ."

II.141. <u>ghosts of the mighty dead</u>: As *1989* suggests, the phrase occurs in James Montgomery's "Ode to the Volunteers of Britain on the Prospect of Invasion" (in *The Wanderer of Switzerland and Other Poems* [1806], 133), but *ghost, mighty,* and *dead* were favorite words in PBS's vocabulary throughout his poetic career. Cf. **"Ghosts of the dead!"** (the second poem in **St.Irv**) and "the tombless ghosts of the guilty dead" in line 56 of **The Spectral Horseman,** the fourth poem in **PF.**

II.182. <u>sea-mew</u>: Though the name is that of the common sea-gull, the phrase <u>sea-mew</u> took on symbolic significance from Milton's *Paradise Lost* XI.829–38, in which Michael tells how the Mount of Paradise will be washed down to "an Island salt and bare, | The haunt of Seals and Orcs, and Sea-mews' clang." Cf. also **Euganean Hills,** line 125.

II.192. In *1829E* there is a closing quotation mark after "there" that signals the end of its excerpt; the same mark is found in *1831F* and might simply reflect its dependence on *1829E,* since there is no opening quotation mark to which it corresponds. Neither text uses quotation marks to set off the Song (**II.161–92**) as a whole, or any of its stanzas.

II.193–98. <u>She ceased . . . their close</u>: These lines, in Medwin's *Life,* ed. Forman, in a footnote on pages 40–41, are collated as *1913;* Medwin claimed that **lines 196–97** were judged by Thomas Campbell to be the "only two good lines" in the entire poem (40).

II.193–227. *1829E* replaces this passage with the following summary: "At the conclusion of the song, Paulo declares his intention to relate to Rosa and Victorio, who is also with him, his past adventures, which he accordingly does in the next canto. Cantos third and fourth are by far the finest; but our extracts having been so copious already, we must postpone their consideration till next Saturday, when we promise our readers several passages of thrilling power and beauty."

II.220. With: The unwarranted change to "Wild" in *1887D* has been followed by most subsequent editors.

III. Epigraph. Taken from Milton's *Paradise Lost* (I.591–94, 600–602), this passage describes the fallen host's perception of Satan, "Thir dread commander" (I.589), as he prepares to address them for the first time since their expulsion from Heaven.

III.1–8. "'Tis sixteen hundred . . . riven womb: *1829E* substitutes for this passage the following summary:

> We resume with much pleasure our analysis of this truly interesting poem.
> We have already given some account of the two first Cantos. The third is occupied with a retrospective view of the hero's fortunes and wanderings, which he relates to his bride Rosa, and the noble Italian Victorio. We look upon the following passage, with which he commences his narrative, as worthy of the most attentive perusal, being peculiarly striking, both on account of its own intrinsic merits, and in reference to the tenets subsequently disseminated by its author: . . .

From the Wandering Jew's claim that he left Israel sixteen hundred years ago (just after the Crucifixion), the setting of the poem can be dated ca. 1630.

III.9–117. Medwin claimed that the Crucifixion scene was "altogether a plagiarism from a volume of Cambridge Prize Poems" (*Life*, ed. Forman, 40), a poem identified by Dobell in *1887D* as the "Seatonian poem for 1765, called 'The Crucifixion,' by Thomas Zouch" (xxix). Although *WJ* shares a few similarities with *The Crucifixion* (see the cross-referenced passages at **III.24–39** and **40–47**), these seem based less on direct influence than on a mutual reliance on the conventional topoi concerning the Crucifixion and its aftermath, several of which are touched upon in Richard Polwhele's *The English Orator: A Didactic Poem* (London: C. Dully, 1786), in which the fourth book, "On the Eloquence of the Pulpit," instructs would-be pulpit-orators as follows:

> If thy Speech
> The stronger Passions shall address, behold
> The everlasting Gospel brings to view,
> Amid the Horrors of the spreading Gloom
> Miraculous, a dying Saviour nail'd
> Upon the Cross, while in the midst is rent
> The Temple's Veil; and the pale Vaults resign

> Their dead! Behold, the Gospel blazons forth
> The Dissolution of a World in Flames;
> Pictures the bloody Sun; the rushing Spheres,
> The Elements that melt with fervent Heat;
> Portrays the Throne of Judgment and the Crowds
> That meet their Doom eternal—some ingulph'd
> In fiery Depths sulphureous; others high
> Among the Saints, and crown'd with starry Light.
> (IV.622-36)

1989 points out a few relevant parallels in phrasing between *WJ* and Richard Cumberland's *Calvary; or, The Death of Christ* (1792), but not enough to substantiate the hypothesis that Medwin had confused Zouch's poem with Cumberland's.

III.16-22. <u>I mock'd . . . return again</u>: The underlying source for this version of the story is Roger of Wendover, who claims that it was told to him by an Armenian archbishop: "When therefore the Jews were dragging Jesus forth, and had reached the door, Cartaphilus, a porter of the hall in Pilate's service, as Jesus was going out of the door, impiously struck him on the back with his hand, and said in mockery, 'Go quicker, Jesus, go quicker, why do you loiter?' And Jesus looking back on him with a severe countenance said to him, 'I am going, and you will wait till I return'" (*Roger of Wendover's "Flowers of History,"* trans. J. A. Giles [1849; Felinfach: Llanerch, 1996]: II, pt. 2, 513. The account PBS provides here of the Wandering Jew's crime and punishment differs from both of the other accounts he offers in *QM* (see our note for *QM* VII.67).

III.17. <u>he said</u>: The change in *1831F* to "said he" was to create a rhyme with "see" (**III.23**), as *1989* notes.

III.24-39. <u>His perforated . . . trembled</u>: Cf. the following lines in *The Crucifixion* (Cambridge: T. and J. Merrill, 1765):

> The solemn scene on Calv'ry's mount,
> Where frighted nature shakes her trembling frame,
> And shudders at the complicated crime
> Of deicide.—The thorn-encircled head
> All pale and languid on the bleeding cross,
> The nail-empierced hand, the mangled feet,
> The perforated side, the heaving sigh
> Of gushing anguish, the deep groan of death,
> The day of darkness, terror and distress . . .
> (8-9)

III.37-41. <u>Convulsed . . . dead</u>: rewritten in *1831F* so as to form rhyming couplets:

> Convulsed, all nature shook with fear,
> Earth trembled as if the end was near.
> Rent was the Temple's vail in twain—
> The graves gave up their dead again.

III.40–47. <u>Rent</u> . . . <u>yell</u>: Cf. *The Crucifixion:* "Whilst ruin bursts the Temple's inmost veil, | And 'midst surrounding scenes of horror roam | The grisly spectres, as at midnight hour . . ." (16). PBS's spelling "vail" instead of "veil" in line 40 is an alternative authorized by *Entick's New Spelling Dictionary* (1805) as well as a pocket edition of Johnson's *Dictionary* (1803).

III.42–57. <u>Whilst ghosts</u> . . . <u>my brain</u>: *1831F* omits 42–48 and compresses 49–57 as follows:

> 'Twas then I felt the Almighty's ire—
> Those words flashed on my soul, my frame,
> Scorched breast and brain as with a flame
> Of unextinguishable fire!

III.58–159. This passage is replaced in *1829E* with the following summary: "In the pages which succeed this fine passage, Paulo goes on to describe at some length the misery he suffered, not only from the consciousness that he lay under the curse of the Almighty, but from the knowledge that it was impossible for him ever to find refuge from his sufferings in death. Years and generations pass away,—all around him changes,—new forms, and customs, and governments, arise,—he alone is strange, weary, and hopeless. His excited feelings almost amount to madness, and induce him to seek for death in every hideous shape. There is a great deal of power in the passage which we subjoin: . . ."

III.63–65. <u>grasp of death</u> . . . <u>dews of poppy</u>: The poppy is traditionally associated both with Thanatos and Hypnos, "Death and his brother Sleep," as they are called in the second line of **QM**.

III.94. <u>duskness</u>: We retain the reading in *1831F*, our copy-text for this portion of the poem. The conjectural emendation in *1887D* to "darkness" (followed by most subsequent editors) is possible, especially because <u>duskness</u> may have been a change initiated in *1831F* to prevent the repetition of <u>Darkness</u>, which appears in the preceding line. On the other hand, PBS might have chosen <u>duskness</u> for precisely the same reason. In any case, the two words would have looked quite similar in PBS's hand. The word *duskness* does not appear in any of PBS's other published poems, and none of the *OED*'s citations of the word are taken from poetry.

III.114. <u>disparted</u>: moved apart.

III.115. <u>sulphureous tide</u>: Cf. the description of Hell in Edward Young's *A*

Poem on the Last Day: "A furnace formidable, deep, and wide, | O'er-boiling with a mad sulphureous tide" (III.108–9).

Although the spelling "sulphurous" appears elsewhere in *WJ* (**I.205, III.203**), sulphureous was an acceptable alternative in PBS's day (and the one given in *Entick's New Spelling Dictionary* [1805]). We have preserved the inconsistencies of our copy-text, which also uses sulphureous in the prose **footnote** to **III.197** detailing the Wandering Jew's history, suggesting that PBS used *sulphurous* as a metrical abridgment.

III.122. burning cross . . . brow: Lewis introduced this detail in the fourth chapter of *The Monk*, about which an admiring S. T. Coleridge comments in the *Critical Review* for February 1797: "The tale of the bleeding nun is truly terrific; and we could not easily recollect a bolder or more happy conception than that of the burning cross on the forehead of the wandering Jew" (194). Coleridge, with grave reservations about *The Monk* as a whole, comments that Lewis's Wandering Jew is "a mysterious character, which, though copied . . . from Schiller's incomprehensible Armenian [in *Der Geisterseher* (1786–89); translated into English, 1795], does, nevertheless, display great vigour of fancy" (194).

In noting that the burning cross of the Wandering Jew resembles the mark of Cain, Anderson claims that "its being cruciform may have been suggested by the tradition alluded to in Pierre Bayle's famous *Dictionnaire historique et critique* (1697), which insisted that the Mark of Cain was also in the form of a cross" (*Legend/WJ*, 179).

III.130. I cursed . . . birth: repeated at **III.283,** a good example of the many repetitions within the text, perhaps a result of its manifold stages of revision.

III.136–37. Vain . . . my own misery: echoes Satan's speech in *Paradise Lost* IV.73–78, which PBS quotes as his epigraph to the first canto.

III.152. sacred temple: the temple at Jerusalem.

III.158. last setting: "lasting setting" in *1989* is apparently an error.

III.160–96. For these 37 lines, *1831F* substitutes the following 24 lines:

> How have I longed to plunge beneath
> The mansions of repelling death
> Where earthly sorrows cease!
> Oft have I rushed to the towering height
> Of the gigantic Teneriffe,
> Or some precipitous cliff,
> All in the dead of the stormy night,
> And flung me to the seas.
> The substantial clouds that lower'd beneath,

Bore my detested form;
They whirl'd it above the volcanic breath,
And the meteors of the storm.
Hark to the thunder's awful crash!
Hark to the midnight lightning's hiss!
At length was heard a sullen dash,
Which made the hollow rocks around
Rebellow to the awful sound,
The yawning ocean opening wide,
Received me in its vast abyss,
And whelm'd me in its foaming tide—
My astounded senses fled!
Oh—would that I had waked no more,
But wild surge swept my corpse ashore—
I was not with the dead!

III.169. Teneriffe: the largest of the Canary Islands, opposite the northwest coast of Africa in the Atlantic Ocean. Teneriffe was known in PBS's day for a volcanic explosion that occurred early in the eighteenth century and buried much of the northern coast of the island under lava. It continued to be volcanically active. Rees's *Cyclopædia,* one of PBS's key sources for the notes to *QM,* gives the "Peak of Teneriffe" as 12,236 feet high, in a table listing the highest mountains of the world, and provides the following relevant description:

The historical celebrity of this island has been very much owing to its *Peak,* elevated to a considerable height from a base lying a little to the S.W. of its centre.... the crater of the Peak is a perfect solfatara or laboratory of sulphur.... On the edges of the crater, and particularly towards the lowest part, are several apertures or vents, exhaling watery and sulphuric acid vapours.... Although the vortex appears sharp, and of the exact resemblance of a cone, yet it is flat for the extent of an acre of ground, in the centre of which is a dreadful volcano, which frequently breaks out into flames, so violent as to shake the whole island with an incredible force. Smoke constantly issues from the mountain, near its summit, but no eruption has occurred since the year 1704....

III.178. electric flame: lightning. Cf. Erasmus Darwin's *The Botanic Garden* I.551–52: "Nymphs! o'er the soil ten thousand points erect, | And high in air the electric flame collect."

III.197. Footnote. scattered oak: an unusual but plausible phrase in *1831F* that has led some editors to conjecture "shattered oak" and *1989* to emend to "scathed oak," either of which is possible, given PBS's hand. PBS uses the word scathed to describe a pine tree in both **III.215** and **III.218,** and in *QM* the Wandering Jew compares himself to a "giant oak, which heaven's fierce flame | Had scathed in the wilderness" (VII.259–60).

III.212. pangs: Although the change in *1887D* to "pains" is unwarranted, it is followed by most subsequent editors.

III.213, 215–23. An epigraph to Chapter 10 of **St.Irv** is collated as *1811* (186). These lines also appear separately as "Fragment from the Wandering Jew" ("The Elements respect their Maker's seal!") in several major editions that do not contain **WJ** proper, including *1870*, *1876*, *1904*, and *1970*. In *1927*, they appear both within **WJ** and as a separate lyric. The text in *1870*, which does not begin until **line 215,** departs from our text by treating "tempests" as singular in **line 216** and by replacing scathed with "shattered" (**218**) and rears with "raises" (**223**). All the other editions omit line 214 and give "flame" for fire (**217**). *1904* additionally replaces bickering with "flickering" (**217**).

Medwin quotes **lines 215–33** in a footnote (*Life*, ed. Forman, 42), which we collate as *1913*.

III.232–71. These lines are omitted in *1829E*, which provides the following comment:

> In a note, Shelley acknowledges that many of the ideas in the above passage [III.160–231] were suggested to him by a German author, who has written upon the same subject. It will be recollected by the readers of "Queen Mab," that he has casually introduced Ahasuerus, or the Wandering Jew, in a very sublime manner, in that poem, and that he there also acknowledges his obligations to the same German author, and quotes a part of his work, different, however, from that to which he alludes in the volume before us.
>
> Death being the predominant thought in the mind of Paulo, as well as his great aim and object, the following incident is finely introduced: . . .

III.232. intellectual eye: For a similarly penetrating "intellectual eye," cf. James Thomson's "To The Memory of Sir Isaac Newton," in which Newton is described as "All intellectual eye" (line 39) and "Nature herself | Stood all subdued by him, and open laid | Her every latent glory to his view" (lines 36–38; *The Poetical Works of James Thomson*, London: William Pickering, 1830). PBS also uses the phrase "intellectual eye" in **QM** II.98.

III.238. The past, the present, and to come: A formulation for prophetic vision since antiquity, the phrase appears notably in Virgil's *Georgics* IV.387, in a reference to Proteus that reads, in Dryden's translation: "With sure foresight, and with unerring doom, | He sees what is, and was, and is to come" (*The Complete Poetical Works of Dryden*, ed. George R. Noyes [Boston: Houghton Mifflin, 1909], 483). In a letter to Thomas Hookham written 18 August 1812, PBS announced that "The Past, the Present, & the Future are the grand & comprehensive topics of" **QM** (**Letters** I, 324), a point restated by Mab herself within the poem proper: "Spirit, come! | This is thine high reward:—the past shall rise; | Thou shalt behold the present; I will teach | The secrets of the future" (II.64–67).

III.242–47. Awed by the Cross . . . command: The Wandering Jew in *The Monk* (and in **Ghasta** in *V&C*) similarly possesses occult powers and similarly produces awe and horror through his mark. The ghost of the Bleeding Nun finally submits to him only because "I tremble at that mark!—I respect it!—I obey you!" (Lewis, ed. H. Anderson, 172).

III.261. Wolga's shore,: The period after "shore" in *1831F* reflects the editor's penchant for breaking up PBS's long sentences into shorter units; here, however, it severs the dependent clauses that follow from the rest of the sentence.

It is not clear exactly when and why Victorio fought on the banks of the Wolga or Volga. The first third of the seventeenth century was tumultuous in Russian history, particularly before 1613, a period of dynastic confusion, civil wars, and foreign invasions known as "the Time of Troubles." This period was marked by an influx of foreigners into Muscovy, especially of those serving as military personnel and mercenaries, many of whom congregated around the Volga, where much fighting occurred. As a soldier from Catholic Italy, Victorio might have served with the Catholic Poles who, with the blessing of the Pope, attempted to enforce the claims to the throne of the "False Dimitry," a converted Catholic through whom, it was hoped, all Muscovy could be converted and would subsequently join in the fight against the Turks and Tatars. Tensions between the Poles and Russians continued to grow, however, and on 19 March 1611, the Poles burned Moscow. The troubles of Muscovy were related in England in such contemporary narratives as *The reporte of a bloudie and terrible massacre in the citty of Mosco, with the fearefull and tragicall end of Demetrius the last Duke, before him raigning at this present* (London: Samuel Macham & Mathew Cooke, 1607). For a detailed survey of Russian history at this time, see S. F. Platonov, *The Time of Troubles: A Historical Study of the Internal Crisis and Social Struggle in Sixteenth- and Seventeenth-Century Muscovy*, translated by John Alexander (Wichita: UP of Kansas, 1970).

The association of Victorio with the Volga might also be related to Schiller's treatment of the Wandering Jew legend in *Der Geisterseher,* in which the Wandering Jew figure appears as a Russian army officer (see G. Anderson, *Legend/WJ*, 175–77).

III.274. sightless fiends: invisible. Cf. the opening lines of the epigraph to Chapter 7 of **St.Irv** (*1811*, 123): "Yes! 'tis the influence of that sightless fiend, | Who guides my every footstep, that I feel. . . ."

III.290. stave: stanza or set of verses.

III.300–349. *1829E* substitutes for this passage the following summary: "Finding that Heaven would not interfere to shorten his probation, and having made himself familiar with all the secret arts of necromancy, he resolves to call the powers of the lower world to his aid, and is more than once on the very point of selling his soul to purchase the happiness of death. Upon one occasion the Prince of Darkness appeared to him after the following manner: . . ."

III.302. calcined: destroyed by fire.

III.319. marked a circle: The Wandering Jew in *The Monk* similarly marks a circle in his exorcism of the ghost of the Bleeding Nun: "He next drew from the Chest a covered Goblet: With the liquor which it contained, and which appeared to be blood, He sprinkled the floor, and then dipping in it one end of the Crucifix, He described a circle in the middle of the room. Round about this He placed various reliques, sculls, thigh-bones &c . . ." (Lewis, ed. H. Anderson, 171). PBS, of course, had his own experience at trying to raise ghosts and devils. See, for instance, Hogg's description of PBS's ventures in the occult and Hogg's relation of his own schoolboy experience within a magic circle (*Life*, ed. Wolfe, I, 36–40).

III.327. night raven . . . flitted by: Cf. Southey, *The Vision of the Maid of Orleans:* "The plumeless bats with short shrill note flit by, | And the night-raven's scream came fitfully, | Borne on the hollow blast" (I.39–41).

III.335. lightnings gleam: We retain the reading of *1831F*, in which *lightnings* is plural and *gleam* is a verb (cf. **I.211**: "Red lightnings gleam from every cloud"), but "lightning's gleam," the emendation in *1989* that parallels "meteor's glare" in the preceding line, is another possible reading, given PBS's penchant for omitting the apostrophe from possessives.

III.338–428. As Cameron has pointed out, this long phantasmagoric temptation scene parallels Ginotti's dream at the end of Chapter 10 of *St.Irv* (*YS*, 35), a chapter, moreover, headed by an epigraph from *WJ*. The primary differences are that the pleasing form that tempts Ginotti begins as male (though it also dissolves into a demonic form) and that Ginotti is finally terrified into yielding at the end of his dream. Behind both of these scenes, Zimansky notes ("Borrowings," 601–2), is a passage from *The Monk* in which Matilda conjures Satan before a terrified Ambrosio:

What was his surprize, when the Thunder ceasing to roll, a full strain of melodious Music sounded in the air. At the same time the cloud dispersed, and He beheld a Figure more beautiful, than Fancy's pencil ever drew. It was a Youth seemingly scarce eighteen, the perfection of whose form and face was unrivalled. He was perfectly naked: A bright Star sparkled upon his fore-head. . . . His form shone with dazzling glory: He was surrounded by clouds of rose-coloured light, and at the moment that He appeared, a refreshing air breathed perfumes through the Cavern. . . . Yet however beautiful the Figure, He could not but remark a wildness in the Dæmon's eyes, and a mysterious melancholy impressed upon his features, betraying the Fallen Angel, and inspiring the Spectators with secret awe. (Lewis, ed. H. Anderson, 276–77)

Later in *The Monk*, the narrator comments that Lucifer had "borrowed the Seraph's form to deceive Ambrosio" (433).

III.339. ear: The reading "air" in *1892W* appears to be a misprint.

III.346. insubstantial: a synonym for *unsubstantial*, as conjecturally emended in *1887D*.

III.355. wreath: a contemporary alternative spelling for the verb.

III.383–86. scroll . . . blood: Zimansky ("Borrowings," 602) notes the parallel between this part of *WJ* and Ambrosio's attempt at the end of *The Monk* to escape the Spanish Inquisition by selling his soul to the Devil, who "in one hand . . . held a roll of parchment, and in the other an iron pen" that he struck "into a vein of the Monk's left-hand. It pierced deep, and was instantly filled with blood" (Lewis, ed. H. Anderson, 433, 435).

III.387. then: first altered to "when" in *1887D*, a conjectural emendation that gratuitously changes the meaning of the line. The Devil is claiming that after the Wandering Jew sells his soul by signing the volume with his blood ("then"), he will at last be able to die. As the Wandering Jew ultimately seems to understand this offer, however, it would provide peace only for the interval between his immediate death and Judgment Day, when he would be consigned forever to Hell (see **III.403–4**). A contemporary Anglican discussion of death and Judgment Day (*The New Whole Duty of Man, containing The Faith as well as Practice of A Christian* [Published by the King's Authority; London: W Bent, and (9 other booksellers), 1805]) offers a similar understanding:

Notwithstanding . . . that there is a *particular* judgment passed upon all men; forasmuch as good men, when they die, pass into a state of happiness, and bad men into a state of misery; yet all the declarations of our Saviour and his apostles, concerning judgment . . . plainly refer to the last and *general* judgment: for it is only in that day that the whole man shall be completely happy, or completely miserable; for in that day it is that the bodies of men shall be raised; and as they have been partakers with the soul, either in obeying or offending God, so shall they then share in the rewards and punishments of it; and in that day only can the degrees and measures of their happiness and misery be adjusted; for, even after death, the effect of men's good or bad actions may add to their punishment, or increase their reward, by the good or bad examples they have given, by the foundations they have established for piety and virtue, or by the customs they have introduced to countenance immorality and vice. (110–11)

For an excellent discussion of the debate in nineteenth-century Anglican theology about what happens to the body and soul after death and before Judgment Day, see Linda E. Marshall, *Victorian Newsletter* 72 (1987): 55–60.

The pact with the Devil signed in blood is, of course, a longstanding rite in demonology, widely disseminated in various incarnations of the Faust legend.

III.406. coursed: followed.

III.421–22. Thunders . . . ire: In *The Monk*, after Ambrosio refuses to sell his soul to the Devil, "Instantly the Thunder was heard to roll horribly: Once more the earth trembled with violence . . . and the Dæmon fled with blasphemy and curses" (Lewis, ed. H. Anderson, 435).

III.429–55. *1829E* substitutes the following note, with its special pleading, for the concluding lines of Canto III:

Having so far gained a victory over himself and his tempters, he contrived to drag on a wretched existence for sixteen hundred years, about the expiration of which period he had met with Rosa, and in her deep confiding affection found a temporary solace for his griefs. His narrative and third canto conclude together.

The fourth canto opens in a strain of truly elevated morality and piety, which shows how much of good there must always have been at Shelley's heart: . . .

III.439–42. a tale disclose . . . shrink to hear: echoing the gist of *Hamlet* I.v.15–18: "I could a tale unfold whose lightest word | Would harrow up thy soul, freeze thy young blood, | Make thy two eyes like stars start from their spheres, | Thy knotted and combined locks to part. . . ." PBS quotes these lines in the epigraph to Canto II of *WJ* and echoes them also in **II.208–9**.

IV. Epigraphs. The first epigraph is from Aeschylus's *Eumenides* (V.48–49, 53–54) and reads in translation: "No! women they were surely not, Gorgons I rather call them. Nor yet can I liken them to forms of Gorgons either. . . . sable, and altogether detestable. Their snorting nostrils blow forth fearsome blasts, and from their eyes oozes a loathly rheum." The omitted passage (V.50–52) reads: "Once ere this I saw some pictured creatures carrying off the feast of Phineus—but these are wingless, . . ." (trans. Herbert Weir Smyth [Cambridge: Harvard UP, 1926], II, 277). For PBS's subsequent interest in the Eumenides or Furies, see especially the first act of **Prom;** for his abiding interest in the Gorgons and Medusa, in particular, see the fragment conventionally titled **On the Medusa of Leonardo da Vinci in the Florentine Gallery** (1819).

The second epigraph is taken from Banquo's encounter with the witches in *Macbeth*, I.iii.39–43.

IV.1–37. This opening stanza advocates a piety unusual in PBS's poetry, climaxing in **lines 19–23,** which berate humankind for railing "at Heaven" and opposing "the Almighty Cause." Such a statement appears to be in tension with PBS's alternative title for *WJ:* "Victim of the Eternal Avenger." Dobell, noting that the passage has no integral "connection either with what has preceded or with what follows it," goes so far as to suggest that it is imported from the draft of an unknown poem by PBS in which "the question as to man's relations with the Deity should be discussed between two speakers," with these lines spoken by an orthodox speaker. PBS thus inserted it in *WJ* because "he did not like to lose it" (*1887D,* 111–12).

However, nothing in this passage goes beyond Deism, a position PBS was advocating, for instance, in December 1810, in a letter to "Wedgewood," the still unidentified correspondent with whom he was debating theology and attacking Christianity. See B. C. Barker-Benfield's *Shelley's Guitar,* in which Jones's transcription of "?Revd" is corrected to "Deism" (22) in a letter of 20 December 1810 that PBS wrote to Hogg about the "Wedgewood" correspondence (**Letters** I, 28). Two weeks later, PBS confesses to Hogg that "Pope's 'all are but parts of one tremendous whole' . . . has ever been my favourite theory," even as he curses Christianity (**Letters** I, 35). In this same letter, with the Wandering Jew in mind, he interestingly claims: "For the immoral 'never to be able to die, never to escape from some shrine as chilling as the clay-formed dungeon which now it inhabits' is the future punishment which I believe in" (**Letters** I, 35; PBS's quotation, which is not identified in **Letters,** is paraphrased from the Schubart translation in *La Belle Assemblée;* see *SC* II, 650). Cf. also *A Sabbath Walk* in *Esd.*

IV.8. garniture of . . . fields: ornaments of the landscape. Cf. James Beattie, *The Minstrel; or, The Progress of Genius:* "The pomp of groves, and garniture of fields . . ." (I.76; *Poems on Several Occasions* [Edinburgh: W. Creech, 1776]).

IV.12. from whom these blessings flow: an echo of the opening of the Doxology (praise to God) by Thomas Ken (1637–1711; Anglican bishop and hymn writer), which is still frequently sung in Protestant church services: "Praise God, from whom all blessings flow. . . ."

IV.38–85. In omitting this passage, *1829E* substitutes the following summary: "Victorio is now brought more prominently into notice. It appears that he has conceived an unlawful passion for Rosa, and his mind, tempest-tost between his duty to his friend, and his burning anxiety to possess Rosa, at whatever cost, is driven almost to distraction. In a fit of despair he determines on committing suicide. The following passage is a noble one: . . ."

IV.60. soul-harrowing: We have inserted a hyphen, omitted in *1831F,* for the compound adjective.

IV.79. melancholy nightshade: The poisonous woody nightshade (*Solanum dulcamara*, or bittersweet) appears several times in PBS's poetry, in which it is often associated with passion.

IV.99. o'er: Victorio is no doubt "suspended o'er" (*1831F*), rather than "suspended on" (*1829E*) "the yawning flood"; PBS's handwriting was liable to misreading on this point, especially because he omitted apostrophes.

IV.114–15. death angel . . . wave: a probable reference to Mors, known as the destroying angel and described in Lempriere's *Classical Dictionary* (1820) as a daughter of Night, worshiped by the Lacedæmonians, but represented by moderns as "a skeleton armed with a scythe and a scymetar." According to the entry on "Death" in Rees's *Cyclopædia*, "The face of Mors seems . . . to have been of a pale, wan, dead colour. The poets . . . seem to give her black robes and dark wings, and represent her often as of an enormous size. Statius gives her arms and a sword, exhibiting her like a destroying angel, where he is describing a pestilence. The ancient poets sometimes represent her as coming to the doors of mortals, and thundering at them, to demand the debts they owe her: sometimes approaching to their bedsides, and leaning over them: and at other times, pursuing her prey, or hovering in the air, and ready to stoop upon it."

If PBS is indeed referring to Mors, he thinks of her as male. Cf. also the unattributed epigraph for Chapter 2 of ***St.Irv*** (*1811*, 44): "The fiends of fate are heard to rave, | And the death-angel flaps his broad wing o'er the wave." He may therefore have been conflating Mors with the decidedly male angel of death Azrael, who appears in both Jewish and Islamic traditions, with various iconographic attributes. The medieval Death with his deadly dart and Milton's Death in *Paradise Lost* could also have contributed to the masculinity of PBS's "death angel."

IV.149–402. This long passage is replaced in *1829E* with the following summary:

Thus diverted from his purpose, his [Victorio's] passion for Rosa retains as fierce a hold of his bosom as ever. Before he reaches his own castle, the Witch of the Alps presents herself before him, and promises him the accomplishment of his desires provided he consents to surrender his soul to her. Victorio agrees; and the Witch, having led him to her cell, pronounces "Some maddening rhyme that wakes the dead;" and after an incantation scene of considerable length, the whole of which is exceedingly powerful, Victorio receives a drug from the hand of a fiend, which he is ordered to mingle with Paulo's wine, whose death will be the certain consequence. The drug is infused, but the wine is drunk by Rosa instead of Paulo, who is thus lost to both her lovers. What becomes of Victorio we are not told; but the poem concludes with these lines. It is Paulo who is supposed to speak: . . .

Note, however, that the designation "Witch of the Alps" may be *1829E*'s gratuitous borrowing from Byron's *Manfred* and that the action is more ambiguous than the summary represents. The Witch offers to provide Victorio a love potion; it is unclear whether Victorio is able to hear the Devil tell the Witch that the drug he has concocted will bring death to the one who drinks it. There is a longstanding demonological tradition that witches cannot kill other humans, "unless it be those witches which kill by poison, which either they receive from the devil, or he teacheth them to make" (see Rossell Hope Robbins, *The Encyclopedia of Witchcraft and Demonology* [New York: Bonanza Books, 1959], 369–70).

IV.171–78, 180–90. These lines appear in Medwin's *Life*, ed. Forman (39–40), where they are described as versified almost verbatim from a "wild and extravagant" prose romance entitled *Nightmare* that Medwin and PBS supposedly wrote, "in alternate chapters," during the winter of 1809. No trace of this romance survives, nor is there evidence for its existence beyond Medwin's own account. We collate the lines from *Life* as *1913*.

IV.182. rocks,: The semicolon following "rocks" in *1831F* unnecessarily obscures the syntax of the sentence.

IV.186. Were: Rogers in *1972* emended to "Was," because the grammatical subject of the verb is fold (**185**), but the logical subject is weeds (i.e., clothes), a figurative appositive for locks (**181**). If we assume an error, it may have resulted from compression through omission in *1831F.*

IV.189. "Grinned . . . ghastly smile": slightly misquoted, perhaps from memory, from *Paradise Lost* II.845–46, in which "Death | Grinn'd horrible a ghastly smile. . . ."

IV.196. weird female: "witch," recalling the "weird sisters" in *Macbeth,* to whom Macbeth addresses the question quoted in the epigraph for this canto. Medwin claims that *Nightmare* contained "a hideous witch [who] played the principal part, and whose portrait—not a very inviting one—is given in *The Wandering Jew* . . ." (*Life,* ed. Forman, 39). PBS's portrait of the witch may be compared to Southey's memorable witch Lorrinite, the subject of Book XI of *The Curse of Kehama* (1810), who "haunted" PBS, according to Medwin (44). Although PBS does not make us privy to his witch's motives, Southey provides the following analysis of Lorrinite:

> She hated men because they lov'd not her,
> And hated women because they were lov'd.
> And thus, in wrath and hatred and despair,
> She tempted Hell to tempt her; and resign'd
> Her body to the Demons of the Air. . . .
>
> (XI.37–41)

Southey completed *Kehama* on 25 November 1809, but it was not published until December 1810, and therefore could have influenced *WJ* directly only if the extant text includes later revisions—for example, those possibly made in the MS that PBS left with Ballantyne in Edinburgh during the summer of 1811. PBS was certainly eager to read *Kehama:* in a letter of 2 December 1810, in which he asks Stockdale to send him back a copy of *WJ* for corrections, he also asks: "When do you suppose that Southey's Curse of Kehama will come out, I am curious to see it . . ." (***Letters*** I, 24). He quite possibly read *Kehama,* then, in time to influence *WJ,* especially the heavily revised Canto IV.

IV.227–28. putrefaction's power . . . blue mist: The blue mist might be a phenomenon of bioluminescence, which *The Britannica Online* (1997) describes as "the emission of light by an organism . . . [including] the ghostly glow of bacteria on decaying meat. . . ."

IV.242. curled clouds: Cf. Ariel's offer to serve Prospero by riding "On the curl'd clouds" (*The Tempest,* I.ii.192). The ability to raise storms through spells and intermediary spirits has long been accounted an attribute of witches in folk tradition and was accepted in the thirteenth century as true by such Church authorities as Thomas Aquinas and Bonaventure. See Robbins, *Encyclopedia of Witchcraft,* 487–89.

IV.262. secret power is mine: As Zimansky points out, Victorio's resort to a witch who will in turn call upon the Devil to create a "philtre" that will make Rosa love him is reminiscent of Ambrosio's resort in *The Monk* to Matilda, who summons the Devil to deliver a "phial" that will cause Antonia to sleep helplessly while Ambrosio rapes her ("Borrowings," 606).

IV.270. to one, who: We retain this comma in *1831F* as indicative of a rhetorical pause after one.

IV.271–331. *Edinburgh Literary Journal,* which omitted these lines in its text of *WJ* proper, gives them as a separate poem, "An Incantation Scene.—a Poem, hitherto unpublished, By Percy Bysshe Shelley," in the issue for 26 December 1829 (collated above as *1829Inc*). For the discrepancies between *1829Inc* and *1831F,* see the section, "Editorial Analysis, Copy-Text, and Emendations," above.

IV.271. The charm begins: This line begins "An Incantation Scene" in *1829Inc*. In placing the first three words of the line into the same sentence as the last three, *1829Inc* alters PBS's syntax; the only such alteration (so far as we can determine) in the *Edinburgh Literary Journal*'s treatment of *WJ.*

IV.276. dark: We follow the reading in *1829Inc,* though "dank" in *1831F* is also possible. It would be difficult to tell the difference between the two words in PBS's hand.

IV.277–79. threw ... blue ... flew: A curly brace in *1829Inc* marks the triple rhyme.

IV.291–300. But when ... their eyes: This passage, which was probably drawn from a heavily revised section of PBS's MS, appears in a briefer and quite different form in *1831F*:

> His horrid form obscured the cell.
> Victorio shrunk, unused to shrink,
> E'en at extremest danger's brink;
> The witch then pointed to the ground,
> Infernal shadows flitted around,
> And with their prince were seen to rise,

Because Victorio's great courage as a soldier was stressed earlier (he is called fearless, **III.258**), it is possible that *1831F* provides the more accurate rendering of these lines.

IV.306–7. Words ... flood: The Witch is engaged in coprolalia, a demonic version of glossolalia (speaking in tongues), in which the speaker obsessively vocalizes obscenities, a condition that was often linked to demonic possession and which is inspired here by the presence of the devil and his minions. See Matthew J. Bowyer, *Encyclopedia of Mystical Terminology* (New York: A. S. Barnes, 1979), 53.

IV.329. basiliskine eye: The gaze of the legendary basilisk was reputed to be fatal; PBS may have coined the adjective, which does not appear in the *OED*.

IV.315–31. *1831F* omits **lines 318–33** and gives **315–17** as follows:

> Along the rocks a death-peal rang.
> In accents hollow, deep, and drear,
> They struck upon Victorio's ear.

IV.340–41. Between these lines there is an apparent abridgement of the text. The omitted passage may have included the three lines described in the introductory essay of *1831F* as "a pretty, affecting passage at the end of the fourth canto," and quoted as follows:

> 'Tis mournful when the deadliest hate
> Of friends, of fortune, and of fate
> Is levelled at one fated head.

The essayist in *Fraser's* goes on to apply these lines "to the cloud of family misfortune in which he [PBS] was then [in his youth] enveloped" (536), raising the interesting possibility that the lines may be dated after PBS's expulsion from Oxford and, perhaps, after his elopement with Harriet

Shelley. *1989* conjectures that these three lines may have been located between **IV.370** and **371**.

IV.341. Footnote. This note, presumably by PBS, is drawn from Sin's speech to Satan about the birth of Death, *Paradise Lost* II.787–89.

IV.370. philtre: love potion or charm.

IV.377–78. Which . . . yon hill: *1892W* transposes these two lines. There is no precedent for the reading "the hill" (*1989*).

IV.383–90. These lines were quoted in full and praised by M. J. Jewsbury in *The Athenæum* for 16 July 1831 (457) as providing "a tone of that perfect song, 'I awake from dreams of thee' " (i.e., "I arise from dreams of thee," the lyric first published by MWS in *1824* as "Lines to an Indian Air"). They have been excerpted as a separate lyric, "Song from the Wandering Jew" ("See yon opening flower," or "See yon opening rose") in several major editions, including *1870, 1876, 1904,* and *1970;* in *1927* they appear both as part of *WJ* proper (see Historical Collations) and as a separate lyric. *1870* and *1927* replace "flower" with "rose" (**383**) and "blast" with "gale" (**384**), altering as well the order of words in **line 386** ("fast—is pale" for "pale, is fast"). We collate as *1913* these lines as they appear in Medwin's *Life*, ed. Forman, page 41.

IV.394. Lara's castled height: As *1989* points out, although PBS places Lara in Italy, the name itself is probably Spanish, derived from a Castilian family named in the chronicles of "El Cid" and later evoked in Byron's *Lara*. PBS may have come across the name in Southey's 1808 *Chronicles of the Cid* (London: Longman, Hurst, Rees, & Orme), in which a long endnote gives the history of the "Infantes of Lara," who are described as "among the most celebrated heroes of the popular Ballads of Spain" (389).

IV.413. Enthroned: "Enthrones" in *1831F* is probably a typo.

IV.419–28. Ah! . . . pangs I feel: These lines appear in a different, compressed form in *1831F* from what may have been a heavily revised portion in PBS's MS:

> Ah! I have felt his burning ire,—
> Wild anguish glooms my brow;
> His flaming mark is fixed on my head,
> And must there remain in traces dread;
> I feel—I feel it now!

IV.433. After this concluding line of the poem, *1829E* adds:

We have thus presented our readers with a good number of the most striking passages in this poem; and we are satisfied that none who take delight in such matters can have perused them without a very high degree of interest and satisfaction. That so elaborate and valuable a work, by one of the first poets of our times, should have existed entirely unknown to his nearest surviving friends and relatives, cannot fail to be of itself regarded as a circumstance well worthy of commemoration. That it should have fallen to our lot to be the first to intimate the existence of this important literary curiosity, and to present to the public, through the pages of the *Literary Journal,* various selected portions of its contents, must always remain with us a subject of pleasant retrospection and self-congratulation. It is not impossible that the whole poem may be afterwards published in a separate shape, but of this we are not yet aware. In conclusion, we have only to hope, though we can scarcely promise, that in the prosecution of our labours, we shall occasionally be enabled to offer to our readers literary matter of as novel and interesting a nature as that to which we have now directed their attention.

Posthumous Fragments of Margaret Nicholson

As Denis Florence Mac-Carthy first noted (*Early Life*, 39), the earliest contemporary evidence for the existence of this odd collection is a notice on 17 November 1810 in the *Oxford University and City Herald*, advertising its sale for two shillings at J. Munday (also publisher of the Oxford weekly paper). On 21 November 1810, PBS wrote to Edward Fergus Graham in London: "You heard from me last night, & were doubtlessly surprised at the enclosure. I wish you would advertise it in all the papers which I mention.... Nothing is talked of at Oxford but Peg Nicholson, I have only printed 250 copies & expect a second edition soon" (**Letters** I, 21–22). Graham must have hinted that he needed money to pay for the advertisements, for PBS wrote to him in his next letter, 30 November 1810: "I enclose a 5 £ note which is all I can immediately spare; I shall see you in a fortnight." **Posthumous Fragments of Margaret Nicholson** (**PF**) was not reviewed, perhaps because PBS believed that the scandalous nature of the poems would make favorable reviews unlikely but would facilitate their sale by word of mouth. In his 30 November letter, he assured Graham that the "indelicacy" of the ***Epithalamium*** would have no ill consequences for himself, but would make the book "sell like wildfire, and as the *Nephew* is kept a profound secret, there can arise no danger from the indelicacy of the Aunt—It sells wonderfully here, & is become the fashionable subject of discussion—" (**Letters** I, 23).

PBS's letters to Graham remained unpublished till much later (three of them first in H. B. Forman's *The Shelley Library* [1886] and others in Ingpen's 1909 edition of PBS's *Letters*), and two other early friends provided the first known mentions of ***PF*** after 1810. Thomas Medwin was characteristically imprecise in his "Memoir of Shelley," first published in the weekly *Athenæum* in July–August 1832 (here quoted from *The Shelley Papers*, 1833). After mentioning PBS's expulsion from Oxford, Medwin wrote: "During the last term he had published also a strange half-mad volume of poems, entitled 'Posthumous Works of my Aunt Margaret Nicholson,' in which were some panegyrical stanzas to the memory of Charlotte Corday; the poetry was well *worthy* of the subject—probably the copy I have is the only one existing" (11). In his *Life of PBS* (60–62), Medwin repeats the same account—adding only the misinformation that *PF* was published by Parker (another Oxford bookseller)—before quoting much of T. J. Hogg's story of *PF* from *Shelley at Oxford* (1833; ed. R. A. Streatfeild [1904]). Medwin's copy of *PF* has not come to light.

In 1833, Hogg wrote that he had found PBS reading proofs of some very bad poems and suggested that, instead of publishing them anonymously, PBS should make them a little worse and turn them into amusing burlesques of radical poetry. The two first-year students therefore decided to attribute them to an appropriate persona: "A mad washerwoman, named Peg Nicholson, had attempted to stab the king, George the Third, with a carving-knife; the story has long been forgotten, but it was then fresh in the recollection of every one. . . . The poor woman was still living, and in green vigour within the walls of Bedlam; but since her existence must be uncomfortable, there could be no harm in putting her to death, and in creating a nephew and administrator to be the editor of his aunt's poetical works" (Streatfeild, ed., 200–201). Mac-Carthy enumerates several errors in Hogg's retrospective account, demonstrating that Hogg was not PBS's close friend when the *PF* volume was conceived, but rather that *PF* was being put together by the time the two young men first met (*Early Life*, 34–40). Cameron, though warning that we cannot trust Hogg's highly colored account, credits Hogg's claim that he supplied the title, because his hometown in County Durham was near Nicholson's birthplace (*SC* I, 36fn). Yet, as Hogg himself notes, her name was widely known at the time—she had appeared in the Whig satires of the royal family by John Wolcot ("Peter Pindar"), which PBS read; there is also evidence that others besides Hogg made suggestions for *PF*. Two brief notes that PBS sent to James Roe of Trinity College—one asking Roe to return a "poetical scrap" because he wished to continue to work on it and the other inviting Roe to his room at teatime for "wine & Poetry"—may, as Cameron suggests, date from the period when *PF* was in proof (*SC* II, 639–41).

As we note in discussing the poems in *St.Irv*, PBS himself was probably ambivalent about the quality of his poetry during his first term at Oxford, and as his letter to Graham indicates, he may have initiated such a defensive maneuver as Hogg describes. But he may also have adopted the pseudonymous persona of "Margaret Nicholson" not simply because the poetry was bad but because he and his Oxford friends feared, like Graham, that it was likely to get PBS into trouble with the authorities. Hogg stated that "there was no lack of beardless politicians amongst us. Of these, some were more strenuous supporters of the popular cause in our little circles than others; but all were abundantly liberal" (Streatfeild, ed., 122). These "little circles," however, obviously shared the secret with others outside their sympathetic coterie. Charles Kirkpatrick Sharpe (?1781–1851, *DNB*), a Tory Scot who was a fellow of Christ Church, Oxford, wrote at least two letters to friends about PBS's literary exploits before his expulsion; in the one that survives (altered to an undeterminable extent by its survival only in Lady Charlotte Campbell's semifictionalized *Diary Illustrative of the Times of George IV* [1838] and included in *Letters from and to Charles Kirkpatrick Sharpe*, ed. A. Allardyce [1888]), Sharpe wrote on 15 March 1815:

> we have lately had a literary Sun shine forth upon us here, before whom our former luminaries must hide their diminished heads—a Mr Shelley, of University College, who lives upon arsenic, aquafortis, half-an-hour's sleep in the night, and is desperately in love with the memory of Margaret Nicholson. He hath published what he terms the Posthumous Poems, printed for the benefit of Mr Peter Finnerty, which, I am grieved to say, though stuffed full of treason, is extremely dull; but the author is a great genius. . . . Shelley's style is much like that of Moore burlesqued; for Frank [i.e., Ravaillac] is a very foul-mouthed fellow, and Charlotte, one of the most impudent brides that I ever met with in a book. (I, 442–43)

Sharpe's allusions to PBS's chemical experiments and mishaps (later described by Hogg in *Shelley at Oxford*) and to his efforts to reduce his sleeping time show that Sharpe had been informed of PBS's private doings as well as his publishing exploits. PBS wrote in his 21 November letter to Graham, "I now do not take more than three hours sleep, & feel quite pleased at the idea that I shall soon be able to live without that *morbid suspension of every energy*—" (**Letters** I, 22). In this connection, note that Southey's memoir introducing *The Remains of Henry Kirke White* (1807), which PBS had probably read by this date, attributes the early death of White (1785–1806) to his strict regimen of study and prayer at Cambridge that allowed him only five hours of sleep per night (I, 45–50).

Slatter's Testimony

Additional information on the composition and publication of **PF** first appeared in the notes at the end of the fourth edition of Robert Montgomery's *Oxford: A Poem* (Oxford: Henry Slatter, 1835), page 165, in a memoir-letter by Henry Slatter, the junior partner in the firm of J[ohn] Munday (later Munday and Slatter) that printed and published **PF**. Slatter recounts that when Timothy Shelley brought PBS to Oxford, the father lodged in the home of Henry's brother John Slatter, with whose family he had lived when *he* had been a student.

> While lodging there with the son of his former host he [Timothy Shelley] . . . learned that one of the sons was about embarking as partner with a bookseller and printer; thither Sir Timothy repaired with his son, and gave him a particular injunction to buy whatever he required in books and stationery of the aforesaid parties; Sir Timothy moreover, said "My son here," pointing to him, "has a literary turn, he is already an author, and do pray indulge him in his printing freaks"—one of the works alluded to was his romance of "St. Irvyne, or The Rosicrucian;" [A

footnote keyed here identifies the publisher as J. J. Stockdale and the date as 1811; actually, PBS had published **Zastrozzi,** rather than **St.Irv,** by Oct. 1810. Slatter's memory of the latter title probably came from Stockdale's account of **St.Irv** in *Stockdale's Budget,* to which Slatter alludes to remind the public of another publisher who had lost money by trusting PBS and Timothy Shelley.] he [PBS] soon put the parties to the test by writing some fugitive poetry, entitled, "Posthumous Fragments of Margaret Nicholson," a work almost still-born, and directing the profits to be applied to Peter Finnerty; the ease with which he composed many of the stanzas therein contained, is truly astonishing; when surprised with a proof from the printers, in the morning, he would frequently start from the sofa, exclaiming, that that had been his only bed, and, on being informed that the men were waiting for more copy, he would sit down and write off a few stanzas, and send them to the press, without even revising or reading them,—this I have myself witnessed.

On PBS's poetic facility, our analysis of the plagiarized **Saint Edmond's Eve** in **V&C** and some of his privately released lyrics suggests that young PBS cultivated an air of *sprezzatura* by first memorizing verses (written by himself or others) and then pretending to compose them extemporaneously. But in **PF** there are passages, especially in **Fragment ("Yes! all is past"),** that show signs of haste, and **The Spectral Horseman,** which is unrhymed, frenetically paced, and leaves one line incomplete, may have been composed in the manner Slatter describes.

Slatter emphasizes how much money his firm and other printers and publishers lost because of PBS's irresponsible publishing schemes in order to shame Timothy Shelley into paying PBS's debt for **PF.** He may therefore both magnify his losses and overstress Sir Timothy's desire that Munday and Slatter "indulge" PBS in "his printing freaks"—a story that does not jibe with Stockdale's portrayal of Timothy Shelley as one who kept his son on a short leash financially. Thus Slatter's claim that **PF** was "almost stillborn" sounds like special pleading. Slatter does not describe **PF**'s format as a printed book, and when he wrote, he seems to have had no remaining copy of the volume that he says sold so badly. Munday and Slatter must, therefore, have sold the extra copies of the work in some fashion—at least as scrap paper—or this title would not be one of PBS's rarest. If not widely sold, it must at least have circulated from hand to hand, for we have Kirkpatrick Sharpe's letter dated four months after its publication to support PBS's contemporary testimony and Hogg's recollection that the work attracted considerable attention at Oxford. Though we may question Slatter's testimony on matters pertaining to the sales and financial rewards of **PF,** his account, which provides the only eyewitness evidence about the publication of **PF** other than Hogg's clearly fantasized version, effectively contradicts the claim that Hogg supervised the publication of the volume.

Slatter's narrative shares with Sharpe's letter of 1811 the idea that PBS directed "the profits [of **PF**] to be applied to Peter Finnerty" (?1766–1822,

DNB). Mac-Carthy and Cameron (*YS* 49–51) quote an advertisement of 9 March 1811 in the *Oxford University and City Herald* (also published by J. Munday) that names *A Poetical Essay on the Existing State of Things* as the poem from which Finnerty, an Irish journalist, was to receive the profits. (If this work was ever published, no copy has been located; see Appendix C.) Finnerty was tried and convicted of slandering Lord Castlereagh, but not until February 1811. How, then, could **PF**, as originally published in November 1810, have been written for his benefit? Did PBS or Slatter reissue **PF** under a new title in the spring, just before PBS's expulsion? Or do the statements of Sharpe and Slatter that **PF** was the work alluded to in the advertisement simply mean that they, never having seen *A Poetical Essay on the Existing State of Things,* assumed that the publication advertised in March was really **PF**?

Margaret Nicholson and Eleanor Nicholls

As Hogg contends, the name of Margaret Nicholson (?1750–1828, *DNB*) was familiar to the upper classes of the day as the "mad washerwoman" who on 2 August 1786 attacked King George with a dessert knife, wounding him slightly, and who was thereafter judged insane and incarcerated in "Bethlem" or "Bedlam"—that is, Bethlehem Hospital. For example, Kirkpatrick Sharpe's March 1811 letter (quoted above) to Lady Charlotte Campbell, lady-in-waiting to Caroline, Princess of Wales, shows no need to identify the madwoman. While at Eton, PBS could have heard from his mentor Dr. James Lind more of Nicholson's story than Hogg ever knew; Lind (1736–1812, *DNB*), a physician in the household of King George III, certainly knew colleagues who treated the king's madness, one of whom—Dr. Willis—PBS names both in an April 1811 letter to Hogg ("I wish you would allow me to be your Dr. Willis" [**Letters** I, 74]) and in **Peter Bell III** (line 474), and Lind may also have consulted at Bedlam. Stories about Nicholson probably also appeared in the newspapers from time to time, since she continued in her delusion that she was a member of the royal family and repeatedly sent letters of petition to the King and the Prince of Wales (see *SC* I, 34–38, 88–89), including at least one autograph manuscript poem of four irregular quatrains (unpublished; now in Pfz), which appeals to the king—"Justice with Mercy I so to Balance the scale I that Charitys Excellence I may never fail I . . . So the force of temporal power I But mitigate my plea I according to gods attribute I Thus redeem my pergery . . ."—and concludes, "So Subscribe myself I your Royal Highnesses I Most devoted I and Most Humble Servant I Margaret Nicholson." Lind (a free-thinking correspondent of David Hume and Benjamin Franklin) may have mentioned such verses to PBS, or contrasted the fate of this woman, confined to the sad precincts of Bedlam for a feeble attempt on the life of one person, with that of George III, who still lived in splendor, though his "liberticide" wars had killed thousands. She thus provided a convenient authorial persona to whom to attribute poems condoning regicide that PBS may have judged too dangerous to publish under his own name. Moreover, *The Life and Transactions of Margaret Nicholson,* written by her landlord Jonathan Fisk and published in 1786 (in Ashley, BL), mentions a love affair between her and a Swiss valet who, after promising to marry her, had abandoned her for another woman. If PBS, through his omnivorous reading, or Lind, or one of his Oxford friends, was aware of this aspect of Nicholson's life, he could have seen in her another dimension that sanctioned publishing his own poems about disappointed love that his developing literary aspirations and improving critical standards deemed to be, like the poems in *St. Irv,* unworthy of his name.

Even if PBS's knowledge of the would-be regicide was neither detailed nor specific, PBS may have seized upon the name Nicholson for personal reasons: (1) his grandfather Sir Bysshe Shelley had a mistress named Eleanor Nicholls, who lived at Lambeth, Surrey, and whose two sons and two daughters Sir Bysshe acknowledged and provided for in his will (see *SC* III, 444–45); (2) the elder of these sons was named John and the younger Bysshe (Sir Bysshe's legitimate sons being Timothy and John); and (3) PBS's father also had an illegitimate son (first name yet undiscovered) who was older than PBS and whom Timothy Shelley acknowledged and reputedly liked better than PBS (see J. Bieri, *Keats-Shelley Journal* 39 [1990]: 29–33). Nothing has yet been discovered of Nicholls's origins, and the mother of Timothy Shelley's natural son remains unidentified, but in naming the "editor" of **PF** "*John* Fitzvictor" (the prefix "Fitz" being the patronymic traditionally given to acknowledged illegitimate children of the royal blood), PBS may have played not only upon *Victor,* his nom de plume for *V&C,* but also on *John:* combined with Nicholson, the editor's name may well incorporate family jokes in Timothy Shelley's household about Sir Bysshe's mistress, his younger legitimate son, John, and his illegitimate son of the same name. Hogg and PBS's other Oxford friends, ignorant of this familial subtext, may have seen in the name Fitzvictor an allusion to Mrs. Fitzherbert, the Prince Regent's favorite mistress, whom he had actually married, according to contemporary rumor that historians have since confirmed (see note to **DW,** lines 67–70).

The personae whom PBS chose as the author and the editor of **PF** thus potentially meld public themes and semipublic gossip about the royal family with such personal matters as the illegitimate children of PBS's father and grandfather, and his method in constructing **PF** seems to involve a nexus of mutually supportive public and private associations that anticipates (albeit in a crude form) the complex intertwining of traditional myth, literary precedent, historical allusion, scientific knowledge, and personal emotion that characterizes his mature poetry. In critiquing *PF* and its constituent poems, we focus on two primary areas: first, the probable origins and occasion of each of the six individual poems, and, second, the extent to which each poem expresses PBS's own ideas and feelings and in what measure those ideas and expressions are modified by the volume's fictive structure, by representing the emotional outpourings of a mad laundress and would-be regicide, arranged by her nephew.

Motivation, Emphasis, and Effect

PBS's letters to Graham give more attention to the sexually free aspects of *PF* than to its political dimensions; he writes that "the [latter] part of the Epithalamium . . . is omitted in numbers of the copies,—that which I sent to my Mother of course did not contain it" and adds, "to my Father Peg is a profound secret" (*Letters* I, 23; no copies of PBS's poems belonging to his mother have surfaced and no copy of *PF* located to date omits any text). But, as PBS himself surely recognized, both the first, untitled poem—which some scholars believe was the one he later alluded to as *Essay on War* (see Appendix C)—and the assassination theme of the *Epithalamium,* which purports to celebrate the spiritual union of a regicide and the assassin of a republican demagogue, provide transgressions much more likely to trouble the Oxford authorities than was evidence of student prurience. Both PBS's letters and the Advertisement to *PF* also ignore the personal elements in the third, sixth, and perhaps fourth poems, which seem to reflect bitter disappointment in love and probably originated as reactions to the Grove family's decision to break off the tacit engagement of Harriet Grove to PBS. Only *The Spectral Horseman,* an imitation of the poems of "Ossian," might have seemed conventional enough to prevent the Oxford establishment from imputing to its author either a subversive purpose or a troubled mind, and even that poem can be interpreted as a call for rebellion in Ireland.

Although most poems in *PF* were probably written with a serious intent, the form that the published volume took has the air of a defiant undergraduate prank in which PBS, egged on by friends or (perhaps) by student provocateurs who wished him trouble, tried to offend almost everyone, especially the Oxford authorities and the adults in the Grove and Shelley households. In entitling the volume *Posthumous Fragments,* as with *Original Poetry,* PBS seems to have been playing a game of misnomers: Margaret Nicholson was not dead, and only two of the six poems in *PF* are presented as fragmentary (though the final word is omitted from **line 59** of *Spectral Horseman*). One likely explanation for these anomalies, given his treatment of the poems in *St.Irv,* is that he was apologizing for the imperfect quality of all the poetry, the sentimentally personal as well as the prurient or political.

Given the complexity of PBS's motives and the circumstances of the publication of *PF,* attempts to find ideological or artistic coherence in the volume have met with frustration. In *YS,* Cameron reads *PF* ideologically, finding evidence of PBS's growing radicalization and republicanism, but he treats only the first two poems. He sees **"Ambition, power, and avarice"** as an attack on "George III and his ministers as the instigators of the war with France" (54; see also 318–19). In *The Romantic Fragment Poem* (139–50), Marjorie Levinson tries to solve the unstated problem in Cameron's treatment of *PF* by showing that when the persona of Margaret Nicholson is regarded as a unifying dramatic element throughout the entire volume, the political message is dissipated by the merely personal problems of unhappy love bemoaned by Nicholson in the third, fourth, and sixth poems.

Readers who do not believe either that politics was PBS's primary passion during his first term at Oxford or that a simulacrum of Margaret Nicholson was in his mind when he wrote each of these poems may regard the personae of this woman and her nephew simply as carnivalesque masks employed to shield the young poet from taking full responsibility for his opinions, his emotions, and (perhaps) his imperfect versification. Such dodges had been a staple of English antiestablishment literature from the beginning and had gained momentum during the century from Swift's *Modest Proposal* and *The Drapier's Letters* through the letters of "Junius" and down to Byron's use of the mask of "Horace Hornem, Esq.," to attack the Prince Regent in *Waltz* (1812). PBS himself was later to employ similar fictions in **Peter Bell III**, in **Swellfoot,** and—more relevant to the personal poems in *PF*—in **Epipsychidion.** One way to read *PF* as a coherent whole that successfully fulfills its author's intention is to see it simply as a sophomoric prank by a precocious freshman.

Bibliographical Description

According to T. J. Wise's *A Shelley Library* (31), there were just six surviving copies of the first edition. We have located and collated five copies of *1810PF:* BL, Ashley (from Wise's collection, also at BL), Pfz (the copy in the Pforzheimer Collection, New York Public Library, previously owned by Hogg and H. B. Forman), Tx (the Stark copy, completely uncut and unopened), and Htn. (Though we queried a large number of other libraries, surveyed via OCLC's WorldCat, that listed copies of *1810PF* in their catalogues, all those copies proved to be facsimiles of *1810PF* rather than the original.)

In order to reduce such confusion in the future, we include a detailed bibliographical description of *1810PF.* This volume is a large quarto, the British Library's cut-and-bound copy measuring 21.6 × 27.8 centimeters, while the totally uncut and unopened Stark copy at the University of Texas *1810PF* Tx) measures about 29 × 23 cm. The complete volume (exemplified by *1810PF* Ashley) consists of four quires: A_{1-4} includes the half-title (verso blank), title page (verso blank), Advertisement (verso blank), and the beginning of the first poem on the quire's final leaf, recto and verso, the last page of which is numbered "8." The first leaf of quire B (pp. 9–10) concludes the text of the opening poem. The subsequent three leaves (pp. 11–16) contain the bulk of **Epithalamium**, which concludes on page 17, the first page of quire C (verso blank); C_2 (pp. 19–20) contains the complete text of **Despair**; folio C_3 (pp. 21–22) contains the text of the **Fragment** (*"Yes! all is past"*), and C_4 (pp. 23–24) begins the text of **The Spectral Horseman**, which concludes on page 25 (D_1 recto; verso blank). D_2 and the recto of D_3 (verso blank) contain **Melody to a Scene of Former Times** and (as the law prescribed) the printer's colophon, which had to appear on the last page containing text. The verso of D_3 and both sides of D_4 are blank; the final blank leaf is present only in the Ashley and Tx copies, having been discarded from the rebound copies.

The British Museum acquired its rebound copy of *1810PF* relatively early (accessioned "28 JU [18]59"); perhaps this BL copy was the model for the first reasonably accurate witness to the original text, a careful typefacsimile edition prepared by R. H. Shepherd that W. M. Rossetti first saw at Swinburne's house sometime before November 1868 (see *Rossetti Papers* [1903], 335), but T. J. Wise's suggestion that Shepherd's facsimile edition dated from ca. 1870 (Wise, 32), may mean that Rossetti saw a preliminary proof that was not perfected and circulated until later. Both Forman in *The Shelley Library* and Wise in *A Shelley Library* distinguish this facsimile from *1810PF* by its lack of the 1807 watermark in the paper, its misprinting of hateful streams for baleful streams on page 8 (*"Ambition, power, and avarice,"* **line 24**), and a different line break on the "dropped head" (second line of the title) of **Epithalamium**; Granniss adds that the paper of the facsimile is thicker than that of the original and that two rules on its title page differ from the original fancy rules of *1810PF*. Our computer collation of the two texts has turned up three additional minor textual differences between *1810PF* and Shepherd's facsimile: In **line 41** of the first poem, there is a comma after pride in *1810PF* that *c.1870 PF* omits; in the **Epithalamium**, **line 6**, Kings is followed by a semicolon in *1810PF* and by a comma in the facsimile; and slumb'ring in **line 11** of the final poem is spelled slumbering in the facsimile. Otherwise, Shepherd's edition is a reasonable duplicate of the original and, in the absence of the latter, can be a useful check on the accuracy of other texts.

Textual Authorities and Later Editions

There survive no holograph textual corrections in the extant copies of *1810PF* (not even in Hogg's copy, now at Pfz) and no unambiguous references to the volume after PBS's expulsion from Oxford. Unless there should surface another printing of the first, untitled poem under the title *An Essay on War* (see note below), or a copy of that poem, cut out of **PF** and emended for Godwin, *1810PF* provides the sole textual authority.

In *1870*, Rossetti omitted the first poem entirely on the grounds of Hogg's unsupported remark (Streatfeild, ed., 203) that it "had been confided to Shelley by some rhymester of the day," and Rossetti or the publisher—possibly to save space—ran together some of the lines of the poems from **PF** that he did publish, as well as making his usual massive changes in punctuation and orthography (changes not materially corrected in Rossetti's revised edition of *1878*).

We collate Shepherd's facsimile text (based on copies at Bod and Tx) as a primary textual witness, denominated *c.1870PF*. Three other separate editions of **PF** that claim to reproduce the original text literatim are of less interest. One by Forman (1877) consisted of copies of his accurate text of **PF** from Volume IV of his Library Edition (1876–77), which were offprinted for separate sale. A second facsimile mentioned in Wise's *Shelley Library* (31) was an abortive effort by Forman and Wise to produce an exact facsimile more accurate than Shepherd's; according to Wise, a single copy only was printed for them and is in his collection. This item (BL Ashley 5025) proves to be a copy of page proofs (printed on one side only) of Forman's undated facsimile. Finally, a copy in the Avon Books series (1911), though purporting to be a line-for-line reprint, was set in a much smaller format than *1810PF* and is riddled with textual errors. Most collective editions of PBS's poetry follow the poetic texts in **PF**, though with varying faithfulness and accuracy (see Historical Collations beginning on p. 375).

Advertisement

By using the first paragraph of John Fitzvictor's introduction here to call attention to the untitled first poem on the evils of war, PBS suggests that the volume's primary focus is political. The second paragraph, which promotes a possible sequel volume, raises the question of whether PBS had additional poems to use for such a purpose. Several times during his career, he asked his publishers to advertise or prepare for works that he had only begun to write or conceive, but he also had additional poems from the Oxford period that he later copied into **Esdaile Notebook (Esd)**. The last sentence, on the inchoate state of Margaret Nicholson's MSS, may be either an attempt to add substance to the fiction of the poems' authorship or a defense designed to limit the responsibility of the "editor" and to excuse the imperfections of the poetry, as well as its extreme opinions and sentiments, as the ravings of a deranged mind.

"Ambition, power, and avarice"

This poem is without a title in *1810PF*, though some later editors entitled it "War." Frederick L. Jones (**Letters** I, 231n) and the editors of *1989* (I, 114) suggest that this was PBS's *Essay on War* that he later promised to send to Godwin (PBS to Godwin, 16 Jan. 1812; **Letters** I, 231). This supposition remains likely as long as there can be identified no separate volume entitled *War* or *Essay on War* published at Oxford or London in 1810–11, and thus far nobody has claimed to have seen one. If PBS sent a copy of *"Ambition, power, and avarice"* to Godwin, he may have removed it from **PF** to keep his mentor from seeing the sophomoric sexual jokes in **Epithalamium** and the personal laments later in the volume. Shelleyans should remain alert, however, for the belated reappearance (in some newly computerized library catalogue?) of another poem on war that may prove to be a lost work by PBS.

If PBS did write a lost poem on war, *"Ambition, power, and avarice"* still could provide clues to the tone and possibly some of the contents of that work. Though Nathaniel Bloomfield (the shoemaker brother of the popular self-taught poet Robert Bloomfield) wrote his *Essay on War* (1803) in blank verse, a poem named "Essay" in PBS's day was more likely to be written in heroic couplets—a convention established by Pope's *An Essay on Criticism* and *An Essay on Man* and reinforced by such intervening poems in the "middle" or "legislative" style on the nature of man in society as Johnson's *The Vanity of Human Wishes* (1749), Goldsmith's *The Traveller; or, A Prospect of Society* (1764), and a series of poems by Cowper—*The Progress of Error, Truth, Expostulation,* etc. Any work by PBS entitled *Essay on War* would have castigated monarchs and statesmen for initiating wars that caused suffering for their people: among his surviving early poems that contain such attacks are **To the Emperors of Russia and Austria, The Monarch's Funeral Anticipated**, and others that focus on the victims of imperial wars, including **Zeinab and Kathema, The Voyage, Henry and Louisa,** and **A Tale of Society as It Is**—all in **Esd**, as well as **Falshood and Vice**, which PBS first included in **Esd** and, when he failed to publish that volume, added to the notes of **Queen Mab (QM)**.

Antiwar sentiments, found in European literature throughout the eighteenth century (e.g., in *Gulliver's Travels* and *Candide*), gained strength during the wars of Europe's monarchies against republican France. Joseph Fawcett (d. 1804; *DNB*), a schoolmate of Godwin and a Dissenting clergyman whose liberal lectures at London's Old Jewry influenced both young Wordsworth and Hazlitt (and whose later disillusionment with the French Revolution may have made him one of the models of Wordsworth's "Solitary"), published pacifist poems in *The Art of War* (1795) and *War Elegies* (1801). In 1803 Nathaniel Bloomfield published his book-length *An Essay on War*, which was praised by Henry Kirke White in Southey's edition of

White's *Remains* (II, 252–55). Other likely sources for PBS's ideas include Godwin's essay entitled "Of Trades and Professions" in *The Enquirer* (1797) and some of the numerous antiwar poems in the public press between 1808 and 1810 (specimens of which appear in *British War Poetry in the Age of Romanticism,* ed. Betty T. Bennett, 1976).

But poems that expatiated upon the evils created by kings who send their subjects to war could still be considered treasonous by a monarchy fighting for its survival, and PBS's attack goes beyond the popular antiroyalist and antiministerial feeling generated by such military debacles as the Walcheren expedition of 1809, or the Foxite Whigs' politically motivated advocacy of peace after Napoleon's defeat of the Austrians led to the Treaty of Schönbrunn (Oct. 1809), which renewed the subservience to Napoleon of all Britain's continental allies except Portugal and the Spanish rebels. PBS's poem condemns *all* wars as exploitations of common people by self-indulgent rulers and seems to hint that regicide was the surest cure for the disease. There is no evidence, however, that PBS wrote this poem to represent the views of the historical Margaret Nicholson, who neither was politically active nor held antimonarchical sentiments. On the contrary, her delusion was that *she* was the rightful monarch of England.

Textually, ***"Ambition, power, and avarice"*** presents few problems. The likely errors in *1810PF* are (1) some apparently inconsistent punctuation in **lines 12–13** and **49–52**, (2) a failure to include commas to set off <u>Oppressors of mankind</u> and <u>Heaven</u> in **lines 23** and **34,** and (3) a failure to indent **line 63** (the first line on p. 10 in *1810PF*) to show that it begins a new verse paragraph following the Alexandrine in **line 62**. We have left a line space between **62** and **63** but have not otherwise emended, because these oversights seem unlikely to confuse readers and others may identify reasons for these anomalies in PBS's text that have eluded us. Although the poem is untitled in *1810PF,* the half-title for the entire volume, "Posthumous Fragments," appears just above it.

line 2. <u>bleeding world</u>: Cf. Charlotte Smith's indictment of "Wise Politicians" who "consign | To tears and anguish half a bleeding world!—" (*The Emigrants* II.321; *The Poems of Charlotte Smith,* ed. Stuart Curran [New York: Oxford UP, 1993]).

line 5. <u>avenger's</u>: i.e., Satan's.

line 9. Here *hectic* is a noun ("a fever"—*Entick's . . . Dictionary,* 1795) and *does . . . flush* a verb.

line 14. As PBS's line suggests, at this period the government provided no support for "dependants of military casualties" (*1989*).

line 16. <u>their listless ear</u>: Throughout this poem, singular nouns appear with collective plural intent, as here, where *ear* (with a plural adjective) implicates the dual ears of several kings. PBS never totally gave up this old-fashioned usage (e.g., **Athanase,** line 72), perhaps reinforced by his tutors at Eton and Oxford, but it appears less often in his mature poems.

line 24. baleful may come from relevant contexts in Milton's *Comus:* "*Circe* with the Sirens three, . . . Culling their Potent herbs, and baleful drugs" (253–55), *Paradise Lost:* "four infernal Rivers that disgorge | Into the burning Lake thir baleful streams" (II.575–76), or Goldsmith's *The Traveller:* "Yes, brother, curse with me that baleful hour, | When first ambition struck at regal power" (lines 393–94). In *c.1870PF* Shepherd accidentally substituted "hateful" for baleful.

line 27. Here, many a widow (grammatically singular) dropping a single tear is a variant of the idiom described in the note to **line 16,** above.

lines 29, 35. The widow's appeal represents God in depersonalized deistic terms as an Almighty Power rather than a "Heavenly Father," just as the author (or typesetter) fails to capitalize he in **35,** where the pronoun refers to this ultimate force in the universe. PBS's diction and orthography may subtly reinforce his antitheistic message.

line 37. Did PBS write parts of this poem at a level of abstraction that betrayed him into using the singular pronoun thine for a collectively plural monarchs; is thine a solecism introduced to represent the poem as the work of semiliterate Nicholson; or is monarchs simply a copying or typographical error?

line 51. Though it is not clear to us why there is a semicolon after sway and periods at the ends of the previous and the following lines, we have left this evidence of what may be a hasty revision of the text at this point (by PBS or the compositor), an unnoted grammatical usage that signals the compression of the subject into the relative pronoun (i.e., Who sees for "[He] . . . | Who sees"), or perhaps another solecism by "Margaret Nicholson."

line 58. The Latinate inversion of subject and predicate nominative here tends to muffle PBS's—or Nicholson's—meaning.

lines 59–62. last eventful day: Though the echo of "dust to dust" from the burial service suggests simply the leveling of kings to common humanity through natural death, eventful and the image of the sword-wielding warrior suggest the apocalyptic final battle between Good and Evil.

lines 62–63. See Commentary to this poem on the possible significance of the Alexandrine at the end of a page in *1810PF.* A space between these lines alerts readers to the probable beginning of the final verse-paragraph.

lines 68ff. Fear, War, Woe, Terror, and Ruin are here capitalized, presumably to emphasize—or personify—them (as Byron capitalizes similar abstractions in *Childe Harold* I.xxxviii–xl). The practice of the Romantics (as in W. Wordsworth's and S. T. Coleridge's early volumes) may derive partly from the Greek habit of personifying human emotions (as in Homer and Hesiod) and partly from the traditional typographical practice of using capitals for emphasis (as Pope does consistently). The succession of George I to the British throne reinforced the native practice with the German usage of capitalizing all nouns. Byron's MSS show more frequent use of capitals for emphasis than do those of PBS, but neither poet's practice has been fully analyzed.

lines 73–76. The image of Ruin as a charioteer careening in the wake of Fear foreshadows the chorus in **Hellas** (711ff.) in which "The world's eyeless charioteer, | Destiny" is led by Ruin and followed by Renovation.

line 77. smoking: a common, though old-fashioned, contemporary spelling.

lines 79–83. In *1892W*, Woodberry adds quotation marks to mark the first half of **lines 79** and **80–82** (along with the first half of **83**, which *1810PF* enclosed in quotes) as direct quotations of words spoken by a voice (**79**). Though Woodberry's reading seems a likely one, the interpretation has such far-reaching implications that we prefer to advance it in this note, rather than to emend the sole textual authority, thereby foreclosing other possible interpretations.

line 85. enthusiast: This rare adjectival use of the word may follow William Collins's *Ode to Pity* 29; in PBS's day the noun *enthusiast* tended to have positive connotations for religious Dissenters and political liberals but negative ones for Anglicans and Tories. Cf. PBS's clearly positive use of the word at *QM* I.49.

line 87. Since the hated cause of the work of hell (**86**) is clearly said to be the Monarch (**78, 83**), to advocate the removal of that cause, if human agency were involved, might suggest that the poem advocates regicide.

line 88. Though in **lines 68–76** PBS capitalized the nouns discussed above, he did not always personify or emphasize either similar negative nouns (e.g., those in **1–2, 32, 41**, and **44**) or even such positive ones as peace, innocence, and love in the final line. We are not certain whether the MS copy, the typesetting, or PBS's proofreading was haphazard, or whether he intended to leave such inconsistencies as attributes of "Nicholson's" irregular habits of composition.

Fragment. Supposed to Be an Epithalamium of Francis Ravaillac and Charlotte Cordé

This poem, which PBS discussed in his letters to Graham, is one that Hogg and other Oxford friends of PBS may have altered, introducing little jokes that turned a serious poem depicting tyrannicides as saints into a sexually risqué schoolboy burlesque. Its "plot" begins as Margaret Nicholson's vision of the afterworld (**lines 1–68**) and then turns into an erotic lyric dialogue between François Ravaillac and Charlotte Corday d'Armans, the hero and heroine of "Nicholson's" vision. Traditional epithalamia celebrate the fleshly pleasures of newlyweds, but the thematic keynote of PBS's radical statement appears in **lines 42–45**:

> Congenial minds will seek their kindred soul,
>   E'en though the tide of time has roll'd between;
> They mock weak matter's impotent control,
>   And seek of endless life the eternal scene.

Corday (b. 1768 of a noble family in Normandy) was inspired by Girondin refugees from the Assembly to travel from Caen to Paris on behalf of the Girondin cause; on the pretext of informing on the Girondins at Caen, she obtained an interview with Jean Paul Marat, the leading Jacobin journalist, confined to his bathtub by a skin disease, and stabbed him in the heart (13 July 1793). Corday was guillotined on 17 July 1793. In 1811, PBS was unlikely to have known Southey's poem celebrating "Corde" published in the Tory *Morning Post* on 13 July 1798, which Southey apparently believed was the fifth anniversary of her execution (see *Contributions of Robert Southey to the* Morning Post, ed. K. Curry [1984], 73–75). But as Gary Kelly notes (*Women, Writing, and Revolution;* 1993), Corday is a heroine of Helen Maria Williams's *Letters Containing a Sketch of the Politics of France . . .* (1795 et seq.; I, 126–38), which PBS almost certainly did know. There PBS would have found a woman of principle, courage, and dignity, as well as a male admirer who felt himself drawn to Corday as by an elective affinity: in a long footnote, Williams tells how a young man named Adam Lux fell in love at first sight with Corday as "he accidentally crossed the street as she was passing on her way to execution"; he promptly published "a pamphlet, in which he proposed raising a statue to her honour," was imprisoned for this provocation, and thereafter talked of nothing but Charlotte Corday and "the guillotine; which . . . appeared to him transformed into an altar," until he, too, was "executed as a counter-revolutionary" (I, 134–35).

Historically, François Ravaillac (1578–1610) gained notoriety by assassinating King Henri IV of France (14 May 1610), who, as Henry of Navarre, leader of the Huguenot faction in the French civil wars, won the throne of France when he conciliated Roman Catholic moderates by converting to

Catholicism. After gaining military control of the country, he issued the Edict of Nantes (1598), which granted religious and political rights to the Protestant minority. Voltaire's *Dissertation sur la mort de Henri IV* (*Oeuvres complètes* [La Société Littéraire-Typographique, 1785], X, 339–54) insists that Ravaillac, though influenced by the rhetoric of militants among Henry's enemies in the Catholic League, acted alone. After tortures failed to force Ravaillac to reveal any accomplices, he was (according to a contemporary account) executed by being dragged and pulled apart by horses, after which his limbs and torso were burned and his ashes scattered to the winds.

Given this background, it becomes clearer why PBS, either in his own persona or, indeed, in that of Nicholson, with her pretentions to royalty, might have begun the poem as an attempt to versify the love of Adam Lux for Charlotte Corday than why he should involve Ravaillac. Both "Nicholson" and PBS, with his aristocratic bias against demagogues, were likely to sympathize with Corday, an idealistic young woman who gave her life to avenge the slaughter of the September Massacres (though since the immediate consequence of Marat's assassination was the Reign of Terror, it would be hard to argue that the end justified her means). But while in *Political Justice* Godwin names Ravaillac among those assassins who, though misguided, "seem to have been deeply penetrated with anxiety for the eternal welfare of mankind" (II.iv; 3rd ed., ed. Priestley [1946], I, 153), we have found no purely historical sources likely to have convinced PBS that Ravaillac's assassination of Henri IV ended a tyranny. Still if PBS began with Lux as his hero, the name <u>Francis</u> does provide an exact metrical substitute for *Adam*.

Moreover, even if PBS in fact knew all about Ravaillac, he may have decided to use him for one or another of these reasons: (1) to forestall extreme actions by readers of his attack on kings in **"Ambition, power, and avarice"** by stigmatizing violence through choosing at least one unpalatable French assassin to appeal to British readers' prejudice against the terrorism of the French Revolution—thus according with the views of Godwin and the mature PBS that political violence leads ultimately to military tyranny, as in Napoleonic France; (2) to focus on reactionary, rather than radical terrorists, to implicate the evil of such other bloody episodes as the royalist counterrevolution in the Vendée that the English supported; (3) simply to illustrate "Nicholson's" mental confusion; or, (4) because the total destruction of Ravaillac's body, which historical sources reported in great detail— for example, in Simon Vigor's *Les canons des conciles de Tolede, de Meaux, de Mayence, d'Oxfort, & de Constance* (1615)—adds thematic resonance to PBS's claim that <u>congenial minds</u> can overcome the forces of <u>weak matter</u>.

Finally, Nora Crook has suggested to us that "both Ravaillac and Corday were idealists . . . whose violent acts unleashed worse violence. . . . PBS is writing a vindication; though misguided, their idealism and willingness to pay the price for it, no matter how cruel, should be rescued from the opprobrium which attaches itself to assassins and leads them to be dismissed as fanatics" (personal communication).

Even more ambiguous than the political implications of the poem are its sexual elements. As Matthews and Everest note in *1989*, the tyrannicides are welcomed into a "Heaven" that consists of "limitless sensual indulgence" (I, 118). PBS's first letter to Graham about **PF** mentions that "the latter part of the Epithalamium was composed in compliance with the desires of a poetical friend" (***Letters*** I, 22)—possibly Hogg; in his next letter, PBS tells Graham a less credible story, probably to protect himself and his accomplice: "The part of the Epithalamium which you mention, (i.e., from the end of Satan's triumph[)] is the production of a friend's *mistress;* it had been concluded there [i.e., at **line 68** or **73**] but she thought it abrupt & added this" (***Letters*** I, 23). The first statement—that PBS composed the section at the request of "a poetical friend"—is probably as close to the truth as we can get, for both entries in the notebook (now at Pfz) that Hogg kept at Oxford in 1810–11 and the sexual fantasies that fill his romance *Memoirs of Prince Alexy Haimatoff* (1813) suggest that if Hogg did contribute to **PF** (as he claims in *Shelley at Oxford*), his mark would most likely be found in the lubricious lines in this poem—including, perhaps, a faked typographical error in **line 109**. For PBS's critique of the male erotic fantasies in *Alexy Haimatoff*, see his anonymous review of Hogg's novel, published in the *Critical Review* for 1814 (***Prose***/EBM I, 140–46, esp. 142).

Whoever may first have suggested ending the **Epithalamium** with this love duet, PBS himself composed it—though not without models. White (*Shelley* I, 93) suggests parallels with the odes of Catullus, staples of the Latin grammar school education, that (as Matthews notes in "Shelley's Lyrics," rpt. *1977*) also provided models for epithalamia that PBS wrote in 1821. Crook and Guiton (*Shelley's Venomed Melody* [1986], 42–43 and n.) point to lines from John Nott's "a fragment to Lydia," an imitation of the Renaissance Latin erotic lyric "Lydia, bella puella candida" by Cornelius Gallus. Nott (uncle of the clergyman of the same name who castigated PBS at Pisa in 1821) included this imitation in his anonymous translations and imitations of the *Basia* ("Kisses") by Johannes Secundus (see below). The relevant lines from "To Lydia" are quoted in the footnotes to John Mason Good's translation of Lucretius's *De Rerum Natura* (1805–7), a parallel text that PBS bought in 1815:

> Let a warmer crimson streak
> The velvet of thy downy cheek:
> Let thy lips that breathe perfume,
> Deeper purple now assume;
> Give me now one *humid kiss,*
> Now repeat the melting bliss;

> Soft, my Love!—my Angel, stay!
> Soft! you suck my breath away.
> (Good's Lucretius II, 191)

Crook and Guiton conjecture that PBS may have been familiar with Good's Lucretius earlier than 1815, inasmuch as Medwin says that PBS "deeply studied" Lucretius at Eton (Medwin, *Life*, ed. Forman, 50). Alternatively, he may have read "To Lydia" in Nott's *Kisses*, which reads in the four most relevant lines differently from Good's version:

> Give me little billing kisses,
> Intermix't with mur'mring Blisses.
> Soft! my love!—my Angel, stay!—
> Soft!—you suck my Breath away,
> (1778 [3rd ed.])

Nott's *Kisses* was again reprinted in 1803, with no substantive changes in these lines.

Two sentences in PBS's 21 November 1810 letter to Graham suggest another likely influence on the form of ***Epithalamium:*** "I have some songs which if Woeffl wants I will enclose. What have you done about the Opera?" (**Letters** I, 22; *corrected from MS*). Was this opera a joint undertaking, with music by Graham and lyrics by PBS? Even if not, the antiphonal songs of Charlotte and Francis may have grown out of PBS's knowledge of—or experimentation with—the writing of operatic lyrics.

The headnote to this poem in *1989* (I, 117–18) cites several other possible influences: the expression of ideals through dream-visions goes back at least to Cicero's "Scipio's Dream," which outlines the cosmology from Plato's *Timæus*, including the music of the spheres. Though Angelo Mai did not publish until 1823 the main text of Cicero's *De Re Publica* (which he rediscovered in 1819–20, as the undertext of a palimpsest), the "Somnium Scipionis" from Book VI had also survived in manuscripts of both Cicero and Macrobius, who wrote a commentary on it; the text appears in early nineteenth-century school selections of Cicero's writings available to PBS. Other influences suggested by *1989* include Volney's *Ruins* IV, Southey's *Joan of Arc* IX (1795; though if PBS did not read this edition, he could not have seen this section, which Southey excised from the 2nd ed.), and *The Grecian Girl's Dream* . . . from Moore's *Epistles, Odes and Other Poems* (1806 and ff.). But PBS's imagination has fused all such possible influences into something new, for ***Epithalamium*** resembles none of these works in thought, form, diction, or tone.

Textually, *1810PF* requires emendation only at **line 70.** Other apparent errors in **lines 66, 101,** and **109** may be relevant to PBS's intention.

lines 1–68. Although some diction in this induction to the dream-vision suggests self-parody (e.g., **line 2**), such ideas as the woes of lost mankind and the ceaseless rage of Kings (**5–6**) are basically those that PBS expressed in *QM* and, in less blatant forms, throughout his poetry.

Except for **lines 10–23**, the induction consists of stanzas with eight lines of iambic pentameter followed by an Alexandrine, rhymed *ababcdcdD*. We have not succeeded in identifying an earlier model for this precise form, and it may reflect young PBS's difficulty with composing in the more complexly rhymed Spenserian stanza (*ababbcbcC*).

line 8. mazy: By PBS's day, hedge mazes had been a feature of landscaping and a source of popular entertainment for at least two centuries; *mazy* appears in poems by Spenser, Milton (twice), Pope (three times), Gray (*Progress of Poesy*, four times), Johnson, Cowper, Moore, and dozens of others read by PBS, though Coleridge's *Kubla Khan* (not published till 1816) was probably not one.

line 34. Sylph of symmetry: Since the use of guardian Sylphs derives from Pope's mock-heroic *Rape of the Lock*, the reference may be intended to set a tone for the poem to extenuate its political extremism.

line 66. thou despots: Several editors, noting the grammatical solecism, emend thou to "ye," but PBS may have intended to characterize the limitations of his washerwoman persona.

lines 68–74. Although the four rows of asterisks may suggest that four lines in the last nine-line stanza have been censored, the existing rhymes here show that PBS simply failed to complete the stanza. This lapse, in turn, suggests that PBS invented his stories that a friend requested this passage, or that a mistress wrote the following lyrics, to cover up his own failure to complete the poem in a uniform stanzaic pattern.

line 70. angels': We have emended from "angels" (*1810PF*).

lines 74–113. Not only were these antiphonal solos and choruses written by PBS, but they mark, perhaps, the first time that he discovered his personal lyric voice, which would achieve its greatest successes in the choruses and lyrics of the **Prometheus** volume and the choral sections of **Hellas**. As noted above, there were precedents for these antiphonal erotic dialogues in Latin lyric poetry and in Italian opera. Even if PBS began with a satirical view of his characters, he may simply have been carried away by his own lyric impulse and created one of his finest early compositions.

lines 82–90. SYMPHONY, as used before **line 82**, probably should be defined as "Music . . . sung . . . by a number of performers with pleasing effect; concerted or harmonious music" (*OED* 4). Among the antecedents to this passage in the *Basia* ("Kisses") of the Dutch neo-Latin poet Johannes Secundus, see especially "Kiss V": "While you, sweet Nymph! with Am'rous Play, | In kisses suck my breath away;" and "Kiss XIX": "But still, YE BEES well-favour'd prove; | . . . If e'er I claim . . . | To share those Lips, those honied Lips! with you | Nor suck INSATIATE all their Balm away, | And to your bursting Cells the Sweets convey" (*Kisses: A Poetical Translation of the BASIA of Joannes Secundus* . . . 2nd ed.; London: printed for J. Bew, 1778). See also "A Kiss after the Manner of Secundus: To Cynthia," pages 236–38 in *Kisses,* 3rd ed., with additions (London: printed by D. Bond for J. Bew, 1778 [engraved title dated Jan. 1779]). In Regency slang (as in nineteenth-century French), "kiss" as a verb could mean to have sex or reach orgasm. Eric Partridge, *Dictionary of Slang* (8th ed., updated by P. Beale) notes that kiss "As the sexual favour" is a usage from "S[tandard] E[nglish].—2."

line 90. death: a literary double entendre for orgasm.

line 101. lye: This archaic spelling for "lie" may include a submerged pun, alluding to the "author's" occupation as a washerwoman.

line 109. Though the typographical anomalies here seem to result from loosening of the types, the evidence is ambiguous. The five copies of *1810PF* examined (BL, Ashley, Htn, Pfz, Tx) have identical literals and similar spacing; none shows a space between "w" and "a" of wat, as should appear if the "h" fell out accidentally. Perhaps PBS altered the type to create the sophomoric visual pun t wat. Yet a similar gap between the "wa" and "t" in *1810*Tx and similar slippage in the "r" in "ea r" in BL, Htn, Pfz, and Tx show that some type was loose in the chase. One explanation that accounts for this evidence is that the type at the end of the line moved after PBS or the printer altered the first two words. A note by Hogg shows his interest in names for female genitalia: "*Pullet,* a woman's *belle chose* so called— at Leeds — proved upon oath in a rape cause at York" (f. 2 verso in a college notebook of Hogg's, now at Pfz, that also contains PBS's poem beginning **"Oh wretched mortal"**), and the vulgarism twat, as Robert Browning learned to his sorrow, is a seductively poetic word. (Browning used it in the first edition of *Pippa Passes,* thinking that it named part of the costume of a nun; see *OED.*) Though Hogg may have suggested inserting this word in **Epithalamium** by means of a faked typo, PBS (who, as we noted in the commentary to **V&C,** had learned to set type) was more likely either to have carried out the scheme or persuaded someone at Munday and Slatter's printshop to do so. PBS's familiarity with slang terms for female sexual organs is apparent in his professing to be shocked at Hogg's York address in Coney Street: "I blush when I write the directions to you.—How salacious a street" (**Letters** I, 78).

One of PBS's motives for carrying out such a prank may have been to distract the attention of the Oxford authorities from the call for tyrannicide in **lines 109–12**, for any accusation on political grounds would inevitably have become entangled with the vulgar pun. But PBS had another defense as well: his lines on tyrannicide here echo closely Scott's early ballad "Cadyow Castle" where the hero Bothwellhaugh begins to recount his assassination of the Regent Murray, whose men had burned Bothwellhaugh's house and murdered his wife:

> Sternly he spoke—"'Tis sweet to hear
>   In good greenwood the bugle blown,
> But sweeter to Revenge's ear,
>   To drink a tyrant's dying groan."

(quoted from *Minstrelsy of the Scottish Border* [2nd ed., 1802–3], III, 392). The same verbal text reappears in Scott's *Ballads and Lyrical Pieces* (4th ed., 1812, 51).

Despair

Unlike the first two poems in the volume, this poem and two of those that follow were probably personal in origin, rather than being written specifically as part of the Margaret Nicholson hoax (though, as noted in the introduction to the volume, Nicholson was reputed to have experienced such disappointments). **Despair** seems to embody PBS's feelings of rejection at the growing split between himself and Harriet Grove (see the poems and notes in *V&C*). After the death of her sister Louisa on 19 June 1810, Harriet's diary records the waning of her emotional involvement with PBS; and after the publication of *V&C*, with its indiscreet references to her sister Charlotte, she turned away from PBS and toward her parents and siblings for emotional support. Although the text is thus meaningful when read in the context of PBS's life, Levinson (*Romantic Fragment Poem*) reads this and the other personal poems as the work of Nicholson, contending that they illustrate the subjective weakness of that "poet's" political ideology and, hence, "her" sanity.

In **Despair** the poet (whether seen to be PBS or Nicholson) wonders why Nature and the world of spirits do not empathize with the pain of his (her) loneliness and destroy him (her). Thematically the poem thus explores the relationship between Nature and the suffering human individual later developed in **Alastor, Mont Blanc, [Stanzas written in Dejection near] Naples—December 1818,** and **Adonais.** Formally, PBS employs the same non-Spenserian nine-line iambic stanza ending in an Alexandrine that he used in the first part of **Epithalamium.**

line 22. tempest's lacks an apostrophe in *1810PF;* we (like other editors) emend to the possessive singular, rather than plural, because of the parallels with tide and lightning in adjacent lines.

line 30. The commas after <u>peace</u> and <u>joy</u> seem to be rhetorical or metrical (i.e., to mark pauses in reading the line), rather than syntactical.

line 36. In the final line, though the poet plans to curse God (here an impersonal "power"), as Job's friends urged him to do, he also testifies that the "power" never made anything in vain. PBS seems to be saying that God—perhaps viewed as an impersonal Necessity—created him to curse his creator. Given this as PBS's recurrent self-image, such figures as Satan, Cain, Job, the Wandering Jew, Prometheus, Faust, and, peripherally, even Nicholson herself became appropriate imaginative surrogates of the poet.

Fragment ("Yes! all is past—swift time has fled away")

Again PBS employs his quasi-Spenserian stanza in a personal poem to express a mood of despair, concluding with a frenetic dialogue between the poet and a <u>maniac</u> who is his alter ego (cf. ***Julian and Maddalo***). Perhaps this was one of the poems that PBS dashed off while Henry Slatter waited for additional copy for the press, though if so, it may have been an uncompleted poem that PBS had well enough in mind to set down and complete hastily when called upon to supply more verse.

lines 10–11. The poet here contemplates suicide by drowning to actualize the figurative death recorded in **line 4**, which presumably resulted from rejection by a beloved and/or by society more generally.

lines 19–22. When the poet meets a <u>maniac</u> double (<u>he</u>) in **19** and addresses him, PBS (unlike W. Wordsworth) does not think of the person as homeless or *physically* outcast but as a psychologically alienated person who chose to leave <u>home</u> because of an unsympathetic family. The poet's speech clearly ends with **line 22**, where we, like other editors, have added closing quotation marks that are not present in *1810PF*.

lines 23–27. The poet, who in the first stanza was imagined as dead from rejection, here imagines the <u>maniac</u>'s beloved to be dead from coldness. The <u>maniac</u> will resurrect her by sleeping in <u>her grave</u>, after which the lovers' ghosts will ride the storm together, as the narrators in *Wuthering Heights* later imagine the spirits of Heathcliff and Cathy walking the moors or flying up to knock on the outside of upper-storey windows.

lines 28–31. The poet, too emotionally drained to weep, will instead <u>rest</u> on the maniac's <u>bier</u> and <u>shriek in horror</u>. PBS, having raised the volume of this "theatrically exaggerated 'mad song' " (*1989*) to a full <u>roar</u>, ends the poem precipitously. Again, his improving taste during his first months at Oxford may have begun to outstrip his limited artistry.

The Spectral Horseman

The Ossianic form of this poem is packed with "as many miscellaneous gothicisms as possible" drawn from several cultures (*1989* I, 125). One can almost imagine a group of undergraduates each adding a few lines to a collective horror poem, or PBS improvising a few lines on each topic suggested by his friends; but Hogg would hardly have omitted such a story, and the poem's individual features can all be traced to PBS's list of favorite authors at that time—especially works by Scott, Southey, and Moore. The poem also bears the stamp of PBS's individual poetic imagination. He may have written it hastily in the manner described by Henry Slatter (see general commentary on **PF** above). The tetrameter lines are basically anapestic, though irregular both as to number of syllables and placement of stresses—almost a ballad without rhyme.

line 5. It is the: "It is not the" in *1870;* "Is it the" in *1989*. Neither of these emendations (or errors) is based on documentary authority.

The phrase Benshie's moan derives from Scott's *The Lady of the Lake* (1810), and the following description of Brian the Hermit, Clan Alpine's evil cheerleader—a figure almost outcast enough to provide an analogue to the Wandering Jew in PBS's poetry—may have suggested the entire **Spectral Horseman:**

> The only parent he could claim
> Of ancient Alpine's lineage came.
> Late had he heard, in prophet's dream,
> The fatal Ben-Shie's boding scream;
> Sounds, too, had come in midnight blast
> Of charging steeds, careening fast
> Along Benharrow's shingly side,
> Where mortal horseman ne'er might ride; . . .
> (2nd ed., 1810, 106; III.vii.17–24)

As Scott noted, a "Ben-Shie" (banshie) was "the female Fairy whose lamentations were often supposed to precede the death of a chiefton of particular families" (346).

line 13. vampire: This reanimated corpse that extends its life by sucking blood from living people (or, figuratively, exploits others to sustain its life) originated in middle European folk myths but was familiar enough in eighteenth-century England for Goldsmith to refer to it casually in *The Citizen of the World* (1762, Letter LXXX), in describing a corrupt and bloodthirsty magistrate. The *OED* cites earlier discussions of the vampire in travel books on the Balkans, but as *1989* suggests, PBS's reference here derives directly from Book VIII of Southey's *Thalaba* (1801), with its series of extended notes on reports of "Vampirism" in Transylvania and Greece, the passage most relevant here being: "In a certain town of *Hungary*, . . . a part of *Transylvania* . . . The people . . . believe that certain dead persons, whom they call Vampires, suck the blood of the living, insomuch that these people appear like skeletons, while the dead bodies of the suckers are so full of blood, that it runs out at all the passages of their bodies, and even at their very pores" (Vol. II, 106–7). *Vampire* probably became part of young PBS's judgmental vocabulary, for after he left Harriet Shelley she referred to him in a letter to Catherine Nugent as a vampire (see **Letters** I, 421 fn.). PBS used the word again in **Prometheus Unbound** (III.iv.147).

lines 14, 16. seven years' end: As *1989* notes, John Leyden's *The Elfin-King* in M. G. Lewis's *Tales of Wonder* contains this exact phrase (twice) within a narrative that closely parallels this passage. Also relevant to PBS's theme of apocalyptic upheaval in the cause of justice is the biblical Year of Jubilee, in which the land was to be allowed to lie fallow for renewal every seventh year (the basis of academic sabbatical leaves) and slaves were to be freed after seven times seven years (Leviticus 25).

line 31. snows of Nithona: This reference sounds as if it comes from one of the Ossianic sagas, and *1989* cites the name Inisthona ("Island of Waves") in Ossian's "War of Inis-thona" and Ithona in his "Conlath and Cuthóna." PBS's copy of *The Poems of Ossian*, "translated by" James Macpherson, Esq. (2 vols., London: Cadell & Davies, R. Faulder [etc.], 1807), survives (Pfz), with PBS's signature and "1810" on the title page of each volume. In this edition, "The War of Inis-thona" appears at I, 413–22, and in "Conlath & Cuthona" (no accent in this edition) mentions "I-thona" and in a note at the foot of the page defines it as *"island of waves;* one of the uninhabited western isles," at II, 252. There may also be an echo of the River Nith in Scotland.

line 35. Inisfallen: Ireland; in *1989*, Matthews and Everest give as a literal translation of the Gaelic, "island of the Fa-il, or Falans."

line 41. meteors of midnight: the lightning bolts alluded to in **39**; a meteor was any sublunar aerial phenomenon, including rain, clouds, etc.

lines 47–49. The main clause (Then does the dragon . . . moan and yell) is interrupted by a parenthetical comment on the dragon (who chain'd . . . curses the champion of Erin). Though *1989* cites the victory of Cuchullin over "a worm or dragon which rose from a lake," no source for PBS's knowledge of this battle has been found. His images may, instead, conflate the myth of St. George, patron saint of England, who slays the dragon, with a story in which suppressed dragon powers, like the conquered Titans buried under volcanos in Greek myth, fulminate and threaten to overthrow the champion (i.e., the conqueror) of Ireland—perhaps Lord Castlereagh, whose role in the bloody repression of the United Irishmen in 1798 was being publicized by the Irish journalist Peter Finnerty about the time **PF** was published. PBS's sympathy for the cause of the Irish, evident as early as *The Irishman's Song* in *V&C*, was natural for the scion of a Whig family allied with the Duke of Norfolk, one of the Howard family who had remained Roman Catholics for generations after the Reformation.

line 59. In *1810PF* nothing follows gigantic except the two asterisks, which PBS or the compositor added to mark the place where a word was missing; they may either provide evidence of the haste with which PBS composed this piece, or (as Jack Stillinger suggests to us) presage the "ineffably gigantic" that was to reappear in **Prometheus** as Demogorgon, whose "dreaded name" (according to a note in Peacock's *Rhododaphne* [1818]) "was so sacred among the Arcadians, that it was held impious to pronounce his name" (180).

Melody to a Scene of Former Times

Here the poet (PBS or "Nicholson") laments the loss of a lover's (probably Harriet Grove's) affection; the dash in **line 11** may represent the name Harriet, though not even iconoclastic PBS would have used her name publicly in this context. As in other poems of this period, the indentations of these irregularly rhymed iambic tetrameter lines indicate the location of rhymed lines, rather than breaks in the thought: there are no stanzas or verse paragraphs.

line 20. This line remains unrhymed until **lines 45** and **46.**

line 28. Two years of speechless bliss: If the poem is read as PBS's poem about the end of Harriet Grove's attachment to him, the two years are those between their first serious recorded correspondence, late in 1808, and the apparent rupture between them after the publication of *V&C,* in the autumn of 1810 (Hawkins, *First Love,* 11, 45–51).

Poems from
St. Irvyne; or, The Rosicrucian

John Joseph Stockdale, who undertook the sale of **Original Poetry** "by Victor and Cazire" (**V&C**), only to suppress it because of the plagiarism from *Tales of Terror*, was impressed enough with PBS to publish the young man's second Gothic romance, **St. Irvyne** (**St.Irv**), and, apparently, to consider publishing **The Wandering Jew** (**WJ**) as well. Writing to Stockdale from Oxford on 14 November 1810, PBS enclosed his corrected proofs of **St.Irv** (**Letters** I, 20); perhaps these proofs were long "slips," like modern galley proofs, because had the proofs been set in pages, PBS would have known how many pages there were and should not have expressed surprise less than a week later "that the romance would make but one small volume" (I, 21). By 2 December he was asking Stockdale impatiently, "When *does* St. Irvyne come out?" (I, 24).

Printing and First Distribution

The printing of **St.Irv** was complete, and PBS had received a few copies by 18 December 1810, when from Field Place (his home) he inscribed a copy (now at Berg) to his uncle Robert Parker. Though PBS did not emend the text of any of the poems in that copy, a change in the prose—a careted insertion of *again* before "seek the gaming table" (p. 80, line 10)—seems to be in his hand. PBS also wrote to Stockdale, approving his "advertisement of the Romance" and asking that copies be sent to Thomas Jefferson Hogg, Thomas Medwin, and "Miss Marshall, Horsham Sussex" (**Letters** I, 24). James Bieri has identified the last as Elizabeth Marshall (later Mrs. Clough, d. 1830), daughter of a friend of Timothy Shelley who was curate of the Horsham Church attended by the Medwins and the Shelleys; according to E. J. Lovell, "this church, specifically, and its curate of thirty-five years, the Rev. George Marshall, . . . provided the irritant which was eventually to produce *Queen Mab* and Shelley's other attacks upon organized Christianity" (*Captain Medwin* [1962], 7). On 11 January PBS, still at Field Place, asked Stockdale to "send a copy . . . to Miss Harriet Westbrook" (**Letters** I, 40), the school friend of his sisters whom he later married. His cousin and old love Harriet Grove may not have received one, though her diary does record that she read an unnamed "novel" 22–24 December 1810.

In his 18 December 1810 letter to Stockdale, PBS wrote, "Mr. Munday of Oxford will take some Romances," before concluding the paragraph, "I will enclose the Printers account for yr. inspection in a future letter" (I, 25). Though this might suggest that PBS engaged the printer, Samuel Gosnell, whose shop on Little Queen Street was near Lincoln's Inn Fields (where PBS often stayed with his cousin John Grove), Stockdale states in his memoir of PBS that the "manuscript of St. Irvyne, The Rosicrucian ... I promised to revise and print for him" (*Budget* [20 Dec. 1826], 9); that is, Stockdale had agreed to engage a printer and see the manuscript through the press. Because Gosnell, who had been in business at the same address since 1790, frequently printed books for Stockdale, the bookseller probably selected him, while PBS remained responsible for paying the costs, for PBS told Stockdale on 14 November, "I would wish it to be published on my *own* account" (**Letters** I, 20). Perhaps PBS sent "the Printers account" to Stockdale simply to make sure that Gosnell was not cheating him (PBS to Stockdale, 18 Dec. 1810 and 11 Jan. 1811; **Letters** I, 25, 40). Stockdale ultimately claimed that he had been left holding the bag for the printer's bill, though his assertion that he lost some £300 on **St.Irv** seems inflated, even when his costs and accumulated interest until 1827 were added, for the number of surviving copies of the two issues of **St.Irv** (dated 1811 and 1822, when Stockdale reissued the original sheets with a new title page) suggests that he sold most of the copies.

Stockdale and Gosnell (who later printed Hogg's *Memoirs of Prince Alexy Haimatoff*) not only transposed PBS's loose orthography and punctuation into the house style, but the printer used every typographical means to reduce the number of pages and thus the cost of paper and imposition. Stockdale and Gosnell also altered PBS's spelling and capitalization and heavily punctuated the text of **St.Irv** according to the best conservative conventions of that day, and PBS (perhaps aware of his errors and solecisms in **V&C**) accepted their guidance. As he returned the proofs to Stockdale, he replied thus to what must have been strictures on the state of his original press copy: "I return you the Romance by this day's coach. I am much obligated by the trouble you have taken to fit it for the press. I am, myself, by no means a good hand at correction, but I think I have obviated the principal objections which you allege" (14 Nov. 1810; **Letters** I, 20).

Poetry in Shelley's Gothic Romances

The only poetry that PBS included in **Zastrozzi** (1810), his first publication, is found in epigraphs, which cast light on PBS's favorite authors and works of the period. These epigraphs and their locations in **Zastrozzi** are: *Paradise*

Lost II.368–71 (title page), *Macbeth* I.vii.39–44 and I.v.45–50 (Chaps. 9 and 15), Scott's *Lay of the Last Minstrel* III.ii.7 (9) and *Marmion* III.xiii.3–4 (16), Thomson's *Seasons: Spring*, 990–92 (13), and Horace's *Odes* III.iii.7–8 (17); this last, significantly for the future author of **Prometheus Unbound** (**Prom**), appears in Horace's description of the "man tenacious . . . in a righteous cause" who "is not shaken . . . by the mighty hand of thundering Jove. <u>Were the vault of heaven to break and fall upon him, its ruins would smite him undismayed</u>" (the underscored words translate the Latin epigraph itself).

St.Irv also includes epigraphs from *Paradise Lost* II.681–83 (Chap. 3) and Scott's *Lay* (12)—the same line ("For love is heaven, and heaven is love") that he used in **Zastrozzi** and that Byron later employed quite differently in *Don Juan* XII.xiii.1–2. PBS also used tags from lesser-known works, one entirely unlabeled. That for Chapter 8 is from his own (then unpublished) **WJ** (II.74, 102–10). In *1989* (I, 83–84), Matthews and Everest identify three other epigraphs as the work of PBS, but the epigraph for Chapter 9—"If Satan had never fallen, | Hell had been made for thee" (a distich that PBS also uses in his 23 April 1810 letter to Edward Fergus Graham; **Letters** I, 9)—actually comes from Edward Young's verse tragedy *The Revenge* (1721), slightly altered (see Appendix E, 469). Epigraphs to Chapters 4 and 7 of **St.Irv** labeled "Olympia" and the unlabeled couplet that heads Chapter 2 may either be the work of PBS (as *1989* suggests) or come from another unidentified author. These epigraphs are discussed in Appendix D, "Dubia."

Besides these poetic epigraphs, six original poems and fragments are scattered through the text of **St.Irv**, just as lyrics are distributed throughout both *The Monk* by Matthew G. Lewis and *Confessions of the Nun of St. Omer* (1805) by Charlotte Dacre ("Rosa Matilda"), a clear influence on PBS's romance. (Dacre's *Zofloya*, which provided plot elements for both **Zastrozzi** and **St.Irv**, has poetry only in its epigraphs.)

Time of Composition

Though the publication date of **St.Irv** is clear, the period of its composition is less certain. Cameron (*YS*, 302–3) dated it between September 1809 and April 1810, with additional tinkering before it was published by 18 December 1810. But he and others later noted that some poems in **St.Irv** were composed after April 1810. Since these poems appear throughout the text of the printed book, PBS either did *not* complete his romance before August 1810, or else he later revised it extensively to integrate the poetry. Cameron also argues in *YS* that PBS's reading of William Godwin caused him to lose interest in this second Gothic romance and that Stockdale had to goad him into completing it. Though PBS was being radicalized while at Oxford, he did not therefore immediately cease to be a "votary of Romance" (PBS to Godwin, **Letters** I, 227), for *St. Leon,* Godwin's most Gothic work, was one model for *St.Irv* (**Letters** I, 21). PBS had begun, however, to consider poetry and other types of fiction to be more satisfactory genres than "romance"; on the day that *St.Irv* was published, he wrote to Stockdale that he was writing "a Novel . . . principally constructed to convey metaphysical & political opinions by way of conversation" (**Letters** I, 25), thus contrasting this "Novel" of ideas with *St.Irv,* which he always calls a "romance." Late in 1810, PBS was also revising *WJ*—a very Gothic poem that he tried to persuade Stockdale to publish as soon as *St.Irv* was off his hands—and composing **Posthumous Fragments of Margaret Nicholson** (*PF*), which PBS arranged to publish at Oxford while *St.Irv* was going through the press in London. Both *WJ* and *PF* also attempt to embody radical themes within a spirit of imaginative "romance" rather than the realistic "novel."

Shelley's Self-Parody

PBS's self-critical denigration of his early writings may have arisen not so much from his political radicalism as from a growing dissatisfaction with their aesthetic quality. He presents the entire *PF* volume and most of the poems in *St.Irv* within dramatic contexts, as though authored by and representing the tastes of limited characters in specific dramatic situations; and he shows himself—not only in his roles as the omniscient narrator of *St.Irv* and the "editor" of *PF,* but even through the thoughts of some of the characters who write or recite poems within *St.Irv*—as being ashamed of the quality of the verses. In *St.Irv,* PBS had no need (as he did with *PF*) to screen himself from responsibility for politically subversive ideas or sexually charged themes, for the poetry of *St.Irv* never violates the accepted norms of contemporary Gothic romances.

Thus, *St.Irv,* like *PF,* includes elements of parody that may signal PBS's awareness that these poems failed to meet his own standards for poetry. He assigns the first two poems to Wolfstein and Megalena, his anti-hero and anti-heroine, who feel such doubts about the worthiness of their poems that they destroy them before anyone except the omniscient narrator (and thus his readers) can see them. The third and longest poem in *St.Irv*—the Gothic **Ballad** recited by one of the outlaws—appears as a peasant's tale praised by a band of cut-throats; in PBS's aesthetic, this meant that the poem pandered to low and corrupted tastes. Only the last three poems— each entitled **Song** and rendered by Eloise de St. Irvyne, the over-innocent heroine—seem to have PBS's approval, but even one of these proves to be a pastiche taken from two distinct poems that PBS had earlier written to Harriet Grove, and there may be elements of parody in the settings and occasions upon which Eloise sings the other two (see the notes below). PBS at age nineteen thus asks us to refrain from judging his sensibility by the poems in **St.Irv**—or by his Gothic romances themselves. Later PBS was very disparaging of both **Zastrozzi** and **St.Irv** to everyone except his father, to whom PBS would never concede failure, and Stockdale, his publisher, whom he was encouraging to sell enough copies of **St.Irv** to pay the printer's bill.

In PBS's second letter to Godwin (10 Jan. 1812), when the young man promised to send his mentor copies of his two Gothic romances, he added that Godwin should not "consider this as any obligation to yourself to misapply your valuable time" (**Letters** I, 227) and assured him in his next letter that "Zastrozzi and St. Irvyne were written prior to my acquaintance with your writings" (I, 231). By 1817, PBS was even more embarrassed by these works: Leigh Hunt told Browning that he had discovered a copy of **St.Irv** "in Shelley's own library at Marlow once, to the writer's horror & shame—'He snatched it out of my hands'—said H—" (*The Brownings' Correspondence* XI, ed. Philip Kelley & Scott Lewis [1993], 108; see also 106).

Reviews

If, as we believe, PBS had doubts about the merits of **St.Irv** when he published it, the three surviving contemporary reviews (all in periodicals that also reviewed *V&C*) would have tended to deepen those misgivings. In January 1811, the Tory *British Critic* dismissed the romance in short order by quoting its first sentence, stating that those readers who decide to read further "will find the Cavern of Gil Blas with very little variation of circumstance, a profusion of words which no dictionary explains, such as *unerasible, Bandit, en-horrored*, descriptions wilder than are to be found in Ratcliffe, and a tale more extravagant than the St. Leon of Godwin"; the notice concludes by wishing that "this gentleman of Oxford had a taste for other and better pursuits" (see *Romantics Reviewed* [*RR*], C, I, 204). The *Literary Panorama* for February 1811 devoted two full pages to **St.Irv** but denigrated it effortlessly by adding these headings to its quotations from the book's opening and its conclusion: "HOW TO BEGIN A ROMANCE. A.D. 1811.", and "HOW TO END A ROMANCE.—A.D. 1811." (*RR*, C, II, 542–43). Finally, a full year later, in January 1812, the rabidly Tory *Antijacobin Review*, which had reviewed *V&C* in October 1810, included two and a quarter pages that take the ideas in **St.Irv** seriously enough to condemn its teachings on marriage and on the judgment of Wolfstein's soul (*RR*, C, I, 31–32). None of these reviews alludes to the poetry.

Textual Authorities

Since PBS, whatever his misgivings, read proofs and chose to accept the text of *1811* as his public work (e.g., not emending the poems when he sent a copy of ***St.Irv*** to his uncle Robert Parker), we have followed that printing as our copy-text, collating the poetic texts in the following copies of ***St.Irv*** (*1811*): Berg (presentation copy from PBS to Parker); Bod 1 (= Shelley-Rolls copy, Shelley adds. e. 23); Bod 2 (= Huth copy, Don.e.322); BL; Tx (Stark); Pfz 1 (bookplate of George Allison Armour, but with blue slipcase in style of Forman's cases for his Shelley first editions); Pfz 2 (= John Spoor & Frank Hogan copy); and Htn. Though imprecise inking has left a few marks of punctuation ambiguous in some copies, we have found no textual variants in the poetry of these seven copies of *1811*.

In 1822, Stockdale reissued the unsold sheets of *1811* with a new title page (see Forman, *Shelley Library*, 15), probably to take advantage of the publicity surrounding PBS's death in order to recover his cost for the printing. We have collated the *1811* text of the poems with two copies of the 1822 issue that are at Tx, again without identifying any variants. Other primary authorities have been collated with individual poems: for the first poem, we collate the version in ***V&C*** *1810;* for the second poem, Medwin's quotation of it in his letter in the notes to Robert Montgomery's *Oxford, a Poem* (*1835*); and for the fourth and fifth poems, the versions in PBS's letters to Graham of 22 April and 14 September 1810 (***Letters*** I, 7–8 and 16).

"'T was dead of the night"

Virtually the same poetic text appears as the final poem in ***Original Poetry*** "by Victor and Cazire" (***V&C***) under the title ***Fragment, or The Triumph of Conscience.*** Did PBS first include it in an early draft of ***St.Irv*** and borrow it from that unpublished manuscript to fill up two blank pages at the end of ***V&C?*** Or did he write it in August 1810, as it is datelined in ***V&C***, to help fill out that volume and then insert it later in the romance? In either case, by the time ***St.Irv*** went to press, PBS's dissatisfaction with the quality of the fragment may be seen in the way he first introduces and then disposes of it in Chapter 1. Wolfstein, the anti-hero, "sank on a mossy bank, and, guided by the impulse of the moment, inscribed on a tablet the following lines; for the inaccuracy of which, the perturbation of him who wrote them, may account"; immediately after the poem is presented, "Overcome by the wild retrospection of ideal horror, which these swiftly-written lines excited in his soul, Wolfstein tore the paper, on which he had written them, to pieces, and scattered them about him" (***St.Irv***, 17–18).

St.Irv went to press in November 1810, after unfavorable reviews of ***V&C*** appeared in the October issues of the *Antijacobin Review* and the *Literary Panorama*, and PBS may also have heard that volume criticized by Stockdale and by earlier friends and acquaintances also at Oxford, such as George Marshall of Horsham, Elizabeth's brother, who was then twenty-three and a fellow of Wadham College (see White, *Shelley* I, 82). PBS seems never to have mentioned *V&C* to his new friend Hogg, indicating that he already had qualms about its poetry and plagiarisms by the time they met sometime in October. Thus, the narrator's negative view of some poems in *St.Irv* probably reflects PBS's personal feelings about them.

Since the printers of *St.Irv* took great pains to correct PBS's errors and inconsistencies, we can gauge the idiosyncrasy of his own punctuation and orthography by comparing the two texts of this poem printed three months apart. As the texts of the poems in the **Esdaile Notebook** (**Esd**) and PBS's letters and other privately released MSS show, he punctuated more lightly than was characteristic of "learned" poetry of the day and he used more archaic forms of orthography than were current in London printshops. The notes to **lines 1–8** below highlight differences between the two versions in their first two stanzas.

lines 1–3. The version of the poem that appears in *St.Irv* changes the orthography by replacing *V&C*'s "'Twas" and "sate" with 'T was and sat; *St.Irv* also adds a comma after night, changes *V&C*'s terminal comma (**line 1**) and comma plus dash (**2**) to semicolons, and adds a comma after Around (**3**).

lines 4–5. *St.Irv* adds a dash to *V&C*'s comma (**4**), changes the stanza's final exclamation to a period, and alters *V&C*'s "presaged" to presag'd (**5**) so as to mark the elision of the final *e*.

line 6. *St.Irv* changes *V&C*'s comma after started to an exclamation mark plus a dash, but leaves the following the uncapitalized.

line 7. lightning, which danc'd in the sky; *St.Irv*
lightning that danced on the sky, *V&C*
The change from "on" to in probably corrects a typographical error in *V&C*; PBS to the end of his career, when revising his texts, almost invariably replaced *that* with *which*, the sound of which he clearly preferred.

line 8. *St.Irv* adds a comma after me; rolling is followed by a comma in both *1811* and *1822*, though in some copies, bad inking makes it appear to be a period. (Hereafter, these notes will record only verbal differences between **St.Irv** and *V&C;* consult the collations below the text of the poem for additional variants in punctuation and orthography.)

lines 10, 12–13. The imperfect rhyme of war with ear and fear is not authorized by the tables of rhymes in Bysshe, *Art of English Poetry* (1705), or *Entick's New Spelling Dictionary*. However, in John Walker's *A Rhyming Dictionary . . . of the English Language* (2nd ed., London: J. Johnson, J. Walker, G. Wilkie and J. Robinson [etc.], 1806),—a "reverse dictionary" that alphabetizes words in the order of their final rather than their initial letters—

words ending in *-ear* are listed between those ending in *-dar* and *-far*, thereby giving the impression that *ear* should rhyme with *jar*. See also lines 10 and 12 in **"Ghosts of the dead!"** and note, below.

lines 15–17. The rhyming of <u>upholding</u> and <u>holding</u> provides one of the few instances in PBS's early versification of *rime riche*—the repetition of the same exact accented syllable in the rhyming words. Forman, in his edition of Medwin's revised *Life of PBS* (1913), accepts Medwin's change of <u>upholding</u> in **15** to "upfolding" as "an authentic correction" of the text (51n and 52). We believe, however, that the sense of **15–16** is <u>The ghost of . . . Victoria then strode, upholding her form on the whirlwind</u>, with <u>upholding</u> having the fifth sense of the transitive verb "uphold": "to raise or lift up; to direct upwards" (*OED*). To substitute "upfolding" here seems to increase, rather than solve the syntactical difficulties. We would be unlikely, in any case, to emend on the authority of Medwin, whose published quotations of PBS's texts are notoriously unreliable (partly, no doubt, because his handwriting is very difficult to decipher).

line 16. <u>The ghost of the murder'd Victoria</u>: PBS's early poems are filled with women seduced or raped and then abandoned or murdered. Though this theme was common in the literature of the eighteenth and early nineteenth centuries, from Samuel Richardson's *Clarissa* through Lewis's *The Monk* and Dacre's romances, PBS's youthful attention to the woman's dilemma probably relates both to his personal role-playing as victim and his sensitivity to the feelings of oppressed women that later led him repeatedly either to attempt their rescue from the "tyranny" of parents or other authority figures or to represent such tyranny and escapes in his poetry. These feelings may signal some personal trauma in his youthful experience—possibly his humiliations at school, or animosity toward his older, illegitimate half-brother (see James Bieri, *KSJ* 39 [1990]: 29–33)—but they probably originated in the petty despotism of Timothy Shelley over PBS, his mother, and his sisters, including Timothy Shelley's threat to have PBS confined as a madman (the fate of Sir Bysshe Shelley's older brother). Whatever their sources, PBS later transformed his feelings into sympathy for suffering victims and subtle portraiture of the psychology of oppression in **The Cenci** and **Prom.**

"Ghosts of the dead!"

Later in Chapter 1 of **St.Irv**, Megalena, whom Wolfstein finds imprisoned by the robber band that he has joined, is left alone and thinks of her father, the Count de Metastasio, who had been murdered by these bandits: "Again her thoughts recurred to her father: tears bedewed her cheeks; she took a pencil, and, actuated by the feelings of the moment, inscribed on the wall of her prison these lines: [the poem follows; then—] Here she paused, and, ashamed of the exuberance of her imagination, obliterated from the wall the characters which she had traced: the wind still howled dreadfully: in fearful anticipation of the morrow, she threw herself on the bed, and, in sleep, forgot the misfortunes which impended over her" (38–40).

The poem's central conception may derive (as *1989* suggests in a note to **line 14**) from James Macpherson's note to "Ossian's" *Conlath and Cuthona:* "It was long thought, in the north of Scotland, that storms were raised by the ghosts of the deceased.... the vulgar ... think that whirlwinds ... are occasioned by spirits, who transport themselves, in that manner, from one place to another." In PBS's copy of *The Poems of Ossian* (London: Cadell and Davies [etc.], 1807) in Pfz, this note appears at II, 253.

lines 1–2. In a letter in the notes to Robert Montgomery's *Oxford, a Poem* (*1835*, 164), Thomas Medwin observed that these lines imitate lines 17–18 of Byron's *Lachin y Gair,* which PBS knew from *Poems, Original and Translated* (1808), the edition of Byron's early poems that he probably owned (see note below to **"How swiftly through heaven's wide expanse," lines 17–18**). Byron's text reads: "Shades of the dead! have I not heard your voices | Rise on the night-rolling breath of the gale?" If PBS consciously plagiarized here, the words may possibly contain an element of parody.

line 1. dead!: An exclamation mark was the conventional contemporary mark of punctuation to indicate the vocative case (i.e., when a person or personification was addressed directly). Used thus, the mark might—but did not necessarily—suggest heightened emotion. Stockdale or Gosnell, the printer, followed the convention consistently here, but elsewhere PBS does not, reserving the ! to express emotion, rather than to indicate grammar and syntax.

line 2. night-rolling: reverberating by night.

line 4. past: This common contemporary variant spelling of the past participle of *pass* emphasizes the elision of the last syllable and the unvoiced pronunciation of its final consonant.

line 5. Jura: a range of mountains running northeast from the eastern end of Lake Geneva to the Rhine near Basle, along the modern border between France and Switzerland.

line 8. The mark of punctuation at the end of **line 8** is a comma in *1811*, though in a few copies poor inking may suggest that it is a period.

lines 8, 16. Whilst: This variant form, pervasive in this poem, seems to have been PBS's preferred form throughout his early manuscripts. In *Esd* MS Pfz, *whilst* appears 35 times to 13 appearances of *while* as a conjunction or an adverb, besides a few times as a noun. Nora Crook also informs us that "PBS seems to have had a mania for changing MWS's 'while' into 'whilst' in *Frankenstein*" (personal communication).

line 12. jar (like war in line 10 of the previous poem), rhymes imperfectly with ear. PBS, who often contorted the syntax in his early poems to achieve exact rhymes, left all rhymes in the middle two stanzas of this poem inexact: Jura/fury, beneath/death, howling/rolling (a rhyme that also appears in lines 6, 8 of the previous poem), and ear/jar. Was he trying to imitate (or parody) the imperfect rhymes of the ballad revival, or—as Crook suggests to us—equating free rhyming with artistic and (later) with moral and political liberty? (See also Claire Clairmont, *Journals*, ed. Marion Kingston Stocking [1968], p. 195.)

line 16. In *1811*, this line is not indented (as the pattern of indentations suggests it should be). In the volume's small 12mo format (i.e., having twelve leaves in each gathering of the printed book), if this long line had been indented, it would have spilled over, adding an extra line to page 39 and causing it to end with the first half of a hyphenated word. We have restored this indentation to remove an anomaly introduced by compositorial expedience.

Ballad ("The death-bell beats!—")

In Chapter 2 of *St.Irv*, while the bandits drink at midnight, their leader, Cavigni, exclaims: "Steindolph, you know some old German stories; cannot you tell one, to deceive the lagging hours?" (46). Then the narrator continues:

> Steindolph was famed for his knowledge of metrical spectre tales, and the gang were frequently wont to hang delighted on the ghostly wonders which he related.
> "Excuse, then, the mode of my telling it," said Steindolph, "and I will with pleasure. I learnt it whilst in Germany; my old grandmother taught it me, and I can repeat it as a ballad."—"Do, do," re-echoed from every part of the cavern.—Steindolph thus began:

The **Ballad** then follows. "As Steindolph concluded, an universal shout of applause echoed through the cavern" (47–51).

That Steindolf's old grandmother's tale is applauded by bloodthirsty bandits makes PBS's attitude toward this **Ballad** suspect. Moreover, the poem takes its plot from *The Black Canon of Elmham; or St. Edmond's Eve*, which PBS had earlier plagiarized from Lewis's *Tales of Terror* and republished in *V&C* as **Saint Edmond's Eve** (q.v.). *Tales of Terror* itself was a take-off on *Tales of Wonder* by Lewis, Scott, and Southey, and there may well have been a parodic intent behind PBS's scene in which bandits drawn from

Schiller's *Die Räuber* (1781–82) are entertained by a pseudo-German verse tale à la Lewis, under the watchful eye of Wolfstein, a guilt-ridden stranger, and Ginotti, who proves to be the Wandering Jew. This tendency toward parody also emerges in the language, where in several places (noted below) PBS seems to have carried the tone past the "Gothic sublime" into the ridiculous.

The headnote in *1989* suggests as a principal source for this poem *The Mad Monk* (sometimes claimed for Wordsworth, but usually attributed to Coleridge as a parody of Wordsworth; see Coleridge, *Essays on His Times*, ed. D. V. Erdman III, 291). We find this connection weak; Lewis's *The Monk* and *The Black Canon* provide stories of guilt-ridden men who break religious vows by impregnating maidens and murdering them, whereas *The Mad Monk* murders Rosa (a name obvious for poems with continental settings) because she loved another and resisted the monk. Not only does PBS's poem differ from *The Mad Monk* in rhyme scheme, structure, and tone, but he could never have seen *The Mad Monk* unless he had read either the *Morning Post* for 13 October 1800, or else *The Wild Wreath* (1804; *NSTC* #1330), a rather obscure poetic miscellany featuring poems by Mary "Perdita" Robinson—poet, actress, and mistress of the Prince Regent (ed. M. E. Robinson, Perdita's daughter).

line 4. dark monk may parody "black canon" in **Saint Edmond's Eve.**

lines 26-29. These lines have an air of parodic fun, especially when the monk stamp'd on the ground like Rumpelstiltskin.

line 39. to: compared to.

lines 42-46. In *1811*, the typography suddenly reverses the pattern of indentation here, probably because the compositor, by indenting the shorter rather than the longer lines, could avoid several spill-overs and complete stanza 8 on page 48, the final page of signature C. We have left the indentation of this stanza as in *1811*, for PBS in reading proofs may have agreed that it was better to reverse all the indentations than to spill-over his longer lines.

line 52. Monk!: On the use of the exclamation point to signal vocatives, see the note to line 1 of the previous poem.

lines 61, 67. The marks of punctuation ending these two lines appear to be regular colons in most copies that we have examined but are doubtful in *1811* Tx. (In *1811* BL and *1822* Tx [= Wrenn] only the colon in **67** appears irregular.) But under magnification, these types are all colons, their apparent irregularity being due to imperfect inking or imposition.

line 70. enhorror'd: Though not in the *OED* and ridiculed by the review in the *British Critic* as a neologism (see Reviews, above), this word occurs in crucial passages of two romances by Charlotte Dacre ("Rosa Matilda"): *Confessions of the Nun of St. Omer* (1805; II, 105) and *Zofloya* (1806; ed. Montague Summers [London: Fortune Press, n.d.], 259, in the fourth paragraph from the end of the romance). Apparently coined on the analogy of such participles as *emboldened, enchanted, enraptured, enthralled*, it does not appear in *Entick's New Spelling Dictionary*, which, however, lists several similar verbs equally unfamiliar to us—for example, *endew* ("to disgorge, throw up"), *enercate* ("to kill, butcher"), *enfetter, engaol, engrapple, enwheel*, and *enwomb* (128–32).

line 71. PBS approved fiend's as a possessive singular (rather than a nominative plural, as most editions emend the word), because rave here is not a verb, but a noun—once a very rare functional shift, according to *OED*, though now common whenever a play receives "raves" from critics.

line 73. The comma following shadows, which is parallel to rave (71)—the two nouns form the compound subjects of linger—is a typical contemporary mark of rhetorical rather than grammatical punctuation, designed to elicit a pause in the reading of the line, even though it separates subject from verb.

lines 74–78. Although the Monk tries to repent, his awareness of the weight of his sins makes him (like Ambrosio in *The Monk*) both despair of salvation (76) and compound his crime by desecrating Rosa's grave.

lines 82ff. *1811* indents **82, 83,** and **85;** presumably the compositor indented **82** before realizing that **84** was too long to indent without causing a spill-over line; when he then decided to indent the stanza's "b" rhymes instead of the "a" rhymes, he forgot to reset **82** to the left margin. PBS, who read proofs, may have accepted this printer's expedient to forestall the need to add extra pages to the volume by reducing the number of spill-over lines.

Since the shorter lines, with the "b" rhyme, are indented in the final three stanzas, we have moved **line 82** to the left margin as the simplest way of restoring indentation as a guide to the rhyme scheme.

line 85. Gosnell's compositors regularly used apostrophes to mark the elision of the *-ed* in past participles (e.g., Mix'd in **83**), but the convention seems not to apply to Whistled (**85**). Poets from Pope through Cowper used the apostrophe to represent elision of syllables, but PBS (apparently following another orthographical convention) more often changed the spelling of the word—"passed" to "past," "lightning" to "lightening," "mixed" to "mixt"—to represent its intended pronunciation. (Later editors often imposed on his poetry still a third convention—one foreign to it—

by adding an accent mark above the final *e* of any past participle that is to be pronouncèd.)

line 88. Rosa's <u>half-eaten eyeballs</u> (like <u>her skeleton lungs</u> in **96**) achieve a parodic quality that (it is charitable to believe) was part of PBS's intention.

line 91. <u>brain</u>: In *1811* the final letter of this word is a damaged type, broken at the top, so that in some copies (e.g., Bod 1) it appears to be a *u* (or an *n* turned upside down) until it is magnified.

line 94. <u>mine</u>] my *1989:* Matthews and Everest, either inadvertently or to modernize according to the Longman series guidelines, changed the once-standard alternative form for the first person singular possessive pronoun when it was used before a word beginning with a vowel or an unaspirated *h*.

line 99. <u>And as</u>] As *1927*/III: This reading in the Poetry section of the Julian Edition is simply an error, since the reading remains unchanged where it appears in the romance ***St.Irv***, in the Julian Edition's text of the prose (*1927*/V).

Song ("How swiftly through heaven's wide expanse")

The textual history of this poem illustrates the intricate relationship between private and public poetry in PBS's canon. The text in ***St.Irv*** is a corrupt redaction of the poem of ten quatrains that PBS wrote to Harriet Grove during her visit to Sussex and London in April 1810 and also sent to Graham in a letter dated 22 April 1810 (= MS PMgn; ***Letters*** I, 7–8). The version that appears in ***St.Irv*** (132–33) consists of the first four stanzas of that private love lyric, rounded off with two stanzas, the final one being a variant of the second stanza of *"Song ("Come—————! sweet is the hour")* from ***V&C***. In the letter containing MS PMgn, PBS authorized Graham to set the lyric to music, but he may have considered that version too personal to publish in a book that his family and friends would know that he had written. Still more likely, PBS may have truncated the original love poem and added the conclusion about a lover with <u>torn, despis'd, neglected and forlorn</u> <u>heart</u> sinking <u>in death</u> in reaction to news that the Grove family had decreed an end to his relationship with Harriet. On the other hand, PBS may have melded the ***St.Irv*** version out of the two disparate parts to parody the poetry in the sentimental novels that he had once enjoyed but now was beginning to outgrow. For an earlier personal poem that also associates Grove with the ruins that PBS calls "St. Irvyne," see the final poem in ***Esdaile Notebook*** in Volume II of this edition.

Chapter 7 of ***St.Irv*** (which follows directly after Chap. 4, thereby illustrating either PBS's Shandean sense of humor or his cavalier carelessness about this romance) provides a setting for the poem quite different from the tête-à-tête between PBS and Harriet Grove that gave rise to the earlier version of *"How swiftly."* Here Eloise de St. Irvyne recalls a time when a treacherous postilion led her and her mother from their broken carriage to a mountain house filled with bandits. (PBS here combines two distinct situations, involving different characters, from Lewis's *The Monk*.) A bandit of "gigantic stature" but with a "countenance of excessive beauty" and "an expression of superhuman loveliness" (i.e., Ginotti, the Wandering Jew) asks Eloise if she can sing. "'I can,' replied Eloise; 'and with pleasure.'" The *Song* follows; and after it, we find: "She ceased;—the thrilling accents of her interestingly sweet voice died away in the vacancy of stillness;—yet listened the charmed auditors; their imaginations prolonged the tender strain" (131–33). Again, excesses in both the plot and the diction suggest that PBS was parodying, as well as imitating, his Gothic and Sentimental models.

line 8. moonbeams rest] moonbeam's rest   MS PMgn, *1913, 1964J, 1989*. Though moonbeam appears in the singular in **lines 3** and **14,** it seems less jarring to allow the variety here (since either a single moonbeam, several moonbeams, or a generic moonbeam could represent PBS's varied intentions) than to twist the syntax by following *1989* in reading rest as a noun. This is especially true because how fair . . . the trees! (**7–8**) echoes *Merchant of Venice* V.i.54: "How sweet the moonlight sleeps upon this bank!" PBS, following the schoolboys' tradition of changing a few words while plagiarizing their compositions in Latin verse from classic authors, has altered "moonlight sleeps" to moonbeams rest.

See notes to line 1 of **Song. To ────── ("Ah! sweet is the moonbeam")** in *V&C* and to the letter version of *"How swiftly through Heaven's wide expanse"* (in **Ten Early Poems [1809–1814]**, pp. 301–5 below).

line 13. Irvyne's tower: PBS gave this romanticized name to Hills or Hill Place, the seat of Lady Irwin, which (according to Paterson's *Roads* [1808], 34) was located at Broadbridge Heath, just south of Warnham and across the Dorking-to-Arundel road from Field Place. Hawkins notes that Lady Irwin's "ruined house was said to be Elizabethan, the grounds laid out by Capability Brown" (*First Love*, 33). For Lady Irwin as the political rival of the Duke of Norfolk and his supporter Timothy Shelley, see William Albery, *Parliamentary History of . . . Horsham* (1927).

lines 17–18. As many have noted, these lines duplicate two lines in stanza 3 of Lord Byron's *Stanzas* (*"I would I were a careless child"*), first published in *Fugitive Pieces* (1807; suppressed) and subsequently included in his *Poems on Various Occasions* (1807), *Hours of Idleness* (1807), and *Poems, Original and Translated* (Newark: S. and J. Ridge, and London: B. Crosby, Longman [etc.], 1808). Harriet Westbrook Shelley copied into her commonplace book (ff. 26r–27v) "The Tear" by Byron, which appeared in the same collections; since her transcript lacks the Latin epigraph from Gray found in *Hours of Idleness* and her punctuation and orthography agree with those in *Poems, Original and Translated*, that was probably the edition of Byron's early poems that PBS owned. Byron's corresponding lines in 1808 (169) read: "Ah! why do dark'ning shades conceal | The hour when man must cease to be?" with not the smallest difference between it and PBS's borrowing.

lines 19–20. Though the first two lines of this stanza were cribbed from Byron, the final two, in which the speaker seeks to <u>unveil</u> . . . <u>futurity</u>, seem peculiarly Shelleyan. PBS employed the image of <u>unveil</u>ing ultimate reality throughout his career; though the *Shelley Concordance* records only four other uses of the word—all in early poems up through ***Dæmon of the World***—*futurity* appears later in his prose, his most famous uses being in the penultimate sentence of ***Defence of Poetry*** and the second note to ***Hellas***. Though the word is not found in the original poetry of Spenser, Milton, or Pope, and though only Blake among PBS's major contemporaries used the word in published poetry before he did, there were precedents: Shakespeare used *futurity* once (*Othello* III.iv.117); it appears in Dryden's translation of the *Aeneid* VI.101 and Pope's *Statius His Thebais*, 552, in an eighteenth-century translation of Cicero, Hartley's *Observations on Man*, and Richardson's *Pamela* (*OED*), as well as in more than 332 collections of English poetry in Chadwyck-Healey *Lion*. Among PBS's precursors, likely influences include Gray (*The Bard*, 134), Young (7 uses in *Night Thoughts*), Johnson's poems (2), Cowper's (3), and Chatterton's (4); among his contemporaries, they include Samuel Rogers, Joanna Baillie (who uses the phrase "dark futurity" three times in one of her early plays), Leigh Hunt in his *Juvenilia*, Southey (15 uses in all), and Henry Kirke White (3 uses).

lines 21–24. In remodeling this stanza from the second stanza of ***Song ("Come————! sweet is the hour")*** (the fourth poem in ***V&C***), PBS alters the meter from that poem's anapestic trimeter to iambic tetrameter.

Song ("How stern are the woes of the desolate mourner")

PBS included this poem in his letter to Graham of Friday, [14 Sept.] 1810 (Bodleian MS. Shelley adds. b.2, ff. 4–5 = MS Bod; ***Letters*** I, 16), where the poem begins immediately after "Dear Graham | This is the other song" and occupies the rest of page 1 and the first three lines of page 2 of the MS. In the same letter PBS mentions a "farce" that he "anxiously" desires to have accepted for production or publication; this may be the same unrecovered farce that Hellen Shelley later remembered as the joint production that PBS and his sister Elizabeth submitted to Charles Mathews (1776–1835, *DNB*); see Commentary to ***V&C*** and Appendix C.

In ***St.Irv***, PBS entitled the poem ***Song*** (which W. M. Rossetti later altered to "Bereavement"). Though some orthography and much punctuation in ***St.Irv*** were probably added by Stockdale and the printer, this version remains the form that PBS (who both supplied copy and read proofs) approved as his public text. In MS Bod, the stanzas are numbered "1" and "2"; Gosnell's compositor may have dropped these numbers to save lines, so that the poem would fit on page 171 of ***St.Irv***, but we accept the omission because: (1) of PBS's published lyric poems, only in the dedication poem "To Mary" and the lyric hymn within Canto Fifth of ***Laon and Cythna*** are the stanzas numbered with arabic numerals; the others that have stanza numbers seem to use roman numerals, whether the poems were written in the more formal genres—epic-romance (***Laon*** itself), ode (***West Wind***, ***Liberty***), or classical elegy (***Adonais***)—or in more modern stanzaic patterns, such as he used in ***Witch of Atlas*** and ***Fugitives*** (both in ***Posthumous Poems***); (2) the stanza numbers in MS Bod may have been meant simply to clarify for Graham where the break came between the stanzas; and, therefore, (3) PBS may not have numbered the stanzas in the manuscript that he sent to press (now lost).

The poetic stanza and meter of this and the following poem—eight lines of anapestic tetrameter lines rhymed *ababcccb*—follow the model of Scott's *Helvellyn* (1805), which tells the romantic story that also inspired W. Wordsworth's *Fidelity* (written 1805; published 1807) of a traveler who died in a fall among the Westmorland mountains and whose faithful dog guarded his corpse for months until later climbers found them there. Readers of the diaries of Harriet Grove may agree with us that, as the editors of *1989* suggest, PBS wrote the poem in memory of Grove's younger sister Louisa, who died on 19 June 1810 (later than Cameron's suggested date for the completion of ***St.Irv***). But PBS also uses the name *Louisa* in the following poem and in ***Song. To*——— ("Stern, stern is the voice")** (the thirteenth poem in ***V&C***) and in ***Henry and Louisa*** (***Esd***), and it is both a variant of the name of ***St.Irv***'s heroine Eloise and a generally popular poetic name (cf. Wordsworth's *Louisa*, pub. 1807) that fits anapestic meter.

In Chapter 9 of ***St.Irv***, young Eloise, now orphaned, friendless, and far from her home, walks from her mother's funeral to a ruined abbey near Lake Geneva at dusk "to meet the strange one who professed himself to be her friend.... The abbey brought to her recollection a similar ruin which stood near St. Irvyne [her family home]; it brought with it the remembrance of a song which Marianne [her sister] had composed soon after her brother's death. She sang, though in a low voice:" [here follows the Song; then:] "She ceased: the melancholy cadence of her angelic voice died in faint reverberations of echo away, and once again reigned stillness" (170–72).

line 3. enanguish'd: another of the en- and em- words favored in PBS's early poetry that does not appear among the many such words in *Entick's New Spelling Dictionary*. The final *-ed* is spelled out in both MS Bod and in line 14 of **Melody to a Scene of Former Times,** the fifth and final poem in **Posthumous Fragments of Margaret Nicholson (PF)**.

line 6. on: The reading of *1811* makes more sense than the "oer" in MS Bod.

line 7. while] time MS Bod. The sounds of while meld with those of lull'd, providing a reason for PBS's revision in *1811*.

line 9. The figure of night of the grave looks backward to the eighteenth-century "graveyard school" featuring Young's *Night Thoughts* and Blair's *The Grave,* and forward to the relationship between sleep and death that opens **QM.** For this specific language, *1989* cites James Beattie's *The Hermit* ([1766], 31–32); Beattie's entire stanza—eight lines of anapestic tetrameter, but rhymed *ababcdcd*—articulates the lament of the *Pervigilium Veneris* that nature is cyclically renewed, while the individual human life is finite: "I mourn, but, ye woodlands, I mourn not for you; | . . . Kind Nature the embryo blossom will save. | . . . But when shall spring visit the mouldering urn! | O when shall it dawn on the night of the grave!" (*The Minstrel . . . with Other Poems* [London, 1811], 60). Here, as in **Adonais,** PBS suggests a solution to this problem through imagery of transcendence.

lines 11–13. The idiom is unusually compressed here: Heaven will save the spirit that [seemingly] faded away when a dying person's breath faded; Eternity now points to the spirit's ultimate destination in its [i.e., Eternity's] amaranth bower after woe fades away (**16**).

Though in modern botanical parlance, the Amaranthus family includes such species as "pigweed" and "love-lies-bleeding," the classical literary associations of *amaranth* come from the Greek *amarantos,* which means "unfading"; this etymology, in turn, suggested to poets an imaginary flower that never faded or died, symbolic of eternal life. Among many possible sources for PBS's usage the most relevant are *Paradise Lost* III.352ff., where Milton mentions "Amarant, a Flow'r which once | In Paradise, fast by the Tree of Life | Began to bloom, but soon for man's offense | To Heav'n remov'd" and later, at XI.78, where he tells how, at the sound of God's trumpet convening a heavenly Synod, the angels all hastened "from thir blissful Bow'rs | Of *Amarantin* Shade"; Pope uses the phrase "Amarathine bowers" in both *Ode . . . St. Cecilia's Day,* line 76, and *Winter,* line 73; Cowper, who speaks of Hope plucking "amarathin joys from bow'rs of bliss" (*Hope* 164), also writes: "The only amaranthine flow'r on earth | Is virtue" (*The Task* III: "The Garden," 268–69). PBS used *amaranth* at least once more as an adjective, in ***Rosalind and Helen*** 1308, and three times as a noun—***QM*** I.108, ***Prom*** II.iv.61, and among drafts for ***Athanase***.

line 14. The final word of this line in MS Bod (the first line on p. 2 of the letter) is lost because of the tear made by the seal when the letter was opened. The text in ***St.Irv*** is not in doubt at this point, and editors of the ***Letters*** have added "[lower]" at the point of the seal tear in the MS. Since that tear in MS Bod (along the top edge of the centerfold between pp. 2 and 3 of the letter) does not seem to affect page 2 enough to obliterate so long a word, either PBS omitted it entirely, or else he ran it across the fold, into the larger section of missing paper on page 3. Since the context suggests, however, that there is also text missing from the sentence that continues from the bottom of page 2 to the top of page 3, the MS may well have omitted the final word of the line; that is, PBS may not have decided on the rhyme word to be used here when he sent the poem to Graham. The metrical context seems to require a verb with fewer syllables than *deflower* or *embower*, leaving as the only exactly rhyming alternatives *cower, flower, glower, shower, sour,* and *tower,* none of which seems as likely a choice for a prospect with clouds as is the cliché lower ("lour"), which PBS presumably adopted after seeking a less hackneyed alternative.

In MS Bod there are pencil underlines below oe'r (*sic*) and prospect, but it is unclear whether the underlines are contemporaneous with PBS and Graham or reflect the effort of some over-diligent later owner or scholar to puzzle out the line and recover the lost word at the end.

line 15. Unspeakable: "inexpressible, indescribable, ineffable" (*OED* 1).

line 16. When] Where   MS Bod, *1989*. Because the similarity between *when* and *where* in PBS's MSS often confuses even experienced and alert Shelley scholars, there is a temptation to emend the text in this line to *Where,* the clear reading in MS Bod. Though we accept the possibility of a compositorial error here, that likelihood is not strong enough to require an emendation.

Song ("Ah! faint are her limbs, and her footstep is weary")

In this ballad, a woman, driven from her pitiless home for loving Henry against her family's wishes, hastens to the lakeside to elope in her lover's boat. W. T. Baker first suggested the influence of the form of Scott's *Helvellyn* on this and the previous poem in *Notes & Queries* (7th series, 2 [11 Dec. 1886]: 471–72; reprinted in the *Notebook of the Shelley Society* [1888], 132), while André Koszul (*Athenæum,* 6 May 1905, 561–62) traced PBS's inspiration here to a song from the poems of "Ossian" (see *1989*, 106); either source would account for the mountain and lake setting. PBS—who not only used imaginatively this plot of an escape by water in later poems (notably ***Fugitives*** and ***Epipsychidion***) but personally enacted it in his 1814 elopement with Mary Godwin (later MWS)—probably wrote this ***Song*** in the summer or early autumn of 1810, during the growing estrangement between Harriet Grove's parents and himself; here he seems to imagine Grove choosing to elope with him, though the tale concludes tragically with one of his many portrayals of the death of his persona.

Later in Chapter 9 of ***St.Irv***, Nempere, who is ultimately revealed to be Ginotti (the Wandering Jew), tries to seduce Eloise; when she demurs, he asks her to sing to him: "Willingly did Eloise fetch her harp; she wished not to scrutinize what was passing in her mind, but, after a short prelude, thus began—" [the ***Song*** follows, and then—] "'How soft is that strain!' cried Nempere, as she concluded. 'Ah!' said Eloise, sighing deeply; ''t is a melancholy song; my poor brother wrote it, I remember, about ten days before he died. 'T is a gloomy tale concerning him; he ill deserved the fate he met. Some future time I will tell it you; but now, 't is very late.—Goodnight'" (181–83).

line 5. The whortle or whortleberry plant is a European blueberry, akin to the American huckleberry.

line 6. The European myrtle, traditionally sacred to Aphrodite/Venus and therefore a symbol of sexual love, is a plant with white or pink star-shaped flowers and black berries.

line 7. kirtle: This Old English word with Old Norse analogues had come to mean in different dialects either a man's short ("curt") tunic or a woman's long gown or petticoat (*OED*). Of the many poetic examples we have located prior to PBS, the most likely influences are Spenser's "in a kirtle of greene saye, | The greene is for maidens meete" (*Shepherd's Calendar*, "August," 67–68) and Milton's "Amidst the flowry-kirtl'd *Naiades*" (*Comus*, 254).

The Devil's Walk

The first evidence that PBS had begun this poem appears at the end of his letter to Elizabeth Hitchener of ?16 January 1812 (***Letters*** I, 235–37; BL Add. MS 37,496, f. 80 verso), in which PBS included seven irregular ballad stanzas (49 lines) on the theme of Satan's encounters with members of the British establishment, introducing the poetry thus: "Here follows a few stanzas which may amuse you. I was once rather fond of the Devil."

The stanzas are modeled on *The Devil's Thoughts*, a poem that Southey and Coleridge had composed jointly and published (anonymously) in the *Morning Post*, 6 September 1799. (That text appears in the notes to J. D. Campbell's *Poetical Works of Coleridge* [1893 etc.], 621–22.) PBS probably first read *The Devil's Thoughts* while seeing Southey at Keswick, beginning about Christmas 1811. Before they met, PBS had been prejudiced against Southey by reports that he had grown more conservative, but after they talked a few times, he wrote to Hitchener: "Southey tho' far from being a man of great reasoning powers is a great Man. . . . He is a man of virtue, he never will belie what he thinks" (***Letters*** I, 212). Southey's contemporary letters show that he and PBS discussed the relation of Southey's youthful political and religious beliefs to PBS's current ones. If during these conversations PBS confessed to Southey his school-boy attempts to raise the Devil, Southey likely tried to maintain his rapport with the youthful enthusiast by showing him his own early antiestablishment poems, including *The Devil's Thoughts*.

Other Romantic Devils

The Devil's Thoughts, begun for amusement while shaving, as Southey tells in his extended version (*Poetical Works of Southey* [1838], III, 96), became popular through its many unauthorized reprintings under various titles over the years. Richard Porson (1759–1808), a Cambridge classical scholar who was also a radical Whig apologist, even tried to take credit for composing it. In 1813, Lord Byron wrote *The Devil's Drive* as an imitation of *The Devil's Thoughts*, which he had read in a version misattributed to Porson; Byron, following what he believed to be the spirit and substance of Porson's liberal political views, changes the verse form and adds touches from

Goethe's *Faust* that had come to him via Staël's *De l'Allemagne* (see Byron, *CPW* III, 95–104, 428–30). Finally, in 1827, Southey publicly claimed authorship for Coleridge and himself, while expanding their poem to 57 stanzas and (ignorant of PBS's poem) changing its name to *The Devil's Walk* to distinguish it from the version falsely attributed to Porson.

PBS's **The Devil's Walk** (***DW***) of 1812 openly imitates both the larger conception and some specific details of Southey and Coleridge's original *Devil's Thoughts,* which aims barbs at corrupt or incompetent lawyers, apothecaries, and booksellers, war and its financial burdens, unhealthy prisons that enforce unequal justice, false religion and its support of war, and an unnamed general—probably either Isaac Gascoigne or Banastre Tarleton, both of whom had been "involved in England's suppression of Ireland" and who publicly opposed the abolition of slavery (see M. D. Paley, "Coleridge and the Apocalyptic Grotesque," in *Coleridge's Visionary Languages,* ed. T. Fulford and Paley [1993]). Except for PBS's scathing attack on the Prince Regent, his targets in ***DW*** are similar to those of Southey and Coleridge, for as S. E. Jones observes of PBS's poem, "'derivativeness' is precisely the point. . . . Shelley declares himself to be derived—from . . . the best in the earlier work of the elder poets" (*Shelley's Satire* [1994], 41–42). Often forgotten in commentaries on ***DW*** is its ultimate indebtedness to the Bible and Satan's reply to God—that he comes "From going to and fro in the earth, and from walking up and down in it" (Job 1:7 and 2:2).

Historical Contexts

The draft of ***DW*** in PBS's mid-January 1812 letter to Hitchener (which we print as Supplement to the published version) is far from a finished poem. But by August 1812, PBS had prepared for distribution a fully developed satirical poem of thirty stanzas and had it printed as a broadsheet (arranged in three columns of ten stanzas apiece) entitled **The Devil's Walk, A Ballad.** This poem treats several topics that are absent from his draft in the January letter—some of more recent date. We know that PBS's diabolical ballad was printed after he left Ireland on 4 April 1812, because it was not seized by the customs agent at Holyhead along with **Declaration of Rights** (***DR;*** for this seizure, see E. B. Murray in *Prose* I, 349). PBS thus did not complete the poem or, probably, write his attack on the Prince Regent in **lines 67–79** until after Leigh Hunt and his brother John were charged with seditious libel for publishing a critique of the Prince in the *Examiner* for 22 March 1812 that called him "a corpulent gentleman of fifty," besides alluding to his flaws of character. PBS seconds and extends their attack by calling the Regent a fat-head as well as an obese glutton, but given the Hunts' legal difficulties, PBS probably did not decide to print or circulate ***DW*** to challenge the government until after July 1812, when the ministry postponed the Hunts' scheduled trial, for fear that a regular jury might not convict them (A. Blainey, *Immortal Boy . . . Leigh Hunt* [1985], 54–56).

After the Shelleys crossed from Ireland to Holyhead, they proceeded to Nantgwillt, near Rhayader, Radnorshire (now Powys) by ca. 16 April, and stayed at the estate of PBS's cousin John Grove at nearby Cwm Elan through mid-June, before proceeding to Devonshire by way of Chepstow at the foot of the Wye Valley; they arrived at Lymoth (now Lynmouth), Devon, between 25 and 30 June (see E. Dowden, *Life of PBS* I, 266–79, and **Letters** I, 280–310). The facts of PBS's excursion into Devon are explored, with extended quotations from relevant documents, by Mac-Carthy in *Early Life* (321–53); Richard Holmes captures the human drama in *Shelley: The Pursuit* ([1974], 133–62), and Cameron explores its political implications in *YS* (165–86). In April 1812, Cobbett's *Political Register* reported that there were food strikes and other popular disturbances in Cornwall and parts of Devon, including Barnstaple (*YS*, 175–78). Since PBS regularly read Cobbett's periodical, he probably went to Devon with the idea of stirring those warm ashes, for from the time that he left Keswick, PBS had elected to play the role of outside agitator, hurrying to sites of discontent—first Dublin and then to Devon—to try to redirect the course of those antigovernment feelings. These activities earned him the serious attention of the local authorities.

The context of these political aims seems to explain better than others why PBS should release two more "popular" works in Devon—**DW**, aimed at the lower classes, and **DR**, calibrated for the bourgeoisie—so soon after the failure of his similar efforts in Dublin, where he found that the Irish nationalists did not trust a very young Englishman. The food riots in Devon also provided part of his motivation for satirizing the Prince Regent's gluttony. Though PBS opposed violence as a means of redress on both moral and pragmatic grounds, his theory was to move the discontented people to seek reform by using rational and moral suasion. But since his experience in Dublin made him (like Coleridge and Southey before him) doubt that the common people were well equipped for intellectual and moral conflict, he appealed to them in **DW** (as later in **The Mask of Anarchy**) in doggerel verse-satire based on popular religious symbols. For an analysis of **DW** in the context of PBS's ambivalent feelings toward the whole genre of satire, see Jones, *Shelley's Satire*, 38–48.

Printing and Attempts to Circulate

The papers of Edward Dowden at Trinity College, Dublin, include Mathilde Blind's notes of her 1871 conversations with Mrs. Mary Blackmore, niece of Mrs. Hooper, the Shelleys' landlady at Lymouth, who stated that PBS "had a number of papers printed at Barnstaple" (see *1989* I, 230). Both **A**

Letter to Lord Ellenborough (***LLE***), of which he sent copies to Thomas Hookham on 29 July, and ***DW*** were clearly among those "papers," and the printer was Mr. Syle (J. R. Chanter, *Sketches of the Literary History of Barnstaple* [1866], as quoted in Mac-Carthy, *Early Life,* 345–48). Mary Blackmore said that as a girl she was invited to help the Shelleys cut the printer's name off some work, which was presumably ***LLE***. But our inspections of the sole known copy of ***DW*** itself at the Public Record Office (PRO) confirm the evidence of the photofacsimile in Granniss's *First Editions* that the broadside has not—and never did have—a colophon listing the printer's name and address, as the law required, for the sheet is intact, totally unmutilated. How did PBS evade the law that prescribed very harsh penalties for a printer who failed to list his name and address on the first and last printed leaf of any publication? A recollection of "Mr. Brooke . . . who supervised the printing of the pamphlet" (i.e., ***LLE***) quoted in Chanter's *Sketches of . . . Barnstaple* noted that PBS came to the shop "from time to time to read the copy and correct the press," where it may have been possible for him, by cajolery or bribery, either to set the single page himself and then persuade someone sympathetic to his cause—perhaps Brooke himself?—to print without reading the single sheet, or even to set and print it after hours, without the required colophon. Some egregious errors in the text (noted in the collation and commented upon below) suggest either great haste or an amateur hand involved in the typesetting.

PBS resided at Mrs. Hooper's in the small fishing village of Lymouth for nine weeks and three days (see Godwin's account in ***Letters*** I, 326 fn. 8), from there trying to circulate both ***DW*** and ***DR*** in West Devonshire by hand and to other parts of England by mail. According to a letter dated 20 August 1812 from Henry Drake, Town Clerk of Barnstaple, to Lord Sidmouth, the Home Secretary, the former attempt ended on the evening of 19 August, when PBS's Irish servant Daniel (né Healey) was "observed distributing and posting" ***DR*** at Barnstaple; he was arrested and charged with ten counts of "Publishing and dispersing Printed Papers without the Printer's name being on them [as mandated] under the Act of 39. Geo. 3.c.79." Daniel Hill (as Healey gave his name) was duly tried and convicted by the Mayor of Barnstaple and fined £20 for each offense. Unable to pay the £200, he was incarcerated in "the Common Gaol" of that borough. While Healey (without betraying his master) began to serve six months in Barnstaple jail in lieu of paying the fine, the town officials investigated PBS; Drake's letter notes that "Mr Shelley has been regarded with a suspicious Eye since he has been in Lymouth, from the Circumstance of his very extensive Correspondence and many of his Packages and Letters being addressed to Sir Francis Burdett—and it is also said that Mr Shelley has sent off so many as 16 Letters by the same Post—." Drake goes on to tell of

PBS launching bottles into the Bristol Channel, one of which was found to contain "a seditious Paper" (PRO, H.O. 42/127). That PBS tried to disseminate his broadsheets thus impersonally by sea in bottles and by air in balloons (both launchings are celebrated by sonnets in *The Esdaile Notebook*) seems much less foolish when one considers the penalty for distributing them in person.

After Healey's arrest, the remaining copies of **DW** were probably destroyed or discarded (perhaps PBS cast them into the sea sans bottles) before the Shelleys fled Devon about the end of August. Thus, the single extant copy of **DW** owes its preservation to Drake, the Devonshire Dogberry, whose copies of **DR** and **DW** eventually went from the Home Office into the PRO, where they reside with the letter quoted above and a second letter that Drake wrote to Sidmouth on 9 September 1812.

Textual Transmission

Though W. M. Rossetti, R. Garnett, Mac-Carthy, and Dowden had earlier made copies and published excerpts from PBS's letters to Hitchener, that correspondence, including his letter of ?16 January 1812 containing the early draft of **DW**, was first published in full by T. J. Wise in 1890 (see Seymour de Ricci, *A Bibliography of Shelley's Letters, Published and Unpublished* [1927]; rpt. New York: Burt Franklin [1969], 105, 112). Thus, the public's first knowledge of **DW** came when Rossetti, alerted by someone at PRO to the PBS materials there, published the text of the *1812* broadsheet and its accompanying letters in *Fortnightly Review* for January 1871 (n.s., 9 [15 of full sequence], no. 49, 67–85). H. B. Forman, after checking the text at PRO, included **DW** in his edition of 1876–77 (IV, 371–77). Though Rossetti accepted several of Forman's corrections in *1878* (III, 371–76), he retained much of his own revised punctuation and orthography, rather than returning to that of *1812*. Rossetti's most important innovation was the addition of quotation marks around **lines 45–79,** which embody his insight that these seditious lines were meant to be Satan's words, thereby allowing PBS to evade prosecution by claiming that the attacks on the Regent are presented as being from the lips of the Father of Lies.

Copy-text

The sole textual authority for **DW** remains the single copy of *1812* in the PRO (H.O. 42/127, f. 426 [citation incorrect in *1989*]). The document is a single sheet of wove paper without visible watermark, originally white but aged to yellow-brown, that (when in reading position) measures 18 1/16 inches high by 14 7/8 inches wide (= 45.85 cm. by 36.8 cm.).

line 2. Beelzebub: In the Hebrew Bible (2 Kings 1), *Baalzebub* ("King of the Flies") was a Philistine god; in the Greek New Testament, *Beelzebub* ("Lord of the Dwelling" or "Lord of the Dung") was the ruler of evil spirits (Matthew 10:25, 12:24; Mark 3:22; Luke 11:15ff.). Unlike Milton, who in *Paradise Lost* I–II personalizes Beëlzebub as second in rank to Satan, PBS follows popular tradition by using interchangeably the names Devil, Satan, Beelzebub, and Old Nick.

line 7. Previous editors inserted *a* before Bras Chapeau; chapeau-bras was "a small three-cornered flat silk hat . . . worn by gentlemen at court or in full dress in the 18th century" (*OED*). Years later, in **Peter Bell III,** PBS was to say, "The Devil is a gentleman"; here this "natty . . . *Beau*" (**8**) begins to survey England at Bond-street, site of London's most fashionable tailors and luxury shops.

line 15. St. James's Court: St. James's Palace, built by Henry VIII on the site of a medieval hospital, was still the governing seat of the British monarch in 1812 ("the Court of St. James"); according to *The Picture of London for 1817,* this palace was "used by the king only for purposes of state" (London: Longman [etc.], 84). Major governmental offices (e.g., Whitehall) and the Houses of Parliament are clustered near the palace and St. James's Park.

line 16. St. Paul's Cathedral—near the Bank of England, the East India House, and other centers of British commercial power—symbolized the establishment interests of the Church of England.

in: Other texts substitute *on* for this *1812* reading.

line 17. every Saint: Here PBS implicates both the Anglican religious tradition and the evangelical Parliamentary bloc led by William Wilberforce (1759–1833, *DNB*), known as the Saints; they opposed slavery and supported other reforms, but their ostentatious piety, social conservatism, and support of the censorious Society for the Suppression of Vice offended both the Foxite Whigs and more radical reformers.

line 19. agriculturist: a landed proprietor whose income came from farming—socially superior, in the view of PBS, the heir to such a fortune, to someone whose income came from entrepreneurship or a profession. Nora Crook suggests an allusion to Jesus's parable of the wheat and the tares, with the devil being the enemy who sows tares (Matthew 13:38–39).

line 22. wouldn't: misprinted "would'nt" in *1812*.

line 24. In *1989*, Matthews and Everest follow an apparent typo in *1927* that replaces the semicolon after view at the end of this line with a comma.

lines 25–27. Though as in the letter version (**line 46**) Satan shows his satisfaction by Grinning his applause ("marked approval," *OED*, 2) at those who delighted to do his works, they still fear him.

lines 28–32. These lines satirizing fashionable young ladies may bear sexual implications when Satan pokes into crannies so small (**28**).

line 37. Ah! Ah!: *1812* leaves no space between the first exclamation point and the second *Ah!*

lines 40–41. house was . . . hot: If the Windsor Castle quarters of King George III, who had become incurably insane late in 1811, were kept exceptionally warm for England in that period—knowledge of that was likely available to PBS either from the frequent contact that Etonians had with members of the King's household at nearby Windsor, or from PBS's mentor Dr. James Lind, one of the King's personal physicians. Alternatively, the allusion may derive from (out-of-date) gossip about the Prince Regent: On 5 November 1811, Thomas Creevey noted in his journal that at the Brighton Pavilion, Mrs. Creevey told the Prince that "she was glad on account of his health that he kept his rooms cooler than he used to do, and he said that he was quite altered in that respect—that he used to be always *chilly*, and now was never so—" (*The Creevey Papers*, ed. John Gore [1963], 83).

In *1812* hot as was misprinted "hot at".

line 43. twisted: *1989* emends this word to "twirled" because the editors perceive that to be the reading in the letter text of several months earlier. We read twisted in the letter as well, but even if we agreed with "twirled," we would not emend the reading of the later, clearer, and more authoritative text, which makes perfect sense.

lines 45–79. As we noted above, Rossetti added quotation marks around these stanzas to indicate that they embody Satan's words; we prefer to consider them, more precisely, as what Satan thought (**45**). In either case, PBS evades uttering seditious libel against Castlereagh and the Prince Regent by putting these charges into the mind—or mouth—of the Devil.

line 46. Cattle: "A collective name for live animals held as property" (*OED* II.4.A).

line 48. The end punctuation, which in *1812* slipped low in the type chase, is a comma.

line 50. their was misspelled "thier" in *1812*, where either the compositor slavishly followed PBS's copy, or PBS introduced this characteristic erratum while setting type himself; when correcting this error, most editors through *1972* omit the first as in the line.

lines 51–56. *1989* cites the bloody British siege of Badajos in April 1812; if PBS wrote this passage as late as August 1812, it could also refer to the equally bloody Battle of Salamanca on 22 July. (Though the British and their allies won both battles, British casualties alone were about 5,000 in each.) The Whigs, including Byron, thought that Viscount (later Duke of) Wellington's Peninsular Campaign against the French in Spain was simply an exercise in Tory political aggrandizement; PBS believed that *all* military actions harmed common people and weakened liberty. Southey, who had conveyed a similar message in *The Battle of Blenheim* (1798), was at this time writing a series of poems in which he commemorated each of Wellington's victories in Spain.

line 54. Other editors, seeking rhetorical parallelism, have emended When to "Where"—perhaps because in PBS's handwriting these two words are difficult to distinguish and may have confused a compositor setting from PBS's MS. But here PBS may have set the type himself, and since When adds variety and makes equally good sense, we retain the reading of *1812*.

line 57. Fat—: The initial *F* is a malformed piece of type.

lines 57–59. Robert Stewart (1769–1822), eldest son of the 1st Marquis of Londonderry, though not himself a peer till his father's death in 1821, was known by his courtesy title (i.e., his father's second title) as Viscount Castlereagh. In Parliament, he originally supported enfranchisement of Catholics in Ireland (Erin). But in 1797–98, as chief deputy to the Viceroy of Ireland, he suppressed the rebellion of the United Irishmen by arresting their leaders just before the event, and in 1800 he engineered (through wholesale bribery) the votes by which the Irish Parliament joined Ireland with Great Britain and then dissolved itself.

Atrocities involved in crushing the rebellion in 1798, Castlereagh's harsh methods of interrogating rebel prisoners, and the corruption with which he pushed through the Act of Union earned him the lasting enmity of Irish nationalists. In February 1811 he was pilloried in the London press during the trial of Peter Finnerty, who as part of his defense presented affidavits from Irish prisoners who had been tortured under Castlereagh's direction. These accounts, quoted and discussed in Cobbett's *Political Register* and the Hunt brothers' *Examiner*, probably helped to deepen both PBS's and Byron's hatred of Castlereagh during his years as Foreign Secretary and Tory leader in the House of Commons. For PBS's support of Finnerty, see the discussion of **Poetical Essay on the Existing State of Things** in Appendix C.

lines 60–62. *1989* (I, 235) relates these lines to the death of Robert Emmet in 1803 (see **Esd,** poem 13), and another note (*1989* I, 204) quotes records of the Irish rebellion of 1798 that involved cutting out rebels' hearts. PBS's allusion here, probably informed by many such anecdotes that he heard during his stay in Ireland, is generic, not specific.

line 61. clasp: misprinted as "claps" in *1812*; such an error suggests the clandestine haste involved in the illegal production, whether or not PBS actually set type himself.

line 65. fret their little hour: Cf. Shakespeare, *Macbeth* V.v.25.

lines 67–70. PBS, who like Byron despised the Prince of Wales for his extravagant selfishness and his betrayal of the Whigs and reform when he became Regent, portrays the Prince as a spoiled child. The word maudlin (**67**) and the complicated mixed metaphor in which the gilded toy of **line 68** apparently becomes a sweetmeat in **69**, suggest that PBS is subtly alluding to the Prince of Wales's sentimental love affair with the twice-widowed Maria Fitzherbert (1756–1837), a Roman Catholic whom he could not wed legally without forfeiting the crown. The Prince did, in fact, marry Mrs. Fitzherbert surreptitiously on 15 December 1785 after threatening to stab himself if she would not consent (events retold in the gossip of two generations), but after that marriage took place, he carried on a long series of other love affairs.

lines 71–75. For the specific occasion of this attack on the Prince's obesity, see the Commentary, above. A levee (**72**) was a formal afternoon reception at St. James's Palace at which the ruler received only men. (The name alludes to the origins of the ceremony in the practice of counsellors calling upon the monarch in his bedchamber when he was arising.)

line 76. plenty is the subject of Could make ... start (**79**).

line 80. PBS's parenthetical statement (signaled, according to a practice of the time, with both commas and parentheses) seems to be saying that the Devil is identical to Nature; but the references to Nature in *QM* and other poems of this period suggest that PBS held no such belief at this time. More likely, he is noting that people use "human nature" as their excuse for following their own evil desires—that is, Satan.

line 82. change: PBS alludes to the Prince of Wales's betrayal of his old Whig friends when he became Regent in 1812.

line 83. This line burlesques line 4 in Joseph Addison's "Ode," later the text of a standard hymn, the opening stanza of which follows the thought of Psalm 19, verse 1 ("The Heavens declare the glory of God" etc.): "The Spacious Firmament on high, | With all the blue Etherial sky, | And spangled Heav'ns, a Shining Frame, | Their great Original proclaim" (*The Specta-*

tor, no. 465, 23 Aug. 1712; ed. D. F. Bond IV [Oxford: Clarendon Press, 1965], 144).

lines 84–87. This stanza is the only one that, in both the letter text and the broadside version of PBS's poem, replicates the idea of an entire stanza of *The Devil's Thoughts* by Southey and Coleridge (1799), which reads, in a note to J. D. Campbell's edition of Coleridge (621): "He saw a Lawyer killing a viper | On a dunghill beside his stable; | 'Oh—oh,' quoth he, for it put him in mind, | Of the story of Cain and Abel."

In 84 the medial comma marks a rhetorical pause to indicate the inversion of natural word order at the end of the line.

line 88. yeoman: an independent farmer who owned (rather than leased or rented) the land that he worked.

line 91. The punctuation ending this line is a semicolon, though in facsimiles it might be read as a colon.

line 94. garb of gore: the red coats of the British soldiers.

lines 96–97. Perhaps a reference to those who collect and live on rents, taxes, and tithes.

lines 100–107. That is, Bishops = pigs and Lawyers = cormorants. In *Paradise Lost*, when Satan entered Eden, he "Sat like a Cormorant" upon the Tree of Life (IV.196).

line 106. In the second half of *DW*, we have restored several rhetorical commas found in *1812* but omitted by earlier editors, whom we join, however, in deleting a comma between are and sin-like. Though PBS may have intended this comma to indicate the location of the caesura, it confuses the syntax more than it clarifies the rhythm of the line.

line 114. Statesman: Though *OED* finds positive connotations to this word, opposing it to the modern connotations of "politician," English writers from Dryden through Lockhart frequently used it as a term of contempt: for example, "like Great Statesmen, we encourage those who betray their Friends" (Gay, *Beggar's Opera* II.x); "Tho' equal to all things, for all things unfit, | Too nice [i.e., ethical] for a statesman, too proud for a wit: | . . . And too fond of the *right* to pursue the *expedient*" (from *Retaliation*, Goldsmith's "epitaph" on Burke, 37–40). PBS used *statesman* pejoratively in *QM* at IV.80, 104, 168, and V.93.

line 115. dare is conditional or subjunctive; that is, "The Devil would, could, or might dare. . . ."

line 120. thy: The reading in *1812*, has been emended to *the* by earlier editors; but this phrase, addressing Satan directly, may begin the intentional shift from Satan's perspective to that of the author that carries on in Hark . . . I hear (**128**) and the judgmental final two stanzas.

Stygian: pertaining to the Styx, the river boundary of the classical underworld; hence, hellish. Milton uses the adjective in *L'Allegro*, *Comus*, and five times in *Paradise Lost*.

line 123. gory laurel: Though the reference is generic for honors won in war, it may also allude to poets who praise war and specifically to Southey, who, as PBS would know, was publishing many poems in support of the Peninsular Campaign. Though Southey did not become poet laureate till 1813, he had actively pursued a government sinecure since 1809 to help support his family—and Coleridge's family as well (Jack Simmons, *Southey* [1945], 137ff.). During their frank discussions at Keswick, Southey may have told PBS of his hopes for the laureateship whenever it became time to appoint a successor to Henry James Pye (1745–1813), the laughably bad poet who was the current laureate.

line 128. An early use of PBS's favorite symbolism equating political revolution with earthquake.

lines 140–43. ere (**141**) suggests that the sons of Reason may bring about a millennium before the final apocalypse. It appears here that PBS thought that Earth's destruction was likely to follow from a conflagration generated by the Sun or a wayward comet. The thought he later pursued in *QM* about a millennium introduced by the precession of the equinoxes to the point at which the pole on which Earth rotates would no longer be tilted in relation to the Sun does not seem relevant here, since the Pole is here to be "consumed" or destroyed, rather than realigned. But the main point of interest may be that at this early age, when he was most politically active, PBS was already able to look past the "World's great age" to a return of "hate and death" without abandoning or minimizing the benefits of even temporary political reform and social improvement.

Supplement: Letter Version

lines 1–28. Here we transcribe the original manuscript in PBS's mid-January 1812 letter to Hitchener (BL Add. MS. 37,496, f. 80 verso); there is a facsimile of the portion of that letter containing this poetic text, together with another literal transcription, in *MYR: Shelley* (VIII, ed. Reiman and O'Neill [1997], 50–56).

Although the text of these stanzas in F. L. Jones's **Letters** (I, 235–37) places some characters at the ends of the first 28 lines within brackets, as though they were illegible or missing from the right-hand edge of the manuscript page, the only damage and repairs actually affecting these lines are along the fold of the letter paper at the *left-hand* edge of the column of poetry—at the *beginnings* of those lines. Jones must, therefore, have relied upon an imperfect photocopy of the MS.

line 6. earth: The initial *e* may be a capital letter, written minutely.

line 14. We think that the first word is more likely Grinning—as the editors of the letters have it—than "Receiving" (*1989*). This reading accords with the syntax, since the basic meaning of applause is "approval publicly expressed" and Satan is the active agent throughout this stanza. O'Neill, when transcribing the MS for *MYR: Shelley* VIII, was dubious about the reading but left "Receiving" in the text, while discussing his doubts in a note.

line 16. PBS first underscored they and then canceled the underline.

line 20. PBS left a blank after were to be filled later—presumably by a word rhyming with prayer (**18**).

line 22. thats: *Sic.*

lines 25-28. This is the stanza that PBS directly recollected (though perhaps unwittingly) from *The Devil's Thoughts* (see note to **lines 84-87** of Text). In the letter version, however, PBS miswrote the Devil for "a lawyer" in **line 25**; in **26** his is superimposed on the.

line 29. Beginning with this line, PBS continued his writing on the opposite side of the address panel; from here on, the repair to the worn fold is along the *right-hand* edge of the text, where the damage does affect the final letters of some words.

line 32. twisted: Though *1989* and *MYR*/VIII read this word as "twirled" (and *1989* emends twisted in the final text to "twirled"), the crucial letters *st* now seem to us to be relatively clear in the facsimile.

line 36. humans: PBS canceled the final letter in his draft.

line 41. bond Street beau: *Sic.*

line 42. For: This word might be read as *Nor* were there not an identical For at the beginning of **line 23**.

altho: First two letters are canceled.

lines 43-44. PBS, the son of an M.P., had probably seen Castlereagh in person and would certainly have known political caricatures of him.

line 47. hore, which appears as "horse" in *1927*/VIII and *1964J*, and as "Iron" in *1989* and *MYR*/VIII, is a word directly from Old English. The *OED* gives it only as an obsolete noun meaning "dirt, filth, defilement, foulness," but even though the noun had dropped out of use, probably because of its closeness to *hoar* and *whore,* PBS here seems to use hore adjectively, meaning filthy or foul—a usage that may have persisted in rural Sussex.

The strongest argument in favor of the alternative "Iron" is metrical, for a disyllabic word seems to work better here than a monosyllabic one; the weakest aspect of this reading is that its initial letter must be read as a capital, for which there seems to be no reason.

line 48. and: written minutely and unclearly, but not "&" (as in *1989*).

line 49. After **line 49** is a final short rule parallel with the others below each stanza, here presumably separating the poem from the letter.

Ten Early Poems (1809–1814)

The ten poems and fragments in this group differ from many other poems PBS released, in whole or in part: though he released them privately to friends who preserved the MSS in which they were found, they were never published or otherwise made public during the poet's lifetime. They share, therefore, more informal orthography and punctuation than most of PBS's released poems, partly because he assumed that his intimate friends would be able to comprehend his meaning from their awareness of his speech patterns in conversation or his reading of poetry. Some, moreover, he either composed spontaneously—or wished his friends to believe that he did—under circumstances that did not allow time for studied revision or polishing. In composing these poems, PBS was—or chose to present himself to his close friends as—one of those "Great Wits" of Pope's *An Essay on Criticism,* who "*gloriously offend*" the "*vulgar Bounds*" of common criticism "And *snatch* a *Grace* beyond the Reach of Art" (lines 152–55). When copying into his letter to Elizabeth Hitchener of 7 January 1812 a partial text of a preliminary version of the poem beginning "She was an aged woman" (which he was later to include in a longer and more polished text in ***The Esdaile Notebook*** [***Esd***] under the title ***A Tale of Society as it is from facts 1811***), PBS warned Hitchener not to judge it as she would a published work: "Think of the Poetry which I have inserted as a picture of my feelings not a specimen of my art" (***Letters*** I, 226). In several other instances, the poems he inserted in letters or wrote out for friends in their presence were said by him to be mere extempore effusions or unimproved copies of poems drafted that week, that morning, or a few minutes before he transcribed the copy that has survived.

Whether or not PBS was being candid about his facility in composing poetry, whenever he later prepared such a poem for publication, he revised and polished its text. Like many other poets, he clearly exerted a different level of effort when fashioning a poem that he wished to represent him to the reading public and posterity than he did when copying a draft in a private letter or transcript for the perusal and response of an intimate friend and confidant. For this reason, wherever two authoritative versions of a poem survive—one released privately and the other published or prepared for publication by him—we accord greater authority to the latter version, and we include the private version as a separate text only if there are such significant differences between the versions as to render the two texts distinct compositions, as is true with *"How swiftly through Heaven's wide expanse"* (the second poem in the present group) and with *The Devil's Walk* (q.v.). Because of this disparity between poems released publicly and privately, we do not interfile the two types in a purely chronological sequence, but instead group the less polished texts of privately released poems after the more finished public texts of the same period. Modern readers can best judge distinctions between his publicly and privately released poems after acclimating themselves to the standards of presentation that PBS chose or accepted for the public ones during each stage of his artistic development.

We have arranged these poems in the order of PBS's first release of each poem, as nearly as we can determine that sequence, even though the surviving MSS that provide our copy-texts are sometimes of later date. From the standards that reveal themselves through our analyses of PBS's public poetry, we have endeavored to edit these privately released poems so as to retain the character of their informal, colloquial manuscript originals, while correcting slips of the pen and errors of omission in orthography and punctuation that (as we can surmise from PBS's printed texts) he probably would have corrected, had he noticed them. It is not easy to determine exactly how much punctuation PBS would have added—or even favored—had he revised them during the 1809–14 period, since almost all of his early poems in letters and manuscript transcripts are underpunctuated by the conventions of his day and ours. Later, however, when PBS gave his poems to Jane Williams and other private friends, he attempted to punctuate them more carefully than he did in his early years. Now that the audience for these poems no longer consists of PBS's close friends, who might be expected to intuit his intentions, we have added the minimal punctuation required to achieve readability, while attempting to retain the distinction between his private communications and the publicly released works.

"A Cat in distress"

The text of "A Cat in distress," perhaps the earliest surviving poem by PBS, was first published by Thomas Jefferson Hogg in the opening chapter of his *Life of PBS* from one of several letters of reminiscence sent in 1856–57 by PBS's younger sister Hellen Shelley (b. 26 Sept. 1799) to Lady (Jane) Shelley, who with Sir Percy Florence Shelley, PBS's son, was gathering materials for Hogg's ill-fated "official" biography of the poet. The authority behind Hellen Shelley's text of the poem and our copy-text is the MS in the Pforzheimer Collection (MS Pfz), the only known contemporary textual authority, which is a fair transcription in the hand of PBS's sister Elizabeth

Shelley, headed by a watercolor picture of a tabby cat and followed by a note in an unidentified hand that reads: "Percy Bysshe Shelley written | at 10 years of age to his Sister | at School." MS Pfz is reproduced in black-and-white photofacsimile, transcribed and annotated by Cameron, in *SC* IV (813–19), and as the frontispiece to this volume.

Date of Composition

Elizabeth Shelley's transcription of **"A Cat"** is written on paper watermarked "CHARLES WILMOTT | 1809." In her letter transcribing the poem, Hellen Shelley remarks in a letter to Lady Shelley, which Hogg quotes in his *Life of PBS,* that this "child's effusion about some cat . . . evidently *had* a story, but it must have been before I can remember" (*Life,* ed. Wolfe, I, 29). Cameron takes this to mean that Hellen Shelley was about five years old at the time (i.e., ca. 1804) and, after observing that a notation on MS Pfz in an unidentified hand says that the poem was written by PBS "at 10 years of age" (1802–3), he dates the poem 1803–5 (*SC* IV, 818). Matthews and Everest in *1989* concur with Cameron's dating, focusing on 1804.

Nora Crook, however, in "Shelley's Earliest Poem?" (*Notes and Queries,* n.s. 34 [Dec. 1987]: 486–90), challenged the 1802–5 dating. She observed that the notation, probably added late in the nineteenth century, may have no authority, while Elizabeth Shelley's calligraphic transcription is hardly "unformed" (as Hellen Shelley described it), or the work of a young child. Noting the 1809 watermark on the paper of Elizabeth Shelley's transcription, Crook argued that: (1) Hellen Shelley's statements in middle age about the early composition were merely guesses, based on a subjective impression that the poem seemed juvenile; and (2) Elizabeth Shelley's transcription is roughly contemporaneous with PBS's composition. Using the dates in *SC* for PBS's letters on paper with the same Wilmott watermark, Crook notes that they all emanated from Field Place, the Shelley family home, during 1810–11. In her *N&Q* article, Crook redates the composition of **"A Cat"** to the late spring or early summer of 1811, after PBS's expulsion from Oxford, arguing that PBS, whose father had cut off his income after his expulsion, was himself the Cat in distress.

In a letter to Reiman on 10 July 1994, Crook modified her conclusions, noting that the watermark evidence would also support a date in 1810, when PBS and Elizabeth Shelley were collaborating on **Original Poetry "by Victor and Cazire"** (*V&C*). **"A Cat"** might, therefore, relate to the situation when Timothy Shelley refused to pay the printer's bill for typesetting that volume. Crook also observed that the meter and stanzaic form of the poem resemble those of the third poem in **St.Irv** (**Ballad ["The death-bell beats!—"]**), written in 1810.

We accept Crook's warning against relying blindly on comments on the poem's date quoted as Hellen Shelley's—the more so because, as Carol Thoma (now completing a study of Hogg's *Life of PBS* [*1858*]) reports, her original letters about *"A Cat"* seem not to be extant, leaving us no way to judge the accuracy of Hogg's quotations from them. After the deaths of PBS and Elizabeth Shelley, Hellen Shelley—whose letters concede her ignorance of the poem's origin—may simply have guessed about its date. We also note that PBS's verse letters to Edward Fergus Graham, as well as some of his later ballads (e.g., **The Devil's Walk**) and other "exoteric" poems that aim at unsophisticated readers, show PBS writing with similar abandon well into manhood. After his expulsion from Oxford (25 March 1811), PBS was, however, so angry at his father that he would not, we believe, have exhibited the playfulness found in *"A Cat,"* and if he had disguised his feelings enough to adopt such a light tone during the sundering of the Shelley family, Elizabeth Shelley (who had been forbidden to communicate with her brother and must have been emotionally affected by the trauma) would have been unlikely to copy and illustrate it for display. *"A Cat,"* we believe, was most likely composed between 1809 (the date of the watermark on Elizabeth Shelley's transcript) and PBS's expulsion from University College. Since the transcript shows that PBS *could* have released this poem to his sister as early as 1809, we give its putative term of release as ?1809–early March 1811, making it still possibly PBS's earliest extant poem.

Copy-text and Emendations

Our Text of *"A Cat"* is based on MS Pfz, but we have added punctuation (including the commas, periods, semicolon, and colon at the ends of **lines 2, 3, 6, 9, 12, 15, 18, 21, 24, 27,** and **30**) and the apostrophes that indicate elisions in **20** and **28**, recording all such departures from MS Pfz in the primary collations that accompany the Text. Because the letter used by Hogg as his copy-text for *1858* has not been located, we cannot specify which departures from MS Pfz are attributable to the transcription in Hellen Shelley's letter to Lady Shelley (which served as Hogg's source) and which come from Hogg or his compositor.

While editing *1927*/III, Roger Ingpen saw MS Pfz, which then belonged to Mrs. J. C. Worthington, who had obtained it, by gift or purchase, from a Mrs. Titchurch (see *SC* IV, 817), but Ingpen's opportunity to study it must have been brief. Collation shows that, though he corrected some verbal errors, he introduced a new one in **line 14** and retained most of the orthography and punctuation found in *1858* and later nineteenth-century editions. Matthews and Everest base their *1989* text on Cameron's transcription and the facsimile in *SC*/IV. We therefore collate at the foot of our Text only *SC*/IV and MS Pfz (i.e., our independent transcription of the MS).

Variants from the influential editions of PBS's poetry appear on pages 411–12 as Historical Collations.

Sources and Occasion

The following notes reflect our view that PBS wrote this version of *"A Cat"* between late 1809 and early 1811. One literary model for the poem was Gray's *Ode on the Death of a Favourite Cat,* which PBS had memorized at a very early age, as Hellen Shelley "frequently heard" from their mother (Hogg, *Life of PBS,* ed. Wolfe, I, 23). Though this knowledge may have suggested to Hellen Shelley that *"A Cat"* was a juvenile effort, the diction and rhymes of PBS's poem are far more colloquial than those in Gray's *Ode,* which followed a mock-heroic tradition of laments for pets that is at least as old as Catullus III ("Lugete, o Veneres Cupidinesque") on the death of his beloved Julia's pet sparrow. PBS's colloquial rhymes, such as tell ye and belly (**3, 6**), set his level of style as the familiar, or even burlesque, rather than the elevated diction of mock-heroic poetry assumed by Catullus and Gray.

Stanza 1 suggests that the poem may have been ostensibly about a specific cat that had been troublesome to Elizabeth Shelley, or other members of the Shelley family—perhaps one of many cats likely to have been kept around the Shelley farms at Field Place, or even the cat belonging to their cousin John Grove that is mentioned in **line 40** of Elizabeth Shelley's second verse letter to Harriet Grove in *V&C*. But the fable may also comment upon some disagreement—perhaps financial—between PBS and his father. PBS could well have sent the poem to Elizabeth Shelley from Oxford in the fall of 1810, when Timothy Shelley refused to pay for the printing of *V&C*. (See Commentary, pp. 149–53.) For interpretations based on earlier datings, see *SC* IV, 814–19, and *1989* I, 3–4.

line 4. sinner: This comic rhyme suggests that PBS wrote the poem before Harriet Grove's rejection of him and his expulsion from Oxford led him to adopt a more consciously anti-Christian vocabulary.

line 5. wants in MS Pfz is given as "waits" in texts from Hogg's *1858* through *1927*/III.

line 7. You migh'n': PBS's omission of the *t* in might and *o* in not, with his diminution of its final *t* into a superscript, indicates that the two words are to be pronounced colloquially as a single syllable ("mynt"), thus rendering superfluous emendations to "You would not" (*1858,* etc.) and "You'd not" (*1972*) on the supposition that the line is "unmetrical" (Rogers, *1972* I, 349).

line 11. like many] like so many   *1858* through *1927*/III. The error of adding *so* to this line in *1858* may rest with either Hellen Shelley or Hogg, who based his text in *1858* on her copy of MS Pfz. As the editors of *1989* note, "A pencilled *so* has been added in the transcript" (4), and indeed, such an interlineation appears between like and many not only in MS Pfz itself, but also (though very faintly) in the photofacsimile of the first page in *SC* IV, 815 (though the word is not cited in the transcription, textual notes, or collation accompanying that facsimile). When Matthews and Everest add, however, that this word is "apparently in Elizabeth S.'s hand," we disagree.

There is no particular affinity between the writing of the tiny penciled interlineation and Elizabeth Shelley's formal, calligraphic hand transcription of the poem in ink. The inserted "so" is more likely the work of Hellen Shelley, who wrote of the poem before she transcribed it for Lady Shelley that "there is no promise of future excellence in the lines, the versification is defective" (Hogg, *Life*, ed. Wolfe, I, 26), or of Mrs. Titchurch, Mrs. J. C. Worthington, or a later owner before the Pforzheimer Library acquired the MS from Seven Gables Bookshop (New York) in the late 1960s.

Whoever added "so" to the line belonged to the *dum-de-dum-de-dum* school of scansion. The MS line recorded in ink, though a syllable short of the obvious quota, should be read with a slight pause between Which and like to produce a subtle syncopation that (like a comma) signals the start of the simile. Someone untrained in poetry, perhaps comparing MS Pfz with a printed text deriving from *1858,* may have preferred Hogg's emended version, or may have given precedence to the printed text and, therefore, "corrected" the authoritative MS in pencil.

line 12. With comic incongruity, PBS alludes to the humans, whose behavior he compares with the Cat in distress, as poor dogs. Hellen Shelley or Hogg emended dogs to "souls" to add dignity to the poem.

line 13. As *1989* notes, living here refers to an official appointment to a benefice as tenured pastor of a parish in the established Church, either as a "rector," who received the tithes of the parish directly, or as a "vicar," who was paid a salary by the college, cathedral, landowner, or other individual or institution holding the rights to the tithe income. A "curate," who was paid by and served at the pleasure of a tenured rector or vicar, was not said to have a living in this sense.

lines 14–15. Some scholars read these lines as alluding to Timothy Shelley's desire for the death of Sir Bysshe Shelley, *his* father, so he might inherit his wealth and baronetcy; we believe that they may also reflect PBS's feelings about Timothy Shelley.

line 24. The subtlety of PBS's irregular, colloquial rhythms in *"A Cat"* may have led either Hellen Shelley or Hogg to change require to "want" in *1858*, thus affecting subsequent editions dependent upon Hogg's corrupted text.

line 29. As the Historical Collations show, Ingpen after seeing the MS corrected this line in *1927*/III from its previous reading (by Hellen Shelley or Hogg): "*Some* people had such food," which is certainly unmetrical.

line 30. hold their jaw: Hellen Shelley wrote, "That last expression is, I imagine, still *classical* at boys' schools, and it was a favourite one of Bysshe's, which I remember from a painful fact, that one of my sisters ventured to make use of it, and was punished in some old-fashioned way, which impressed the sentence on my memory" (quoted in Hogg, *Life,* ed. Wolfe, I, 30).

In MS Pfz, this line is followed by an elaborate flourish (probably by Elizabeth Shelley) and then by this note in an unidentified hand: "Percy Bysshe Shelley written | at 10 years of age to his Sister | at School"; this note—which cannot be by Hellen Shelley because of the impersonal way it alludes to both PBS and Elizabeth Shelley—is a later addition; though it may derive from Hellen Shelley's oral recollections, it was just as likely added by a later owner of the MS—Mrs. Titchurch or Mrs. Worthington (see *SC*/IV)—who took up the suggestion from Hogg's *Life of PBS* or a biography deriving from it. Unless the author of the notation can be identified as a contemporary of PBS or a friend of Elizabeth Shelley who could have known directly about the composition of ***"A Cat,"*** the comment has little authority.

"How swiftly through Heaven's wide expanse"

As noted earlier, PBS published another version of this poem in **St.Irv,** where we trace its textual history. This earlier version was privately released to Edward Fergus Graham in a letter of 22 April 1810; in declaring to Graham that the "lines . . . I can assure you are natural" (**Letters** I, 7), PBS intended to convey that they were spontaneous and sincere, rather than artful or artificial—part of his pose that he took little pains with his verses. He had, in fact, carefully structured ***"How swiftly"*** in a form popularized by Thomas Gray's *Elegy Written in a Country Churchyard* (1751), in which the poet, after describing a scene, quotes an inscription on a monument, or the words or imagined sentiments of someone he encounters there—the poet thus objectifying and distancing personal feelings by expressing them through words attributed to another.

Later in 1810, perhaps after Harriet Grove or her family expressed doubts about the proposed match with her cousin, PBS must have recognized that this early version of ***"How swiftly"*** is repetitive, with several awkward stanzas. These he removed in the much-revised version published as the fourth poem in *St.Irv.* But while recontextualizing it within the Gothic novel, he also mutilated the poem's original structure and left it in a somewhat incoherent form—perhaps intentionally so, based on his new satirical intentions, as we suggest in our Commentary to *St.Irv.*

Date and Occasion

PBS wrote this poem to his Wiltshire cousin Harriet Grove, during or immediately after her family's visit to Sussex and London in April and May 1810. Grove's diary shows that she and PBS spent as much time as possible together at this time, and that "they delighted in each other's company as avowed lovers and were recognised as such by their parents" (Hawkins, *First Love*, 38) —perhaps even unofficially engaged—by the end of the visit (see *SC* II, 575–79). No copy of *"How swiftly"* given to Grove has come to light, and this version of the poem survives only in PBS's letter sent to Graham, together with the suggestion that the poem be set to music. There PBS indicates that the poem is too personal, even in its quasi-public form, to show to his family if they knew him to be its author.

Copy-text and Emendations

The chief textual authority for the present version is the holograph letter to Graham, now in the Pierpont Morgan Library (MS PMgn). The paper of MS PMgn, having suffered much damage from folding and wear—at some time having had fragments detached—has been repaired and silked (i.e., supported between two layers of fine, transparent silk or another fabric to hold the fragile paper together). Though the staff at PMgn once considered the MS to be a forgery (see PBS, *Letters* I, 9), not only does the letter boast an impeccable provenance (Seymour de Ricci, *A Bibliography of Shelley's Letters, Published and Unpublished* [1927]; rpt. New York: Burt Franklin [1969], 87–88), but its paper bears the "C WILMOTT | 1808" watermark that was used at Field Place during this period (cf. *SC* II, 621), and the handwriting shows that it is certainly genuine, as Forman indicated by printing it in an appendix to his edition of Medwin's *Life of PBS* (*1913*) and as the editors of *1989* conclude after a long discussion. To the text of MS PMgn we have added minimal punctuation and eliminated apostrophes misused by PBS, basing these changes partly on the authority of the poet's own practice in his published version in *St.Irv.*

line 2. <u>fade</u>: *a* lost to damage in MS PMgn.

line 8. <u>The moonbeams rest</u>: Having learned from *Entick's New Spelling Dictionary* that the apostrophe ought not be used to form the possessive case (see the notes to *V&C*), PBS had difficulty remembering where it should be used. The apostrophes in MS PMgn here and in **lines 9, 14,** and **15** probably all fail to convey PBS's intentions to modern readers. Though *1989* argues that "moonbeam's rest" is a correct possessive followed by a noun ("It is the *repose* of the moonlight that is so beautiful"), PBS more likely intended moonbeams as a plural noun and rest as the verb. All of PBS's uses of this figure—including the revised text of this poem in *St.Irv*— derive from Shakespeare's image in *Merchant of Venice* V.i: "How sweet the moon light sleeps upon this Bank!"—an image that Harriet Westbrook Shelley copied into her Commonplace Book (f. 17v) in 1812–13 and that PBS discussed in an 1822 debate with Byron, as described anonymously in "Byron and Shelley on the Character of Hamlet" (*New Monthly Magazine* 29, Pt. 2 [1830], esp. 330–31; relevant text quoted in Reiman, *Shelley's "The Triumph of Life"* [1965], 99–100; and E. R. Wasserman, *Shelley: A Critical Reading* [1971], 133).

line 9. turret glimmers white: "glimmer's" in MS PMgn also illustrates PBS's unconventional use of the apostrophe.

line 13. Irvyne's tower: This is the imaginative name that PBS gave to Hill Place, the vacant house of Lady Irwin (earlier the political rival of the Duke of Norfolk and his supporter Timothy Shelley; see William Albery, *Parliamentary History of . . . Horsham* [1927]). Hill Place was located at Broadbridge Heath, just south of Warnham and across the Dorking-to-Arundel road from Field Place (Paterson's *Roads* [1808], 34). Hawkins notes that Lady Irwin's "ruined house was said to have been Elizabethan, the grounds laid out by Capability Brown" (*First Love*, 33).

lines 14–15. In MS PMgn these lines read: "The moonbeam pours it's silver ray; | It gleam's upon the ivied bower". PBS's misunderstanding of the use of the apostrophe (see note to **line 8**) produced the erroneous gleam's in **15,** while his use of the apostrophe in "it's" in **14** derives from a common eighteenth-century convention followed for years afterwards in the MSS and books of his contemporaries. Though obsolescent, *it's* was not considered an error in 1810. But PBS soon afterwards accepted the printer's changes of such forms when he published a version of this same poem in *St.Irv,* and we change both words to their modern forms, already dominant in PBS's day.

line 16. in] on   *1927*/ VIII, *1989*. The Julian Edition apparently served as copy-text for *1989;* these editions are the only ones to include this error and to change tumult to "tumults" (**34**).

lines 20, 40. Having in **17–19** introduced a youth as his surrogate, PBS quotes this youth's lament, beginning with **20**. (Though MS PMgn omits closing quotation marks, we supply them at the end of **line 40**.) The obvious model for this oblique structure was Gray's *Elegy*, in which the imagined speech of "some hoary-headed swain" (lines 98–116) and the epitaph of the youth (117–28) conclude that poem (which PBS translated into Latin in 1808 or 1809; see Appendix A). Although both Gray's and PBS's poems also employ quatrains rhymed *abab*, PBS's impassioned tetrameter lines do not resemble Gray's stately pentameter ones.

lines 21–24. The syntax of these lines is difficult: The youth says that he would (i.e., he wills) that fiends should feast on his torn soul and dire fate's ... storm should lower (= lour) over his frail form so that he can prove (i.e., test) the pains of death. PBS later used "frail and wasted human form" while describing the youthful wanderer in **Alastor** (line 350) and repeated frail form when introducing himself as a mourner in **Adonais** (line 271).

line 27. Can stop the bosom's bursting woes] Can still the bursting bosom's woes   *1989*. Matthews and Everest do not annotate this line; though the reading "still" for stop first appeared in *1927*/III, we cannot explain the transposition "bursting bosom's" in *1989*.

line 28. calm] still: In MS PMgn, "stem" is inserted in pencil above. In **line 36**, PBS replaced "still" with calm. Later, either he or Graham, trying to revise lines that were too nearly identical, may have written "stem" as an alternative to calm in **28**; but the penciled word may be, rather, the attempt of some later reader of the MS to transcribe the nearly illegible cancellation. Since we are uncertain that the penciled word is in PBS's handwriting, we follow his original inked text.

frantic grief: This phrase occurs only occasionally in poems before PBS's lyric, but at least two precedents may have influenced him here: first, in line 107 of *The Troubador; or, Lady Alice's Bower*—in M. G. Lewis's *Tales of Terror* (1801, 1808), from which PBS plagiarized **Saint Edmond's Eve** in *V&C*—Lady Alice, at an abbey, experiences "a frantic grief" when she learns that the troubadour whose love she has scorned has languished and died; the phrase also appears, though in a less obvious context, in Book XI, line 18, of Southey's *Thalaba the Destroyer* (1801), a poem that strongly influenced **Queen Mab** and other poems by PBS.

line 30. Though both Forman in Medwin's *Life of PBS* and Jones in **Letters** indicate that the bottom edge of this leaf was missing, this line, which they omit, is now legible at the bottom of page 2 of MS PMgn. Perhaps a fragment—detached when Forman saw the MS on display before its sale at a London auction house, but preserved for the buyer—was later reattached when MS PMgn was restored and silked; Jones may have seen the MS before that restoration, relied on an imperfect photocopy, or followed Forman.

line 35. The dash certainly stands for the name Harriet (pronounced in two syllables). PBS's reluctance to include it in this publicly released version accords with the wish he expressed to Graham that his authorship of the poem be kept secret from his family. If Graham did set it to music, PBS may have asked him to substitute another woman's name, such as "Mary" or "Lucy," to fill the gap.

lines 37–40. We discuss both PBS's borrowing from Byron's "I would I were a careless child" and PBS's uses of the words unveil and futurity in the note to **lines 19–20** of the *St.Irv* version of this poem.

"Oh wretched mortal, hard thy fate!"

This poem, a new addition to PBS's canon, appears in facsimile and diplomatic transcription in *SC* IX. It is written on folio 5 recto of a notebook in the Pforzheimer Collection. This notebook belonged to Hogg while he was a student at Oxford in 1810–11, when he made notes and drafted essays in it; later in 1811 he used it for his private studies at York while he was training to become a lawyer. The MS Pfz text of **"Oh wretched mortal"** is written in faint pencil in PBS's hand, except that someone—perhaps but not certainly PBS himself—has gone over the first two lines with pen and ink and also recrossed the initial *T* of **line 3** in ink.

Provenance and Discovery

In 1961, Cameron visited England and arranged to purchase the notebook from one of Hogg's descendants on behalf of the Carl H. Pforzheimer Library, where it was accessioned as "Hogg 114." Some years later, Reiman, during a periodic review of MSS in the Pforzheimer Library, noticed that this poem was written in the hand of PBS rather than Hogg.

Since that time, both the editorial team of *Shelley and his Circle* and we working on *CPPBS* have checked various sources to ascertain that **"Oh wretched mortal"** is not simply PBS's copy of a text by someone else. A keyword search of the Chadwyck-Healey *Lion* databases of English poetry, drama, and eighteenth-century fiction and American poetry has found no close parallels to the first line of the poem and no earlier occurrences of the phrase *wretched mortal* parallel to its meaning in this poem: in several instances *mortal* is used as an adjective rather than a noun, and in other poems the "mortal" is described as wretched in comparison to God (or classical gods). In none is a mortal portrayed as being wretched simply because he is or has been a lover.

Date and Occasion

PBS wrote *"Oh wretched mortal"* on an early recto page of a college notebook that Hogg began to use in Michaelmas term (Oct.–Dec.) at Oxford in 1810. The main contents of the notebook, written in the same direction as this poem, seem to be Hogg's college exercises and notes on things that interested him during his months at Oxford, some very likely reflecting his early discussions with PBS. Later, after their expulsion from Oxford, while Hogg was studying law at York, he reversed the notebook and utilized it from the other end, writing *reverso* (i.e., upside down and from the back toward the front of the notebook, as he first used it) to record his ideas and pursue his study of Hebrew. *"Oh wretched mortal"* is published in a diplomatic transcription as part of the Retrospective of important early writings that opens Volume IX of *SC,* with a full bibliographical discussion of Hogg's notebook and a circumstantial account of the probable date and situation of the poem's origins.

Though *"Oh wretched mortal"* invokes a theme and ideas common in PBS's early poetry, it lacks the sense of personal emotional engagement that characterizes, for example, his poems of love and longing during his infatuation with Harriet Grove, or the deep-felt anger of the poems in which, after the breaking of their engagement and his expulsion from Oxford, PBS lashed out at Grove's parents, religious bigotry, and his own father. The poem also lacks the more abstract but still pointed sociopolitical tendentiousness of many early poems in *Esd.* The stilted style and moralistic final line of *"Oh wretched mortal"* mark it as an exercise, or tour de force, and from other interactions between PBS and Hogg, we infer that PBS, very early in their acquaintance, picked up Hogg's notebook and dashed off the eight pentameter couplets to impress his new friend with his facility as a poet. PBS's similar performances connected with the publication of *V&C* and *PF* suggest that he may actually have composed the short poem sometime earlier, before he wrote it out flawlessly in the notebook of his new acquaintance as if he were writing extemporaneously. Though he left the poem virtually unpunctuated, perhaps partly to convince Hogg that he was composing spontaneously rather than transcribing from memory, the closure of the poem's rhetoric and a long line firmly drawn with the same pencil across the page just below the last line indicate that PBS regarded it as complete.

Editorial Issues

For this text, the poem's first appearance in a critical edition, we have added such minimal punctuation as appears in his safe-keeping copies of contemporary short poems in *Esd,* where PBS might have included it had he not been at odds with Hogg when he assembled that collection of short poems for publication. We punctuate *"Oh wretched mortal"* so as to convey PBS's intended meaning, while maintaining the light and informal style of pointing characteristic of his other early short poems. These editorial interventions also enable us to show how we interpret various minor cruxes without adding extensive notes.

To Mary who died in this opinion

This poem appears in a letter from PBS to Elizabeth Hitchener dated 23 November 1811 (**Letters** I, 190), which survives as BL MS ADD. 37,496, folio 57 recto. There is a facsimile in *MYR: Shelley* VIII (ed. Reiman and O'Neill [1997], 39–42), with literal transcription and notes by Michael O'Neill. PBS wrote four other poems on the theme of Mary's suicide that appear as poems #37–40 in **Esd**.

Date and Occasion of Composition and Release

In October 1810, soon after PBS met Hogg at University College, Oxford, Hogg told his new friend the story of a young woman he knew in County Durham who was socially ostracized or otherwise persecuted and who, after discussing suicide with Hogg, actually killed herself because of the misery of her situation. In a possibly fictionalized "Advertisement" to the other poems "To Mary" included in **Esd,** PBS wrote: "Mary died three months after before I heard her tale. —" (*SC* IV, 1005). Previously scholars had only the facts on the person behind Hogg's story from Dowden's statement that "Mary was an unhappy girl known to Hogg, who had embodied part of her story in his unpublished novel 'Leonora'" (Dowden, *Life of PBS* I, 155–56 fn.; *SC* II, 774). But, thanks to B. C. Barker-Benfield's "Hogg-Shelley Papers of 1810–12" (*Bodleian Library Record* 14 [Oct. 1991]: 14) we now know that, however much Hogg may have embellished the truth in relating the story to PBS, the original of "Mary" was likely a Miss Dillon, about whom Hogg's father and his friends exchanged letters early in October 1810, making plans to spirit her out of town, to keep her out of Hogg's orbit, lest the two young people become seriously involved before Hogg returned to Oxford.

Though Hogg's copies of PBS's poems "To Mary" have not come to light, PBS's letters make clear that Hogg saw the poems inspired by his story at the time PBS composed them in 1810. Since this poem, unlike its companions in **Esd,** has no publication date to supersede its private release at Oxford, we give **To Mary who died** a putative release date of ca. 1 November 1810, remembering however that PBS may well have revised this version a year later, as he copied it into his letter to Hitchener.

The four poems in **Esd** addressed "To Mary" tell the story in a sequence that would place ***To Mary who died in this opinion*** between the second and third of those poems (see Kenneth Neill Cameron, ed., *The Esdaile Notebook: A Volume of Early Poems by Percy Bysshe Shelley* [1965], 243). Cameron, judging the present poem to be aesthetically superior to others reprinted in ***Esd,*** asks why PBS did not include this one with them. Its context in PBS's letter to Hitchener may provide part of the answer, for as Cameron observes, <u>this opinion</u> in the poem's subtitle refers to Mary's belief in immortality: Earlier in the letter PBS exclaims to Hitchener, "I cannot submit to perish like the flower of the field, I cannot consent that the same shroud which shall moulder around these perishing frames shall enwrap the vital spirit which hath produced sanctified (may I say eternized) a friendship such as ours.—" (***Letters*** I, 188). After continuing in this vein, PBS introduces the poem in these words: "I transcribe a little Poem I found this morning; it was written some time ago, but as it appears to shew what I then thought of eternal life I send it. | To Mary who died in this opinion," and the poem follows (***Letters*** I, 189–90). Thus, PBS tells Hitchener, he had by November 1811 disavowed the opinions in this poem, referring to them as "what I *then* (i.e., in Nov. 1810) thought...." By the end of 1812 and the early months of 1813, after PBS had written most of ***Queen Mab*** and when he was revising and copying his "younger poems" for ***Esd,*** he professed the ideology of French materialists, who denied personal immortality. Perhaps PBS omitted ***To Mary who died*** (in which the poet says that, though he cannot believe in personal immortality, he would <u>barter</u> his <u>existence</u> to have such a <u>dream</u>), because the poem's emotional perspective conflicted with doctrines that he espoused in 1812–13, when he attempted to publish ***Esd*** along with ***QM.***

Provenance and Textual History

Ironically, because ***To Mary who died*** was included in a letter, it was the first of the 1810 poems addressed "To Mary" to appear in print. W. M. Rossetti tells in *Some Reminiscences* (1906) how in 1868 he was introduced to Henry J. Slack, "a legal gentleman" who had in his possession Shelley's letters to Elizabeth Hitchener (now in BL). "Mr. Slack ... was not in an accurate sense their owner. They had been deposited with him as a lawyer, many years previously, by a representative of Miss Hitchener." Rossetti's account (on pp. 364–66) generally corroborates what Reiman had inferred in 1978 from Rossetti's diaries and the accounts of Hitchener by other scholars (see Reiman's Introduction to the poems of Hitchener in a volume of *Romantic Context: Poetry* containing the poems of David Booth and Hitchener). The standard story that Hitchener went abroad and married an Austrian officer, as Slack told T. J. Wise, was not true but was concocted to explain how Slack had come into possession of PBS's letters to Hitchener, which he probably obtained from one H. Holste, a solicitor who was the executor of Hitchener's estate at her death in 1822. Rossetti reports that though Slack permitted him to read and copy the letters, he honored Slack's wish that he not quote them or cite their whereabouts in the memoir of PBS that opened *1870*, but that "a few juvenile poems interspersed in the letters were used in my edition, under the sanction of Mr. Slack." One of these was **To Mary who died.** Later texts follow closely the basic text found in either *1870* or Rossetti's revised text of *1878*, with only minor tinkering and some new input from the texts of PBS's letters since 1907, when the Rev. Charles Hargrove deposited the original MSS of PBS's letters to Hitchener in the British Library, after they had been bequeathed to him by Mrs. Slack.

Copy-text and Emendations

Though the overall theme and emotions of this poem are clear, the syntax is especially difficult and tangled. Coming back to it after a long interval, PBS may not have been able to make complete sense of it, and his ad hoc revisions while transcribing it hastily into the letter may further have muddled it. Our copy-text is MS BL, but we, too, after consulting earlier editions and O'Neill's transcription and notes in *MYR: Shelley* VIII, 37–42, have added limited punctuation, expanded some abbreviations, and emended what we regard as careless miswritings, as well as inferring and supplying letters now missing but perhaps present in the MS when it was seen by Rossetti.

line 5. morn's: The editorially added apostrophe (omitted by PBS) aids understanding of the syntax: the first stanza is a single thought that counsels the young Maiden to draw courage (Firmness . . . borrow) from her wrecked hopes (destiny) because the ray that reveals morn's flower (5) does not have so bright a hue (6) as the ray that mocks concealing (see note to 7) and bathes her in its loveliest light (8).

line 7. mocks concealing: "defies concealment." *Shelley Concordance,* though not glossing the line in **To Mary who died** this way, cites at least seven other places where PBS uses *mock* to mean "scorn," "defy," or "ignore," including three in **QM:** "Fearless and free the ruddy children played, | Weaving gay chaplets for their innocent brows | With the green ivy and the red wallflower, | That mock the dungeon's unavailing gloom" (IX.115–18); "Whose wonders mocked the knowledge of thy pride" (VI.91); and "Mocking my powerless tyrant's horrible curse" (VII.257).

line 12. The *I* of In, written on what is now a fold-crease of the letter, was probably legible to early readers of MS BL but is now lost to damage and repair of the paper.

lines 13–14. In the late eighteenth and early nineteenth centuries, *tho* (or *tho'*) was a viable alternative spelling for *though* in printed texts as well as MSS. We have tried to clarify the compressed syntax by adding a comma after fainting to set off fair one (i.e., Mary) and parentheses and an apostrophe in **14** to show that this line is an aside, depicting a personified "Sorrow" who has itself delivered to Mary either a symbolic cup of bitterness or a literal one of poison.

line 20. affection's . . . shrine] affections . . . shine   MS BL. We first tried to make sense of these words as PBS wrote them in the MS by adding commas to render **line 20** in apposition to **line 19**: "And smile to die a martyr, | On affections bloodless shine,"—a reading that would have the speaker say: "I would trade my existence to have a dream [i.e., belief in immortality] like yours, and—having that faith—I would smile to die as a martyr, [or] to shine on bloodless affections." When this expedient created more problems than it solved, we emended both affections and shine, as previous editors had done. See note to **line 23**.

line 22. and: This word is malformed in MS BL.

line 23. PBS's miswriting in MS BL of enshrined as "enshined" here tends to confirm that "shine" in **20** also exemplifies PBS's miswriting or miscopying, rather than his tortured syntax.

line 24. Such as: These first words of the line do not now appear in MS BL because when Hitchener opened the letter, the sealing wax or wafer seal tore away the portion of the letter on which the missing words were written, and that seal, with whatever fragment of paper adhered to it, is no longer with MS BL. In *1870*, Rossetti printed the first text of the poem from the MS, and as Matthews and Everest remark in *1989*, the words *Such as* may have been present then (though only if the seal and the portion of the MS adhering to it were there). Since Rossetti inclined, however, to correct what he regarded as PBS's omissions and errors in other texts, his inclusion of this phrase does not guarantee that PBS wrote Such as; the phrase may be simply Rossetti's shrewd guess about what the poet would have written.

  thine: The antecedent is heart (**line 23**).

"Why is it said thou canst but live"

This poem appears in the second of two letters that PBS wrote to Hogg on 8 May 1811 (see Cameron's commentaries in *SC* II, 769–79). PBS probably began this letter at his lodgings in Poland Street, which he and Hogg had shared after their expulsion from Oxford before Hogg capitulated to his father's proposals and went to study law at York. PBS completed the letter—and added the poem—while he was at the home of Eliza and Harriet Westbrook (later Shelley) on Chapel Street, in London's West End.

Context and Occasion

In the letter, after discussing possible financial settlements with his father, PBS declares that money means nothing to him personally, though it would be a useful thing to have if one planned to marry: "well do I see why you would not reject it;—you think it would possibly add to the happiness of some being to whom you cherish some remote hope of approximation, union . . The indissoluble sacred union of love[.]" Then follows the poem ***"Why is it said."*** When PBS resumes the letter, he writes: "Excuse this strange momentary mania. I am now at Miss Westbrooke's and she is reading Voltaires Philosophique Dictionnaire," and he ends with a discussion of the hypocrisy and other evils of the institution of marriage (*SC* II, 776–77).

PBS's comments on money and marriage obviously applied to his own situation at least as much as to Hogg's, for PBS soon opened negotiations with his father in which, without renouncing any of his declared beliefs, he won an agreement that provided him with £200 per year. Soon after that, he eloped with Harriet Westbrook. PBS probably wrote this poem for Harriet, but however much she fascinated him, it would not have been appropriate, in his penniless state before the settlement with his father, for him to give her a poem about the enduring quality of love. While her older sister and chaperon Eliza Westbrook, the "Miss Westbrooke" of PBS's letter ("Miss" always designating the older or oldest sister), labored to endear herself to PBS by reading Voltaire aloud, he transcribed the poem (which he may have prepared in advance and memorized) as an extempore effort to impress not only Hogg but, first, Harriet Westbrook, who may have watched him write it out (with just a few minor cancellations) while they listened to Eliza's reading from across the room.

Copy-text and Textual History

Though Harriet Westbrook probably read the poem, the scenario outlined above suggests why PBS may not have given her a copy of it; and since it was—or was alleged to be—an extempore composition, he probably kept no draft. And after PBS broke off with Hogg in September 1811 over his friend's attempt to seduce Harriet Westbrook Shelley at York, he lacked access to a copy of ***"Why is it said"*** when he collected his other early poems while he was isolated at Tanyrallt (near Tremadoc in North Wales) during the winter of 1812–13. The only authority for ***"Why is it said"*** is thus PBS's letter to Hogg (MS Pfz), in which the poem appears on pages 2–3; Hogg first published it (with several verbal errors) in Chapter 11 of his *Life of PBS* (*1858*), from which all subsequent texts of the poem derived until 1961, when a diplomatic transcription of MS Pfz appeared in *SC* (II, 776), showing that PBS's only marks of punctuation are a period and dash at the end of **line 10** and a long dash after **14**. The poem is untitled both in MS Pfz and in Hogg's *Life;* but in *1870,* Rossetti entitled it "Love," a name accepted by most subsequent editors. We have followed MS Pfz, adding punctuation with a sparing hand, so as not to obliterate the poem's (?calculated) air of spontaneity.

line 6. vermeil: PBS here spells correctly this variant of vermillion, in which he usually reversed the *e* and *i;* perhaps Harriet Westbrook helped with the spelling while he wrote out the poem.

lines 7–10. The probably meaning of these lines is: even death, victor over time, confesses [that] . . . Love [thou] retains its unchanging bloom, even in the tomb. Hogg, apparently confused by the syntax, changed the first word of **line 7** from Since to "Nor."

line 10. We retain the period of MS Pfz, rather than change it to a question mark as *1989* does. PBS characteristically supplied queries and exclamation points where he felt they were needed, and because the mood of the long rhetorical period in the first ten lines quickly changes from interrogative to declarative, a query after **10** would undermine his probable intention.

lines 11–12. blest reviving: alludes to the Anglican doctrine of the Last Judgment, when the righteous will arise from their graves (see the Commentary to **V&C** and the note to **Ghasta 94**). Here PBS asserts that love is the power that will revive them.

The phrase *day star* also appears in **QM** (I.128), ***To the Republicans of North America*** (***Esd*** poem 17, line 41), and ***"Death-spurning rocks!"*** (***Esd*** poem 22, line 28: "The daystar shines, the daybeam dawns"); it derives ultimately from Milton's *Lycidas,* 168, where it refers to the sun, but PBS's four uses of the phrase refer to the morning star (*Shelley Concordance*), both usages being noted in *OED*. Some other poets used the phrase in ways that, though perhaps meant to echo Milton's usage, may have led PBS to think they meant *day star* to signify Lucifer, the morning star: for example, R. Burns's "On the Death of a Favourite Child," line 8; T. Campbell's *The Exile of Erin,* 5 (in *Gertrude of Wyoming and Other Poems,* 1809, etc.); and S. T. Coleridge's *To an Unfortunate Woman at the Theatre* (pub. 1797 and 1800), 31.

line 14. We have added a period after this line, in addition to the very long dash that PBS used to mark the major break in thought after **14**, after which the mood does remain interrogatory to the end.

lines 15ff. The thou addressed is no longer "love" but Hogg or any reader of the poem. Matthews and Everest comment on this change in the meaning of thou after **14** in *1989*. Such a bifurcated structure is not uncommon in PBS's poems, which frequently begin with a metaphysical problem (e.g., the dangers of isolation to the idealist in **Alastor**, or the unjust sufferings and early deaths of the righteous in **Adonais**) that he answers, not by metaphysical argument, but appeal to his personal desires, feelings, and experience. In **"Why is it said"** the problem seems broader than the nature of "Love" (rendering Rossetti's title inadequate). Perhaps the poem raises and attempts to answer the question, What is the source of human hopes for beatitude? **Lines 1–14** express the hopes of a devotee of love, but the concluding lines appeal to an almost mystical experience of inspiration to validate such aspirations.

line 19. noonday dream: PBS repeats virtually the same phrase in two later poems: "It circles round | Like the soft wavy wings of noonday dreams, | Inspiring calm and happy thoughts, like mine" (**Prom** III.iii.144–46), and "I bear light shade for the leaves when laid | In their noon-day dreams" (**The Cloud** 4). In fact, PBS used *noon, noonday,* and *noontide* and their variants far more frequently than other poets: the printed concordances list 112 uses by PBS, compared with 50 in S. T. Coleridge's similar quantity of poetry, 29 in Byron's much larger oeuvre, just 19 in Milton's poetry, and none at all in Spenser's. Moreover, *noon* usually carries a special symbolic significance in PBS's work, for example, in **Lines written among the Euganean Hills**, 285–320 (see section 5 of Reiman's essay on this poem, *PMLA* 77 [1962]: 404–13) and **Prom** II.iv.173 and II.v.10.

lines 20–24. Though *silence* occurs over 100 times in PBS's poetry, this personification of Silence, in a simile (**16–18**) picturing a scene of languor rather than activity that evokes an indistinct rapturous thrill (**15**), may seem to some readers un-Shelleyan and more in the languourous vein identified with Keats's *Ode on Indolence* or *To Autumn*. Though *1989* suggests line 12 of Gray's *Elegy* as a verbal source for **24**, "The mopeing owl" complaining to the moon of people who "near her secret bower, | Molest her ancient solitary reign" (Gray, *Works* [1807] I, 59) does not match the effect of PBS's figure, while Chadwyck-Healey *Lion* yields no closer verbal parallel.

"As you will see I wrote to you" [To EFG #1]

We designate this poem, the first of two verse letters to Edward Fergus Graham, **To EFG#1**. It survives in the Henry W. and Albert A. Berg Collection at the New York Public Library; a facsimile of MS Berg appears in *MYR: Shelley* VIII (10–16). Jones dates this verse letter 14 May 1811 (**Letters** I, 86–88), assuming that the note to Graham, dated only "Field Place" but announcing PBS's agreement with his father for an income of £200 per year (85) was the cover franked by "Timothy Shelley, M.P." to which PBS alludes in **line 3** of this verse letter. (There is no visible postmark date on this note, now at Harvard.) The verse letter itself indicates that PBS wrote it probably on 14 or 15 May 1811, immediately after he returned to Field Place, upon extracting a financial agreement from his father. PBS soon learned that, though in his letter containing **"Why is it said"** he had affected to scorn money, £200 a year was insufficient to support him and his enthusiasms in the style to which they had become accustomed.

To EFG#1 was first published in full by Ingpen in the Julian Edition (*1927*)—not with the letters issued in 1926 (Vols. VIII, IX, and X), but with the early poems published in 1927 (III, 92–94). There Ingpen's note contextualizes the tone of the poem: "We are apt to forget, and Shelley helps us to forget except in this instance, in some parts of *Margaret Nicholson* and in *Swellfoot the Tyrant*, that he lived in the days of the Regency and of Peter Pindar, when profligacy was a common subject for coarse satire among versifiers. From the reference to 'Peter Pindar' in Shelley's letter to Graham of July 15, 1811, it is probable that he was familiar with his verse" (*1927*/III, 320).

John Wolcot (1738–1819, *DNB*), who used *Peter Pindar* as his principal nom de guerre, was a Whig satirist whose mock-heroic odes, epistles, and a mock epic entitled *The Lousiad* attacked his political and personal enemies, including King George III, Lord Liverpool, Pitt, Canning, and William Gifford. Wolcot's satires appeared almost annually from the 1780s through 1814 (see *NCBEL* and the Commentary for **On a Fête at Carlton House** in Appendix C). PBS, the scion of a Whig political family, could hardly have missed reading some of them, and MWS records in her journal that on 28 September 1816, "Shelley reads P. Pindars works aloud."

In *Liberty's Last Squeek* (1795, but reprinted frequently), PBS would have encountered two references to Margaret (Peg) Nicholson and her knife (see "Pindar's" *Works* [1802] IV, 48, 55). While we agree with Ingpen that the tone of satires like Wolcot's provides a contemporary context for PBS's tone in his two verse letters to Graham, PBS's satire here is much more intimately personal and slanderous than almost any publications of the period, and its tone has strongly affected the printing history—or lack thereof—of these two poems.

Provenance and Public Knowledge

Several Shelleyans had seen **To EFG#1** prior to its full publication in *1927*. In Rossetti's "reminiscences of Graham" (as quoted by Ingpen), he wrote that when he was about fifteen years old, Graham (an old friend of Rossetti's father, Gabriele Rossetti) showed him among his letters from PBS "two very early verse-compositions, addressed to himself, by Shelley—one of them, I think, remains still unpublished" (see *1927/* VIII, xxiv–xxv), and Rossetti notes having seen this verse letter again and copied it out in May 1869 at the home of Frederick Locker—later Locker-Lampson (*The Rossetti Papers, 1862–1870* [1903], 392), and his letter of 1 May 1878 to Richard Garnett mentions the verse letter, but declares it unfit to appear in his proposed collective edition of PBS's letters (*Letters about Shelley* [1917], 60). Dowden mentioned **To EFG#1** only as a "poetical epistle to Graham" by PBS "referring to his father in odious terms" (*Life* I, 131n). In the introduction to his Aldine Edition, Forman described the poem as "characterized by a certain adolescent wantonness ... but distinctly clever" with "ribald allusions to Mr. Timothy Shelley," but he quotes just four innocuous lines (*1892F* I, xix). During the centennial year of PBS's death, this game of restrained allusion became almost an editorial strip-tease. The *London Mercury,* in its "Bibliographical Notes and News" column for August 1922 (VI, 418), while discussing the contents of a sale catalogue issued by the American collector (and writer of musical comedies) Harry B. Smith and his brother R. B. Smith, not only published **lines 1–10, 18–28,** and **51 to the end** of the poem, but it also characterized the sections not quoted, in which PBS calls his father "Killjoy," describes him as a hateful coward (**11–17**), and explores the likelihood of an affair between PBS's mother and Graham (**29–50**). The provenance of MS Berg given in *MYR: Shelley* VIII mentions neither the Harry B. Smith sale of 1922 nor the quotation of much of the text in *London Mercury* (*1922/LMer*).

Although publication of **To EFG#1** in 1927 finally ended censorship of the poem, Ingpen tucked it amid the poetic juvenilia in the third volume of the expensive, ten-volume limited edition; and during the subsequent forty years, the poem was known, if at all, by rich collectors or dedicated Shelleyans. It goes unmentioned in both White's *Shelley* and Cameron's *YS*, perhaps because its coarse Regency humor does not mesh with White's efforts to rehabilitate PBS as a philanthropic moralist or with Cameron's picture of him as a serious-minded radical from an early age. In *The Nascent Mind of Shelley* (1947), the contemporaneous British study of PBS's early life, A. M. D. Hughes alludes to "Julian Shelley, iii.92," in a note keyed to a comment about PBS's attitude toward his mother and Graham (110), but fails to indicate that a poem is involved. **To EFG#1** first received attention after its inclusion in **Letters** (*1964J*) and, subsequently, in the chronological editions of PBS's early poems by Rogers (*1972*) and Matthews and Everest (*1989*). By the latter date, Rogers's intervening publication in 1973 of PBS's second, equally salacious verse letter to Graham beginning **"Dear dear dear dear dear dear Græme"** (**To EFG#2**) demonstrated that **To EFG#1** was no anomaly.

Biographical and Historical Background

Though PBS combines personal themes with wider political and philosophical issues in this verse letter, as he does in virtually all of his poetry, this poem centers on the domestic politics of his situation vis-à-vis his parents and his older friend and confidant Graham, the music master (for whom, see Commentaries in *SC,* esp. II, 621–25, and those of the "Retrospective" that opens *SC* IX).

Having reached a financial settlement with Timothy Shelley, PBS now set himself to take control of the family at Field Place itself. In the undated cover letter, PBS told Graham: "We had this morning a letter addressed to my Father accusing him & my mother of <ge>tting drunk, & the latter of being <m>ore intimate with *you* than with my father himself. We all laughed heartily & thought it a good opportunity of making up. But he [i.e., Timothy Shelley] is as inveterate as ever" (***Letters*** I, 85). Cameron (*YS,* 344) and Gelpi (Barbara Charlesworth Gelpi, *Shelley's Goddess: Maternity, Language, Subjectivity* [1992], 116) both infer that the anonymous letter to Timothy Shelley, alleging misbehavior by his wife and his dependent protégé, was sent by PBS himself, reenforcing what Gelpi considers PBS's even more transgressive proposal to renounce his right to about half of the Shelley estates, entailed to the male heirs, in favor of his mother and sisters—both actions aimed at driving a wedge between Timothy Shelley and the women in the family (109–11). If we accept the idea that PBS, once he had been granted an income, embarked upon a strategy of dividing to conquer, one can view his two May 1811 verse letters to Graham as calculated to escalate the tensions among Timothy Shelley, Graham, and Elizabeth Pilfold Shelley, thus leaving his father without any allies in his own household.

EFG#1 emphasizes how Timothy Shelley hates both PBS and Graham and connects Timothy Shelley's jealousy of Graham with what seems to be his dislike of Gen. Thomas Graham (later Baron Lynedoch; 1748–1843, *DNB*), who on 5 March 1811 defeated the French at Barossa, on Spanish fields in the Peninsular War (see **lines 8, 17**). Though Edward Fergus Graham's family background is obscure, there is no known connection between him and General Graham; but since the latter served as a Whig M.P. for Perthshire, 1794–1807, Timothy Shelley must have known Thomas Graham and may have disliked him personally. PBS himself opposed the Peninsular War (see ***Devil's Walk***) and, indeed, all British foreign wars, and his linking of his father's anger at E. F. Graham with his father's dislike of General Graham's fame may be significant: if E. F. Graham was the lover of Timothy Shelley's wife (and thus the seducer of PBS's mother), both Timothy Shelley and PBS—if he believed the charge—may have borne an animus toward Graham for his erotic conquest, just as they did toward General Graham for his military one. PBS may thus be projecting onto his father his own feelings toward both Grahams. In any case, the verse letter incriminates E. F. Graham, forcing him to try to make his peace with Timothy Shelley, PBS, and, possibly, Elizabeth Pilfold Shelley as well.

Editorial Issues

The limitations of MS Berg, the sole textual authority, are apparent from the facsimile, diplomatic transcription, and notes by Reiman in *MYR: Shelley* VIII (7–17). PBS wrote his poem carelessly, perhaps to prevent anyone unfamiliar with his hand from reading it, once Graham had opened the letter. Moreover, during nearly two centuries the MS has also become worn, with the text obscured or even obliterated in some places. We have tried to clarify the text according to our understanding of the sometimes ambiguous evidence in MS Berg, recording in the primary collations all of our emendations of the MS. Besides expanding three ampersands and other abbreviations and correcting a few misspelled or miswritten words, we have minimally supplemented PBS's sparse punctuation to clarify what we believe his intentions to have been, discussing both our departures from the MS and our reasons for not emending elsewhere. PBS himself included only the following marks of punctuation in this 60-line poem: **line 3:** comma after frank; **line 5:** exclamation mark at end; **7:** comma after Graham; **11:** short dash after Fear; **21:** comma at end; **23:** comma after globe; **24:** comma after Peace; **28:** period at end; **35:** comma after famed; **42:** semicolon at end; **47:** semicolon after sin; **54:** comma after Græme and period at end; **57:** comma at end; **60:** exclamation mark after Oh; and final stop at **61.**

line 3. What appears to be a dot above the comma to form a semicolon is actually a tiny hole in the MS.

line 5. so blue: In his cover letter to Graham, PBS comments, "he [Timothy Shelley] looks rather blue today . . ." (***Letters*** I, 85); below, in **line 16,** Timothy Shelley is said to be "hot with envy blue."

line 7. Graham: This word was pronounced as two syllables; PBS spelled the name "Græme" in **line 17** (and in ***To EFG#2***) where the name was to be pronounced in the Scottish way, as a monosyllable rhyming with "fame." Compare "Lochinvar" in Scott's *Marmion* (V.xii): "There was mounting 'mong Græmes of the Netherby clan; | Forsters, Fenwicks, and Musgraves, they rode and they ran."

line 8. Spanish: The *S* may be lowercase in MS Berg.

line 11. In MS Berg, a short dash after Fear (which appears as a hyphen, but was intended to function like a comma) may, in a photocopy, have suggested to *1989* that the word was "Fierce."

line 12. usurps: "Of feelings, passions, etc.: To take possession of, ... or assume predominance in" (*OED* def. 2.c, with examples from 1759–1853).

lines 14–15. if you ... tale to you: Although we retain the punctuation of MS Berg, this aside could be placed within parentheses.

line 17. Because PBS often omits commas conventionally used both to set off vocatives and to separate three or more parallel substantives in a series, one cannot be certain whether Græme me or you addresses Graham as "Græme" (as in **line 54**), or whether Græme refers to General Graham as a third person whom Timothy Shelley could not bear. Other editors punctuate here as though the second alternative is correct; we leave the options open by retaining the punctuation of MS Berg.

line 19. This is the last line on page 1 of MS Berg; page 2 ends with **40**.

line 20. may justly be] may be justly be   MS Berg. The duplication of *be* suggests that PBS copied MS Berg from a draft with interlinear insertions.

line 21. After seeking a precedent for the spelling "Satian" (MS Berg), we conclude that it is simply PBS's miswriting of Satan.

line 24. PBS's comma after Peace (MS Berg) indicates the placement of the caesura and thus clarifies the rhythm of the line.

line 25. Where: probable reading; in MS Berg a later hand has written "When" above line in pencil, but *when* and *where* (as we have noted) are sometimes indistinguishable in PBS's handwriting.

line 29. Fargy is PBS's spelling in several other letters of the pronunciation of "Fergy" (for Fergus, Graham's middle name); the joke may have arisen because Graham pronounced the *e* before *r* like the *a* in "far" (as in the British pronunciations of *Berkeley*, *clerk*, *Derbyshire*, *Hertford*).

line 31. courtship: "courtsip" (MS Berg) is clearly a slip of the pen.

line 34. forty eight: Elizabeth Pilfold Shelley was born in 1763 (d. 1846).

line 35. Ninon (i.e., Anne) de Lenclos (1620–1705), celebrated Parisian hostess and center of an intellectual salon, was a freethinker who chose a sequence of lovers from among the most distinguished men of France, while resisting churchmen and others who tried to take advantage of her situation. The ultimate source of PBS's reference to her is probably the famous letter by Voltaire to J. H. S. Formay (ca. 1 May 1751), in which, during a long account of Lenclos (whom his father knew well), Voltaire tells how she had to resist the advances of a nineteen-year-old, with tragic consequences. This youth, whose father, M. de Villarceau, had not told him his true parentage, fell in love with Ninon (his real mother) and confronted her when she was at a restaurant with a party of her friends: "Ce jeune homme lui fit dans le jardin une déclaration si vive et si pressante que m^lle de Lenclos fut obligée de lui avouer qu'elle était sa mère. Aussitôt ce jeune homme, qui était venu au jardin à cheval, alla prendre un de ses pistolets à l'arçon de la selle, et se tua tout roide. Il n'était pas si philosophe que sa mere" (*Voltaire's Correspondence,* ed. Theodore Besterman, XIX [1956], 125).

PBS may have misremembered this account, or his errors may be due to someone else's garbled retelling of the anecdote, for Ninon was part of student folklore at Eton; John Richardson, PBS's contemporary there, compares an Eton "dame" (housemother) with Ninon in respect to youthful beauty: "at sixty" this woman "looked little older than thirty" (*Recollections . . . of the Last Half-Century* [London: C. Mitchell, 1856], I, 87–88).

line 40. We have added parentheses to clarify the intended syntax.

line 42. cornuting: crowning with horns, cuckolding (from the Latin *cornu,* horn).

line 43. corageous: PBS's spelling here is probably not an accidental use of an obsolete English spelling but a Latinate pun, conflating the root *cor* (heart) with *cornu* found in the previous line.

line 46. A crease along this line has torn with wear, causing it to appear as a cancel line in the facsimile of MS Berg in *MYR: Shelley* VIII.

line 48. temptation: In MS Berg, the letters *pt* are written as a single character, which is crossed. This was probably a simple miswriting, rather than a spelling error.

line 50. sinning sake: This solecism in MS Berg may evidence careless writing or PBS's unconventional understanding of the English possessive.

line 52. But: In MS Berg, this word has been rendered virtually illegible by damage and repair of the paper.

line 53. Before and face are marred in MS Berg by damage and repair.

line 57. A dear delightful red faced brute: PBS's ambivalence toward his only legitimate brother—the family baby—is palpable here, as it is in Hellen Shelley's reminiscences, where PBS's interactions with little John Shelley while he was still "a child in petticoats" consist of PBS's "pushing him gently down to let him rise and beg for a succession of such falls," causing him to cry by tipping him out of a carriage, and teaching him the word *Devil* (Hogg, *Life,* ed. Wolfe, I, 23–24).

line 58: setting is written in pencil above the line in MS Berg; though PBS's word appears more like *altering* or *uttering,* it is so dubious that we, like other editors, follow the hint of that unknown nineteenth-century transcriber, who saw the MS when it was in better condition and whose choice makes sense in the context (as would *sending*).

parachute: "An apparatus for descending safely from a great height in the air, esp. from a balloon; it is constructed like a large umbrella, so as to expand and check the velocity of descent by means of the resistance of the air" (*OED* 1, with examples as early as 1785 and 1796). PBS probably made a toy parachute for his little brother John, or Jack, (b. 1806) from a small piece of cloth with its corners fastened to a weight; when thrown into the air, the cloth is caught by the wind and floats down slowly, some distance from its launch site. (Reiman's father once made him such a parachute from a handkerchief and a golf ball.)

line 60. Oh! Fargy (Fargy is not capitalized in MS): The exclamation point following Oh may have been PBS's attempt to punctuate for the vocative of direct address, for which contemporaries placed an exclamation point *after* the name of the person addressed.

wonderous: This unconventional spelling indicates that PBS means the word to be pronounced in three syllables.

line 61. This final line is probably not, technically, part of the poem, but PBS's prose comment on it, as he ended abruptly to seal his letter and take it to his father to be franked. In *1989* Matthews and Everest read the final word as "para" (a truncation of *parachute*); though the word is obscurely written, we think poem is the more likely transcription, even though "para" may make just as good sense.

"Dear dear dear dear dear dear Græme" [To EFG#2]

PBS's second verse letter to Edward Fergus Graham was first published by Neville Rogers in *KSMB* XXIV ([1973], 20–24), with an accompanying fold-out facsimile. Matthews and Everest in *1989* relied on the facsimile to correct some of Rogers's errors and add valuable notes, before the MS was auctioned with other autographs collected by Richard Monckton Milnes, 1st Baron Houghton (1809–85, *DNB*), and purchased by the Pforzheimer Foundation for the Carl H. Pforzheimer Collection of Shelley and His Circle (Pfz) at the New York Public Library. MS Pfz, the sole authority and our copy-text, appears in both facsimile and diplomatic transcription in the "Retrospective" of early MSS that opens *SC* IX.

Biographical Issues

In *SC* IX, the Commentary on MS Pfz explores its biographical implications, including the significance of a note in the hand of PBS's mother,

Elizabeth Pilfold Shelley, to Graham. This note, written sideways on page 1 of MS Pfz, which contains **lines 1–38** of *To EFG#2,* reads: "B. [i.e., Bysshe] intends seeing | Merle do you think | there is any harm in | the Man, tell me when | you write next- let your | letter be directed as the last[.]" Though Elizabeth P. Shelley probably did not read the offensive parts of PBS's verse when she wrote her note at right angles to the poem in the blank margin to the right of **lines 1–10,** PBS may have wished Graham to think that she had done so, perhaps to ascertain from Graham's reaction whether or not his mother and Graham actually were having an affair. In exploring Graham's possible motives for saving (and showing to young Rossetti in the 1840s) the two verse letters that implicate him in a possible betrayal of his patron, SC suggests that the musician and would-be composer of operas may have seen himself as a Figaro who does a star-turn while outsmarting his master, or as an amorous Cherubino, comforting his beloved mistress after she has been mistreated by her husband.

Date, Occasion, and Structure

To EFG#2 was written on or about 7 June 1811, when PBS returned to Field Place after visiting his uncle John Pilfold at Cuckfield. Awaiting him on his return was the response from Graham provoked by *To EFG#1,* which PBS here answers with carefully structured rhetoric, disguised as spontaneous effusion.

Though MS Pfz shows no formal divisions, the poem's versification breaks it into three distinct parts: **Lines 1–8,** which are in iambic tetrameter rhymed *aabccddb,* form a prologue, suggesting that it would be counterproductive for Graham to be penitent before Timothy Shelley. There follow ten rhymed couplets in anapestic tetrameter (**9–28**) specifying aspects of Timothy Shelley's sadistic temperament and behavior towards his wife and daughters. The final twelve anapestic lines (**29–40**), varied between tetrameter and pentameter, comprise three quatrains, in each of which the first and third lines are internally rhymed and the second and fourth are rhymed with each other. The last two of these lines appear on the verso of the letter sheet where, after it was folded and sealed, they could be seen by Timothy Shelley, to whom PBS (or his mother) took the letter to be franked; PBS clearly wrote them to tantalize his father by mentioning <u>Godwin</u> and suggesting that there was <u>fun</u> inside the letter that he was not permitted to see. Adding to PBS's <u>fun</u>, perhaps, was his success in maneuvering his mother into writing a note to Graham near the lines in which PBS urges Graham to sleep with her. PBS, as he frequently did, disguised his art by leaving the punctuation of his poem sparse and informal; we have supplemented the pointing editorially, recording the variants from MS Pfz below the Text.

line 1. By using <u>dear</u> six times, PBS signals his tone as one of amused condescension. For <u>Græme</u> as a Scottish (and monosyllabic) variant spelling of "Graham," see note to *EFG#1*, line 7.

line 2. PBS had visited his uncle Capt. John Pilfold at the nearby village of <u>Cuckfield</u> from 21 May till 4 June 1811, during which time he began his philosophical discussions with Elizabeth Hitchener.

line 14. <u>Catalani</u>] Calatani   MS Pfz. PBS here misspelled (unintentionally, we believe) the name of the great Italian soprano Angelica Catalani (1780–1845), who starred at the opera in London from 1806 to 1813.

line 18. This line contains erasures, overwriting, and several nearly illegible words.

line 20. [<u>When</u>]: conjectural because the paper has been torn by the seal; <u>passion condenser</u>: that is, Timothy Shelley's anger and jealousy become more concentrated and stronger when he sees others happy. We add the question mark.

lines 21–28. These lines provide in miniature a portrait of the sadist at home that suggests the reason for PBS's later fascination with the account of the Cenci family.

line 21. The second <u>a</u> is marred by damage and repair of the paper.

line 26. <u>their</u>: appears in MS as "thier" (one of PBS's most characteristic misspellings).

lines 27–28. These lines parallel the aphorism that defines a sadist as one who is kind to masochists; <u>be't</u> reduces *be it* to a monosyllable.

line 36. <u>when they're wanted</u>] when there wanted   MS Pfz. This long line of verse almost reached the edge of the paper before PBS began to write these words. Perhaps in his concern to squeeze them down the right-hand margin, he—guided by the aural aspects of the words as he shaped his versification—neglected to consider which spelling of *there/they're* was appropriate here. And, as in many cases in PBS's holograph MSS, *when* could easily be read *where*, with context guiding the transcriber's choice.

"Sweet star! which gleaming oer the darksome scene"

PBS included this poem—or (more likely) this uncompleted fragment—in a letter that he wrote to Hogg from Field Place on 18–19 June 1811 (*SC* II, 809–12; *Letters* I, 106–8). This letter also contains fragments of two other poems, beginning **"Hopes that bud"** and **"How eloquent are eyes!"**, both of which he included, in revised and extended texts, in *Esd.*

Date and Occasion

After reaching the financial settlement with his father and returning home about 14 May 1811, PBS apparently expected his mother and his sisters to remain his allies, as they had been before his expulsion. Though his younger sisters were at school in London, his sister Elizabeth Shelley, whom he had for some months been trying to interest in Hogg, was at home, just recovering from scarlet fever. On his first or second day at home, PBS amused himself by writing his first verse letter to Graham (**To EFG#1:** *"As you will see"*), in which he said that Elizabeth Pilfold Shelley, his mother, and Graham had been accused of being overly intimate; that letter (about which PBS's mother may have learned from Graham) and, likely, PBS's demeanor of general contempt for his elders seem to have quickly alienated his mother. After just a week at home, he therefore returned to the home of his uncle John Pilfold at Cuckfield on 21 May, extending his stay there after he met Elizabeth Hitchener. But when PBS returned to Field Place on 2 June 1811, he again faced virtual isolation. Writing to Hogg on 18–19 June, he said that he and his mother were now reduced to speaking only about the weather, "upon which she is irresistibly eloquent   otherwise all deep silence" (*SC* II, 810). Though recalling the eloquent ending of *"Why is it said"* (above) that features a favorably personified Silence, this thought foreshadows, rather, the many appearances in PBS's poetry of *silence* and *silent* as adjuncts, not of bliss, but of vacancy and death.

Although Matthews and Everest argue that *"Sweet star!"* was written "to titillate Hogg's imagination by picturing Field Place as an ideal setting for romance" with Elizabeth Shelley (*1989* I, 177), the surrounding letter suggests to us something quite different. After failing in his persistent attempts to interest Elizabeth Shelley in his friend and when his efforts had become a source of conflict between PBS and his sister, he was now trying to get Hogg to forget his unrequited love for Elizabeth Shelley (whom Hogg had not yet seen). While cut off from his family and living as "a perfect hermite," PBS seems to have focused his daydreams on *The Missionary* by Sidney Owenson (later Lady Morgan), which he describes to Hogg as "really a divine thing." He praises in particular the character of "Luxima the Indian [who] is an Angel," and exclaims, "What pity that we cannot incorporate [i.e., give bodies to] these creations of Fancy; the very thought of them thrills the soul. Since I have read this book I have read no other—but I have thought strangely." PBS then sends *"Sweet star!"* to Hogg as part of "a strange melange of maddened stuff which I wrote by the midnight moon last night" (**Letters** I, 107). *"Sweet star!"* might thus be understood as a poem originally inspired by the poet's own yearning for an unattainable ideal, rather than a prank to titillate Hogg. But since he could not "incorporate" this phantom, the young man's fancy soon turned to thoughts of Harriet

Westbrook, with whom he communicated while she was at Miss Fenning's school, through the mediation of "Miss Westbrook"—that is, Eliza W.

"Sweet star!" breaks off in the middle of a line, perhaps indicating that PBS had not developed it fully, or that he had continued it with sentiments he did not wish to share with Hogg. For, though PBS had urged Hogg to fall in love with his sister Elizabeth Shelley, who was said to look as much like PBS as if they had been twins (see the opening of the Commentary to *Song ("Cold, cold is the blast")*, the third poem in *V&C*), he avoided telling him about his infatuation with Westbrook until after he had eloped with her. In copying his poems for Hogg, therefore, PBS probably omitted any lines that would have revealed his love for a real woman.

Hogg's homoerotic feelings for PBS can be more fully explored since Cameron in *SC* and Jones in **Letters** undid Hogg's alterations of the texts of PBS's letters to him as they appeared in Hogg's *Life of PBS;* there Hogg changed many pronouns from "I" to "you" and "you" to "I" to confuse readers about whether he or PBS had expressed certain sentiments. Though some psychoanalytic critics who relied on these corrupt texts concluded that PBS was probably in love with Hogg, in fact these roles were reversed. PBS's efforts to interest Hogg in Elizabeth Shelley and her in Hogg; the latter's attempt to seduce Harriet Shelley soon after she married PBS; the abortive ménage-à-quatre in 1814 that involved the two young men, MWS, and Claire Clairmont; and Hogg's later courtship and union with Jane Williams probably all involved either PBS's attempts to deflect the passion he sensed in Hogg's friendship for him or Hogg's (probably subconscious) efforts to achieve vicarious sexual intimacy with PBS. Even Hogg's later nastiness toward his friend, particularly in his *Life*, while partly justified by PBS's frequent use of him as a cat's paw, may also be seen as resulting, in part, from the fury of a lover scorned.

In MS Pfz, its only surviving authority, *"Sweet star!"* breaks off in the midst of the fifteenth line of unrhymed iambic pentameter; in its present, probably truncated form, it approximates a blank-verse sonnet in the manner of Keats's "What the thrush said," with a quiet tone not dissimilar to the sonnet beginning, "Bright star" that was once thought to be Keats's last poem. Though, as it stands, *"Sweet star!"* exemplifies PBS's early experimentation with traditional poetic forms, to which he (unlike Keats) adhered more rigorously the longer he wrote and the greater mastery he achieved, there may originally have been more lines than survive. PBS released the poem in this form to Hogg, whose omission of <u>love</u> from **line 11** muddled all the texts through *1927*. We—lacking any superseding authority—include it here among his early privately released "poems," rather than among his fragmentary "poetry," following MS Pfz except in a few minor features discussed below.

line 2. fling'st: In MS Pfz, PBS began to write "fligh" (for *flight*?) but canceled the *gh* before completing the word. This slip of the pen indicates that he was probably copying the lines from an earlier draft.

line 3. veil] viel   MS Pfz. We correct PBS's frequent misspellings of "ie" for "ei" (and vice versa), just as he did—or allowed others to do—when publishing his poems.

line 6. Since **lines 1–6** contain no unsubordinated verb, we add a dash, rather than more definite punctuation, at the end of this line.

line 10. Favonius, the personification of the spring west wind (equivalent to the Greek Zephyrus) that appears in Latin poetry (e.g., Horace, *Odes* I.iv.1 and III.vii.2, and Catullus XXVI.2), may be relevant to PBS's conception of the West Wind in his later **Ode**.

line 11. The full stop just before art seems grammatically superfluous in the poem as it survives: one cannot capitalize art, the independent verb for which the Sweet star! (addressed twice) has been waiting, and the dash provides closure for the parenthetical remark (begun by the comma and dash in **line 8**) that names the exceptions to the evening's silence. That PBS seems to intend no full stop to the breathless end of the poem as we have it may mark *"Sweet star!"* as a fragment or a stylistic experiment.

aught] ought   MS Pfz. We follow all other editors in altering the reading in PBS's MS, even though that variant is marginally defensible on the basis of acknowledged contemporary usage: a pocket *Dictionary of the English Language compiled from Dr. Johnson* (6th ed., London, 1803) lists "Ought, s[ubstantive]. *more properly* Aught, any thing."

love: omitted by Hogg's text in *1858* and all texts dependent upon it.

line 12. slaves of interest: those motivated by a desire for personal gain, particularly regarding money and material concerns. Cf. James Thomson, *To the Nightingale:* "But we, vain slaves of interest and of pride" (line 13).

line 13. could] cd.   MS Pfz. Here, as elsewhere, we expand the abbreviations that PBS expanded when his writings were published.

line 15. unnerved] enamoured   *1858 through 1927*. The word *unnerved*, meaning enfeebled or weakened, does not appear in the *Shelley Concordance*, because of Hogg's misreading of the scrawled writing in MS Pfz, but the word, though found in 61 English poets of the eighteenth and nineteenth centuries (Chadwyck-Healey *Lion*), is restricted partly because the verb *to unnerve* was becoming obsolescent by PBS's time. In reprints of the popular dictionaries of the period, we can trace the replacement of *unnerve* (*Johnson's*, 1803 and *Entick's*, 1808) with *enervate* (*Bailey's*, 1823). Precedents that PBS may have known include four uses in James Thomson's poetry (three in *Liberty*), Dr. Johnson's *Irene* V.48, Henry Kirke White's *Christiad* I.120, and, most likely, "Unnerv'd is the hand of his minstrel, by death"—line 12 of Byron's *On Leaving Newstead Abbey:* This poem opens Byron's *Poems, Original and Translated* (1808), a volume probably in PBS's library by this date (see note to lines 17–18 of the **St.Irv** version of *"How swiftly through Heaven's wide expanse"*), and would undoubtedly strike a chord in PBS's mind when he returned to Field Place after exile from *his* ancestral home. (The only other major Romantic poet to use the word was Keats, in *Eve of St. Agnes,* 280.)

"Bear witness Erin! when thine injured isle"

This fragment of a poem not otherwise extant appears in PBS's long letter to Elizabeth Hitchener dated from a Dublin address on 14 February 1812, soon after he, Harriet Shelley, and her sister Eliza Westbrook arrived in Dublin on the evening of 12 February 1812 (see **Letters** I, 250–55). The original survives at BL, with PBS's other letters to Hitchener there catalogued as ADD. MS 37,496, in which these lines appear on folio 90 recto. PBS's letter of 14 February also contains the 40-line poem honoring a revolution in Mexico, beginning *"Brothers, between you and me,"* that PBS later included in **Esd** as **To the Republicans of North America** (*Esd* #17), and the poetic prose lines beginning *"The Ocean rolls between us"* (see Appendix B for this non-poem and its complex textual history, which became entangled with that of *"Bear witness Erin!"*). Since *"Bear witness Erin!"* does not appear in **Esd,** either as an independent short poem or as part of a larger one, it was likely a fragment that PBS failed to develop, rather than a finished piece.

That PBS took time, immediately after his arrival in Dublin, to compose (or copy out) these celebrations of revolutions and to reflect on the solidarity of libertarians separated by the Irish Sea speaks to the self-dramatizing character of PBS's expedition to Ireland. But why did PBS (who had already notified Hitchener of their safe arrival at Dublin in a short note dated 13 Feb.) report to her so frequently and usually at great length during 1811–12, and why did he insist that she come to join his household? Though the answer must remain conjectural, PBS began his lengthy and candid correspondence with Hitchener just when his relationship with his mother Elizabeth Pilfold Shelley was rapidly deteriorating, and we therefore support Gelpi's suggestion that Hitchener became his "mother surrogate" (*Shelley's Goddess,* 125)—the first of a series of older women in whom he confided, as he had earlier confided in his mother. After reassuring Hitchener of his safety, about which she had expressed concern in her letters that awaited him at Dublin, PBS urges her to give up her teaching post at the end of the school year and join their household: "We will meet you in

Wales, and *never part again*"—a thought he repeats later in the letter, but with a specific time for their reunion: "—Dearest friend come to us all,— at *midsummer* never to part again—" (***Letters*** I, 251–52).

Whistling in the dark is a valid recourse for antiestablishment activists with enough imagination to see the potentially unpleasant consequences of their activities, but PBS may have retreated to pen and ink also because of the disgust he expressed in his letters from Dublin at the poverty and degradation he found in its streets. Having arrived there in the bleak heart of winter, he imagines the rural scenes and uncontaminated waters of his own youthful home as symbols of virtue and renovation and foresees better days for Ireland by representing it as a fruitful tree, capable of reviving with the turn of the seasonal cycle. This imagery is either echoed or foreshadowed by a passage in PBS's ***Proposals for an Association of Philanthropists . . .*** , the prose tract that he began to write soon after his arrival in Dublin. To the intended readers of ***Proposals***—the middle and upper classes, including members of the Protestant ascendancy, he echoed a familiar concept from the Bible (Matthew 7:15–20 and Luke 3:9): "The tree is to be judged of by its fruit. I regard the admission of the Catholic claims, and the Repeal of the Union Act, as blossoms of that fruit, which the Summer Sun of improved intellect and progressive virtue are destined to mature" (***Prose***/EBM I, 43).

line 1. Bear witness Erin!: The text in MS BL is here damaged beyond legibility by wear and repair, to read "Be<   >tness Erin!"

line 5. oer: Because the omission of the apostrophe, though informal, can neither confuse the meaning nor lead to mispronunciation of the verse, we retain this form when PBS used it in these privately released poems.

line 6. This line exemplifies one habitual irregularity in PBS's punctuation of his MSS: he frequently fails to supply commas between a series of parallel substantives. We leave the line as he wrote it in this fragment to call attention to this idiosyncrasy, which underlies the variable punctuation of such series in both first and later editions of his writings.

beauty is superimposed on "freshness" in MS BL.

line 7. The long dash here indicates that the line is incomplete; therefore, these lines probably represent an early stage in the development of a poem, rather than an excerpt from one that PBS had completed.

lines 9–10. The cold hand that gathers the scanty fruit of Ireland—a tree in PBS's metaphor (5)—represents England and the Anglo-Irish absentee landlords.

line 10. its] it's   MS BL. Here we drop the apostrophe so as not to puzzle readers.

"Thy dewy looks sink in my breast"

This poem—or, perhaps, this surviving fragment of a longer poem—was written in March 1814, thus being the last known example of poetry that PBS released privately before he became involved with Mary Wollstonecraft Godwin (later MWS). *"Thy dewy looks"* was addressed to Cornelia de Boinville Turner, the daughter of Harriet Collins de Boinville. The mother and her sister Cornelia Collins Newton (wife of John Frank Newton, the vegetarian upon whose *Return to Nature* Shelley drew heavily in his notes to **Queen Mab**) were co-heiresses of a West Indies sugar fortune and cultivated devotees of philosophy, the arts, and liberal politics. PBS was introduced to their circle, which also included the vegetarian physician William Lambe, in November 1812, immediately after his first meeting with Godwin (see Dowden, *Life of PBS* I, 306ff.). During 1813–14, PBS, Hogg, and Peacock spent much time in the coterie centered on the Newtons and Harriet de Boinville (whose French husband died that year during Napoleon's retreat from Moscow); according to Hogg, PBS flirted with several younger women in the circle, one certainly being Cornelia Turner, who in 1812 had married Thomas Turner, a young lawyer and disciple of Godwin.

Context and Occasion

In the orbit of the Newton-Boinville group, PBS increasingly came to feel that Harriet Shelley had lost interest in his intellectual pursuits. According to Hogg, when the Shelleys returned to London after the birth of their daughter Ianthe in June 1813, Harriet Shelley gave up her previous interest in study, and instead of pursuing her old pastime of reading good books aloud during Hogg's visits, she would propose walks that "commonly conducted us to some fashionable bonnet-shop" (Hogg, *Life of PBS*, ed. Wolfe, II, 128). When PBS spent more time with the Boinville-Newton set, Harriet Shelley (counseled by Eliza Westbrook) became upset by PBS's attentions to these women; and by the time PBS wrote Hogg in March 1814, she had taken the carriage that PBS had purchased for her when she was pregnant and gone to Bath with her sister.

PBS remained in the London area making efforts to borrow money to pay his own and Godwin's debts, perhaps including one for the carriage (*SC* III, 153–66). But to avoid his most importunate creditors, he often resided with the Boinvilles in the village of Bracknell, Berkshire, about 28 miles from London (Paterson's *Roads*, 1808) (now near Heathrow Airport). When PBS apparently declared his love for Cornelia Turner, her mother banned him from the house and arranged for Turner to take his wife away where PBS could not see her. From this abortive affair (which resembles PBS's later infatuation with Jane Williams) at least two poems survive—this pair of quatrains and the better-known *Stanzas: April, 1814*, published with *Alastor*. For more on the Boinville family and PBS in 1814–15, see *SC* III–IV *passim*.

Copy-text

So far as we know, *"Thy dewy looks"* survives only in the letter from PBS to Hogg (*Letters* I, 383–85). It was first published in Hogg's *Life of PBS*, and all other texts have hitherto derived from that one (see the Historical Collations). We base our Text upon the original MS, recently located by James Bieri in the Ogden Collection at University College, London (MS UCL). This MS shows that the poem consists of two quatrains, rather than one eight-line stanza, thus mooting Matthews's speculation that *"Thy dewy looks"* is the second stanza of a poem, the first 8-line stanza of which appears as a draft on page 3 of Bodleian MS Shelley adds. e.12 (see *1989*, Appendix C, I, 588–89). Nancy Goslee, in her edition of the Bodleian Notebook in question, reads the name in the putative first stanza as "Emilia" (*BSM* XVIII [1996], 5), rather than Matthews's "Priscilla" and thereby supports Ingpen's association of the drafted lines with Teresa Viviani (*Verse and Prose*, 5), while casting doubt on Matthews's dating of them and his entire argument. Since *"Thy dewy looks"*—or a longer poem of which this poignant lyric outcry may well have been only a part—could also have been sent or given to Cornelia Turner, another holograph or contemporary copy may still survive, either in France or in England, to provide a definitive answer to this speculation. (For the later years in Paris of Harriet de Boinville and Cornelia de Boinville Turner, as well as a portrait of the latter as a young woman, see *SC* VIII, 983–95.)

lines 3–4. rest is the portion (i.e., gift, or inheritance) of despair because a lack of hope prevents further disappointment.

line 7. chains that bind: This imagery derives directly from PBS's association of his infatuation with Cornelia Turner with their reading of an important treatise on crimes and punishments by Cesare Bonesana, Marchese di Beccaria (1738–94); as he wrote to Hogg, shortly before quoting *"Thy dewy looks"*: "I have begun to learn Italian. I am reading 'Beccaria delle delitti e pene'. . . . Cornelia assists me in this language." PBS's phrase may also play off the popular hymn "Blest be the tie that binds," written by John Fawcett (1740–1817), who is not to be confused with Joseph Fawcett, the liberal Dissenting preacher and antiwar poet.

HISTORICAL COLLATIONS

The following Historical Collations have been selected from a broader computer-generated collation of all variants between the Texts in *CPPBS* and the texts of the editions listed at the head of the variants for each individual poem. Because of the large number of variants involved in poems to be included in later volumes of *CPPBS*, our general policy in the edition as a whole is to record only those variants that we judge may have some potential effect on the sound and rhythm of the verse or on its meaning, through either denotation or connotation. However, in Volume I we have provided a much more comprehensive record of variants to convey clearly the editorial policies of the major editions of Shelley's poetry. We discuss at length our rationale for the Historical Collations in the Editorial Overview.

The siglum *omnia* indicates that all editions being collated agree upon the reading. In lemmas concerning variant titles of Shelley's poems, the reading for our Text is shown as *no title* whenever Shelley himself did not entitle the poem.

Original Poetry

by Victor and Cazire

Letter [1] ("Here I sit with my paper, my pen and my ink")

Text collated with *1904, 1927*/I, *1972* (*1989* omits this poem).

Title.   Letter [1]]   I (*follows comment*)   *1904*
                        omitted   *1927*/I
                        I   *1972*
12   nought,] nought.   *omnia*
18   tost;] tossed;   *1904 1972*
19   despair] despair,   *omnia*
42   heart,] heart.   *1927*/I
52   spite,] spite[,]   *1904 1927*/I
53   heaven] Heaven   *omnia*
56   cobler] cobbler   *omnia*
60   cassoc,] cassock,   *omnia*
61   coblers] cobblers   *omnia*
68   every thing] everything   *omnia*
71   not a] not to a   *omnia*

Letter [2] To Miss ——— ——— from Miss ——— ———

Text collated with *1904, 1927*/I, *1972* (*1989* omits this poem).

Title.   TO MISS ——— ———]
                II | To MISS ——————— [HARRIET GROVE]   *1904*
                II | *To Miss* [Harriet Grove]   *1972*
Title.   FROM MISS ——— ———]
                FROM MISS ——————— [ELIZABETH SHELLEY]   *1904*
                from Miss [Elizabeth Shelley]   *1972*
1   ————,] ———— [Hattie],   *1904*
                [Hattie],   *1972*
3   Tho'] Though   *1904 1972*
4   letter,] letter.   *1972*

12   morning-call] morning—call   *1927*/I
13   ───────────] [Charlotte]   *1972*
     ───────────] [Cuckfield]   *1972*
14   pay] pay [───] *1970*
         pay, *1972*
15   the Colonel] [the Colonel]   *1904 1972*
         ─────── *1927*/I
16   sight.] sight,   *1972*
19   mischevious] mischievous   *omnia*
35   croud,] crowd,   *omnia*
41   ───────'s] ─────── [Bysshe's]   *1904*
                 [Bysshe's]   *1972*
44   sun shine] sunshine   *1904 1972*
     rain,] rain.   *omnia*
47   drest,] dressed,   *omnia*
51   tho'] though   *1904 1972*
58   Tho'] Though   *1904 1972*
64   learnt] learned   *omnia*
65   ───────] ─────── [Hattie]   *1904*
                 [Hattie]   *1972*

Song ("Cold, cold is the blast when December is howling")

Text collated with *1858, 1904, 1927*/I, *SC*/II, *1972, 1989*.

Here *1989* provides a reprint of the Hogg MS in a footnote to the Esdaile version of **"Cold, cold."** We collate the reprint and will deal with the Esdaile version in our next volume. In *1858* and *SC*/II, this poem is followed directly by fragments from **Song. To** ─────── ("Ah! sweet is the moonbeam that sleeps on yon fountain") and **Song. To** ─────── ("Stern, stern is the voice of fate's fearfull command").

Title. SONG.] *omitted*   *1858 SC*/II *1989*
            III. SONG   *1904 1972*
1   COLD,] Cold   *SC*/II *1989*
    blast] blast,   *1858*
    howling,] howling   *SC*/II *1989*
2   Man's brow,—] man's brow.   *1858*
              man's brow,—   *1904 1927*/I *1972*
              mans brow   *SC*/II *1989*
3   seas] seas—   *1858*
    rolling,] rolling   *SC*/II *1989*
4   is] *omitted*   *1858 SC*/II *1989*

```
         low; ] low.    1858
                  low    SC/II 1989
 5   thee, ] thee    SC/II 1989
 6   thee, ] thee    SC/II 1989
 7   their ] these    1858 SC/II 1989
     thee, ] thee    SC/II 1989
 8   groans ] groans,    1858 SC/II 1989
     anguish ] anguish,    1858
     flow.— ] flow.    1858 SC/II 1989
              flow—    1904 1927/I 1972
 9   And ] And—    1858
     [Louisa] ] Louisa    1858 SC/II 1989
              ——————    1904 1927/I
     horror, ] horror;    1858
              horror    SC/II 1989
10   fate: ] fate,    1858
              fate    SC/II 1989
11   'Till ] Till    1858 SC/II 1989
     outcast ] outcast,    1858
     sorrow, ] sorrow    SC/II 1989
12   gate— ] gate.    1858
              gate    SC/II 1989
13   betrayer, ] betrayer    SC/II 1989
14   laughing ] callous    1858 SC/II 1989
     moans ] moan    1858
     prayer, ] prayer,—    1858
              prayer    SC/II 1989
15   nothing, ] nothing    SC/II 1989
     hair, ] hair    SC/II 1989
16   mountain ] mountain's    1858
     side, ] side    SC/II 1989
     tho' ] though    1904 1927/I 1972
              tho    SC/II 1989
     late. ] late    SC/II 1989
     stanza break ] omitted    1972
17   wild . . . dark ] dark summit of huge    1858 SC/II 1989
     Penmanmawr, ] Penmanmauer    1858
              Penmanmawr    SC/II 1989
18   [Louisa] ] Louisa    1858 SC/II 1989
              ——————    1904 1927/I
     reclined; ] reclined,    SC/II 1989
19   afar, ] afar    SC/II 1989
```

20   gust] gusts *omnia*
       wild sweeping] wild-sweeping *1858*
       wind.—] wind. *1858*
            wind SC/II *1989*
21   "I] I SC/II *1989*
       rocks] clouds, *1858*
           ~~rocks~~clouds *inserted* SC/II
           clouds *1989*
       thunder peals] thunder-peals *1858*
       rattle,] rattle SC/II *1989*
22   "I] I *1858 1904* SC/II *1972 1989*
       clouds] rocks, *1858*
           rocks SC/II *1989*
       battle,] battle SC/II *1989*
23   "But] But *1858 1904* SC/II *1972 1989*
       thee,] thee SC/II *1989*
       cruel [Henry]] perjured Henry, *1858*
             cruel———— *1904 1927*/I
             perjured Henry SC/II *1989*
       unkind!—"] unkind!" *1858*
             unkind!"— *1904 1927*/I *1972*
             unkind SC/II *1989*
24   mountain,] mountain SC/II *1989*
25   And] And, *1858*
       laughing,] laughing SC/II *1989*
       entwined,] entwined SC/II *1989*
26   o'er] oer SC/II *1989*
       fountain,] fountain SC/II *1989*
27   And] And, *1858*
       laving] leaving *1904 1927*/I *1972*
       wind.] wind SC/II *1989*
28   "Ah! go,"] "Ah, go!" *1858*
           "Ah! go" SC/II *1989*
       exclaimed,] exclaimed SC/II
       "when . . . yelling,] "where . . . yelling; *1858*
             "where . . . yelling SC/II *1989*
29   "'Tis] 'Tis *1858 1904* SC/II *1972 1989*
       swelling,] swelling; *1858*
           swelling SC/II *1989*
30   "But I left,] But I left, *1858 1904 1972*
           But I left SC/II *1989*
       pityless outcast,] pitiless outcast, *1858 1904 1927*/I *1972*
             pityless outcast SC/II *1989*

dwelling,] dwelling;   *1858*
             dwelling   SC/II *1989*
31 "My] My   *1858 1904* SC/II *1972 1989*
    torn, so] torn—so,   *1858*
             torn so   SC/II *1989*
    say] say,   *1858*
    mind—"] mind."   *1858*
             mind"   SC/II *1989*
32 [Louisa], but] Louisa—but   *1858* SC/II *1989*
             ———, but   *1904 1927*/I
33 yew,] yew   SC/II *1989*
34 rave,] rave   SC/II *1989*
35 peace] Peace   *1858* SC/II *1989*
    dew.] dew   SC/II *1989*
36 mid] 'mid   *1858*
    heather,] heather   *1858* SC/II *1989*
37 Tho'] Though   *1904 1972*
             Tho   SC/II *1989*
    is] be   *1858* SC/II *1989*
38 perfidy,] Perfidy,   *1858*
             perfidy   SC/II *1989*
    traveller!] traveller,   *1858*
             traveller   SC/II *1989*
    her,] her   *1858* SC/II *1989*
39 tears,] tears   *1858* SC/II *1989*
    due.—] due!   *1858*
             due   SC/II *1989*
Dateline.   JULY, 1810.] *omitted*   *1858* SC/II *1989*

Song ("Come ——————! sweet is the hour")

Text collated with *1904, 1927*/I, *1972, 1989*.

Title.   SONG.] IV. SONG   *1904 1972*
1   Come ——————!] COME [Harriet]!   *1904 1972*
             COME ——————!   *1927*/I *1989*
2   Zephyrs] zephyrs   *1989*
3   flower,] flower   *1989*
5   torn,] torn   *1989*
7   forlorn,] forlorn   *1989*
9   woe,] woe   *1989*
11 low,] low   *1989*

17   ———!] [Harriet]!   *1904 1972*
      dearest] dearest,   *1989*
18   I] I,   *1989*
Dateline.   APRIL, 1810.] *omitted*   *1989*

Song. Despair

Text collated with *1904, 1927/I, 1972, 1989.*

Title.   SONG.] V. SONG   *1904 1972*
2   breast,] breast   *1989*
3   faultering,] faltering,   *omnia*
4   tho'] though   *1904 1972 1989*
      rest.—] rest;   *1989*
5   wildered] 'wildered   *1904 1927/I 1972*
6   glance,] glance;   *1989*
8   trance.] trance;   *1989*
9   around] around,   *1989*
11   tho'] though   *1904 1972 1989*
12   sooth] soothe   *omnia*
19   memory,] memory   *1989*
24   hour.—] hour.   *1904 1927/I 1972*
27   sigh,] sigh   *1989*
Dateline.   JUNE, 1810.] *omitted*   *1989*

Song. Sorrow

Text collated with *1904, 1927/I, 1972, 1989.*

Title.   SONG.] VI. SONG   *1904 1972*
4   blissfull] blissful   *omnia*
5   view,] view   *1989*
6   Shewed] Showed   *1904 1972 1989*
8   cloy:] cloy;   *1904 1927/I 1972*
12   Fading] Fading,   *1989*
13   throng,] throng   *1989*
14   give,] give[,]   *1904 (1970 omits brackets around comma)*
18   console,] console?   *1989*
20   'Till] Till   *1972 1989*
22   tell;] tell   *1989*
28   lightening's] lightnings   *omnia*

32   bid ungrateful] bid the ungrateful   *1989*
Dateline.   AUGUST, 1810.] *omitted   1989*

Song. Hope

Text collated with *1904, 1927*/I, *1972, 1989.*

Title.   SONG.] VII. SONG   *1904 1972*
4   shrine.—] shrine—   *1927*/I
          shrine?—   *1989*
6   light] light;   *1904 1927*/I *1972*
7   Mountain's] mountain's   *1989*
     brow,] brow.   *1904 1927*/I *1972*
8   shews] shows   *omnia*
     bright——] bright?—   *1989*
9   'Tis] Tis   *1904 1927*/I (*1970 reads* 'Tis)
     ray,] ray   *1989*
10   shews] shows   *1904 1972 1989*
11   day,] day   *1989*
12   flowers,—] flowers.—   *1989*
13   vermeil tinted] vermeil-tinted   *1989*
     blossom,] blossom;   *1904 1927*/I *1972*
          blossom   *1989*
14   anew.] anew,   *omnia*
15   Then] Then,   *1989*
     deceiver] deceiver,   *1989*
17   believe,] believe   *1989*
18   peace,] peace;   *1989*
21   tho'] though   *1904 1972 1989*
22   Tho'] Though   *1904 1972 1989*
24   shews] shows   *omnia*
Dateline.   AUGUST, 1810.] *omitted   1989*

Song, Translated from the Italian

Text collated with *1904, 1927*/I, *1972, 1989.*

Title.   SONG,] VIII. SONG   *1904 1972*
          SONG.   *1927*/I *1989*
2   ambitious] ambition's   *1989*
6   tho'] though   *1904 1972 1989*
     fare,] fare?   *1989*

11   fast falling] fast-falling   *1972*
Dateline.   JULY, 1810.] *omitted   1989*

Song. Translated from the German

Text collated with *1904, 1927/I, 1972, 1989.*

Title.   SONG.] IX. SONG   *1904 1972*
5   hero,] hero   *1989*
   youth,] youth   *1989*
7   swell,] swell   *1989*
8   judgment] judgement   *1904 1927/I 1972*
11   clangor] clangour   *omnia*
   arms,] arms   *1989*
13   extatic] ecstatic   *1904 1972 1989*
   sip,] sip   *1989*
15   prove,] prove   *1989*
Dateline.   OCTOBER, 1809.] *omitted   1989*

The Irishman's Song

Text collated with *1904, 1927/I, 1972, 1989.*

Title.   THE IRISHMAN'S SONG.] X | THE IRISHMAN'S SONG   *1904*
                                    X. THE IRISHMAN'S SONG   *1972*
11   clangor] clangour   *omnia*
13   heroes!] heroes?   *1972*
   triumphant] Triumphant   *1972*
14   blood sprinkled] blood-sprinkled   *1972 1989*
15   Or] As   *1989*
Dateline.   OCTOBER, 1809.] *omitted   1989*

Song ("Fierce roars the midnight storm")

Text collated with *1904, 1927/I, 1972, 1989.*

Title.   SONG.] XI. SONG   *1904 1972*
1   storm,] storm   *omnia*
5   height,] height   *1989*
9   howl,] howl   *1989*
11   roll,] roll   *1989*
23   die,] die   *1989*
Dateline.   DECEMBER, 1809.] *omitted   1989*

Song. To ——— *("Ah! sweet is the moonbeam that sleeps on yon fountain")*

Text collated with *1858, 1927*/I, *1904, SC*/II, *1972, 1989*.

1858 and *SC*/II consist of lines 1–5 only, where these lines are preceded directly by **Song** *("Cold, cold is the blast")* and followed directly by a fragment of **Song. To** —— *("Stern, stern is the voice")*.

Title.   SONG. To ————] *omitted*   *1858 SC*/II
　　　　　　　　　　　　XII. SONG | To————[HARRIET]   *1904*
　　　　　　　　　　　　SONG | To——   *1927*/I
　　　　　　　　　　　　XII. Song | To [Harriet Grove]   *1972*
　　　　　　　　　　　　Song: To ——   *1989*

1　Ah!] Oh!   *1858*
　　　　Ah   *SC*/II
　fountain,] fountain   *SC*/II
2　soft-sighing] soft sighing   *SC*/II
　breeze,] breeze   *SC*/II
3　dimly-seen] dimly seen   *SC*/II
　mountain,] mountain   *1858 SC*/II
4　trees.] trees;   *1858*
　　　　trees   *SC*/II
　stanza break] *omitted*   *1858 SC*/II
5　all . . . affection,] all——   *1858 SC*/II
6　eve,] eve;   *1989*
7　recollection,] recollection   *1989*
8　————] [Percy]   *1904 1972*
11　hope-winged] hope-wingèd   *1904 1972 1989*
13　thou] thou,   *1989*
　friend] friend,   *1989*
14　fast rolling] fast-rolling   *1989*
　year,] year;   *1989*
15　one] one,   *1989*
　Oh!] oh,   *1989*
Dateline.   AUGUST, 1810.] *omitted*   *1989*

Song. To ———— *("Stern, stern is the voice of fate's fearfull command")*

Text collated with *1858, 1927/*I, *1904,* SC/II, *1972, 1989.*

1858 and SC/II consist of lines 9–18 only, where these lines are preceded directly by **Song** (*"Cold, cold is the blast"*) and a fragment of **Song. To** ——— (*"Ah! sweet is the moonbeam"*).

Title. SONG. To —————] *omitted   1858* SC/II
       XIII. SONG | To ————
       [HARRIET]   *1904*
       SONG | To ————   *1927/*I
       XIII. Song | To [Harriet Grove]   *1972*
       Song: To ————   *1989*

1 fearfull] fearful   *1904 1927/*I *1972 1989*
3 land,] land   *1989*
4 dear,] dear;   *1989*
7 wending,] wending   *1989*
8 appear—] appear.—   *1989*
  stanza break] *omitted   1970*
9 And] And,   *1858*
  he] she   *1858* SC/II
  heart-stricken] heart-shocked   *1858*
       heart stricked   SC/II
  quarry,] quarry   SC/II
10 friend] scenery   *1858* SC/II
  affection] childhood   *1858* SC/II
  farewell,] farewell   SC/II
11 He] She   *1858* SC/II
  so] all   *1858* SC/II
  gory,] gory   SC/II
12 He] She   SC/II
  drear passing] drear-passing   *1858*
  knell,] knell.   *1858*
    knell   SC/II
    knell—   *1972*
    knell;   *1989*
13 is] are   *1858* SC/II
  grief] woes   *1858* SC/II
  death couch] death-couch   *1858*
  reposing,] reposing   *1858* SC/II

14   closing!] closing,   *1858*
             closing   *SC*/II
15   outcast] outcast———   *1858*
             outcast—   *SC*/II
     whose . . . losing,] *stanza break*   *1858 SC*/II
     losing,] losing   *1989*
16   The . . . swell!] *omitted*   *1858 SC*/II
17   tones] notes   *1858 SC*/II
     soft,] sad   *1858*
             soft   *SC*/II
     sad,] soft,   *1858*
             sad   *SC*/II
     that] that,   *1858*
     never,] never   *1858 SC*/II *1989*
18   Can] May   *1858 SC*/II
     Memory's] memory's   *1858 SC*/II
     ear,] ear!   *1858*
             ear   *SC*/II
             ear;   *1989*
19   Nature] nature   *1989*
     ever,] ever   *1989*
Dateline.   AUGUST, 1810.] *omitted*   *1858 SC*/II *1989*

Saint Edmond's Eve

Text collated with *1904*, *1927*/I, *1972*. *1989* omits this poem.

Title.   SAINT . . . EVE.] XIV. SAINT . . . EVE   *1972*
                           XIV I SAINT . . . EVE   *1904*
1   black] Black   *1904 1972*
9   wailings] wailing   *omnia*
13   strong,] strong   *omnia*
21   faultering] faltering   *omnia*
33   strait] straight   *omnia*
35   "The] The   *omnia*
36   "At] At   *omnia*
38   "Keen] Keen   *omnia*
39   "The] The   *omnia*
40   "'Till] 'Till   *omnia*
41   to night,] to-night,   *omnia*
42   "You've] You've   *omnia*
43   "To-morrow] To-morrow   *omnia*

44	"That] That *omnia*	
	aisle."] aisle. *1904 1927*/I	
46	"Yet] Yet *omnia*	
47	"Yet] Yet *omnia*	
48	"Must] Must *omnia*	
49	delay,—] delay, *1972*	
50	"For] For *omnia*	
51	"A] A *omnia*	
52	"O] O *omnia*	
65	cloisters] cloisters' *omnia*	
66	"Conceals] Conceals *omnia*	
67	"Within] Within *omnia*	
68	"The] The *omnia*	
72	calls] call *omnia*	
73	"The] The *1904 1972*	
74	"As] As *omnia*	
75	"From] From *omnia*	
76	"And] And *omnia*	
78	"What] What *omnia*	
79	chancels] chancel's *omnia*	
80	"No] No *omnia*	
	bears"—] bears.' *1972*	
83	door] doors *omnia*	
87	enter] enter, *omnia*	
	Canon"] Canon,' *omnia*	
94	thro'] through *1904 1972*	
	chancels] chancel's *omnia*	
95	skeletons] skeleton's *omnia*	
99	black] Black *1904 1972*	
100	"And] And *omnia*	
104	monks] Monk's *omnia*	
	grey] gray *1904 1972*	
107	black] Black *1904 1972*	
115	monks] Monks *1904 1972*	
118	thro'] through *1904 1972*	
	gloom] loom *1904* (*1970 reads* gloom)	

Revenge

Text collated with *1904, 1927/I, 1972, 1989.*

Title. REVENGE.] XV. REVENGE   *1904 1972*
2   "Its] Its   *omnia*
3   "The] The   *omnia*
4   "You] You   *omnia*
    me] me,   *1972 1989*
    love.—"] love."—   *1927/I 1989*
5   "I] I   *1904*
    must] must,   *1927/I 1989*
6   "I] I   *omnia*
    Strasburg] Strasbourg   *1989*
7   "I] I   *omnia*
    ancestors'] ancestor's   *1972*
8   "And] And   *omnia*
10 "And] And   *omnia*
    'till] till   *1989*
11 "And] And   *omnia*
12 "So] So   *omnia*
    farewell dearest Agnes] farewell, dearest Agnes,   *1989*
    away,—] away;—   *1989*
14 "Or] Or   *omnia*
15 "And] And   *omnia*
    breath,] breath   *1989*
16 "Than] Than   *omnia*
    death,] death;   *1972*
17 madness] madness,   *1989*
    Agnes I] Agnes,—I   *1989*
18 "My] My   *omnia*
19 "This] This   *omnia*
20 "Alone] Alone   *omnia*
    all conquering] all-conquering   *1989*
    maw"—] maw.'—   *1972 1989*
21 no] no,   *1989*
        no   *1904 (1970 reads* no!*)*
    Adolphus thy] Adolphus—thy   *1972*
                Adolphus, thy   *1989*
    share,] share   *1972 1989*
22 "In] In   *omnia*
    there,] there;   *1972 1989*

Historical Collations for Pages 24–28   347

23   "I] I   *omnia*
     spirit,—I] spirit, I   *1972*
24   "My] My   *omnia*
     save—] save"—   *1904 1927*/I
                save!'—   *1972*
25   "Nay] 'Nay,   *1989*
26   "But] But   *omnia*
27   "For] For   *omnia*
     day,] day   *1989*
28   "If] If   *omnia*
     away"—] away.'   *1972*
                away.'—   *1989*
29   bleak] bleak;   *1989*
30   ground,] ground;   *1989*
31   flit,—and] flit and   *1972*
32   gate.—] gate.   *1972*
40   advanced—tall] advanced, tall   *1972*
     form—fierce] form, fierce   *1972*
45   Thy] 'Thy   *1989*
46   well,] well;   *1989*
47   son,] son,—   *1989*
49   I] 'I   *1989*
51   hurled,] hurled   *1989*
52   world,—] world.—   *1989*
53   Now] 'Now,   *1989*
     Adolphus] Adolphus,   *1989*
56   bride—] bride.   *1972*
                bride.'—   *1989*
58   stride,] stride;   *1989*
59   Agnes—he] Agnes, he   *1972*
60   sky—] sky.   *1972*
                sky.—   *1989*
61   silent,—and] silent, and   *1972*
62   gloom,—] gloom,   *1904 1927*/I
                gloom;   *1989*
Dateline.   DECEMBER, 1809.] *omitted*   *1989*

Ghasta; or, The Avenging Demon!!!

Text collated with *1833, 1847, 1870, 1876, 1892W, 1904, 1904frag, 1913, 1927*/I, *1927*/III, *1972, 1972frag, 1989.*

A variant on the first stanza of **Ghasta,** *1833, 1847, 1870, 1876, 1892W, 1904frag, 1913, 1927*/III, and *1972frag* consists of lines 1–4 only. This fragment was first published in Medwin, *Shelley Papers* (*1833*) and reprinted in *1847*, *1870*, *1876*, and *1892W* without **Ghasta**. *1927*/I offers the full text of **Ghasta** while the fragment appears in *1927*/III. Since *1904* and *1972* include both the fragment and **Ghasta,** we have used "*1904frag*" and "*1972frag*" to refer to the fragment in these editions. In some editions, a series of asterisks (Text, *1989*) or periods (*1904*, *1927*/I, *1972*) occurs between lines 28 and 29. All of these editions except *1989* contain two rows of these fragment markers.

Title.   GHASTA;]   *omitted*   *1833 1847 1913*
                   FRAGMENT.   *1870 1876*
                   OMENS   *1892W*
                   XVI. GHASTA   *1904 1972*
                   GHASTA   *1927*/I
                   FRAGMENT: OMENS   *1904frag 1927*/III
                   Fragment: Omens   *1972frag*
Subtitle.   OR, . . . DEMON!!!]   *omitted*   *1833 1847 1870 1876 1892W*
                   *1904*frag *1913 1927*/III *1972frag*
                   or . . . Demon!!!   *1989*
PBS's headnote.   *The idea . . . lie.*]   *omitted*   *1833 1847 1870 1876 1892W*
                   1904frag 1913 1927/III *1972*frag
                   1989

1   Hark!] HARK;   *1927*/III
   her] his   *1833 1847 1870 1876 1892W 1904frag 1913 1927*/III
       1972frag
   wing,] wings   *1833 1847 1870 1876 1892W 1904frag 1913 1927*/III
       1972frag
       wing   *1989*
2   beneath,] beneath;   *1847 1876 1892W 1904frag 1913 1972frag*
       beneath!   *1870*
3   Hark!] Hark;   *1927*/III
   night . . . loudly] 'tis the night-raven   *1833 1847 1870 1876 1892W*
       1904frag 1913 1927/III *1972frag*
   sing,] sings   *1833 1847 1870 1876 1892W 1904frag 1913 1927*/III
       1972frag
       sing   *1989*
4   despair and] approaching   *1833 1847 1870 1876 1892W 1904frag*
       1913 1927/III *1972frag*
   death.—] death.   *1833 1847 1876 1892W 1904frag 1913 1927*/III
       1972frag
       death!   *1870*
       death:—   *1989*
5   Horror] 'Horror   *1989*

8   soon—] soon.'—   *1989*
13 bell,] bell   *1989*
16 Goblins] goblins   *1904 1927/I 1972*
    roam—] roam.—   *1989*
18 way,] way;   *1989*
23 pains,] pains   *1989*
25 toil,] toil   *1989*
28 storm.—] storm.   *1904 1927/I 1972 1989*
31 Majestic,] majestic,   *1989*
    stride,] stride;   *1989*
32 sate,] sat,   *1989*
    name—] name.—   *1989*
33 blaunched] blanched   *1904 1927/I 1972 1989*
38 "Tell] Tell   *1904 1927/I 1972 1989*
39 "Or] Or   *1904 1927/I 1972 1989*
    light,] light   *1989*
40 "Where] Where   *1904 1927/I 1972 1989*
42 "Fiercer] Fiercer   *1904 1927/I 1972 1989*
43 "Fiercer] Fiercer   *1904 1927/I 1972 1989*
    fire,] fire   *1989*
44 "When] When   *1904 1927/I 1972 1989*
    past—"] past'—   *1904 1927/I 1972*
            past.'—   *1989*
46 scowl,] scowl;   *1989*
47 die,"] die"   *1989*
48 soul.—] soul.   *1904 1927/I 1972*
49 Stranger!] "Stranger!   *1927/I 1989*
    whosoe'er] whoso'er   *1904 1927/I 1972*
51 Horrors] Horrors,   *1989*
    stranger] stranger,   *1989*
53 O'er] 'O'er   *1989*
55 observed,] observed   *1989*
57 Light] 'Light   *1989*
59 bog,] bog   *1972 1989*
60 hangs] hangs,   *1972 1989*
61 Horror] 'Horror   *1989*
62 eye,] eye.   *1972*
63 speak,—In] speak,—in   *1989*
64 fly—] fly.—   *1989*
65 At] 'At   *1989*
    form,] form   *1989*
69 In] 'In   *1989*
71 thro'] through   *1904 1927/I 1972 1989*

72	around.] around:	*1989*
73	"Thou] '"Thou	*1989*
74	"'Till] 'Till	*1904 1972*
	Till	*1989*
75	"I] I	*1904 1972 1989*
76	"'Till] 'Till	*1904 1972*
	Till	*1989*
	hurled——] hurled—	*1989*
77	"Strong] '"Strong	*1989*
	fate] fate,	*1904 1972*
78	"Which] Which	*1904 1972 1989*
79	"Breaks] Breaks	*1904 1972 1989*
	gate,] gate	*1989*
80	"Where] Where	*1904 1972 1989*
	yell,] yell;	*1989*
81	"Haply] '"Haply	*1989*
82	"From] From	*1904 1972 1989*
83	"Haply] Haply	*1904 1972 1989*
84	"On] On	*1904 1972 1989*
	flowry,] flow'ry,	*1904 1927/I 1972*
85	—"But] '"—But	*1989*
	disclose,] disclose	*1989*
86	"Of] Of	*1904 1972 1989*
87	"On] On	*1904 1972 1989*
88	"But] But	*1904 1972 1989*
89	"Now] '"Now	*1989*
90	"Lay] Lay	*1904 1972 1989*
91	"My] My	*1904 1972 1989*
	prove,] prove	*1989*
92	"Where] Where	*1904 1972 1989*
93	"For] '"For	*1989*
	mine,] mine	*1989*
94	"'Till] 'Till	*1904 1972*
	Till	*1989*
	judgment] judgement	*1904 1972*
95	"I] I	*1904 1972 1989*
	thine,] thine	*1989*
96	"Night] Night	*1904 1972 1989*
97	Still] 'Still	*1989*
101	Restless,] 'Restless,	*1989*
102	bed,] bed	*1989*
105	Slow] 'Slow	*1989*
109	At] 'At	*1989*

113	In] 'In *1989*	
114	it] its *1904 1927*/I *1972*	
115	What] That *1972*	
	And *1989*	
117	Her] 'Her *1989*	
	head,] head *1989*	
120	roll—] roll.— *1989*	
121	Months] 'Months *1989*	
122	comes,] comes; *1989*	
124	roams—] roams.— *1989*	
125	Stranger!] 'Stranger! *1989*	
	thee,] thee *1989*	
127	me,] me *1989*	
128	scape] 'scape *1904 1927*/I *1972*	
	Hell—] Hell?'— *1904 1989*	
	Hell[?]— *1927*/I	
	Hell?— *1972*	
129	Warrior!] 'Warrior! *1989*	
132	me.] me— *1904 1927*/I *1972*	
	me.' *1989*	
133	wing,] wing *1989*	
135	sing,] sing: *1989*	
136	Mortal] Mortal! *1904 1972 1989*	
137	clear,] clear *1989*	
138	trode,] trod, *1904 1927*/I *1972 1989*	
145	head,] head *1989*	
150	"Bring] Bring *1904 1972 1989*	
151	"Quickly] Quickly *1904 1972 1989*	
152	"Ghasta!] Ghasta! *1904 1972 1989*	
153	grey,] gray, *1904 1972*	
	grey *1989*	
156	"Come] Come *1904 1972 1989*	
165	Phantom] 'Phantom *1989*	
	Theresa] Theresa, *1989*	
	say,] say *1989*	
168	flame,—] flame.'— *1989*	
169	"Mighty] Mighty *1904 1972*	
	one] one, *1989*	
170	"Mightiest] Mightiest *1904 1972 1989*	
171	"Know] Know *1904 1972 1989*	
172	"Know] Know *1904 1972 1989*	
173	"That] That *1904 1972*	
174	"From] From *1904 1972 1989*	

175 "My] My   *1904 1972 1989*
176 "Mighty] Mighty   *1904 1972 1989*
     well."—] well.—   *1904 1972*
177 Ghasta!] 'Ghasta!   *1989*
181 Thou] 'Thou   *1989*
     dead,] dead   *1989*
184 die.] die.'   *1989*
185 there,] there   *1989*
187 hair,] hair   *1989*
189 warrior] Warrior   *1989*
     upwards] upward   *1989*
195 dew,] dew   *1989*
199 "Mortal!] 'Mortal!   *1904 (1970 reads* Mortal!*)*
Dateline.   JANUARY, 1810.] *omitted   1989*

Fragment, or The Triumph of Conscience

Text collated with *1904, 1927*/I, *1972*. (See also Historical Collations for **"'T was dead of the night,"** the version of this poem that appears in **St.Irv**, p. 387.)

At the poem's end, after line 19, two rows of asterisks appear in the Text; in *1904, 1927*/I, and *1972* periods replace the asterisks.

Title.   FRAGMENT,] XVII. FRAGMENT,   *1904 1972*
11   mountain tops] mountain-tops   *omnia*
14   *stanza break*] *omitted   1904 1927*/I
17   blood reeking] blood-reeking   *1972*
18   *stanza break*] *omitted   1904 1927*/I

The Wandering Jew;
or, The Victim of the Eternal Avenger

Text collated with *1887D*, *1892W*, *1913*, *1927*/IV, *1972*, and *1989*. *1913* (Medwin's *Life*, ed. Forman) contains only II.193–98, III.215–23, and IV.171–78, 180–90, and 383–90. *1887D* gives prefatory material in the introduction. In *1989*, the epigraph appears after the Preface.

Title. The Wandering . . . Avenger] THE WANDERING JEW *1887D*
      1892W 1927/IV *1972*
    date "1810" *given after title 1972*
    or,] or *1989*
Epigraph. "If] If *1972*
      thee?—follow] thee? Follow *1887D 1927*/IV *1972 1989*
      me." St.] me."—St. *1927*/IV
        me." *1887D 1892W*
        me.—St. *1972*
    St. John,] St. John *1989*
        22d chapter of St. John *1892W*
    xxi.22.] *omitted* *1892W*
Dedication. *omitted* *1972*
Preface. to the public any thing] anything to the public *1887D*
                                1892W 1927/IV *1972*
    authorize] authorise *1887D 1927*/IV *1972*
    J—— C——,] J[esus] C[hrist], *1972*

Canto I

Epigraph. *Lost.*] *Lost,* II.73. *1927*/IV
        Lost. [iv73–8] *1989*
2 a mellow] a *omitted* *1887D 1892W 1927*/IV *1972*
   ray] ray, *1887D 1972*
5 height] height, *1887D 1892W 1927*/IV *1972*
7 And,] And *1887D 1927*/IV
8 Tipp'd] Tipt *1887D 1927*/IV *1972*
       Tipped *1892W 1989*

355

9   below.] below;   *1887D 1892W 1927*/IV *1972*
11 linger'd] lingered   *1892W 1989*
12 fair,] fair.   *1887D 1892W 1972*
13 there even luxury to grieve;] luxury even, there to grieve.   *1887D*
                    1892W 1927/IV
                    luxury even, there to grieve;   *1972*
16 Paradise,—] Paradise,   *1892W*
17 splendour] splendor   *1892W*
18 repose;—] repose.   *1892W 1972*
21 a distant] a *omitted*   *1887D 1892W 1927*/IV *1972*
22 ear,] ear   *1887D 1972*
23 Echo's] echo's   *1887D 1927*/IV
    pleased] charmed   *1887D 1892W 1927*/IV *1972*
25 glow'd] glowed   *1892W 1989*
26 bestow'd;] bestowed;   *1892W 1989*
29 clouds,] clouds   *1887D 1892W 1927*/IV
    gay,] gay   *1892W*
30 Hung] Hung,   *1887D 1892W 1927*/IV
    array] array,   *1892W*
31 sky;] sky: *1887D 1927*/IV *1972*
34 nigh;] nigh: *1887D 1927*/IV *1972*
            nigh.   *1892W*
35 sound,] sound   *1892W*
36 The smooth turf trembling as] O'er the smooth, trembling
                    turf   *1887D 1892W 1927*/IV *1972*
    bound,] bound!—   *1972*
38 harmony!] harmony;   *1887D 1927*/IV
41 dew-drops] dewdrops   *1887D 1892W 1927*/IV *1972*
    morn] morn,   *1887D 1892W 1927*/IV *1972*
42 blossom'd] blossomed   *1887D 1892W 1927*/IV *1972 1989*
43 pow'r] power   *1892W*
    stanza break] *omitted 1887D 1892W 1927*/IV *1972*
45 alloy,] alloy,—   *1972*
46 on,—ye] on, ye   *1972*
    hours,] hours!   *1972*
50 favour'd] favored   *1892W*
            favoured   *1989*
57 around.] around!   *1972*
61 below:] below.   *1892W*
66 far off] far-off   *1972*
69 glow'd] glowed   *1892W 1989*
70 on—] on;   *1892W*
75 grey.] gray.   *1892W*

77   spell—] spell!   *1892W*
79   sound:] sound;   *1892W*
80   again:] again;   *1892W*
82   past,] passed,   *1892W 1972 1989*
89   entered;] enterèd;   *1892W 1927/IV 1989*
91   saint-cipher'd] saint-cyphered   *1887D 1892W 1927/IV 1972*
              saint-ciphered   *1989*
     panes,] panes;   *1887D 1927/IV*
              panes   *1972*
92   Or,] Or   *1887D*
94   gliding,] gliding   *1887D 1892W 1927/IV 1972*
95   aisle,] aisle;   *1887D 1892W 1927/IV 1972*
96   striding] striding,   *1887D 1927/IV*
97   coignes] coigns   *1989*
     pillar'd] pillared   *1989*
     pillar'd pile;—] gothic pile.   *1887D 1892W 1927/IV*
              Gothic pile.   *1972*
Footnote. Buttress] '"Buttress   *1989*
           nor] or   *1892W 1927/IV*
           coigne] coign   *1892W 1927/IV*
           'vantage.—*Macbeth.*] vantage.—*Macbeth.*   *1887D 1972*
                       vantage. *Macbeth.*   *1892W 1927/IV*
                       'vantage"—*Macbeth* [I vi 7]'
                            added   *1989*
103 past] passed   *1892W 1972 1989*
105 day.] day   *1887D*
110 floats—] floats;   *1892W*
112 choir,] choir   *1927/IV*
113 desire;] desire,   *1892W 1927/IV*
118 ran,] ran   *1892W 1927/IV 1989*
123 chaunted] chanted   *1892W*
124 said,] said   *1892W*
138 knew,] knew   *1892W 1927/IV 1989*
142 aisle—] aisle.   *1892W*
147 bear—] bear;   *1892W*
148 fled,] fled   *1887D 1892W 1972*
150 confest,] confessed   *1892W*
              confessed,   *1989*
158 there,] there;   *1892W*
159 fix'd] fixed   *1892W 1989*
162 Novices] novices   *1887D 1892W 1927/IV 1972*
163 strew'd] strew   *1887D 1892W 1927/IV 1972*
              strewed   *1989*

	ground,] ground:	*1887D 1927*/IV *1972*
	ground;	*1892W*
164	array'd;] arrayed,	*1887D 1892W 1927*/IV *1972*
	arrayed;	*1989*
165	Three] Nine	*1887D 1892W 1927*/IV *1972*
166	Sabean] Sabæan	*1887D 1892W 1927*/IV *1972 1989*
175	Thro'] Through	*1892W 1972 1989*
	man,] man;	*1892W*
176	clamours] clamors	*1892W*
	ran,] ran—	*1892W*
189	throng,] throng—	*1892W*
198	prest,] pressed,	*1892W 1989*
203	hark!] Hark!	*1887D 1892W 1927*/IV *1972*
209	loud,] loud,—	*1892W*
222	storm.] storm;	*1892W*
	storm,	*1972*
224	The] Came the	*1972*
	sea mew] sea-mew	*1887D 1892W 1972*
225	flew;] flew,—	*1892W*
226	blast] blast,	*1892W*
227	past;] passed,	*1892W*
	passed	*1972*
	passed;	*1989*
229	by,] by,—	*1892W*
232	form,] form;	*1892W*
233	fear.] fear;	*1892W*
	fear—	*1972*
Footnote.	"Behold] '"Behold	*1989*
	vi. 8] vi. 8'	*1989*
240	gaze,] gaze,—	*1892W*
242	light.] light,	*1892W 1989*
245	dead,] dead	*1989*
246	Drest] Dressed	*1892W 1989*
247	sight—] sight;	*1892W*
248	sustain,] sustain	*1892W 1927*/IV *1989*
250	o'er,] o'er;	*1892W*
255	ear,] ear	*1972 1989*
256	hear;] hear,	*1972*
258	fly,] fly	*1892W*
261	"And, ah!"] And, 'Ah!'	*1989*
262	frame,] frame	*1892W 1927*/IV *1989*
263	flame—] flame!	*1972*
269	heart.] heart!	*1972*

270 vain,] vain   *1892W 1927/IV 1989*
271 grief;—] grief,—   *1887D 1972*
           grief;   *1892W*
275 reign—] reign.   *1892W*
277 Ever] Ever,   *1989*
     stanza break] *omitted 1892W 1927/IV*
279 past,] passed,   *1892W 1972 1989*
289 pityless] pitiless   *1892W 1972 1989*
291 wave;—] wave;   *1892W*
294 here,] here   *1892W*
295 swelling] swellings   *1927/IV*
298 earth,] earth   *1892W 1927/IV 1989*
300 above,] above   *1892W 1927/IV 1989*
303 past;] past,   *1892W*
           passed;   *1989*
305 fly:] fly.   *1892W*
307 night,] night;   *1892W*
309 grave.—] grave;   *1892W*
           grave!   *1972*
310 hurled—] hurled   *1892W*
           hurled,   *1972 1989*
313 sky:] sky;   *1892W*
314 th'] the   *1892W*
316 etherial] ethereal   *1892W 1972*
317 give,—] give,   *1892W*
318 receive,] receive,—   *1892W*
319 measure."] measure!'   *1972*
321 gaze:] gaze.   *1892W*
329 flame,] flame   *1892W 1989*
335 thee] these   *1989*
337 rest] rest,   *1892W*
338 And] And,   *1892W*
339 harm:] harm.   *1892W*
340 sea,] sea,—   *1892W 1972*

Canto II

Epigraph.   combined] combinèd   *1892W 1927/IV*
            porcupine." | *Hamlet.*] porcupine."—*Hamlet,* 1.5   *1927*
                        porcupine."—*Hamlet.*   *1887D 1972*
                        porcupine." | *Hamlet* [i v 15–20]   *1989*
1 nightly] mighty   *1887D 1892W 1972*

2	tempest clouds were past,] tempest clouds, were passed—	*1892W*
	tempest-clouds were past	*1972*
4	fled,] fled *1892W 1989*	
7	vapours] vapors *1892W*	
8	rosy tinted] rosy-tinted *1972*	
9	grey] gray *1892W*	
10	rise,] rise *1892W*	
13	rocks—the] rocks, the *1892W*	
17	drest.] dressed; *1892W*	
	dressed. *1989*	
20	colours] colors *1892W*	
	hue.] hue, *1887D 1989*	
	hue; *1892W 1972*	
24	cliff's] cliffs' *1887D 1927/IV 1989*	
26	shore.] shore! *1972*	
27	To-day—scarce] To-day scarce *1972*	
28	seas] seas, *1892W 1972*	
30	serene,] serene; *1892W*	
	serene! *1972*	
35	went,] went; *1892W*	
42	vassals,] vassals *1892W 1927/IV 1972 1989*	
44	scorned,] scorned *1892W*	
45	woe:] woe; *1892W 1927/IV*	
46	sate,] sate *1892W 1989*	
48	And] And, *1892W*	
51	wood,] wood; *1892W 1972*	
53	high,] high,— *1892W*	
61	prey,] prey; *1892W*	
64	*stanza break*] *page break 1887D 1972*	
	omitted 1892W 1927/IV	
68	day:] day. *1892W*	
75	fly,] fly *1892W*	
76	beam] beams *1887D 1892W 1972*	
77	bestow,] bestow *1892W 1927/IV*	
79	vast,] vast *1972*	
80	past,] past *1892W*	
83	o'erspread,] o'erspread *1887D 1892W 1972 1989*	
88	lour.] lower. *1892W*	
94	gush'd] gushed *1892W 1989*	
95	mutter'd] muttered *1892W 1989*	
	ear?—] ear? *1892W*	
96	smother'd] smothered *1892W 1989*	
	sigh?—] sigh? *1892W*	

101 burn'd] burned   *1892W 1989*
     flame;] flame,   *1887D 1972*
103 labour'd] labored   *1892W*
              laboured   *1989*
107 death,] Death,   *1972*
112 deform'd] deformed   *1892W 1989*
117 eye,] eye   *1892W 1927/IV*
120 siren] syren   *1887D 1927/IV 1972*
121 Lull'd] Lulled   *1892W 1989*
     rest.] rest,   *1887D*
              rest;   *1892W 1927/IV*
123 fled:] fled;   *1892W*
124 life,] life   *1887D 1927/IV 1972*
126 lapt] lapped   *1892W 1989*
129 Howl'd] Howled   *1892W 1989*
133 flash,] flash.   *1887D 1927/IV*
              flash   *1972*
134 gleam'd] gleamed   *1887D 1892W 1927/IV 1972 1989*
136 lash'd] lashed   *1892W 1989*
137 mutter'd] muttered   *1892W 1989*
141 talk'd] talked   *1892W 1989*
     dead,] dead,—   *1892W 1972*
144 phantasy,] fantasy,   *1892W 1989*
146 flash'd] flashed   *1887D 1892W 1927/IV 1972 1989*
147 stalk'd] stalked   *1892W 1989*
150 Retain'd] Retained   *1892W 1989*
151 love?—] love?   *1972*
157 wings,] wings   *1892W 1927/IV 1972 1989*
158 melodies,] melodies;   *1892W 1972*
159 ebb'd] ebbed   *1892W 1989*
160 listen'd] listened   *1989*
161 What] "What   *1887D 1927/IV 1972 1989*
165 Nightly] 'Nightly   *1989*
167 cliff-embosom'd] cliff-embosomed   *1892W 1989*
169 Now] 'Now   *1989*
173 Oft] 'Oft   *1989*
     Abbey's] abbey's   *1887D 1892W 1927/IV 1972*
174 high;] high,   *1972*
175 lour,] lower,   *1892W*
177 That] 'That   *1989*
     maid,] maid   *1972*
179 madden'd] maddened   *1892W 1989*
     obey'd,] obeyed,   *1892W 1989*

180	cliff] cliffs	*1887D 1892W*
	plunged] plung'd	*1887D 1927/IV 1972*
181	There] 'There	*1989*
185	Yet] 'Yet	*1989*
186	its] it	*1989*
189	That] 'That	*1989*
	Abbey] abbey	*1887D 1892W 1927/IV 1972*
191	darken'd] darkened	*1892W 1989*
192	there.] there."	*1887D 1927/IV 1972 1989*
194	died;] died—	*1913*
196	some] an	*1913*
197	the] a	*1913*
	symphony;] symphony:	*1913*
198	close,] close.	*1913*
201	*stanza break*] *page break 1887D*
		omitted 1892W 1927/IV 1972
204	blood—] blood,	*1972*
211	Scenes,] Scenes	*1972*
	now,] now	*1972*
216	trace,] trace	*1892W 1927/IV 1989*
217	destiny.] destiny!—	*1972*
220	With] Wild	*1887D 1892W 1972*
221	dashing;] dashing,	*1892W 1972*
223	soul.] soul!	*1972*
227	me."] me!'	*1972*

Canto III

Epigraph.	*Paradise*] —*Paradise*	*1887D 1927/IV 1972*
	Lost.] *Lost*, I. 591.	*1927/IV*
	Lost [i 591–4, 600–2]	*1989*
1	"'Tis] 'Tis	*1892W*
4	hand,] hand	*1892W*
9	"How] How	*1892W*
13	'Twas on that day, as] As dread that day, when	*1887D 1927/IV*
	As dread that day, when,	*1892W*
16	mock'd] mocked	*1887D 1892W 1927/IV 1972 1989*
17	'Go! go!'] Go, go,	*1887D*
	"Go, go,"	*1892W 1927/IV*
	"Go, go."	*1972*
	go,' he said,] go,' said he,	*1887D 1892W 1927/IV 1972 1989*
18	invite,] invite;	*1887D 1892W 1927/IV 1972*

19   blest] blessed   *1989*
     light;] light   *1887D 1892W 1927/IV 1972*
20   go—but] go, but   *1887D 1892W 1927/IV 1972*
     remain,] remain—   *1887D 1892W 1927/IV 1972*
21–22   Nor . . . day | Till . . . again."]
           Thou diest not till I come again'—   *1887D 1892W 1927/IV*
           Thou diest not till I come again!"   *1972*
25   madden'd] maddened   *1892W 1989*
     stands,] stands.   *1887D 1927/IV*
           stands;   *1892W*
27   anguish'd] anguished   *1892W 1989*
     tear;] tear.   *1887D 1892W 1927/IV*
28   Hark] Hark,   *1887D 1892W 1927/IV*
     groan! He dies, he dies!] groan!—he dies—he dies.   *1887D 1927/IV*
           groan!—he dies—he dies,—   *1892W*
30   enemies!] enemies.   *1887D 1892W 1927/IV*
31   noonday] noon-day   *1887D 1927/IV 1972*
32   shrouded;] shrouded.   *1887D 1892W 1927/IV*
34   beaming,] beaming;   *1887D 1892W 1927/IV*
36   night;] night.   *1887D 1892W 1927/IV 1972*
39   trembled;] tremblèd;   *1989*
40   vail,] veil;   *1892W*
           veil,   *1972 1989*
45   fiends] fiends,   *1972*
     array'd] arrayed   *1892W 1989*
     light,] light   *1892W 1989*
47   shriek'd] shrieked   *1892W 1989*
48   shriek'd] shrieked   *1892W 1989*
51   despised,] despised   *1887D 1927/IV*
     alas!] alas,   *1972*
53   Flash'd] Flashed   *1887D 1892W 1927/IV 1972 1989*
54   scorch'd] scorched   *1892W 1989*
59   Heaven.] Heaven;   *1972*
60   Time,] Time   *1892W 1927/IV 1989*
69   prolonging,] prolonging   *1892W*
70   "Methought,] Methought   *1892W*
71   light,] light   *1892W*
           light—   *1972*
72   skies,] skies,—   *1892W*
73   rise.] rise!   *1972*
74   bled!] bled!—   *1972*
77   eye?] eye,   *1972*

90   King.] King!   *1972*
91   "But,] But   *1892W*
     instant,] instant   *1892W*
     sight,] sight   *1892W*
94   duskness] darkness   *1887D 1892W 1972*
     covered] cover'd   *1887D 1927/IV 1972*
112 weight. I] weight—I   *1972*
114 wide,] wide   *1892W*
115 sulphureous] sulphurous   *1887D 1892W 1927/IV 1972 1989*
118 "Yet] Yet   *1892W*
119 mind,] mind   *1892W*
123 grey,] gray,   *1892W*
126 fire.] fire: *1972*
129 "A] A   *1892W*
131 land.] land!   *1972*
135 woe.] woe—   *1972*
137 misery.] misery!   *1972*
138 "Since] Since   *1892W*
     when,] when   *1972*
     deathlike] death-like   *1887D 1892W 1972*
139 Past,] Passed,   *1892W 1972 1989*
     past,] passed,   *1892W 1972 1989*
140 me,] me;   *1892W 1972*
141 When] Then, all at   *1972*
     once] once,   *1972*
     fondly] *omitted 1972*
142 place.] place,   *1887D 1892W*
         place—   *1972*
143 Jerusalem, alas!] Jerusalem—alas!   *1892W*
     name,] name—   *1892W*
         name: *1972*
145 trace.] trace;   *1972*
146 Her pomp—her splendour—was no more.]
             Her pomp, her splendour, was no more.   *1887D*
             Her pomp, her splendor, was no more.   *1892W*
             Her pomp, her splendour, was no more;   *1972*
147 rise,] rise   *1892W*
148 skies.] skies,—   *1892W*
         skies;   *1972*
149 bust,] bust   *1892W 1972*
150 dust.] dust,   *1972*
151 gore.] gore,   *1887D 1892W 1972*
153 blood.] blood;   *1972*

154   since,] since   *1892W*
156   spear,] spear—   *1972*
158   last] lasting   *1989*
160   "Rack'd] Racked   *1892W*
161   long'd] longed   *1892W 1989*
162   death!] death,   *1972*
164   cease.] cease!   *1892W 1972*
172   "I] I   *1892W*
174   lower'd] lowered   *1892W 1989*
176   whirl'd] whirled   *1892W 1989*
       breath,] breath   *1892W*
179   Scorch'd] Scorched   *1892W 1989*
185   wide,] wide   *1892W 1927/IV 1989*
187   whelm'd] whelmed   *1892W 1989*
191   Dash'd] Dashed   *1892W 1989*
194   hell!] hell   *1972*
196   soul.] soul!   *1887D 1892W 1972 1989*
       stanza break] *omitted 1927/IV*
197   "I] I   *1892W*
Footnote.
Sentence 2   billows,] billows   *1887D 1972*
Sentence 4   Vesuvius,] Vesuvius;   *1892W*
              again,] again   *1887D 1972 1989*
              parched up] up *omitted*   *1927/IV*
              flesh,] flesh   *1887D 1892W 1972*
              chain] chains   *1927/IV*
Sentence 5   thunderbolt] thunderbolt,   *1892W*
Sentence 6   scattered oak,] scattered [? shattered] oak,   *1887D 1892W*
                            1927/IV
                        shattered oak,   *1972*
                        scathed oak,   *1989*
              for ever.] forever.   *1892W*
Sentence 9   endeavoured] endeavored   *1892W*
198   doom] doom,   *1887D 1927/IV 1972*
201   'Mid] Mid   *1989*
202   'Mid] Mid   *1989*
       fire,] fire   *1887D 1892W 1972*
203   whirl'd] whirled   *1892W 1989*
204   scorch'd] scorched   *1887D 1892W 1927/IV 1972 1989*
205   Parch'd] Parched   *1892W 1989*
206   rack'd] racked   *1892W 1989*
       pains;] pains,—   *1892W*
207   hurl'd] hurled   *1892W 1989*

208   what] that   *1927/IV*
212   pangs] pains   *1887D 1892W 1927/IV 1972*
214   head.] head!   *1972*
215   "Still] Still   *1892W 1913*
      scathed] scathèd   *1892W 1972 1989*
      pine-tree's] pine tree's   *1913*
216   tempests] tempest   *1913*
      night] night,   *1892W*
            night;   *1913*
217   fire.] fire—   *1913*
            fire,—   *1972*
218   scathed] scathèd   *1892W 1972*
            shattered   *1913*
      pine] pine,   *1913*
221   heath,] heath;   *1913*
222   even] e'en   *1913*
223   rears] raises   *1913*
224   roar,] roar   *1887D 1892W 1927/IV*
228   doom'd] doomed   *1892W 1989*
232   "I] I   *1892W*
      eye,] eye   *1927/IV 1989*
237   birth:] birth;   *1892W*
239   sight:] sight;   *1892W*
240   spell,] spell   *1989*
244   noon,] noon   *1892W*
245   moon.] moon—   *1887D 1892W 1927/IV 1972*
            moon,   *1989*
247   command."] command.—   *1892W*
249   grey] gray   *1892W*
250   cross] Cross   *1887D 1892W 1927/IV 1972*
251   colour] color   *1892W*
261   Wolga's] Volga's   *1989*
      shore,] shore.   *1887D 1892W 1927/IV*
267   Wolga's] Volga's   *1989*
      strand;] strand,   *1887D 1892W 1972*
268   cry.] cry,   *1887D 1892W*
271|272   [PAULO]   *stage direction added 1892W*
272   "Once] Once   *1892W*
274   tempests] tempest   *1989*
275   storm-blacken'd] storm-blackened   *1892W 1989*
276   glare,] glare   *1887D 1892W 1972*
280   drench'd] drenched   *1892W 1989*
281   bid] bade   *1887D 1892W 1927/IV 1972*

284	madden'd] maddened	*1887D 1892W 1972 1989*
294	hurl'd,] hurled,	*1892W 1989*
299	loud yelling] loud-yelling	*1972*
	stanza break] *page break*	*1887D*
	omitted	*1892W 1927/IV*
300	"Ah!] Ah!	*1892W 1927/IV*
301	Chaos] chaos	*1887D 1892W 1972*
303	nod!"] nod!—	*1892W*
310	"Oft] Oft	*1892W*
314	—Once] Once	*1892W*
317	calm,] calm	*1887D 1892W 1972*
	breast,] breast,—	*1892W*
	breast—	*1972*
318	Death] death	*1887D 1892W 1972*
	resolved—intent,] resolved, intent,	*1972*
320	reliques] relics	*1892W 1989*
321	reliques] relics	*1892W 1989*
323	*stanza break*] *page break*	*1887D*
	omitted	*1927/IV*
324	"All] All	*1892W 1927/IV*
328	silver winged] silver-winged	*1972*
	winged] wingèd	*1892W 1927/IV 1989*
	mew] mew,	*1892W*
329	screams] screams,	*1892W*
334	glare,] glare	*1887D 1892W 1927/IV 1972*
335	lightnings] lightning's	*1989*
338	"A] A	*1892W*
339	ear,] air;	*1892W*
346	insubstantial] unsubstantial	*1887D 1892W 1972*
	night,] night	*1892W 1927/IV*
349	vapours] vapors	*1892W*
355	mists,] mists	*1989*
	wreath,] wreathe,	*1927/IV 1989*
359	stream'd] streamed	*1892W 1989*
362	deck'd] decked	*1892W 1989*
363	Bloom'd] Bloomed	*1892W 1989*
365	Pour'd] Poured	*1892W 1989*
367	play'd,] played,	*1892W 1989*
368	pourtray'd] portrayed	*1892W 1989*
	portray'd	*1972*
371	brow] brow,	*1887D 1892W 1927/IV 1972*
372	mark'd] marked	*1892W 1989*
373	deepen'd] deepened	*1892W 1989*

376 conceal'd;] concealed;   *1892W 1989*
378 Conscience,] Conscience   *1892W 1927/IV*
379 betray'd,] betrayed,   *1892W 1989*
380 reveal'd.] revealed.   *1892W 1989*
384 Crimson'd] Crimsoned   *1892W 1989*
387 said,] said   *1892W 1972*
    then] when   *1887D 1892W 1972*
388 cease;] cease,   *1892W 1972*
390 tomb;] tomb,   *1892W*
391 lull'd] lulled   *1892W 1989*
392 labouring] laboring   *1892W*
    breath;] breath,   *1892W*
395 oh,] O,   *1892W*
396 scroll;] scroll!   *1972*
401 lightnings] lightnings,   *1892W 1972*
402 Flash'd] Flashed   *1892W 1989*
407 labour'd] labored   *1892W*
    laboured   *1989*
411 shriek'd] shrieked   *1892W 1989*
412 peal'd] pealed   *1892W 1989*
413 scatter'd] scattered   *1892W 1989*
415 touch'd] touched   *1887D 1892W 1972 1989*
416 roll'd] rolled   *1892W 1989*
417 Reveal'd] Revealed   *1892W 1989*
419 Gleam'd] Gleamed   *1892W 1989*
421 dead,] dead   *1892W 1927/IV 1989*
423 rush'd] rushed   *1892W 1989*
424 fill'd] filled   *1892W 1989*
428 near.] near!   *1972*
429 "Here] Here   *1892W*
431 faint:] faint;   *1892W*
443 no."—] no—"   *1887D 1972*
    no—   *1892W*
448 demon's] Demon's   *1892W*
    form.] form?   *1892W 1972*
455 reality.] reality   *1887D 1892W*

Canto IV

Epigraph 1   48.] 48–54.   *1972*
Epigraph 2   "———What] "What   *1892W*
    th' inhabitants] th'inhabitants   *1989*

        on 't?—Live] on't?—Live   *1887D 1892W 1927/IV 1972*
                                                                      1989
            Macbeth.] *Macbeth* I. 3.   *1927/IV*
                     Macbeth [I iii 39–43]   *1989*

3   confest] confessed   *1892W 1989*
4   first—the] first, the   *1972*
     noblest—and] noblest, and   *1972*
     best;] best,   *1892W*
         best—   *1972*
5   vast—whose] vast, whose   *1972*
     eye,] eye   *1927/IV 1989*
6   sky,] sky—   *1972*
15 woe,] woe?   *1887D 1892W 1927/IV 1972*
17 heav'nly] heavenly   *1892W*
19 Heaven,] Heaven;   *1887D 1892W 1927/IV*
21 laws,] laws;   *1887D 1892W 1927/IV*
23 state,] state;   *1887D 1892W 1927/IV*
25 die.] die!   *1972*
27 heighten'd] heightened   *1892W 1989*
     rays,] rays;   *1887D 1892W 1927/IV*
         rays!—   *1972*
29 bliss,] bliss;   *1892W*
         bliss!   *1972*
31 wind,] wind;   *1887D 1892W 1927/IV 1972*
32 hush'd] hushed   *1892W 1989*
33 breast,] breast;   *1887D 1892W 1927/IV*
35 pride,] pride;   *1887D 1892W 1927/IV*
         pride,—   *1972*
36 overwhelm'd] overwhelmed   *1892W 1989*
42 happiness.] happiness;   *1972*
43 blest] blessed   *1892W 1989*
50 face;] face,   *1972*
52 desire;] desire?—   *1972*
55 labouring] laboring   *1892W*
     breath—] breath?—   *1972*
56 death.] death: *1972*
57 eye,] eye,—   *1972*
61 supprest—] suppressed—   *1892W 1989*
68 fear;] fear!   *1972*
70 sound,] sound   *1989*
71 ear.] ear!   *1972*

76	high,] high	*1892W 1927*/IV
82	disk,] disc,	*1989*
89	reach'd] reached	*1892W 1989*
90	head,] head	*1887D 1892W 1927*/IV *1972*
93	air,] air;	*1892W 1927*/IV
94	call'd] called	*1887D 1892W 1927*/IV *1972 1989*
103	dimm'd] dimmed	*1892W 1989*
114	death angel] death-angel	*1927*/IV
115	blacken'd] blackened	*1892W 1989*
	wave.] wave!	*1972*
117	on;] on!	*1972*
121	song,] song	*1892W*
128	past,] passed,	*1892W 1989*
	pass'd,	*1972*
129	lengthen'd] lengthened	*1892W 1989*
130	Till] Till,	*1892W 1972*
138	shudder'd] shuddered	*1892W 1989*
146	throbb'd] throbbed	*1892W 1989*
148	rush'd] rushed	*1892W 1989*
149	thro'] through	*1892W 1989*
150	glare,] glare;	*1892W 1972 1989*
158	crost.] crossed.	*1892W 1989*
162	mists,] mists	*1892W*
165	What] "What	*1892W*
166	despair?] despair?"	*1892W*
170	*stanza break*] *omitted 1972*	
171	Suddenly] When suddenly,	*1913*
	glare,] glare	*1913 1989*
172	air;] air,	*1913*
173	through] thro'	*1913*
174	on] from	*1913*
	Witch's] witch's	*1913*
	broke,] broke:	*1913*
	broke!	*1972*
	broke;	*1989*
175	herculean] Herculean	*1913*
176	flame;] flame—	*1913*
177	eyes] eyes,	*1913*
178	filled.] filled,	*1913*
	filled;	*1972*
179	They . . . night,] *omitted 1913*	
182	rocks,] rocks;	*1887D 1892W 1927*/IV
	rocks—	*1913*

184	trail;] trail: *1913*	
	trail. *1972*	
186	Were] Was *1972*	
188	hide—as] hide, as *1913*	
189	"Grinned] Grinned *1913*	
	smile"] smile," *1892W*	
	smile, *1913*	
190	demon] hideous *1913*	
	stanza break] *page break 1887D*	
	omitted 1927/IV	
192	lime leaves] lime-leaves *1927*/IV *1972*	
194	Swam—Vainly] Swam—vainly *1892W 1927*/IV *1989*	
	Swam. Vainly *1972*	
197	thro'] through *1892W 1989*	
208	thro'] through *1892W 1989*	
210	rays,] rays *1887D 1892W 1927*/IV *1972*	
215	flame—a caverned] flame, a caverned *1892W*	
216	hell,] Hell, *1892W*	
226	dead;] dead *1887D 1972*	
232	thro'] through *1892W 1972 1989*	
	air:] air, *1892W*	
	air *1972 1989*	
235	night,] night; *1972*	
236	eye] eye, *1892W 1927*/IV	
237	stare,] stare *1887D 1972*	
238	radiancy;] radiancy— *1972*	
240	heath;] heath, *1972*	
241	form,] form *1989*	
250	*stanza break*] *omitted 1892W*	
255	light] light, *1892W 1989*	
256	brow,] brow *1892W 1989*	
263	"Give] Give *1892W*	
265	command.] command! *1972*	
268	land."] land. *1892W*	
	land!' *1972*	
269	"Calm] Calm *1892W*	
270	one,] one *1989*	
271	begins." I —An] begins." I An *1887D 1927*/IV *1972*	
	begins.— I An *1892W*	
273	air,] air; *1887D 1892W 1927*/IV	
274	fix'd] fixed *1887D 1892W 1927*/IV *1972 1989*	
	stare;] stare: *1887D 1927*/IV	
	stare, *1972*	

275 floor,] floor;   *1972*
276 Around,] Around   *1887D 1892W 1927/IV 1972*
    dark] dank   *1887D 1892W 1927/IV 1972*
    vapours] vapors   *1892W*
    lower;] lower: *1887D 1927/IV*
277 threw;] threw,   *1887D 1892W 1927/IV*
278 by] with   *1887D 1892W 1927/IV 1972*
279 flew;—] flew;   *1887D 1892W 1927/IV*
280 soul!—] soul;   *1887D 1892W 1927/IV*
            soul!   *1972*
281 Then . . . round] Around strange fiendish laughs   *1887D 1892W*
            1927/IV 1972
283 In . . . ground.] At fits was heard to float around.   *1887D 1892W*
            1927/IV 1972
284 utter'd] uttered   *1887D 1892W 1927/IV 1972 1989*
286 fiend] fiend,   *1887D*
287 bend.] bend;   *1887D 1892W 1927/IV*
290 Hell!] Hell—   *1887D 1892W 1927/IV 1972*
291 But . . . his] His horrid   *1887D 1892W 1927/IV 1972*
    cell,] cell.   *1887D 1892W 1927/IV*
        cell!   *1972*
292 What . . . tell,] Victorio shrunk, unused to shrink,   *1887D 1892W*
            1927/IV 1972
293 The . . . look!] E'en at extremest danger's brink;   *1887D 1892W*
            1927/IV 1972
294 witch's] witch   *1887D 1892W 1927/IV 1972*
    heart, . . . shrink] then pointed to the ground,   *1887D 1892W 1972*
            then pointed to the ground;   *1927/IV*
295 Even . . . brink,] Infernal shadows flitted around,   *1887D 1927/IV*
            1972
            Infernal shadows flitted around   *1892W*
296 With . . . shook!] *omitted 1887D 1892W 1927/IV 1972*
297 Prince] prince   *1887D 1927/IV 1972*
    rise] rise,   *1887D*
        rise;   *1892W 1927/IV 1972*
298–300 *omitted 1887D 1892W 1913 1927/IV 1972*
302 Which,] Which   *1887D 1972*
303 tempest-waves.] tempest waves.   *1887D 1892W 1927/IV 1972*
304 wrapt] wrapped   *1892W 1989*
305 strange] strange,   *1887D 1892W 1927/IV 1972*
    and . . . enchantress] the awful being   *1887D 1892W 1927/IV 1972*
    stood;—] stood.   *1887D 1892W 1927/IV*

306   came,] came   *1892W*
307   flood,] flood   *1892W 1972*
308   lips—array'd] lips,—array'd   *1887D*
                    lips, arrayed   *1892W*
                    lips,—arrayed   *1927/IV*
                    lips—arrayed   *1989*
309   livid,] livid   *1887D 1892W 1927/IV 1972*
      joy—] joy;   *1887D 1892W 1927/IV*
310   dropp'd] dropped   *1887D 1892W 1927/IV 1972 1989*
311   now,] now   *1927/IV*
      wide,] wide   *1927/IV*
      display'd] displayed,   *1887D*
                displayed   *1892W 1927/IV 1972 1989*
312   blue.] hue,   *1887D 1892W*
            hue,—   *1927/IV*
313   cry,] cry   *1892W 1927/IV 1972*
314   sang,] sang;   *1892W*
315   The . . . with] Along the rocks   *1887D 1892W 1927/IV 1972*
      death-peal,] death-peal   *1887D 1892W 1927/IV 1972*
      rang,] rang.   *1887D 1927/IV*
            rang;   *1892W 1972*
316   And . . . accents,] In accents hollow,   *1887D 1892W 1927/IV 1972*
317   Struck] They struck   *1887D 1892W 1927/IV 1972*
      terror on the dark night's ear!] upon Victorio's ear.   *1887D 1892W*
                    1927/IV
                upon Victorio's ear;   *1972*
319   power,] power   *1892W*
320   shrieks;—the] shrieks; the   *1892W*
      disperse;—] disperse;   *1892W*
322   confest!] confessed!   *1892W*
327   appall'd] appalled   *1887D 1892W 1927/IV 1972 1989*
331   *stanza break*] omitted *1887D 1892W 1927/IV*
336   tide,] tide   *1927/IV*
337   dead."] dead!"   *1972*
339   past,] passed,   *1892W 1989*
            pass'd,   *1972*
Footnote.   death."] Death!"   *1927/IV*
            —Paradise] Paradise   *1892W 1927/IV*
            Lost.] Lost, II.787.   *1927/IV*
                  Lost [ii 787–9]   *1989*
342   ground,] ground;   *1892W 1927/IV 1989*
            ground,—   *1972*

Historical Collations for Pages 82–84   373

344   fell;] fell.   *1972*
346   glance,] glance—   *1972*
              glance;   *1989*
350   "Receive] Receive   *1892W*
355   thine."] thine.   *1892W*
              thine!'   *1972*
358   around,] around   *1892W*
360   terror—thro'] terror—through   *1892W 1972 1989*
362   And] And,   *1892W 1927/IV*
368   frame;] frame,   *1989*
377   Which . . . by,] Are wafted from yon hill;   *1892W*
378   Are . . . hill:] Which on the blast that passes by,   *1892W*
        yon] the   *1989*
        hill:] hill;   *1887D 1927/IV 1972*
380   ear;] ear: *1887D 1927/IV 1972*
              ear,—   *1892W*
383   flower] rose   *1913*
384   blast;] gale!   *1913*
385   hour,] hour!   *1913*
386   pale, is fast.] fast—is pale—   *1913*
387   maiden;] maiden,   *1913*
388   decay;] decay—   *1913*
389   laden,] laden   *1913*
390   death away.] death—away.   *1913*
393   ear,] ear   *1892W*
397   past?] passed?   *1892W 1989*
              pass'd?   *1972*
400   nature] Nature   *1892W*
403   "Lies] Lies   *1892W*
        devour,] devour?   *1972*
404   hour,] hour?   *1972*
421   fix'd] fixed   *1892W 1989*
422   dread;] dread!   *1972*
424   Griefs] griefs   *1927/IV*
        burn,] burn   *1892W*
425   heal!] heal?   *1972*
428   feel!"] feel?'   *1972*
432   hollow] hollow,   *1972*
433   misery."] misery!'   *1972*

Posthumous Fragments of Margaret Nicholson

Stanza Breaks

1904, *1927*/I, and *1972* show stanza breaks by indentation rather than by line breaks.

Advertisement

Text collated with *1870*, *1876*, *1892W*, *1904*, *1927*/I, *1972*, *1989*.

1989 includes the Advertisement in the editors' notes; in all other witnesses, the Advertisement prefaces the poems.

Paragraph 1   *Fragments,*] Fragments   *1870 1892W 1904 1927*/I *1972*
                 Public] public   *1870 1904 1927*/I *1972*
                 Notice.] notice.   *1870 1904 1927*/I *1972*
                 and] and,   *1870*
                 genius,] genius   *1870*
                 had] has   *1876 1892W 1904 1972*
                 phrenzy] frenzy   *1870 1892W 1904 1972 1989*
Paragraph 2   *Public*] public   *1870 1904 1972*
                 Poems,] poems,   *1870 1904 1972*
                 possession,] possession   *1870 1904 1927*/I *1972*
                 arrangement;] arrangement: *1870*

"Ambition, power, and avarice, now have hurl'd"

Text collated with *1876*, *1892W*, *1904*, *1927*/I, *1972*, *1989*. This poem is omitted from *1870*. The following editions do not give quotation marks at the beginnings of lines 12–20: *1892W*, *1904*, *1972*, *1989*.

Title.   *Untitled*] WAR   *1892W 1904 1972*
              [WAR]   *1927*/I
1   hurl'd] hurled   *1892W 1904 1927*/I *1972 1989*
3   lie,] lie!   *1892W*

4   thro'] through   *1892W 1904 1927/I 1972 1989*
    sky;] sky!   *1892W*
6   stage:] stage.   *1892W*
7   groan, an] groan—an   *1892W*
    anguish'd] anguished   *1892W 1904 1972 1989*
10 speak—] speak:—   *1892W*
11 "Oh] "O   *1892W*
    children—Monarch] children! Monarch,   *1892W*
                       children—Monarch,   *1989*
16 dull'd] dulled   *1892W 1904 1927/I 1972 1989*
17 moan,] moan;   *1892W*
18 anguish'd] anguished   *1892W 1904 1927/I 1972 1989*
21 reclin'd] reclined   *1892W 1904 1927/I 1972 1989*
23 mankind] mankind,   *1892W 1989*
26 Snatch'd] Snatched   *1892W 1904 1927/I 1972 1989*
29 thine,] Thine,   *1904 1927/I 1972*
31 thy] Thy   *1904 1972*
33 Form'd] Formed   *1892W 1904 1972 1989*
    approv'd?—it] approved?—it   *1892W 1904 1972 1989*
34 me] me,   *1904 1972 1989*
    warp'd] warped   *1892W 1904 1927/I 1972 1989*
35 not—he] not—He   *1904 1927/I 1972*
36 triumph'd] triumphed   *1892W 1904 1972 1989*
    hell—] hell.   *1892W*
50 all.] all,—   *1892W*
       all,   *1972 1989*
51 Swell'd] Swelled   *1892W 1904 1972 1989*
52 unmov'd] unmoved   *1892W 1904 1972 1989*
    away.] away,   *1892W 1989*
56 clamours] clamors   *1892W*
57 pleas'd] pleased   *1892W 1904 1972 1989*
58 smile—] smile.   *1892W*
62 ensanguin'd] ensanguined   *1892W 1904 1972 1989*
    brand.] brand   *1927/I*
63 Oh!] O   *1892W*
    peace,] Peace,   *1892W 1904 1972 1989*
    for ever] forever   *1892W*
    gone,] gone?   *1892W*
64 for ever] forever   *1892W*
67 Alas] Alas,   *1904 1972*
69 War,] War   *1892W*
    Woe,] Woe   *1892W*
    Terror,] Terror   *1892W*

71 Then] Then, *1892W*
   ensanguin'd] ensanguined *1892W 1904 1972 1989*
72 hell] Hell *1904 1927/I 1972*
   death.] Death. *1904 1927/I 1972*
73 blood-stain'd] blood-stained *1892W 1904 1972 1989*
   car,] car; *1892W*
75 destruction] Destruction *1904 1972*
   career,] career; *1892W*
77 ruin'd] ruined *1892W 1904 1972 1989*
   smoaking] smoking *1892W 1904 1927/I 1972 1989*
   tell,] tell *1989*
78 hell.] Hell. *1904 1972*
79 It] "It *1892W 1904 1927/I 1972 1989*
   work!] work!" *1892W 1904 1927/I 1972 1989*
   repeat,] repeat. *1989*
80 Shakes] "Shakes *1892W 1904 (1970 reads:* Shakes)
83 "It] It *1892W*
   Monarch;"] Monarch." *1892W*
   now] Now *1892W*
84 fainter] fainter, *1876 1904 1972*
   around,] around; *1892W*
86 heaven,] Heaven, *1904 1972*
   hell,] Hell, *1904 1972*
88 innocence,] innocence *1892W*

Fragment. Supposed to be an Epithalamium of Francis Ravaillac and Charlotte Cordé

Text collated with *1870, 1876, 1892W, 1904, 1927/I, 1972, 1989.*

Two editions—*1870* and *1892W*—do not give quotation marks at the beginning of lines 67–68 or in lines 82–90 and 91–102. Three editions—*1904, 1972,* and *1989*—provide quotation marks at line 68 and at the opening and closing of the two speeches in lines 82, 90, 91, and 102.

Title. . . . CORDÉ.] . . . CORDAY. *1870 1892W 1904 1972*
Stanza marker. *none*] 1. *1870*
1 now—athwart] now. Athwart *1870*
  air,] air *1870 1892W*
3 glare,] glare,— *1870*
4 shews] shows *1870 1892W 1904 1972 1989*
  stanza break added *1904 1972*
5 ponder'd] pondered *1870 1892W 1904 1972 1989*

6   ponder'd] pondered   *1870 1892W 1904 1972 1989*
    Kings;] kings;   *1870 1892W*
9   brings.] brings   *1927/I*
Stanza marker.   *none*] II.   *1870*
10 yell—it] yell! It   *1870*
    knell,] knell   *1870*
12 swell,] swell   *1870 1892W*
14 death's] Death's   *1870*
15 shore;] shore: *1870*
18 sleep] sleep,   *1870*
    lines 18 and 19 run together   *1870*
19 That] that   *1870*
21 soul,] soul;   *1870*
    lines 21 and 22 run together   *1870*
22 And] and   *1870*
    control,] control   *1870 1892W 1989*
Stanza marker.   *none*] III.   *1870*
24 Methought] Methought,   *1870 1972*
    enthron'd] enthroned   *1870 1892W 1904 1972 1989*
25 'mid] mid   *1892W 1904 1927/I 1972 1989*
    light;] light,   *1870 1892W 1972 1989*
26 form] form,   *1870*
    æther] ether,   *1870*
        ether   *1892W 1989*
27 spurn'd] spurned   *1870 1892W 1904 1972 1989*
28 ravish'd] ravished   *1870 1892W 1904 1972 1989*
    ears,] ears!   *1870*
30 spheres,] spheres—   *1870*
31 by,] by—   *1870*
32 æthereal] etherial   *1870 1989*
        ethereal   *1892W*
34 Sylph] sylph   *1870*
37 Enthron'd] Enthroned   *1870 1892W 1904 1972 1989*
38 Strew'd] Strewed   *1870 1892W 1904 1972 1989*
43 roll'd] rolled   *1870 1892W 1904 1972 1989*
    between;] between: *1870*
46 death's] Death's   *1870*
    die,] die;   *1870*
47 nature's] Nature's   *1870 1892W 1904 1972*
    decay—] decay: *1870*
        decay.   *1892W*
48 tie] tie,   *1972*

49 clay,] clay   *1870*
51 Yes] Yes,   *1870 1892W 1904 1972 1989*
52 heart-strings] heartstrings   *1892W*
   breast,] breast;   *1870 1892W*
53 gore,] gore   *1870 1892W 1989*
54 rest;] rest:—   *1870*
55 lov'd] loved   *1870 1892W 1904 1972 1989*
58 mock,] mock   *1870*
   smiles,] smiles   *1870*
59 'mid] mid   *1892W 1904 1927/I 1972 1989*
61 shades.] shades!   *1870*
64 plain;] plain—   *1870 1892W*
65 hell.] hell:—   *1870*
        hell;   *1892W*
        Hell.   *1904 1972*
66 "Welcome] "Welcome,   *1870 1892W 1904 1927/I 1972*
   thou] ye   *1904 1972 1989*
   despots] despots,   *1870 1892W 1904 1972 1989*
   domain,] domain!   *1870 1892W*
          domain;   *1989*
67 anguish'd] anguished   *1870 1892W 1904 1972 1989*
68 well."] well!"   *1870*
Stanza marker.   *none*] IV.   *1870*
69 Hark! to those notes, how sweet, how thrilling sweet] Hark to those notes! How sweet, how thrilling sweet,   *1870*
70 angels'] angels   *1876 1892W*
   feet.] feet!   *1870*
Stanza marker.   *none*] V.   *1870*
71 Oh] Oh!   *1870*
        Oh,   *1892W*
72 bed.] bed!   *1870*
73 Oh haste—hark!] Oh! haste!... Hark,   *1870*
             Oh, haste—hark!   *1892W*
   hark!—they're] hark!... They're   *1870*
   gone.] gone!   *1870*
        gone.'   *1989*
Stanza marker.   *none*] VI.   *1870*
74 STAY] Stay,   *1870 1892W 1904 1972*
        STAY,   *1927/I*
        Stay   *1989*
75 erasing,] erasing!   *1870*
        erasing;   *1892W*

Historical Collations for Pages 95–97

76   Stay] Stay,   *1870 1892W*
77   pleasing.] pleasing!   *1870 1892W*
     stanza break] *omitted*   *1972*
78   And] And,   *1870*
     near,] near   *1870*
81   ice-drop] icedrop   *1870*
Stanza marker.   *none*] VII.   *1870*
82   angel] angel,   *1870 1904 1927/I 1972 1989*
     stay,] stay!   *1870*
83   away;] away!   *1870*
84   on, suck on,] on, suck on!   *1870*
86   soul.] soul!   *1870*
87   kiss,] kiss—   *1870*
88   bliss,] bliss!   *1870*
89   breath,] breath!   *1870*
90   death."] death.   *1870 1892W*
Stanza marker.   *none*] VIII.   *1870*
91   "Oh!] Oh   *1870*
     yes] yes!   *1870*
          yes,   *1892W 1989*
92   form;] form.   *1870*
94   warm.] warm!   *1870*
          warm   *1927/I 1972*
          warm,   *1970*
96   thee.] thee;   *1870 1892W 1904 1927/I 1972*
101 lye] lie   *1870 1892W 1904 1972 1989*
102 long,] long   *1870*
     bliss."] bliss.   *1870 1892W*
     rule added below this line   *1892W*
Stanza marker.   *none*] IX.   *1870*
103 Spirits!] Spirits,   *1870*
106 sigh;] sigh,   *1870*
109 Bu t] But   *omnia*
     wa t] what   *omnia*
     revenge's] Revenge's   *1870*
     ea r] ear   *omnia*
112 knell.] knell!   *1870*
Stanza marker.   *none*] X.   *1870*
113 I wake—'tis] I wake! . . .'Tis   *1870*
     o'er.] o'er!   *1870*
          over.   *1904 1972*
          over . . .   *1927/I*
          o'er . . .   *1989*

Despair

Text collated with *1870, 1876, 1892W, 1904, 1927/I, 1972, 1989.*

Stanza marker. *none*] I. *1870*
1   can'st] canst   *1870 1892W 1904 1972 1989*
3   flow'rets,] flowerets,   *1870 1892W*
4   'Mid] Mid   *1892W 1904 1927/I 1972 1989*
5   you] you,   *1870*
7   hill,] hill?   *1870*
8   And,] And   *1870*
    sky,] sky   *1870*
Stanza marker. *none*] II. *1870*
10   zephyr's] Zephyr's   *1870*
    wing,] wing!   *1870*
        wing—   *1892W*
11   sky;] sky!   *1870*
12   touch'd] touched   *1870 1892W 1904 1972 1989*
    string—] string!   *1870*
13   die,] die,—   *1870*
        die.   *1892W 1904 1972*
        die;   *1989*
14   agony.] agony;   *1892W*
15   Now—now] Now, now,   *1870*
    swells—again] swells! again   *1870*
16   melody.] melody: *1870*
        melody;   *1892W*
18   bitterer,] bitterer   *1870*
    tide,] tide   *1870*
    flow.] flow!   *1870*
    stanza break] *omitted*   *1927/I*
Stanza marker. *none*] III. *1870*
19   Arise] Arise,   *1870 1892W*
20   aërial] aëreal   *1904 1927/I 1972*
    song,] song!   *1870*
22   tempest's] tempests   *1876*
    along.] along!   *1870*
23   forked] forkèd   *1870 1892W 1904 1972 1989*
24   cloud-form'd] cloud-formed   *1870 1892W 1904 1972 1989*
    roar;] roar,   *1870*
25   whirlwind—and] whirlwind, and   *1870*
26   shore,] shore!   *1870*
        shore,—   *1892W 1904 1927/I 1972*

27   life] life,   *1870*
     more.] more!   *1870 1892W*
Stanza marker.   *none*] IV.   *1870*
28   Yes!] Yes,   *1870*
     dead;] dead.   *1870*
29   fate] Fate,   *1870 1904 1972*
          fate,   *1892W 1989*
          Fate   *1927/*I
     obey,] obey: *1870*
          obey!   *1892W*
30   peace,] peace   *1870*
     joy,] joy   *1870*
31   power,] Power,   *1870*
     away.] away,   *1876*
32   ruin'd] ruined   *1870 1892W 1904 1972 1989*
     hell,] Hell,   *1904 1972*
33   triumph,] triumph   *1870*
34   And] And,   *1870 1892W*
     heart-strings] heartstrings   *1870 1892W*
36   power] Power   *1870*
     vain.] vain!   *1870*

Fragment ("Yes! all is past—swift time has fled away")

Text collated with *1870, 1876, 1892W, 1904, 1927/*I, *1972, 1989*.
   The following editions do not give quotation marks at the beginning of lines 21–22, 24–27, and 29–31: *1870, 1892W, 1904, 1972, 1989*.

Stanza marker.   *none*] I.   *1870*
1   Y<small>ES</small>!] Y<small>ES</small>,   *1870*
    past—swift] past! swift   *1870*
2   mind;] mind.   *1870 1892W*
4   dead, and] dead,—and   *1870*
    behind.] behind!   *1870*
5   Oh!] O   *1870*
    fate,] Fate!   *1870*
         Fate,   *1904 1972*
    spell,] spell!   *1870*
6   be,] be,—   *1870*
7   hell;] hell: *1870*
         Hell;   *1904 1972*
8   Ah! no,] Ah no!   *1870*

heaven] Heaven   *1904 1972*
me;] me: *1870*
9   fate,] Fate,   *1870 1904 1972*
seal'd] sealed   *1870 1892W 1904 1972 1989*
Stanza marker.   *none*] II.   *1870*
10   surge,] surge;   *1870 1892W*
11   sigh'd] sighed   *1870 1892W 1904 1972 1989*
woes,] woes: *1870*
         woes;   *1892W*
14   madden'd] maddened   *1870 1892W 1904 1927/I 1972 1989*
main,] main,—   *1870*
15   glare;] glare.   *1870*
16   Still'd] Stilled   *1870 1892W 1904 1972 1989*
strain,] strain   *1870 1892W 1989*
17   Swell'd] Swelled   *1870 1892W 1904 1972 1989*
'mid] mid   *1904 1972 1989*
air,] air:—   *1870*
Stanza marker.   *none*] III.   *1870*
19   maniac, like] maniac,—like   *1870*
         maniac—like   *1892W 1904 1927/I 1972 1989*
me,] me.   *1870*
         me;   *1892W*
20   said—"Poor] said: "Poor   *1870*
victim] victim,   *1870 1892W 1904 1972 1989*
22   home?"] home?   *1876*
23   "Ah] "Ah!   *1870*
         "Ah,   *1892W 1989*
sleeps:] sleeps!   *1870*
cold] Cold   *1870*
25   madden'd] maddened   *1870 1892W 1904 1972 1989*
26   sweep] sleep   *1870*
wilder'd] wildered   *1870 1892W 1904 1972 1989*
wave;] wave: *1870*
Stanza marker.   *none*] IV.   *1870*
28   "Ah! no,] "Ah no!   *1870*
tear,] tear: *1870*
29   more;] more.   *1870*

The Spectral Horseman

Text collated with *1870, 1876, 1892W, 1904, 1927/*I, *1972, 1989.*

1   fancy's] Fancy's   *1904 1972*
5   It is the] It is not the   *1870*
         Is it the   *1989*
6   that] that,   *1870 1892W*
    sin,] sin   *1989*
8   Wing'd] Winged   *1870 1892W 1904 1972 1989*
9   plain.] plain?   *1989*
10 hell] Hell   *1904 1972*
11 night;] night: *1876 1904 1927/*I *1972*
13 gore;] gore.   *1870*
14 aye] aye,   *1870*
    end,] end   *1892W*
15 storm] storm;   *1870*
         storm,   *1892W 1904 1972 1989*
16 aye] aye,   *1870*
18 Awakens] Awakens,   *1870*
19 man,] man   *1870*
22 chill,] chill;   *1870 1892W*
23 soul.] soul;   *1870*
24 death-demon's] Death-demon's   *1870*
         death-daemon's   *1904 1972*
26 hell.] Hell.   *1904 1972*
27 form,] form.   *1870*
28 sprite;] sprite: *1870*
29 mountain,] mountain   *1870*
31 *his*] his   *1870*
    Nithona] Nithona,   *1904 1927/*I *1972*
32 winter] Winter   *1870*
34 Yet] Yet,   *1870*
35 Inisfallen,] Inisfallen,—   *1870*
36 'mid] mid   *1904 1972 1989*
39 heaven] Heaven   *1870 1904 1972*
40 fear,] fear   *1870*
41 figure,] figure;   *1870 1892W*
42 wildered] 'wildered   *1904 1972*
    peasant] peasant,   *1892W 1904 1972*
    by,] by   *1870 1989*
43 thro'] through   *1870 1892W 1904 1972 1989*
    form:] form;   *1892W*

44   though] tho'   1927/I
47   who] who,   1870 1892W 1904 1927/I 1972
      chain'd] chained   1870 1892W 1904 1927/I 1972 1989
50   wreathes] wreaths   1870 1892W 1904 1927/I 1972 1989
      demons;] daemons;   1904 1972
51   eye-balls,] eyeballs,—   1870
                  eyeballs,   1892W 1904 1972 1989
52   wilder'd] wildered   1870 1892W 1927/I 1989
                  'wildered   1904 1972
      die!] die.   1870
55   vain;] vain.   1870
59   gigantic * *] gigantic . . . ;   1870
                  gigantic . . .   1892W 1904 1972

Melody to a Scene of Former Times

Text collated with *1870, 1876, 1892W, 1904, 1927/I, 1970, 1972, 1989*.

The following editions do not give quotation marks at the beginning of lines 43 and 44: *1870, 1892W, 1927/I, 1972, 1989*.

1   for ever] forever   1892W 1904 1927/I 1972
      gone,] gone—   1870
2   For ever,] Forever,   1892W 1904 1927/I 1972
4   all,] all   1870
5   given,] given?   1870
6   heaven,] Heaven,   1904 1972
7   hell?] Hell?   1904 1972
8   thee] thee,   1870 1892W 1904 1927/I 1972 1989
      dear!] dear: 1870
9   Ah! no,] Ah no!   1870
                  Ah, no!   1904 1972
10   brain] brain,   1870 1892W 1904 1972
11   slumb'ring] slumbering   1870 1892W
12   heaven] Heaven   1870 1904 1972
13   heaven] Heaven   1870 1904 1972
      still,] still—   1870
                  still,—   1892W
14   sick'ning] sickening   1870 1892W
      thrill,] thrill   1870
15   judgment] judgement   1904 1927/I 1972
16   memory;] memory,—   1870
18   blest] blessed   1870
19   ecstacy] ecstasy   1870 1904 1972 1989

20 knew,] knew   *1972*
21 away.] away!   *1870*
22 liv'd] lived   *1870 1892W 1904 1972 1989*
    before,] before! . . .   *1870*
23 more.] more!   *1870*
24 And] And,   *1870*
25 thee] thee,   *1870 1892W 1904 1972*
    love; ah] love,—ah   *1870*
              love; ah,   *1904 1972*
26 anguish'd] anguished   *1870 1892W 1904 1972 1989*
28 gone,] gone:—   *1870*
              gone,—   *1892W*
29 thee] thee,   *1870 1892W 1904 1972*
    dearest] dearest,   *1870 1892W 1904 1972*
30 night—what] night: what   *1870*
33 by.] by,   *1892W*
34 Oh!] O   *1870*
    hours] hours,   *1870 1892W 1904 1972*
    fly!] fly!—   *1870*
35 lengthen'd] lengthened   *1870 1892W 1904 1972 1989*
36 tomb;] tomb: *1870*
37 lowering] louring   *1870*
41 tone.] tone:—   *1870*
42 say,] say: *1870*
    "confide] "Confide   *1870 1904 1972 1989*
45 awak'ning] awakening   *1870 1892W*
46 enanguish'd] enanguished   *1870 1892W 1904 1972 1989*
47 fiercer,] fiercer   *1870*
    FINIS.] *omitted*   *1892W 1927/I 1970 1972 1989*
              [End of Margaret Nicholson.]   *1870*
              [End of Posthumous Fragments of Margaret Nicholson]   *1904*

Poems from
St. Irvyne; or, The Rosicrucian

"'T was dead of the night, when I sat in my dwelling"

Text collated with *1847, 1870, 1876, 1892W, 1904, 1913, 1927*/III, *1927*/V, *1972, 1989*.

Editors have inserted asterisks (*1876* and *1989*) or periods (*1892W, 1904, 1927*/III, and *1972*) at the poem's conclusion.

Title.   *none*] SONG.   *1847 1913*
        VICTORIA.   *1870*
        NUMBER 1.   *1876*
        I | VICTORIA   *1892W 1927*/III
        I.—VICTORIA   *1904 1972*
        Fragment, or the Triumph of Conscience   *1989*
        "1810" *given on line after title*   *1927*/III

Stanza marker.   *none*] I.   *1870 1876 1892W 1904 1927*/III *1972*
1 'T was] 'Twas   *1847 1870 1876 1892W 1904 1913 1927*/III *1927*/V *1972 1989*
   night,] night   *1870*
   dwelling;] dwelling   *1847 1913*
2 low;] low,   *1847 1913*
3 swelling,] swelling;   *1870*
4 yelling,—] yelling,   *1847 1913*
        yelling—   *1870*
5 presag'd] presaged   *1847 1870 1892W 1904 1913 1927*/III *1927*/V *1972 1989*
   woe.] woe: *1847 1913*

Stanza marker.   *none*] II.   *1870 1876 1892W 1904 1927*/III *1972*
6 'T was] 'Twas   *1847 1870 1876 1892W 1904 1913 1927*/III *1927*/V *1972 1989*
   started!—the] started! the   *1847 1913*
        started! The   *1870*
   howling,] howling;   *1870*
7 seen,] seen   *1847 1870 1892W 1913*
   lightning,] lightning   *1847 1870 1892W 1913*

which] that   *1870*
danc'd] danced   *1847 1870 1892W 1904 1913 1927*/III *1972 1989*
sky;] sky.   *1847 1913*
8   me,] me   *1870 1892W*
rolling,] rolling;   *1870*
9   low,] low   *1847 1870 1913*
murmurs,] murmurs   *1847 1870 1892W 1913 1989*
Stanza marker.   *none*] III.   *1870 1876 1892W 1904 1927*/III *1972*
10   sank] sunk   *1847 1913*
me—unheeded] me, unheeded   *1847 1913*
me;—unheeded   *1870*
11   clouds,] clouds   *1847 1870 1892W 1913 1989*
mountain-tops,] mountain tops   *1847*
mountain-tops   *1870 1892W 1913 1927*/III *1989*
broke;—] broke,   *1847 1913*
broke;   *1870 1892W*
broke—   *1927*/V
12   thunder-peal] thunder peal   *1847*
crash'd] crashed   *1847 1870 1892W 1904 1913 1972 1989*
ear—] ear,   *1847 1913*
ear.   *1870*
13   fear;] fear: *1870*
fear,   *1989*
14   low,] low   *1870*
Stanza marker.   *none*] IV.   *1870 1876 1892W 1904 1927*/III *1972*
15   'T was] 'Twas   *omnia*
that] that,   *1870 1892W 1913*
form] form,   *1847*
on] in   *1847 1913*
upholding,] upfolding,   *1847 1913*
16   murder'd] murdered   *1847 1870 1892W 1904 1913 1972 1989*
strode;] strode,   *1847 1913*
strode: *1870*
17   hand,] hand   *1847 1870 1892W 1913*
holding,] holding   *1847*
holding: *1870*
holding;   *1892W*
18   advanc'd] advanced   *1847 1870 1892W 1904 1913 1927*/V *1972 1989*
lonesome] lonely   *1847*
abode.] abode   *1927*/III
Stanza marker.   *stanza break omitted*   *1847 1927*/V
none] v.   *1870 1876 1892W 1904 1927*/III *1972*

19 call'd] called   *1847 1870 1892W 1904 1913 1972 1989*
    bear] hear   *1870*
    me——] me.—   *1847 1913*
            me | ... | 1808.   *1870*
            me—   *1892W 1904 1927/*III *1972 1989*

"Ghosts of the dead! have I not heard your yelling"

Text collated with *1847, 1870, 1876, 1892W, 1904, 1913, 1927/*III, *1927/*V, *1972, 1989.*

Title.   *none*] SONG.   *1847 1913*
            THE FATHER'S SPECTRE.   *1870*
            NUMBER 2.   *1876*
            II | "ON THE DARK HEIGHT OF JURA"   *1892W*
            II.—'ON THE DARK HEIGHT OF JURA'   *1904 1972*
            II | ON THE DARK HEIGHT OF JURA   *1927/*III
            'Ghosts of the dead!'   *1989*
Stanza marker.   *none*] I.   *1870 1876 1892W 1904 1927/*III *1972*
1 yelling] yelling,   *1847 1913*
2 Rise] Ride   *1847*
3 ether] aether   *1904 1972*
   is] was   *1847 1913*
4 thunder-peal] thunder-peals   *1847 1913*
   past?] past.   *1847 1913*
            passed?   *1870 1892W 1904 1972*
Stanza marker.   *none*] II.   *1870 1876 1892W 1904 1927/*III *1972*
5 Jura,] Jura   *1870*
7 brav'd] braved   *1847 1870 1892W 1904 1913 1927/*V *1972 1989*
8 me,] me   *1847 1913*
   thought,] thought   *1847 1913*
   echo'd] echoed   *1847 1870 1892W 1904 1913 1972 1989*
Stanza marker.   *none*] III.   *1870 1876 1892W 1904 1927/*III *1972*
9 now,] now   *1847 1913*
10 father!] Father!   *1847 1913*
   ear;] ear.   *1847 1870 1913*
11 air] air,   *1847 1913*
12 elements'] element's   *1847 1913*
Stanza marker.   *none*] IV.   *1870 1876 1892W 1904 1927/*III *1972*
13 mountain] mountain,   *1847 1913*
14 dead;] dead,   *1847 1913 1989*
            dead,—   *1870 1892W*
            dead: *1972*

15   fountain,] fountain,—   *1870*
16   a] the   *1927*/III
      vapour] vapor   *1892W*
Dateline. | 1809. *added*   *1870*

Ballad ("The death-bell beats!— ")

Text collated with *1847, 1870, 1876, 1892W, 1904, 1913, 1927*/III, *1927*/V, *1972, 1989*.

Title.   BALLAD.] SISTER ROSA.   *1870*
         NUMBER 3.—BALLAD.   *1876*
         III | SISTER ROSA: A BALLAD   *1892W 1927*/V
         III.—Sister Rosa: A Ballad   *1904 1972*
         III | SISTER ROSA | A BALLAD   *1927*/III
         Ballad: 'The death-bell beats!'   *1989*
Stanza marker.   I.] *omitted*   *1847 1913*
                 1.   *1989*
1   beats!—] beats,   *1847 1913*
     no line break; line 2 runs into line 1   *1870*
2   The] the   *1870*
3   knell;] knell: *1870*
4   monk] Monk   *1870 1904 1913 1927*/III *1972 1989*
     now] now,   *1972*
     no line break; line 5 runs into line 4   *1870*
5   Wraps] wraps   *1870*
Stanza marker.   II.] *omitted*   *1847 1913*
                 2.   *1989*
7   death] Death   *1870*
     no line break; line 8 runs into line 7   *1870*
8   Chills] chills   *1870*
     breath,] breath   *1870 1989*
9   lay] lay,   *1847 1892W*
10   *no line break; line 11 runs into line 10*   *1870*
11   As] as   *1870*
12   day.] day;   *1870*
13   *no line break; line 14 runs into line 13*   *1870*
14   When] when   *1870*
     fates] Fates   *1847 1870 1913*
Stanza marker.   III.] *omitted*   *1847 1913*
                 3.   *1989*

16   past;] past,   *1847*
         past: *1870*
         past   *1913*
     no line break; line 17 runs into line 16   1870
17   And] and   *1870*
     last] last,   *1847*
18   monk's] Monk's   *1870 1904 1913 1927/*III *1972 1989*
     brain.] brain;   *1847 1892W 1913*
19   tears,] tears   *1847 1870 1892W 1989*
     eyes,] eyes   *1847 1870 1892W 1989*
     gush'd] gushed   *1870 1892W 1904 1972 1989*
     fast;] fast,   *1847 1870 1989*
20   *stanza break*] *omitted   1847*
Stanza marker.   IV.] *omitted   1847 1913*
             4.   *1989*
21   dash'd] dashed   *1847 1870 1892W 1904 1913 1972 1989*
     floor,] floor   *1870 1927/*V
22   ear.] ear—   *1847 1913*
         ear,—   *1892W*
         ear.—   *1904 1972*
         ear,   *1927/*V *1989*
23   Delight] "Delight   *1847 1870 1892W 1904 1913 1927/*III *1972*
             1989
     no line break; line 24 runs into line 23   1847 1870 1913
24   For] for   *1847 1870 1913*
     evermore;] evermore,   *1847 1913*
             evermore—   *1870*
             ever more;   *1927/*III
25   But] But,   *1870*
     me] me,   *1870*
     fear.] fear."   *1847 1892W 1904 1913 1927/*III *1972 1989*
         fear!"   *1870*
Stanza marker.   v.] *omitted   1847 1913*
             5.   *1989*
26   roll'd,] rolled,   *1847 1892W 1904 1913 1972 1989*
         rolled   *1870*
     no line break; line 27 runs into line 26   1870
27   When] when   *1870*
     toll'd,] tolled,   *1847 1870 1892W 1904 1913 1972 1989*
28   rag'd] raged   *1847 1870 1892W 1904 1913 1927/*V *1972 1989*
     woe.] woe;   *1847 1892W 1913*
         woe,   *1870*

29   stamp'd] stamped   *1847 1870 1892W 1904 1913 1972 1989*
     ground,—] ground,   *1847 1913*
               ground;   *1870*
     no line break; line 30 runs into line 29   *1870*
30   But] but,   *1870*
         But,   *1892W*
     ceas'd] ceased   *1847 1870 1892W 1904 1913 1927/V 1972 1989*
               ceasèd   *1927/III*
     sound,] sound   *1927/V*
31   began] begun   *1847 1913*
Stanza marker. VI.] *omitted*   *1847 1913*
               V.   *1972*
               6.   *1989*
32   *no line break; line 33 runs into line 32*   *1870*
33   Chill'd] Chilled   *1847 1892W 1904 1913 1972 1989*
               chilled   *1870*
     care,] care;   *1870*
34   sate] sat   *1927/V 1989*
     still;] still: *1847 1913*
               still   *1870*
35   through] thro'   *1847 1913*
     air,] air   *1927/V*
36   moon-beam] moonbeam   *1847 1870 1892W 1904 1913 1927/III*
               1927/V 1972 1989
     hill.] *omitted*   *1847*
Stanza marker. VII.] *omitted*   *1847 1913*
               7.   *1989*
37   cell:—] cell,   *1847 1870 1913*
               cell,—   *1892W*
     no line break; line 38 runs into line 37   *1870*
38   And] and   *1870*
39   delights] delights,   *1870*
     agoniz'd] agonised   *1847 1913*
               agonized   *1870 1892W 1904 1927/V 1972 1989*
     pain.] pain,   *1847 1876 1904 1913 1972*
               pain;   *1870 1892W*
40   pray'd] prayed   *1847 1870 1892W 1904 1913 1972 1989*
     spell,] spell   *1870 1989*
41   for] *omitted*   *1847 1913*
     for ever] forever   *1892W*
Stanza marker. VIII.] *omitted*   *1847 1913*
               8.   *1989*
42   pray'r] prayer   *1847 1870 1892W 1913 1927/V*

        on] to   *1847*
43   abbey] Abbey   *1927*/III
     abbey bell] abbey-bell   *1870*
     One:] one;   *1847 1892W 1913*
            one.   *1870*
44   sound:] sound,   *1847 1913*
            sound;   *1870 1892W*
45   A voice hollow and] And a voice hollow,   *1847*
                        And a voice—hollow,   *1870*
     horrible murmur'd] horrible, murmured   *1847*
                         horrible—murmured   *1870*
     murmur'd] murmured   *1892W 1904 1913 1972 1989*
     around—] around,   *1847 1913*
            around   *1870*
            around,—   *1927*/V
46   done!"] done."   *1847*
Stanza marker. IX.] *omitted*   *1847 1913*
                9.   *1989*
47   night;] night—   *1870*
     no line break; line 48 runs into line 47   *1870*
48   The] the   *1870*
     moon-beam] moonbeam   *1847 1870 1892W 1904 1913 1927*/III
                              1927/V *1972 1989*
49   Wax'd] Waxed   *1847 1870 1892W 1904 1913 1972 1989*
50   And,] And   *1847 1870 1892W 1913*
     hill,] hill   *1847 1870 1892W 1913*
     no line break; line 51 runs into line 50   *1870*
51   Went] went   *1870*
     still,—] shrill—   *1847*
            still: *1870*
            still—   *1913*
52   "Monk!] "Monk,   *1870*
     die."] die!"   *1870*
Stanza marker. X.] *omitted*   *1847 1913*
                10.   *1989*
53   *no line break; line 54 runs into line 53*   *1870*
54   And] and   *1870*
56   *no line break; line 57 runs into line 56*   *1870*
57   O'er] o'er   *1870*
     grew;] grew,   *1870*
58   shudder'd] shuddered   *1847 1870 1892W 1904 1913 1972 1989*
Stanza marker. XI.] *omitted*   *1847 1913*
                11.   *1989*

Historical Collations for Pages 111–112   393

59   *no line break; line 60 runs into line 59*   *1870*
60   Rav'd] Raved   *1847 1892W 1904 1913 1927/*V *1972 1989*
           raved   *1870*
61   gloom:] gloom;   *1847 1870 1913*
62   *no line break; line 63 runs into line 62*   *1870*
63   To] to   *1870*
     wind,] wind   *1870 1989*
     high,] high   *1870 1989*
64   search'd] searched   *1870 1892W 1904 1927/*V *1972 1989*
Stanza marker. xii.] *omitted*   *1847 1913*
               12.   *1989*
65   forms,] forms   *1847 1913*
          the forms   *1870*
     high,] high   *1847 1870 1913*
     no line break; line 66 runs into line 65   *1870*
66   Seem'd] seemed   *1870*
           Seemed   *1892W 1904 1972 1989*
67   blast:] blast;   *1847 1870 1913*
           blast,—   *1892W*
68   *no line break; line 69 runs into line 68*   *1870*
69   Half-seen] half-seen   *1870*
     fall,] fall   *1870 1927/*III
70   As] And   *1847*
         As,   *1892W*
     enhorror'd] enhorrored   *1870 1904 1972 1989*
             enhorrored,   *1892W*
     pass'd.] passed.   *1870 1892W 1904 1972 1989*
Stanza marker. xiii.] *omitted*   *1847 1913*
               13.   *1989*
71   storm-fiend's] storm fiends   *1847*
             storm-fiends   *1870 1892W 1904 1927/*III *1972 1989*
     no line break; line 72 runs into line 71   *1870*
72   O'er] o'er   *1870*
     new-made] new made   *1847 1913*
73   shadows,] shadows   *1847 1870 1892W 1904 1927/*III *1972 1989*
     around.] around,   *1847 1913*
          around;—   *1892W*
74   Monk] monk   *1847*
     call'd] called   *1870 1892W 1904 1972 1989*
75   And,] And   *1847 1870 1913*
     horror,] horror   *1847 1870 1913*
Stanza marker. xiv.] *omitted*   *1847 1913*
               14.   *1989*

76 nerv'd] nerved   *1847 1870 1892W 1904 1913 1927/V 1972 1989*
   arm] arm,   *1847 1913*
   no line break; line 77 runs into line 76   *1870*
77 To] to   *1870*
78 asunder.] asunder;   *1870 1892W*
79 *no line break; line 80 runs into line 79*   *1870*
80 More] more   *1870*
   fell,] fell   *1989*
81 peal'd] pealed   *1870 1892W 1904 1972 1989*
Stanza marker. XV.] *omitted*   *1847 1913*
                15.   *1989*
82 laugh'd,] laugh'd   *1847*
            laughed   *1870 1892W*
            laughed,   *1904 1972 1989*
   joy,] joy   *1847 1870 1892W*
   throng,] throng   *1989*
83 Mix'd] Mixed   *1870 1892W 1904 1972 1989*
   dead:] dead;   *1847 1870 1892W 1913*
84 wings,] wings   *1870*
   along,] along   *1870*
Stanza marker. XVI.] *omitted*   *1847 1913*
                16.   *1989*
86 Nun] nun   *1847*
   rear'd,] reared,   *1870 1892W*
            reared   *1904 1972 1989*
87 dripp'd] dropped   *1870*
            dripped   *1892W 1904 1972 1989*
   hell.] hell;   *1870 1892W*
88 eyeballs] eye-balls   *1847 1913*
   appear'd,] appeared,   *1870 1892W 1904 1972 1989*
89 And] But   *1847 1913*
   Monk] monk   *1847*
   glar'd,] glared   *1870*
            glared,   *1892W 1904 1927/V 1972 1989*
Stanza marker. XVII.] *omitted*   *1847 1913*
                17.   *1989*
91 brain;] brain,   *1847 1870 1892W 1913*
92 nerv'd] nerved   *1870 1892W 1904 1927/V 1972 1989*
   fear.—] fear.   *1870*
            fear,—   *1892W*
93 never,] never   *1870*
   henceforth,] henceforth   *1870*
   again;] again: *1870*

Historical Collations for Pages 112–114   395

94 mine] my *1989*
    anguish'd] anguished   *1870 1892W 1904 1972 1989*
    pain.—] pain;   *1847 1913*
        pain: *1870*
        pain.   *1892W*
95 yawns,—we] yawns—we   *1847 1870 1913*
Stanza marker. XVIII.] *omitted*   *1847 1913*
        18.   *1989*
97 lone,] lone   *1892W*
    fell,] fell   *1892W*
98 shudder'd] shuddered   *1870 1892W 1904 1972 1989*
    ground;] ground,   *1847 1913*
        ground: *1870*
99 And] And,   *1870 1892W*
    And as] As   *1927*/III
100 answer'd] answered   *1870 1892W 1904 1972 1989*
    hell.] Hell!   *1847 1913*
        Hell.   *1870*
Dateline. | 1808. *added*   *1870*

Song ("How swiftly through heaven's wide expanse")

Text collated with *1847, 1870, 1876, 1892W, 1904, 1909, 1913Irv, 1913EFG, 1927*/III, *1927*/V, *1927*/VIII, *1964J, 1972, 1989*. Medwin *Life*, ed. Forman (*1913*) contains texts of all six poems from **St.Irv** ("How swiftly" on pp. 54–55, denoted here *1913Irv*). Forman printed for the first time the text of Shelley's letter to E. F. Graham dated 22 April 1810, containing the original lyric from which the version in **St.Irv** derives (pp. 452–54, denoted *1913EFG*).

    The two different versions of this poem, the one from **St.Irv** and the one from the 22 April 1810 letter from PBS to EFG (MS PMgn), have been presented by different editors in various fashions:

    Stanzas 1 through 4 are parallel in both letter and **St.Irv** versions.

    The **St.Irv** version has six stanzas: stanza 5 begins "Ah! why do dark'ning shades conceal," and stanza 6 begins "The keenness of the world hath torn."

    The letter version omits stanza 6 and inserts between stanzas 4 and 5 five additional stanzas (here designated A through E):

        A begins "For there a youth with darkened brow"
        B begins "O'er this torn soul, o'er this frail form"
        C begins "Ah! why do prating priests suppose"

D begins "Within me burns a raging Hell—"
E begins "No power of Earth, of Hell or Heaven"

Stanza 5 ends the letter version.

We publish the letter version in the "Ten Early Poems" section. See pages 412–15 for the collation of the letter version, including the additional stanzas A–E from *1909*, *1913EFG*, *1927/*III, *1927/*VIII, *1964J*, *1972*, *1989*.

We offer here a breakdown of the various editions according to the way they incorporate the different stanzas:

- 5, 6 (***St.Irv*** version): *1847*, *1870*, *1876*, *1892W*, *1904*, *1913Irv*, *1927/*V
- 5, 6 (then A, B, C, D, E renumbered and labeled "additional stanzas"): *1972*
- A, B, C, D, E, 5 (letter version): *1913EFG*, *1927/*VIII
- A, B, C, D, E, 5 (letter version) with 6 in a footnote: *1964J*, *1989*
- (A, B, C, D, E in brackets) and then 5, 6: *1927/*III

Stanzas A through E and 5 only were reprinted in the *Athenæum* (5 June 1909).

Title.   SONG.] ST IRVYNE'S TOWER.   *1870*
           NUMBER 4.—SONG.   *1876*
           IV | ST. IRVYNE'S TOWER   *1892W*
           IV.—ST. IRVYNE'S TOWER   *1904 1972*
           omitted   *1909 1913EFG 1927/*VIII *1964J*
           IV | SONG. ST. IRVYNE'S TOWER   *1927/*III
           SONG   *1927/*V
           'How swiftly through Heaven's wide expanse'   *1989*

Stanza marker.   *none*] I.   *1870 1876 1892W 1904 1927/*III *1972*

1 swiftly] softly   *1870*
   heaven's] Heaven's   *1847 1904 1913Irv 1913EFG 1927/*VIII *1964J 1972 1989*
2 day's] days   *1913EFG 1927/*VIII *1964J*
   colours] colors   *1892W 1913EFG 1964J*
   fade!] fade   *1913EFG 1927/*VIII *1964J*
       fade,   *1989*
4 tint] teint   *1913EFG 1927/*VIII *1964J*
   St.] St   *1870*
   Irvyne's] Iroyne's   *1847*
       Irvynes   *1913EFG 1927/*VIII *1964J*
   glade!] glade   *1913EFG 1927/*VIII *1964J*
       glade.   *1989*

Stanza marker.   *none*] II.   *1870 1876 1892W 1904 1927/*III *1972*

5 air,] air   *1847 1870 1913Irv 1913EFG 1927/*VIII *1964J 1972 1989*
6 borne] bourne   *1927/*VIII
     breeze;] breeze.   *1870*
          breeze,   *1913EFG 1927/*VIII *1964J*
7 scene!] scene,   *1913EFG 1927/*VIII *1964J 1989*
     scene! how] scene—how   *1870*
8 moonbeams] moonbeam's   *1913EFG 1964J 1989*
     trees!] trees   *1913EFG 1927/*VIII *1964J*
          trees.   *1989*
Stanza marker. *none*] III.   *1870 1876 1892W 1904 1927/*III *1972*
9 white,] white;   *1870*
        white   *1913EFG 1927/*VIII *1964J*
10 mournful] gloomy   *1847 1913Irv*
     owl;] owl,   *1847 1913Irv*
         owl   *1913EFG 1927/*VIII *1964J*
11 night,] night   *1847 1870 1892W 1913EFG 1927/*VIII *1964J 1989*
12 roll.] roll   *1913EFG 1927/*III *1927/*VIII *1964J*
Stanza marker. *none*] IV.   *1870 1876 1892W 1904 1927/*III *1972*
13 Irvyne's] Iroyne's   *1847*
        Irvyn's   *1927/*VIII
     tower,] tower   *1847 1870 1892W 1913Irv 1913EFG 1927/*VIII *1964J 1989*
14 silver moonbeam pours her] moonbeam pours its silver   *1913EFG 1927/*VIII *1964J 1989*
     ray;] ray   *1847*
        ray: *1870 1989*
15 gleams] gleam's   *1913EFG 1964J*
     bower,] tower,   *1847*
         bower   *1913EFG 1927/*VIII *1964J*
16 in] on   *1870 1927/*VIII *1989*
     spray.] spray   *1913EFG 1964J*
         spray,   *1989*
Stanza marker. *none*] V.   *1870 1876 1892W 1904 1972*
         follows stanzas A-E   *1909 1913EFG 1927/*VIII *1964J 1989*
            X   *1927/*III *stanzas v–ix are from letter version and are in brackets*
17 "Ah!] Ah!   *1870*
        Ah   *1909 1913EFG 1927/*VIII *1964J*
       'Ah,   *1989*
     dark'ning] darkening   *1847 1870 1892W 1909 1913Irv 1927/*V *1989*
           darkning   *1913EFG 1964J*

Song. ("How stern are the woes of the desolate mourner,")

Text collated with *1847, 1870, 1876, 1892W, 1904, 1913, 1927*/III, *1927*/V, *1927*/VIII, *1964J, 1972, 1989*.

Title.   SONG.] BEREAVEMENT.   *1870*
     NUMBER 5.—SONG.   *1876*
     V | BEREAVEMENT   *1892W 1927*/III
     V.—BEREAVEMENT   *1904 1972*
     omitted   *1927*/VIII *1964J*
     Song: 'How stern are the woes'   *1989*
Stanza marker.   *none*] 1.   *1876 1892W 1904 1927*/III *1972*
      1.   *1927*/VIII *1964J 1989*
1 mourner,] mourner   *1870 1964J 1989*
2 o'er] oer   *1964J*
  hallowed] hallowèd   *1870 1904 1927*/III *1972*
  bier,] bier   *1964J*
3 enanguish'd] ensanguined   *1847*
     enanguished   *1870 1892W 1904 1913 1927*/VIII *1964J*
     1972 1989
  scorner,] scorner.   *1927*/VIII
    scorner   *1964J 1989*
4 drops,] drops   *1847 1870 1892W 1913 1927*/VIII *1964J 1989*
  perfection's] Perfection's   *1847 1904 1913 1927*/VIII *1964J 1972*
    1989
  remembrance,] remembrance   *1847 1870 1892W 1913 1927*/VIII
    1964J 1989
  tear;] tear.   *1927*/VIII
    tear   *1964J*
  stanza break added   *1847*
5 cheek] cheeks   *1847 1870*
  streaming,] streaming   *1964J*
6 on] o'er   *1927*/VIII *1989*
    oer   *1964J*
  beaming,] beaming   *1964J*
7 Or,] Or   *1847 1913 1927*/VIII *1964J 1989*
  lull'd] lulled   *1847 1870 1892W 1904 1913 1927*/VIII *1964J 1972*
    1989
  a while,] awhile,   *1870 1904 1927*/III *1927*/V *1972*
    a time,   *1927*/VIII *1964J 1989*
  dreaming,] dreaming   *1927*/VIII *1964J 1989*
8 dear.] dear   *1964J*

Stanza marker. *none*] 11. *1876 1892W 1904 1927*/III *1972*
                            2. *1927*/VIII *1964J 1989*
9   Ah!] Oh!   *1927*/VIII *1964J 1989*
    grave,] grave   *1964J*
10 death?] death;   *1927*/V
                Death,   *1927*/VIII
                Death   *1964J*
                Death?   *1989*
11 awhile,] awhile   *1927*/VIII *1964J*
    victim,] victim!   *1847 1870 1913*
        victim   *1927*/VIII *1964J*
    and] &   *1964J*
    Heaven] heaven   *1847 1913*
    save] save,   *1927*/VIII
12 spirit,] spirit   *1847 1870 1892W 1913 1927*/VIII *1964J 1989*
    breath.] breath   *1964J*
13 points] points,   *1870*
    in] to   *1847 1927*/VIII
    bower,] bower   *1870 1964J 1989*
14 o'er] oe'r   *1964J*
    lower,] lour,   *1870*
            [lower,]   *1927*/VIII
            [lower]   *1964J*
            lower   *1989*
15 pleasure,] pleasure   *1927*/VIII *1964J*
    dower,] dower   *1964J*
16 When] Where   *1927*/VIII *1964J 1989*
    of] on   *1927*/VIII *1964J 1989*
    heath.] heath   *1964J*
Dateline. | 1808. *added*   *1870*

Song ("Ah! faint are her limbs, and her footstep is weary")

Text collated with *1847, 1870, 1876, 1892W, 1904, 1913, 1927*/III, *1927*/V, *1972, 1989*.

Title. SONG.] THE LAKE-STORM.   *1870*
            NUMBER 6.—SONG.   *1876*
            VI | THE DROWNED LOVER   *1892W 1927*/III
            VI.—THE DROWNED LOVER   *1904 1972*
            Song: 'Ah! faint are her limbs'   *1989*
Stanza marker.   1.] *omitted*   *1847 1870 1913*
                    1.   *1989*

1   Ah!] Oh!   *1847*
2   roam;] roam,   *1847 1913*
          roam: *1870*
7   kirtle,] kirtle: *1870*
8   lake,—dearest] lake, dearest   *1847 1913*
                lake: dearest   *1870*
    Henry,] Henry!   *1847 1913*
    come."] come!"   *1847 1870 1913*
Stanza marker.   II.] *omitted*   *1847 1870 1913*
                2.   *1989*
9   swell'd] swelled   *1847 1870 1892W 1904 1913 1972 1989*
    affection,] affection   *1927/V*
11 recollection:] recollection,   *1847 1913*
                recollection:—   *1870*
                recollection;   *1876 1892W 1904 1927/V 1972*
12 thee."] thee!"   *1847 1870 1913*
16 fate] Fate   *1870*
    flee!] flee.   *1847 1913*
Stanza marker.   III.] *omitted*   *1847 1870 1913*
                3.   *1989*
17 lower'd] lowered   *1847 1892W 1904 1913 1972 1989*
                loured   *1870*
18 gleam'd] gleamed   *1847 1870 1892W 1904 1913 1972 1989*
    air;] air,   *1847 1913*
          air.   *1870*
19 fond] false   *1870*
20 Oh!] Oh   *1847 1913*
21 laving,] laving;   *1870*
22 O'er] On   *1847 1913*
    raving;] raving,   *1847 1913*
                raving.   *1870*
23 But,] But   *1847 1870 1892W 1913 1989*
    spirit;] spirit!   *1847 1870 1913*
    thy] Thy   *1870*
    saving,] saving   *1870*
24 bowers,] bower,   *1847 1913*
                bowers   *1870*
Dateline. | 1808. *added*   *1870*

The Devil's Walk,
A Ballad

Text collated with *1871* (*Fortnightly Review*), 1876, 1892W, 1904, 1927/I, 1972, 1989.

In *1876, 1892W, 1904,* and *1927/I,* the stanzas are numbered with roman numerals.

Title.   THE DEVIL'S WALK] *The Devil's Walk* | . . . | II   *1972*
         A BALLAD.] *omitted   1972*
1   ONCE,] Once   *1871*
2   Beelzebub] Beëlzebuth   *1871*
     arose,] arose;   *1871*
6   claw,] claw;   *1871*
7   Bras Chapeau,] a *bras chapeau;*   *1871*
                    a *Bras Chapeau,*   *1876 1892W 1904 1927/*I *1972*
8   *Beau,*] beau   *1871*
             Beau   *1892W 1904 1927/*I *1972 1989*
9   Bond-street] Bond Street   *1871 1989*
11   ray,] ray.   *1871*
              ray;   *1892W 1904 1927/*I *1972*
12   favourite] favorite   *1892W*
     chat,] chat   *1989*
13   religion,] religion   *1871*
15   court] Court   *1871 1904 1927/*I *1972*
16   in] on   *1871 1876 1892W 1904 1927/*I   *1972*
     way,] way;   *1871 1892W 1904 1927/*I *1972*
17   Saint,] saint,   *1871*
18   Tho'] Though   *1892W 1904 1927/*I *1972 1989*
19   Devil] devil   *1871*
     agriculturist,] agriculturist: *1871*
20   And] And,   *1871*
21   wist] wist,   *1871 1892W 1904 1927/*I *1972*
24   live stock] live-stock   *1871 1876 1892W 1904 1972*
              livestock   *1989*

view;] view.   *1871*
     view,   *1927*/I *1989*
25 shewed] showed   *omnia*
    claws,] claws;   *1871*
26 sight,] sight   *1871 1989*
27 works] work   *1871 1876 1892W 1904 1927*/I *1972*
28 small,] small   *1871 1892W 1904 1927*/I *1972 1989*
30 lambkins!] lambkins,   *1972*
    all,] all   *1892W 1904 1927*/I *1972 1989*
31 dress] dress,   *1871*
    ball,] ball;   *1871*
32 Devil] devil   *1871*
33 Priest,] priest,   *1871*
    the Devil] he   *1871*
    prayer,] prayer   *1871 1892W 1904 1972 1989*
35 Declared,] Declared   *1871 1892W 1904 1972*
    that] that,   *1871 1892W 1904 1972*
    tempter] Tempter   *1904 1972*
36 abide;] abide.   *1871 1876 1892W 1904 1972*
37 Ah! Ah!] "Ah! ah!"   *1871*
          Ah! ah!   *1892W 1904 1927*/I *1972*
    that's] "that's   *1871*
    trick,] trick;   *1871*
38 Devil,] devil,   *1871*
    O!] O   *1871 1892W 1904 1927*/I *1972*
    favourite] favorite   *1892W*
    evil,] Evil,   *1904 1972*
39 ride.] ride."   *1871*
40 King,] king,   *1871*
41 own,] own.   *1871*
        own;   *1892W 1904 1972*
42 imps] Imps   *1904 1972*
    wing,] wing;   *1871*
43 twisted] twirled   *1989*
44 Throne.] throne.   *1871*
45 Ah,] "Ah!   *1871*
        Ah!   *1904 1927*/I *1972*
    ha!] ha!"   *1871*
        ah!   *1904 1927*/I *1972*
    the] "the   *1871*
46 Cattle] cattle   *1871*
    others,] others;   *1871 1892W 1904 1972*
49 bed;] bed: *1871*

50 as fat] fat   *1871 1876 1892W 1904 1927/I 1972*
51 Fat] "Fat   *1871*
    fiends] Fiends   *1904 1972*
52 Spain,] Spain,—   *1871*
53 ruin] Ruin   *1904 1972*
    way,] way   *1989*
54 When] Where   *1871 1892W 1904 1972*
55 Victor's] victor's   *1871*
57 Fat—as the] "Fat as   *1871*
    death birds] death-birds   *1871 1876 1892W 1927/I 1989*
              Death-birds   *1904 1972*
60 Patriot's] patriot's   *1871*
    his] his   *1871*
63 Fat—as] "Fat as   *1871*
    reptiles] Reptiles   *1904 1972*
    tomb,] tomb   *1871*
67 Fat] "Fat   *1871*
    Prince's] prince's   *1871*
    brain,] brain   *1871*
68 Which] Which,   *1871 1892W 1904 1972*
70 humoured] humored   *1892W*
71 For] "For   *1871*
    fat, his] fat; his   *1871*
              fat,—his   *1892W 1904 1927/I 1972*
73 paunch,] paunch;   *1892W 1904 1927/I 1972*
74 half moons,] half-moons   *1871 1904 1927/I 1972*
    moons,] moons   *1876 1892W*
76 How] "How   *1871*
78 twenty,] twenty   *1871 1989*
79 pantaloon seams] pantaloon-seam   *1871*
    start.] start."   *1871*
80 Devil,] devil   *1871*
              Devil   *1892W 1904 1927/I 1972 1989*
    nature,)] Nature)   *1871*
              nature),   *1892W 1927/I*
              Nature),   *1904 1972*
              nature)   *1989*
82 change,] change   *1871 1876 1892W 1904 1927/I 1972*
    feature,] feature   *1871*
84 lawyer,] lawyer   *1871 1892W 1904 1927/I 1972 1989*
    slay,] slay   *1871*
85 table,] table;   *1871*
86 marvellously,] marvellously   *1871 1892W 1904 1927/I 1972 1989*

88   wanders,] wanders   *1871 1892W 1904 1972 1989*
92   thro'] through   *1892W 1904 1972 1989*
94   well,] well   *1871 1892W 1904 1927/I 1972*
     gore,] gore   *1871 1892W 1904 1927/I 1972 1989*
95   livery,] livery;   *1871*
96   well,] well   *1871 1892W 1904 1972*
     poor,] poor   *1871 1892W 1904 1972 1989*
97   penury,] penury.   *1927/I*
98   store,] store   *1871 1904 1972 1989*
100 Bishops] bishops   *1871*
     tho'] though   *1892W 1904 1972 1989*
     big,] big;   *1871 1892W 1904 1927/I 1972*
101 tho'] though   *1892W 1904 1927/I 1972 1989*
102 gown,] gown   *1871*
     wig,] wig   *1871*
105 Altho'] Although   *1871 1892W 1904 1972 1989*
107 Altho'] Although   *1871 1892W 1904 1927/I 1972 1989*
111 skips,] skips   *1871*
     wing,] wing,—   *1871*
112 sidles,] slides,   *1871*
113 dares,] dares   *1871*
     is,] is   *1871*
114 Statesman] statesman   *1871 1876 1892W 1904 1972*
     pass'd—alone] passed:—alone   *1871*
                    passed—alone   *1892W 1904 1972 1989*
     him,] him   *1871 1989*
115 uncover,] uncover,—   *1871*
119 King,] king;   *1871*
120 fiend] Fiend   *1904 1972*
     thy] the   *omnia*
     night,] night   *1871 1989*
122 guilt steeled] guilt-steeled   *1871 1892W 1904 1972 1989*
     brow,] brow   *1871 1989*
123 crowned:] crowned;   *1871*
124 hell-hounds,] hell-hounds   *1871*
     Want] Want,   *1871*
125 For ever] Forever   *1892W 1904 1927/I 1972*
     hungering] hungering,   *1904 1927/I 1972*
126 food,] food,—   *1871*
128 Hark,] Hark!   *1871 1892W 1904 1927/I 1972*
          Hark   *1876*
     hear,] hear;   *1871*
          hear,—   *1892W 1904 1972*

129 Conquerors] conquerors *1871*
    start,] start; *1871*
132 fiends] Fiends *1904 1972*
    revelry,] revelry *1892W 1904 1927*/I *1972*
133 King's] king's *1871*
134 sire] Sire *1904 1972*
    see,] see *1871 1892W 1904 1927*/I *1972*
136 But] But, *1871*
    keen,] keen *omnia*
138 Majesty] Majesty, *1871*
    ween,] ween *1989*
139 joy.] joy *1927*/I
140 Reason] reason *1871*
    see,] see *1871 1892W 1904 1927*/I *1972 1989*
141 That] That, *1871 1892W 1904 1972*
    Pole,] pole, *1871*
142 Tyrant's] tyrant's *1871*
    be,] be *1871 1904 1972 1989*

Supplement: Letter Version

Text collated with *1890, 1927*/I, *1927*/VIII, *1964J, 1972, 1989*.
In *1890, 1927*/I, and *1927*/VIII, the stanzas are numbered with roman numerals.

Title. *omitted*] I *added* *1972*
1 a walking] a-walking *1890 1927*/I *1927*/VIII *1972*
   day] day, *1890 1927*/I *1927*/VIII *1972*
2 Hell] Hell. *1890 1927*/I *1927*/VIII *1972*
3 array] array; *1890 1927*/I *1927*/VIII *1972*
4 drest] dressed *1890 1927*/I *1927*/VIII *1972*
5 pry, whether] pry whether *1972*
          pry | Whether *1890 1927*/I *1927*/VIII
6 well] well. *1890 1927*/I *1927*/VIII *1964J 1972*
7 small] sma[ll] *1964J*
8 w^d.] would *1890 1927*/I *1927*/VIII *1972*
       wd. *1964J 1989*
   there] there, *1890 1927*/I *1927*/VIII *1972*
         ther[e] *1964J*
9 creatures] creatures! *1890 1927*/I *1927*/VIII
            creatures, *1972*
   all] all, *1890 1927*/I *1927*/VIII
       a[ll] *1964J*

10   dress] dress,   *1890 1927*/I *1927*/VIII *1972*
     ball] ball: *1890 1927*/I *1927*/VIII *1972*
          ba[ll]   *1964J*
11   —The] The   *1890 1927*/I *1927*/VIII *1972*
     there] there.   *1890 1927*/I *1927*/VIII *1964J 1972*
12   stole] stole,   *1890 1927*/I *1927*/VIII *1972*
          sto[le]   *1964J*
13   view] view.   *1890 1927*/I *1927*/VIII *1972*
14   Grinning] Receiving   *1989*
     applause, he] applause | He   *1890 1927*/I *1927*/VIII *1972*
     shews] shows   *1890 1927*/I *1927*/VIII *1972*
     claws] claws: *1890 1927*/I *1927*/VIII *1972*
          claw[s]   *1964J*
16   fright,] fright   *1890 1927*/I *1927*/VIII *1972*
     fright, from] fright | From   *1890 1927*/I *1927*/VIII
     his] his   omnia
17   do] do.   omnia
18   whom] whom,   *1890 1927*/I *1927*/VIII *1972*
     prayer] prayer,   *1890 1927*/I *1927*/VIII *1972*
          praye[r]   *1964J*
19   devil] Devil   *1890 1927*/I *1927*/VIII *1972*
     sate] sat   *1964J*
     side] side,   *1890 1927*/I *1927*/VIII *1972*
20   that] that,   *1890 1927*/I *1927*/VIII *1972*
     devil] Devil   *1890 1927*/I *1927*/VIII *1972*
     were] were [there],   *1890 1927*/I *1927*/VIII *1972*
          were [there]   *1964J 1989*
21   couldnt] couldn't   *1890 1927*/I *1927*/VIII *1972*
     abide,] abide.   *1890 1927*/I *1927*/VIII *1972*
22   Ha ha] "Ha ha!"   *1890 1927*/I *1927*/VIII *1972*
     old] Old   *1890 1927*/I *1927*/VIII *1972*
     Nick, thats] Nick, | "That's   *1890 1927*/I *1927*/VIII
          Nick, "That's   *1972*
          trick
     very stale ∧] very stale trick: *1927*/I *1927*/VIII *1972*
23   For] For,   *1890 1927*/I *1927*/VIII *1972*
     Devil, ô] Devil, | O   *1890 1927*/I *1927*/VIII
          Devil, O   *1964J 1972*
     favorite] favourite   *1890 1927*/I *1927*/VIII *1972*
     evil] evil,   *1890 1927*/I *1927*/VIII *1972*
24   ride] ride!"   *1890 1927*/I *1927*/VIII *1972*
          ride.   *1964J*

25 the Devil] the Devil [? a Lawyer]   *1890 1927/*I *1927/*VIII *1964J*
        a Lawyer   *1972*
        the Devil [*for* a lawyer]   *1989*
26 table] table: *1890 1927/*I *1927/*VIII *1972*
28 Abel] Abel.   *1890 1927/*I *1927/*VIII *1964J 1972*
29 Brainless] brainless   *1890*
    King] king;   *1890*
        King;   *1927/*I *1972*
        King,   *1927/*VIII
30 In . . . own] Many imps he saw near there on the wing: *1890*
    own] own.   *1927/*I *1927/*VIII *1972*
31 Many . . . wi[ng]] In a house as hot as his own.   *1890*
    wi[ng]] wing: *1927/*I *1927/*VIII *1972*
        win[g]   *1964J*
        wing   *1989*
32 pennon] pennon,   *1890 1927/*I *1927/*VIII *1972*
    and] &   *1989*
    twiste[d]] twisted   *1890 1927/*I *1927/*VIII *1972*
        twirle[d]   *1989*
    sting] sting,   *1890 1927/*I *1927/*VIII *1972*
33 throne] throne.   *1890 1927/*I *1927/*VIII *1964J 1972*
34 Ah! Ah] "Ah ah!"   *1890 1927/*I *1927/*VIII *1972*
    Satan] Satan,   *1890 1927/*I *1927/*VIII *1972*
    the] "the   *1890 1927/*I *1927/*VIII *1972*
    go[od]] good!   *1890 1927/*I *1927/*VIII *1972*
        good   *1964J 1989*
35 <u>here</u>] here   *1890*
        here   *1927/*I *1927/*VIII *1964J 1972 1989*
    oth[ers]] others!   *1890 1927/*I *1927/*VIII *1972*
        others   *1989*
36 food,] food   *1972*
    food, news] food | News   *1890 1927/*I *1927/*VIII
    humans] human   *omnia*
    blood] blood: *1890 1927/*I *1927/*VIII *1972*
37 &] and   *1890 1927/*I *1927/*VIII *1972*
    dead] dead,   *1890 1927/*I *1927/*VIII *1972*
38 bed] bed,   *1890 1927/*I *1927/*VIII *1972*
39 W^{ch}.] Which   *1890 1927/*I *1927/*VIII *1972*
        Wch.   *1964J*
        Wch   *1989*
    brothers .] brothers."   *1890 1927/*I *1927/*VIII *1972*
        brothers.   *1964J 1989*

40 Park] Park,   *1890 1927/*I *1927/*VIII *1972*
41 bond] Bond   *1890 1927/*I *1927/*VIII *1972*
    beau] beau: *1890 1927/*I *1927/*VIII *1972*
42 For altho] Nor, although   *1890*
                 Nor, tho'   *1927/*I *1927/*VIII *1972*
                 Nor tho   *1964J*
                 For tho   *1989*
    dark] dark,   *1890 1927/*I *1927/*VIII *1972*
43 wide] wide,   *1890 1927/*I *1927/*VIII *1972*
    out] out,   *1890 1927/*I *1927/*VIII *1972*
44 snout] snout,   *1890 1927/*I *1927/*VIII *1972*
45 calld] called   *1890 1927/*I *1927/*VIII *1964J 1972*
    so, so . .] so-so.   *1890 1927/*I *1927/*VIII *1972*
                 so, so.   *1964J 1989*
46 wide] wide,   *1890 1927/*I *1927/*VIII *1972*
47 &] And   *1890 1927/*I *1927/*VIII *1972*
    shew] show   *1890 1927/*I *1927/*VIII *1972*
    hore] horse   *1890 1927/*I *1927/*VIII *1972*
         [? horse]   *1964J*
         Iron   *1989*
    within] within?—   *1890 1927/*I *1927/*VIII *1972*
48 Nine and ninety] Nine-and-ninety   *1890*
                     Nine & ninety   *1989*
    side] side,   *1890 1927/*I *1927/*VIII *1972*
49 reckoning—] reckoning!   *1890 1927/*I *1927/*VIII *1972*

Ten Early Poems (1809–1814)

"A Cat in distress"

Text collated with *1858, 1870, 1876, 1892W, 1904, 1927*/III, *1972, 1989*. Stanza numbers are given as roman numerals in *1870, 1876, 1892W, 1904, 1927*/III, *1972*.

Title. *none*] VERSES ON A CAT.   *1870 1876 1892W 1904 1927*/III
    1972
    'A Cat in distress'   *1989*
    "1802" *given on line after title*   *1927*/III *1972*
Stanza marker.   1.] *omitted*   *1858*
1 Cat] cat   *1858 1870 1876 1892W 1904 1927*/III *1972*
   distress] distress,   *1858 1870 1876 1892W 1904 1927*/III *1972*
2 more] more,   *1858 1870 1876 1892W 1904 1927*/III *1972*
   or] nor   *1858 1876 1892W 1904*
   or less,] nothing less:—   *1870*
   less,] less;   *1858 1876 1892W 1904 1927*/III *1972*
3 folks] folks,   *1858 1870 1876 1892W 1904 1927*/III *1972*
4 sinner] sinner,   *1858 1870 1876 1892W 1904 1927*/III *1972*
5 wants] waits   *1858 1870 1876 1892W 1904 1927*/III
Stanza marker.   2.] *omitted*   *1858*
7 You migh'n^t] You'd not   *1972*
   migh'n^t] would not   *1858 1870 1876 1892W 1904*
      mightn't   *1927*/III *1989*
9 earth,] earth;   *1858 1876 1892W 1904 1927*/III *1972*
10 evils] evils,   *1858 1876 1892W 1904 1927*/III *1972*
11 Which] Which,   *1870*
    like many] like so many   *1858 1870 1876 1892W 1904*
    devils] devils,   *1858 1870 1876 1892W 1904 1927*/III *1972*
12 dogs] souls   *1858 1870 1876 1892W 1904*
    birth:] birth.   *1858 1870 1876 1892W 1904 1927*/III *1972 1989*
Stanza marker.   3.] *omitted*   *1858*
13 require] require,   *1858 1870 1876 1892W 1904 1927*/III *1972 1989*
14 And others] And some others   *1927*/III

15 way,] way;   *1858 1876 1892W 1904 1927/III 1972*
              way: *1870*
17 guessed] guessed,   *1858 1870 1876 1892W 1904 1927/III 1972*
Stanza marker. 4.] *omitted*   *1858*
19 society] society,   *1858 1876 1892W 1904 1927/III 1972 1989*
              society,—   *1870*
20 T'other] Another   *1858 1876 1892W 1904*
              Another,   *1870*
              Tother   *1927/III 1972*
       variety] variety,   *1858 1876 1892W 1904 1927/III 1972 1989*
              variety,—   *1870*
21 Others] Others,   *1870*
       life;] life,   *1989*
22 food] food,   *1858 1876 1892W 1904 1927/III 1972 1989*
              food;   *1870*
23 Others] Others,   *1858 1870 1876 1892W 1904 1927/III 1972*
       good] good,   *1858 1870 1876 1892W 1904 1927/III 1972*
24 require] want   *1858 1870 1876 1892W 1904*
Stanza marker. 5.] *omitted*   *1858*
25 Cat] cat   *1858 1870 1876 1892W 1904 1927/III 1972*
26 rat] rat,   *1858 1876 1892W 1904 1927/III 1972*
              Rat   *1989*
27 maw,] maw;   *1858 1876 1892W 1904 1927/III 1972*
              maw: *1870*
28 'twere] it were   *1858 1870 1876 1892W 1904*
29 Had . . . food] *Some* people had such food,   *1858 1876 1892W 1904*
              Some people had such food   *1870*
              Had some people such food,   *1927/III 1972*
30 hold . . . jaw.] *hold their jaw!*   *1858 1876 1892W 1904*
              "hold their jaw."   *1870*
              hold their jaw!   *1927/III 1972*

"How swiftly through Heaven's wide expanse"

Text collated with *1909, 1913EFG, 1927/III, 1927/VIII, 1964J, 1972, 1989.* See also Historical Collations for the version of this poem in **St.Irv.**

Title. *none*] IV I SONG. ST. IRVYNE'S TOWER   *1927/III*
              IV.—*St. Irvyne's Tower*   *1972*
Stanza marker. *none*] I   *1927/III 1972*
1 Heaven's] heaven's   *1927/III*
2 day's] days   *1913EFG 1927/VIII 1964J*
       colors] colours   *1927/III 1927/VIII 1972 1989*

       fade,] fade   *1913EFG 1927/*VIII *1964J*
            fade!   *1927/*III *1972*
4   teint] tint   *1927/*III *1972 1989*
       Irvyne's] Irvynes   *1913EFG 1927/*VIII *1964J*
       glade.] glade   *1913EFG 1927/*VIII *1964J*
            glade!   *1927/*III *1972*
Stanza marker. *none*] II   *1927/*III *1972*
5   air] air,   *1927/*III
6   borne] bourne   *1927/*VIII
       breeze,] breeze;   *1927/*III *1972 1989*
7   scene,] scene!   *1927/*III *1972*
8   moonbeams] moonbeam's   *1913EFG 1964J 1989*
       trees.] trees   *1913EFG 1927/*VIII *1964J*
            trees!   *1927/*III *1972*
Stanza marker. *none*] III   *1927/*III *1972*
9   grey] gray   *1913EFG 1927/*III *1964J 1972*
       white,] white   *1913EFG 1927/*VIII *1964J*
10 owl;] owl   *1913EFG 1927/*VIII *1964J*
11 night] night,   *1927/*III *1972*
12 roll.] roll   *1913EFG 1927/*III *1927/*VIII *1964J*
Stanza marker. *none*] IV   *1927/*III *1972*
13 Irvyne's] Irvyn's   *1927/*VIII
       tower] tower,   *1927/*III *1972*
14 moonbeam pours its silver] silver moonbeam pours her   *1927/*III
                         1972
       ray;] ray: *1989*
15 gleams] gleam's   *1913EFG 1964J*
       bower,] bower   *1913EFG 1927/*VIII *1964J*
16 in] on   *1927/*VIII *1989*
       spray.] spray   *1913EFG 1964J*
            spray,   *1989*
Stanza marker. *none*] V   *1927/*III
              additional stanzas   *1972*
17 For] [For   *1927/*III
       darken'd] darkned   *1909 1913EFG 1964J*
                dark'ned   *1927/*III *1927/*VIII
                darkened   *1972 1989*
18 long lost] long-lost   *1927/*III *1927/*VIII
       mourn:] mourn   *1909 1913EFG 1927/*VIII *1964J*
             mourn,   *1927/*III
             mourn,—   *1972*
             mourn.   *1989*
19 bosom's] bosoms   *1909 1913EFG 1964J*

   woe—] woe, *1927*/III
     woe *1927*/VIII
     woe: *1972*
20 "Ah!] Ah! *1927*/VIII
  those] these *1927*/III *1927*/VIII
  return?] retur[n?] *1909 1913EFG 1964J*
    return. *1927*/III
    return *1927*/VIII
Stanza marker. *none*] VI *1927*/III
21 O'er] "O'er *1927*/III *1972 1989*
  soul,] soul *1909*
  form] form, *1972*
22 love—] love *1909 1913EFG 1927*/VIII *1964J*
    love, *1927*/III *1989*
    love!— *1972*
23 lower] hover *1927*/III *1927*/VIII
  storm,] storm *1927*/VIII *1989*
    storm!— *1972*
24 would] would, *1989*
  prove.] prove[.] *1909 1913EFG 1964J*
    prove *1927*/VIII
    prove! *1972*
Stanza marker. *none*] VII *1927*/III
25 Ah!] "Ah! *1927*/III *1972 1989*
  suppose,] suppose *1927*/III *1927*/VIII *1972 1989*
26 relief,] reli[ef,] *1909 1913EFG 1964J*
    relief? *1927*/III
    relief *1927*/VIII
    relief?— *1972*
27 stop] still *1927*/III *1927*/VIII *1989*
  bosom's bursting] bursting bosom's *1989*
  woes] woes, *1927*/III *1972*
28 Or calm] Or ~~stop~~ calm *1913EFG 1964J*
  grief?] grief[?] *1909 1913EFG 1964J*
    grief *1927*/VIII
Stanza marker. *none*] VIII *1927*/III
29 Within] "Within *1927*/III *1972 1989*
  Hell;] Hell *1909 1913EFG 1927*/VIII *1964J*
    Hell— *1972*
    Hell. *1989*
30 Fate] Fate, *1927*/III *1927*/VIII *1972 1989*
  farther] further *1927*/III *1927*/VIII

   power,] power. *1927/*III
     power *1927/*VIII
     power! *1972*
  line cut away with foot of leaf *1909 1913EFG 1964J*
31 Fate] Fate! *1972*
     Fate, *1989*
   spell] spell, *1927/*III *1972 1989*
32 hour.] ho[ur.] *1909 1913EFG 1964J*
     ho[ur] *1927/*VIII
     hour! *1972*
Stanza marker. *none*] IX *1927/*III
33 No] "No *1927/*III *1972 1989*
   Heaven,] Heaven *1909 1913EFG 1927/*III *1927/*VIII *1964J 1972*
34 tumult] tumults *1927/*III *1927/*VIII *1989*
   brain:] brain *1909 1913EFG 1927/*VIII *1964J*
     brain. *1927/*III
     brain; *1989*
35 ———'s] [Harriet's] *1972*
36 To calm] To take calm *1913EFG 1964J*
   pain.] pain *1909 1927/*VIII
     pain.] *1927/*III
     pain.' *1972*
Stanza marker. *none*] X *1927/*III
     V *1972*
37 Ah] "Ah! *1927/*III *1972*
     'Ah, *1989*
   darkning] darkening *1909 1989*
     dark'ning *1927/*III *1927/*VIII *1972*
38 hour] hour, *1927/*III *1972*
   man . . . be?] ma[n must cease to be?] *1909*
     Man . . . be? *1927/*VIII *1989*
39 minds unveil] min[ds unveil] *1909*
40 dark shade] dim mists *1927/*III *1972*
   futurity?"] fu[turity?] *1909*
     futurity? *1913EFG 1927/*III *1927/*VIII *1964J 1972*
     futurity?'— *1989*

"Oh wretched mortal, hard thy fate!"

No historical witnesses.

To Mary who died in this opinion

Text collated with *1870, 1876, 1892W, 1904, 1927*/III, *1927*/VIII, *1964J*, *1972, 1989*.

Title. "1810" *given on line after title*   *1927*/III
   "c. 1810–11" *given after title*   *1972*
Stanza marker.   *omitted*] 1.   *1876 1892W 1904 1927*/III *1972*
                              [1]   *1964J*
 2   eye:] eye;   *1892W*
        eye   *1964J*
 4   destiny;] destiny   *1964J*
 5   morn's] morns   *1964J*
 7   concealing] concealing,   *1870 1876 1892W 1904 1927*/III *1927*/VIII *1972*
 8   you.] you   *1964J*
Stanza marker.   2] *omitted*   *1870 1927*/VIII *1989*
10   bliss:] bliss?   *1870 1876 1892W 1904 1927*/III *1927*/VIII *1972*
        bliss   *1964J*
        bliss;   *1989*
11   broken hearted] brokenhearted   *1870*
                broken-hearted   *1904 1927*/III *1927*/VIII *1972 1989*
12   this?] this!   *1870 1876 1892W*
        this   *1964J*
13   Yet] Yet,   *1870 1876 1892W 1904 1927*/III *1927*/VIII *1972*
     tho] though,   *1870 1876 1892W 1904 1927*/III *1927*/VIII *1972 1989*
     fainting,] fainting   *1870 1876 1892W 1904 1927*/III *1927*/VIII *1964J 1972 1989*
     one] one,   *1870 1876 1892W 1904 1927*/III *1927*/VIII *1972 1989*
14   (Sorrow's ... given),] Sorrow's ... given,   *1870 1876 1892W 1904 1927*/III *1927*/VIII *1972 1989*
        Sorrows ... given   *1964J*
15   one] one,   *1870 1876 1892W 1904 1927*/VIII *1972*
16   part] part,   *1870 1876 1892W 1904 1927*/III *1927*/VIII *1972 1989*
     Heaven.] heaven.   *1870 1876 1892W*
        Heaven   *1964J*
Stanza marker.   3] *omitted*   *1870 1927*/VIII *1989*
17   would] w[oul]d   *1927*/VIII
        wd.   *1964J*
18   thine,] thine   *1964J*

20 affection's] affections   *1964J*
    shrine:] shrine.   *1870 1876 1892W 1904 1927*/III *1927*/VIII *1972*
        shrine   *1964J*
        shrine;   *1989*
21 would] *would*   *1927*/III *1927*/VIII
        wd.   *1964J*
    pleasure] pleasure   *1870 1876 1892W 1904*
        pleasure   *1927*/III *1927*/VIII *1964J 1972 1989*
22 cheek] cheek,   *1870 1876 1892W 1904 1927*/III *1927*/VIII *1972*
24 [Such as]] Such as   *1870 1876 1892W 1904 1972 1989*
    break.] break   *1964J*

"Why is it said thou canst but live"

Text collated with *1858, 1870, 1876, 1892W, 1904, 1927*/III, *1927*/VIII, *1964J, 1972, 1989*.

Title. *none*] LOVE.   *1870 1876 1892W 1904 1927*/III *1972*
        "1811" *given on line after title*   *1927*/III *1972*
1   but] not   *1858 1870 1876 1892W 1904 1927*/III *1927*/VIII
2   and] &   *1964J*
    fair:] fair,   *1858 1870 1876 1892W 1904 1927*/III *1927*/VIII *1972 1989*
        fair   *1964J*
3   give,] give—   *1870*
        give   *1964J*
4   forever] for ever   *1858 1870 1876 1904 1927*/III *1927*/VIII *1972*
    there,] there?   *1858 1876 1892W 1904 1927*/III *1927*/VIII *1972*
        there—   *1870*
        there   *1964J*
5   possesses] possest,   *1858 1876 1927*/III *1927*/VIII
        possessed,   *1870 1892W 1904*
        possesses,   *1972 1989*
6   Age] age,   *1858 1870 1876 1892W 1904 1927*/III *1927*/VIII *1972*
        Age,   *1989*
    hue,] hue   *1964J*
7   Since] Nor   *1858 1870 1876 1892W 1904 1927*/III *1927*/VIII *1972*
    time's] Time's   *1870*
    victor] victor,   *1858 1870 1876 1892W 1904 1927*/III *1927*/VIII *1972*
    death] death,   *1858 1876 1892W 1904 1927*/III *1927*/VIII *1972*
        Death,   *1870*

confesses] confess'd,   *1858 1876 1927*/III *1927*/VIII
                confessed,   *1870 1892W 1904*
                confesses,   *1972*
8   Tho] Though   *1858 1870 1876 1892W 1904 1927*/III *1927*/VIII
        1972 1989
    bathed] bathèd   *1989*
    poison] posion   *1927*/VIII
    poison dew,] poison-dew?   *1870*
    dew,] dew?   *1892W*
        dew   *1964J 1989*
9   retainst] retain'st   *1858 1870 1876 1904 1927*/III *1927*/VIII *1972*
        retainest   *1892W*
    bloom] bloom,   *1858 1870 1876 1892W 1904 1927*/III *1927*/VIII
        1972
10 Fixed] Fix'd   *1858 1876 1927*/III *1927*/VIII
        Fixed,   *1870 1892W*
    tranquil] tranquil,   *1858 1870 1876 1892W 1904 1927*/III
        1927/VIII *1972*
    tomb.—] tomb.   *1858 1870 1876 1892W 1904 1927*/III *1927*/VIII
        1972
        tomb?—   *1989*
    stanza break added   *1870*
11 And] Ah   *1927*/VIII
    blest] blessed,   *1870*
        blest,   *1892W 1904 1972*
    reviving] reviving,   *1870 1892W 1904 1927*/III *1972*
12 day star] day-star   *1858 1870 1876 1892W 1904 1927*/III *1927*/VIII
        1972 1989
    love,] Love,   *1870*
        love   *1964J*
13 soul surviving] soulsurviving   *1870*
14 vivid] vivid,   *1858 1876 1904 1927*/III *1927*/VIII *1972*
    above.———] above,   *1858 1870 1876 1892W 1904 1927*/III
        1927/VIII *1972*
        above—   *1964J 1989*
15 thrill] thrill,   *1858 1870 1876 1892W 1904 1927*/III *1927*/VIII
        1972
16 breath] breath,   *1858 1876 1892W 1904 1927*/III *1927*/VIII *1972*
    fly] fly,   *1858 1870 1876 1892W 1904 1927*/VIII *1972*
17 Oer] O'er   *1858 1870 1876 1892W 1904 1927*/III *1927*/VIII
        1972 1989
    steal] steal,   *1858 1870 1876 1892W 1904 1927*/III *1927*/VIII *1972*

18   die—] die?   *1858 1876 1892W 1904 1927*/III *1927*/VIII *1972*
         die?—   *1870*
         die   *1964J*
         die,   *1989*
19   dream] dream,   *1858 1870 1876 1892W 1904 1927*/III *1927*/VIII
         1972
20   stream] stream,   *1858 1876 1892W 1904 1927*/III *1927*/VIII *1972*
21   says] says,   *1858 1876 1892W 1904 1927*/III *1927*/VIII *1972*
         1989
     mine] Mine   *1858 1876 1892W 1927*/VIII *1989*
         "Mine   *1870 1904 1927*/III *1972*
     dell,] dell;   *1858 1876 1892W 1927*/VIII
         dell,"   *1870*
         dell";   *1904 1927*/III *1972*
         dell   *1964J*
22   plain] plain,   *1858 1870 1876 1892W 1904 1927*/III *1927*/VIII
         1972
23   fell] fell,   *1858 1870 1876 1892W 1904 1927*/III' *1927*/VIII *1972*
24   reign?] reign.   *1858 1870 1876 1892W 1904 1927*/III *1927*/VIII
         1972
         reign   *1964J*
Dateline.   April 1811. *added*   *1870*

"As you will see I wrote to you" [To EFG #1]

Text collated with *1892F, 1892W, 1917, 1922LMer, 1927*/III, *1964J, 1972, 1989*. *1892F* and *1892W* consist of only lines 55–58; *1917* of only 55–58, 60–61; and *1922LMer* of only 1–10, 18–28, 51–61.

Title.   *none*] A LETTER TO EDWARD FERGUS GRAHAM   *1927*/III
         To EDWARD FERGUS GRAHAM, London   *1964J*
         Letter to Edward Fergus Graham   *1972 1989*
         1811 *given on line after title.*   *1927*/III
         [Field Place, ? 14 May 1811] *given on line after title.*   *1964J*
         [?] 14 May 1811 *given on line after title.*   *1972*
1   see] see,   *1927*/III *1972 1989*
     wrote] write   *1922LMer 1927*/III
2   fitting,] fitting   *1922LMer 1927*/III *1964J 1972*
     and] &   *1964J*
     due] due,   *1927*/III *1972 1989*
3   frank,] frank;   *1927*/III *1972 1989*

4   Jealousy,] jealousy,   *1922LMer*
              jealousy.   *1927/III*
              Jealousy   *1964J*
              jealousy.—   *1972*
5   brows] brow   *1922LMer 1927/III*
    dark,] dark   *1922LMer 1964J*
    blue!] blue—   *1972*
6   this] his   *1927/III*
    you.] you   *1922LMer 1964J*
         you!   *1972*
7   Yes] Yes,   *1927/III 1972 1989*
    name] name,—   *1927/III*
          name,   *1972*
8   fame] fame,—   *1927/III*
         fame,   *1972*
9   which] with   *1927/III*
    sickening] sickening,   *1927/III*
10 fear.] fear   *1964J*
         fear!   *1972*
11 Fear,] Fear   *1964J*
          Fierce   *1989*
    hatred] hatred,   *1927/III 1972*
    have] have;   *1927/III*
         have,   *1972 1989*
12 brave] brave.   *1927/III*
          brave;   *1972*
          brave,   *1989*
13 And] And,   *1927/III 1972*
    therefore] therefore,   *1927/III 1972 1989*
    Graham] Graham,   *1972 1989*
14 You] You,   *1927/III 1972 1989*
    don't] dont   *1964J*
    well] well,   *1927/III*
15 you] you: *1927/III*
         you,   *1972 1989*
16 Killjoy,] Killjoy   *1964J 1989*
    blue,] blue   *1964J 1989*
17 bear] bear,   *1972 1989*
    Græme] Graeme,   *1989*
    Græme me] Graeme, me,   *1927/III 1972*
    you.] you   *1964J*
         you!   *1972*

18 him,] him   *1922LMer 1964J*
         him;   *1927/III 1972*
19 idiot's] idiots   *1964J*
    won't] wont   *1964J*
    him,] him.   *1922LMer 1927/III*
         him   *1964J*
20 justly be] be [*sic*] justly be   *1964J*
    Hell,] Hell   *1922LMer 1927/III 1964J 1989*
21 'twas] twas   *1964J*
    Pride] pride   *1922LMer 1927/III 1972*
    fell,] fell.   *1922LMer 1927/III 1972*
22 conquerors] conqueror   *1922LMer 1927/III*
23 Oer] O'er   *1922LMer 1927/III 1972 1989*
24 Peace,] peace,   *1922LMer 1927/III*
         peace   *1972*
         Peace   *1989*
25 Hatred] hatred   *1972*
    dwell:] dwell   *1922LMer 1927/III 1964J*
         dwell—   *1972*
         dwell,   *1989*
26 its] it's   *1964J*
    way,] way   *1922LMer 1964J*
         way;   *1927/III*
         way.   *1972*
27 wretch] wretch,   *1927/III 1972*
28 prey.] prey!   *1927/III 1972*
29 you] you,   *1972 1989*
    Fargy] Fergy   *1927/III*
         Fargy,   *1972 1989*
31 courtship] courts[h]ip   *1964J*
32 flames,] flames   *1927/III 1964J*
         flames,—   *1972*
34 forty eight] forty-eight   *1927/III 1972 1989*
    queen] queen,   *1972*
36 ninety two] ninety-two   *1927/III 1972 1989*
38 Grandson's] grandson's   *1927/III 1972 1989*
    heart,] heart   *1964J*
         heart,—   *1972*
39 We] All   *1927/III*
    soul] soul,   *1927/III 1972*
         soul—   *1989*

40 (Tho ... roll)] Though ... roll,   *1927*/III *1972*
                        Tho ... roll   *1964J*
                        Though ... roll—   *1989*
42 Killjoy's] Killjoys   *1964J*
43 'twere] twere   *1964J*
   corageous] courageous   *1927*/III *1972 1989*
            co[u]rageous   *1964J*
44 adorn:] adorn   *1927*/III *1964J*
            adorn!   *1972*
            adorn.   *1989*
46 fell] full   *1927*/III
   there.] there   *1964J*
            there!   *1972*
47 sin] sin;   *1927*/III *1964J 1972 1989*
   altho'] although   *1972 1989*
   there's] theres   *1964J*
48 temptation] temptation,   *1972 1989*
49 'twere] twere   *1964J*
50 sinning] sinning's   *1927*/III *1972*
            sinning['s]   *1964J*
   sake.] sake   *1964J*
            sake!   *1972*
51 Yet] Yet,   *1972*
   this] the   *1922LMer 1927*/III
52 and] &   *1964J*
53 adieu] adieu,   *1972*
54 wish] wish,   *1972 1989*
   Græme,] Graeme,   *1927*/III *1972 1989*
54-55 ———] *Extended dash occurs between lines 54 and 55.*
            omitted   *1922LMer 1927*/III *1972 1989*
55 high] high,   *1927*/III *1972*
   and] &   *1964J*
56 green,] green—   *1892F 1892W*
            green   *1922LMer 1964J*
57 dear] dear,   *1917 1972*
   delightful] delightful,   *1917*
   red faced] red-faced   *1892F 1892W 1922LMer 1927*/III *1972 1989*
            redfaced   *1917*
   brute,] brute   *1917*
            brute;   *1927*/III *1972*
58 parachute;] parachute."   *1892W*
            parachute.   *1917 1922LMer*
            parachute   *1927*/III *1964J 1972 1989*

59 played] played.   *1927*/III *1972 1989*
   line omitted   *1917*
60 Oh!] Oh   *1917*
   Fargy] — —   *1917*
      Fergy,   *1922LMer 1927*/III
      fargy   *1964J*
      Fargy,   *1972 1989*
   wonderous] wondrous   *1917 1927*/III *1972 1989*
   made.] made   *1964J*
61 poem] *omitted*   *1917*
      poem?   *1922LMer 1927*/III *1972*
      para   *1989*

"Dear dear dear dear dear dear Græme!" [To EFG #2]

Text collated with *KSMB/1973* and *1989*.

Title. *none*] Second Letter to Edward Fergus Graham   *1989*
1 Dear dear dear dear dear dear] Dear, dear, dear, dear, dear,   *KSMB/1973*
   Græme!] Graeme!   *KSMB/1973 1989*
3 letter,] letter.   *KSMB/1973*
4 prevail] prevail,   *KSMB/1973*
5 avail,] avail—   *KSMB/1973*
6 relenting—] relenting!   *KSMB/1973*
      relenting.   *1989*
8 temper-whetter,] temper-whetter;   *KSMB/1973*
9 repent,] repent   *KSMB/1973*
   demands] demands,   *KSMB/1973 1989*
10 submit,] submit   *KSMB/1973*
   the] he   *KSMB/1973*
   commands] commands,   *KSMB/1973 1989*
11 joy's] joys   *KSMB/1973*
      joy   *1989*
   so] to   *KSMB/1973*
   divine] divine,   *KSMB/1973*
      divine!   *1989*
12 will he want] he desires   *KSMB/1973*
14 Catalani's] Catalini's   *KSMB/1973*
   squall—] squall: *KSMB/1973 1989*
15 hears] hears,   *KSMB/1973*
17 sounds] sound   *KSMB/1973*

woe] woe?   *KSMB/1973*
       woe,   *1989*
18 bid satire] had [?] [?]   *KSMB/1973*
    flow,] flow?   *KSMB/1973*
20 [?When]] [? Than]   *KSMB/1973*
       [When]   *1989*
    passion condenser?] passion-condenser?   *KSMB/1973 1989*
21 But] [ ]!   *KSMB/1973*
    give] Give   *KSMB/1973*
    throne] throne,   *1989*
22 alone:] alone!   *KSMB/1973*
       alone,   *1989*
23 crammed] crammed—   *KSMB/1973*
       crammed,   *1989*
24 damned;] damned!   *KSMB/1973*
       damned,   *1989*
25 wife,] wife—   *KSMB/1973*
26 life] life!   *KSMB/1973*
       life,   *1989*
27 way,] way   *KSMB/1973 1989*
28 obey.] obey!   *KSMB/1973*
29 horn,] horn   *1989*
30 daring] dancing   *KSMB/1973*
    attempted?] attempted?—   *1989*
31 age] age,   *KSMB/1973 1989*
32 exempted:] exempted.   *KSMB/1973 1989*
33 squire,] squire   *KSMB/1973 1989*
34 implanted—] implanted!   *KSMB/1973*
35 exactly,] exactly;   *1989*
    he'd] he'll   *KSMB/1973*
    directly] directly—   *KSMB/1973*
       directly,   *1989*
36 wanted.] wanted: *KSMB/1973*
       wanted;—   *1989*
37 drive,] drive   *KSMB/1973 1989*
38 His] The   *KSMB/1973*
    whim.] whim!   *KSMB/1973*
39 done, for] done—for   *KSMB/1973*
40 Godwin.] Godwin!   *KSMB/1973*

"Sweet star! which gleaming oer the darksome scene"

Text collated with *1858, 1870, 1876, 1886, 1892W, 1904, 1927*/III, *1927*/VIII, *1964J, 1972, 1989*.
1886 consists of lines 13–15 only.

Title.   none] TO A STAR.   *1870 1876 1892W 1904 1927*/III *1972*
        'Sweet star!'   *1989*
        "1811" *given on line after title*   *1927*/III *1972*
1   star!] star,   *1858 1876 1892W 1904 1927*/III *1927*/VIII *1972*
        star   *1870*
  which] which,   *1870*
  oer] o'er   *1858 1870 1876 1892W 1904 1927*/III *1927*/VIII
        1972 1989
  scene] scene,   *1870*
2   Thro'] Through   *1858 1870 1876 1892W 1904 1927*/III *1927*/VIII
        1972 1989
        Thru'   *1964J*
  radiance] radiance,   *1989*
  fling'st] flyest,   *1858 1876 1892W 1927*/VIII
        fliest!   *1870*
        fliest,   *1904 1927*/III
        flingst   *1972*
3   Spanglets] Spanglet   *1858 1870 1876 1892W 1904 1927*/III
        1927/VIII
  veil] veil,   *1858 1876 1892W 1904 1927*/III *1927*/VIII *1972*
4   day beam] day-beam   *1858 1876 1892W 1904 1927*/III *1927*/VIII
        1964J 1972 1989
        daybeam   *1870*
  lake,] lake   *1964J*
5   love,] love;   *1858 1876 1892W 1904 1927*/III *1927*/VIII *1972*
  love, more] love,—more   *1989*
6   morn-star's] moon-star's   *1964J*
        Morn-star's   *1989*
  fires—] fires.   *1858 1876 1892W 1927*/III *1927*/VIII
        fires!   *1870*
        fires:—   *1904 1972*
        fires   *1964J*
        fires: *1989*
7   when] When   *1858 1876 1892W 1904 1927*/III *1927*/VIII *1972*
  nature] Nature   *1858 1876 1892W 1904 1927*/III *1927*/VIII *1972*
  sleep] sleep,   *1858 1870 1876 1892W 1904 1927*/III *1927*/VIII *1972*

8 hushed,—all] hushed,—all, *1858 1876 1892W 1904 1927*/III
    1927/VIII *1972*
   hushed—all *1870*
 love,] Love, *1858 1876 1892W 1904 1927*/III *1927*/VIII *1972*
11 ear] ears *1927*/III
 stillness,—art] stillness, art *1858 1876 1892W 1904 1927*/III
   1927/VIII
   Stillness—art *1870 1989*
   stillness.—art *1964J*
 aught] ought *1964J*
 love] Love *1972*
  love, *1989*
  omitted *1858 1870 1876 1892W 1904 1927*/III *1927*/VIII
12 repose] repose, *1870*
13 With . . . oh! I could look] "Oh, I would look *1886*
 mild] mild, *1858 1876 1892W 1904 1927*/III *1927*/VIII *1972*
 gaze . . oh!] gaze! Oh, *1858 1876 1892W 1927*/III *1927*/VIII
   gaze?—Oh! *1870*
   gaze? Oh, *1904 1972*
   gaze—oh! *1964J*
   gaze? . . . oh! *1989*
 could] would *1858 1870 1876 1892W 1904 1927*/III *1927*/VIII
  cd. *1964J*
14 On] In *1858 1870 1876 1886 1892W 1904 1927*/III *1927*/VIII
 'till] till *1858 1870 1876 1886 1892W 1904 1927*/III *1927*/VIII
  1972 1989
15 unnerved. . . . .] enamoured—— *1858 1876 1892W 1904 1927*/III
   1927/VIII
   enamoured! | 1811. *1870*
   enamoured." *1886*
   unnerved—— *1964J*
   unnerved. *1972*
   unnerved . . . *1989*

"Bear witness Erin! when thine injured isle"

Text collated with *1870, 1872, 1876, 1892W, 1904, 1927/*III, *1927/*VIII, *1964J, 1972, 1989*.

Title.   *none*] TO IRELAND.   *1870 1872 1876 1892W 1904 1927/*III
  1972
  [To Ireland]   *1927/*VIII *1964J*
  'Bear witness, Erin!'   *1989*
  "1812" *given on line after title*   *1927/*III *1972*
1 Bear witness] Bear witness,   *1870 1872 1876 1927/*VIII *1989*
  I | Bear witness,   *1892W 1904*
  II | Bear witness,   *1927/*III *1972*
  Be{ar witn}ess   *1964J*
  isle] isle,   *1872*
2 smile,] smile   *1964J*
4 deep—] deep.   *1870 1872 1876*
  deep!   *1892W 1904 1927/*III *1972*
  deep.—   *1927/*VIII
  stanza break added   *1989*
5 oer] o'er   *1870 1872 1876 1892W 1904 1927/*III *1927/*VIII *1972*
  1989
6 Peace] Peace,   *1870 1872 1876 1892W 1904 1927/*III *1927/*VIII
  1972 1989
  wealth] wealth,   *1870 1872 1876 1927/*VIII
  beauty] beauty,   *1870 1876 1892W 1904 1927/*VIII
  wave] wave,   *1870 1872 1876 1892W 1904 1927/*III *1972*
  wave.   *1927/*VIII
7 ———its] . . . its   *1870*
  . . . . its   *1872*
  its   *1876 1892W 1904 1927/*III *1927/*VIII *1972*
  fade] fade,   *1870 1876 1892W 1904 1927/*III *1927/*VIII *1972 1989*
  fade;   *1872*
8 shade] shade;   *1870 1872 1876 1892W 1904 1927/*III *1972*
  shade,   *1927/*VIII *1989*
9 fruit] fruit,   *1870 1872 1876 1892W 1904 1927/*VIII
10 its] it's   *1964J*
Dateline.   *February* 1812. *added*   *1870*
  Dublin, February, 1812. *added*   *1872*

"Thy dewy looks sink in my breast"

Text collated with *1858, 1870, 1876, 1886, 1892W, 1904, 1911, 1927*/III, *1927*/IX, *1964J, 1972, 1989*.

Title.   *none*] Stanza, written at Bracknell   *1876 1904 1911 1972 1989*
        FRAGMENTS. | I. | To———.   *1870*
        STANZA | WRITTEN AT BRACKNELL   *1892W*
        LINES WRITTEN AT BRACKNELL   *1927*/III
        (March 1814) *added after title*   1911
1   Thy] "Thy   *1858*
    breast,] breast;   *omnia*
2   there:] there;   *1858 1876 1886 1892W 1904 1911 1927*/III *1927*/IX *1964J 1972 1989*
4   despair.] despair!   *1858 1876 1886 1892W 1904 1911 1927*/III *1927*/IX *1964J 1972 1989*
    stanza break] omitted   *omnia*
5   Duty's] duty's   *1870*
    control] control,   *1858 1870 1886 1892W 1904 1927*/IX *1964J 1989*
        controul,   *1876 1911 1927*/III
6   lot:] lot;   *1870 1927*/IX
8   then—but] then, but   *1870 1886*
    not.] not."   *1858*

APPENDIXES

Line engraving by E. J. Roberts of John Martin's painting *Sadak in Search of the Waters of Oblivion*, published in *Keepsake* for 1828. With kind permission of Archives and Special Collections, Amherst College Library.

In these appendixes, we discuss a number of works either written by the young PBS or attributed to him, but which—for reasons that we will adduce—do not belong in the canon proper. In later volumes, we will treat poems problematically attributed to the mature PBS, including "The Calm," "The Creator," "The Dinner Party Anticipated," "The Magic Horse," "Shadows of the Soul," "Vox et Practerea Nihil," and "What Mary is."

We shall also publish in a later volume PBS's early poetic translation of about a third of Goethe's *Faust,* written on English paper watermarked "1810." A photofacsimile and transcription of this translation are available in *BSM* XXI (ed. E. B. Murray [1995], 120–80). Because no other known literary MS from PBS's youth has survived, Murray believed that the *Faust* translation might have been written after PBS eloped with MWS, sometime between 1814 and 1818 (476). In 1997, Nora Crook and Timothy Webb in their edition of *The* Faust *Draft Notebook* (*BSM* XIX), which contains PBS's later translations from Goethe's drama, call Murray's discussion of the dating "full and balanced" (lvii). On the other hand, Joseph Gibbons Merle reported that, after being expelled from Oxford, a financially desperate PBS unsuccessfully attempted to raise money by offering prose translations, two of which were from German tales, to several different publishers ("A Newspaper Editor's Reminiscences," *Fraser's Magazine* 23 [June 1841], 703). Because the *Faust* translation MS is a fair copy that might similarly have been shown to (and perhaps left with) a prospective publisher in the spring of 1811, we tend to agree with Leland R. Phelps's article "Goethe's *Faust* and the Young Shelley" (in *Wege der Worte,* ed. Donald C. Riechel [Cologne and Vienna: Böhlau, 1978], 304–12) that it could have been written as early as 1810 or 1811, its MS perhaps preserved by the publisher to whom PBS offered it (just as the Ballantynes kept the MS of *WJ*). The text of this early *Faust* translation will appear, however, as Supplement to PBS's mature translations from *Faust* composed in 1822, where its history and significance can be explored in greater detail.

Appendix A. Latin School Exercises

Sir John Rennie recalls the young PBS composing English and Latin verse at Syon House Academy (*Autobiography* [London: E. & F. N. Spon, 1875], 2); PBS's early facility at translating verse into and out of Latin is also commented upon by both Thomas Jefferson Hogg and Thomas Medwin. In his *Life of Percy Bysshe Shelley*, Medwin demonstrates PBS's "great skill in the art of versification" by presenting two "specimens I kept among my treasures, which he gave me in 1808 or 9. The first is the Epitaph in Gray's *Elegy Written in a Country Churchyard* [***Epitaphium***], probably a school task." The other poem, ***In Horologium***, Medwin describes as "of a totally different character," and observes that it "shows a considerable precocity" (*Life*, ed. Forman, 35–37). There are no extant MSS for either poem, and although the attribution of the two translations to PBS might well be correct, Medwin is not only an unreliable witness but the text of ***Epitaphium*** changed each time he published it.

Epitaphium

Epitaphium, a translation into Latin of lines 117–28 of "Elegy Written in a Country Churchyard," was first printed in Medwin's 1847 *Life* and was reproduced in an altered, heavily revised version in Medwin's *Nugæ* (Heidelberg, 1856), for which, see *Life*, ed. Forman, 35–36n. Forman's text in *Life* offers ***Epitaphium*** in yet a third version, presumably based on changes Medwin made while revising the first edition.

While English poets generally use Latin to condense English phrases, PBS instead expands Gray's elegy into Latin Sapphic stanzas. The meter of the verse, Sapphic/Adonic, was used by Horace in the formal odes of the fourth book and in the *Carmen Saeculare*. Horace's influence on the poem is further apparent in two echoes: "popularis . . . aurae" in lines 3–4 (*Odes* 2.4.22) and "fuge suspicari" in line 18 (*Odes* 3.2.20). Despite the Horatian influence on the translation, Late Latin rather than classical spelling is used throughout (e.g., "cespitis" for *caespitis*, "cœlum" for *cælum*, and "Cæteras" for *Ceteras*). For a basic list of PBS's uses of Horace in his poetry, see Mary Rebecca Thayer, *The Influence of Horace on the Chief English Poets of the Nineteenth Century* (1916; rpt. New York: Haskell House, 1965), 85–92.

Epitaphium appears in the following collective editions: *1870*, *1876*, *1878*, *1892W*, *1904*, *1927*, and *1972*. All texts of the translation are ultimately derived from Medwin's in *1847M* (I, 48–49), which we reproduce below without emendation, except for the change of "Longivus" to <u>Longius</u> (line 17), which was in the errata list of *1847M*. Rossetti first altered <u>mæstis</u> to "mœstus" (line 13) and <u>Cælo</u> to "Cœlo" (line 15). The collective editions insert stanza numbers and lighten the punctuation throughout the poem.

EPITAPHIUM.

Hic, sinu fessum caput, hospitali,
Cespitis, dormit juvenis, nec illi
Fata ridebant, popularis ille
    Nescius auræ.

5   Musa non vultu, genus, arroganti,
Rusticâ natum grege despicata,
Et suum, tristis, puerum, notavit
    Sollicitudo.

Indoles illi bene larga, pectus
10   Veritas sedem sibi vindicavit,
Et pari, tantis meritis, beavit
    Munere, cœlum.

Omne, quod mæstis habuit, miserto
Corde, largivit lacrymam, recepit,
15   Omne, quod Cælo voluit, fidelis
    Pectus amici.

Longius, sed tu, fuge, curiosus,
Cæteras laudes, fuge, suspicari,
Cæteras culpas, fuge, velle tractas
20   Sede tremendâ.

Spe tremescentes, recubant, in illâ
Sede, virtutes, pariter que culpæ,
In sui, Patris gremio, tremendâ
    Sede, Deique.

In Horologium

Denis Florence Mac-Carthy first noted that although Medwin evidently considered *In Horologium* to be "not only precocious, but original, with Shelley ... Something of the precocity is explained ... and all of the originality removed, by a reference to *The Oxford Herald* of Saturday, September 16th, 1809," which contains an English epigram entitled "On seeing a French Watch round the Neck of a Beautiful Young Woman," upon which *In Horologium* is based:

> Mark what we gain from foreign lands,
>   *Time* cannot now be said to linger,—
> Allow'd to lay his two rude hands
>   Where others *dare* not lay a finger.

Mac-Carthy concludes justifiably that "Shelley's Latin lines are simply a translation of this epigram, which he most probably saw in *The Oxford Herald*, but may have read in some other paper of the time ..." (*Early Life*, 27).

In Horologium appears in the following collective editions: *1870, 1876, 1878, 1892W, 1904, 1927,* and *1972*. Our Text is unemended from Medwin's 1847 *Life* (I, 49). Rossetti in *1870* first corrected Quà to "Quas" (line 3), and Rogers in *1972* corrects the gender of marmoreas to "marmoreos," speculating that it might be an error in copying (*1972*, I, 350; the change creates agreement with the masculine gender of colles).

The meter of the Latin translation is elegaic couplet (dactylic hexameter in the first line and pentameter in the second).

IN HOROLOGIUM.

Inter marmoreas, Leonoræ, pendula colles,
Fortunata nimis, Machina, dicit horas.
Quà *manibus,* premìt illa duas, insensa, papillas,
Cur mihi sit *digito* tangere, amata, nefas.

Appendix B. Prose Treated as Poems

"The Ocean rolls between us"

The lines beginning "The Ocean rolls between us," which appear in most collective editions as either a discrete poem or as part of a larger lyric ("To Ireland"), in fact originated as a prose passage in a letter PBS wrote to Elizabeth Hitchener on 14 February 1812. In this letter, now at the British Library (ADD. MS 37,496, folios 89–90), PBS copied two lyrics: ***"Brothers, between you and me"*** (first titled "The Mexican Revolution" in *1870;* see ***Esd***) and ***"Bear witness Erin!"*** (first titled "To Ireland" in *1870;* see p. 145). Ranging into the text of the letter preceding these poems, Edward Dowden, in his 1886 *Life of PBS,* observed a passage in which PBS's "ecstatic protestations of eternal friendship, though written as prose, assume consciously or unconsciously the form of blank verse . . ." (I, 247), a point Dowden highlights by setting **lines 15–18** of our transcription on page 441 as four lines of blank verse:

> Thou art a conqueror, Time; all things give way
> Before thee but 'the fixed and virtuous will;'
> The sacred sympathy of soul which was
> When thou wert not, which shall be when thou perishest.

Dowden adds in a footnote: "A few of the lines which precede may be given here to show that the blank verse can hardly have been an accident," and he prints as verse **lines 6–10** of our transcription:

> I could stand
> Upon thy shores, O Erin, and could count
> The billows that, in their unceasing swell,
> Dash on thy beach, and every wave might seem
> An instrument in Time, the giant's grasp,
> To burst the barriers of Eternity.
> Proceed, thou giant, conquering and to conquer;
> (I, 247–48)

The first editor to act upon Dowden's observation was Woodberry, who in *1892W* created an entirely new work in PBS's poetic canon under Rossetti's title "To Ireland" by adding Dowden's blank verse as a second stanza to the rhymed couplets of *"Bear witness, Erin!"* and filling in some of the lines that Dowden had omitted (**lines 10–15** of our transcription):

TO IRELAND

I

Bear witness, Erin! when thine injured isle
Sees summer on its verdant pastures smile,
Its cornfields waving in the winds that sweep
The billowy surface of thy circling deep!
Thou tree whose shadow o'er the Atlantic gave
Peace, wealth and beauty, to its friendly wave,
                    its blossoms fade,
And blighted are the leaves that cast its shade;
Whilst the cold hand gathers its scanty fruit,
Whose chillness struck a canker to its root.

II

              I could stand
Upon thy shores, O Erin, and could count
The billows that, in their unceasing swell,
Dash on thy beach, and every wave might seem
An instrument in Time, the giant's grasp,
To burst the barriers of Eternity.
Proceed, thou giant, conquering and to conquer;
March on thy lonely way! The nations fall
Beneath thy noiseless footstep; pyramids
That for millenniums have defied the blast,
And laughed at lightnings, thou dost crush to nought.
Yon monarch, in his solitary pomp,
Is but the fungus of a winter day
That thy light footstep presses into dust.
Thou art a conqueror, Time; all things give way
Before thee but 'the fixed and virtuous will;'
The sacred sympathy of soul which was
When thou wert not, which shall be when thou perishest.

In *1904*, Hutchinson simply followed the lead of Woodberry, but Ingpen in *1927* was more textually adventuresome, reversing the order of the stanzas in "To Ireland," so that *"Bear witness, Erin!"* becomes the second stanza rather than the first, and preceding the blank verse lines fashioned from PBS's prose in *1892W* with eight more lines newly excavated from PBS's letter (**lines 1–6** of our transcription below):

The ocean rolls between us. O thou ocean,
Whose multitudinous billows ever lash

Prose Treated as Poems   439

> Erin's green isle, on whose shores this venturous arm
> Would plant the flag of liberty, roll on!
> And with each wave whose echoings die amid
> Thy melancholy silentless [*sic*, for "silentness"] shall die
> A moment too—one of those moments which
> Part my friend and me!

In *1972*, Rogers follows *1927*, though he notes Jones's objection in **Letters** to the yoking of *"Bear witness, Erin!"* and the lines fashioned from PBS's prose as a single continuous poem (I, 353; and see **Letters** I, 254 n. 13)—an objection with which Matthews and Everest agree in *1989*, where the two sections are printed as separate poems: *"The Ocean rolls between us"* and *"Bear witness, Erin!"*

However, given that PBS only produced and released the lines now known as *"The Ocean rolls between us"* as prose within a letter, no matter how poetic they might be, we do not print them as a separate poem, nor as part of a larger poem coupled with *"Bear witness, Erin!"* Instead, we transcribe the relevant portion of PBS's letter to Hitchener (folio 89; mistakenly cited in *1989* as folio 90), for readers to judge the evidence for themselves. A photofacsimile of the MS of *"The Ocean rolls between us"* with an accompanying transcription by Michael O'Neill is available in *MYR: Shelley VIII*, 57–62. O'Neill notes that the question of whether this passage "should be set out as verse is a ticklish editorial decision" and that "what sways me in favour of doing so is PBS's apparent use of commas to indicate line-breaks" (57). But is PBS indicating line breaks with the commas, or simply rhetorical pauses? Should we be systematically scouring PBS's prose for evidence of other such "poems"? This is a particularly slippery slope, down which one can slide to near absurdity, as recently demonstrated by William H. Shurr's so-called "discovery" of 498 "new" poems in Emily Dickinson's letters (*New Poems of Emily Dickinson* [Chapel Hill: U of North Carolina P, 1993]). Nora Crook ingeniously has suggested the possibility that PBS embedded these lines in prose purposely to test Hitchener's ability to discover the concealed poetry and that, therefore, an important part of their meaning inheres in their embodiment as prose. Whatever the case, one cannot but look askance at their transmission history.

The full text of the letter in which *"The Ocean rolls between us"* appears can be found in **Letters** I, 250–55. The entire passage was quoted as prose in 1892, about the time of Woodberry's edition, by W. G. Kingsland, who commented that it "must surely have roused the prosaic soul of Elizabeth Hitchener to something akin to enthusiasm . . ." (*Poet-Lore* [July 1892]: 312).

Text: BL ADD. MS 37,496, folio 89 (line for line as it appears in MS).

...— The ocean
rolls between us. O thou Ocean, whose multitudinous billows ever
lash, Erin's green isle on whose shores, this venturous arm would
plant the flag of liberty. Roll on! and with each wave whose echoings
die, amid thy melancholy silentness shall die a moment too — one   5
of those moments, which part my friend and me. I could stand, upon
thy shores, o Erin, and could count the billows that in their unceasing
swell, dash on thy beach, and every wave might seem, an instrument
in Time the giant's grasp, to burst the barriers of Eternity
Proceed thou giant conquering and to conquer. March on thy lonely   10
way — the Nations fall beneath thy noiseless footstep — pyramids
that for milleniums have defied the blast, and laughed at lightnings thou
dost crush to nought. Yon monarch in his solitary pomp, is but the
fungus of a winter day that thy light footstep presses into
dust — Thou art a conqueror Time! all things give way before   15
thee, but "the fixed and virtuous will," the sacred sympathy of soul
which was when thou wert not, which shall be when thou perish
est.—

"Oh Ireland!"

In their commentary to *"The Ocean rolls between us,"* Matthews and Everest observe that "a passage of similar imperfect blank verse occurs at the end of the fourth paragraph of ***An Address to the Irish People***" (1812), which they provide in the form of a poem by way of illustration:

>   Oh Ireland!
> Thou emerald of the ocean, whose sons
> Are generous and brave, whose daughters are
> Honourable and frank and fair, thou art the isle
> On whose green shores I have desired to see
> The standard of liberty erected—a flag of fire—
> A beacon at which the world shall light
> The torch of Freedom!

As PBS published it in ***An Address to the Irish People*** (p. 4) the passage appears as follows:

> Oh! Ireland, thou emerald of the ocean, whose sons are generous and brave, whose daughters are honorable, and frank, and fair; thou art the isle on whose green shores I have desired to see the standard of liberty erected, a flag of fire, a beacon at which the world shall light the torch of Freedom!

Appendix C. Lost Works

Joseph Gibbons Merle mentions that PBS published at his grandfather's expense "many of his fugitive pieces," which were "issued from the press of a printer at Horsham named Phillips" ("A Newspaper Editor's Reminiscences," 702). Although none of these miscellaneous early poems has yet been identified, Merle's account is credible. An aspiring poet himself, this friend of Graham worked as corresponding clerk for Ackermann's *Poetical Magazine* and admired PBS's work; Merle would thus have had reason to note these fugitive publications and the means by which they were produced. The printing firm of the Horsham Phillips's sons, C. and W. Phillips of Worthing, certainly produced for PBS, at the very least, **V&C** and **The Necessity of Atheism.** In fact, when descendants of the Phillips family removed to New Zealand, they transported a copy of **The Necessity of Atheism** now in the Robert H. Taylor Collection at the Firestone Library, Princeton University. We believe that among the other "fugitive pieces" that C. and W. Phillips might have printed for PBS are **Essay on War** and **On a Fête at Carlton House** (for each of which, see below), as well as a volume of poems that Cameron claims was jointly produced by Hellen Shelley and PBS but subsequently suppressed (*YS,* 301 n.109). As Hellen Shelley makes clear, however, this volume contained her poems alone; PBS's role was confined to assigning her the subjects of several poems and to arranging for the printing, which came as a surprise and somewhat of a shock to Hellen Shelley. She recalled, "When I saw my name in the title page . . . I felt much more frightened than pleased, and as soon as the publication was seen by my superiors, it was bought up and destroyed" (Hogg, *Life,* ed. Wolfe, 26). Because of PBS's connection to Merle and his expressed interest in having work published in Ackermann's *Poetical Magazine* (**Letters** I, 14–15), we have checked all four volumes of the *Poetical Magazine* (first published in May 1809) for verse by PBS but have found no likely candidates, though we did note poems by "Clio" Rickman, Phillis Wheatley, and Felicia Dorothea Browne (later Hemans).

Among other possible lost poetry by PBS is a poem that Hellen Shelley remembered as "illustrating some thing unfavourable to a French teacher," as well as a play that she claimed was coauthored by PBS and Elizabeth Shelley (Hogg, *Life,* ed. Wolfe, 25, 26). Although PBS alludes to this "farce" (see Commentary to *"How stern are the woes"* in *St.Irv*), he also mentions in a letter to Graham a tragedy upon which he was at work and that he planned to submit to the "managers of the Lyceum Theatre . . ." (***Letters*** I, 14)—perhaps entitled *Olympia* (see Unattributed Epigraphs to *St.Irv* in Appendix D). And according to Andrew Amos, PBS's classmate at Eton, in his reminiscences in the *Athenæum* for 15 April 1848, the two boys while at Eton "used to amuse ourselves in composing plays . . ." (390). It is unclear whether any of the plays PBS apparently composed were in verse.

Besides the shadowy works just enumerated, the following five poems were probably written by the young PBS, but subsequently lost.

Satirical Poem on "L'infame"

In a letter written 20 December 1810 to Hogg, PBS comments: "I am composing a *Satirical Poem* on L'infame, I shall print it at Mundays, unless I find from you that Robinson is ripe for printing whatever will sell—In case of that he is my man—" (***Letters*** I, 28). No such poem has yet been identified successfully, and the attempts of earlier editors to do so were compromised by their dependence on a text of this letter as silently expurgated by Hogg in *Life* (1858) that omitted the Voltairian phrase "on L'infame" and, hence, disguised the fact that Christianity was the primary target of PBS's lost satire.

Mac-Carthy, for example, states that the ***Poetical Essay on the Existing State of Things*** is the satirical poem PBS refers to in his letter to Hogg (*Early Life*, 103), a claim he probably would not have pressed had he known the full text of PBS's letter, since he recognized that the title, dedication, and epigraph to the lost ***Poetical Essay*** all indicate that its main subject was politics, not Christianity as such, with England's treatment of Ireland a likely focus (see discussion of ***Poetical Essay***, below). Forman, similarly hampered, speculates in *The Shelley Library* ([1886], 23–26) that what he calls the "Missing Satire of 1811" was eventually published as *Lines Addressed to His Royal Highness, The Prince of Wales, on His Being Appointed Regent* (for which, see Appendix E, Misattributions), a conjecture he hardly would have made had he known the full text of PBS's letter. Restoring the phrase "on L'infame" undercuts Forman's related and otherwise unfounded supposition that the "Missing Satire" was the unnamed work that PBS tried unsuccessfully to publish with Rowland Hunter in the spring of 1811 (23–24). For our argument that the unnamed poem that PBS brought to Hunter was actually ***The Wandering Jew***, a work we know PBS tried several times to publish during this same period, see the Commentary for *WJ*, page 195.

Lady (Jane) Shelley prepared a corrected text of PBS's letter, used by both Koszul in *La jeunesse de Shelley* (1910) and Ingpen and Peck in *1927*, which nonetheless apparently still omitted "on L'infame." However, since

1964, when Jones published the full text in **Letters,** no likely identification of the poem has been made. If PBS ever did complete the poem, he seems to have had no luck finding a publisher, and the MS was probably lost or destroyed. Another possibility, of course, is that the poem was never finished. PBS's letter to Hogg is filled with impassioned imprecations against Christianity, and while beginning such a satire may have relieved the tensions of the moment, the poem could have remained, like other of his attempts at satire, an abortive fragment. He was, however, to use Voltaire's slogan "*Ecrasez L'infame*" as one of the epigraphs for **QM,** and perhaps some drafts from this satire were later reworked in the attacks on Christianity in Canto VII of **QM.**

Poetical Essay on the Existing State of Things

Cameron has appropriately labeled **Poetical Essay** "one of the unsolved mysteries of Shelley bibliography" (*YS,* 316 n.62). Questions remain about whether Shelley wrote such a poem and about whether it was ever actually printed or published, although the former is more easily resolvable than the latter.

On 9 March 1811, as Mac-Carthy first discovered (*Early Life,* 100), the following ad appeared in the *Oxford University and City Herald,* a newspaper in which PBS had advertised, in advance of publication, **The Necessity of Atheism** exactly one month earlier:

Literature.

Just published, Price Two Shillings,

A POETICAL ESSAY

ON THE

Existing State of Things.

AND FAMINE AT HER BIDDING WASTED WIDE
THE WRETCHED LAND, TILL IN THE PUBLIC WAY
PROMISCUOUS WHERE THE DEAD AND DYING LAY,
DOGS FED ON HUMAN BONES IN THE OPEN LIGHT OF DAY.
Curse of Kehama.

By A

GENTLEMAN *of the University of Oxford.*

For assisting to maintain in Prison

Mr. Peter Finnerty,

IMPRISONED FOR A LIBEL.

London: Sold by B. Crosby and Co.,

and all other Booksellers.

1811.

No copy of this "Just published" poem has yet been located, but there are good reasons to think that PBS may have been its author. Not only had he used the pseudonym "A Gentleman of the University of Oxford" for *St.Irv* (published the previous December), but also he was an active supporter of the Irish journalist Peter Finnerty, whose highly publicized trial for libel against Viscount Castlereagh in 1811 further exposed Castlereagh's responsibility for the torture and abuse of Irish prisoners during the 1798 uprising (see Commentary to **The Spectral Horseman,** lines 47–49, and **The Devil's Walk,** lines 57–59). In the weeks immediately preceding the 9 March ad for **Poetical Essay,** the *Oxford Herald* followed the lead of Sir Francis Burdett and Leigh Hunt in London by opening a subscription for Finnerty (23 February), to which PBS was listed as one of four contributors on 2 March.

Subsequent ads for *Poetical Essay* in the *Morning Chronicle* for 15 and 21 March and in *The Times* for 10 and 11 April 1811 all claim that the poem was published "for assisting to maintain in prison Mr. Peter Finnerty, imprisoned for a libel." About Finnerty's trial, PBS later writes in *An Address to the Irish People* (1812): "But Mr. Finnerty, much as he has lost, yet retains the fair name of truth and honor. He was imprisoned for persisting in the truth" (*Prose*/EBM, 33).

One important contemporary source connecting PBS with a poem in support of Finnerty is the *Dublin Weekly Messenger* for 7 March 1812, which claims:

Mr. Shelly [*sic*] commiserating the sufferings of our distinguished countryman, Mr. Finerty, whose exertions in the cause of political freedom he much admired, wrote a very beautiful poem, the profits of the sale of which we understand, from *undoubted*, authority, Mr. Shelly remitted to Mr. Finerty;—we have heard they amounted to nearly an hundred pounds.—This fact speaks a volume in favour of our new Friend. (*Prose*/EBM, 298)

PBS clipped this article from the newspaper and sent it to Godwin in a letter of 8 March 1812 (see *Letters* I, 268–69), proof that he was at least claiming to have written a poem the profits of which went to Finnerty.

It remains unclear how "very beautiful" a poem the *Poetical Essay* would have been: the dedication to Finnerty, as well as the epigraph taken from one of PBS's favorite poems, *The Curse of Kehama*, with its references to "famine" and a "wretched land," imply that the poem addressed the troubles in Ireland, quite possibly in the form of political satire, as Mac-Carthy conjectures (*Early Life,* 103). On the other hand, at the beginning of the nineteenth century *beautiful* could still mean "fine" or "admirable." Mac-Carthy further suggests that the volume was bought in great numbers, "not for the sake of the verse, but for the sake of the cause" (104), noting that advertising for *Poetical Essay* stopped abruptly, after only a month, "by which time, it may be presumed, the whole impression was bought up" (105–6). However, as Forman points out, for a two shilling poem to raise £100, it must sell at least 1,000 copies (*The Shelley Library,* 21), which considering the relatively dormant sales of PBS's other works would have been extraordinary. And if 1,000 copies had indeed been sold, it is likely that at least one of them would be known today. Quite possibly, then, the *Dublin Weekly Messenger* (following PBS's assertions?) exaggerates the amount of money that PBS directed to Finnerty. Otherwise, it refers either to yet another unknown poem by PBS or to the proceeds from *PF,* which PBS's printer, Slatter, states went to the aid of Finnerty (in the notes to the fourth edition of Robert Montgomery's *Oxford: A Poem* [1835], 165), a claim also made by PBS's Oxford contemporary, Charles Kirkpatrick Sharpe (*Letters From and*

To Charles Kirkpatrick Sharpe, Esq., ed. Alexander Allardyce [Edinburgh: William Blackwood, 1888], I, 442).

Whether or not the *Poetical Essay* is the work to which the *Dublin Weekly Messenger* actually refers, Sharpe's own testimony is one of two contemporary comments that independently confirm PBS as the author of the poem. In a letter dated 15 March 1811, less than a week after the 9 March ad describing *Poetical Essay* as just published, Sharpe writes that "Shelley's last exhibition is a poem on the State of Public Affairs" (I, 443). Less than two weeks later, on 27 March 1811, just two days after PBS and Hogg were expelled from Oxford, a Bodleian assistant and Fellow of St. John's named Philip Bliss (later a distinguished bibliographer) compiled the earliest known bibliography of PBS's works, which includes as the fourth item the following entry: "*A Poetical Essay on the existing State of Things*—4°. Oxford 1811" (Bod MS Top. Oxon. e. 51, pp. 160–61; see B. C. Barker-Benfield, *Shelley's Guitar* [1992], 31). Bliss's description of the volume as a quarto is the best evidence that the published poem was actually seen by someone, unless Bliss was merely conjecturing or had heard second-hand about the format. *PF,* the only other poetic volume in Bliss's brief bibliography, as he notes, had also been printed as a quarto.

White has surmised that *Poetical Essay on the Existing State of Things* may never have been written, "but was a fiction to support interest in Finnerty's case" (*Shelley* I, 108), a possibility that cannot yet be disproved. However, sufficient evidence exists to indicate that PBS did indeed write such a poem, and possibly that it was published as a quarto sometime in March 1811, just prior to PBS's expulsion from Oxford. By 11 April 1811 when the advertising for the volume stopped, PBS had removed to London with Hogg and was not only severely short of cash (see *Letters* I, 59, 61), but also in the midst of fraught negotiations with his father about his future. The ads for *Poetical Essay* may have stopped in mid-April simply because PBS could no longer afford them. However, an explanation that would account for all of the evidence is that the ads stopped and no extant copies of the poem have been found, either because PBS withdrew the volume from the press or because the printer refused to produce the book on credit, as was likely if PBS took it to one like Munday, to whom he already owed money.

In actively supporting Finnerty, PBS was taking an extreme political position, far enough to the left of the Whigs for Cameron to suggest that PBS's efforts "played a part in his expulsion" from Oxford (*YS,* 51). Given his lack of funds and alienation from his father after being sent down, he may have tried to avoid straining past the breaking point his deeply imperiled relations with Timothy Shelley, a stalwart Whig. Indeed, in April 1811 the Duke of Norfolk, political patron of Timothy Shelley and a Whig leader, intervened in the heated negotiations between father and son, unsuccessfully attempting to lure PBS into the political arena (see White, *Shelley* I, 135). Whatever PBS's actual motives, **Poetical Essay,** if he succeeded in having it published, was probably suppressed by mid-April, when the ads for it cease.

Dowden (*Life* I, 110–11), A. M. D. Hughes (*The Nascent Mind of Shelley* [1947], 174–75), and Matthews and Everest in *1989* (I, 266) all speculate that PBS reworked **Poetical Essay** for Cantos III and IV of **QM,** which focus on the present state of society, but there is, of course, no hard evidence of this. With just as little evidence but more self-assurance, Forman claims:

> To save the risk of disappointment in the *Poetical Essay,* let us clearly understand that, when that "very beautiful poem" does turn up, it will assuredly be found to be in the very beautiful taste of the eighteenth century—probably a little less hollow and trifling than the *Posthumous Fragments of Margaret Nicholson,* and somewhere midway between that level and the precarious altitudes of *Queen Mab,* wherein the still young muse of Shelley thought itself seriously occupied in the interests of posterity. (*Shelley Library,* 22)

The proof of such conjectures awaits that time when a copy of **Poetical Essay** finds the light of day.

On a Fête at Carlton House

PBS appears to have written a short satirical poem about the notorious fête the Prince Regent held at Carlton House (his official residence) on 19 June 1811, at which some 2,000 English nobles and gentry, as well as the entire royal family of France, were entertained lavishly at tremendous cost, while many throughout England were suffering from economic deprivation and the cumulative effects of the war with France. In a letter to PBS's younger sister Hellen Shelley, written 25 February 1857, Charles Grove recalls:

> during the early summer which Bysshe spent in town, after leaving Oxford [in 1811], the Prince Regent gave a splendid fête at Carlton House, in which the novelty was introduced of a stream of water, in imitation of a river, meandering down the middle of a very long table, in a temporary tent erected in Carlton Gardens. This was much commented upon in the papers, and laughed at by the Opposition. Bysshe also was of the number of those who disapproved of the fête and its accompaniments. He wrote a poem on the subject of about fifty lines, which he published immediately, wherein he apostrophized the prince as sitting on the bank of his tiny river; and he amused himself with throwing copies into the carriages of persons going to Carlton House after the fête. (Hogg, *Life,* ed. Wolfe, II, 157–58)

During the spring and early summer of 1811, Charles Grove was one of PBS's main confidants, and the circumstantiality of his story is persuasive, especially because we do know that PBS was outraged by accounts of the fête in the newspapers, where he could have found detailed reports in such likely sources as the *Morning Chronicle* for 15 and 20 June, *The Times* for 20 June, and the *Oxford University and City Herald* for 22 June. Almost certainly he read the *Morning Chronicle* for 15 June, which, in an article headlined "*The PRINCE REGENT'S FETE*," describes preparations for the fête in words PBS was to echo:

> The whole of this promenade (the aisle) will resemble an Allee-vert, or green-walk. . . . The *chef d'œuvre* of the whole will be a serpentine bubbling brook of real water, occupying a centrical [*sic*] space down the Prince's table, 170 feet in length, and 14 inches in depth. It will be a running stream, produced by a reservoir at one end, and waste pipes at the other. This canal, which will be filled with gold and silver fish, will meander over weeds, congenial to the soil, artificially constructed. A space in each side is allotted for moss and flowers, to give the banks an appearance of an enamelled mead, the bubbles in the water will be produced by square blocks of wood, placed at equi-distances at the bottom, and painted a lead colour, so as to resemble a natural appearance.

PBS writes to Hitchener on 20 June 1811:

> What think you of the bubbl{ing} *brooks, & mossy banks* at Carlton House—the allee-verts &c—it is said that this entertainment will cost 120,000£; nor will it be the last bauble which the nation must buy to amuse this overgrown bantling of regency. How admirably this growing spirit of ludicrous magnificence tallies with the disgusting splendors of the stage of the roman Empire, which preceded its destruction! Yet here are a people advanced in intellectual improvement, willfully rushing to a Revolution, the natural death of all great commercial Empires, which must plunge them in the barbarism from which they are slowly arising. (**Letters** I, 110)

PBS's reference in this letter (which would not have been known to Charles Grove) to the "*mossy banks*" at Carlton House foreshadows the "mossy brink" in the first line of the poem as Grove remembered it (see below), adding further credibility to *his* overall account.

Throughout May and June of 1811, PBS lived at Field Place, but both Charles Grove and his brother John were in London, where, according to Hawkins, "they were able, by the influence of the Duchess of Rutland, to visit Carlton House" (*First Love*, 91), a visit that must have come up in the various exchanges between PBS and the Groves. If Charles Grove is correct about PBS's immediately "publishing the poem" and "throwing copies into the carriages of persons going to Carlton House after the fête," PBS probably had the poem printed as a broadside somewhere in Sussex—perhaps by C. and W. Phillips at Worthing, the printers of *V&C* and **The Necessity of Atheism**. He could then have brought the copies with him to London, where he spent several days between 4 and 15 July on his way to Wales from Horsham, and when he would have been able to fling copies of the poem into the carriages of surprised visitors to Carlton House.

Beyond Charles Grove's account, there is one other probable reference

Lost Works 449

to the poem. PBS writes in a letter to Graham that is dated 19 June 1811 by Jones:

> If Graham, within that democratical bosom of thine, *yet* lingers a spark of loyalty, if a true & firm Kings man ever found favor in thy sight, if thou art not totally hardened to streamlets, whose mossy banks invite the repose of the wanderer.... Then, Graham do I conjure thee, by the great George our King, by our noble Prince Regent & our inimitable Commander in chief... that thou wilt assist me... in my loyal endeavours to magnify, if magnification be possible, our noble Royal Family. High let them soar, high as the expanse of the empyrean & may no invidious louse dare to interrupt the reveries of pensive enthusiasm—In fine, Græme, thou hast an harp of fire, & I a pen of honey. Let then the song roll, wide let it roll. Take then thy tuning fork, for the ode is coming. Lo! Fargy thou art as the bard of old, I as the poet of other times. (***Letters*** I, 105–6)

PBS signed this letter "Philobasileus" and added his translation of nine lines of the *Marseillaise* as a postscript. His reference to "streamlets" with "mossy banks" indicates that the satirical "ode" he was writing and wanted Graham to set to music had been provoked by the Prince Regent's fête, and unless it is yet another lost satire, it is probably the same satirical poem on the fête described by Charles Grove.

Forman, who incorrectly identifies *Lines, Addressed to His Royal Highness The Prince of Wales, on His Being Appointed Regent* as the poem to which PBS alludes in his letter to Graham (see Appendix E, Misattributions), notes two other published poems on the Prince Regent's fête: *Carlton House Fête; or, the Disappointed Bard ... by Peter Pindar, Esq.* and *The Regent's Fête or the Prince and his Country. By E. Fitzgerald, Esq.* (Shelley Library, 26, 23). A review in the *Poetical Register* for 1810–11 describes "Peter Pindar's" (i.e., John Wolcot's) *Carlton House Fête* as "past all comparison, the best poem which he has written for many years. We cordially recommend it to our readers, in full confidence that it will afford them amusement, and that, this time, they will laugh *with* the old Bard, and not *at* him" (628). According to Robert L. Vales, in *Peter Pindar (John Wolcot)* ([1973], 159), *Carlton House Fête* was, in fact, the last satire Wolcot ever published under that pseudonym. For PBS's knowledge of "Peter Pindar's" work, see page 314.

Charles Grove claimed to recall four of the fifty lines of PBS's poem, which he recited to Richard Garnett some forty-six years after the fête. Although there is no way to gauge the accuracy of Grove's memory of the poem, the lines he recalls do, at least, have an archly Shelleyan flavor. Garnett subsequently made his transcription available to Rossetti, who first printed the lines in *1870*, and they have since been included in all major collective editions of PBS's poetry.

Text: From *1870*.

ON A FÊTE AT CARLTON HOUSE.
(Fragment).

By the mossy brink,
With me the Prince shall sit and think;
Shall muse in visioned Regency,
Rapt in bright dreams of dawning Royalty.

Essay on War

PBS's only mention of the **Essay on War** appears in a letter of 16 January 1812 to Godwin: "I have desired the publications of my earlier youth to be sent to you, you will perceive that Zastrozzi and St. Irvyne were written prior to my acquaintance with your writings. The Essay on War a little Poem, since" (***Letters*** I, 231; Bod MS Shelley c.1, f. 57). But Hogg, who first published this letter in 1858 (*Life*, ed. Wolfe, I, 309), gave "Essay on Love" for "Essay on War," an error (assuming it was unintentional) easy to make given the hastily scrawled appearance of "War" in the MS. Hogg's reading of "Love" was perpetuated by subsequent editors and scholars until F. L. Jones corrected it in the *Times Literary Supplement* for 4 July 1952 (437).

Before Jones's correction, Mac-Carthy had surmised that because PBS did not mention to Godwin the ***Poetical Essay on the Existing State of Things***, the "Essay on Love" might have been an alternative title for ***Poetical Essay***, adding that "The word 'Essay' gives great probability to this supposition" (*Early Life*, 105). Mac-Carthy's conjecture remains no less possible given the actual title "Essay on War." Forman, who without elaboration finds Mac-Carthy's hypothesis "highly improbable," offers instead the possibility that "*An Essay on Love* was one of the occasional trifles which 'A Newspaper Editor' [i.e., Gibbons Merle] believed to have been printed at Horsham at the cost of Sir Bysshe" (*Shelley Library*, 16). It is unlikely, however, that PBS, who was trying to impress Godwin with a work produced after he had become acquainted with Godwin's writings, would have sent one of his "occasional trifles."

After Jones's correction of the title, the fruitless scholarly search for an "Essay on Love" written by the young PBS was altered to an equally fruitless search for any evidence that a poem entitled "Essay on War" was published in Oxford or London in 1810–11. In *TLS*, Jones suggested that "Essay on War" was, in fact, the untitled opening poem of **PF** (***"Ambition, power, and avarice"***), which was first titled "War" by Woodberry in *1892W*. If so, however, PBS sent Godwin either a transcript or a copy of the printed poem removed from the volume (with "Essay on War" written in as the title), since he clearly did not send the **PF** volume but a separate poem. Although

Matthews and Everest accept without comment Jones's conjecture (*1989*, I, 114), the identification of **Essay on War** as *"Ambition, power, and avarice"* remains purely speculative. See the Commentary for *"Ambition, power, and avarice,"* page 245, for a more detailed discussion of this issue.

God Save the King

Although evidence is scant, PBS may have written and had printed a now lost poem entitled **God Save the King,** as White surmises (*Shelley* I, 279–80). PBS mentions this work in only two surviving letters, both written to Thomas Hookham. In the first letter, written in mid-November 1812, PBS writes: "Oh! & is God Save the King done. My loyal soul pants for its arrival" (**Letters** I, 332). In the second, written less than a month later, he asks: "When does God save {the King [tear in paper]} I am anxious for th {[tear in paper]}" (**Letters** I, 334). If this indeed refers to one of his own poetic works, PBS must have sent it to Hookham to have it printed in London. As both the title and PBS's tone suggest, the poem was probably both satiric and subversive, perhaps a broadside like **The Devil's Walk** that similarly risked prosecution. Of course, as Cameron notes, **God Save the King** could simply be the name of a work that Hookham had told PBS about, or "one that Hookham was himself publishing" (*YS,* 382).

There is, however, one other intriguing possible reference to **God Save the King.** In a postscript to a letter PBS wrote from Dublin on 30 March 1813 to John Williams in Tremadoc, Harriet W. Shelley asks Williams to forward a box for the Shelleys to her father's house in London, rather than directly to the Shelleys in Ireland. She explains that if the box "came to us the Custom house men would take it as it contains G{[tear in paper]}" (**Letters** I, 364). During the Shelleys' return from their first trip to Ireland, PBS's seditious Irish writings were confiscated by Customs at Holyhead and a report was filed to the Home Secretary. The Shelleys were thus understandably reluctant to have that experience repeated with the seditious material contained within the box in question. In *SC* IX, the editors speculate that the part of the letter that was torn out contained the rest of the title "God Save the King," which Williams tore out to protect himself from being implicated in the publication of a seditious work. If the box did contain copies of **God Save the King,** they were probably destroyed by either John Williams or PBS, for no copy of such a work has subsequently been identified.

Appendix D. Dubia

The following poems have been attributed inconclusively to PBS.

Poems in the *Oxford University and City Herald*

In *Early Life*, Mac-Carthy identifies six poems published in the *Oxford University and City Herald* (*OxH*) between 22 September 1810 and 9 March 1811 as possibly being by PBS. The first of these, "*Ode, to the Breath of Summer*," is unsigned and appears before PBS actually arrived in Oxford for the beginning of term. The others include four translations from the Greek Anthology, two of which are signed "S." and two "Versificator," and one translation, also signed "Versificator," from the Latin of Vincent Bourne (1695–1747, *DNB* [more under "Translation of an Epigram," below]). Mac-Carthy has argued that Timothy Shelley probably subscribed to the *OxH*, which was liberal in its politics and widely circulated in the southern counties of England; he suggests that issues arrived weekly at Field Place for years before PBS left for Oxford (*Early Life*, 26). The *OxH* was printed by J. Munday (later Munday and Slatter), the publisher of *PF*, and PBS not only advertised in its pages and subscribed to its fund for Peter Finnerty while he was at Oxford (see the discussion of **Poetical Essay on the Existing State of Things**, above), but we now know that several years later he contributed **To Constantia,** which appeared in *OxH* on 31 January 1818.

Beyond these connections between PBS and the *OxH*, Mac-Carthy accurately notes that coincident with PBS's arrival in Oxford, the *OxH* began publishing original verse (some signed with the letter "S"), an initiative that ceases about the same time as PBS's expulsion. He thus concludes about the six poems: "The signature attached to them, the time at which they appeared, the journal in which they were published, and the course of his studies at the time, all create an amount of presumptive evidence that justify me in offering them here as having in all probability been written by Shelley." Mac-Carthy does distinguish, however, between "*Ode, to the Breath of Summer,*" which he finds "essentially Shelleyesque both in the language and the ideas," and the five translations, in which he can find no stylistic evidence of PBS's authorship (58).

While the "Ode" is certainly more "Shelleyesque" than the translations, there is insufficient evidence from their content or style to attribute any of these poems to PBS, even given the circumstantial connections made by Mac-Carthy. Indeed, after the MS for *Early Life* had gone to the press, Mac-Carthy himself turned up a final piece of evidence that undermined his entire argument. He adds in a note: "Since this page was in type I have found in *The Oxford Herald* another translation from Vincent Bourne, signed 'S.S—— Edmonton' [printed on 9 Feb. 1811, though Mac-Carthy does not give the date]. Whatever effect this may have on the suggestion thrown out above, it is only right that it should be mentioned" (61–62n). Because Mac-Carthy had argued that all five of the translations were produced by a single author who used both "S." and "Versificator" as signatures, his discovery of the other translation from Vincent Bourne leads to the possibility that at least those signed "S" were written not by PBS, but by "S.S——" of Edmonton. Nonetheless, given the interactivity between reader-contributors and periodicals of the early nineteenth century, the possibility remains strong that more than one author was involved in composing the group of translations, perhaps in emulatory rivalry, as Reiman has suggested (*Romantic Texts and Contexts* [1987], 46).

The translations appear in the following sequence: two from the Greek Anthology, signed "S." (5 and 12 Jan.); one from Vincent Bourne signed "S.S——Edmonton" (9 Feb.); another from Bourne, signed "Versificator" (23 Feb.); and two from the Greek Anthology, signed "Versificator" (9 Mar.). This sequence breaks into two symmetrical groupings, the first comprising two translations from the Greek Anthology followed by one from Bourne (all possibly by "S.S——"), the second, one translation from Bourne followed by two from the Greek Anthology (all by Versificator). This symmetry suggests that two or possibly three (if "S." and "S.S——" are different) writers (who may have known each other) were responsible for the translations. Due to the wealth of circumstantial connections between PBS and the *OxH,* as well as the appearance of the translations while PBS was at Oxford, we provide texts for all of these poems below (with the exception of the Bourne translation by "S.S——Edmonton") on the chance that any or some of them may be by PBS.

Rogers in *1972* is the only editor of a collective edition to provide texts for the five translations, which he includes among PBS's "Early Shorter Poems and Translations, 1802–1812" (I, 6–8); he does not comment upon Mac-Carthy's discovery of the second translation of Vincent Bourne. Rogers neither prints "*Ode, to the Breath of Summer*" nor explains why he omits it. In small headnotes, we provide the source of our Text. For translations, we cite a source for the text of the original. All citations for the Greek Anthology are from the Loeb edition (*The Greek Anthology*, ed. W. R. Paton [Cambridge: Harvard UP, 1958 and 1960]).

Ode, to the Breath of Summer

Text: *OxH*, 22 September 1810, page 2 (top of col. 4). Erroneously titled "Ode to the Death of Summer" by Mac-Carthy in *Early Life* (59).

ODE,
TO THE BREATH OF SUMMER.

ZEPHYR, whither art thou straying,
    Tell me where;
With prankish girls in gardens playing,
    False and fair
A butterfly's light back bestriding,   5
Queen bees to honey-suckles guiding,
Or in a swinging hair-bell riding,
    Free from care?

Before Aurora's car you amble,
    High in air;   10
At noon, when Neptune's sea-nymphs gambol,
    Braid their hair:
When on the tumbling billows rolling,
Or on the smooth sands idly strolling,
Or in cool grottoes they lie lolling,   15
    You sport there.

To chase the moon-beams up the mountains,
    You prepare:
Or dance with elves on brinks of fountains,
    Mirth to share.   20
Now seen with love-lorn lilies weeping,
Now with a blushing rose-bud sleeping,
While fays from forth their chambers peeping,
    Cry, oh rare!
                [no signature]

The Grape. From the Greek Anthologia

Text: Mac-Carthy, *Early Life*, 60. Translation of *Gr. Anth.* IX.375; Loeb III, 204–7. First published in *OxH*, 5 January 1811, an issue we have been unable to locate; it is missing in both hard copy and microfilm from the copies of *OxH* held by Htn, BL, Bod, and the Oxford County Library.

THE GRAPE.
From the Greek Anthologia.

<pre>
     This grape, of future wine the store,
     Who from the tree unripen'd bore?
     And, loathing its yet acid taste,
     Thus on the ground half-eaten cast?
5   To every footstep passing by
     The spurn'd remains obnoxious lie;—
     To him, the foe of mirth and love,
     May Bacchus ever hostile prove,
     As to the barb'rous prince of yore
10   Who Thracia's blooming vines uptore:—
     This grape, thus wantonly abus'd,
     When in the sparkling glass infus'd,
     This might have warm'd some poet's lay,
     Or chased corroding care away!   S.
</pre>

Epigram, from the Greek Anthologia

Text: *OxH*, 12 January 1811, page 74 (back page). Translation of *Gr. Anth.* VI.345; Loeb I, 482–83.

EPIGRAM,
FROM THE GREEK ANTHOLOGIA.

Supposed to be spoken by some Roses on the Birth-day of a Beautiful Girl, who was on the point of Marriage.

—

<pre>
We that were wont in Spring's soft lap to bloom,
Now early blush, 'mid Winter's dreary gloom,
And on this day we smiling hail thy charms,
That soon sweet maid, shall bless a husband's arms;
More pleased thy lovely temples to adorn,
Then wait the rising of the vernal morn.   S.
</pre>

Translation of an Epigram of Vincent Bourne's

Vincent Bourne was a distinguished English Latinist and though an "indolent" usher at Westminster School when William Cowper studied there, he was rated by Cowper a great Latin poet, nearly equal to Ovid (see Cowper's comments on the title page and on page v of *The Poetical Works, Latin and English, of Vincent Bourne* (Cambridge: W. P. Grant, 1838). Several of Bourne's Latin poems were translated by Cowper and others by Charles Lamb, who wrote to W. Wordsworth on 16 April 1815 about Bourne's poetry: "What a heart that man had, all laid out upon town scenes, a proper counterpoise to *some people's* rural extravaganzas. ... what a sweet unpretending pretty-mannered *matter-ful* creature—sucking from every flower, making a flower of every thing—his diction all latin and his thoughts all English——. Bless him, Latin was'nt [*sic*] good enough for him, why wasnt he content with the language which Gay & Prior wrote in——" (*The Letters of Charles and Mary Lamb*, ed. Edwin W. Marrs Jr. [Ithaca: Cornell UP, 1978], III, 140).

Text: *OxH*, 23 February 1811, page 4 (bottom of col. 2). Text in Latin appears in *Poematia latine partim reddita partim scripta a Vincentio Bourne* (ed. John Mitford [London: G. Pickering, 1840], 248).

TRANSLATION OF AN EPIGRAM OF
VINCENT BOURNE'S.
—x—

Down the river's gentle tide,
As to London bridge we glide,
Hark! the bells of Mary's tow'r,
Sweetly warbled music pour!
With what harmony and grace   5
Each preserves its stated place!
While the air, above, around,
Trembles with the varied sound!

Merry changes ceaseless glide
To old Thames's willow'd side;   10
Still recede; and sweeter still,
Through the raptur'd breast they thrill.
Such the pleasure to our hearts,
Distant melody imparts—
Enter once within the tow'r,   15
All the harmony is o'er.
                    VERSIFICATOR.

Two Epigrams from the Greek Anthology: "On Old Age" and "Venus and the Muses"

Text: *OxH*, 9 March 1811, page 4 (top of col. 1). Translation of *Gr. Anth.* IX.54; Loeb III, 28–29.

ON OLD AGE,
FROM THE GREEK ANTHOLOGY

Mortals for age, when distant, pray,
Age, when at hand, they wish away;
The thing of which we're not possest,
We constantly esteem the best.

VERSIFICATOR.

Text: *OxH*, 9 March 1811, page 4 (top of col. 1). Translation of *Gr. Anth.* IX.39; Loeb III, 22–23.

VENUS AND THE MUSES
FROM THE SAME

The Queen of love once threat'ning vow'd,
Unless the Nine her sway allow'd,
That Cupid's never-erring dart
Should quickly pierce them to the heart.
Then they: "On Mars your menace try,
The little urchin we defy."

VERSIFICATOR.

Unattributed Epigraphs to St. Irvyne

To Chapter 2:

> The fiends of fate are heard to rave,
> The death-angel flaps his broad wing o'er the wave.

This unattributed epigraph to Chapter 2 of ***St.Irv*** appears to be drawn from PBS's draft of **The Wandering Jew** (***WJ***), for it closely resembles two different pairs of lines in that poem as it was first published in the *Edinburgh Literary Journal* (*1829E*); first a couplet: "When the sightless fiends of the tempests rave, | And hell-birds howl o'er the storm-blacken'd wave" (III.274–75); and then an unrhymed pair of lines: "Hark! the death angel flaps his wing | O'er the blacken'd wave" (IV.114–15).

To Chapter 4:

> ——Nature shrinks back,
> Enhorror'd from the lurid gaze of vengeance
> E'en in the deepest caverns, and the voice
> Of all her works lies hush'd.
>
> OLYMPIA.

To Chapter 7:

> Yes! 't is the influence of that sightless fiend
> Who guides my every footstep, that I feel:
> An iron grasp arrests each fluttering sense,
> And a fell voice howls in mine anguish'd ear,
> "Wretch, thou mayst rest no more."
>
> OLYMPIA.

A character named Olympia appears in Chapter 4 of the prose romance *St.Irv* itself. Otherwise, searches of both print bibliographies such as *NUC* and *NSTC* and searchable on-line bibliographies, including *OCLC* and Chadwyck-Healey *Lion,* have failed to reveal a poem or poetic drama titled *Olympia* (or having an "Olympia" as a major character) from which these lines were taken. Thus, we can support the hypothesis of Matthews and Everest, who attribute these epigraphs to PBS. His possible authorship is supported by the diction of the lines, which include some favorite words and phrases found in his early poetry: *enhorrored* (in **St.Irv**, see **Ballad,** line 70 and Commentary); *lurid* (in **PF**, first line of **Epithalamium** and nine times in **WJ**); *deepest caverns* (cf. **Spectral Horseman,** line 47 in **PF**); *sightless fiend* (the exact phrase appears at **WJ** III.274, while *sightless*—with the same meaning of "invisible"—also appears in line 19 of **Despair** in **PF**); and *fluttering sense* (cf. "fluttering breath" in line 15 of the poem **Revenge** in **V&C** and at **WJ** III.62). Even if these two fragments were composed by PBS, it is impossible to determine whether he composed them as epigraphs for **St.Irv**, salvaged them from drafts of **WJ** or another published poem, or took them from an otherwise unknown, unpublished, and probably unfinished work that he entitled *Olympia.*

While we believe that PBS probably wrote these lines, we do not judge that, though occupying a humble place in PBS's prose romance, they deserve a separate place in his poetic canon, as *1989* gives them for the first time (I, 83). Moreover, they still may turn up in a work entitled *Olympia* by another author steeped in the clichés of the Gothic mode.

Sadak the Wanderer. A Fragment

Sadak the Wanderer. A Fragment, perhaps the most promising of these poems attributed to PBS, first appeared anonymously in the *Keepsake* for 1828 (117–19), where, as one of three interrelated works about Sadak, it is joined by the succeeding prose tale "The Deev Alfakir" and by E. J. Roberts's line engraving of John Martin's stunning oil painting entitled *Sadak in Search of the Waters of Oblivion* (1812). Based on Davidson Cook's arguments in *TLS* (16 May 1936, 423), Rogers incorporated *Sadak* into PBS's poetic canon first, in *1972;* Matthews and Everest followed his lead in *1989.* By 1936, Cook had purchased a volume of original autograph MSS comprising the contents of the 1828 *Keepsake,* which was owned previously by J. Dykes Campbell (editor of S. T. Coleridge) and, before him, by the great manuscript collector Dawson Turner. In *TLS,* Cook explained that this volume originally had contained an autograph manuscript of *Sadak* "in the hand of the poet [i.e., PBS] or possibly transcribed by his second wife." However, although an index at the beginning of the volume identifies PBS as the author of *Sadak,* the MS of *Sadak* itself had been removed sometime prior to Cook's possession of the volume, and its present location is unknown. To what extent, then, can this attribution be credited? Important evidence, some of which was first discussed in Reiman's review of *1972* (*Romantic Texts and Contexts,* 47), casts serious doubt that *Sadak* is indeed by PBS. Because his authorship has, however, recently become widely accepted, it is worthwhile to sketch the arguments involved.

The original source of the Sadak story is James Ridley's popular two-volume *Tales of the Genii* (1764; often reprinted, including editions in 1805, 1808, ?1810, and 1814 [*NSTC*]), whose title page employs the ruse that the whole is translated from the Persian by "Sir Charles Morell, FORMERLY AMBASSADOR FROM THE BRITISH SETTLEMENTS IN INDIA TO THE GREAT MOGUL." "Sadak and Kalasrade" appears as Tale 9 in Volume II (London: James Wallace, 1805, 97–271). The story concerns the triumph of love and patient heroism over tyranny, and it is easy enough to see why PBS might have been attracted to it. The Sultan Amurath becomes jealous of the domestic happiness that Sadak, a military hero, enjoys in retirement with his beloved wife Kalasrade and their family. Amurath, who becomes enamored of Kalasrade, contrives to have her kidnapped and brought to his seraglio, where, in order to fend off the tyrant's insistent advances, she agrees to be his, but only after she is able to drink from the fabled waters of oblivion, which will allow her to forget her ties to Sadak. Ingeniously, Amurath forces Sadak himself to seek these waters, knowing that no one has ever returned alive from such a quest. With the support of the spirit Adiram, Sadak survives a furious storm at sea, the plague, evil genii, a whirlpool in a cave, and a harrowing ascent up a towering volcanic mountain to return after successfully completing his quest. To ease his own guilty conscience (the better to enjoy Kalasrade), Amurath drinks first of the enchanted water and—to the surprise of all—dies, thereby allowing for the happy reunion of Kalasrade with Sadak, who becomes the new sultan in Amurath's place.

While staying true to the spirit of the Sadak story, which it truncates radically (hence its subtitle "A Fragment"), the *Keepsake* poem focuses exclusively on the arduous final stage of Sadak's quest, ending with the foreshadowing of his eventual success and his regaining of "young Kalasrade." Beyond omitting much of the tale proper, the poem makes a few other significant changes, the first two of which are noted in *1989:* while the original Sadak fended off starvation by eating his belt, the first stanza of the poem in the *Keepsake* recounts in detail how Sadak resorted to killing and eating wild animals; unlike the Sadak of the story, the Sadak of the poem descends into an active volcano as part of his quest; and unlike the Kalasrade of the story, who is old enough to have adult children—though her charms are described as "yet undiminished by age"—the Kalasrade of the poem is "young."

Cook's argument for attributing *Sadak* to PBS rests primarily on the identification in the *Keepsake* index, but he also notes that MWS was a friend of William Harrison Ainsworth, the editor of (only) the *Keepsake* for 1828, and was a known contributor of both her own and PBS's work to later *Keepsakes* (under the succeeding editor, Frederick Mansel Reynolds), which published in 1829 three poems by PBS (**Summer and Winter, The Tower of Famine**, and **The Aziola**) and his essay **On Love**. In addition, Cook argues that the "character of 'Sadak the Wanderer' . . . is very much akin to that of 'The Wandering Jew'—a great favourite with Shelley. . . ." Rogers accepts and repeats these arguments. Matthews and Everest, cognizant of Reiman's counterarguments, more cautiously note that in the absence of the missing MS, PBS's authorship cannot be definitely established; but they conclude that internal evidence "favours S[helley]'s claim," adducing PBS's abiding interest in volcanoes and the following list of "favourite Shelleyan themes . . . introduced in this Tale: Adiram's overshadowing pinions ('Hymn to Intellectual Beauty' (Text B) 1–12; *Mask of Anarchy* 110–17), and the fountain in the cave; Sadak foreshadows Ahasuerus (*WJ; Q Mab* vii 49–275; *Hellas* 738–861), as Amurath foreshadows the tyrant Othman in *L&C;* and the quest within the volcano suggests Asia's visit to Demogorgon in *PU* II" (I, 6).

For all of their citation of Shelleyan elements in *Sadak,* Matthews and Everest, like Cook and Rogers, take as their principal authority the uncontroverted evidence of the *Keepsake* index; they claim in *1989* that, although Richard Garnett knew of this ascription, "there is no evidence that he or any other editor actually saw the MS, which was bought by J. Dykes Campbell at the Dawson Turner sale, and had been abstracted from the file by

1936" (I, 6). In fact, however, both Garnett and Rossetti not only knew of the ascription but actually examined the MS and judged that it was not in the hand of PBS, MWS, or Medwin. Two pieces of evidence document the exchange between Garnett and Rossetti. The first is a letter (of which Matthews and Everest were aware) written by Rossetti to Garnett on 21 June 1870:

> A Mr. J. D. Campbell writes me from the Mauritius on 2 or 3 Shelley points (showing him to be well informed)—one of them being that he bought at Dawson Turner's sale a MS. vol. of "MSS. to Keepsake 1828," including "Sadole [sic] the Wanderer," wh[ich] the index ascribes to "P.B. Shelley." I must look up this tale in the Keepsake: cant at present imagine that there is any ground for connecting it with Shelley, but it is a point worth enquiry. May it possibly be by *Mrs* Shelley? (*Letters about Shelley Interchanged by Three Friends*, ed. R. S. Garnett [London: Hodder and Stoughton, 1917], 36)

The key evidence that Rossetti actually did pursue the ascription of *Sadak* has been overlooked, but can be found in his journal entry for "Tuesday 4 June" 1872:

> Mr. Walter Besant brought me round the MS. (belonging to Mr. [J. Dykes] Campbell, of the Mauritius, who has written me letters on the subject) containing the originals for writings published in *The Keepsake* for 1828. One of these is a "poem" named *Sadok the Wanderer* [sic], notified in the Index to the MS. as being by Shelley. I am quite certain it is neither the composition nor the handwriting of Shelley, and pretty certain that it is not the handwriting of Mrs. Shelley. Garnett (Somerset House) [i.e., Garnett called on Rossetti where he worked] does not suppose it to be Medwin's. (*The Diary of W. M. Rossetti: 1870–1873*, ed. Odette Bornand [Oxford: Clarendon Press, 1977], 206)

As the only editors of PBS's work actually to have seen the *Sadak* MS, the judgments of Rossetti and Garnett are crucial in evaluating the claims of the *Keepsake* index. Of all the early Shelley scholars and editors, Garnett most worked with the MSS themselves. His apparent agreement with Rossetti suggests the likelihood that whoever wrote the ascription in the index was either mistaken or misinformed, as Reiman had surmised before knowing about Rossetti's diary entry (*Texts and Contexts*, 47). The confidence with which Rossetti disavowed the authenticity of the *Sadak* MS must also have convinced J. Dykes Campbell himself, who appears never to have claimed that PBS was the author of *Sadak* to his friend and scholarly correspondent Dowden, who produced the first official biography of PBS as well as an edition of the poetry (*1890*).

With the ascription of the hand in the *Sadak* MS put into serious doubt, the case for PBS's authorship of the poem becomes much weaker, resting primarily on MWS's connection with the *Keepsake* and on what Matthews and Everest call "internal evidence." But MWS's only known contributions to the *Keepsake* began in 1829, under a different editor using very different policies than had MWS's friend Ainsworth (see Peter J. Manning, "Wordsworth in the *Keepsake*," in *Literature in the Marketplace*, ed. John O. Jordan and Robert L. Patten [1995], 44–73). Moreover, Cook evades an important question: if MWS contributed *Sadak*, why did she not publish it in *1839*, as she did all the other poems by PBS that she contributed to the *Keepsake*? And why is there no MS of the poem at the Bodleian or Huntington Libraries, along with all the other MSS from which MWS drew her texts for the posthumous publications of PBS's verse? For MWS to have contributed the poem to the *Keepsake*, the following would have to be the case: (1) *Sadak* was composed after the Shelleys eloped in July 1814 (MWS had no MSS of PBS's poems predating the elopement), (2) MWS sent her only MS of the poem to the *Keepsake*, and (3) she subsequently forgot about the poem or for some reason thought it was not worthy of publication in *1839*. While this sequence of events is possible, it is not likely, and the fact remains that there is no hard evidence whatsoever that MWS believed that PBS wrote *Sadak*, or that she contributed anything of PBS's to the *Keepsake* for 1828, weakening another link in the chain of attribution.

Matthews and Everest, in particular, note a few salient Shelleyan features of *Sadak*, but any attribution of the poem based on such internal evidence is vexed, because the poem could have been written at any time before the end of 1827, and its Shelleyan elements may simply reflect PBS's influence upon its author, as is the case with the Shelleyan "The Deev Alfakir," the tale that accompanies *Sadak* in the *Keepsake*. Moreover, in drawing comparisons between *Sadak* and PBS's other work, Cook and Matthews and Everest minimize significant differences. For instance, their comparison of Sadak to Ahasuerus (PBS's Wandering Jew) exaggerates minor similarities; the two characters share almost nothing except their oppression (by very different types of tyranny) and their wandering. Unlike the isolated and aimless Ahasuerus, who seeks only death, Sadak wanders on a specific quest accompanied by two sons (one of whom dies along the way), and he returns home a successful questor, whose very success depends upon his religious piety—not a particularly Shelleyan virtue in a hero. And, however much the Amurath of the original prose tale "foreshadows the tyrant Othman" in **Laon,** as suggested in *1989*, the *Sadak* poem itself treats Amurath in only two lines, whereas one would expect PBS to have developed the contrast between the heroic Sadak and the tyrannical Amurath more extensively. Finally, Sadak's killing of wild animals and meat-eating in the first stanza, are unlikely elements for PBS to have added gratuitously to the story, especially after March 1812 when he began to practice vegetarianism and advocate its utopian possibilities.

Those arguing for PBS's authorship of *Sadak* do not agree on when he composed it. Although Cook does not directly attempt to date the poem, he suggests that it was influenced by John Martin's painting (a problematic assumption; see below), which would place it no earlier than May 1812; and his belief that MWS contributed the poem to the *Keepsake* requires a date of composition after July 1814. Rogers, who accepts Martin's painting as a possible influence, nonetheless dates the poem "?1810–12," without providing any rationale for his conclusion. Matthews and Everest speculate that *Sadak* might be the poem on "an excellent subject" PBS promised to J. T. Tisdall in a letter written 7 April 1809 (*Letters* I, 4), and that the "happy ending foreseen after separation might then reflect S.'s hopeful situation in relation to Harriet Grove in Spring 1809" (*1989* I, 6). But this is sheer guesswork, without any substantiating evidence. Neither Medwin nor Hogg records PBS's ever mentioning *Sadak,* much less writing a poem on the subject. The problem of dating *Sadak* is inextricably linked to one of the key arguments for attribution, since those who believe that *Sadak* is an early poem cannot posit that MWS contributed it to the *Keepsake.* And the question remains, if *Sadak* is an early poem by PBS, why did he not collect it in *Esd,* where he gathered most of his early poems, several no better than *Sadak?*

Given the absence of *Sadak* from both *Esd* and MWS's editions, if PBS were its author, the most likely date of composition would be 1813–14, after he had sent *Esd* to Hookham for publication and before he eloped with MWS. This is a time of high general interest in the *Sadak* story, marked both by John Martin's painting, which was displayed in the anteroom of the Royal Academy of Arts in 1812, and by the staging at Covent Garden in April 1814 of *Sadak and Kalasrade, or, The Waters of Oblivion: A Grand Romantic Drama in Two Acts,* with original music by Henry Rowley Bishop (1786–1855, *DNB*), who was musical director of Covent Garden and acclaimed in his day as "the English Mozart." The possible influence of Martin's picture on the poem *Sadak,* in particular, is worth entertaining. Thomas Balston notes that this large and ambitious painting "is a grand design of mountains, more rugged than any he [Martin] can have seen, with flashes of lightning playing among peaks which overhang a pool. From the pool great cataracts descend, and between them, desperately struggling to climb on to a rocky ledge, is the small, half-naked figure of Sadak, occupying not more than a hundredth part of the picture" (*John Martin, 1789–1854: His Life and Works* [Gerald Duckworth, 1947], 33). This striking scene is suffused with glowing volcanic reds of an almost apocalyptic intensity, much like the *Keepsake* poem, with its "fiery land" and "iron torrent red" fed by "a thousand fountains." Perhaps most important, the painting and the poem focus on virtually the same moment in the overall *Sadak* story and the same landscape. Whoever wrote the *Sadak* poem, then, may well have been influenced by Martin.

However, even the most likely scenario for PBS's authorship of *Sadak* is deeply problematic. To propose that PBS composed the poem at a peak of popular interest in the Sadak story, sometime after he had seen Martin's painting but before his elopement, one has to assume that (1) he actually saw the painting, which turns out to be highly unlikely: completed in April 1812, the painting—as we have recently discovered—was on exhibit at the Royal Academy only from 1 May through 20 June 1812 (Council Minutes for 1812 of the Royal Academy), while PBS was in Wales; he did not return to London until the following fall; (2) someone other than MWS possessed a MS of the poem and later contributed it to the *Keepsake;* and (3) at the dawn of his own self-conscious commitment to vegetarianism, PBS added to his hero's actions the killing and eating of wild animals. If one accepts the influence of the Martin painting on the *Sadak* poem in the *Keepsake,* one has to assume that PBS was not its author, but that it, like "The Deev Alfakir," was written either by someone who had firsthand knowledge of the painting, or someone who was commissioned to "illustrate" Roberts's engraving of Martin's *Sadak in Search of the Waters of Oblivion,* which also was produced specifically for the *Keepsake.* Such intertextual play between words and images was a standard feature of this giftbook, which was founded and owned by the engraver Charles Heath.

One indication of the general popularity of the story of Sadak and Kalasrade during the Romantic period can be gleaned from the Advertisement to the 1814 production at Covent Garden: "The Juvenile frequenters of the Theatre will ... experience as much pleasure in the *representation* of the trials of *Sadak and Kalasrade,* as they invariably do *in perusing them;*—and those of maturer age, perhaps, will not be displeased at having the tales of their infancy again brought before their imaginations" (Bod Shelfmark: Harding D343). A popular bedtime story for over two generations by 1814, *Sadak and Kalasrade: or the Waters of Oblivion* had earlier been adapted for the stage by Thomas Dibdin as "A grand seriocomic pantomime" in 1797 (see BL Crachl.Tab.4.b.43.[14]) and was to be staged again in 1835 as a "Romantic Opera, In Two Acts" written by Mary Russell Mitford. Songs from the 1814 production even found their way into such collections of popular ephemera as *Momus's New Comic Tickler for 1815!* (London: J. Walton, 1815). The story was also reprinted in Henry Weber's three-volume *Tales of the East* ([Edinburgh: John Ballantyne, 1812]: III, 521–56), which was on MWS's reading list for 1815 (*MWS, Journals* I, 92). Given the pervasiveness of the Sadak story, PBS was likely to have known it, but so were most of his contemporaries, any number of whom could have written the poem in the *Keepsake.* A possibility remains that PBS could have authored *Sadak the Wanderer,* but with the attribution in the *Keepsake* archive discredited by Rossetti and with the other subsidiary evidence so highly questionable, unless and until more persuasive evidence is brought forward, we believe that the poem does not belong within PBS's canon proper.

Our text of *Sadak* reproduces without emendations that of the *Keepsake* for 1828; a page break in the *Keepsake* at line 20 may possibly camouflage a stanza break. Rogers in *1972* bases his text, not on the *Keepsake*, but on Cook's text in *TLS*, from which he reproduces Cook's only substantive error: "footsteps" for "footstep" (line 51). Matthews and Everest base their text in *1989* on the *Keepsake*, which they emend substantively in line 45 from "sheltr'd brow" to "shattered brow," presuming that "shelter'd" is a "misreading of S.'s orthography."

SADAK THE WANDERER.
A FRAGMENT.

* * * * * *
* * * * * *

He through storm and cloud has gone,
To the mountain's topmost stone;
He has climb'd, to tear the food
From the eagle's screaming brood;
5   By the turbid jungle tide,
For his meal the wolf has died;
He has brav'd the tiger's lair,
In his bleeding prey to share.
Hark! the wounded panther's yell,
10 Flying from the torn gazelle!
By the food, wild, weary, wan,
Stands a thing that once was man!

Look upon that wither'd brow,
See the glance that burns below!
15 See the lank and scatter'd hair!
See the limb, swart, wither'd, bare!
See the feet, that leave their mark
On the soil in bloodstains dark!
Who thus o'er the world doth roam,
20 With the desert for his home?
Hath he wander'd with the brand
Of the robber in his hand?
Hath his soul been steep'd in crime
That hath smote him in his prime?
25 Stainless as the newborn child,
Strays this wanderer through the wild;
Day by day, and year by year,

Must the pilgrim wander there;
Through the mountain's rocky pile,
Through the ocean, through the isle,   30
Through the sunshine, through the snow,
Still in weariness, and wo;
Pacing still the world's huge round,
Till the mystic Fount is found,
Till the waters of the Spring   35
Round the roofs their splendours fling,
Round the pearl-embroider'd path,
Where the tyrant, Amurath,
Leaves the haram for the throne:—
Then shall all his wo be done.   40

Onward, Sadak, to thy prize!
But what night has hid the skies?
Like a dying star the sun
Struggles on through cloud-wreaths dun;
From yon mountain's shelter'd brow   45
Bursts the lava's burning flow:
Warrior! wilt thou dare the tomb
In the red volcano's womb!
In he plunges: spire on spire
Round him shoots the living fire;   50
Rivers round his footstep pour,
Where the wave is molten ore;
Like the metal in the mould
Springs the cataract of gold;
O'er the warrior's scorching head   55
Sweeps the arch of burning lead;
O'er the warrior's dazzled glance
Eddying flames of silver dance;
By a thousand fountains fed
Roars the iron torrent red;   60
Still, beneath a mighty hand,
Treads he o'er the fiery land.
O'er his head thy purple wing,
Angel spirit of the Spring!
Through the flood, and through the field, 65
Long has been the warrior's shield.

Never fell the shepherd's tread
Softer on the blossom'd mead,

	Than, thou man of anguish! thine,
70	Guided through this burning mine.
	Hanging now upon the ledge,
	That the precipice doth edge;
	Warrior! take the fearful leap,
	Though 't were as the ocean deep:
75	Through the realm of death and night
	Shall that pinion scatter light,
	Till the Fount before thee lies.
	Onward, warrior, to the prize!
	Till thy woes are all repaid:
80	Thine, all thine, young Kalasrade!

Appendix E. Misattributions

The following poems have been erroneously attributed to the young PBS.

Epigraph: "If Satan had never fallen"

This two-line epigraph prefixed to Chapter 9 of *St.Irv* was first misattributed to PBS by Matthews and Everest in *1989*, with a presumed date of composition of ca. April 1810. As Matthews and Everest note, PBS playfully quotes these lines in a letter to E. F. Graham dated 23 April 1810 (***Letters*** I, 9). Although *1989* states that "Nothing is known of 'The Revenge,' perhaps a title arbitrarily attached to a casual epigram" (I, 84), PBS actually took his epigraph from Edward Young's verse tragedy, *The Revenge* (1721) — a crude yet popular imitation of *Othello* set in Spain, in which Zanga, a Moorish Iago, betrays his master, the Spanish general Alonzo. The two half-lines in PBS's epigraph are slightly altered from Alonzo's cry near the end of Act 5, after Zanga has revealed his villainy: "Had Satan never fell, | Hell had been made for me" (*The Revenge*, ed. Elizabeth Inchbald [1806], 61).

Text: ***St.Irv***, epigraph to Chapter 9.

> If Satan had never fallen,
> Hell had been made for thee.

Lines, Addressed to His Royal Highness The Prince of Wales, on His Being Appointed Regent

In a circumstantial but misleading discussion in *The Shelley Library*, Forman makes the case that PBS's "missing satire of 1811" might be *Lines, Addressed to His Royal Highness The Prince of Wales, on His Being Appointed Regent*, by "Philopatria, Jun.," which was published in 1811 by Sherwood, Neely, and Jones, and printed by Hamelin and Seyfang. Forman explains: "Some years ago . . . I found at a bookseller's shop a thin pamphlet [containing a preface of 4 pages and 18 pages of text] which I picked out from a large number of such things because it commended itself to me as having the general air of a juvenile work of Shelley's" (25). In connecting this volume to PBS,

469

Forman adduces the following evidence: (1) there is a resemblance between PBS's mock signature "Philobasileus" in his 19 June 1811 letter to Graham and the pseudonym "Philopatria, Jun."; (2) Sherwood, Neely, and Jones would later publish **Laon** (1817); (3) Seyfang would later print *Swellfoot the Tyrant* (1820), which is another PBS satire aimed at George IV; and (4) the motto for the volume, taken from Horace's *Odes* I.ii, introduces a note of "ironical adulation" that is pursued by "Philopatria, Jun." in his poem, which "might well be the 'ode' with which Philobasileus threatened the devoted Graham" (26).

These points, though interesting, are far from persuasive, especially in light of the poetry itself, which Forman neglects to mention. First, we know from the restored text of PBS's letter of 20 December 1810 to Hogg that the "missing satire of 1811" was about Christianity, not the Prince Regent (see "Satirical Poem on 'L'infame'" in Appendix C, Lost Works). Second, the resemblance between "Philobasileus" and "Philopatria, Jun." is superficial, especially given the frequency with which such pseudonyms were assumed in PBS's day; see, for example, *An Essay on Government* (1808), by "Philopatria" (Rachel Fanny Antonia Lee). Third, while PBS had later dealings with the publisher Sherwood, Neely, and Jones, he had no known contact with them until well after 1811. And, as Forman knew, Horace Smith or Johnston, the piratical publisher, not PBS, arranged for Seyfang to print *Swellfoot the Tyrant* in 1820, while PBS was in Italy. Fourth, Horace's *Ode* I.ii is addressed to Octavian as a plea to stabilize the nation during a dark time, which is why "Philopatria, Junior" mines it for a motto (printed all in capitals "SERUS IN CŒLUM REDEAS; DIUQUE | LŒTUS INTERSIS POPULO QUIRINI" ("late mayest thou return to the skies and long mayest thou be pleased to dwell amid Quirinus' folk" [lines 45–46; *Horace: The Odes and Epodes,* trans. C. E. Bennett {Cambridge: Harvard UP, 1968}, 9–11). "Philopatria, Junior" quotes Horace's hope that Octavian will live long among the Romans, to parallel the turbulence of post-Actium Rome with England's traumas during the Napoleonic wars. In each case, the poet in panegyrical tones calls upon the heir of a fallen leader to stabilize a nation in crisis. As "Philopatria, Junior" puts it in his introduction, he looks to the Prince Regent "as the Saviour of a Nation which has been for a series of years harrassed by difficulties, and depressed by misfortunes" (ii). The connection between the Prince Regent and Octavian is made explicitly within the poem itself, in "Philopatria, Junior's" hope for the future: "A second CÆSAR! GEORGE in Britain reign . . ." (line 200). There is, in fact, apparently nothing "ironical" about the adulation "Philopatria" has for the Prince Regent and the royal family, nor, for that matter, about Horace's adulation for Octavian, on whom Horace was dependent. Indeed, the single most important objection to Forman's attribution is the style and content of "Philopatria, Junior's" poem itself.

One look at the actual text of *Lines, Addressed to His Royal Highness* is enough to discredit the possibility that PBS wrote it. Written in heroic couplets in a neoclassical diction completely uncharacteristic of PBS, the poem celebrates British nationalism, commerce, the Tories, and Britain's naval might, as well as George III and the Prince Regent. "Philopatria Junior" states in the Introduction his "love for the throne," as well as his hope that his "zealous enthusiasm and admiration of the Regent's qualifications, will not be mistaken for servility or flattery, against which he loudly protests" (ii, iii). If there is irony in any of these statements, it is impenetrable. Take, for example, the following typical lines of the poem proper:

> So, PRINCE, dost thou thy SIRE's experience bind,
> To steer the bark with an enlighten'd mind.
> Taught by experience, we thy ascent hail!
> Pilot, well taught to stem the boist'rous gale!
> (lines 37–40)

It strains credulity and the notion of ironic subtlety to imagine that these lines could have been written by the young PBS. His own characterizations of the Prince Regent during this period are broad and bawdy, as in **The Devil's Walk.**

Forman himself must have recognized that *Lines, Addressed to His Royal Highness* was not by PBS, despite his attribution in *The Shelley Library*. He never attempted to print it in any of his editions (nor in any other format) and apparently made no attempt to answer the following interrogation of his argument made in the *Notebook for the Shelley Society* for 1888 (1888; rpt. New York: AMS Press, 1975), in a section called "Queries and Answers" (p. 149):

Have any fresh facts regarding the *Lines addressed to His Royal Highness the Prince of Wales,* by Philopatria Jun., been brought to light since the publication of the first part of Mr. Buxton Forman's *Shelley Library?* In that book (pp. 23–26) Mr. Forman endeavours to identify the pamphlet in question with Shelley's supposed missing Satire of 1811, but fails altogether to establish his case. It would be interesting, however, to know whether any fresh information has come to hand which goes to decide the question either way. J. F. (*Exeter*).

All of the queries surrounding J. F.'s are answered and the silence here of Forman, who helped produce this Shelley Society volume, is telling. We know of no subsequent editorial discussions of the poem. In the past, Forman's claims were impossible to verify because he owned the only known copy of *Lines, Addressed to His Royal Highness,* which we have located at the Huntington and from which we reprint the full text below, so that others can come to their own conclusions.

TO THE PUBLIC.

It may, perhaps, be deemed superfluous, for the Author to state his reasons, and the principles which suggested the following Lines, and caused him to introduce them to the Public attention; but as there is, in the present day, an universal spirit of enquiry into the motives, as well as the character, of the Individual, he thinks it may not be improper to make a few observations upon the subject. He acknowledges, with candour, that he is actuated by no other motive, than that which so eminently characterises every native of Great Britain. The love of their Sovereign (from the most dignified personage, down to the meanest subject,) is too well known to be disputed. He therefore, in unison with the feelings of every Briton, claims a portion of that spirit, which admires whilst it supports the throne; and he has adopted this mode, of expressing his Loyalty in the following humble effusion. To his love for the throne, he acknowledges also an individual respect for the exalted Character who is now appointed to discharge the duties of the kingly office. To him he looks up as the Saviour of a Nation which has been for a series of years harrassed by difficulties, and depressed by misfortunes. From the period of his accession he dates the commencement of an æra of exquisite happiness and unprecedented prosperity. He admits and bends to the urbane and merciful disposition of the Royal Parent; yet, when he looks to the Son, and beholds the same Virtues amalgamated with superior powers of mind, and enlightened by philosophical investigation, he cannot refuse that tribute which his virtues and his talents deserve. The author hopes that his zealous enthusiasm and admiration of the Regent's qualifications, will not be mistaken for servility or flattery, against which he loudly protests. Further, he (as is generally the case) does not regret that his subject has not fallen into abler hands; for by that means, the opportunity is given him of stating his sentiments, which, with pride he adds, are the general sentiments of a whole empire.- - -For the learned and ingenious, there still lies open a wide field wherein they may display their superior talents and acquisitions, without this being a stumbling-block in their way. Fully acquainted with the patronizing disposition of his countrymen, and sensible that their love of justice will not allow them to condemn without sufficient cause for condemnation, his knowledge of the frailty of human nature forbids him to hope that his Address will be found entirely destitute of errors; yet still, with all its faults, relying upon their generosity, he commits it to the perusal of a liberal and enlightened people!

LINES,
ADDRESSED
TO HIS ROYAL HIGHNESS
THE
PRINCE OF WALES.

HAIL! scenes of joy, which from Contentment's shade,
Burst with glad wing, and ev'ry soul pervade;
That cheer the mind, that fill the flowing vein,
Each pipe awake, and sound in ev'ry strain.
Blest Muse! the Bard with genial thoughts inspire; 5
With pow'rs new brace him, and with ardour fire;
Open Pieria's sweet and lucid rill,
And from its fount thy richest drops distill.
Buoy'd up thro' crowds, on Fame or Friendship's wing,
The Bard, unfledg'd, a Regent's worth will sing. 10
    Though Panegyric echoes through his lays,
The cautious Muse instruction blends with praise.
Flatt'ry may fawn, to court a Prince's smile,
And round his heart, like basking serpents, coil:
But I such motives and such minds disdain; 15
Virtue elicits, Conscience grants my strain.
The sordid Muse may patron acts deny,
Motives degrade, and princely deeds decry,
But whilst his hand is open'd to diffuse
Mankind his blessings, and enrich the Muse, 20
Ne'er will the Bard his Laureat-song forego,
To praise, whilst Mercy stills the throbs of woe.
    O'er Europe's face what varying views disclose,
An Empire's greatness, or a Nation's woes;
In southern climes, what vasty dangers press, 25
And plunge their wretched subjects in distress.
There the dread torch of war the Furies light,
And guide to fields of slaughter thro' the night;
With harpy aspect, and with dismal glare,
Hurl at one blow a nation to despair. 30
    On ALBION's cliff now sinks the glowing blaze,
And the Sire Bird in Honor's lap decays.

From parent dust behold the Phœnix rise,
Fledg'd with new pow'rs, and wing towards the skies.
35 No winds, how strong so e'er, can stop his course;
Uncurb'd he flies with new-gain'd GIANT force:
So, PRINCE, dost thou thy SIRE's experience bind,
To steer the bark with an enlighten'd mind.
Taught by experience, we thy ascent hail!
40 Pilot, well taught to stem the boist'rous gale!
Should tempests rise, and wash the pitchy deck,
Whilst the scar'd sailors dread approaching wreck,
Thou wilt with skill the dreaded ills prevent,
And stop the chasms which storms and winds have rent.
45 Thy art from rocks our bark shall safely guide,
And, free from harms, 'mid tempests proudly ride.
    When Night appears with gas-condensed head,
And sombre clouds her length protracted spread,
In gloom enwrapt, Sol hides his gloomy face,
50 Nor even glimmers thro' the murky haze.
But when these fogs, these mists, disperse away,
From clouds emerg'd, he shines more bright, more gay;
With genial pow'rs embraces Mother Earth,
And gives the embryon germ of Nature birth.
55   Ages have pass'd, unknown have poets sung,
Pleasure and use their varying themes have rung.
Merit, unnotic'd, oft penurious died,
And want a sous, who states and nations guide.
But now that patronage (so long withheld) bestow'd,
60 Will ease the man of mis'ry's pond'rous load;
As fields more verdant grow from gentle dews,
Thy beams increase the blessings of the Muse.
No more desponding shall she droop her head,
Foster'd in Honor's lap, by Merit fed.
65 These still her throbs, these give her pains relief,
Her anguish banish, and remove her grief,
Fill the bright youth with Fancy's varying fire,
And bid his embryon pow'rs to fame aspire,
    No more shall poets on rude mattress lie,
70 Unhonor'd drag a life,—unnotic'd die;
Whilst living, wretched; no one told his name,
When dead, his relics gave immortal fame.
THOU mak'st this source of sorrow cease to flow,
Its pregnant streams of grief, despair, and woe!

Pluck'st with kind hand from Poverty's cold cell, 75
And bidd'st the Muse in vales of comfort dwell.
    Whilst Desolation grumbles from afar,
And neighb'ring nations feel the ills of war;
Whilst conflagrations make whole empires smoke,
And princes kneel to kiss a tyrant's yoke, 80
Let Wisdom's voice avert from ALBION's shore
These wild commotions,—Disaffection's roar.
Let Justice in thy courts unbiass'd shine,
And Learning prop it, as the oak the vine;
Drive from thy presence sycophants and knaves, 85
Courtiers, who fawn, despise; and flatt'ring slaves,
Who strive by fraud t' obscure each worthier name,
And tear the laurels from the brows of Fame;
Thwart their vile crafts; around the vet'ran brows,
Bind the green wreath, an opiate for past woes. 90
    Across the plain the fiery courser flies,
That judg'd the best which wins the golden prize,
Whilst the old Nag, worn out, but trots the plain,
The younger courser cuts the wind in twain.
Match not to run the old unmettled dame; 95
The young is fleet, and doubtless seals thee fame.
The plate is won by nimbleness and speed—
Trust then to youth, discard the spavin'd steed;
So then will honors round thy table rise,
And the Muse hail thee chosen of the skies. 100
Now rob'd with pow'r, which virtuous acts create,
Upheld by Fortune, and secur'd by Fate,
Ne'er let thy heart a parent's deeds despise,
But hold them *sacred,* and account them *wise.*
Although the Council which advis'd his throne 105
Are not the people which direct thine own,
Be thou not biass'd by ambitious tools,
To spurn at *Tories* as a host of fools.
    So when fell ILIUM, in ill-fated hour,
And sunk in dust, to Greece's vengeful pow'r, 110
ROME's early parent wing'd his first born care,
To snatch an aged PARENT from despair.
Midst Grecian troops which crowded ILIUM's plain,
Midst scenes of horror, and midst heaps of slain,
ÆNEAS his sire upon his shoulders bore, 115
And convoy'd safe to LATIUM's distant shore.

          Turn to Iberia, that insulted state!
          And there, behold! thy FATHER's mind is great:
          For when a Tyrant press'd her sacred shore,
120   And strew'd her vineyards and her fields with gore;
          When intrigue, craft, and cunning, pav'd the way,
          Their king made pris'ner, and his throne a prey,
          FREEDOM, to BRITAIN ever hail'd and dear!
          Heard the sad news, and pitying dropt a tear—
125   Nor wept alone. They Britain's aid implore,
          To drive the traitors from their blood-stain'd shore.
          GEORGE hears what patriots and what men require,
          Yields to their wish, and grants what they desire.
          See yet they fight, and struggle with the foe,
130   And hope, still hope, to lay the tyrant low.
          Look at their wants, do thou thine aid extend,
          At once be BRITAIN's and IBERIA's friend.
          While England waves her sceptre o'er the sea,
          The World in fetters bends the neck to thee!
135   Towards COLUMBIA be thy wisdom bent,
          To heal the wounds which factious fools have rent.
          A cordial balm of soothing pow'rs apply,
          Assuage the tumor, and the ulcers dry.
          In War's dread columns and in hostile rage,
140   Ne'er let the sire to meet a son engage;
          Ne'er let contending parricides be found,
          Again to violate Columbia's ground.
          Send then the dove the wide Atlantic oer,
          And plant the olive on Columbia's shore.
145   But why should I suspicions entertain,
          Or treat his worth with sceptical disdain.
          Full well I know his principles possess'd
          The glowing fire which animates his breast.
          The Country's weal his patriot bosom warms,
150   Its riches please him, and its honor charms.
          The joyful mien, which all around reveals,
          The hopes, the pleasures, every subject feels,
          Urge each alike, this first, this laureat theme,
          To hail with joy Anticipation's dream.
155   Minds that Ne'er felt the kind, the genial rays,
          Which bright PHILOSOPHY's expanding blaze
          Pours thro' the sense, enriching ev'ry pore,
          And bursts th'arcanean bolts to Nature's store,

Bigots throughout, with sanctimonious face,
For boyish faults would seal a man's disgrace. 160
What are thy faults? possest by all mankind,
Themselves possess; with zeal to this they're blind.
Contemn their mean insinuating ways,
Which Virtue scorns, as Vice degen'rate pays.
We own thy merits, and admiring see 165
A HENRY's virtues concentrate in thee!
   ROME, once the empress of the world, in state,
By wisdom propp'd, she stood sublimely great.
Her senatorial bands, by friendship join'd,
Spoke each the dictates of a lofty mind: 170
Still might have rul'd Creation to this hour,
In grandeur equal, and confirm'd in pow'r.
Neer had she sunk in superstition's shade,
Had but AUGUSTUS, or a TRAJAN sway'd.
When wisdom quits, when vice to worth succeeds, 175
Power sinks to nought, as wounded virtue bleeds.
From Rome's dread fall what great examples flow,
To rule a nation, and chastise a foe.
From Wisdom's fount, the luscious potion sip,
And catch the sounds from Ciceronian lip; 180
Whilst fawning myriads round thy footstool bend,
And loud requests with pompous praises blend,
Hear their requests, but grant with cautious care,
Yet keep the sinking subject from despair.
Now shall thy worth a nation's lot decide, 185
With mind determin'd, and with manly pride.
Thought into act, with nervous strength shall fly
To bless a race, and seal a nation's joy.
Behold deserted Commerce abject bend,
Bemoan disasters, and implore a friend; 190
Her votaries sing beneath increasing pain,
And ask thy aid; ne'er let them ask in vain.
The country's love, by thee so strong possess'd,
Will ope the passage to thy aching breast.
Through the fine vein of love, thy hand bestows 195
The just petition, and removes their woes.
Show them that BRITAIN's weal thy thoughts inspire,
Grant them but PEACE, and consummate desire.
Virtues like thine empyreal honors rais'd
To Cæsar's name! ROME's sacred altars blaz'd! 200

A second CÆSAR! GEORGE in Britain reign
Lov'd by thy people, ruler of the main;
Then shall thy fame till time expires remain.

Blest Isle! protected by a prince like thee,
205   Long will she prosper, powerful, great, and free.
Long shall the world, transcendent merits own,
And bend obsequious to thy GOLDEN THRONE.

When Mars' dread clangor sounds with loud alarms
And tells thy subjects—Fly to arms! to arms!
210   Anxious they meet with martial steel in hand,
To guard their REGENT and defend their land.
Patriots, to death, or victory they rush,
And fall; or, conqu'ring, hostile armies crush.
So o'er Oceana's billows proudly ride
215   Our Nation's batt'ries and our Country's pride.
Laws to the world our naval pow'rs proclaim,
And Neptune yields his realms for ALBION's fame.
Whilst Ocean's waves encompass Britain's shore,
Wash her white sides, and guard with dreadful roar,
220   Great and sublime she lifts her tow'ring head,
And owns her pow'r is Neptune's wat'ry bed.
Internal blessings GEORGE's hand bestows,
And grants by Peace a Nation's wish'd repose.
Ye heav'nly Pow'rs, which rule the world above,
225   O'er BRITAIN shed your lasting rays of love:
O'er her lov'd PRINCE your arms protecting spread,
And blessings heap upon his royal head;
Midst mighty Monarchs may he mightiest shine,
And teach them this,—his GUARDIAN IS DIVINE!

The Modern Minerva; or, The Bat's Seminary for Young Ladies. A Satire on Female Education. By Queen Mab

Copies of this work at BL and Cam are listed by *NSTC* simply under the pseudonym "Mab" (M52), but James Bieri pointed out to us that a 1909 index to Sotheby catalogues recorded a sale of the volume in 1896 as "Probably written by P.B. Shelley" on the grounds that "he commenced to write his 'Queen Mab' in 1809, and, being mixed up with school girls his own age, he might have written this squib at their suggestion. At page 10 are eight lines against fagging. Everybody remembers Shelley organized a rebellion against fagging at Eton in 1806." Luckily, the Pforzheimer Library in 1977 (i.e., prior to moving to NYPL) had purchased a copy of this poem, published in 1810, to help the editors of *SC* assess the use of the character Queen Mab in the period prior to PBS's selection of that title for his attack on the British social order, as well as for its possible interest as a commentary on women's education in the wake of Wollstonecraft.

The poem, a slim quarto of twelve leaves (22 numbered pages) dated "London | Printed by Macdonald and Son, 46 Cloth Fair, | West Smithfield. | 1810," is a clever satire about Miss Bat, who ran an expensive and pretentious girls' school devoted to fashion, rather than learning. (According to contemporary penciled marginal annotations in the copy at Pfz, the poem apparently satirizes a Miss May, who kept her school in a house that she had enlarged and stuccoed.)

An epigraph on the title page from Pope's *The Rape of the Lock* (V.21–22) sets the tone: "Who would not scorn what housewife cares produce, | Or who would learn one earthly thing of use?" The poem proper, written in anapestic tetrameter couplets that exhibit some wit and skill of execution, may be the work of an alumna of the school, a disgruntled parent, or a competing schoolmistress (or her friend). The first lines are:

> Near the forest frequented by juvenile fowl,
> Who composed "the Academy kept by an Owl,"
> In a ruin o'ershaded with ivy-boughs, sat
> A modern Minerva, the prudent Miss Bat;
> Who, observing the Owl's sudden progress in pelf,
> Form'd a similar plan for enriching herself:
> But decided in favour of female tuition,
> As better adapted to her erudition.
>
> (3)

Miss Bat finds that she can attract a more fashionable clientele by changing her name to Madam Chauvesouris. She then hires "Weazle" and Mouse as assistants and, as an underassistant, Mole, "a pennyless orphan," who becomes "a fag to the rest"—i.e., does all the unpleasant work for them (9–10).

Much of the poem is a rather light-hearted, moralized beast-fable that is good fun, but it has no connection with PBS, either in subject matter, printer, diction, or tone. Since Queen Mab was not only the subject of Mercutio's eulogy in Shakespeare's *Romeo and Juliet* (I.iv.53–94) but (as Reiman and Powers note) often appeared in the titles of eighteenth-century children's books (see *1977* 14 fn.), any number of people could have used the pseudonym when writing such a satire. But PBS, who made the Queen Mab in his radical didactic poem of 1813 a philosophical demiurge—whom he calls in his redaction of the poem, "Queen of the Universe"—probably would not have used the name both here and in that quite different work, even had he been capable, at the very dawn of his poetic career, of writing with such lightness and wit as appear in *The Modern Minerva*.

Anecdotes of Father Murdo

The *National Union Catalog of Printed Books* (*NUC*) attributes to PBS a work entitled *Anecdotes of Father Murdo* (*Pre-1956 Imprints*, vol. 542, p. 664, col. 3). This slim volume was published by John Joseph Stockdale in two editions in 1813, the first an octavo and the second a quarto, according to the *NSTC* (#0267). We have located at Cam a copy of the second edition, which runs twenty-four pages and is titled in full: *Anecdotes of Father Murdo, a Poet of the eighteenth century: to which is added (supposed to be written by him), Irish Night Thoughts, or A Complaint Against The Heretics and Their Bible*. Priced at one shilling, most of the volume consists of the prose apparatus with which the anonymous editor surrounds "Irish Night Thoughts," a forty-eight line poem to the tune of "Sheelin-o-Gera" that supposedly parodies a sermon preached by "Father Murdo O'Lavery" against a proposal to translate the New Testament into Irish. According to the editor, O'Lavery was a convivial parish priest in Northern Ireland, who was known as the Falstaff of his neighborhood. We note the publication in 1747 (*ESTC*) of *Purgatory Proved,* another parody, which is supposedly based on a funeral sermon of Father "Murtagh O'Lavery," in which O'Lavery (also called "Morgan O'Lavery") is described as a "priest of the parishes of St. John's, Dromore, and Marlin" (all in Northern Ireland).

The *NUC* probably attributed *Anecdotes of Father Murdo* to PBS because the work was published in 1813 by PBS's former publisher Stockdale, it addresses the Irish public, it attacks Catholicism, and is in parodic verse. However, from Stockdale's own account in *Stockdale's Budget,* we know that by the "Spring of 1811, all friendly intercourse, between the Shelleys [both Timothy Shelley and PBS], and me, . . . ceased" and that by 11 April 1811, Stockdale had already met PBS "for the last time" (31 Jan. 1827, 59; 17 Jan. 1827, 42). PBS thereafter avoided Stockdale, to whom he still owed money for the publication of *St.Irv* in 1811 (a debt that he never repaid). Moreover, as the introduction and extensive notes of *Anecdotes of Father Murdo* make clear, the editor is an English or an Irish Protestant who objects to Catholicism, but not to Christianity itself. There is nothing Shelleyan about the editor's theology or introductory prose. Among the targets of the editor's attack are the celebration of "divine service in an unknown tongue" (17), belief in Purgatory (18–19), the need for prayers to saints, angels, and the Virgin Mary (19), the sale of indulgences (20), the doctrine of transubstantiation (21), the practices of confession, penance, and absolution (22), and the infallibility of the Church (23). The editor's self-identification as a Protestant is explicit throughout and includes statements such as "They [i.e., Catholics] often ask us, where was our religion before Luther? We answer: wherever Christianity was. We may ask them, was it Luther who invented the creed, the *ten* commandments, and the sacraments?" (22). Finally, there is not a single identifiable Shelleyan element in the poem itself, which we print below.

Text: taken from the second edition of *Anecdotes of Father Murdo* (1813).

IRISH NIGHT THOUGHTS; OR, LILY TRIUMPHANT;
Or, A Panegyric on "As In Præsenti."[1] *Being the Substance of a Sermon preached at ——, by Father O'Lavery, against the Use of the Bible in the vulgar Tongue. Addressed to all good Christians.*

TUNE—Sheelin-o-Gera.

Good Christians all, of this Catholic Nation,
I rise to address you in great tribulation—
We are horribly used by an heretic squad,
Whose vile machinations have put me half mad.
They would rob you of LATIN, and teach you to pray   5
In barbarous English, the Protestant way;
But stick to the language your Fathers have sent you,
And I will instruct you in—*As in Præsenti.*

2.
They tell of a parcel of Jewish Imposters,
Who would rob you of *Aves,* and sweet Paternosters;   10
Their Samuel and Daniel, Isaiah, and Moses,
Would drench you, instead, with most terrible doses.
Their Proverbs, their Gospels, their Psalms, and Epistles,
Are scarce worth a dozen of halfpenny whistles.
But mind your bog Latin, that well may content ye—   15
The true way to Heaven is by—*As in Præsenti.*

3.
Their Luke, and their John, and their Matthew, and Mark,
Would lead you, like Will-o'-the-wisp, in the dark;

---

[1] *As in Præsenti* is a school-boy term, for a noted part of Lily's Latin Grammar, introduced here for the purpose of recommending that language in preference to English, for obvious reasons.

  Of Virtue they babble, of Faith and Repentance,
20 But, of *after Purgation,* they don't say one sentence,
  They tell you of trials, and conflicts, and nonsense,
  But Indulgence and Bead-work's sufficient in conscience.
  Then pray well, and pay well, no sins will prevent ye,
  Of a passport to Heaven, thro'—*As in Præsenti.*

4.

25 Your pledge of Salvation you get at the Bakers,
  They furnish the Dough, but the Priests are the makers,
  In the hands of the holy you're taught to adore it,
  And you lift up your hearts, when you're prostrate before it.
  O, Moses! O, Moses! how could you pretend,
30 That to worship a Wafer, was Heav'n to offend,
  No, such precepts as this from Mound Sinai was sent ye,
  Nor a word of an Idol in—*As in Præsenti.*

5.

  Of Mahomet's Ass they repeat a curs'd lie,
  That it carried him up in a whiff to the Sky;
35 But—*As in Præsenti,* when saddled by me,
  And bridled by Lily, is brisk as a bee.
  Tho' it looks like a Grammar, all sheep-skin and paper,
  Transmuted by me, it will scamper and caper,
  And bear you to Heaven, before you'd count twenty:
40 No Pegasus equals my—*As in Præsenti.*

6.

  O, Dominic, Francis, and sweet Virgin Mary,
  Will you suffer your votaries thus to miscarry;
  If you slumber much longer, those vagabond Jews
  Your Temples will burn and your Statues abuse.
45 Bestir you in time, or, like Nebo and Baal,
  Osiris and Apis, the Gods of the Stall,
  You'll sink from your stations of peace and of plenty,
  In spite of my labours, and—*As in Præsenti.*

To the Queen of My Heart

"To the Queen of My Heart" was printed as one of PBS's works in Medwin's *The Shelley Papers* (1833), from which MWS reprinted the text (with the error of "rising" for "shining" in line 33) in *1839*. She placed "To the Queen of My Heart" among the poems of 1822, apparently assuming that it was of a piece with PBS's emotional lyrics to Jane Williams that were first published by Medwin in the *Athenæum* and were previously unknown to her. However, in *1840* MWS withdrew the poem from her edition, remarking: "It was suggested that the Poem 'To the Queen of my Heart,' was falsely attributed to Shelley. I certainly find no trace of it among his papers, and as those of his intimate friends whom I have consulted never heard of it, I omit it" (xi). In *1876,* Forman nonetheless printed the poem among PBS's juvenilia, finding MWS's "negative evidence quite insufficient for so judicial an occasion. It is to my mind almost inconceivable that even the careless Medwin can have 'falsely attributed to Shelley' these verses, which, judged on their merits, are quite as good as most things to be found among the *Juvenilia,* and bear strong enough marks of Shelley's youthful hand" (IV, 369).

Forman, however, clearly had not seen a review article published in 1851 in the *Eclectic Review* (n.s., vol. 2) that describes "To the Queen of My Heart" as a hoax perpetrated by James Augustus St. John (1801–75, *DNB*) on a group of literary friends. The anecdote appears as a digression within an anonymous review of R. P. Gillies's *Memoirs of a Literary Veteran. Including Sketches and Anecdotes of the Most Distinguished Literary Characters from 1794 to 1849.* Although it is long, we quote it in full because of its importance to the textual history of "To the Queen of My Heart":

But to show that even authors themselves are not always infallible judges, we will relate an anecdote which has never yet been made public; though having received it from an undoubted source, we venture to vouch for its veracity. Shelley, whose poems many years ago were so much read and admired, necessarily excited much discussion in literary circles. A party of literary men were one evening engaged in canvassing his merits, when one of them declared that he knew the turns of Shelley's mind so well, that amongst a thousand anonymous pieces he would detect his, no matter where published. Mr. James Augustus St. John, who was present, not liking the blustering tone of the speaker, remarked, that he thought he was mistaken; and that it would, amongst so many, be difficult to trace the style of Shelley. Every one present, however, sided with his opponent, and agreed that it was perfectly impossible that any one could imitate his style. A few days after, a poem entitled 'To the Queen of my Heart' appeared in the 'London Weekly Review,' with Shelley's signature, but written by Mr. St. John himself. The same coterie met and discussed the poem brought to their notice, and prided themselves much upon their discrimination; said, they at once recognised the 'style of Shelley, could not be mistaken, his soul breathed through it—it was himself.' And so 'The Queen of my Heart' was settled to be Shelley's! and to this day it is numbered with his poems [see Shelley's Works, edited by Mrs. Shelley, vol. iv. p, 168. It deceived even his wife.], and very few are in the secret that it is not actually his. The imitation was perfect, and completely deceived every one, much to the discomfiture of all concerned. (66–67)

As detailed in the *Bookman* of October 1891 (p. 20), an editor for the *Bookman* discovered this anecdote in the *Eclectic Review* and forwarded it to PBS's biographer and editor Dowden, asking for a response. Dowden acknowledged that "I printed it [in his 1890 edition of PBS's works], but with great misgivings, and with a footnote to warn the reader that it is of doubtful authenticity, placing it, as Forman does, among the *Juvenilia*. It ought never to have been mistaken for a poem of Shelley's maturity, and Medwin's authority is the only ground for admitting it among Shelley's poems. I do not believe he wrote it." Dowden, nonetheless, did not remove "To the Queen of My Heart" from the many subsequent reissues of *1890*; Hutchinson published it among PBS's *Juvenilia* in *1904* and all subsequent reprintings of his popular Oxford Standard Authors edition until *1970*, when Matthews excised it from the corrected OSA edition. Woodberry omits the poem in *1892W* but mentions it in a section "Doubtful Poems," where he reprints relevant passages from the *Eclectic Review* and the *Bookman* without any accompanying commentary. "To the Queen of My Heart" is omitted without comment by Locock in *1911* (which does not contain any of PBS's shorter juvenilia) and by Ingpen and Peck in *1927*. None of these editors, however, pursues the reliability of the anecdote in the *Eclectic Review*—the single most conclusive piece of evidence concerning the authorship of "To the Queen of My Heart."

In 1851, James Augustus St. John, a distinguished man of letters, was still very much alive and active on the London literary scene, and he presumably would have been able to contest the account in the *Eclectic Review* had it been untrue. Moreover, St. John in 1827 founded and began editing the *London Weekly Review and Journal of Literature and the Fine Arts* (*LWR*, 1827–29), which would have made it easy for him to have published "To the Queen of My Heart" there, as stated in the *Eclectic Review*. The best proof of the anecdote, however, is that, just as reported in the *Eclectic Review*, "To the Queen of My Heart" "By Percy Byshe Shelley" (*sic*) does indeed appear in the *LWR*, in the issue for 3 May 1828, on page 283. Given this evidence, there is little reason to doubt that "To the Queen of My Heart" was written by St. John as a hoax in 1828.

We can thus reconstruct the early textual history of "To the Queen of My Heart." Someone probably brought the poem in the *LWR* to the attention of Medwin after he began publishing the series of PBS's poems and essays that appeared in the *Athenæum*, between 21 July and 24 November 1832 (with an additional installment on 20 April 1833), but before he published *The Shelley Papers* in 1833 (for more on the *Athenæum* poems, see Fraistat, *"Prometheus Unbound" Notebooks*, xlix). This would explain why "To the Queen of My Heart" appears in the latter but not the former. Medwin would have had little reason to doubt the attribution in the *LWR* of a poem that seemed so Shelleyan, and Forman's conviction that Medwin would not knowingly have sponsored an outright fraud would thereby be vindicated. A collation of the *LWR* text with Medwin's in *1833* reveals only two small differences: *1833* uses small capitals in the initial word of the poem and hyphenates "night-air" (line 35), both of which reflect the printer's house style. The agreement of the two texts in virtually every other detail suggests that Medwin, whose handwriting was nearly illegible, may have sent to the press a copy of the poem directly clipped from *LWR*.

Whoever told MWS that "To the Queen of My Heart" was not by PBS may well have been in on the original hoax; perhaps Augustus St. John, an avid admirer of PBS, did so himself, after discovering in a copy of MWS's 1839 edition that he was an unacknowledged contributor to the *Poetical Works by Percy Bysshe Shelley*. We reproduce below, for the first time, the text of "To the Queen of My Heart" as it appeared in the *London Weekly Review*.

TO THE QUEEN OF MY HEART.
By Percy Byshe Shelley.

Shall we roam, my love,
To the twilight grove,
   When the moon is rising bright;
Oh, I'll whisper there,
In the cool night-air,   5
   What I dare not in broad day-light!

I'll tell thee a part
Of the thoughts that start
   To being when thou art nigh;
And thy beauty, more bright   10
Than the stars' soft light,
   Shall seem as a weft from the sky.

When the pale moonbeam
On tower and stream
   Sheds a flood of silver sheen,   15
How I love to gaze
As the cold ray strays
   O'er thy face, my heart's throned queen!

Wilt thou roam with me
To the restless sea,   20
   And linger upon the steep,
And list to the flow

　　　　　　Of the waves below
　　　　　　　　How they toss and roar and leap?

25　　　　　Those boiling waves,
　　　　　　And the storm that raves
　　　　　　　　At night o'er their foaming crest,
　　　　　　Resemble the strife
　　　　　　That, from earliest life,
30　　　　　　　The passions have waged in my breast.

　　　　　　Oh, come then and rove
　　　　　　To the sea or the grove
　　　　　　　　When the moon is rising bright,
　　　　　　And I'll whisper there
35　　　　　In the cool night air
　　　　　　　　What I dare not in broad day-light.

Index of Titles

An asterisk marks titles that have been used in other editions but differ from those in this edition.

"A Cat in distress"	135
"Ambition, power, and avarice, now have hurl'd"	93
Anecdotes of Father Murdo	480
"As you will see I wrote to you"	140
Ballad ("The death-bell beats!—")	111
"Bear witness Erin! when thine injured isle"	145
*Bereavement	115
"Dear dear dear dear dear dear Græme!"	142
Despair	99
Epigram, from the Greek Anthologia ("We that were wont")	456
Epigraph: "If Satan had never fallen"	469
Epitaphium	435
*Epithalamium	95
Essay on War	451
Fragment, or The Triumph of Conscience	37
Fragment. Supposed to be an Epithalamium of Francis Ravaillac and Charlotte Cordé	95
Fragment ("Yes! all is past—swift time has fled away")	100
Ghasta; or, The Avenging Demon!!!	30
"Ghosts of the dead! have I not heard your yelling"	110
God Save the King	452
"How swiftly through Heaven's wide expanse"	136
In Horologium	437
Letter [1] ("Here I sit with my paper, my pen and my ink")	7
Letter [2] To Miss—— ——From Miss—— ——	9
*Letter to Edward Fergus Graham	140
Lines, Addressed to His Royal Highness The Prince of Wales, on His Being Appointed Regent	469
*Lines Written at Bracknell ["Thy dewy looks"]	145
*Love	139
Melody to a Scene of Former Times	102
Ode, to the Breath of Summer	455
"Oh Ireland!"	441
"Oh wretched mortal, hard thy fate!"	138

*Olympia [epigraphs to Chapters 4 and 7]	459
On a Fête at Carlton House	448
On Old Age, from the Greek Anthology	458
*On the Dark Height of Jura	110
Poetical Essay on the Existing State of Things	444
Revenge	28
Sadak the Wanderer. A Fragment	460
Saint Edmond's Eve	22
*St. Irvyne's Tower	114
Satirical Poem on "L'infame"	443
*Second Letter to Edward Fergus Graham	142
*Sister Rosa. A Ballad	111
Song ("Ah! faint are her limbs, and her footstep is weary")	116
Song ("Cold, cold is the blast when December is howling")	11
Song ("Come————! sweet is the hour")	13
Song. Despair	14
Song ("Fierce roars the midnight storm")	19
Song. Hope	16
Song ("How stern are the woes of the desolate mourner")	115
Song ("How swiftly through heaven's wide expanse")	114
Song. Sorrow	15
Song. To———— ("Ah! sweet is the moonbeam that sleeps on yon fountain")	20
Song. To———— ("Stern, stern is the voice of fate's fearfull command")	21
Song. Translated from the German	17
Song, Translated from the Italian	17
*Stanza, written at Bracknell ["Thy dewy looks"]	145
"Sweet star! which gleaming oer the darksome scene"	144
The Devil's Walk, a Ballad	123
The Devil's Walk, Supplement: Letter Version	128
*The Drowned Lover	116
The Grape. From the Greek Anthologia	456
The Irishman's Song	18
The Modern Minerva; or, The Bat's Seminary for Young Ladies. A Satire on Female Education. By Queen Mab	478
"The Ocean rolls between us"	438
*The Revenge	469
The Spectral Horseman	101
The Wandering Jew; or, The Victim of the Eternal Avenger	39
"Thy dewy looks sink in my breast"	145
*To a Star	144
*To Ireland ["Bear witness Erin!"]	145
To Mary who died in this opinion	138
To the Queen of My Heart	482
Translation of an Epigram of Vincent Bourne's	457

"'T was dead of the night, when I sat in my dwelling"	109
Unattributed Epigraphs to St. Irvyne	458
Venus and the Muses, from the Same	458
*Verses on a Cat	135
*Victoria	109
*War	93
"Why is it said thou canst but live"	139

Index of First Lines

A Cat in distress	135
Ah! faint are her limbs, and her footstep is weary	116
Ah! grasp the dire dagger and couch the fell spear	17
Ah! quit me not yet, for the wind whistles shrill	28
Ah! sweet is the moonbeam that sleeps on yon fountain	20
Ambition, power, and avarice, now have hurl'd	93
And can'st thou mock mine agony, thus calm	99
And said I that all hope was fled	16
Art thou indeed for ever gone	102
Ask not the pallid stranger's woe	14
As you will see I wrote to you	140
Bear witness Erin! when thine injured isle	145
By the mossy brink	451
Cold, cold is the blast when December is howling	11
Come———! sweet is the hour	13
Dear dear dear dear dear dear Græme!	142
Down the river's gentle tide	457
Fierce roars the midnight storm	19
For your letter, dear———, accept my best thanks	9
Ghosts of the dead! have I not heard your yelling	110
Good Christians all, of this Catholic Nation	481
Hail! scenes of joy, which from Contentment's shade	473
Hark! the owlet flaps her wing	30
Here I sit with my paper, my pen and my ink	7
He through storm and cloud has gone	466
Hic, sinu fessum caput, hospitali	436
How stern are the woes of the desolate mourner	115
How swiftly through heaven's wide expanse	114
How swiftly through Heaven's wide expanse	136
If Satan had never fallen	469
Inter marmoreas, Leonoræ, pendula colles	437
Maiden, quench the glare of sorrow	138
Mortals for age, when distant, pray	458
——Nature shrinks back	459
Near the forest frequented by juvenile fowl	479
Oh! did you observe the black Canon pass	22
Oh! Ireland, thou emerald of the ocean	441

Oh! what is the gain of restless care	17
Oh wretched mortal, hard thy fate!	138
Once, early in the morning	123
Shall we roam, my love	485
Stern, stern is the voice of fate's fearfull command	21
Sweet star! which gleaming oer the darksome scene	144
The brilliant orb of parting day	44
The death-bell beats!—	111
The Devil went out a walking one day	128
The fiends of fate are heard to rave	458
—The ocean rolls between us.	441
The Queen of love once threat'ning vow'd	458
The stars may dissolve, and the fountain of light	18
This grape, of future wine the store	456
Thy dewy looks sink in my breast	145
'Tis midnight now—athwart the murky air	95
To me this world's a dreary blank	15
'Twas dead of the night when I sate in my dwelling	37
'T was dead of the night, when I sat in my dwelling	109
We that were wont in Spring's soft lap to bloom	456
What was the shriek that struck fancy's ear	101
Why is it said thou canst but live	139
Yes! all is past—swift time has fled away	100
Yes! 't is the influence of that sightless fiend	459
Zephyr, whither art thou straying	455

DONALD H. REIMAN, Adjunct Professor of English at the University of Delaware, has since 1965 been the editor (now co-editor with Doucet Devin Fischer) of *Shelley and His Circle*, a catalogue-edition of relevant manuscripts in the Carl H. Pforzheimer Collection at the New York Public Library. He is also co-editor of *Shelley's Poetry and Prose*, which he and Neil Fraistat are updating for a second edition. He compiled and edited *The Romantics Reviewed* (9 volumes) and *The Romantic Context: Poetry* (128 volumes) and served as general editor, as well as editor or co-editor of eight volumes, of *Manuscripts of the Younger Romantics* (29 volumes) and *The Bodleian Shelley Manuscripts* (23 volumes).

Since earning his academic degrees at the College of Wooster and the University of Illinois, Reiman has taught the Romantics at Illinois, Duke, Wisconsin-Milwaukee, City University of New York, Columbia, St. John's, University of Washington, and New York University and has lectured at universities in the United States, Canada, and the United Kingdom. His other books on Shelley and the Romantics include *Shelley's "The Triumph of Life," Percy Bysshe Shelley, Byron on the Continent* (with D. D. Fischer), *English Romantic Poetry, 1800–1835, Intervals of Inspiration: The Skeptical Tradition and the Psychology of Romanticism, Romantic Texts and Contexts,* and *The Study of Modern Manuscripts,* the last based on the Lyell Lectures in Bibliography that he delivered at Oxford University in 1989. He co-edited *The Evidence of the Imagination: Studies of Interactions between Life and Art in English Romantic Literature* and has contributed some 150 essays and reviews to multiauthored books, encyclopedias, and scholarly journals on subjects ranging from *Beowulf,* Chaucer's *The Clerk's Tale,* and Shakespeare's *Richard II* to the prose of Matthew Arnold, Henry James, and J. D. Salinger and the poetry of G. M. Hopkins, W. B. Yeats, and A. R. Ammons.

In addition to serving on the editorial boards of several scholarly periodicals, Reiman was a founding director of the Wordsworth-Coleridge Association, the Byron Society of America, and the Society for Textual Scholarship and a director of the Keats-Shelley Association of America.

NEIL FRAISTAT, Professor of English at the University of Maryland and a founder and general editor of the *Romantic Circles* Website, received his

Ph.D. from the University of Pennsylvania. He has published *The Poem and the Book: Interpreting Collections of Romantic Poetry*, *Poems in Their Place: The Intertextuality and Order of Poetic Collections*, and *The "Prometheus Unbound" Notebooks*. He is editing, with Donald H. Reiman, the second edition of *Shelley's Poetry and Prose;* with Elizabeth B. Loizeaux, a collection of essays entitled *Textual Studies in the Late Age of Print;* and, with Susan S. Lanser, an edition of Helen Maria Williams's *Letters Written in France.*

Fraistat's online editions of Percy Bysshe Shelley's *The Devil's Walk*, co-edited with Reiman, and *The Medusa of Leonardo Da Vinci*, co-edited with Melissa J. Sites, can be found on *Romantic Circles*. He has published widely on Romantic Period literature and culture in such journals as *PMLA, JEGP, Studies in Romanticism, Keats-Shelley Journal, The Wordsworth Circle,* and *Publications of the Bibliographical Society of America;* and he is a member of the editorial board for *Studies in Romanticism, Keats-Shelley Journal, Romanticism, Romanticism on the Net,* and the Emily Dickinson Editing Collective. He was awarded the Society for Textual Scholarship's Fredson Bowers Memorial Prize for Most Distinguished Essay on Textual Scholarship and the Keats-Shelley Association Prize.

Library of Congress Cataloging-in-Publication Data
Shelley, Percy Bysshe, 1792–1822.
[Poems]
The complete poetry of Percy Bysshe Shelley / edited by
Donald H. Reiman and Neil Fraistat.
   p. cm.
   Volume 1.
   Includes index.
   ISBN 0-8018-6119-5 (alk. paper)
   I. Reiman, Donald H.   II. Fraistat, Neil, 1952–
III. Title.
PR5402 2000
821'.7—dc21   99-15163
                                                    CIP

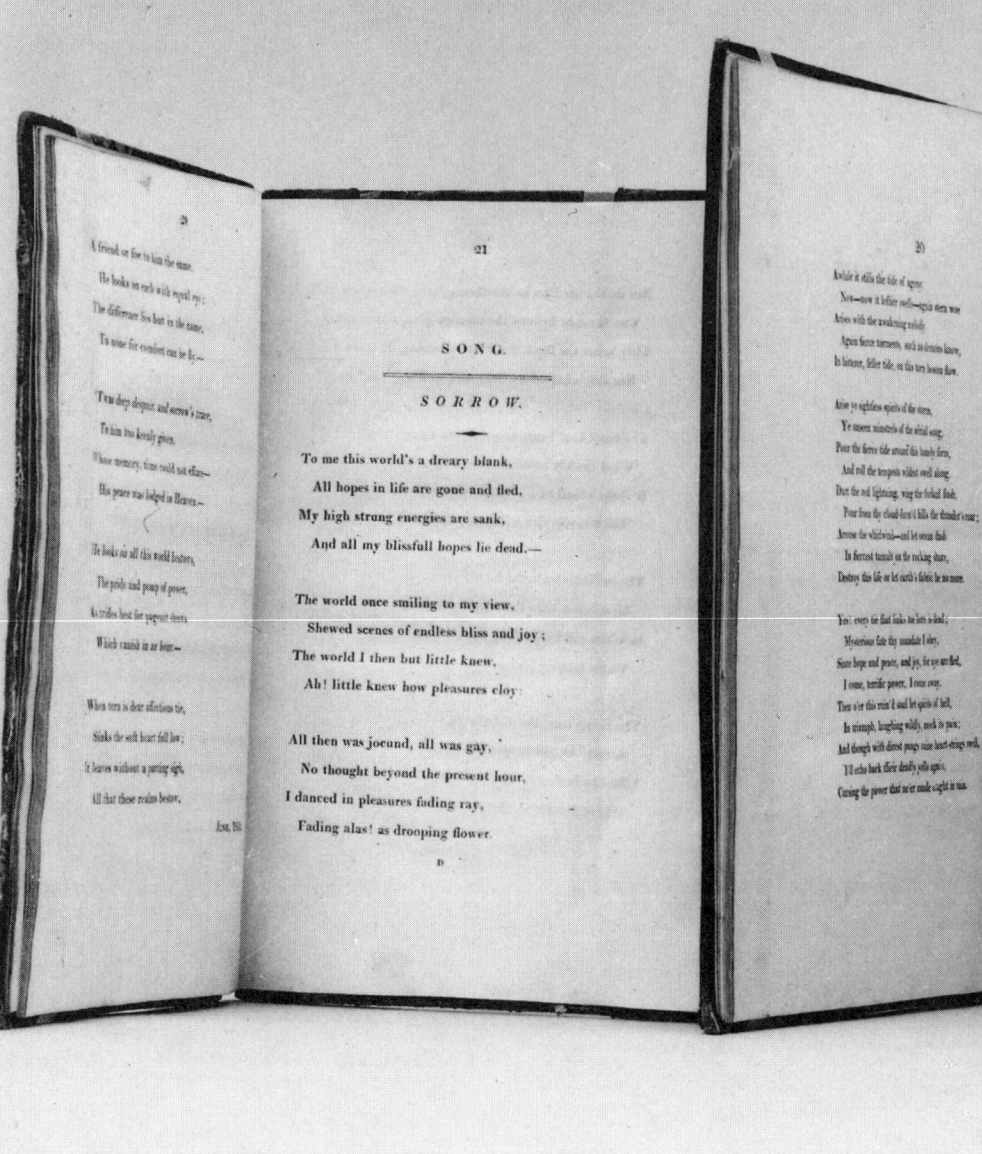

SONG.

SORROW.

To me this world's a dreary blank,
  All hopes in life are gone and fled,
My high strung energies are sank,
  And all my blissfull hopes lie dead.—

The world once smiling to my view,
  Shewed scenes of endless bliss and joy;
The world I then but little knew,
  Ah! little knew how pleasures cloy:

All then was jocund, all was gay,
  No thought beyond the present hour,
I danced in pleasures fading ray,
  Fading alas! as drooping flower.